THE MINERS:

YEARS OF STRUGGLE

by the same author

THE MINERS

Being Volume One of

A HISTORY OF THE MINERS' FEDERATION OF GREAT BRITAIN

———————————

FACTS FROM THE COAL COMMISSION

THE POLITICS OF OIL

THE GENERAL STRIKE MAY 1926: ORIGIN AND HISTORY

WILLIAM MORRIS: A VINDICATION

A SHORT HISTORY OF THE RUSSIAN REVOLUTION

THE DURHAM MINERS' GALA
by Charles Cundall, R.A.

THE MINERS:

YEARS OF STRUGGLE

*A History of the Miners' Federation
of Great Britain
(from 1910 onwards)*

BY

R. PAGE ARNOT

REPRINTS OF ECONOMIC CLASSICS

AUGUSTUS M. KELLEY • PUBLISHERS
NEW YORK • 1966

FIRST PUBLISHED IN 1953

PRINTED IN GREAT BRITAIN
in 12 point Baskerville type
BY UNWIN BROTHERS LIMITED
WOKING AND LONDON

FOREWORD

WE are happy and proud to present this, the second volume of the history of the British Miners, to the public of Britain and to the miners of all lands. The first volume met with a general welcome and we are certain that this volume has been awaited with an eagerness that will not be disappointed.

Our miners are now recognised to be of the greatest importance so far as the general economic welfare of the country is concerned. This was not always the case as a perusal of this history will show.

We, who feel honoured to be the elected leaders of this great body of workers, look back over the years at the bitter struggles and un-flinching courage of those who made our great organisation and this history possible, and we send forth this volume as a lesson, and we hope an inspiration, to workers everywhere, of the power of organisation to protect and advance the welfare of the working class.

President.

Vice-President.

Secretary.

NATIONAL UNION OF MINEWORKERS
July 1952

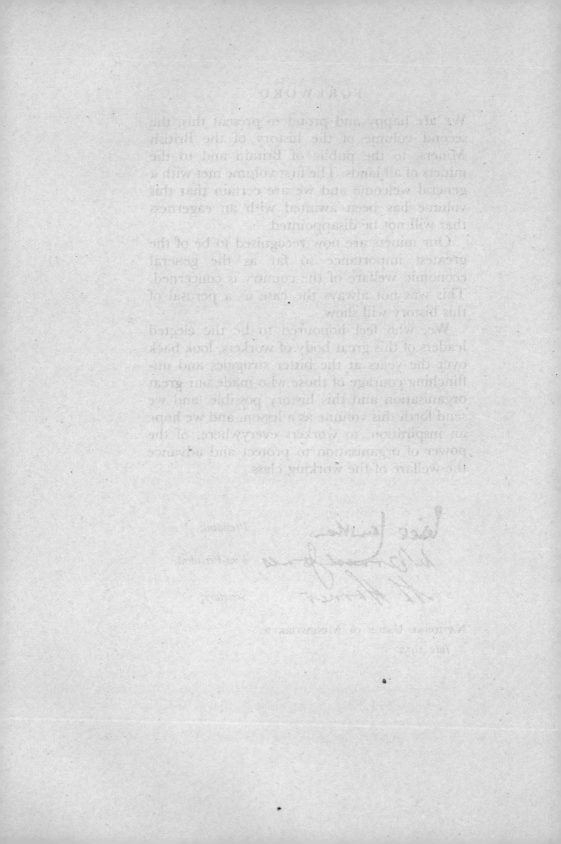

PREFACE

THE main events in this history take place within the short scope of fifteen years from 1912 onwards, years of such turbulence as neither the mining industry nor the successive Cabinets concerned with it had hitherto experienced. But these great strikes and lock-outs, involving each time the almost exclusive attention for weeks on end of His Majesty's Government, were only part of the experience and the activity of the miners and their unions. From 1910 onwards the Miners' Federation of Great Britain had such an immense spread of activities and was concerned with so much that happened in Europe as to bring matters of both domestic and foreign policy within its range. Moreover this million miners, this mining community of some four or five million people, exceeding in size the contemporary total population of several European states, was not a paper grouping like the members of an age-group in the census. Their trade union was a common bond of such strength that if need be they would all jeopardise their livelihood to carry out its decisions arrived at democratically. Hence their relation to the political, legal and social institutions of Britain had an impact that affected all the rest of the population.

To deal with all this would compel me to handle the history of Britain. I have therefore limited myself to telling that story from the miners' standpoint, as set forth in their own reports and documents. These, however, are so voluminous as sometimes to contain over a million words in a single year. To make a history out of the multitudinous facts recorded has caused me to ponder much what to put in and what to leave out. If any complain that this or that is omitted, I assure them that it was not done through lack of thought.

The manuscript was complete in 1949, with a fullness of detail and documentation which would have made the price nearly double that of the first volume of this history. In an endeavour to keep down the price I undertook to reduce the size. I omitted many documents available elsewhere, gave only selective and summary treatment to the concluding chapter, and took out much laborious chronicle of the less momentous months. In the end, however, it meant I had largely to rewrite the book—an ungrateful task which was completed by the summer of 1951—only to find that the unprecedented sevenfold rise in the price of paper had made it a vain endeavour.

Two duties of thanks: first to those who were members of the Miners' Federation of Great Britain (now the National Union of

Mineworkers) for their courtesy and helpfulness; and second to the friends, also too numerous to name, for their great help and advice.

Lastly, I should like to quote Sir Samuel Hoare, now Lord Templewood, who was in a position to know full well what a struggle there was between the Miners' Federation and the British Government in the crucial years of this history. For he was, as he says, "thirty-four years in the House of Commons, four times Air Minister, First Lord of the Admiralty, Secretary of State for India, Foreign and Home Affairs, Lord Privy Seal in the War Cabinet" and finally Ambassador on Special Mission. In his book on this last office he tells that in his wide political experience he had learned that there were "three institutions most difficult to defeat; the British Treasury, the Miners' Federation and the Vatican." When I read these words by one who had so long and so often been their opponent I exclaimed, "Is Saul also amongst the prophets?": and I conclude this preface to a book that recounts temporary set-backs of what is now the N.U.M. with his prophetic words:

"The Miners' Federation . . . most difficult to defeat."

R. PAGE ARNOT.

45 Fitzroy Road, London, N.W.1.
August 1, 1952.

CONTENTS

ACKNOWLEDGEMENTS

To Messrs. Heinemann Ltd. for permission to quote from *The Truth About Reparations and War Debts*, by David Lloyd George.

To Messrs. Routledge and Kegan Paul Ltd. for permission to quote from *The British Coal Trade*, by H. S. Jevons.

To Messrs. Hutchinson Ltd. for permission to quote from *Annals of an Active Life*, by Sir Nevil Macready.

To G. A. Hutt for permission to quote from his *The Post-War History of the British Working Class.*

To the Labour Research Department for permission to quote from its publications and for the courtesy and help of its staff.

To the National Coal Board for help in supplying illustrations.

To *Picture Post* photographic library for their courtesy in supplying reproductions of the illustrations facing pages 16, 17, 33, 81, 272, 464, 465, 496.

To the *Illustrated London News* for permision to use the illustration facing page 49.

To *The Yorkshire Post* for permission to use the illustration facing page 32.

To the trustees and staff of the British Museum for their courtesy and help in the matter of books and prints.

To D. N. Pritt, Q.C., for permission to use as frontispiece the reproduction of "The Durham Miners' Gala" by Charles Cundell, R.A.

ILLUSTRATIONS

CHAPTER I

THE PASSING OF AN EPOCH

WITH the closing months of the reign of Edward VII the Miners' Federation of Great Britain entered on its twenty-first year and became adult in more senses than one. The reign of Edward had appeared as an appendix to the late Victorian era. All seemed peaceful and prosperous in what was still "Liberal England." Abroad, there was the same air of undisturbed continuity with the past. Throughout the Old World the ancient monarchies ruled from the Pacific to the Atlantic: a Mikado of Japan, an Emperor of China, a Sultan of the Ottoman Empire, a Tsar of all the Russias, Emperor Francis Joseph since 1848 head of the dual monarchy or Austria-Hungary, a Hohenzollern Kaiser in the German Empire, and elsewhere other emperors, kings and sultans, emirates and principalities. France was still the only republic in Europe, apart from the Swiss cantons, and a powerful faction there was seeking for the return to monarchy. Whatever internal changes had been brought by a century and more of capitalism, the countries of Europe and Asia still wore on their outer garments all the blazonry of feudalism.

In what was still called the New World, the score of states broken away from the British, Spanish and Portuguese Empires maintained republican forms beyond an ocean that took all but the fastest vessels over a week to cross. The Concert of Europe, comprising the Great Powers, had for nearly a century charged themselves with composing differences between states through occasional conferences, to the most recent of which the United States of America had been for the first time admitted. The powers of Europe had only just completed "the opening-up of Africa"—their motto that of Ancient Pistol

> Why then the world's mine oyster
> Which I with sword will open.

In the centre of the British Empire the brilliant Court of

St. James reflected the prosperity of Britain, the prosperity of Europe. Its gaieties were adorned with rank and beauty. Titled hostesses gave balls during "the Season" at their town houses in Belgravia and Mayfair, and each morning, in the Row, well-groomed riders were bowing to marchionesses and other leaders of society. For Rotten Row then seemed to be utterly permanent, something that had always been and ever would be. Permanence and high respectability shone from the cylindrical top hat, worn on special occasions by the middle classes throughout the island and regularly by Members of Parliament, professional men and all the busy throng of the City.

To all this splendour and fair seeming of peace and prosperity there was another side. At the very beginning of the reign of Edward VII the representative of a mining constituency (Merthyr Tydfil) had moved in the House of Commons a resolution which was a challenge, and also (had Honourable Members but known it) a portent for the future like the hand that wrote on the wall at the feast of Belshazzar. This was Keir Hardie, solitary voice of Socialism in that House of Commons, and one of the only two successful candidates of the newly-formed Labour Representation Committee. Proposing his motion on a Socialist Commonwealth,[1] Keir Hardie stated that "the growth of our national wealth, instead of bringing comfort to the masses of the people, is imposing additional burdens on them. . . . There was more happiness, more comfort and more independence before machinery began to accumulate wealth." Then he spoke of the "alarming growth of trusts and syndicates," named a series of trusts and gave an instance of their "most scandalous and shameless persecution of workmen" and finally[2] declared for Socialism. Scant attention was paid to this by the Con-

---

[1] See Appendix to this chapter, Keir Hardie's Motion.

[2] In his closing words Keir Hardie said: "This House and the British nation know to their cost the danger which comes from allowing men to grow rich and permitting them to use their wealth to corrupt the Press, to silence the pulpit, to degrade our national life, and to bring reproach and shame upon a great people, in order that a few unscrupulous scoundrels might be able to add to their illgotten gains. The war in South Africa is a millionaires' war. Our troubles in China are due to the desire of the capitalists to exploit the people of that country. . . . The pursuit of wealth corrupts the manhood of men. We are called upon at the beginning of the twentieth century to decide the question propounded in the Sermon on the Mount as to whether or not we will worship God or Mammon. The present day is a mammon-worshipping age. Socialism proposes to dethrone the brute-god Mammon and to lift humanity into its place."

WIGAN COLLIERY DISASTER, AUGUST 1908
Wives and relatives waiting for news

HAMSTEAD COLLIERY DISASTER, GREAT BARR, BIRMINGHAM, FEBRUARY 1908
The crowd outside the gates

servatives, Liberals and Irish Nationalists who made up that
House of Commons. In 1901 it was but "a little cloud out
of the sea, like a man's hand."

But from 1910 onwards the storm clouds were gathering.
The epoch of monopoly capitalism, coincident with the
twentieth century, was now made visible by many signs and
tokens. The growing rivalry of the Great Powers had taken
shape in the two armed camps: the Triple Alliance headed
by Germany and the Triple Entente headed by Great Britain.
In Asia the peoples were stirring from their age-long slumber
and with the Chinese Revolution of 1911 were awakening
to political life. At home there were signs of a new epoch
in the militant suffragettes resorting to violence, in the House
of Lords rejecting the Lloyd George Budget and so bringing
on a "constitutional crisis," in the threat from Northern
Ireland that Home Rule legislation would be met by armed
rebellion—to which a climax was to be provided by the
Curragh officers' mutiny in 1914.

The same new turbulence was also to be manifested from
1910 onwards within the Labour movement. Amalgamation
or closer federation of existing trade unions, together with
the formation of new unions in trades hitherto unorganised,
all contributed to such an increase in membership (from two
millions in 1905 and 2½ millions in 1910 to *four millions* in
1913) as had never been known before. In three years trade
unionism had doubled its members and more than doubled
its influence within the body politic. A wave of great strikes
marked the upsurge of trade union activity, while novel
doctrines such as syndicalism[1] added to the growing ferment
of opinion. Amongst the many factors of these new developments two may be singled out, one economic and one political.
The overriding economic factor was the growing dominance
of monopoly capital. A consciousness of this, reflected at the
time in a flood of progressive literature and in such books
as H. G. Wells's *Tono-Bungay* and Bernard Shaw's *Major
Barbara*, was found amongst a number of Socialist and trade
union leaders and certainly provided an impetus both to the
fusion of existing unions into larger units and to the widespread discussion of the need for new policies. But the changing

[1] See Chapter IV.

conditions were brought home to the working class by the rapid rise in prices. Since 1902 prices had been rising, as may be seen from the table given below.

TABLE
INDEX OF PRICES[1]

Year			
1900	..	..	100·0
1901	..	..	96·7
1902	..	..	96·4
1903	..	..	96·9
1904	..	..	98·2
1905	..	..	97·6
1906	..	..	100·8
1907	..	..	106·0
1908	..	..	103·0
1909	..	..	104·1
1910	..	..	108·8

When the economic crisis of 1908–1909 was succeeded by the prosperity of the next five years the workers found their demands for a wage increase, to improve their standard of life or merely to cope with the higher costs of living, meeting with a resistance from many of the employers. Hence the growth of trade unionism, the wave of strikes or in the cant term of those days, "industrial unrest."

On the other hand there was manifest at the same time a phase of disillusionment with parliamentary activity. The 1906 General Election and the appearance in the House of Commons of the Labour Party twenty-nine strong together with fifteen miners' M.P.s had raised hopes that were not justified in the event. The Labour Party, though accepted into the Socialist International, had not yet as far as many of its representatives were concerned cut the umbilical cord from Liberalism: and after 1910 its leader Ramsay MacDonald concerned himself with the problem of maintaining the Liberal Government's majority in the division lobbies of the House of Commons. The new leaders in the unions began to be impatient of a policy that no longer yielded the results which (like the Trade Disputes Act of 1906) had followed on the mere first appearance of the Labour Party in Parliament. At the same time such I.L.P. leaders as Fred Jowett and George Lansbury were heading a

[1] *Labour Year Book*, 1916.

minority in protest against the official policy of their own organisation.

It was in this new stage of the economic and political life of Britain that the Miners' Federation entered on its twenty-first year. It was now fully grown, comprising the hewers' trade unions in every coal-field, negotiating with coal-owners through established conciliation machinery in every county, wielding the largest single vote inside the Trades Union Congress, exercising a strong and growing influence on Government departments and in part through Parliament with its fifteen or more mining representatives. Within its score of affiliated districts were mustered nearly three-quarters of a million miners, equal in 1910 to over a quarter of the two million and more trade unionists of Great Britain. It had become a power in the land. Throughout the first decade of the twentieth century and indeed ever since 1893 it had pursued as a federation a relatively peaceful path. District and local disputes there were in plenty, but a clash on a national scale had been sedulously avoided.

In all this the Miners' Federation was still under the guidance of its founding fathers. No member of the Executive Committee was a newcomer. Most of them had been leading in the work of their county unions for twenty or thirty years. But just because of their long experience their average age was now much higher; and some of them, like Dr. John Wilson, of Durham, were now well stricken in years. Moreover, in the course of years a large proportion of the founding fathers had been elected to Parliament. Eight Members of Parliament sat on the Executive Committee. This was found to be a great advantage. But it had its negative side, which led in after years to a self-denying ordinance to exclude all parliamentarians. For the time, however, it served them well enough. Most of those elected in December 1910 had already served in the first Parliament of Edward VII and had sat there as members of the Liberal Party.

One very remarkable feature of the Executive Committee was that, in England at any rate, most of these founding fathers were Methodists. Enoch Edwards, M.P., Secretary since 1877 of the North Stafford Miners' Federation, President since 1886 of the Midland Miners' Federation, Treasurer of

the Miners' Federation of Great Britain from its formation in
1889 till he became its second President in 1904, was also
a leading figure in the Primitive Methodist Church. It was
a far cry from the days when in 1739 John Wesley had
preached to the colliers of Kingswood Chase and enrolled
among "the people called Methodists" only those who had
"a desire to flee from the wrath to come, to be saved from
their sins." But the rise of the Primitive Methodist connection
was not so remote. Enoch Edwards had been born the same
year as saw the death of Hugh Bourne (1772–1852) the mill-
wright who, from his Methodist society in Burslem, had carried
his gospel to the colliers of Kidsgrove and Harriseahead,
and who along with William Clowes (1780–1851) of Burslem
had held the first "camp meeting" on Mow Cop. Often must
Enoch in his youth have heard of those two men and of their
followers who, schooled in self-expression, had played a part
in leading strikes and building trade unions. And now, within
sight of the lofty Mow Cop, the Mecca of Primitive
Methodism, Enoch Edwards preached in the chapel every
Sunday that he was at home in Burslem. So too did the others
of the Executive Committee who were local preachers,
charged "to spread Scriptural holiness over the land." It
was the same in Wales, where the prevalence of Noncon-
formity (Methodist, Baptist, Congregationalist, Salvationist)
in the mining valleys was reinforced by a nationalist feeling
against the dominion of the Church of England. Thus
treasurer William Abraham, Member of Parliament since
1885, and a leader of the miners since the early 'seventies
when he signed the treaty with the owners that fastened the
sliding scale for nigh thirty years upon South Wales, was also
much sought after as a preacher and singer from which last
was derived his name of Mabon or "the bard." The Scots,
with a different religious tradition, were ready nevertheless
to agree with any opposition to the Church of England,
which they regarded as prelatical or heretical according as
the representatives were Presbyterians or Roman Catholics.
From all these Robert Smillie (1857–1940) stood apart. He
was first and foremost a Socialist, was indeed one of the
pioneer Socialists of a quarter of a century earlier; and
because of it had repeatedly suffered exclusion from the

Vice-Presidency, to which the invalid, Sam Woods, was regularly elected. But now the exclusion could not be maintained; for a year he had been Vice-President and his qualities were gaining him an ascendancy over the other leaders and among all the miners of the United Kingdom.

The fourth office-bearer was the venerable secretary Thomas Ashton, a man whose voice was never heard in public meeting or conference. He was sage in counsel, skilful with his pen, a campaigner with an exact foresight of the moves the owners would make. "His letters to us," recalled one county secretary a generation later, "were like the directives issued by a general in a campaign."[1] He had little sympathy with the Liberalism of his colleagues (privately he leaned to Conservatism like so many Lancashire miners of Victorian days), but most districts of the Federation put their trust in his long trade union experience—he had first been a branch secretary in 1866—and were ready to call upon him in times of need. Enoch Edwards and Tommy Ashton had been the companions-in-arms of Ben Pickard even before the Miners' Federation was formed in 1889. Pickard's testament had been to preserve the unity of the Federation : and this aim these two old veterans upheld, amid the many divergent interests of the constituent district unions. For this reason they were always ready to go to any district where there was a dispute or a threatened dispute. Their intervention more than once served to bring the owners into a more accommodating mood, especially as they bore the authority of a national body federated for wage purposes, while the owners had no corresponding national organisation for negotiations with the men.

The office-bearers and the others of the founding fathers could look back in 1910 upon much accomplished. After twenty years' persevering agitation they had won the Eight Hours' Day (though not the Eight Hours' Day from Bank to Bank as set forth in their objects) and they had obtained other legislation affecting miners. From 1887 they had sought for a better Mines Act : and now they were in full career to obtain such a measure of safety against accidents. With this activity we begin our history.

[1] Fred Swift in an interview, September 1945.

Keir Hardie's Motion (House of Commons, April 23, 1901)

A SOCIALIST COMMONWEALTH

That, considering the increasing burden which the private ownership of land and capital is imposing upon the industrious and useful classes of the community, the poverty and destitution and general moral and physical deterioration resulting from a competitive system of wealth production which aims primarily at profit-making, the alarming growth of trusts and syndicates able by reason of their great wealth to influence Governments and plunge peaceful Nations into war to serve their interests, this House is of the opinion that such a condition of affairs constitutes a menace to the wellbeing of the Realm, and calls for legislation designed to remedy the same by inaugurating a Socialist Commonwealth founded upon the common ownership of land and capital, production for use and not for profit, and equality of opportunity for every citizen.

(MR. KEIR HARDIE, Merthyr Tydfil.)

CHAPTER II

A DANGEROUS TRADE

I. ACCIDENTS AND DISASTERS

MINING has always been one of the more dangerous trades. Roman poets and the earliest English poetry (as in *The Seafarer*) have told of the perils of the sea. But have they amounted to so much more in loss of life and bodies maimed than the perils of the mine? For many years more accidents were reported in mines than in all the factories and workshops of the United Kingdom. The families of the miners live at all times under the shadow of calamity, great or small. The total number killed annually in the mines in the period from 1880 to 1910 was for most years between 1,000 and 1,500. On the average four miners were killed every day in the British coal-fields. But though the total figure of deaths remained very high during these years—and actually increased in the decade up to 1920—there had been a fall in the *rate* of fatal accidents. From 1890, when the number of persons killed per 100,000 employed underground was 206, there was a gradual fall until 1910, when the fatal accidents were 191·7 per 100,000 employed underground and until 1913 when the rate was 173·6 per 100,000 employed underground.

The non-fatal accidents also run to a high figure. For every man killed, a hundred and more were injured. The number of persons injured by non-fatal accidents at mines, reported under the Notice of Accidents Act, 1906, was:

143,258 in 1908
154,740 in 1909
160,638 in 1910
168,360 in 1911
152,302 in 1912
178,962 in 1913

These figures, applying to injuries which caused disablement for more than seven days, amounted to from 14 per cent to 15 per cent of the total number employed—and, of course, to a considerably higher percentage of those employed underground. After 1923 accidents which disabled for more than

PRINCIPAL COLLIERY DISASTERS

CAUSED BY EXPLOSION OF FIRE-DAMP OR COAL DUST

IN THE YEARS 1890 TO 1913

Year	Date		Name of Colliery	County	No. of Killed
1890	February	6	Llanerch	Monmouth	176
	March	10	Morfa	Glamorgan	87
1891	April	2	Apedale, Sladderhill Pit	Stafford	10
	August	31	Malago Vale	Somerset	10
1892	August	26	Nth. Navigation, Park Slip	Glamorgan	112
1893	July	4	Combs	York	139
1894	June	23	Albion	Glamorgan	290
1895	April	26	Quarter	Stirling	13
1896	January	26	Tylorstown	Glamorgan	57
	April	13	Brancepeth	Durham	20
	April	30	Micklefield	York	63
1899	August	18	Llest	Glamorgan	19
1901	May	24	Universa	Glamorgan	81
1902	September	3	McLaren No. 1 Pit	Monmouth	16
1905	January	21	Elba	Glamorgan	11
	March	10	Cambrian	Glamorgan	33
	July	11	National	Glamorgan	119
1906	October	10	Wingate Grange	Durham	25
1908	February	20	Washington, "Glebe"	Durham	14
	April	9	Norton Hill	Somerset	10
	August	18	Maypole	Lancaster	75
1909	February	16	West Stanley	Durham	168
	October	29	Darran	Glamorgan	27*
1910	May	11	Whitehaven, Wellington Pit	Cumberland	136
	December	21	Hulton, No. 3 Bank Pit	Lancaster	344
1912	July	9	Cadeby Main	York	88†
1913	October	14	Senghenydd	Glamorgan	439

* Including five persons killed during rescue operations.
† There were two explosions on the same day. As a result of the first 35 persons were killed, the second explosion causing the loss of 53 members of the rescue parties.

three days were made reportable: and the percentage then rose to from 16 per cent to 18 per cent of all employed at mines. In the reports of H.M. Chief Inspector for Mines the causes of accidents are distinguished according as they occur on the surface or below ground. The accidents below ground are classified into those caused by explosions of fire-damp or coal dust, falls of ground, shaft accidents, haulage accidents, and others. Within these main classifications, more fatal accidents and more injuries come from falls of ground than from any other cause.

Every few years an explosion occurs of such magnitude as to bring home to the public the risks run by miners. The list of colliery disasters caused by explosions is melancholy reading; but it was these disasters rather than the daily tale of killed and injured which resulted in Parliament taking steps to introduce safety measures in the mines.

From the beginning the Miners' Federation of Great Britain was closely concerned with these explosions, as well as with accidents from other causes. At miners' conferences, national and international, disasters, wherever they occurred, immediately found a place on the agenda. Of the original seven objects of the Federation, no less than three bore upon this matter: for example, the sixth object ran as follows:

6. To deal with and watch all inquests upon persons killed in the Mines where more than three persons are killed by any one accident.

These objects were faithfully carried out. To each Executive Committee meeting any such accidents were reported. Regularly members of the Executive were sent to watch the inquests, a painful duty which usually took up several weeks' time in each year. Often, too, especially where numbers of men were known to be trapped underground, members of the Executive sped to the scene of the disaster and helped in the work of rescue. But apart from the attention paid by members of the Executive Committee to these disasters, who can find language to speak the praise of miners who face the terrors of a fearsome death in the effort to save their stricken comrades? Great stories are told, and high honour paid to men risking their life in battle to aid comrades in distress. But never in the history of war was there heroism that called for greater courage, a more iron resolution and more complete unselfish service than has been shown time and time again by the ordinary rank and file in the coal-fields when their mates were in danger deep in the bowels of the earth.

The first occasion on which the newly-formed Miners'

Federation was called upon to carry out its sixth object was the Llanerch Colliery explosion (176 killed), two weeks after the first Annual Conference in 1890. At the Executive Committee a fortnight later, it was resolved "that two persons be appointed from this Federation to conduct the Enquiry on behalf of the Widows, the Monmouth District, and this Federation." The subsequent report, by Ned Cowey and W. Whitefield, is addressed to the "Committee and Members of the Miners' Federation of Great Britain":

Gentlemen

In accordance with your instructions we attended the Coroner's Inquiry into the cause of the Explosion at the said Colliery, which was opened for full inquiry, on February 25th, 1890, and continued the whole of that week, up to late on the Friday, when the Court adjourned until the 25th of March.

The conditions of those days and the type of difficulty encountered, as well as the painstaking manner in which this duty was carried out, are shown in their opening statement:

On the day we were appointed by you, viz. the 18th February, we resolved that one of us should go to Abersychan, the village where the greater number of relatives of the killed lived; accordingly we attended a meeting at Abersychan on the 21st February. We fully explained to the meeting your object in sending us; we pointed out the great need there was of anyone of them coming forward as witnesses who could throw any light on the cause of the explosion, especially if they knew of any laxity prior to the explosion likely to account for it. . . . The meeting by a unanimous vote expressed a desire that we should act in the matter; the resolution was put into writing and signed by the Chairman, which was accepted by the Coroner as a sufficient mandate, without question. . . . Prior to the Court opening we took the common precaution of taking down in writing the evidence of those whom we called to give evidence in the case.

The Report of the Deputation selects some of the main points from the evidence given, notes down facts of importance brought out in their examination of the witnesses, and brings forward proposals on particular points as well as recording the verdict of the jury. For example, the fireman had given in evidence that "the working places were free from explosive gas," but when questioned about 47 disused stalls in that division, which is 36 per cent of the total number, he said he did not examine them; he was not therefore able to say, whether those stalls were free from gas on the morning of February 6th. The certificated manager, Mr. Morgan, when questioned on this point, was not aware that such stalls were not examined by the fireman each morning; he thought they ought to have been examined.

The fireman stated he had at times found gas, but did not enter an account of it into the report book. It is not only our opinion that he ought to have done so, but it is clearly defined in the General Rules of the Coal Mines Regulation Act, as the duty of an examiner to enter into the report book any gas he finds during his examination.

Thirty-five years before this, an Act of Parliament had set forth a series of General Rules, afterwards added to, for prevention of accidents. The eighth General Rule laid it down that no lamp or light other than a safety lamp should be allowed "in any place in a mine in which there is likely to be any such quantity of inflammable gas as to render the use of naked lights dangerous." It was clear that this General Rule had been infringed. Moreover, months earlier (in October 1889) the Inspector of Mines had called the attention of the colliery company to the need for its enforcement. Weeks had gone past and then on December 5th the director of the colliery company had concluded a letter to the Inspector with the words:

The increased wages for working with locked lamps, although amounting to 7½ per cent, shall not, of course, stand in the way when locked lamps become necessary, but at present we think the colliery is thoroughly well ventilated and safe to work with naked lights, and I anticipate you will, on your next visit, be of the same opinion. Very faithfully yours, E. Jones.

To this letter the Mines Inspector straightway replied on December 6th, 1889:

Allow me to point out that because naked lights have been in use in the past is no reason that their abolition should not be desirable in the future. The use of safety lamps is not in lieu of ventilation, but only a safeguard in such cases as may be exceptional, as Mr. Jones admits was the case on the occasion of the recent explosion at the colliery.

And to this the Inspector added an emphatic postscript:

P.S.—Under all circumstances I expect that the requirements of the 8th General Rule should be strictly complied with and enforced.

On the cause of these 176 deaths two months later the Coroner's jury had to give their verdict in accordance with the evidence. Was anyone to blame? And if so, would a prosecution follow? On this the jury held there was "not sufficient proof to attach culpable liability to anyone for the disaster, nor sufficient general probability of the explosion occurring from naked lights to hold anyone primarily responsible for the habitual use before the explosion." Nevertheless, they added a rider that "in future locked safety lamps of the very best description be used throughout the whole of the workings in the colliery."[1]

The Report of this 1890 Deputation was printed and circulated, as were the many other reports on accidents occurring throughout the 'nineties. At the Thirteenth Annual Conference, October 1901, a resolution was passed which relieved the Executive of the duty of sending deputations to each and every inquest where more than three had been killed, and empowered them in the case of explosions and other serious accidents to consider all cases on their merits, and determine whether "representatives shall be appointed to attend the inquest and make full enquiry into such case, and report to the first Board meeting." In practice, however, the Executive Committee did not limit itself thereafter to enquiry into colliery disasters only, but sent deputations when three men were killed if there appeared to be any circumstances which warranted an enquiry.

The result of this activity, carried on for the first twenty years (and also in the subsequent history of the Federation), was to build up a body of expert knowledge in the Executive Committee of the Federation, extending far beyond the experience sadly gained by each member of the Executive in his life as a working collier. No manager or coal-owner could afford to treat them lightly in this matter. Their watchful presence and their probing of witnesses when disaster happened was meant as a guard against the indif-

[1] An official of the National Union of Mineworkers writes:—"The section on the Llanerch explosion has a special interest for me, because my mother's father and two brothers were killed in that explosion. It also turned out that although I had worked in a number of slants or drifts, this was the first shaft I went down, which caused my mother many horrible moments. Many times she stopped me going to work (without any explanation) after a nightmare or some dream or other. But, of course, one had to work somewhere."

ference of an official overcome by the profit motive that drove the industry and against any laxity or complaisance on the part of a Home Office inspector. Together with local agents and secretaries they were a company of men to whom care for the lives and limbs of their members had become a primary duty.

2. THE WHITEHAVEN DISASTER

But when the first M.F.G.B. Special Conference of the year 1911[1] assembled at the end of January it met in a sombre atmosphere. They had just emerged from a year when more men had been killed in the mines than ever before. Had all their watchfulness at inquests and enquiries, all their recommendations to the owners and the authorities been of so little avail? No less than 1,818 miners had lost their lives in 1910. Of these, 501 had perished through explosions of fire-damp and coal dust, 658 through falls of ground, 286 through haulage accidents; and from each of these causes the deaths were at a higher figure than had been recorded since 1872. There had been two major colliery disasters: one an explosion of coal dust at Hulton in Lancashire whereby 344 were killed; the other an explosion of fire-damp at Whitehaven in Cumberland whereby 136 miners were killed. In the latter case there had been evidence of negligence as the Conference delegates were only too well aware from the public enquiry as well as from the report[2] of the Executive's Deputation.

The Wellington Pit on the shore at Whitehaven, 150 fathoms deep at the main shaft, had a main haulage road driven four miles due west under the sea with a dip of one inch per yard. Some of the farthest workings would be at 250 fathoms deep. On May 11, 1910, at about 7.40 p.m., a set of workmen at the end of their shift had arrived near the

[1] This year, in addition to the Annual Conference, there were seven Special Conferences.
[2] The Richards–Smith Report, from which all quotations in this section are taken. The full title is *Wellington Colliery, Whitehaven, Explosion and Underground Fire. Report to the Executive Committee of the Miners' Federation of Great Britain by Thomas Richards, M.P., and Herbert Smith.* Smith was afterwards fourth President, M.F.G.B., and Richards (in 1910 Secretary of the South Wales Miners' Federation) fifth President.

pit bottom and were walking towards the shaft when they felt the air becoming reversed and raising large clouds of dust behind them. They informed the under-manager, whom they found at the pit-top, that "something serious had taken place in the workings." The under-manager went down the pit, and along with one workman proceeded down the incline, leaving the bottom of the shaft at 7.45 p.m. They never reached the scene of the fire. "Without undue haste and going direct," says the report, "they could have been at the scene of the fire at 8.30 p.m." They arrived at a point between three or four hundred yards from it at nearly 10.30 p.m. Where had they been? How had they spent the time? "What they stated was that they were engaged with two workmen they discovered unconscious on the ground, performing artificial respiration upon them for more than an hour." Meantime over four score men in two districts of the mine were not being reached. Yet nearly two hours after the explosion "the workmen in the No. 5 District were alive and well" when two of their number left them at 9.30 p.m., and these two "were able to pass the fire at the friction gear at about 10 p.m., two hours and twenty minutes after the explosion."

By 10.30 p.m., the manager and a large number of officials and workmen arrived and attempts were made to reach the scene of the fire at the friction gear. Many made the attempt at the imminent risk of their lives. But by this time it was too late. The fire was gaining. Next day, May 12th, the heat had become so intense that H.M. Inspector of Mines, who had arrived in the afternoon, withdrew all employed from the shaft. That night it was decided it was now too dangerous to make any further attempt to reach the entombed work-men, and that air-tight stoppings should be put upon the intake and return airways to shut off the ventilation from the fire. This was done by mid-May and the workings remained thus sealed up till the end of September. The rest of the story may be told mainly in the words of the Richards–Smith report. This tells first how "the workmen expressed a strong desire that we should attend the re-opening of the colliery and accompany the exploring party." On September 29, 1910, they went down the shaft, together with two of

H.M. Inspectors of Mines, the manager, under-manager and other officials, a miners' agent and some workmen. They reached the scene of the explosion. Then they came to places where men had chalked up messages such as "All's well in this air-way at 4 o'clock,[1] 35 men and boys.—J. Moore." At this point was the air-way which conveyed the ventilation from the No. 6 District to the No. 5 District:

About 25 yards in this airway from the level, we found the 35 bodies of the workmen who, uninjured in any degree by the explosion, had been the victims of the appalling indifference and cruel neglect of any precautionary preparations at the collieries for dealing with the after effects of an explosion or fire. . . . It is perfectly clear that with but a very little organisation of those informed as to what to do and how to do it, even without any apparatus of any description, the lives of the 87 workmen of the No. 5 and 6 Districts would have been saved. . . .

Had the under-manager displayed ordinary intelligence and fore-thought in taking with him all the workmen available at the bottom of the shaft, eight in number, proceeded down the incline at a pace warranted by the circumstances, left a couple of their number to attend to the two workmen, who were only suffering from shock, and hurried on inbye, they could have extinguished the fire and easily have reached the No. 5 workmen before Weir and Kenmore left, and with but very little risk or danger rescued the No. 5 and No. 6 District workmen.

This was only the beginning of their sad task. It was at first impossible to get into the No. 3 District where the explosion of fire-damp had taken place, because of the quantities of gas. Day after day attempts were made until as the Report says:

Under considerable difficulty and risk we eventually made a complete examination of the whole district, having been engaged in the pit altogether for 23 days.

The M.F.G.B. Deputation called in the expert assistance of Professor Galloway,[2] one of the foremost mining engineers in the country. At the Joint Inquest and Enquiry opening on November 15, 1910 (the Chief Inspector of Mines joining the Coroner as provided for by the Coal Mines Regulation Act of 1887), Professor Galloway's evidence, which was

[1] Four p.m. of May 12th—more than twenty hours after the explosion.
[2] Sir William Galloway, author of the coal dust theory of colliery explosions and formerly one of H.M. Inspectors of Mines, died in November 1927.

mainly accepted by the Home Office officials, gives a very vivid picture of what happens in a pit explosion.[1]

The cause of the explosion of fire-damp was made clear. But why were there such quantities of gas? On this point the pit officials were subjected to a gruelling enough examination by the barrister representing the Home Office by the M.F.G.B. representatives and by the Coroner (and defended arduously but ineffectively by Mr. Rigby Swift, barrister for the coal-owners) from all of which it became clear there had been such a negligent attitude to gas as justified the statement in the Richards-Smith report:

We cannot too strongly denounce the reckless indifference displayed generally by the officials at this colliery to the danger of fire-damp and coal dust. From the reports of the deputies it was impossible for the Manager day by day to have correct knowledge as to the state of the workings of the colliery: and we have been appalled by the admission that work has been continued at this colliery in an atmosphere that might at any moment have been made an explosive mixture. To quote again Mr. Blair: "7 per cent is explosive. I do not see where the danger comes in so long as we keep below that."

Starting with a wrong calculation we have the Assistant Manager of several large collieries employing thousands of workmen satisfied that there is no danger in carrying on the ordinary work of the colliery with the ventilating current impregnated with fire-damp, but a few degrees removed from explosive point, with no margin of safety left, for sudden outburst of fire-damp, fall on the airways, sudden severe fall in the barometer, irregularity of the fan, or the fall in the goaf that they depend upon as the explanation of this explosion. The general practice appeared to have been not how far can we keep the workings from any source of danger, but how near can we approach that danger without a catastrophe.

It is scarcely necessary to go into detail in accounting for this explosion after the foregoing general description of this colliery.

Finally, Professor Galloway, after referring to a lamp with a badly cracked glass found by Mr. Herbert Smith as the likely source of the disaster[2] concluded with these words:

Nothing can be said in palliation of the state of affairs shown to have existed before the explosion. The safety of the men, which must

---

[1] See Appendix to this chapter.

[2] Nearly forty years later there was again a disaster at Whitehaven and by a remarkable enough coincidence it was once again the trade union representatives (in this case Mr. Abe Moffatt, President of the Scottish Miners, and Mr. Alwyn Machen, of Yorkshire) who discovered the immediate cause of the explosion.

RESCUER RETURNING FROM DISASTER

TESTING FOR GAS

be the paramount consideration in all mining operations, imperatively demands the absence of explosive gas from the neighbourhood in which they are at work; and a return to conditions the same as or similar to those which formerly obtained in this mine must, by some means or other, be made absolutely impossible in the future.

It may be imagined what effect the tale of this and other disasters had upon the miners and their representatives. But all that the Conference delegates could hope for as they mourned their dead was the effectiveness of new legislation. All their lives they had striven for "a better Mines Act." They had heard from their fathers of the stirrings of an earlier generation. To the history of this struggle we must now turn.

3. MINING LEGISLATION UP TO 1850

Before 1800 there were Acts of Parliament dealing with miners, but not with their conditions of work. Between 1800 and 1842 the extremely rapid growth of the industry multiplied and made more conspicuous the risk run by the miners. Workings became deeper, colliery disasters happened more often and took a terrible toll of the mining community. In the coal-fields wives and mothers lived in a constant state of dread. The scientist Sir Humphry Davy, brought into consultation, devised improvements in the existing safety lamp which thereafter came to be called the Davy lamp. But the widespread use of the "Davy" did not meet expectations. The mines were driven deeper and operations were carried on with a recklessness greater than before. Evidence was given in 1829 before a Select Committee of the House of Commons that the loss of life had increased since the introduction of the Davy lamp.[1] Another Select Committee, appointed in 1835 "to enquire into the nature, cause, and extent of those lamentable catastrophes which have occurred in the mines of Great Britain, with the view of ascertaining and suggesting the means of preventing the

---

[1] "The inventors had provided the miner with a weapon of defence; armed with it he was led forward to meet fresh perils. They had sought to bring security of life: they achieved an increase in the output of coal. . . . How far the labours of Davy and Stephenson fall short of fulfilling the high expectations that were aroused in 1815 is amply demonstrated on almost every coalfield of our own day."—*The Coal Industry of the Eighteenth Century* by T. S. Ashton and J. Sykes (1929).

recurrence of similar fatal accidents," suggested better systems of ventilation; safety lamps; and accurate plans of the entire workings. The Select Committee was also in favour of education for miners, of visits to the mines by distinguished scientific and philanthropic persons, and of owners not neglecting their responsibilities. No recommendations, however, were made as to legislation, and the Committee in concluding their enquiry expressed the fear that they had "in great measure failed in devising adequate remedies for the painful calamities they had to investigate." In fact there was little attempt at ameliorative legislation until the pitmen themselves began to send forth "a voice from the coal-mines." The public concern over colliery disasters, though genuine enough on each occasion, was fleeting: but concern in the ruling circles over the growth first of trade unionism and then of Chartism was more grave—and more lasting. It was at the height of the Chartist agitation and in the year after the Chartist rising in Monmouthshire that Lord Shaftesbury was moved to bring forward his motion which resulted in the famous Royal Commission (1840–42) to enquire "into the employment of children of the poorer classes in mines and collieries." The Report[1] and the reports of the sub-commissioners for the various coal-fields revealed conditions that exceeded the most dismal surmises. Not only children under ten years of age, but mere infants were taken down the pit. These last cases were indeed exceptional, but as the Commissioners said in their summary of conclusions:

Instances occur in which children are taken into these mines to work as early as four years of age, sometimes at five, and between five and six, not infrequently between six and seven, and often from seven to eight, while from eight to nine is the ordinary age at which employment in these mines commences.

The Report of the Royal Commission showed "a state of things not only disgraceful but perilous to the country," said Lord Shaftesbury on June 7, 1842, as he presented his measure to forbid the labour of women underground or of boys below ten years of age. A different view was taken by the Marquis of Londonderry who fought the Bill tooth and nail: "the measure," he said, "might be regarded as the commencement

[1] See *The Miners*, by R. Page Arnot (1949), Chapter I.

of a series of grievances which would be got up for the purpose of working upon that hypocritical humanity which reigned so much." This was too much for the Bishop of Gloucester who in the House of Lords, on July 14, 1842, asked Lord Londonderry to withdraw the words "hypocritical humanity." But the most noble Marquis, who had stated that "some seams of coal required the employment of women," was not thus to be put down by his spiritual peer: he continued his opposition to the last, and the Bill was returned to the Commons House so altered as to be, in the words of Lord Shaftesbury, "invalidated in principle and made inoperative." The Bill became law on August 10, 1842.

This Act of 1842 prohibited the employment underground of females and of males under the age of ten, the payment of wages in public-houses and the care of winding-engines by persons under fifteen years of age. "None but the most glaring abuses which clearly required reform was suppressed," wrote a mining engineer,[1] "but even this fragment of legislation met with the disapprobation of colliery owners." He adds that, on the other hand, "the measure was received almost with indifference by the colliers . . . the measure, in fact, did not touch many of the grievances under which the colliery populations had been suffering for a long period." In addition that year wages were lowered and many were discharged. The discontent, ascribed to the influence of Chartism,[2] led in the autumn and winter of 1842 to disturbances, which were suppressed by the use of soldiers, while a special commission was set up to try "the ring-leaders." Once the strikes and disturbances had been quelled a coal-owners' move to reintroduce female labour underground was brought up in the House of Commons (in February 1843), but the 114 votes for this proposal left its sponsors in a minority.

[1] Coal Pits and Pitmen, by R. N. Boyd (1892), p. 74.
[2] R. N. Boyd, op. cit., writes: "Meantime the opportunity was seized by the Chartists to spread their doctrines, while fomenting a spirit of discontent among the unsettled working population. . . . The colliers were not exempt from the excitement, and strikes and riots took place in many of the districts, but notably in the Midland counties, where the hungry and unoccupied colliers became easy converts to the new principles at the bidding of the ranting demagogues who came among them in search of proselytes. Not that the colliers were ever enthusiastic Chartists, in a political sense, for they were too ignorant to understand the meaning of the doctrines preached to them. The Chartism of the colliers consisted in a desire to have their grievances remedied; and the Chartist leaders had adopted the device of dilating on these topics, and promising them a speedy remedy as soon as the new political faith should have been adopted by the country. Some of the complaints were reasonable and just."

The miners, however, now kept sending in petitions to Parliament while they were joining in great numbers the Miners' Association of Great Britain and Ireland headed by Martin Jude. After the great strike of 1844,[1] this activity continued. For example the petition presented to the House of Commons in April 1847 by T. S. Duncombe, Member for Finsbury, "HUMBLY SHEWETH,—That your petitioners are COLLIERS, working in the Coal-Mines" of England, Wales and Scotland with the following submissions (partly summarised):

1. "To direct the attention of your Honourable House to the many deaths continually happening from bad ventilation in the mines, and also to the distressing accidents . . . [which] unfortunately for your petitioners do not come before the public unless they occasion death." Here follow instances of the neglect causing accidents of this kind; and a statement that "many of your petitioners have been neglectful and over-confident; but they are many of them very poor, and their position with their masters does not often allow them to speak freely of facts as they really are."

2. "That Inspectors should be appointed to visit all the mines, and that some of these Inspectors should be men practically acquainted with colliery work. . . . That penalties of One Hundred Pounds at the least, should be inflicted in case of any deviation from the orders of such Inspector. . . . Your petitioners submit that small fines in these cases are not felt and are no use whatever. . . ."

3. "Your petitioners submit to your Honourable House that the appointment of Inspectors would not only ensure a better system of ventilation, but would also remove or lessen many other causes of death—such as roofs falling—water rushing in—defective chains and engines. These and many other instances of want of due caution would become much less frequent if proper Inspectors were appointed to visit the mines, and were invested with sufficient power to enforce a compliance with their directions; such Inspectors giving no notice of their intention to visit the mines, and at all times going there when they were not expected. . . ."

4. "Your petitioners have observed with much satisfaction the laws compelling the masters in factories to provide some amount of education for the children who work there, and your petitioners submit to your Honourable House that a similar plan would be of great use to the children of colliers. . . . As the colliers are placed— and your Honourable House will, on consideration, see the truth of this assertion—the difficulty of obtaining education for their children is much greater than ever it was for the parents of factory children."

[1] See *The Miners*, Chapter I.

5. "Many accidents occur in the mines from persons being entrusted with the care of the engines who have served no regular apprenticeship." The conclusion is that an engine-man should be adult, apprenticed for three years and the holder of a certificate after examination by an Inspector.

6. "Your petitioners ask your Honourable House to inquire into the truck system and the manner in which the law made for the purpose of putting down that system is evaded. . . ."

7. "To make a law that wages should be paid every week, or at not greater intervals than once a fortnight. . . ."

8. "That the colliers should be paid for their work by weight and not by measure . . . and that coals be weighed by beams and scales."

The feelings of the colliers at this time on the north-east coast was expressed in rough verses by a local poet:[1]

> Think on us hinnies, if you please,
> An' it war but to show yor pity;
> For a' the toils and tears it gi'es
> To warm the shins o' Lunnun City.
>
> The fiery "blast" cuts short wor lives,
> And steeps wor hyems in deep distress;
> Myeks widows o' wor canny wives
> And a' wor bairns leaves faitherless.
>
> The wait'ry "wyest," mair dreadful still,
> Alive oft barries huz belaw;
> Oh dear! it myeks wor blood run chill,
> May we sic mis'ry nivver knaw.
>
> To be cut off frae kith and kin,
> The leet o' day te see ne mair,
> And left, frae help and hope shut in,
> To pine and parish in despair.
>
> If ye could on'y tyek a view,
> And see the sweet frae off us poorin'—
> The daily dangers we gan through,
> The daily hardships we're endurin!
>
> Ye wad send doon, aw ha'e ne doubt,
> Some chaps on what they call a "mission,"
> To try if they could ferret out
> Somethin' to better wor condition.

[1] Quoted in Fynes' *History of the Northumberland and Durham Miners*, p. 122.

T. S. Duncombe, M.P., followed up the presentation of the petition of the Miners' Association of Great Britain by bringing in two successive Bills on the subject in the summer of 1847. Each was rejected: but the need of inspection underground was being brought to the fore. The Government, though withstanding these Bills, was now being subjected to considerable pressure, which mounted on each occasion of a disaster. After the explosion at the Haswell Colliery in the Durham-Northumberland coal-field by which ninety-five lives were lost on September 28, 1844, a petition from the men drawn up by W. P. Roberts, the Chartist legal adviser of the Miners' Association of Great Britain, had been sent to the Home Secretary; and on this urgent appeal and in view of the great loss of life the Government commissioned the great scientist Michael Faraday and Professor Lyell, the geologist, to enquire into and report upon the cause of the accident. According to one chronicler "the appointment of the two professors caused almost as great a sensation amongst colliery-owners and viewers as the accident itself," and when their report was issued Faraday and Lyell were "criticised in pamphlets and newspaper articles in a tone more or less adverse to scientific suggestions in a matter so practical as coal-mining."[1] But work of fundamental value was carried out when these two scientists, together with Sir Lyon Playfair and Sir Henry de la Beche (afterwards Chief of the Geological Survey), acted as Commissioners of Enquiry into a series of colliery disasters and published the first scientific reports on causes and remedies.

Thus with the pressure mounting throughout the 'forties from the Miners' Association of Great Britain and reinforced by numerous petitions, by recommendations of men of science and by reports of departmental and parliamentary committees, the Government at last yielded. The principle of inspection of coal-mines was conceded by the Act of 1850.

This was quite different from what had been called "inspection" in the 1842 Act, wherein were provisions for the appointment of "Inspectors" to visit mines and collieries (but not to go underground) and to report from time to time to the Home Office. The first of these was Mr. Seymour

Tremenheere. His reports for a period of some sixteen years have been treated as a main source of information on the moral and material conditions of the mining population. Tremenheere gave full emphasis in his reports to the activities of "model employers," especially educational work. He cited one colliery in the West Riding where the members of a musical society composed of the younger generation of miners had become "able to sing with correctness and expression selections from the compositions of Handel, Haydn, Mozart, Spohr, etc.," and he added "Some of the collier boys may be heard as they pass through the village singing and whistling the beautiful airs from the works of these Masters." This, however, as Tremenheere admits, was exceptional; in general the material and moral conditions are described as unsatisfactory. They were intensified by the truck system still largely found in the Midlands in spite of its prohibition in an Act of 1831; by the butty system; by fraudulent weighing; and long intervals between wage payments. Tremenheere was bitterly opposed to trade unions. In one report he says:

The strike of 1844 was organised by delegates of the miners' union. The object of their union was to stop all the manufactories in the kingdom until they could secure the rate of wages they demanded. The colliers were under the instigation of the Chartist delegates, Local Preachers—chiefly Primitive Methodists or Ranters—and showed a strong disposition to violence.

It appears that Tremenheere relied chiefly for his information on colliery officials. The miners were well aware of his bias. Martin Jude, founder in 1842 of the Miners' Association, writes:

Tremenheere did not come to get a correct report, or at all events if he did, he had not gone the way to get one. Instead of taking evidence from all parties, he only went among the petty officials who had been raised up into situations, some of them from working men, and who were now cutting high capers over the poor miners; the commissioner was shown over the houses these little bodies were then living in, taken to the colliery office, and courteously escorted to the station by the officials; but the men were not in any single instance consulted. He took it for granted, that all the agents told him was true, and as such presented it to Her Majesty's Secretary of State for the Home Department, perhaps to form the basis of future legislation for all he knew or cared.[1]

[1] Fynes, *op. cit.*, Chapter XXVII.

While Tremenheere continued to make reports on moral and material conditions, the principle of a true Inspectorate was at last laid down in the new Act of 1850 "to provide for the Inspection of Coal Mines in Great Britain." This Act, described by the Marquis of Londonderry as "the most mischievous and unjust measure that could possibly be imagined," gave the inspectors powers to go underground and imposed penalties for obstruction by mine-owners, who were required to provide and exhibit accurate plans to inspectors. The Act also required colliery proprietors, under penalty of £10 to £20 fine, to notify fatal accidents[1] within twelve hours to the Secretary of State. This last provision indicates that there must have been some amongst the coal-owners who could now echo the words of Hamlet's uncle:

> . . . we have done but greenly,
> In hugger-mugger to inter him.

4. MINES ACTS AFTER 1850

The sixty years from 1850 to 1910 were seen in the memory of the older miners as one long history of struggle for "a better Mines Act." While the coal trade was growing at unexampled speed, the colliers from their lodges and then from their County Associations were striving for the aims set by the earlier unions in Chartist days. The "voice from the coal-mines" was heard in meetings and demonstrations, in petitions to Parliament and deputations to ministers. Evidence was given to Select Committees of the House of Commons and before successive Royal Commissions: and gradually measures of change were won—but only in the teeth of bitter opposition from the coal-owners.

The Act of 1850 had done little more than establish the principle of underground inspection. Ill-received by colliery owners, it soon became a dead letter. But colliery disasters led to the appointment in 1852 of a Select Committee of the House of Commons. Its recommendation for doubling the number of inspectors, from six to twelve, did not satisfy the

---

[1] Coroners were bidden under the Act to give two days' notice of inquests. Before 1815 it had not been considered necessary to hold inquests on colliers killed in the pit.

workmen, who continued the agitation for more inspectors, with greater powers and chosen from their own class. It was clear that at this time they had little confidence in the colliery officers, who had only too often exhibited ignorance and incapacity, as was shown by the disclosures made at inquests. The disquieting increase in the death-roll in mines led to another Select Committee in 1853 which took much evidence and reported in 1854 in such terms as influenced the Home Secretary, Lord Palmerston, who had backed the Act of 1842. Earlier, in his reply to a deputation of workmen's delegates on July 26, 1853 (there were also at this time frequent demonstrations in the coal-fields and many petitions to Parliament or to the Home Secretary), Lord Palmerston indicated that a measure would be introduced. Accordingly an Act was passed in 1855 "to amend the law for the inspection of coal-mines in Great Britain." Seven General Rules to be observed at collieries, as suggested by a conference of coal-owners, were set out; and these, together with Special Rules that might be made for particular collieries, were required to be posted in a conspicuous place in every mine. The number of inspectors was increased from six to twelve and the country divided into twelve Inspection Districts. The penalties for breach of the Act were of a double kind. Owners on conviction paid £5 and thereafter were liable to be fined £1 per day until the law had been complied with, after notice of breach of its provisions had been called to their attention by an inspector. Workmen were liable not only to a fine of £2 but "to be imprisoned, with or without hard labour, in the jail or house of correction for any period not exceeding three calendar months" if they neglected or ignored any of the Special Rules set up at any colliery.

"The Act of 1855 may not improperly be denominated a master's measure."[1] This sentence, from a pen uniformly hostile to trade unionism, was justified not only by these discriminatory penalties. In its application, some coal-owners included in their sets of rules under the Act such matters as the price of labour power or even penal provisions against colliers who did not "attend Divine service at least once on the Lord's Day." Protest strikes compelled the cancellation

---

[1] R. N. Boyd, *op. cit.*

of obnoxious Special Rules: and all the more therefore the aroused colliers at the same time pressed for a better Mines Act. They demanded more inspectors with greater powers; that coals wrought should be paid for by weight and not by measure; and that a Minister of Mines should be created. Alexander McDonald was now carrying on his agitation amongst the miners with great effect. The Act of 1855 was due to expire after five years and when in the spring of 1860 a Bill for a new measure was brought in, there were sent up to Parliament no less then twenty-five petitions in support, signed by over 300,000 colliers. In this Bill there was an education clause. This in particular was opposed in counter-petitions by the colliery owners, who also made a determined attack in the Commons Committee. There they were defeated: but in the House of Lords they succeeded in mutilating the Bill. "The House of Commons," said Mr. Clive, "had carefully considered the clauses of the Bill for sixteen hours, and the whole of their work was undone by the House of Lords in sixteen minutes."

The chief provisions of this Act of 1860 "for the Regulation and Inspection of Mines," which repealed the Act of 1842 except as regards the employment of women underground, were (a) General Rules (now fifteen in number) for better ventilation, care of safety lamps, regulation of haulage and winding; (b) greater powers to inspectors; (c) educational certificates for boys under twelve years of age; and (d) true weighing. It was provided that where persons engaged in mining were paid by weight, the material gotten by them should be duly weighed at the pit bank; and further, they were empowered to appoint a person at their own charge to take account thereof.

Two years later the terrible disaster occurred at the Hartley Colliery, by which 204 lives were lost through lack of an up-cast shaft. An Act was passed immediately making it unlawful to work a mine without two outlets.

No law affecting mines was passed in the next ten years although colliery disasters unprecedented in number and magnitude occurred. Amongst these was the explosion on December 12, 1866, at the Oaks Colliery in Yorkshire whereby 361 lives were lost, and the explosion on November 8, 1867, at Ferndale, in Glamorgan, by which 176 lives were lost. The Miners' National Union, founded in 1863 for the purpose of gaining legislative changes, organised a petition to Parliament in 1864. This led to the appointment in 1864 of a Select Committee of the House of Commons. The Select Committee was not in agreement with the Miners' National Union on many of its demands (such as, that inspectors should be drawn from the same class as the miners; or that a proportion of the Coroner's Jury inquiring into fatal accidents in mines should be working miners) but, after sitting through three parliamentary sessions, they recommended in 1867 that the age limit should be raised, that the provisions against truck should be made more stringent, and that weights and measures used at collieries should come under the survey of the Inspector of Weights and Measures, together with a number of other suggestions. Nothing was done immediately by the Disraeli administration, but during the Gladstone administration from December 1868 onwards, the Government introduced Bills in three successive years. Each Bill was hotly contested by the mine-owners, who objected to a number of provisions and particularly those on weighing and checkweighing, as well as to the appointment of additional inspectors. The Bills had each in turn to be withdrawn, but the agitation led by Alexander McDonald continued: and at last in 1872 a new law was made. By this Coal Mines Regulation Act the principle was established that in future all coals (except in special circumstances) were to be paid by weight, and the system of checkweighing was extended and placed on a sounder basis. The interests of employers, however, were protected by a provision that deductions might be made where tubs of coal were sent up mixed with "dirt" or "dross" (in most coal-fields the fullest advantage has always been taken of this provision). Other provisions increased the General Rules to thirty-one in number, including a requirement that for the future all mine-managers must hold a Certificate of Competency under the Act, to be granted after examination by Boards appointed by the Secretary of State. Powers were given to enquire into cases of negligence or incompetence, with cancellation of certificates. The Act was followed by the appointment of sub-inspectors, which enabled inspection of mines to be more frequent and more thorough. Of this Act Thomas Burt, Secretary of the Northumberland Miners' Mutual Confident Association, took a very favourable view and in a letter where he paid tribute to the ability of McDonald, he wrote:

Never before in the history of British legislation did any section of the working classes so thoroughly leave their impression on an Act of Parliament. All the chief principles sought for by the miners they have gained. What is the secret of this success? . . . They have succeeded because they have looked after their own business; they have sent their own representatives, and have not trusted others to look after their affairs. . . . No class of working men are better united than the miners, none are more public-spirited, and they have certainly brought the power of their unions to bear on this question . . . one voice, demanding in tones clear and strong, that the life of the miner should be protected. The splendid meetings held within a few weeks of each other at Stirling, Blyth, Durham, Barnsley, Leeds, and other places, were evidence of a power which no government could afford to despise or ignore.

But how little this new Act availed to end the dreadful tale of colliery disasters was shown five years later by "The Blantyre Calamity," the most serious explosion ever known in the Scottish coal-fields. Yet it was only one of a series of disastrous colliery explosions, and this despite the operation of the new General Rules. Widespread scientific interest was aroused and there was considerable public discussion stimulated largely by the growing influence of the trade unions. As a result of this public discussion and of much criticism of the administration of the 1872 Act, a Royal Commission, with Thomas Burt, now an M.P., as one of its members, was appointed in 1879 to enquire into accidents in mines. An interim report in 1881 was followed by five more years of enquiry, and in 1886 the Royal Commission issued its final report. They had had to take into account amongst disasters caused by explosions the following which had occurred before they were appointed:

Date	Colliery	Killed
Dec. 6, 1875	Swaith Main, Yorks	143
Oct. 2, 1877	Blantyre, Lanarkshire	207
June 7, 1878	Haydock Wood Pit, Lancaster	189
Sep. 11, 1878	Abercarn, Monmouth	268

During the course of enquiry, there were the following principal disasters causing loss of life of over one hundred on each occasion:

Date	Colliery	Killed
July 15, 1880	Risca, Monmouth	120
Sept. 8, 1880	Seaham, Durham	164
Dec. 10, 1880	Naval Steam Coal, Glamorgan	101
June 9, 1885	Clifton Hall, Trencherbone Seam, Lancaster	178

The final report of the Commissioners contained a comprehensive statement of existing knowledge on the subject of mine gas, and on the subject of the dangerous properties of coal dust which by a series of elaborate experiments they proved could cause or propagate explosions. They recommended the use of high explosives as opposed to gunpowder and electric shot-firing; and in their suggestions for ambulance work and central stations for rescue work they were far ahead of contemporary legislators. An Act was passed of a temporary nature in 1886 which provided that the checkweigher need not be in the employment of the coal-owner, and adjusted the law on inquests upon persons killed in mines. This Act, together with the Act of 1872, was repealed by the Coal Mines Regulation Act of 1887, which was to remain in force for another quarter of a century. It forbade the employment of boys underground below the age of twelve and regulated their employment between the ages of twelve and sixteen. The checkweighing provisions were extended, and though not yet made entirely satisfactory to the miners were considerably improved. The Certificates of Competency were divided into two classes; eight new General Rules were added, one of which raised the minimum age for winding-enginemen from eighteen to twenty-two. A provision in the Act of 1886 for special Courts of Enquiry into accidents, to be set up by the Secretary of State, was re-enacted.

The Acts for the next twenty years were of subordinate importance. In 1891 a further Royal Commission was appointed specially for the purpose of enquiring "into the effect of coal dust in originating and extending explosions in mines, whether by itself or in conjunction with fire-damp"; and also into "any practicable means of preventing or mitigating" such dangers. The Commission reported in 1894 and was followed two years later by the Coal Mines Regulation Act of 1896 which empowered the Secretary of State to issue Special Rules on such questions as explosives, safety lamps, plans of mines whether at work or abandoned, etc. Since then, the Home Office for many years issued a series of Explosives in Coal Mines Orders. This is an early example of that "delegated legislation" which was later to become usual enough, and against which Lord Chief Justice Hewart, a generation later, was to issue his fulminations: echoes of these have been heard in Parliament from 1945 onwards.

Still another measure was passed in 1894 "to amend the provisions of the Coal Mines Regulation Act, 1887, with respect to checkweighers," providing penalties for any interference with the election of checkweighers. This short Act was necessary because of the resentment with which a whole generation of coal-owners viewed the system of checkweighing. Eleven years later the Coal Mines (Weighing of Minerals) Act, 1905, provided for the appointment of deputy checkweighers and regulated the method of their election.

The Mines (Prohibition of Child Labour Underground) Act of 1900, raising the age to thirteen, completed the list of statutes which during the long reign of Victoria had gradually and partially ameliorated some of the conditions of child labour in mines.

5. THE ROYAL COMMISSION ON MINES

The unremitting attention paid by the Miners' Federation of Great Britain to the need for increased safety in coal-mines, carried on persistently for fifteen years, had a considerable effect on the Home Office. Not for a moment was the Home Secretary allowed to forget the demands of the Miners' Federation of Great Britain, while Parliament more and more became a sounding board which roused echoes through the country. The growth in the number of miners' representatives gave a further impetus to the parliamentary fight, and to the feeling that was being aroused in every coal-field as well as amongst the people of the country as a whole. Matters were raised in Parliament as well as through every other available channel. The great increase in the January 1906 election in the number of mining M.P.s also had its effect. Vast though the scope had been of the Royal Commission of 1879 to 1886, the increase in scientific knowledge as well as the increased power of the workers underground to have their grievances and difficulties examined, had made it desirable to have yet another full examination of the problem. Accordingly in the summer of 1906 the Chairman and Treasurer and one other member of the Executive Committee of the M.F.G.B. found themselves upon a new Royal Commission.

The Commissioners, appointed June 7, 1906, "under His Majesty's Royal Sign Manual" were: Baron Monkswell, Chairman; Sir Lindsay Wood; Henry Hardinge Samuel Cunynghame, Assistant Under-Secretary at the Home Office; William Abraham; Frederick Lewis Davis, Chairman of the South Wales Conciliation Board; Enoch Edwards; Thomas Ratcliffe Ellis, Secretary of the Mining Association of Great Britain; Dr. John Scott Haldane, Fellow of the Royal Society; and Robert Smillie, President of the Lanarkshire Miners' Union.

Their task, as set forth in formal wording, "Whereas We have deemed it expedient that a Commission should forthwith issue to inquire into and report on certain questions relating to the health and safety of miners, and the administration of the Mines Acts, namely:—" covered such questions as compulsory watering of the roads in dry and dusty mines; the forms of safety lamp; the better prevention of accidents; the work of rescue; the present system of investigation and enquiry into accidents; a standard of ventilation; the disease known as ankylostomiasis (miners' worm); the adequacy of the administration of the Mines Acts; examination for Managers' and Under-Managers' Certificates of Competency; "and whether certificates granted by Colonial Governments should not be accepted in this country." It ended with the usual formula:

Now KNOW YE that We, reposing great trust and confidence in your knowledge and ability have authorised and appointed, and do by these Presents authorise and appoint you, . . . to be our Commissioners for the purposes of the said inquiry.

AND for the better effecting the purposes of this Our Commission, We do by these Presents give and grant unto you, or any three or more of you, full power to call before you such persons as you shall judge likely to afford you any information upon the subject of this Our Commission.

From the composition of the Commission it will be seen that an endeavour was made to secure changes in the law with the maximum agreement of both coal-owners and coal-miners. The same intention was carried out in the detailed examination of no less than 134 witnesses over a period of three years, including 57 representatives of the workmen, 35 of the coal-owners, and 8 representatives of the National Association of Colliery Managers. Members of the Commission visited France and Germany to obtain comparisons with safety methods used in those countries. A whole series of experiments was carried out at the request of the Commission and in some of these no conclusion was reached (e.g. on the question of watering the mines to deal with coal dust) until further experiments could be made: that is to say, the utmost care was observed in reaching conclusions on the part of the scientific member of the Commission.

One of the first questions tackled was the adequacy of inspection. In the four volumes of evidence striking examples were given on point after point on which the miners themselves gave their reasons why inspection was not adequate. The Home Office evidence, and that of several of the twelve inspectors, showed that inspection only took place "by sample," and was not a complete and thorough examination of all the underground workings of a mine. For example, Tom Richards, M.P., from South Wales, said:

We have several seams being worked in the same mine and it is possible for things to be alright in one seam, whereas they might be quite contrary in the other. I think it gives a false sense of security to both workmen and owners that Inspectors should visit a colliery in this way, because they may base their calculations that everything is alright on the inspection, whereas the Inspector is only inspecting a very small portion of the colliery.

J. G. Hancock of Nottingham said, "I cannot admit that inspecting a certain area and accepting that as a criterion of the whole colliery is satisfactory, reliable, or safe." Similar

WHITEHAVEN A HUNDRED YEARS AGO

CASTLE COLLIERY, WHITEHAVEN

views about the "sample system" were given by John Wilson, M.P., Durham, Harry Twist of Lancashire, and by representatives from Yorkshire and Scotland. On the other hand, the representatives of the owners and managers were agreed in thinking that inspection "by sample" was the only practicable method and was sufficiently effective. To them it appeared the cheapest method and the one that interfered least with the ordinary routine of the pit.

The same difference arose on the question of frequency of inspection. The question of examination of mines on behalf of the workmen by persons appointed directly by the workmen caused much discussion. This provision of the 1887 Act had, it appeared, been largely a dead letter. The Commission recommended an increase in the staff of Government Inspectors and an improvement in their qualifications. But they disagreed with the three mining members who wished the French system to be adopted, by which safety delegates were elected from the workmen employed for a period of several years and were, during this period, paid directly by the Government from moneys contributed by the mine-owners.

Connected with the question of safety was the question of qualifications of firemen or deputies on which Miners' Federation witnesses gave evidence that these were often not high enough. The Commission recommended that no one should be eligible for this post unless over twenty-five years of age, with five years' practical experience and possessed of a Certificate from a Mining School.

On accidents in coal-mines, the Commission, starting with the evidence afforded by mortality tables that the "occupation of a coal-miner is healthy but dangerous," recorded a striking decrease in the death rate by accidents from 1851 onwards. For underground accidents only, the death rate per thousand was reduced from $5 \cdot 149$ to $1 \cdot 473$ during the fifty years from 1851 to 1900.

How did this compare with the accident rate in the nearest coal-producing countries in Europe and with the U.S.A.? The Commission found that the British figures were higher than those of France and Belgium, but lower than those of Germany and far lower than those of the United States where under an almost uncontrolled "free private enterprise," the death rate from accidents in coal-mines was rising.

This is seen from the following table:

COMPARATIVE DEATH RATES FROM ACCIDENTS PER 1,000 PERSONS EMPLOYED

Year	Great Britain	France	Belgium	Germany	U.S.A.
1897	1·34	1·07	1·03	2·25	2·40
1898	1·28	1·07	1·40	2·87	2·61
1899	1·26	1·29	0·97	2·21	3·07
1900	1·30	1·42	1·05	2·19	3·29
1901	1·36	1·21	1·02	2·22	3·10
1902	1·24	1·09	1·07	1·93	3·26
1903	1·27	1·02	1·14	2·00	3·11
1904	1·24	1·07	0·93	1·90	3·35
1905	1·35	1·04	0·91	2·05	3·37
1906	1·29	7·17*	0·95	1·88	3·21
Persons employed in 1906	882,345	178,431	139,394	569,745	640,780

* This high figure is accounted for by the Courrières disaster.

But the accident rate in the United Kingdom was still much too high and the Commission conducted painstaking and complicated investigations into all matters that seemed then to bear upon the health and safety of miners. The Coal Mines Act of 1911, which followed hard upon the final report of the Commission, passed through Parliament with less opposition than usual and still governs the industry. Its provisions (in four parts and nearly a hundred sections— too elaborate and detailed to be summarised here) made it at the time the most advanced ameliorative mining law in Europe or America. It was a far cry from the meagre provisions of the 1850 Act to this most extensive detailed and technical state regulation of the daily working of a great industry.

This elaborate Act was in itself a magnificent tribute to the work of the Miners' Federation and to the unity of the miners which made it possible for the leaders to carry on in the country and in the House of Commons the campaign that was responsible for bringing it into being. It was the reward of twenty years of mounting agitation. It marked a great step forward.

It is, however, one thing to secure the passage of an Act of Parliament; it is quite another to ensure its proper administration, or the full functioning of its provisions, including the imposition of penalties for breaches of the Act. This truism was to be tragically exemplified a few months after the Act came finally into operation.

6. SENGHENYDD

The Coal Mines Act had been passed in 1911. Two years later there occurred at the Senghenydd Pit, in Glamorgan, the worst explosion in the history of coal-mining in Britain. On October 14, 1913, no less than 439 lives were lost in this pit. It was a pit in which previously (1901) there had been an explosion with considerable loss of life because of the gaseous nature of the seams. As late as 1910 there had been an outburst of gas which was not got under control for four days and it had been necessary to withdraw men from the pit. It was thus known to be amongst the more dangerous mines in this country. In spite of this the owners or their agent, who was also the manager, had taken no special precautions. More than that, he had not even taken the minimum precautions enjoined on all managements by the 1911 Act. The Court of Enquiry[1] set up by the Home Secretary (but only after repeated representations from the Executive Committee of the Miners' Federation of Great Britain) was unable to fix with complete certainty the cause of the explosion. But it was able to show that the provisions of the 1911 Act had not been carried out in a number of important respects as well as in a number of lesser matters. "The Report of the Enquiry," wrote Jevons at the time,[2] "bristles with evidence of infractions of the Act." The failure to provide apparatus by which direction of the currents of air throughout the mine could be immediately reversed was probably responsible for a large number of the deaths; for had this apparatus

[1] Reports to the Secretary of State for the Home Department on the Causes of and Circumstances attending the Explosion which occurred at the Senghenydd Colliery on Tuesday, October 14, 1913, by R. A. S. Redmayne, C.B., H.M. Chief Inspector of Mines (Commissioner) and Evan Williams (Chairman, S. Wales and Monmouth Coalowners' Ass.), and Robert Smillie, President, M.F.G.B. (Assessors)—(Cd. 7346).
[2] H. S. Jevons, *The British Coal Trade* (1915).

been installed, some of the miners who had been cut off by the fire that broke out after the explosion from the intake air-current, could have got fresh air. Again, the coal dust had not been dealt with properly, a matter of which the Chief Inspector of Coal Mines took a most serious view at the enquiry. On one matter, the question of the danger of unprotected electrical signalling apparatus, a special circular had been sent out by the Home Office some months earlier; on this, too, the owners had taken no steps. Not only were there these serious failures to carry out the Act, but it almost seemed on certain points as though there had been no intention to carry out the Act. For example, under the Act means of reversing the air-current should have been provided by January 1, 1913, which was already more than twelve months after the passing of the Act. This had not been done. Moreover, in April 1913 the manager applied for an extension of time. This led to correspondence and a visit from a Sub-Inspector for the mine. Eventually an extension of time was granted, up to September 30th, by which time the apparatus should have been installed. When the explosion occurred a fortnight later, no work had even begun for installing the apparatus. No wonder that Commissioner Redmayne referred in his report to "disquieting laxity in the management of the mine."

On behalf of the Home Office, the Divisional Mines Inspector for Wales prosecuted the owners and the manager of Senghenydd Colliery for breaches of the Act. There were four charges against the company and seventeen against the manager, of which seven were dropped. The case was tried by three of the local magistrates. They immediately acquitted the company of all charges; they dismissed several of the charges against the manager, including the charge that coal dust had not been systematically cleared, a matter on which the Chief Inspector took a very grave view. On the most serious charges, (i) that he had failed to provide a means of reversing the air-current, the sentence was £10 or one month's imprisonment; and (ii) that he had failed to make a daily report on conditions as to coal dust, the manager was fined £5 or fourteen days. On other failures, or rather breaches of the law, he had to pay fines of £5 and £2. Altogether, there were convictions on five charges: and total fines so small that the local Labour paper headed its report "MINERS' LIVES AT 1S. 1¼d. EACH."

If indignation had been roused in the coal-fields by the knowledge that the appalling loss of life in this disaster could have been prevented had the law been carried out by the coal-owners and their agent, it was nothing to the wide-spread fury that followed the announcement of this verdict and sentence. It was felt immediately that the local magistracy were exhibiting the same partiality as had been notorious in the first half of the nineteenth century. The Home Office took measures to appeal against two of the decisions of the magistrates, in which they had dismissed the charges, namely, the charge against the owners that they had not provided within the stipulated time the apparatus for reversing the air-current (by which alone perhaps one hundred lives might have been saved); and the charge against the manager that he had failed to clear accumulations of coal dust (which, if done, would certainly have diminished the force of the explosion).

On the utterly insufficient sentences ("1s. 1¼d. a life"), there was, however, no appeal lodged, nor was it possible. Not only in the mine-fields but throughout a large section of the population there was strong feeling that the colliery directors should have been brought to trial for manslaughter. After all, some score years earlier, when danger was appre-hended from the racing carried out between two rival railway companies on the lines to Scotland, the Home Secretary had formerly intimated that if an accident involving fatal injuries to passengers were to occur the directors would be prosecuted for manslaughter. It was obvious that the penalties inflicted by the magistrates for breaches of mining law bore no relation to the gravity of the offences committed by mine-owners and their managers; nor were they on such a scale as to be an effective deterrent. This can be seen from the appended table of prosecutions of owners, agents and managers for offences under the Coal and Metalliferous Mines Regulation Acts in 1913.

The occurrence of this Senghenydd disaster also raised questions of the efficacy of the Act and of the administrative machinery by which it had to be carried out. The total inspectorate had bit by bit been raised from its original dozen to thrice the number and then, following on the Act of 1911, to fourscore. This small number was responsible for over 3,000 coal-mines and many more metalliferous mines and quarries. Under these conditions it is clear that inspection could not possibly be as thorough as was both desirable and necessary. Much consideration was given by the Miners' Union to questions of this kind in the two years following the passing of the Act.

Appendix A

WHITEHAVEN: PROFESSOR GALLOWAY'S EVIDENCE (EXCERPT)

The firedamp was ignited at a damaged or defective safety lamp at 7.45 p.m. Judging now by my own observation of what took place in a damp mine in which I was an eye-witness of a firedamp explosion, the flame spread rapidly, but by no means with lightning-like rapidity, along the under surface of the nearly pure, and, therefore, inexplosive firedamp in the goaf consuming that portion of it which was sufficiently mixed with air to burn. At this stage there was a pause of some duration.

In the case which came within my own experience the pause lasted long enough to enable me and two companions to crawl back some 12 or 15 feet through a small partially obstructed passage about 4 feet square which constituted the only entrance to a large chamber 60 or 70 yards long by 15 feet wide, to run a short distance sideways from the direct line of the passage, to turn round when we came to the solid coal which barred further progress, and to wait several seconds longer before a large blue flame shot out as if through the nozzle of a blow-pipe to a distance of 30 or 40 feet, or more, with a roar like thunder. Having continued for perhaps 10 or 15 seconds the flame was sucked in backwards out of sight, followed by a supply of fresh air; then after a similar interval it shot out a second time, was again drawn back, and shot out a third time, each succeeding time more feebly than the first, and finally disappeared. Mr. Rider Haggard has accurately described the same phenomenon in *She* which appeared some years later.

I wish to draw very particular attention to this pause. It was then that the great body of inexplosive firedamp was being heated, agitated, and expanded by the combustion of the comparatively thin layer of inflammable air and gas going on underneath it. It was then that Macquilliam and his comrades and others near the Dilly, having seen the first flash, fled from their working places. I can see no other feasible explanation of their absence at such a distance from them. After flowing and ebbing, the firedamp, having become mixed with air in the process, emitted a rush of flame which created an airwave. The latter licked up the coal dust from the floor, and mixed it with the air through which it passed. The flame of the firedamp passed directly into the fresh fuel thus prepared for it, and following closely behind the airwave, pressing forward with ever-increasing force, swept through the whole district, and burst into the main engine plane at the friction gear.

It is a popular error to suppose that firedamp is an explosive substance like gunpowder or dynamite, and that it will explode on the application of a flame. It cannot explode or even burn unless it is mixed with air. The mixture that explodes with the greatest violence contains about $9\frac{1}{2}$ per cent of firedamp and $90\frac{1}{2}$ per cent of air; one containing 16 per cent which is the upper limit, or 6 per cent the lower limit will burn quietly without explosion. No mixtures containing more than 16 per cent or less than 6 per cent will burn at all.

Coal dust, on the other hand, is perfectly harmless so long as it lies on the floor. Like firedamp it must be mixed with air before it can burn or explode. The mixture must contain so much coal dust as to be suffocating; and its ignition must be effected by means of a large flame, such as that of a firedamp explosion or a blasting shot.

Appendix B

TABLE OF PROSECUTIONS OF OWNERS, AGENTS AND MANAGERS, FOR OFFENCES UNDER THE COAL AND METALLIFEROUS MINES REGULATION ACTS IN 1913

Prosecutions	Convictions	Cases Withdrawn or Not Proven	Cases Dismissed	Total amount of Fines and Costs Imposed
170*	102	5	63	£337 12s. 7d.

* The number of separate firms proceeded against was 31 in 1913. This table shows that 102 out of 170 prosecutions, or 60 per cent, resulted in convictions. The average amount of fines and costs imposed was £3 6s. 2d., as compared with £2 19s. 10d. in 1912 and £2 8s. in 1911.

CHAPTER III

STRIFE, 1910–1911

I. ABNORMAL PLACES

THE Annual Conference of the Miners' Federation in October 1910 decided that

the miners of Scotland, England and Wales be requested to meet their respective employers and demand a fair living wage to be paid to all miners working in abnormal places.[1]

The question of abnormal working places was an old cause of dispute which had been becoming more acute. The relation of the hewers' piece-work rate to the day wage was always a matter for negotiation. There were variations from District to District and from pit to pit. But in the course of years a relation had been established, though not necessarily one satisfactory to either side. What, however, was to happen when through no fault of his own the coal-hewer found himself working under such conditions[2] that he could not gain a living wage? What, in short, was to be his wage when working in an "abnormal place"?

For many years it had been the custom to meet this by payment of a consideration (usually called "con"). These "considerations" were sometimes included in the pit price list and would be paid as a matter of course. But sometimes the workman had to make a claim and following on the claim had to bargain with the overman or under-manager. This often led to dissatisfaction. Moreover in the early part of this century there had been a growing tendency to reduce or evade payment of consideration money. Wages form the greatest part of the monthly or annual expenditure of a

---

[1] The question of abnormal places had come up earlier that year when deadlock in the negotiations for a new Conciliation Board in South Wales had been referred to an M.F.G.B. Special Conference on March 9, 1910.

[2] Due to the state of the seam (geological conditions) or the state of equipment and organisation (management conditions). Jevons, *op. cit.*, itemises over twenty such conditions.

colliery company. Once Conciliation Boards had begun to
function in every coal-field it was less easy to make a cut
in the district rate and coal-owners, anxious to reduce expenditure, found it easier to cut consideration payments where
they were dealing not with the whole mass of colliers but
with a few individuals. The great struggle that developed
on the question of abnormal places became possible when
the unions were strong enough to regard an injury to one
as an injury to all.

Some of the bigger companies, beginning to apply cost
accounting to their properties, set under-managers and over-
men to compete for lowest costs on what was called "dead
work." "In some companies," says Jevons, "severe pressure
was put upon the managers to cut down costs, and those who
failed had to make room for others. It is not, therefore, surprising that some of the managers showed no fine discrimina-
tion in carrying out the new policy of drastic reduction of the
cost of dead-work." In this way there was no provision for
ensuring that justice was done. In some collieries owners
simply set a fixed maximum total of consideration payments
for each "measuring-up day" (usually fortnightly), beyond
which the manager could not go, no matter how many
justified claims were put in by the men. "It was stated to
me," says Jevons, "by miners who worked in one of the pits
concerned that the manager would make fairly reasonable
allowances to three-fourths or more of the men, namely, those
to whom he happened to come first on his round, but the
rest had to go without anything. He would say quite frankly :
'Sorry, boys, but I have not got a penny left for allowances.' "
Again, the manager might find that he could not pay what
he had promised; and would then strike out the allowances
of those he considered the less deserving; or "sometimes it
was the men who he thought would give least trouble or
could be most easily intimidated who would go short."[1] In
many cases such men, always afraid of being "sacked," were
hesitant about a protest when they received treatment of this
kind.

With these changes in the first decade, men would in many
cases simply work harder, sometimes beyond their strength,

[1] Jevons, *op. cit.*

when they found themselves in an abnormal place. With the passing of the Eight Hours' Act, they had less time in which to put forth their effort. The consideration payments, too, were less, particularly where the owners had been fiercely opposed to the Eight Hours' Act. As a result many men were seriously over-worked. The agitation for a fixed minimum daily earning for piece-workers, which had been going on for the whole decade and had caused not a few stoppages, therefore came to a head.

2. TONYPANDY

Among all the valleys of Glamorgan the musical name of the Rhondda has been famous, at one time for the beauty of its tree-clad hillsides, later for the strife between the masters of its mineral wealth and the men by whom the coal was gotten. By the time the trees were gone from the mountain to become pit-props, the steep slopes were lined with rows of colliers' houses looking down into the valley bottom studded with workings. In this valley, or rather the twin valleys, of the Rhondda there took place the long Cambrian Combine Strike which affected the policy of the Miners' Federation of Great Britain.

The trouble began over the price list for a new seam in the Ely pit of the Naval Colliery Company. This company was controlled by the Cambrian Collieries Ltd., whose Chairman was the masterful D. A. Thomas, afterwards Lord Rhondda. The owners offered a piece rate of 1s. 9d. a ton (plus 1d. for dealing with stone) while the workmen, on the ground that it was a particularly difficult seam bound to cause many abnormal places, asked for 2s. 6d. a ton. The haggling over the price went on for a long time, until the owners felt they could wait no longer and decided to force the issue by resorting to a lock-out. On September 1, 1910, they locked-out not only the few dozen who were in dispute with them but the whole eight hundred of the Ely pit, so as to bring pressure to bear on the seventy men to settle on a price that would be satisfactory to the owners. A lock-out of this kind roused resentment in the Rhondda and other valleys: and, by a ballot of the coal-field, the South Wales Miners' Federation called out on strike the whole of the twelve thousand men employed by the Cambrian Combine in the endeavour "to teach that particular company that tyrannical action over certain men to influence others was not a paying policy." The strike notices were handed in on October 1st and by November 1st the Cambrian Combine strike had begun.

Strikes also began in the Aberdare Valley, where the workmen were demanding the remedy of numerous grievances, especially those connected with abnormal places. Other strikes took place in Ogmore Valley. A state of tension began to develop throughout the coal-field. By the end of the first week in November there were 12,000 miners idle in the Rhondda Valley and 11,000 in Aberdare Valley. By midwinter there were some 30,000 locked out or on strike.

Some South Wales coal-owners were possessed by a hope that the place of the strikers would be filled by blackleg labour. On the other side, all miners were fully aware that the Trade Disputes Act of 1906 had restored the right of "peaceful picketing." A clash between these two could be foreseen. The owners placed their trust in the Chief Constable of Glamorgan. Captain Lindsay had several score of foot and mounted police available for the two valleys, apart from the local constables; after consultation with the local magistrates (some of whom were directors or shareholders in colliery companies) he augmented this force by extra police from the cities of South Wales and from Bristol.

By Sunday, November 6th, the workmen discovered that it was the intention of the owners to import blackleg labour for the Glamorgan Colliery at Llwynypia. On the night of Monday, November 7th, a body of strikers surrounded the colliery, and had a sharp brush with a body of police ensconced in the colliery premises. Reinforcements of police were rapidly sent into the valley, where their arrival aroused resentment, especially in Tonypandy, a mile or two down the valley from Llwynypia. Between midnight and 1 a.m. on the morning of November 8th, disturbances broke out with a certain amount of smashing of windows. The police used their truncheons freely and dispersed the miners. While all this was going on, the Chief Constable of Glamorgan tele-graphed to Shrewsbury, Chester and Salisbury Plain for troops and a few hours later followed up telegraphic messages to the Home Office by an urgent personal telephone call to Winston Churchill, then Home Secretary. At this point Tonypandy, from a local disturbance, became a focus of national attention and the subject of conferences at the Home Office, discussions with the War Office, questions and debates in Parliament.

If it was held to be an awkward situation in the Rhondda Valley, it was an awkward situation also for the Liberal Ministers. The last occasion of the employment of troops in South Wales a dozen years earlier had met considerable opposition in Parliament from Liberal members. Now there was a powerful trade union of the Welsh miners and behind them the Miners' Federation of Great Britain. There were nearly a score of mining M.P.s who, together with the other Labour members, made up a contingent on which the Cabinet had to rely (along with the Irish members) for a sufficient majority against the Conservatives. However much the Home Secretary may have chafed at the restraint imposed by these circumstances (and that restraints of this kind irked Mr. Churchill was shown by his behaviour a few weeks later in Sidney Street),[1] he met in a smooth enough manner the representations put to him at the Home Office on Tuesday, November 8th, by W. Abraham, the Chairman of the South Wales Miners' Federation. He promised to do everything he could to prevent the use of the military. Actually, he countermanded the troop movements for a few hours, held up infantry at Swindon station, diverted a force of cavalry

[1] In Houndsditch, armed burglars (in newspaper rumour a band of anarchists led by "Peter the Painter") had resisted arrest and in the struggle had killed three policemen. Two of them were later located in No. 100 Sidney Street, which was then "besieged" by armed police. The house being set on fire, the men shot themselves. It was a shooting affray of a kind since not unknown in the metropolis. What has never been known since was the conduct on this occasion of the Home Secretary. Leaving his office in Whitehall and his place in Parliament, Winston Churchill reappeared in London's East End where, clad in top hat and frock coat, he endeavoured to encourage by his presence the company of the Scots Guards whom he had arranged to have brought from the Tower of London to take part in this "siege" of Sidney Street. This extraordinary behaviour of a responsible Minister—at an epoch when juvenile imaginations had not yet been debauched by gangster–police films from Hollywood—caused much misgiving among Liberal supporters, gave rise to the no doubt mistaken impression that he was temperamentally bloodthirsty and led to his being dubbed "The 'Hero' of Sidney Street" Macready records that on his return to London Churchill self-consciously enquired what the General thought of his prank in Sidney Street.

to Cardiff, and despatched 500 of his Metropolitan police to reinforce the 600 police already at the disposal of the Glamorgan Chief Constable. This brought remonstrances from the coal-owners, and also created a certain amount of confusion in the public mind as to where, on that night of November 8th, the troops either were stationed or were to be stationed. The next day a special conference of the M.F.G.B. on the Osborne Judgment[1] heard a report upon the Tonypandy situation and expressed their opinion that:

This Conference . . . whilst regretting the disturbances which have occurred, considers the civil forces sufficient to deal with such disturbances, and will strongly deprecate the introduction of the military for such a purpose, and if the military have been sent into the districts affected, asks the Home Secretary at once to recall them. (Wednesday, November 9, 1910.)

Churchill perhaps had fully expected to be thus exposed to pressure and criticism from two sides and on the morning of November 8th, he had taken the unprecedented and as it appeared to many at the time melodramatic step of appointing a General to take charge of both civil and military forces if the latter were called upon "to quell disorder." General Macready, on whom his choice fell, had already arrived at Pontypridd at the mouth of the Rhondda Valley on the evening of the 8th.

Nevil Macready, on whom honours were afterwards to be heaped (until he became General the Rt. Hon. Sir Nevil Macready, Bart., C.G.M.G., K.C.B.) for his activity in suppressing the policemen's trade union in 1919 and in commanding the Black-and-Tans in the Irish troubles of 1920–21, was at this time forty-eight years of age. He was a little bit out of the ordinary, as Generals go; he was the son of William Charles Macready, the celebrated actor of early Victorian times, who was already in his seventieth year when his son was born. Amongst his father's friends and acquaintances had been not only the playwrights of those days, but such literary figures as Charles Dickens and Robert Browning. He was a clever and ambitious soldier, prepared to carry out the orders of the Government without deviation. If anybody could sustain the precepts of the Haldane Committee

[1] See *The Miners*, Chapter X.

(on the Featherstone shootings) that the military, whilst protecting property, must not appear to side either with the employers or the workmen, Macready from his family upbringing and training was eminently suited for this task. In his memoirs, written a dozen years later, Macready, while open enough about his own anti-Socialist views, tells of his surprise in finding that the coal-owners regarded him as being in a sense under their orders, and at what pains he was to disabuse them of this notion—in the sense, at any rate, in which they entertained it. He also takes a certain amount of credit for having entered into direct relations with the Strike Committee, establishing with them a permanent liaison officer.

General Macready had all the bias of his caste against the strike leaders, who are set down in his memoirs as "indifferent workmen and generally without any stake in the locality"—though he felt compelled to add: "In justice to the strike committee in the Rhondda Valley I must say that when they gave their word to me to carry out any undertaking it was scrupulously adhered to, a line of conduct which the employers might well have imitated." His disappointment with the employers was due to a whole series of incidents. At his first meeting with directors of collieries he found that "the idea seemed prevalent with them that the military and police were at their disposal, to be increased to any extent they might demand, and to be allocated according to their advice." Further he noted an "inclination on the part of the colliery managers to send in highly coloured and alarmist reports on account of which police and troops might have been needlessly rushed about the country." He gives two examples:

Mr. Hann, the general manager of the Powell–Duffryn Collieries, rang me up on the telephone one evening to say that five thousand strikers were marching down upon his house. He was quite positive about it and in a state of agitation. I asked him to send the officer attached to his area, who was on the spot, to the telephone. The officer, Captain Francis Farquhar, of the Coldstream Guards, who a few years later fell at the head of Princess Pat's Canadian Regiment in France, soon rang through and told me he had heard nothing of any movement in the neighbourhood but would go and look round. Shortly afterwards he rang up again to say that the whole vicinity was absolutely quiet, and that he could find no grounds for the alarm of the mine manager.[1]

The other example, which Macready describes as "a more glaring case" took place at the Cynon Colliery. At the demand of the manager a large force of police had been sent there. "It afterwards transpired," says Macready, "that the police were required to enforce the levying of a fine against the men, who had offered to pay at once 80 per cent of the fine, an offer which had been recommended by the manager but refused by the owners." Certain conditions had been laid down by Macready. He had outlined to the managers the circumstances under which troops and police would provide protection for the continuation or restarting of pumping, and for blackleg labour; but he adds: "I was never free from anxiety that attempts would be made by the managers to circumvent these conditions, an anxiety which was fully justified, as on several occasions serious trouble was with difficulty staved off owing to attempts to start pumping and import labour without my knowledge or consent."

The poltroonery or knavery that Macready encountered among those whose property and strike-breakers he had been sent to protect did not deter him from his purpose. To a large extent he did overawe the valleys: and his clever and careful use of the forces of the state earned him high favour with his political superiors.

By November 12th, Macready was reporting that "the situation from the point of preserving order had considerably cleared up" and "no special outbreak occurred until the 18th, due in a great measure to the cold inclement weather." In the meantime, there were daily questions in Parliament on the position in South Wales, and on November 15th, the first of the two Adjournment Debates on the South Wales coal strike took place. Keir Hardie, who raised the matter, emphasised firstly that the military should not be employed at all:

The military have been called out in connection with this dispute in South Wales, not only without any grave necessity, but without any necessity at all. There has not been any kind of disorder or disturbance with which the police force was not amply capable of

[1] *Annals of an Active Life*, by Sir Nevil Macready, 1924.

COLLIERS LOADING AT NORTH SHIELDS (*early 19th Century*)

OLD LOCOMOTIVE ENGINE

(Constructed by George Stephenson for Killingworth Colliery)

dealing. If you take what is regarded as the very worst case of all, the Tonypandy window-smashing case, the number of men taking part in that window-smashing never exceeded 100. . . . Local opinion is practically unanimous in saying that had there been three or four or half a dozen policemen on duty on the streets when the window-smashing commenced, the whole of the disorder might have been stopped. But the whole of the police at this time, with the exception of a few, were at the colliery guarding the owners' property. . . .

The presence of the military in South Wales in connection with this dispute is regarded as an insult to the law-abiding inhabitants, and is itself a source and cause of irritation, and may in the end lead to disorder which would altogether be obviated if the troops were not there. . . . Their continued presence in South Wales . . . gives the impression that the Government is taking sides with the employers and is sending those men into the colliery field to help to intimidate and overawe the strikers, and thereby make success more difficult for them.

Secondly, he protested at the unnecessary display of violence by the police. As examples of this, Keir Hardie took not Tonypandy, but the incidents of Aberaman, in his own constituency of Merthyr. He had made personal investigations on the spot on the 13th and 14th. He described the scene of the disturbances which was on a canal towing path where practically the whole population of the village had gathered, men, women and children. The police had been ordered to disperse the crowd; but, said Hardie, "They were not content with merely trying to induce the people to leave. There was no resistance, but the police, in the most indiscriminate fashion, commenced to bludgeon the people right and left." Keir Hardie then told of some of the victims:

The first case I enquired into was that of a man up in years who had gone to gather coal from the old pit heap for his fire. He was bringing the coal home in a hand-cart, and when he reached the canal-bank the police charged him, tipped his little hand-cart into the canal, and knocked him in after it. . . .

Next was a boy sixteen years of age who had been playing football and who had come up to see what was going on:

He was beaten across the loins. The police caught him by the legs and threw him into the canal. He got back to the bank. More police came. The boy said "Oh, policeman, don't hit me again. I have done nothing." But they hit him again and again. He raised his hand to protect his head, and the hand was smashed to pieces. . . .

I come now, I think, to the worst case of all, the case of a school child of eleven years of age—a puny little fellow who doesn't look his age. His statement was this: "A policeman pushed me into the canal, and hit me then on the side of the head. This was at half way to the washery." Two policemen followed this boy to the door of his mother's house, and had to be driven back from there to prevent them again attacking him.

His account was confirmed by Edgar Jones, M.P. Then William Abraham, M.P. (Mabon) and G. N. Barnes, M.P., joined in the demand for a full enquiry. Churchill, in a nervous reply, possibly with one eye on the General Election only a few weeks distant, joined with Mabon in praising "the many virtues of the mining population of South Wales," but was "not convinced by the picture which the Hon. Member for Merthyr Tydfil (Mr. Keir Hardie) drew." Churchill, declaring that he "should be no party to any sort of censure upon the police in this matter," declined to order any enquiry. Nor did Keir Hardie get any further satisfaction when he renewed his charges on the 24th. This stubborn refusal to enquire into the conduct of the police brought upon Churchill widespread condemnation in the coal-fields, especially in South Wales where his very name was to be hated for years to come.

During this month of November, the name of Tonypandy became known throughout the Labour movement; the name was also impressed on far wider circles, due to the exaggerated reporting in the newspapers. There was further tumult in Tonypandy and Penycraig on November 21st, when strikers tried to stop the arrival of blackleg labour sanctioned by Macready and therefore afforded military protection. Macready reports that:

During the rioting that occurred on November 21st throughout the Tonypandy Valley the Metropolitan Police while driving the mob before them along the main road were heavily stoned from the side tracks, and suffered severe casualties. In order to counter these tactics on the part of the strikers on the next occasion when trouble was afoot, small bodies of infantry on the higher ground, keeping level with the police on the main road, moved slowly down the side tracks, and by a little gentle persuasion with the bayonet drove the stone-throwers into the arms of the police on the lower road.[1]

[1] Thirty years later Mr. Churchill, in his attempted justification of his conduct in the matter of Tonypandy, curiously omitted to mention his responsibility for the use of bayonets against the Welsh civilians.

After this, however, the dispute settled down into a long and bitter conflict, as we shall recount. By January 5th, Macready had left Pontypridd and returned to London. The troops remained, as did a large force of police; and Tonypandy became a sort of generic name for all troubles in the South Wales coal-field in 1910 that recalled to the older miners the excitement and indignation caused by the Featherstone shooting a generation earlier.

3. THE CAMBRIAN COMBINE STRIKE

The men in the Rhondda valley had settled down to a long strike struggle, in which they had the support of a weekly levy by the other members of the South Wales Miners' Federation. The strike was accompanied by an intense agitation and discussion amongst the men. Leaflets were issued, controversy was carried on in the newspapers, negotiations carried on from time to time were subjected to intense and continuous scrutiny. The Cambrian Combine strikers felt they were the spearhead of the fight on abnormal places and that not only the South Wales coal-field but all coal-fields were affected and should join in. This became the subject of animated discussion. Thus apart from the struggle with the owners, apart from resentment expressed at the use of police and military, there was also a struggle going on inside the South Wales Miners' Federation. This was not limited to the immediate issues, but developed into a sort of ideological warfare as to methods, aims and objects of trade unionism, in which questions of sympathetic action took foremost place.

By the end of the year 1910 the burden of supporting the 12,000 strikers in the Rhondda was beginning to tell upon the South Wales Miners' Federation. At their request an M.F.G.B. Special Conference was called for January 24 to 26, 1911, with W. E. Harvey, M.P., in the chair. William Brace first explained the particular difficulties of abnormal places in South Wales. "Time was," he said, "when a man at work in an abnormal place had not been fairly paid, that we could go to the County Court and get wages awarded by the County Court Judge." But when Judge Williams was succeeded by Judge Bryn Roberts, a decision was given by the latter almost in direct opposition to the practice of Judge Williams, and according to Brace "laid it down as a matter of law that unless we had a provision in the price list which would give the men a right by that provision to a payment for working in an abnormal place, the men had no right whatsoever to any payment other than in accordance with the will of the manager or official." This was the famous case of Walters *v*. the Ocean Coal Company Limited, of September 1907. "If we can settle the abnormal place question," said Brace, "we can settle the dispute. But we cannot, and we are now face to face with having to continue this struggle. . . . We have felt that rather than wait until we have exhausted all our money, we had better come here so that it shall not be said that an affiliated branch of this Association has been beaten to its knees by the want of funds when men would have been ready to help if they had been asked."

Brace then anticipated a criticism which he knew might be made (and indeed had been made at various times in the previous ten years about the lowness of the South Wales union contributions)[1] and said it was "not the fault of the leaders":

We have time and again asked for an increase in the contribution; but you will be sufficiently experienced as leaders and trade union organisers to know it sometimes requires an acute crisis to teach men their obligations and their duty to themselves. Although our men have only been paying 1s. a month, will the Conference please bear with me when I say that they have been paying very substantial levies and have been paying very much more than has been credited in their favour; and I hope if there is any criticism directed against us on this point that you will be kinder in your criticism.

We are faced with a very acute crisis, and only by your assistance can we come out of it with credit to ourselves and to the great organisation to which we belong.

As a result of this appeal, the Conference resolved to contribute £3,000 a week and for this purpose to call a levy of 3d. a member in all coal-fields, the books in South Wales to be examined by General Secretary Thomas Ashton.

---

[1] Threepence a week. Most other Districts paid 6d. per week.

Another resolution urged upon members of the S.W.M.F. "the advisability of increasing their monthly contributions so as to provide a stronger defence for them against any similar attack that may be made upon them in the future, and to secure uniformity in the payment of members of this Federation." To this (carried with one dissentient) an entirely novel answer was given by one of the South Wales delegation. To the astonishment of the older County Associations (and to the consternation of his fellow delegates) young Noah Ablett rose and put a peculiar theory that the men wanted action not finance. But no attempt at action could be carried through without finance, as the Conference minute shows:

MR. LOVATT: I should like to ask one question. Are you opposed to the grant?

MR. ABLETT: No, I am not opposed to the grant. One has general principles.

MR. BARKER: I should like to say that I disassociate myself entirely with the sentiments expressed by Mr. Ablett. I do not see myself how any body of workers, whether they are Socialists, Trade Unionists, or whatever they are, can fight an enemy without ammunition. It is entirely impracticable, and it will defeat the object at which they are aiming. Personally, I think the first duty of the miners of South Wales is to increase their contribution, and if we had been paying 6d. a week since the Federation was founded we should have had a million pounds in our funds today, and probably there would have been no Cambrian dispute at all.

The Conference took the question of abnormal places[1] separately from the Cambrian strike on which, having taken financial responsibility, they now resolved "that Mr. Ashton and Mr. Harvey assist the South Wales Federation to bring about a satisfactory settlement of the dispute if possible."

But the efforts of Messrs. Harvey and Ashton to bring about a settlement met with no success. When the proposed terms of settlement were put to the S.W.M.F. Council Meeting on February 17th, the deputation from the Cambrian men refused the terms. Much hinged upon the significance of a letter from D. A. Thomas, M.P., head of the Cambrian Combine, in which he appeared to give an assurance that piecework earnings would be made up to 6s. 9d. a day in abnormal places. The Cambrian men considered that

[1] See next section.

D. A. Thomas's assurance was valueless in view of their experience of payments for abnormal places. After the dispute had gone on for another two months a Special Conference of the M.F.G.B. decided that the dispute should be settled by arbitration, namely:

That in the opinion of this Conference the matters in dispute in the Bute seam at the Ely Pit of the Cambrian Combine should at once be submitted to arbitration, and this Conference relegates to the Executive Committee of this Federation the taking of immediate steps in the matter. (April 26, 1911).

Before this, the Conference heard Tom Smith of Tonypandy appeal on behalf of the Cambrian Combine men:

If you think that arbitration offered by this Federation is going to be a means of effecting a settlement we offer no objection. . . . If the owners refuse arbitration, then I take it the Federation is going to take up the whole question of the strike, and see it through. In South Wales men are starving, women are starving, children are starving. I can tell you that women are bringing children into the world with not a rag to cover them when they are born. I know of children who have been born in houses where there has been nothing, not a single bit of clothing to put on them. If ever there was intense suffering that suffering is in South Wales. If ever there was intense heroism manifested it has been by the women and children in this struggle. I take it if arbitration is offered by this great Federation, and is refused, then you are not going to allow us to starve any longer.

The South Wales coal-owners refused the proposal for arbitration. They were willing, however, to discuss the matter. After some two weeks' negotiations, proposed terms of settlement were drawn up and signed (May 15, 1911) by four coal-owners' representatives and also by "Enoch Edwards, M.P., Thomas Ashton, Rt. Hon. William Abraham, M.P., and Thomas Richards, M.P." The terms were: (1) that for a trial period of twelve months the company would pay a cutting rate of 2s. $1\frac{3}{10}$d. per ton on the Upper Five Foot seam of the Ely pit (being the amount previously negotiated by Abraham on October 23, 1910) and that elsewhere work would be resumed as soon as places were ready in the pits; (2) that the assurances of January and February 1911 by D. A. Thomas and others (believed by Ashton to be worth

6s. 9d. a shift) would be carried out; (3) that a committee of the Conciliation Board or, should they fail to agree, the Independent Chairman thereof should decide whether or not in any particular case these assurances in fact were being carried out. The M.F.G.B. Executive four days later approved this.

But the terms got anything but a welcome reception in South Wales. Enoch Edwards in his report to the M.F.G.B. Executive said only that at the South Wales council meeting of May 20th, "Mr. Ashton and himself were not received very graciously." Enoch put it very mildly. But Ashton was deeply hurt. A letter from him the next day (May 21st) to Tom Richards showed this:

We have obtained all in the terms of the agreement that we set out for and fully carried out the instructions of the Special Conference, and yet we are told that we have jockeyed and sold the men.

I have worked for the miners 45 years. I have attended on thousands of deputations and assisted in settling hundreds of large and important disputes. Some of these settlements have not always been satisfactory to myself, but no man has ever said I sold them before yesterday.

The Cambrian Combine Committee, to whom the proposed terms were utterly repugnant, now went a step further. They brought out a manifesto which was sent to every lodge in South Wales, and published in every newspaper. In this they said their leaders had been "palpably fooled," called the assurances of D. A. Thomas "spoof assurances," and recounted the cause of the strike.

If we could only tabulate even a part of the suffering and misery endured by our women and children, we feel sure you would agree with us that the fight has gone too far and the suffering too great that we should now be handed over to the mercy of the Combine. We ask you to say, friends, that the time has arrived when the surrender policy of our apologetic leaders must stop.

This circular had an immediate effect inside South Wales where at Cardiff a coal-field conference of 288 delegates on May 27th unanimously rejected the proposed terms and on May 29th passed a resolution recommending the lodges to reconsider "the sectional strike policy hitherto adopted" and to ask the Miners' Federation of Great Britain at its mid-June

conference "to make common cause with these workmen by
declaring a general stoppage throughout the Federation for
the purpose of securing for all colliery workmen a definite
guaranteed minimum wage"; and, failing national action for
this end, the whole South Wales coal-field should be brought
out on strike. But if the Cambrian men could issue a manifesto
before the South Wales conference and by it convince the
delegates, Ashton could also issue a circular before the
M.F.G.B. Special Conference of mid-June. This he did on
June 2nd. In this he recapitulated the course of events and
ended with severe strictures upon some of those in South
Wales who he said "did not want a settlement," but an
extension of the strike to the whole country.

Meantime the Welsh lodges instructed their delegates to
a further Cardiff Conference on June 12th, which confirmed
the decision to press for a stoppage of all coal-fields but
rejected the resolution for action by the South Wales coal-
field alone by 188 votes to 86. This last Conference had been
a stormy one. Strong feeling was expressed not only against
some of the South Wales leaders (Mabon and Hartshorn
were condemned by resolution for unauthorised communications to the newspapers), but also against the secretary of
the M.F.G.B., Thomas Ashton.

On hearing all this, the M.F.G.B. Executive Committee
on June 12th decided, with the South Wales representatives
in a minority (William Brace, M.P., Tom Richards, M.P.
and W. Abraham, M.P.) to confirm their previous resolution, "accept the terms of settlement and also recommend
the Conference to do the same." The National Conference
met the next day. There were bitter words uttered. The older
leaders of the County Associations were shocked that a
District Conference should have passed a resolution condemning the revered Secretary of the Federation. In the
twenty-one years of the Federation there had been many
controversies with those outside it, but never had there been
any such recrimination in public as had now taken place.
George Barker, who had recently been coming to the fore
as a leader of the advanced section in South Wales, said:

Mr. Ashton says, the Cambrian men want force and nothing but
force. I say, if he has said that deliberately, it is untrue. If he has

not said it deliberately, then it is a most unfortunate mistake for him to send out to the coal-fields. Through that unfortunate mistake or falsehood, the case of the Cambrian Combine men has been prejudiced before the men in all the coal-fields. The South Wales Federation passed a resolution unanimously condemning Mr. Ashton for the issue of that circular.

George Barker, three months before, had secured 1,266 votes as against 1,688 votes for Mabon in the election for the Presidency of the S.W.M.F. which was held to be a clear indication that Mabon's position was insecure. Four months later Barker, along with Hartshorn and Stanton, was to displace Onions, Brace and Richards on the South Wales representation in the M.F.G.B. Executive Committee. Barker, thus strongly supported in South Wales, also represented one side of the ideological warfare that was now developing within the Miners' Federation. The other side of this cleavage is shown very clearly in the concluding passages of the disputed circular issued by Thomas Ashton:

These men have only one weapon to fight with, that of "force," which alone means "anarchy" . . . The South Wales dispute will be considered at the special conference on the 14th or 15th June, and it will be seen then whether the principles of trade unionism or anarchy will prevail.

Vernon Hartshorn was careful in the Conference not to follow along the lines of ideological conflict. He omitted all reference to those points on which Ashton had sought to generalise the causes of difference into a difference between "the principles of trade unionism or anarchy." He stressed the belief of the South Wales men that the settlement would not yield the results claimed for it by the Board of Trade officials and by the Chairman and Secretary of the M.F.G.B., and the Chairman and Secretary of the S.W.M.F. On the other hand, he sought to generalise the dispute in a different way and to raise it to the level of a national question of abnormal places and a minimum wage:

We think the assurances are not such as will justify us in recommending the men to return to work. There is one statement in the circular which I think, in fairness to Wales, should be made clear. He says, in his final remarks, that "all along they have been crying for the 20th rule[1] to be put in operation" and he goes on to say: "It was never intended to be used to assist a district to fix prices in a seam at a colliery, or in any case where less than 80 men are directly affected" (Hear, hear). Hear, hear; certainly, and we say amen. I will challenge Mr. Ashton or any other man in this Conference to produce a statement which has ever been made by a responsible leader in South Wales, that we have contended that there should be national action on the question of a price list. Recently it was put to a Welsh Conference and we said "There is no hope of getting national action on the dispute, and even if we could carry the Conference with us it would not be advisable to do it, because if we adopted a national stoppage on a price list the mining industry would be at a standstill."

What we have contended for in this dispute is that we should establish a minimum wage. That is a dispute which is common to all the coal-fields of the United Kingdom. Here we have got a price list which will not meet the normal conditions of the seam. We say that this 2s. $1\frac{3}{10}$d. will not enable men to make a wage under normal conditions. Then the only alternative is to get a guaranteed wage for all the miners who go into the mine. That is common to the whole of the coal-fields of the kingdom; that is something which would benefit the whole community, and which, if the Federation went for, would embrace this Combine dispute, and enable them to go back and try the price list for 12 months. We say that the Federation ought to take national action for settling the minimum wage for all men. It is a matter of common interest and common importance, and we should take united action on it.

These criticisms brought Ashton to his feet. For the first time for many years the older regular delegates to the Federation Conferences heard their taciturn Secretary make a speech in public. It was the more interesting to them as it was also the first time that any action of Ashton, taken on his own initiative, had been challenged in this way. Ashton said:

After the references which have been made, to this pamphlet which I sent out—which I am responsible for myself, and myself only, for I had no one to consult—by Mr. Barker and Mr. Hartshorn, and the remark of the latter to the 20th rule, I must say that my statement is correct. I said, "There are a number of men in South Wales who do not want a settlement of the strike at the Combine Collieries. All along they have been crying for the 20th rule to be

[1] The famous Rule 20 (later renumbered 21) ran as follows:
"That whenever any Federation or District is attacked on the general wage question all members connected with the Society shall tender a notice to terminate their contracts —if approved of by a Conference called to consider the advisability of such joint action being taken."

put into operation. The terms of agreement contain all that has been asked for, and now they are afraid of the settlement." I believed that to be true when I wrote it; I believe it to be true now. I will tell you why. I heard it in the streets of Tonypandy; when Mr. Harvey and myself went there to report to the Combine Committee, the men cried out "We want the 20th rule." We went into the Committee. The same thing was advocated in the Committee. At the last Conference when Tom Smith was speaking, somebody cried out "Give us the 20th rule."

There are some of your representatives who have gone through the length of England, they have preached this doctrine. I have a letter from the Secretary of the London Trades Council suggesting that we should put the 20th rule in force, because the representatives of the Combine men have suggested it. I have another from the Painters suggesting that the 20th rule be put in force. They say they do not know exactly what it is, but they think it will bring about a settlement, and so they suggest that the 20th rule be put in force.

This ended the morning session. It seems to have been considered that Ashton's brief reply made it now possible to come to a decision. A resolution was moved by David Gilmour of Scotland that:

In the opinion of this Conference, the object sought for at the Special Conference at the Caxton Hall, on the 24th of April is secured in the proposed terms of Cambrian Combine, signed by Mr. Edwards, M.P., Mr. T. Ashton, Mr. W. Abraham, M.P. and Mr. T. Richards, M.P., and this Conference now agrees to accept no further responsibility in this dispute.

The bitter denunciations of Thomas Ashton made by Welsh delegates now brought bitter replies. For years there had not been such scenes witnessed at a Federation Conference. One after another the representatives of the English coal-fields spoke against South Wales, several expressing their strong support for Thomas Ashton. . . . "Those of us," said Harvey of Derbyshire, "who have known Mr. Ashton all these many years do not and would not believe that he would misrepresent anyone, that he has lived too long and done too great a service to the mining interest of Great Britain to misrepresent anybody." But when Harvey went on to speak of "wild howling mobs" in South Wales, the Welsh delegation protested, one delegate saying: "I, as a Welshman, stand and refuse to be abused. We may be wild and irresponsible. Mr. Harvey is old and respectable. I hope he will withdraw the term 'howling mobs.'" This Harvey did, but only after his old associate Mabon had appealed to him to do so. The resolution was carried, with South Wales alone voting against.

The next day Conference, in a discussion on amendments to the Mines Bill, entered a calmer atmosphere, and on the third day carried through a preliminary discussion on abnormal places and on this question adjourned for six weeks.

The decision of the M.F.G.B. Special Conference to confirm the proposed terms of settlement and to "accept no further responsibility in this dispute" did not alter the standpoint of the Cambrian men. They continued on strike throughout the whole summer and early autumn of 1911. They were no longer receiving the £3,000 a week, though the Executive had interpreted the Conference decision so that the money did not stop automatically but was continued up to the first week of July. A long correspondence was conducted by Thomas Ashton with D. A. Thomas, Chairman of the Cambrian Combine, who eventually gave the response in a letter of July 6th to Ashton that "if you think there is still any doubt as to my meaning, and that it would, at this juncture, in any way help towards a friendly and permanent settlement of the dispute, were I to repeat explicitly that I consider 6s. 9d. at the present rate of wages the least amount that should be paid at the Naval Collieries to a competent collier working on the coal-face for a fair day's work, I will gladly do so." But the Cambrian men were not satisfied with this assurance, and by one means or another sought desperately to get coal-field action. The Coal-field Conference and the South Wales Council which had at first increased their levies, eventually had to reduce them to 1s. a week. At last, in August, the strike began to end, amid great suffering and misery. It was not until the beginning of October that work was being resumed, and even so, places could not be found for some 3,000 of the men. The Executive Committee of the M.F.G.B., informed of this on October 4th, granted £2,000 in aid of those men. At the end of December, Ashton, on behalf of the M.F.G.B., enquired whether the agreement in the Ely Pit was being carried out by the management and especially whether any man working at the coal-face had received less than 6s. 9d. per day since the resumption of work. The reply was that no case was known of a collier who had received less than 6s. 9d. a day in the Ely Pit and that "most of the men since they resumed work had earned big wages at the tonnage rate."

The Cambrian Combine men had been forced to accept the original terms of settlement of October 1910 as regards the 2s. $1\frac{3}{10}$d. cutting price for the Bute Seam in the Ely Pit of the Naval Collieries. Nevertheless, in the course of their struggle they had raised the question of abnormal places to be a national mining issue and in the later stages had carried this still farther to the issue of a National Minimum Wage. To this they had converted the whole of the South Wales coal-field and were presently to convert the whole of the miners of the United Kingdom. They had lost their local dispute; they had won the desired national movement to settle the wider question. The strike with all its bitter hardship and suffering had not been in vain.

4. NEGOTIATIONS ON ABNORMAL PLACES

When, on June 15th, the Special Conference turned to deal with abnormal places, deliberately separated from the Cambrian strike, they were resuming the thread of debate. For they had already twice discussed the question, once at the 1910 Annual Conference (where it had also been decided that each District should take action "to have fixed an individual minimum day wage for all men and boys who are now being paid by the ton, yard or scorage, etc.") and again at the Special Conference of January 24, 1911, which instructed all Districts to press forward their claims. Moreover, if any District had failed to obtain satisfaction by the expiry of three months, the members of the M.F.G.B. were to be recommended "to consider the advisability of taking national action to endeavour to enforce it" and at the same time each District was to send in information on the "rate of wages at present paid to day-wage men including surface men." Now by midsummer it was discovered that while progress had been made by some of the County Associations, others had little to record in the way of advance. In particular, the Scottish and Welsh coal-owners were obdurate. Nine months had now elapsed and some of the delegates were for initiating a national movement right away, but a majority (98–55) were in favour of moving more slowly. The decision was that the Conference be adjourned to July 28th, "seeing that these reports are incomplete and negotiations with the coal-owners still proceeding."

By the time the adjourned Special Conference met again on July 28th, substantial differences of opinion were developing. On the one hand, Lancashire and Yorkshire supported by South Wales were in favour of an immediate strike ballot. For Lancashire, old Tom Greenall moved, and Herbert Smith of Yorkshire seconded:

That this Conference is of opinion that it is necessary for a ballot vote of the whole of the members of the Miners' Federation of Great Britain to be taken with a view of declaring a national strike unless the coal-owners agree to a definite payment for all abnormal places of 7s. per day or such payment equal to day-wage coaling rate for each respective county or district in this Federation. (July 28, 1911.)

"The owners in every district," said Greenall, "are not prepared to do anything in this matter until they are forced. . . . What we want to do is to arm those who will meet the employers by a ballot vote of the men." After discussion had gone on for some time, an Executive Committee amendment was carried by 82 votes to 54 to arrange a meeting with all coal-owners to consider a District minimum rate for abnormal places before taking a Federation strike ballot.

The officials, in carrying out the resolution, had to meet the difficulty that the representative national body of the coal-owners, the Mining Association of Great Britain, was not empowered to deal with wages questions, but only with matters of legislation, etc. This was an obstacle of long standing, dating back to before the formation of the Miners' Federation. In the early 'eighties requests from the old Miners' National Union to discuss wages had been refused by the Mining Association of Great Britain. In that refusal they had always persisted. Now for the first time, with the consent of all Districts, the Miners' Federation was taking the initiative on a wages question embracing every coal-field.

How was the difficulty to be got over? The M.F.G.B. Executive felt it was for the owners to solve that question. Solve it the owners did, by persisting in the refusal to meet the men as representing the Mining Association of Great Britain but consenting to meet them as "representative coal-owners from different Districts"! But to settle this point of etiquette, as it seemed at the time, took the coal-owners several weeks including preliminary meetings amongst themselves. So it was not until September 29th that there could be held a "Special Joint Meeting of the Coal-owners' and Miners' Representatives of Great Britain, on the Question of Payment for working Abnormal Places, and the low Rate of Wages paid to Day-wage Men."

To the case put forward by Enoch Edwards on behalf of the Miners' Federation, Sir Lindsay Wood replied that the matter could only be dealt with in the Districts. The employers then submitted the following proposals:

(1) The owners recognise the right of workmen who are engaged in places which are abnormal to receive wages commensurate with the work performed. (2) The customs and circumstances of the different districts vary so much that it is, in the opinion of the coal-owners, impossible to deal with the question collectively as applied to the whole kingdom, and therefore the method of dealing with it can only be satisfactorily settled locally in the different districts. (3) This collective meeting of coal-owners therefore recommends the coal-owners in the various districts of the kingdom to meet the representatives of the men in their respective districts when requested to do so.

This would have thrown the miners back to where they were before. It could not be accepted. The phrase in the first clause "wages commensurate with the work performed" was felt to be a formula so elastic as to contain all possible meanings. The miners' representatives submitted, therefore, a counter-proposal:

That this Joint Conference of Coal-owners' and Miners' representatives recognise the right of a miner working at the coal-face at the fixed tonnage rates to receive full wages, if employed in an abnormal place, the rate to be the average rate of *wages previously earned by the workman* under normal conditions, which shall not be less than the recognised minimum, or county average rate, paid in each district. Further, machinery shall be set up in the various districts for the purpose of deciding the question as to whether the place in dispute is abnormal. Pending the settlement of the dispute as to whether the place is abnormal or not, the man to be paid the district rate.

To this the owners could not agree. So the meeting ended in a deadlock. Nevertheless, an advance in policy resulted from the meeting. The proposals, and even more what were regarded as the quibbling arguments of the coal-owners, convinced the Executive Committee of what the South Wales delegation could not convince them in July; namely, that the special claim on abnormal working places should be dropped, or rather, merged in the wider claim for a minimum wage. Consequently, when the Annual Conference of the Federation opened the next week at Southport and had on its agenda various resolutions on the principle of the minimum wage—from Durham, Lancashire and Cheshire, Yorkshire and Somerset—the delegates had no difficulty in reaching unanimity. In any case, there could be no going back on the steps already taken, though in going forward they knew that conflict on a national scale might have to be faced. The famous Rule 20 (now Rule 21) might have to be used. Their decision, on October 6, 1911, ran as follows:

That the Federation take immediate steps to secure an individual District Minimum Wage for all men and boys working in mines in the area of the Federation without any reference to the working places being abnormal. In the event of the employers refusing to agree to this then the amended 21st Rule of the Federation be put into operation to demand the same. That a Conference be called on November 14th for the purpose of taking action under Rule 21.

A consequential resolution instructed the Districts to meet their employers on the question and to send delegates ready to report upon the situation to a Special M.F.G.B. Conference to be held on November 14th. Since the 1910 Annual Conference had demanded "a fair living wage" for all miners working "in abnormal places," a twelve-month had gone past with little to show for all they had tried. Henceforth the demand would be for an individual (District) minimum wage; and the demand would have behind it the "sanction" of a general withdrawal of their labour. Thus the general principle of the minimum wage was for the first time affirmed as the

MINER'S WIFE DRYING WET CLOTHES BEFORE THE KITCHEN FIRE

GLAMORGAN COLLIERY, TONYPANDY, NOVEMBER 1910
Police being fed in the power-house

most urgent and immediate aim of the Federation, of sufficient moment to invoke the "sanctions clause" of their constitution.

But there was something more to be done. The old Rule 20 (renumerated, with slight alteration, as Rule 21 the previous year) had been most strictly defensive in its meaning. Always, the intention had been to resist attack. Moreover it had been limited to wages questions only; conditions of labour were not within its ambit. Now, with the growing strength of the Federation, they were for the first time prepared to pass to the offensive, and not only on behalf of all wage rates but to assist what at any one time was a relatively small section of their members. Accordingly, when Durham moved that conditions of labour (e.g. the disputed three-shift system, which the owners had been seeking to introduce into Northumberland) should be added, and when South Wales pressed for advances in wages as well as resistance to reductions to be included, the Annual Conference altered the rule to read as follows:

That whenever any Federation or District is attacked on the wages question or the conditions of labour or with the approval of the Conference specially called for that purpose has tendered notice to improve the conditions of labour or to obtain an advance in wages a Conference shall be called to consider the advisability of joint action being taken. (October 6, 1911.)

5. THE MINIMUM WAGE PRINCIPLE

The general minimum wage rate expressed as a percentage on the 1888 basis was the principle on which the Miners' Federation of Great Britain had originally been built up. Now a similar principle, that of the individual minimum wage, had been decided by the miners at their Southport Annual Conference to be their immediate demand. At the Special Conference held in London on November 14, 1911, they had as first business to receive reports from Districts on the progress of negotiations with the coal-owners. From each District the report was that the coal-owners had refused. In one or two cases, negotiations were still proceeding on what was now the lesser question of abnormal places, but in others (e.g. Lancashire and South Wales) the owners had declared the demand to be a breach of existing Conciliation Board agreements and would have none of it. A fairly general standpoint of the owners, expressed most clearly in Durham, was that the individual minimum wage was wrong in principle, that payment would be divorced from the stint of work performed, and a premium would be put on inefficiency and shirking. In one or two instances owners began to take up the hallowed old slogan: "A fair day's wage for a fair day's work," and turn it against the advocates of the individual minimum wage: Northumbrian delegates confessed to the Conference their embarrassment when they saw the banner with this old device being waved by their opponents. On the second day, however, the report was given that in the Conciliation Board for the Federated area (covering over one-third of the organised miners), the owners' representatives only four days earlier had stated:

The amended proposal for a minimum wage for coal-getters, which you have placed before us, has had our careful consideration. *Whilst we could recommend the adoption of a minimum wage*, the matter is beyond our power to decide today. We propose to take it to our districts, and suggest an adjournment to the 6th December for that purpose. In the meantime the negotiations in regard to abnormal places and boys' and datallers' wages shall be continued in the various districts.

The debate that followed revealed two trends of opinion. John Cairns of Northumberland had moved that, seeing the owners had refused to grant the request for an individual minimum wage, they should take a ballot vote in which the miners would be asked whether they were in favour of giving in notices "to terminate your hiring to enforce the same." In support of this he related how he had been asked by "one of our big magnates, a big landlord" to give a reason for the industrial unrest, and that he had replied "Our men have been under the thumbs of the schoolmasters from at least 1870 until now and our men are more refined than they were forty years ago; they desire better homes, better food, better clothing, better conditions." After this had been seconded by Tom Greenall of Lancashire (he urged that they should let the owners see "that our men are as determined as the leaders" and he hoped that they were not going "so to conduct this business that the men are going to get out of hand" for, he remarked, "there is a great deal of unrest amongst the men with regard to the way we are dealing with this matter"), Herbert Smith of Yorkshire rose to take "the unpopular side." He said he was not afraid of a fight, but that the ground had changed with the owners in some parts of the country now prepared to recommend the principle of the individual minimum wage. "Let me say first of all," he said, "even if it comes to a fight I think I shall fight as long and probably longer than some people who are shouting." He moved an amendment to defer action and for further negotiations. In the debate, George Barker (South Wales), after saying that the assurances received by Herbert Smith were "delusive and absolutely valueless," went on to give a typical case of low wages in his District:

Take the case of a colliery labourer with a standard of 3s. per day, plus fifty per cent, or 4s. 6d. per shift. This makes for a full week's work 27s., but he does not work full; there is the slack time, trade and general holidays to be taken into account, which will reduce the average from six days to five-and-a-half per week, and reduces his average wages from 27s. to 24s. 9d. per week. Let us look now at the family budget, which will work out at something like this for a family of six persons. Rent 6s. per week, coal 1s. 6d., fuel 1s., clothing and foot-wear per week 5s., club doctor and Federation per week 1s., making a total of 14s. 6d. This leaves 10s. 3d. per week for food to feed six persons for a week. Allowing a bare three meals per day, eighteen meals per week—126 meals—with 123 pence to pay for them, or less than 1d. per meal per head.

Have we overstated the case? No; if anything it is understated. There are thousands in this movement that are existing for less than 1d. per meal per head.

This way of reckoning the close relation of work and wages to the subsistence needs of the miner with his family was a typical argument from South Wales. From Northumberland then came a speech which was more in the traditional manner, if not the policy, of Thomas Burt, who as well as most of the other older leaders was present at this Conference. Indeed, out of the 160 delegates, no less than 10 per cent were Members of Parliament, elected to that position after many years of service in building up the unions. The speaker

for Northumberland on this occasion was William Hogg,
who said that in his District also there was difficulty in keeping
the men in hand, and that he was against an adjournment:

Our difficulties will not be lessened by a policy of adjourning. We
must have the same forward policy, or are we going to continue
sectionally? Condemnations of sectionalism have been on everybody's lips. It is out of date. It has been found to be a useless weapon,
and so far as I can see there will be a lot of dissatisfaction, and maybe
defeat, if you still insist upon delay. . . . You know the old saying,
"Hope deferred maketh the heart sick." My disposition and my
general tendency is towards peace, my friends know it, that is my
record in the past, but it seems to me so far as we are concerned we
shall be nearer a state of war before peace can be obtained.

The debate continued, but after Durham and Scotland had
agreed to support the amendment that came from the
Federated Area, it was clear which way the Conference would
decide. Moreover, there were weighty speeches from Alder-
man House of Durham, from Steve Walsh, M.P., who
undoubtedly had an effect on the Conference though he
could not sway his own District of Lancashire, and from the
Vice-President, Robert Smillie, always cautious, who said:
"I personally believe that no power on earth can prevent
a national strike; because the Welsh employers will not give
way on that question and the Scottish owners will not give
way, it is bound to come. Whether we declare it here today
or leave it for some future occasion, it will come." It was
as part of his strategy for a strike which he believed to be
inevitable that he supported further negotiations, which he
felt should be nationally conducted. The amendment was
carried by 376 votes to 238, with Northumberland, Cumberland, Lancashire, Somerset and South Wales voting in the
minority. It ran as follows:

That this Conference having heard the reports from the Districts
on the Minimum Wage Question is glad to learn that those Districts
and Counties associated with the English Conciliation Board have
obtained from the Committee of the Employers' Side of the Board
the principle of the Minimum Wage for all men and boys working
underground. We, therefore, are of opinion that this Conference
should stand adjourned to a further date so that further efforts may
be made to bring about a satisfactory settlement. (November 15,
1911.)

This decision was regarded in some quarters as a sign that the issue was no longer so serious or so immediately threatening. But that same afternoon another resolution was carried embodying the strategy already proposed by Smillie. It was laid down that the best course was to negotiate nationally and that for this purpose the Executive Committee of the M.F.G.B. should formulate a claim for each District. Armed with this, the Executive should "with additional representatives meet the coal-owners of Great Britain at the earliest date, and report immediately thereafter to a National Conference." This, however, was not to prevent or interfere with the negotiations then being carried on in the various Districts.

When the adjourned Special Conference met again on December 20th all doubts had been dissipated. The issues had become clear to all the delegates. For though the Coal Conciliation Board for the Federated Area had met, it was only to reveal the fact that the owners in other parts of the country had rounded on the fourteen Conciliation Board owners as "bits of blacklegs" for having appeared to give away the principle of a minimum wage. To the request for a national meeting with the coal-owners of all Districts, the reply given had been that "no useful purpose would be served." After some discussion arising from the final reports of District negotiations, Smillie carried the Conference with him when he said:

We are face to face, as the Chairman has pointed out, with the most serious crisis that the miners of this country or any other country have ever met with. We are met with what ultimately may be a life or death struggle, and this is not the time to be fault finding. Every person who has been negotiating locally has done his best to get a settlement on the grounds that would be acceptable to the whole of the British coal-field. . . .

I believe the time of district negotiation has gone, and that negotiations in connection with this question must be taken on national lines. . . .

The owners have been humbugging us when they tell us they think no good can come out of a national meeting so long as local negotiations are going on. That seems to me to be an attempt to humbug us and blindfold us. I think the chairman has hardly put it strong enough—he does his best to put things in a strong way, yet a mild way—but I say that the action of the employers is an insult to the Miners' Federation of Great Britain. We should make it clear that the mine-owners are responsible for any crisis that arises, and not the miners or their leaders, who I think have done their best in this matter.

The next day the Conference passed a series of resolutions as prepared by the Executive Committee:

(1) That a ballot vote be taken.

(2) That the ballot vote be taken on January 10, 11, 12, 1912.

(3) That no half-members be allowed to vote.

(4) That the result of the ballot in each District be sent to Mr. Ashton, Secretary of this Federation, not later than January 16, 1912.

(5) That each District send to Mr. Ashton a tabulated statement of what is desired to be its Minimum Wage, and that the Executive Committee of the Federation meet to consider these statements and to report to a National Conference to be held in Birmingham on January 18 and 19, 1912.

(6) That during negotiations special machinery be set up in each District for dealing with exceptional cases such as old and infirm workmen.

On one recommendation of the Committee, "That in case the ballot results in favour of a national stoppage, notice be given in every district, so as to terminate by the end of February 1912," an alteration—afterwards to be of great significance—was made by the Conference. Dr. John Wilson, M.P., pointed out that his District, which of course was a separate registered trade union, had in its rules a stipulation that no strike should be called unless a two-thirds majority had voted for it: and that a legal difficulty might therefore arise. If there were a majority less than two-thirds in Durham, a member of the Association could easily obtain an injunction from the High Court against the payment of strike pay on the grounds that the rule had been broken. The same would be true for any other County Association having a similar rule. He was strongly supported by Charles Fenwick, M.P., and finally the Conference decided:

(7) That in case the ballot results in a two-thirds majority in favour of a national stoppage, notice be given in every district, so as to terminate at the end of February 1912.

With these seven resolutions the die was cast. After so many months of discussion and fruitless negotiation, a ballot vote was to be taken for or against a national strike of coal-miners. In those days they called it "the appeal to Caesar." As Hogg of Northumberland put it: "Now is the time to let Caesar speak."

RULES OF THE MINERS' FEDERATION OF GREAT BRITAIN
(as amended in 1910)

Name and Place of Business

1. This Federation shall be called "The Miners' Federation of Great Britain," its office or place of business shall be at 925 Ashton Old Road, Manchester, or at such other place as may at times be most convenient. It shall consist of Federations and Districts who are eligible to join, by paying an Entrance Fee of One Pound per Thousand Members, or fractional part thereof, but no section of a County, where a Federation or County Association exists, shall be eligible to join.

2. *Objects of the Federation*
   (1) To provide funds to carry on the business of this Federation, the same to be disbursed as provided in the following rules.
   (2) To take into consideration the question of Trade and Wages, and to protect Miners generally.
   (3) To seek to secure Mining Legislation affecting all Miners connected with this Federation.
   (4) To call Conferences to deal with questions affecting Miners, both of a Trade, Wage, and Legislative character.
   (5) To seek and obtain an eight hours' day from bank to bank in all mines for all persons working underground.
   (6) To deal with cases of accidents, and attend inquests upon persons killed, in and about mines, whenever the Executive Committee considers it necessary to do so.
   (7) To assist all Federations and Districts in law cases, where they may have to appeal, or are appealed against, on decisions of the lower Courts.
   (8) To provide funds to pay for the election expenses of labour candidates, and support members who may be returned to the House of Commons.

Officials and Executive Committee

3. There shall be in connection with this Federation, a President, Vice-President, Secretary and Treasurer, and an Executive Committee of not less than twelve members exclusive of officers.

Election of Officers

4. The Officials of this Federation shall be elected or re-elected annually, at the Yearly Conference. Each Official and Committee shall be duly nominated by a financial Federation or District.

5. No person shall be eligible for election or re-election whose

Federation or District is more than one month in arrears in contributions or levies.

Auditors

6. There shall be two Auditors appointed annually, at the Annual Conference, to Audit the Accounts of the Federation.

Trustees

7. There shall be three Trustees appointed who must be members of the Federation, and shall continue in office during the pleasure of the Federation. In the event of any such Trustees dying or being removed from office, at the first meeting of the Federation after the vacancy has been reported to Districts, another or others shall be appointed to supply such vacancy. They shall do and execute all the functions required of them by the Federation. They shall attend at the Audit, and examine the Treasurer's Bank Books, and Bonds, and Documents of Investments.

Annual Conference

8. There shall be an Annual Conference of this Federation held in the month of October each year.

9. Special Conferences shall be called by the President and Secretary when necessary.

10. That all the Officials' Salaries shall be fixed at the Annual Conference.

Voting at Conference

11. That the voting at all Conferences shall be by show of hands, but, in the event of a District or Federation claiming a vote by numbers, the voting shall be One Vote for every One Thousand financial members or fractional part thereof.

12. No Official shall be allowed to vote at any Conference except the Chairman, and then only when there is a tie, he shall give the casting vote.

Committee Meetings

13. The Executive Committee shall meet when required. The President and Secretary shall call all Committee Meetings.

14. The Executive Committee shall, in the absence of a Conference, take into consideration all questions affecting the Mining interests, appoint Delegates to attend Coroners' Courts, appeal cases, enquire into disputes on general wage questions, and [undertake] the watching of legislation affecting the Members of the Federation. In cases of emergency the President and Secretary shall have power to appoint representatives to attend an inquiry.

Contributions

15. That the ordinary contributions to this Society shall be at the rate of One Penny Per Quarter per member, and that the same be paid the first week in each quarter to the Treasurer. The quarters

to commence, January, April, July, and October in each year. The
Executive Committee shall have power to call levies when necessary.
16. That any Federation or District allowing its contributions or
levies to fall into arrears, shall not be entitled to any financial
support until three months after all arrears have been paid up;
neither shall arrears be paid up at any time for the purpose of
obtaining support in any case from the funds of this Federation.

When support shall be given
17. That whenever any stoppage of collieries occurs, arising out of
any action taken by a Conference, a Special Conference shall be
called to determine whether support shall be given to any Federation
or District.
18. The Conference shall, after duly considering each dispute, have
power to raise by levy upon the members of the Federation such
sum as will meet the requirements.
19. No Federation or District shall receive support unless more than
15 per cent of the said Federation or District is out of work, consequent upon any action taken by a General Conference.
20. Members shall be supported, in accordance with Rules 17 and
18, who may have been out of work twenty-one clear days from the
commencement of the dispute; and that pay at the rate of 7s. 6d. per
week per member shall commence on the first day after the expiration
of fourteen days from the commencement of dispute.

Defensive Action[1]
21. That whenever any Federation or District is attacked on the
general wage question, all members connected with the Society
shall tender a notice to terminate their contracts, if approved of by
a Conference called to consider the advisability of such joint action
being taken.

E. EDWARDS, President.
THOS. ASHTON, Secretary.

[1] For 1911 alteration, see p. 81.

CHAPTER IV

THE MINIMUM WAGE STRIKE
OF 1912

I. STRIKE BALLOT AND SCHEDULE OF CLAIMS

NINETEEN-TWELVE, a momentous year in the history of the miners, began with the pitmen preparing to vote in their lodges for or against a strike "to establish the principle of an individual minimum wage for every man and boy working underground." At the same time, in application of this principle, the claims for each District were to be examined and formulated by the Executive Committee. This was no easy task. In the first place, the seventeen Districts of the M.F.G.B. had different conditions of work, different costs of living, and historic differences in wage rates. Within each District there were further differences according to the classes of pits. In addition, each pit had its own price list for the different jobs to be performed. All this was further complicated by the different kinds of underground workers, with their various and varying rates. There were even considerable differences of terminology from District to District. In the second place, whereas most Districts in their stated claims for the individual minimum wage had sought to gain an advance, Scotland had been against this, on the ground that it would break their Conciliation Board agreement. This matter, fully and even acrimoniously discussed in the November and December Conferences, had been finally left for the Committee to settle.

But first, the result of the ballot vote had to be received. At the Special Conference, assembled in Birmingham, on January 18, 1912, the report was given of a vote of 443,801 for strike and 115,921 against; and the decision followed "that notices be tendered in every district so as to terminate at the end of February." The ballot[1] had shown not only the requisite two-thirds majority, but a four to one majority with some of the largest Districts voting in the proportion of six to one or five to one. Only the small District of Cleveland, where the ironstone miners already had a minimum wage, had voted against. The miners' leaders could go forward in the knowledge that the backing from the members of the Federation was even greater than some of them had supposed. But the door was left open for a peaceful solution. The conference was unanimous in the view that the employers should be told:

that the workmen's representatives are prepared to meet them to continue negotiations in districts, and nationally, with a view to arriving at a satisfactory settlement. (January 18, 1912.)

By the end of January the Committee had devoted a three days' session to prepare the schedule of rates. They decided finally to fix the individual minimum wage for piece-workers in each District at the existing rate of wages "as near as can be ascertained." Accordingly the claims were no longer to include an advance. The difficulty of diversity of conditions, classes of work, rates, etc., especially for day-wage men, was overcome by a decision that the individual minimum wage for all piece-workers other than colliers (that is, coal-getters or hewers) "be arranged by the districts themselves and be as near as possible to present wages"; and that, as the rates for the underground workers who were paid by day-wage were "so complex and difficult to deal with generally," these too be left to the Districts with instructions that they endeavour to arrange minimum rates locally in each District. But they made the stipulation that no adult should receive a rate of less than 5s. per shift and that no boy be paid less than 2s. a day.

[1] The full result of the ballot was as follows:

District	For	Against	District	For	Against
Yorkshire	63,736	10,477	Somerset	3,378	370
Lancashire and Cheshire	50,517	11,393	Scotland	60,611	12,035
Midland Federation	26,069	5,275	South Wales	103,526	18,419
Derbyshire	17,999	6,816	Northumberland	22,595	7,557
Nottinghamshire	17,086	5,386	Durham	57,490	28,504
Leicestershire	3,681	907	Cleveland	2,021	5,225
South Derbyshire	2,178	593	Forest of Dean	1,585	243
North Wales	7,327	1,566			
Cumberland	4,918	813	Totals	445,801	115,921
Bristol	1,084	342			

From this stipulation the small coal-fields of Bristol, Somerset and the Forest of Dean were exempt: for the delegates from these fields had pointed out that a rigid application of the 5s. and 2s. in their case would actually result in men and boys being thrown out of work.

The rates for the coal-getters were fixed at the adjourned Special Conference of February 1st and 2nd as follows:

SCHEDULE OF CLAIMS
MINIMUM DAY-WAGE RATES FOR COAL-GETTERS
(Piece-workers at the coal-face)

Nottinghamshire .. .. 7s. 6d.	South Derbyshire .. .. 6s. 6d.
Yorkshire .. .. .. 7s. 6d.	Durham .. .. .. 6s. 1½d.
Derbyshire .. 7s. 1½d. to 7s. 6d.	North Wales .. .. 6s. 0d.
South Wales .. 7s. 1½d. to 7s. 6d.	Scotland .. .. .. 6s. 0d.
Leicestershire .. .. 7s. 2d.	Cleveland .. .. .. 5s. 10d.
Northumberland 6s. 0d. to 7s. 2d.	Forest of Dean .. .. 5s. 10d.
Lancashire .. .. .. 7s. 0d.	Bristol .. .. .. 4s. 11d.
Midland Federation 6s. 0d. to 7s. 0d.	Somerset .. .. .. 4s. 11d.
Cumberland .. .. .. 6s. 6d.	

The coal-owners were now prepared to meet the Miners' Federation. Accordingly the Executive Committee, together with seventeen additional representatives, one from each District, met the coal-owners' representatives at the Westminster Palace Hotel on Wednesday, February 7th. Enoch Edwards stated very minutely all the details connected with the application for a minimum wage. He recalled the earlier joint meeting in September 1911 to consider abnormal places when he had said that the coal-owners might afterwards regret the decision they then came to. Now it had become a much wider question. The coal-owners' Chairman said the proposal was "an entirely new departure of a most drastic nature" and asked what relation it bore to existing wage agreements. Edwards, in reply, said that the rates proposed were fairly conformable with the agreements, but that in so far as there were no agreements for a fixed minimum wage "it may be suggested that we are rather treating the agreements with scant courtesy": on the other hand, these rates were based on those agreements. At this remark the South Wales coal-owners took umbrage. There was an adjournment. On the resumption the Welsh coal-owners were not to be found; but they had left behind them a note referring to Mr.

Edwards' statement and saying: "This being an intimation of the men's intention to tear up existing agreements, the South Wales coal-owners are unable to take any further part in the proceedings."

A question was put from one of the Districts outside the Federated Area: "Is it contended that the minimum wage has to be paid irrespective of the work done, or should the man do fair work and give a fair reason why it does not amount to the quantity that will give the minimum wage?" To this Edwards replied: "We expect always a man will do his work for the money he is paid, and we expect that the machinery set up in Districts and pits will take care that the man does his work, and will take care too that he is paid when he has done it." After a further long adjournment, the coal-owners tabled their decision in the form of a resolution, which in the main repeated the decision they had given half a year before at the joint meeting on abnormal places, but contained the statement that while each person in their employment should receive "a fair day's wage for a fair day's work," they were convinced that "the principle of payment in proportion to the amount of work performed is the only one which can be applied successfully in the case of coal-getters." At this refusal Enoch Edwards felt and expressed the miners' disappointment. Neither side was anxious to break up, but neither side would move. There was another adjournment. The miners then submitted their resolution, which expressed their regret that the coal-owners had "refused to accept the principle" of an individual minimum wage "as we know that there can be no settlement of the present dispute unless this principle is agreed to." But since they had "no desire for a serious rupture in the coal trade of the country" they were willing to meet the coal-owners again at any time. To this resolution the Chairman of the coal-owners promised "the most careful consideration." And so the meeting ended. The employers at this stage were ready to ignore the fact that in other industries, such as engineering and shipbuilding, while there was "payment for the amount of work performed" through systems of piece-work or bonus systems, there was always a recognised basic wage below which earnings could not fall.

There had been occasions before when a ballot with a majority for strike action had not been followed by a strike. No doubt many of the public had hoped that it would be so on this occasion. But this hope began to wither when the joint meeting resulted in deadlock—when it became clear that the miners were determined to force the issue to a conclusion—and with the owners showing no sign, despite the overwhelming ballot vote, of making any concession on the principle. The miners' leaders now had very little hope of a settlement; and as part of the strike preparations called a meeting of the Miners' International Committee, where the four officers of the Federation met representatives of the organised miners of France, Belgium, Germany and Austria. These were colleagues between whom and themselves there were strong bonds of international confidence and trust, colleagues whom they had met year after year at the Congresses of the International Miners' Federation. Vice-President Smillie explained the minimum wage question and the course of events. He mentioned the complication of there being five main Conciliation Areas, the largest of which was the "English" Conciliation Area where the coal-owners were prepared to accept the principle and to negotiate. This was not the case in Durham and Northumberland, while in the Scottish and Welsh areas the owners were fiercely opposed. The ballot figures represented only the organised miners (exclusive of half-members) and if a strike were to take place it would affect over one million employed in and about the mines. The British leaders did not ask for a sympathetic strike, but desired that not one single pound of coal should come to Great Britain from the Continent, if the British mines were stopped. This, of course, could be easily done by the Continental miners working one day less per week than was their normal. The International Committee were agreed and expressed these points in an unanimous resolution. At the same time they passed a second resolution as follows:

That if the miners in any of the Continental Nations at the present time or in the future agree to demand an individual minimum wage and declare a strike to secure it, or enter upon a strike to remedy any other grievances, the miners' representatives of Great Britain agree to recommend that the output in Great Britain be curtailed as far as possible. (February 22, 1912.)

This resolution, expressing as it did the international loyalty of the British miners, set a standard of conduct for the future.

The conduct of negotiations and the preparation for a strike if negotiation failed was carried on by the Executive Committee which from mid-February onwards began to be in almost permanent session in Westminster during week-days, with its members returning to the coal-fields during the week-ends. Four Special Conferences of the M.F.G.B. were held in February, covering ten days of that month, while eleven days of March were similarly occupied. Thus the four officers and the sixteen members of the Executive Committee kept in the closest touch with the 160 Conference delegates, who in turn were going to and from the coal-fields. At each stage the Executive Committee reported progress to the Conference, which discussed and ratified each step in policy. In this way, the miners maintained their community of interest, and gave an example of how democratic control could combine with the effective working of a vast organisation.

In the trying days that had now come upon them the frequent dissensions that had been a feature of M.F.G.B. Conferences for nearly a couple of years disappeared. Many of the newspapers continued to speculate on the division between the "older and more responsible" officials and the "new and irresponsible" coal-field leaders; but the verbatim reports of the Conferences show that there was a remarkable unanimity, from the moment that the employers' refusal to yield (on February 7th) made everyone realise that there was little hope of avoiding a struggle. Enoch Edwards, reporting on that meeting, was greeted with a resolution confirming the action of the Executive Committee and also adding that the Conference "desires to place on record its appreciation of the able, concise and businesslike manner in which Mr. Edwards put our case before the owners."

2. HIS MAJESTY'S GOVERNMENT INTERVENES

A coal stoppage of a magnitude hitherto unknown in any country was now approaching. Previous lock-outs or strikes had been felt only by a section of the British industry. Even the great lock-out of 1893 had affected no more than the central coal-fields, and not all the miners in that area. But if all the miners in the United Kingdom were at one and the same time to stop their production of coal, whose supply was "in a true and not exaggerated sense of the term, the life-blood of the industry of the country," then the effect would be not only greater than anything hitherto but of a quite different kind. Public concern began to grow rapidly; and the suggestion came from public bodies that the Government should mediate. In the 1893 lock-out, Government intervention had not taken place until after four months. This time it began before the strike. At the end of the third week of February, a letter from the Prime Minister to Thomas Ashton, beginning, "Sir, His Majesty's Government have watched with close attention, and growing anxiety, the development of the present crisis in the coal trade," offered mediation "to avert the disaster of a national stoppage."

There were other reasons for them to be brisk about it. Not only ministers but all the ruling circles of the country had been troubled by the great strikes of 1911, and that not so much for their magnitude (thrice that of two years earlier) as for the kind of strike. It showed a new temper in the working class that boded ill to "constitutionalism." From the seamen's strike in June 1911, nearly all the docks and other transport came to be affected until the ports of London and Liverpool were stopped and the first national railway strike took place in August. The Port of London Authority, having refused to parley, had for a time the support of the Government in this.[1] Meanwhile the Agadir crisis in foreign affairs, which nearly precipitated the European war, was continuing at high tension throughout that summer.

The four officials in a meeting with Prime Minister Asquith made it clear that the Miners' Conference alone had authority in such a matter. Like Mr. Speaker Lenthall in the Long Parliament, they had "neither eyes to see nor tongue to speak in this place, but as this House is pleased to direct." There-

---

[1] "The War Office, at the request of Mr. Winston Churchill, who was then at the Home Office, accumulated troops in London, and actually threatened to put 25,000 soldiers to break the strike by doing the dockers' work—a step that would undoubtedly have led to bloody conflict in the streets." (Webb, *History of Trade Unionism*.)

upon the Prime Minister invited the whole Conference to come to the Foreign Office, there to meet with himself, the Chancellor of the Exchequer, the Foreign Secretary and the President of the Board of Trade. The M.F.G.B. Conference on February 27th discussed and accepted the invitation and proceeded to the Foreign Office.

Asquith, now in his sixtieth year, was at the height of his powers as a persuasive advocate. After a brilliantly successful career at the Bar and in Parliament, he had been Home Secretary in Gladstone's last administration. Then as one of the Liberal Imperialist group (to whom alone within the Cabinet the secret war engagements with France before 1914 were fully known) he had succeeded the Radical Campbell-Bannerman in 1908 as Prime Minister. Like other Liberal Imperialists he was prepared to modify the old *laissez-faire* attitude so far as to admit of welfare legislation but never so as to imperil the existing framework of society or the undisputed private ownership and control of the staple trades. Moreover, as party leader he could not well forget that several of the most prominent coal-owners sat on the Liberal benches. He had already before February 27th had more than one interview with the coal-owners' representatives of whom a big majority were prepared to agree to "the principle" of a minimum wage.

As he surveyed the 170 M.F.G.B. delegates assembled in the Foreign Office, amongst them the known faces of seventeen Members of Parliament, he could see a round dozen who until a couple of years before had been fellow members of the Liberal Party. There, too, sat Thomas Burt, M.P., and John Wilson, M.P., each staunchly Liberal still. Besides, ever since 1910 the Labour members had voted consistently to keep his administration in office and to keep out the Tories. He could remember how nearly twenty years earlier the magic of a meeting at the Foreign Office (its lustre still undimmed) under his old chief the Earl of Rosebery had sufficed to knit up "the ravelled sleeve of care" in the coal-fields. Altogether it was with every hope of gaining his case that Asquith began his speech to the delegates.

With persuasive utterance he explained why there had been intervention, stated the conclusion of the Government that on the principle of the minimum wage the miners were right, informed them that only a minority of the coal-owners were now resisting the principle, and finally besought the delegates to abandon the application of the principle at the figures set forth in the resolution of February 2nd. "There is not a trade, small or great, which employs labour and mechanical appliances, which does not in the long run depend as much on the coal industry as we all of us depend for our daily bread upon the industry of agriculture." Therefore, he said, the Government had intervened "departing from what has been usual and customary," and he with his colleagues after a week's consideration "without any prepossession, prejudice, party or class bias in one direction or the other and with a perfectly open mind" had reached certain conclusions, with the assent

"of a very considerable majority of the employers" that "it is not right, that it is not just, that it is not in the interest of the community that this great interest of yours should be carried on without adequate securities and safeguards for the attainment by underground workers of a reasonable minimum wage. . . ."

He added that since the aim was not to raise the wages of the coal-miners as a whole (most already getting more than the minimum wage) but, in the interests of a minority

it is an unselfish demand on the part of the great bulk of the miners.

The greater part of his speech was then taken up with a plea that the miners should "allow a reasonable latitude for discussion" in regard to particular rates in the Districts. He stressed the "terrible responsibilities" that lay upon the minority of the coal-owners who clung to their particular formula against a minimum wage, or upon the miners if they clung to a particular set of figures. The principle once conceded of "a reasonable minimum wage for underground workers, which the Government makes itself responsible to secure," urged the Prime Minister, "is it not right, is it not fair, is it not commonsense that in regard to this figure or that, there should be at any rate a reasonable latitude of discussion and consideration?"

The delegates to the Special Conference were impressed by the Prime Minister's eloquence, but were not won over.

They made their standpoint clear: most Districts had originally submitted figures on which there could be latitude for discussion. But when they found that the owners in many Districts refused to have discussions and that bargaining was impossible, they themselves as a Federation had deliberately reduced those figures, had cut them to the bone. Any negotiation to bring down those figures would actually mean a reduction of earnings from what was customary in many, if not most, of the pits. No doubt amongst his audience at the Foreign Office that day Asquith saw in many faces an involuntary admiration at the forensic skill with which he presented the Government's case and sought to weaken the standpoint of the miners. But as he ruefully confessed a few days later to the House of Commons, he had failed in his object. He had argued, so he told the House, that it was impossible for Parliament to be asked to coerce the owners

to accept, not merely the principle, but the very figures which had been dictated by the men without inquiry, without negotiation, without any machinery for arriving at an equitable determination.

I put that argument to the men, and though I have in the course of my life, professional and political, had to present many cases . . . it has never been my good fortune to present a case which seemed to me so irresistible from the point of reason, justice and common sense.

As I watched these men, the very flower of the mining industry of this country, while I was speaking—I was over-sanguine—I flattered myself, and I think some of my right hon. Friends shared my opinion, that I had almost persuaded them. Well, I did not.

Meantime, the Chancellor of the Exchequer, in response to a question, had informed the House of Commons of the standpoints expressed by the Government and by the coal-owners and miners in the meetings held on February 27th. The proposals submitted by the Government for settlement of the dispute were as follows:

1. His Majesty's Government are satisfied, after careful consideration, that there are cases in which underground employees cannot earn a reasonable minimum wage, from causes over which they have no control.

2. They are further satisfied that the power to earn such a wage should be secured by arrangements suitable to the special circumstances of each district. Adequate safeguards to be provided to protect the employers against abuse.

3. His Majesty's Government are prepared to confer with the parties as to the best method of giving practical effect to these conclusions, by means of district Conferences between the parties, a representative appointed by the Government being present.
4. In the event of any of the Conferences failing to arrive at a complete settlement within a reasonable time, the representatives appointed by His Majesty's Government to decide jointly any outstanding points for the purpose of giving effect in that district to the above principles.

The Miners' Federation, while in accord with points (1) and (2) of the Government's proposals, stated on point (3) that they would enter into Conferences only on the understanding that the minimum rates for coal-getters should be those as revised and finally adopted at the Special Conference of February. This standpoint consequently applied to point (4), the proposal for arbitration by Government representatives. In point of fact, the M.F.G.B. repeatedly throughout its existence had declared itself against any form of compulsory arbitration and had always formed part of the majority by which the Trades Union Congress had also repeatedly declared against it.

The coal-owners, on the other hand, were, by an overwhelming majority, in favour of accepting the Government's proposals. For example, the employers on the English Coal Conciliation Board (Lancashire, Yorkshire, Midlands, Notts, Derby and North Wales) had answered by a resolution:

1. The coal-owners in the Federated Area accept the proposals put forward by His Majesty's Government.
2. In accepting the proposals the coal-owners expect the Government to make such arrangements as will enable them to look forward with confidence to the due performance of agreements entered into in the future and to secure that such agreements shall be binding on both sides for some considerable period.

The employers from the Durham coal-field reluctantly accepted the following resolution:

The proposals of the Government will impose serious additional burdens on the coal trade, and the coal-owners of the County of Durham, if consulting their own interests, would hesitate to consent to the conditions put forward. In view, however, of the disastrous consequences which must result to the country from a stoppage of work, the owners will be prepared to accept the proposals.

The Cumberland employers also accepted the proposals of the Government, but the Northumberland coal-owners, by a majority, refused to accept them. The Scottish coal-owners' reply was more ambiguous but it was treated as a refusal:

The coal-owners of Scotland regret that they cannot accept the proposals of His Majesty's Government.

They abide by the agreement made at the Board of Trade on July 30, 1909, to which the President and officials of the Board of Trade were parties.

If there are cases in which underground employees do not earn a reasonable wage it is in exceptional circumstances. The coal-owners are prepared to meet the employees' representatives with a representative of the Government to arrange machinery to prevent any injustice and to fix remuneration in abnormal places in cases of dispute.

They are prepared to agree that in the event of such meeting failing to arrive at a settlement the matter should be referred to the decision of a neutral chairman.

There was no hedging, or majority and minority, in the case of South Wales:

The coal-owners of South Wales adhere strictly to their present Agreement, which terminates by notice at the earliest date on March 31, 1915.

After most careful consideration they are unanimous in stating that they cannot agree to the Government's proposals.

Thus the Conferences of the Government in these last hours of February proved fruitless to avert the stoppage. They were continued on the morning of March 1st, but that afternoon the Prime Minister informed the House of Commons that the Government proposals had been declined both by a section of the coal-owners and by the miners. It had come, said Asquith, "not to a breakdown but to a deadlock."

3. THE GREAT STRIKE OF 1912

By Friday, March 1st, the United Kingdom was faced by a situation never before experienced, never even dreamt of. One million miners out on strike: 800,000 that day alone. Such a concerted cessation of work had never before occurred in the

mining or any other industry, in Britain or any other country.[1]
Apart from the "safety men" whose continued employment
had been sanctioned by the Federation, practically all the
miners of the country were out on strike, the Home Office
returns giving the figures, as at December 31, 1911, of:

Underground workers	..	878,759
Surface workers ..	..	210,331
		1,089,090

Throughout the coal-fields of England, Scotland and Wales,
no coal was being gotten or wound to the surface. The wheels
stood idle. The miners in their villages were waiting, confident
that their cause would win. A golden harvest of ready
audiences was furnished to Labour and Socialist speakers,
as well, of course, as to the miners' own trade union representatives as they reported decisions of Conferences. It meant
short rations for weeks ahead since strike pay was a meagre
substitute for full earnings. The miners' wives, while relieved
from the daily tedium of preparing hot water and clean
clothes for their sons and husbands returning from the pits
—(few pit baths in those days!)—had the new anxiety of
how to feed their children, their husbands and themselves
on a few shillings.

Meantime, the other side were also waiting. The coal-
owners, who had no privations to endure, witnessed a rapid
rise in the price of coal from which those who had big stocks
reaped considerable benefit. In certain coal-fields, the owners,
or some of them, appeared to be convinced that only after
the miners' funds were depleted would they be able to reach
a settlement, and for this they too were prepared to wait.

The effect on industry and on the domestic use of coal,
widely felt by the end of the first week of March, increased
thereafter from day to day. Factories began to close down
while others went on short time to conserve coal. The railways
restricted their services, as did other forms of transport.
Express trains were taken off and other train services reduced
by as much as a third or a quarter. Great numbers of rail-

[1] Apart from the General Strike of October 1905 in Russia.

waymen and transport workers, and considerable numbers
in other industries, were thrown out of work. The home fires
were burning low. In residential colleges students were
huddled together to use only the fire in one room out of half
a dozen. Elsewhere similar conditions developed. There was
a gradual slowing down of the pulse of industrial life.

After the strike began public attention on the coal question
rose to a high pitch. All kinds of bodies and agencies interested
themselves. In 1893, four of the chief cities of the Midlands
had, through a meeting of their Lord Mayors, sought to find
a way out of the impasse in the lock-out. This time, in the
last week of February 1912, all the Mayors and Provosts of
Great Britain headed by the Lord Mayor of London held
a meeting and communicated with the disputants. The
miners' leaders sent a courteous reply.

Having failed to secure a settlement, the Government for
a few days hoped that something might come out of the
meetings of the Industrial Council, a transient body appointed
the previous year for "the prevention and settlement of
Labour disputes." The Industrial Council, meeting from
March 4th to March 7th, proved then and thereafter to be

> Like the snowflake on the river
> A moment white, then gone for ever.

In any case the Executive Committee of the M.F.G.B. did
not feel that they could participate "since negotiations with
the Prime Minister and his colleagues are not broken off,
and we know of no higher authority than the Government."
It was a snub to the Government for trying to shuffle off
its responsibilities. On March 7th, the Government publicly
resumed its task. The Executive Committee minutes report
an interview that day with the Prime Minister and three of
his colleagues at 10, Downing Street.

> The Premier asked if there was any change since last week. Did
> the Federation still stand to an irreducible minimum? Mr. Edwards
> assured him that that was so.

At a further meeting the miners made it clear that on any
question of a Joint Meeting with coal-owners there could be
no rediscussion of the principle of the minimum wage. The

Government, while maintaining its own proposals, felt that without mutual discussion between the parties there would be no progress, and therefore had issued an invitation saying: "His Majesty's Government invite both parties to meet them jointly in conference without prejudice, with a view to a free discussion of the whole situation." The Special Conference of March 11th accepted this by resolution which ended with the words "with the understanding that the principle of the minimum wage is excluded from the discussion."

The next day, March 12th, there was a Joint Meeting of coal-owners' and coal-miners' representatives under the chairmanship of Mr. Asquith, which continued on Wednesday, the 13th, and on Thursday, the 14th. Meantime the Conference, in continuous session, heard reports as to the progress of negotiations from the Executive Committee. After the first day of Joint Meeting they passed a resolution expressing their regret that the mine-owners had "not shown any disposition to concede the rates of wages claimed by the workmen." They added that: "Conference cannot advise a resumption of work until a minimum wage is agreed to." They professed willingness, however, to meet the owners at any time for the purpose of securing a settlement.

After the second day of Joint Meeting, the Conference on the morning of Thursday, March 14th, heard read to them a suggestion, made by the Prime Minister the previous evening, that the particular figures with their complex and intricate nature should be discussed separately by the representatives on either side in each coal-field, with some neutral person present in each case. "I have listened," Mr. Asquith had said, "with great interest to the experts of Yorkshire and Northumberland; but a great expert at the other end of the room (Colonel Shaw) said it was all Greek to him, although he is a most experienced coal-owner in Yorkshire." Reasonable though this sounded (and great personal relief as it would have been to the Prime Minister) the Conference saw in it a danger. National negotiations for District schedules had meant "united we stand." Coal-field discussions on coal-getters' rates might bring divisions in their own ranks. Therefore the Conference decided that they could not take negotiations on the main figures out of the hands of the Executive

Committee; but conceded that if those main figures (the colliers'—or coal-getters'—different rates and the 5s. and 2s. for men and boys) were agreed to, they would thereafter accept District negotiations on the minimum rates to be paid to day-wage men and to piece-workers other than colliers. Further, at such District meetings they stated their willingness to agree to "the proposal of the Prime Minister that some neutral person might attend to help to guide the discussions to facilitate an agreement."

Later that Thursday, during the Joint Meeting (which some of the coal-owners refused to attend) the Prime Minister pressed the Executive Committee to go further and to accept arbitration by the "neutral person." To this the miners' representatives, though perplexed by their own inability to put forward definite figures for day-wage men and for piece-workers other than colliers, felt they had no warrant to agree; and the Conference, with its strong repugnance to compulsory arbitration, unanimously confirmed their decision.

Meantime the Ministers had also been making heavy weather with the coal-owners' side. Not only the three-day Joint Meeting, but also the separate discussions with the employers, had failed to bring a settlement. Accordingly, when the Conference reassembled on the evening of Friday, March 15th, it heard of the complete breakdown of the negotiations. "We have had a lengthy day at the Foreign Office," reported Enoch Edwards, "and it has not been a joint meeting between the owners and us, it has simply been your Committee with the representatives of the Government. They . . . have abandoned all hope of ever coming to an agreement with the employers. . . . We have worked hard and deserved better success, but it is the lot of people sometimes to fall short of their deserts. . . . Mr. Asquith has told us that they shall bring in a Bill to compel the owners to pay a minimum wage."

Thus the second attempt at mediation had failed. It was a far cry from the days of 1893 when Mr. Gladstone's letter had come like a summons from lofty Olympus for the sons of men to compose their differences. The road to the summit of the parliamentary Olympus, which had then seemed far away and inaccessible, now lay open before them; and, subjected to ever-increasing watchfulness and sensitive to criticism, His Majesty's Government seemed less majestic.

Nevertheless, for the moment the Executive Committee hoped for much from Asquith's announcement that legislation would be introduced. They handed in to him their stipulations: namely, (1) no resumption of work until the Bill became an Act of Parliament; (2) a time limit thereafter of one month to settle the details; (3) the rates of wages to be retrospective from the date of resumption of work; (4) the 5s. for adult workers and the 2s. for boys' minimum to be in the Bill; (5) a minimum rate in each of the seventeen Districts of the M.F.G.B. On Tuesday, March 19th, the Prime Minister introduced the Minimum Wage Bill for its First Reading in the House of Commons, and explained that the Cabinet had decided not to include any figures in the Bill, but only to embody the minimum wage principle and to set up the District machinery for giving effect to it. On the same day the Attorney-General authorised the arrest of Tom Mann, the stormy petrel of the working-class movement.

The M.F.G.B. Conference, meeting on Wednesday, March 20th, at once passed a resolution that "No Act of Parliament which does not provide for the inclusion of a minimum wage of not less than 5s. per day for all adult workers other than piece-workers, and 2s. a day for boys at fourteen, will be acceptable to the workmen." On this all were agreed. But now there was the first rift in the unanimity that had marked all the Conferences since February 2nd. The Executive Committee's resolution that the Bill "ought to contain the schedule rates for hewers in each separate district" met with opposition. "Not 'ought to' but 'must,'" said Harry Twist of Lancashire, who thought the negotiators were weakening after several weeks' pressure from Asquith and Lloyd George. Twist's amendment was supported by his own county and by Yorkshire, South Wales, Northumberland, Nottinghamshire and others; and on a card vote received 321 votes against 269. So it was decided that not only the 5s. and 2s., but the whole table of figures must be in the Bill, and that the Labour Party be called on to move the amendment for this inclusion. Otherwise the Bill was to be dealt with by the Executive Committee, supplemented by

Members of Parliament representing the Federation, for the purpose of drafting such amendments as would "bring the Bill into harmony with the decision of the Federation."

Next day, Thursday, March 21st, the Bill went to Second Reading and was carried against Conservative opposition by 348 votes to 325. The Labour Party (including the M.F.G.B. Members) voted for the Second Reading but gave notice of amendments. These amendments were presented on Friday, 22nd, and then on the Report Stage on Tuesday, 26th. All important amendments were defeated by the combined vote of Liberals, Conservatives and Irish Nationalists. The inclusion of the schedule of rates, moved by Enoch Edwards, M.P., was defeated on the 23rd, as was the 5s. and 2s. When the Bill was reported back to the House on the 26th, William Brace again moved to insert the 5s. and 2s. During that week the Government, who were also meeting the owners, had held frequent conferences with the miners' representatives, who were thereby led to believe that the figures would be inserted by agreement. Their disappointment was correspondingly great. They felt that all the hints given them and all the assurances had only served "to lead them up the garden." Accordingly the M.F.G.B. Conference in the early evening of Tuesday, March 26th, decided that the Labour Party be advised to vote against the Bill. Late that night the Bill passed its Third Reading by 213 votes to 48, and was sent to the House of Lords. In the House of Lords the Bill passed through Second Reading, Committee and Third Reading in a couple of days. The minor amendments from the Second Chamber were accepted by the Commons; and the Bill became law when the Royal Assent was given on March 29th.

As soon as the Bill, against the will of the Federation, had passed through the Commons the Conference recognised immediately that a new stage had been reached and that their mandate was now exhausted. Therefore, on Wednesday, March 27th, after a resolution of thanks to the Labour Party "for the great help they have rendered," the Conference decided that a ballot vote of the men be taken with the utmost speed on whether or not to go on with the strike. The Conference then dissolved. The Government which had brought in the Act, the coal-owners who had now accepted it, the Parliament which had passed it, the other trade unions which were now paying each week increasing sums in unemployment benefit, awaited the result of the ballot. But not only these: for the whole country, as well as great masses of workers in Europe and the U.S.A., were keenly watching the outcome.

4. DEMOCRATS' DILEMMA

The miners generally believed that they had been tricked. The new law gave no more, they felt, than had already been conceded in the English coal-fields: and the actual wages for which they had come out on strike were still in hazard. This was also the opinion voiced by some Socialist leaders. Politically there was a strong revulsion of feeling against the Liberals, for whom a majority of the workers had voted fifteen months earlier. Abroad, the leaders of the Continental unions were perplexed at the issue. From Paris Lenin commented:

> The Government pretended to be neutral, intervened in the negotiations between the workers and the capitalists, pretended to yield to the workers, secured the recognition in Parliament of the *principle* of the minimum wage, but, *as a matter of fact*, took the side of capital and did not do anything to secure this minimum wage,

and he drew the moral, since it was "obvious whose interests the Liberals were defending," that the English workers "cannot but realise how important a political organisation, a political party is for them."[1]

In great haste and in a bitter mood, the miners recorded their votes. Aware of this mood, the delegates on March 27th had decided that "this Conference does not advise, but leaves the ballot paper, as agreed, for the men to use their own judgment." Therefore the ballot paper put the bare question:

> Are you in favour of resuming work pending settlement of the minimum rates of wages in the various grades by the district boards to be appointed under the Mines Minimum Wage Act?

By Wednesday, April 3rd, the results had reached Ashton.

[1] *Collected Works*, Vol. XV.

The miners had voted to continue the strike by 244,011 to 201,013.

Amongst the larger Districts[1] only the Midlands Federation and South Wales had voted to end the strike. In the Midlands this had meant a relatively small turnover. But why had South Wales changed from nearly a six to one majority for strike in January to a two to one majority against strike in April? Undoubtedly the main reason was the growing hunger in the mining valleys through the exhaustion of strike pay and the fact that, unlike other Districts, South Wales had no convenient industry which could give employment to members of the miners' families. Furthermore, the South Wales Miners' Federation had begun the strike with lower funds per head than any other large coal-field, due partly to the regular contribution being lower than the others and partly to the draining away of resources in the support of the Cambrian Combine and other strikes.

Whatever the reasons for the diverse District votes, the Executive Committee had to consider the total figures and decide on the further steps to be taken. The ballot put them in a quandary. As a committee they were convinced that a continuance of the strike might result in a serious strain on the unity of the Federation—and this not only because the largest District was for a return to work. Under the pressure of a continued strike the District boards might fix the desired minimum in some cases, but in others they might not. In that event it was easy to foresee the disintegration of the national struggle into District fights. On the other hand they were all convinced democrats, accustomed to accept majority decisions. True, there had been a conference decision that the strike notices would be given only if there were a

[1] The votes by District were as follows:

District	For resumption	Against	District	For resumption	Against
Scotland	23,186	30,473	Bristol	772	326
Lancashire and Cheshire	11,334	29,840	Somerset	2,130	1,220
Yorkshire	13,267	43,914	Cleveland	4,919	908
Derbyshire	8,080	13,428	North Wales	7,446	1,190
Nottinghamshire	8,187	8,213	South Derby	1,626	1,090
Midland Federation	18,168	11,278	Forest of Dean	No ballot	
Cumberland	2,980	4,877	Leicester	1,195	3,104
South Wales	62,538	31,127			
Durham	24,511	48,828	Totals	201,013	244,011
Northumberland	10,674	14,195			

two-thirds majority in favour: but this had been entirely against precedent and was accepted by many only because they were so sure that the majority would be overwhelming. In any case, if Scotland and South Wales had got from the Act the enforcement of the principle on their stubborn coal-owners, there had been no such gain in the English coal-fields where the principle was already conceded: and in the English coal-fields the ballot showed a majority of over two-thirds against returning to work. Truly, they were on the horns of a dilemma. Eventually, after very long discussion, they came to a decision to end the strike, in the following form:

Seeing that there is no provision in the rules or regulations of the Federation to guide this Committee as to the majority required to continue the strike, except the resolution passed at the Conference held December 21st, 1911, that a two-thirds majority was required to declare a national strike, we agree that the same majority be required to continue the strike; and seeing that a two-thirds majority is not in favour of the continuance of the strike, and acting upon that vote, we advise the resumption of work. (April 4, 1912.)

Two days later, on Saturday, April 6th, a Special Conference of the M.F.G.B. heard the arguments for this resolution, moved by the Vice-President Smillie and seconded by Straker of Northumberland. Lancashire and Yorkshire were opposed; but the Conference accepted the resolution by card vote of 449,500 against 125,000 for Lancashire and Yorkshire. The strike was to be ended. Already in the Midlands and one or two smaller Districts men had gone back to work. By mid-April resumption of work was general; and by the end of the month practically all the pits were working.

The strike had lasted for about six weeks. It had been fought on a simple issue of trade union principle, on behalf of a minority of the underground workers. It ended with great dissatisfaction amongst the pitmen, who felt that the Government had cheated them of an assured victory. But the struggle had welded the Federation together into a stronger body than ever before and prepared the way for a great advance in the general political growth of the working-class movement.

5. SYNDICALISM?

Throughout the weeks of the strike and amid the protracted negotiations, coal-field discussions and parliamentary debates, the struggle for the minimum wage as a principle and for its concrete application was treated in many quarters as being the outcome of "a revolutionary conspiracy." After this accusation had been current in the newspapers for nearly a month, it was given full expression in the debate of March 19th on the First Reading of the Bill. Lord Robert Cecil, M.P., son of the Conservative Prime Minister Lord Salisbury, and cousin to his successor A. J. Balfour, was well qualified to express the hopes and fears of that group of ruling families whose members had guided British political life for nearly two centuries. To him it was "no ordinary strike" but "part of a great conspiracy," an attempt to gain "dictatorial powers over the industries of this country by a small band of revolutionaries." In proof of this he cited the agitation begun eighteen months earlier by Tom Mann and the unexampled growth since then in the number and size of strikes. He said:

I would rather even that the strike should go on to its bitter end than that we should teach these Syndicalists the lesson that they have merely to hold up the whole industry of the country, that they need merely put a spoke into the wheels of civilisation, for this Parliament to do almost everything they demand.

He ended with an attempt to find the root cause for the "class hostility which is a profound danger to civilisation." It was, he explained to the House of Commons, the wage system.

I submit that the system by which you buy the labour of a fellow creature, without any other element in it than the mere transaction of bargain and sale of another man's labour, is a thoroughly bad system. Perhaps the highest, or rather the lowest, point of this system is reached in the fairs which take place in the northern part of the Kingdom, where farmers hire labourers for the year on a most barbarous system. It is mitigated to a very great degree by what the Honourable Members opposite describe as the feudalism of the South. The personal relationship between employers and employed which prevails in the agricultural industry in the South is an immense mitigation of what this wage system has brought about.

Other speakers in the House of Commons followed suit on Syndicalism. They included in their attack all those who spoke for Socialism, even going so far as to brand Mr. Lloyd George as a Syndicalist. Naturally, this drew from the Labour benches indignant denials of any Syndicalist leanings. The Bill passed without this issue being settled; nevertheless, throughout the whole of the second decade of the twentieth century there was a widespread belief that "industrial unrest" amongst the miners and in other trades was due mainly to what Lord Robert had called, in language which is not unfamiliar, "a band of men with revolutionary and anarchical theories."

What was the origin of all this pother? The word "Syndicalism" came from France and was indeed to begin with no more than the French word for trade unionism. But it came to mean more than that, as the General Confederation of Labour (in whose origins there was a carry-over from anarchist elements) came to its full development in France. The theoretic outlook of the General Confederation of Labour (called for short the C.G.T.) was stated most fully in its Charter of Amiens (September 1906), which at the time came as a shock to leading Socialists in Britain—and was still capable, nearly forty years later, of exciting the Fabian Bernard Shaw to anger in retrospect. The Charter of Amiens affirmed:

In the sphere of everyday demands, Trade Unionism aims at co-ordinating the efforts of the workers and improving their conditions through the realisation of immediate ameliorations, such as the shortening of hours, increase of wages, etc.

But this is only one aspect of its work; Trade Unionism is preparing the integral emancipation, which can be realised only by the expropriation of the capitalist class; it commends, as a means to this end, the GENERAL STRIKE, and considers that the Trade Union, now a grouping for the purpose of resistance, will be in the future the basis of social organisation, as the group for production and distribution. . . .

Moreover, in sharp contrast with the developing trend of the British movement, the French trade unions were to keep strictly aloof from political parties. In the words of the Charter:

Economic action should be exercised directly against the class of employers, and the Confederal organisations must not, as Trade Union bodies, pay any attention to parties and sects which, outside of them and by their side, are at full liberty to work for the transformation of society.

The C.G.T., founded in 1902, inspired on the other side of the Atlantic, in a country with very different conditions, the formation of the I.W.W. (the Industrial Workers of the World), which had an early connection with the Western Federation of Miners. The 1905 preamble of the I.W.W. began with the words:

The working class and the employing class have nothing in common.

There can be no peace as long as hunger and want are found amongst millions of the working people, and the few who form the employing class have all the good things of life.

Between these classes a struggle must go on until all the toilers come together on the political as well as on the industrial field, and take hold of that which they produce by their labour through an economic organisation of the working class, without affiliation with any political party.

How, from these two sources, did Syndicalism come to Britain? Or what was its origin here? The Webbs, in their *History of Trade Unionism*, consider the pioneer to have been James Connolly, afterwards organiser of the Irish Transport and General Workers' Union. Connolly, called by the Webbs "a man of noble character and fine intelligence, whose tragic execution in 1916 after the suppression of the Dublin rising, made him one of the martyred heroes of the Irish race," was a disciple of one of the founders of the I.W.W. and in 1905 he set up a Socialist Labour Party on the Clyde. In one of his pamphlets Connolly wrote:

It is an axiom, enforced by all the experience of the ages, that they who rule industrially will rule politically. . . . That natural law leads us as individuals to unite in our craft, as crafts to unite in our industry, as industries in our class; and the finished expression of that evolution is, we believe, the appearance of our class upon the political battle-ground with all the economic power behind it to enforce its mandates. Until that day dawns our political parties of the working class are but propagandist agencies, John the Baptists of the New Redemption; but when that day dawns our political party will be armed with all the might of our class; will be revolutionary in fact as well as in thought.

Let us be clear as to the function of Industrial Unionism. That function is to build up an industrial republic inside the shell of the political State, in order that when that industrial republic is fully organised it may crack the shell of the political State and step into its place in the scheme of the universe. . . . Under a Socialist form of society the administration of affairs will be in the hands of representatives of the various industries of the nation; . . . the workers in the shops and factories will organise themselves into unions, each union comprising all the workers at a given industry; . . . said union will democratically control the workshop life of its own industry, electing all foremen, etc., and regulating the routine of labour in that industry in subordination to the needs of society in general, to the needs of its allied trades and to the department of industry to which it belongs. . . . Representatives elected from these various departments of industry will meet and form the industrial administration or national government of the country.

It was not until Tom Mann returned to Britain in May 1910 from his eight years' sojourn in the Dominions that the new doctrines began to be widespread or to have a direct effect. With the rise in the cost of living (25 per cent increase in food prices between 1896 and 1910), and with the fall of the high hopes placed in the Labour Party in 1906, the soil was receptive. The hour had come, and with it Tom Mann. A flood of publications and periodicals began to percolate in the mine-fields and amongst the transport workers. Tom Mann himself became once more an organiser of the Dockers' Union and in the summer of 1911, at the head of a Strike Committee, held up the great port of Liverpool for over ten weeks, during which time, despite all the efforts of Home Secretary Winston Churchill in sending gunboats and cavalry to the Mersey, the industrial life of the city moved only by permits from the Strike Committee. So strong was the hold of the Strike Committee on the minds of the dockers that Catholics and Orangemen joined together in a brass band led by a conductor who waved a baton of mingled green and orange.

The Government, aware that Tom Mann's agitation had played a part earlier in 1911 in the Cambrian Combine strike, were somewhat apprehensive as the 1912 coal dispute developed. However much they might be reassured by the benign features and pacific manner of Enoch Edwards, they could forget neither the tumult and use of troops at Tonypandy nor the startling counter to the use of troops—the "Don't Shoot" leaflet[1]—which Tom Mann was now employing. On the one hand this made the Home Office chary of using troops in the coal-fields; on the other, it decided them when the strike was in its third week to effect the arrest of Tom Mann on a charge under the Incitement to Mutiny Act of 1795. Actually, as the narrative has shown, the minimum wage agitation was a normal development of the traditional living wage policy, ripened by the events of 1910–11 in South Wales: and in the conduct of the dispute there was no theoretic affirmation of new doctrine. This did not prevent newspapers and parliamentary orators from ascribing it all to "Syndicalism," or from exaggerating the influence at the time of the small Syndicalist group in the coal-fields.

6. "THE MINERS' NEXT STEP"

During the Cambrian Combine strike a sharp clash of policy developed between the leaders of the South Wales Miners' Federation and the Cambrian Strike Committee. It became a cleavage throughout the Welsh valleys. The strike ended, but the discussions of it went on. Out of these discussions a group called the "Unofficial Reform Committee" produced a suggested scheme for the reorganisation of the Welsh Federation, and published it at the beginning of 1912 under the title *The Miners' Next Step*. This little pamphlet, written with great vigour, was to become well known not only to miners but to all the readers of the more Conservative newspapers (the *Morning Post* never ceased to quote from it

[1] "Men! Comrades! Brothers! You are in the army. So are we. You, in the army of Destruction. We, in the Industrial army of Construction.

"We work at mine, mill, forge, factory, or dock, etc., producing and transporting all the goods, clothing stuffs, etc., which makes it possible for people to live.

"You are Workingmen's Sons.

"When we go on Strike to better Our lot, which is the lot also of Your Fathers, Mothers, Brothers, and Sisters, YOU are called upon by your Officers to MURDER US. Don't do it."

for a dozen years to come) and, though it had small effect on the 1912 strike, the Syndicalist views expressed in it were to exercise an influence later on certain aspects of M.F.G.B. policy, occasionally to the embarrassment of some of those who had been amongst its authors. The pamphlet began with an examination of the methods and policy previously pursued in the South Wales coal-field, and went on to attack, not only the old leaders, but leadership as such ("the remedy is not new leaders") and thereafter set out a programme, a draft constitution, and a statement of policy. It was a curious amalgam: practical proposals for new rules were afterwards to be adopted in South Wales by many who could not accept the new "principles" from which, in the pamphlet, they were derived; and items were woven into the policy of the M.F.G.B. when the strife in South Wales which had given birth to them had passed away.

The programme ran as follows:

ULTIMATE OBJECTIVE.—One organisation to cover the whole of the Coal, Ore, Slate, Stone, Clay, Salt, mining or quarrying industry of Great Britain, with one Central Executive.

That as a step to the attainment of that ideal strenuous efforts be made to weld all National, County or District Federations, at present comprising the Miners' Federation of Great Britain, into one compact organisation with one Central Executive, whose province it shall be to negotiate agreements and other matters requiring common action. That a cardinal principle of that organisation to be: that every man working in or about the mine, no matter what his craft or occupation—provisions having been made for representation on the Executive—be required to both join and observe its decisions.

IMMEDIATE STEPS—INDUSTRIAL.—(i) That a minimum wage of 8s. per day, for all workmen employed in or about the mines, constitute a demand to be striven for nationally at once.

(ii) That subject to the foregoing having been obtained, we demand and use our power to obtain a 7 hour day.

PROGRAMME—POLITICAL.—That the organisation shall engage in political action, both local and national, on the basis of complete independence of, and hostility to all capitalist parties, with an avowed policy of wresting whatever advantage it can for the working class. In the event of any representative of the organisation losing his seat, he shall be entitled to, and receive, the full protection of the organisation against victimisation.

GENERAL.—Alliances to be formed, and trades organisations

fostered, with a view to steps being taken to amalgamate all workers into one National and International union, to work for the taking over of all industries, by the workmen themselves.

Under the heading of "Policy," the following clauses not only startled the leaders of the other County Associations, but also enraged the coal-owners and the newspapers which represented mining interests:

I. The old policy of identity of interest between employers and ourselves be abolished, and a policy of open hostility installed.

X. Lodges should, as far as possible discard the old method of coming out on strike for any little minor grievance; and adopt the more scientific weapon of the irritation strike by simply remaining at work, reducing their output, and so contrive by their general conduct to make the colliery unremunerative.

XIII. That a continual agitation be carried on in favour of increasing the minimum wage, and shortening the hours of work, until we have extracted the whole of the employers' profits.

XIV. That our objective be, to build up an organisation that will ultimately take over the mining industry, and carry it on in the interests of the workers.

Views similar to these, from this time forward, were occasionally found in other industries, especially transport, railways, building and engineering, though the whole gospel of Syndicalism as proclaimed in the United States was never so potent an influence in Britain. Socialist leaders like Philip Snowden thundered against it, but failed to carry conviction amongst those to whom they were already suspect as "reformist Socialists." Indeed, it was not until the artillery of Lenin was brought to bear on it in 1920 that the Syndicalist doctrines were overcome. But for a period of ten years there was a ferment in the trade unions, appearing in a variety of forms: industrial unionism versus craft unionism; the amalgamation drive ("too many unions, too few trade unionists"); the One Big Union; the longing for the General Strike; the demand for workers' control in industry, etc. etc., as well as in a contempt for Parliamentarianism and the older tenets of Socialist teaching. This ferment is found in the *Daily Herald* (making its first appearance in April 1912 just as the 1912 strike was ended), especially in the cartoons of Will Dyson; in the weekly *New Age*, from which developed a "typically British compromise" in the shape of Guild

Socialism, and the numerous books and pamphlets of Mr. G. D. H. Cole; and in the papers of the Shop Steward Movement which grew to a great height during the 1914–18 war. Some of this ferment of new ideas later became linked with big changes in trade unionism (e.g. constitution of the National Union of Railwaymen, all-embracing growth of the Transport and General Workers' Union, creation of the General Council of the Trades Union Congress, and, at a much later date, formation of the National Union of Mineworkers); while some ideas degenerated into a mere obsession with the structure of trade unionism regardless of spirit and content. But it was not until the twentieth-century struggle between the two main tendencies in modern Socialism— between revisionism (also called reformism or opportunism) and revolutionary Socialism—had reached the acutest conflict in the Russian Revolution of 1917 that the main body of Syndicalist doctrine was brought to a test. Syndicalism was called upon to stand and deliver; and then, while its theoretic pretensions were mercilessly exposed by Lenin, who at the same time treated tenderly the spirit of revolt which had inspired so many of its supporters, the practical methods that remained valid resumed their place in the general strategy and tactics of working-class struggle.

Meantime, in the spring of 1912, within the Miners' Federation these ferments had begun to work, with the result that at the October Conference a part of the presidential address was devoted to a repudiation of Syndicalism.

7. THE MINIMUM WAGE ACT

The provisions of the new Act[1] laid down the framework for minimum rates of wages to be settled by Joint District Boards. Once settled, it would be a breach of contract for any employer to pay less than the said minimum: "any agreement for the payment of wages in so far as it is in contravention of this provision shall be void." But under District

---

[1] Coal Mines (Minimum Wage) Act, 1912 (2 Geo. V. c. 2), officially described as "An Act to provide a Minimum Wage in the case of Workmen employed underground in Coal Mines (including Mines of Stratified Ironstone), and for purposes incidental thereto." It stood on the Statute Book until 1947.

rules (i.e. rules made by the Joint District Board) certain classes of workmen might be exempted from the provisions of the Act; and any workman would forfeit his right to the minimum if he failed to comply with conditions as to efficiency and regularity of work, these conditions also to be laid down by District rules. Once settled, the minimum would be retrospective to the date of the passing of the Act, March 29, 1912: and could be varied thereafter either by agreement of both sides, or after the lapse of a year (plus three months for notice) by decision of the District Board. The Act was to have no effect one way or another on Conciliation Board machinery or on existing customary rates above the minimum. Any District Board (eighteen were set up under the Act) had power to make special minima higher or lower than the general District rate, and special District rules for groups or classes of mines to which general rules were not applicable. Each Chairman of the Joint District Boards (to be appointed by the Board of Trade in default of agreement between the two sides) was not only to have a casting vote, but if minimum rates and rules were not fixed within three weeks or a further specified time, had power himself to make all decisions.

From these provisions it is clear that the Act was only a skeleton to be clothed with flesh by the Joint District Boards, and further that nearly everything hinged upon those appointed to be Chairmen. The Chairmen, in most cases eminent lawyers, soon found that they had to take the full responsibility thrust on them by the Act. Only in three instances (Lancashire and Cheshire, South Derby, Forest of Dean) was agreement reached within three weeks on District rules and minimum rates. In Cumberland and Warwickshire agreement was reached in more than three weeks. But in all other Districts the Boards failed to agree: and the Chairmen had to make the settlements of wages and rules. In a few of those cases, the Chairmen, in their legalistic way, assumed sole responsibility as soon as the three weeks had expired: for example, Lord Mersey in Northumberland and Robert Romer (afterwards Lord Romer) in Durham and in Cleveland. In most cases when the Boards failed to agree, extra time had been given to them: in South Wales, for instance, where both sides had agreed on the choice of "Black

Michael"[1] as Chairman, the final determination was not made by this veteran statesman until July 5th after protracted and infructuous Board meetings had failed to settle.

When the first awards of the Joint District Boards became known, they were so far below what the miners had hoped as to cause protests. An M.F.G.B. Special Conference received reports from Districts and then expressed its regret that there were a "number of awards which fix the minimum rates for underground workmen at less than such reasonable living wage," and further, that "in some cases the chairman refused to take into consideration the average wages earned by piece-workers" (as laid down in the second paragraph of Section 2 of the Act). The Conference recorded

its strongest protests against those awards, and calls upon the Government to take such immediate action as will remedy the defects complained of. (May 22, 1912.)

But when the Executive Committee wrote to the Prime Minister for an interview, they were told that Mr. Asquith preferred to wait until all the Joint District Boards had completed their work. This took them to the middle of July. The Executive Committee then put their points to Mr. Asquith: first, that in nearly every instance the Chairman had fixed the minimum rate for day-wage men at less than 5s. whereas the miners' representatives had understood in the March negotiations that no lower rate than 5s. would be fixed by the independent Chairmen of the Joint Boards; second, that while the Joint Boards were required by the Act to have regard to the "average rate of wages" paid in the District, the Chairmen had declined to act upon that direction, and had fixed the minimum rate for coal-getters considerably below the average wages. To this the Prime Minister replied that it must be left to the opinion of the statutory bodies "to whom Parliament has entrusted the administration of the Act to deal with it in the manner they think proper," and finally said:

I cannot sit here as an appeal from these authorities. All I can do is, if a sufficiently strong case is made out to the Government, we must go to Parliament for further legislation. If you show that such

[1] Viscount St. Aldwyn, previously Sir Michael Hicks-Beach, q.v. in *The Miners*, Chapter X.

a case is justified, action could, of course, be taken. But on the points you have put forward, I cannot think that you mean to suggest that Parliament would be justified in ripping up the Act at this stage. On the contrary, I think the Act is working very well, and of this I am certain, that miners have derived enormous benefits from the passing of the Act, and I do not know that either the owners or the consumers are going to suffer in consequence. (July 15, 1912.)

This reply, made with the happy blanditude for which Asquith was famous, left the miners unsatisfied.

A Special Conference a month later, having heard first the report of this interview and then detailed reports from Districts, expressed its "strong dissatisfaction" with the working of the Act, especially:

(a) the fact that with few exceptions no award has provided for the paying of 5s. per day to the low paid wage workmen;
(b) in many instances the Independent Chairmen have not had reasonable regard to the average wages of the piece-workers in fixing the minimum wage;
(c) those awards which require 100 per cent of attendances at work to qualify for the minimum wage;
(d) the serious delay of many owners in paying the arrears of wages due under the awards;

And further strongly condemns the action of those owners who are coercing or bribing workmen to contract out of the provisions of the Act, either by promising or refusing them work or by offering increased tonnage rates or percentages. (August 16, 1912.)

During the whole of the negotiations for a minimum wage and during the strike, Enoch Edwards, though far from well, had remained at his post. But the strain and the overwork had broken him: and after an illness of some weeks he died on June 28, 1912. The delegates to the Twenty-third Conference of the International Miners' Federation on July 5th paid tribute to his memory. Robert Smillie said:

To Mr. Edwards more than anyone else living today, or anyone connected or who has been connected with the Federation, is due the fact that the miners have been for some time now, absolutely solidly organised together in one body. To him is due the fact that what at one time were warring branches who had the same interest at stake, were drawn together.

Persons holding extreme views, in all probability, however honest and anxious they might be to establish a great ideal, might through their very extreme views prevent them getting very far in that direction: but Mr. Edwards had a desire to see the whole mining movement of Great Britain carried forward together under one banner, and he had that peculiar temperament which could overlook to a great degree the extreme views of others, and could work for the purpose of unity. It was due to a great extent to him that we became united North, South, East, and West, under one common banner in the Federation of all miners of the country.

At the Conciliation Board on July 17th, the employers' Chairman said of Enoch Edwards that "there has never been an unpleasant word uttered by him at any of the meetings. He has taken up his own side and advocated it, I need not say with great ability, but he has never put matters in such a way that any one could go away from the meeting and feel he had acted harshly or unkindly in any way. He has been conspicuous by his ability and by his moderation, and by his trying to look at both sides of the question." Ashton, who had worked closely with him for over a third of a century, wrote in his record that:

Mr. Edwards had no enemies. He was respected by all men and women who knew him. He was a leader that the men he represented might trust as being honest, straightforward and reliable in debate and advocacy of their cause. He was a true and faithful comrade and trustworthy colleague.

CHAPTER V

BEFORE THE FIRST WORLD WAR

I. RELATIONS WITH THE LABOUR PARTY

THE Miners' Federation had come out of the strike struggle strengthened in everything but funds. Total numbers increased, inner coherence was greater, the spirit of the members more militant. Its prestige was enhanced. At the Trades Union Congress it occupied once more the leading position it had held from 1894 to 1904. Within the Federation the leaders of the older school could no longer stem the new tides of opinion, while on the other hand the newer leaders had often to "ca' canny" with some of the Districts where the older outlook was still dominant. A great deal now depended upon the composition of the Executive Committee,[1] to which many more problems were referred than in the past, as their common strike struggle had brought the County Associations and Districts closer together. From midsummer 1912 to midsummer 1914 the Executive Committee had to formulate policy for Conferences on a wide range of activity, much of it concerned with legislation. The successive Acts of Parliament so recently passed—Coal Mines (Eight Hours) Act, 1908, operative in 1909 and 1910; Coal Mines Act, 1911; Coal Mines (Minimum Wage) Act, 1912—did not at once run smoothly and were to require many deputations to the Home Office; while proposals for new legislation and new programmes were being elaborated. Of the new legisla-

---

[1] The twenty men elected as the Executive Committee at the Twenty-fourth (Swansea) Annual Conference of the M.F.G.B. on October 1–4, 1912, were: President: Robert Smillie (unanimous); Vice-President: W. E. Harvey, M.P. (369 to 220); Secretary: Thos. Ashton (unanimous); Treasurer: W. Abraham, M.P. (unanimous); Executive Members: W. Brace, M.P., V. Hartshorn and G. Barker of South Wales; H. Smith and S. Roebuck of Yorkshire; H. Murnin and J. Robertson of Scotland; A. Stanley, M.P., of the Midland Federation; A. Sharp of Cumberland; S. H. Whitehouse of Somerset; J. McGurk of Lancashire; J. G. Hancock, M.P., of Nottinghamshire; B. Kenyon of Derbyshire; W. Straker of Northumberland; J. Robson and Dr. J. Wilson, M.P., of Durham.

It will be seen that the "new men" were few and the older leaders of the 'nineties were still the great majority.

tive proposals the most fundamental was a Bill for the nationalisation of coal-mines, while the most urgent was the Bill for reversal of the Osborne Judgment so as to legalise the use of trade union funds for political purposes. Each of these had to be elaborated in conjunction with the Labour Party.

Relations with the Labour Party went smoothly enough, given the difficulties presented by so huge a new affiliation. The Miners' Federation had been its own "labour party" for so many years: its affiliation fees far outstripped the contribution of any other affiliated body; still more, its formidable list of eighteen Members of Parliament as compared with twenty-four for all the other sections of the Labour Party could rock the vessel; and, finally, several of its older leaders had been first elected to Parliament under Liberal auspices (three of them remained members of the Liberal Party) and did not take easily to the discipline of the Labour Party. Up till the entrance of the miners, the Labour Party, though representing the non-Socialist trade unions, had been steered mainly by the I.L.P. leaders (Keir Hardie, MacDonald, Snowden, etc.), while in so far as it was developing a distinctive ideology this was for the most part under Fabian influence. The I.L.P. and the Fabian Society sought gently to commit the Labour Party to this or that item of their respective programmes: and in furtherance of this the I.L.P., at a meeting of the International Socialist Bureau in October 1908, had got a majority decision in favour of admitting the Labour Party to the International Socialist Congress. The incident illuminates the position of the Labour Party, then with 176 affiliated units and a total collective membership of 1,158,565. The meeting took place at Brussels. Leading representatives of the Socialist parties of Europe made up the Bureau of the Socialist International: Kautsky for Germany, Adler for Austria, Lenin for Russia, Vaillant (an old follower of Blanqui) and Roussel (follower of Guesde) for France, and many others. The proposal by Kautsky was that "the British Labour Party be permitted to attend International Socialist Congresses" on the grounds that although it did not directly "recognise the proletarian class struggle" (the stipulation for affiliation to the Socialist

International) it nevertheless "wages the struggle and in fact and by its very organisation, which is independent of bourgeois parties, is adopting the basis of the class struggle." Hyndman, for the Social-Democratic Federation, supported amongst others by Roussel of France, opposed the admission bitterly. Lenin spoke and voted for the admission of the Labour Party but for the distinctive reason, as against Kautsky's argument, that the Labour Party represented "the first step on the part of the really proletarian organisations of England towards a conscious class policy and towards a *socialist* Labour Party." Similar "expectations" of the Labour Party's future, though from a very different standpoint, had been entertained in Britain. The Fabians looked on themselves as the leaven that would work on the whole loaf. But when in 1909 the Miners' Federation entered the Labour Party, some of the Fabians felt that the loaf was altogether too large for their leaven. Some thirty years later Bernard Shaw could write:

I had said repeatedly, when the Miners' Federation joined the Labour Party, and put money and an overwhelming card vote into it, Socialism would have to take a back place in the Party, and the term Socialist would come to mean no more than the term Christian after the Edict of Constantine.

By 1912 these fears were regarded as imaginary by many of the younger miners' leaders, to whom the supposed conflict of Fabian Socialism and Liberal trade unionism was a conflict of back numbers. But that these fears existed at a time when the unions were beginning to turn away from Liberalism is a fact: it bears witness to the prevalence of intermediary and confused outlooks.

There were some difficulties. They arose mainly from questions of electoral organisation outside Parliament; and notably in the cases of J. G. Hancock and Albert Johnson. Friction could scarcely arise in Parliament where, after 1910, J. R. MacDonald was guiding the Labour Party as though it were a wing of the Liberal Party. But such friction as might have developed was anticipated or smoothed over partly through the close relationship between the I.L.P. leaders of the Labour Party and the President of the M.F.G.B. Robert Smillie, elected President in 1912, had for years

exercised a steadily growing influence in the counsels of the
Federation. Born in Belfast in 1857, he had tried his hand at
various trades before he settled down as a coal-miner in
Lanarkshire, where in the late 'eighties he built up a local
trade union in Larkhall. He was a close associate of Keir
Hardie, and was one of the original founders of the I.L.P.
at Bradford in 1893. By the end of the next year he had
become President of the newly-formed Scottish Miners'
Federation and was thereafter regularly elected to the
Executive Committee of the M.F.G.B. Smillie proved himself
as a pioneer Socialist fighter. Again and again he contested
parliamentary seats, no matter against what odds. Defeated
time after time at by-elections or general elections, he never
quailed before difficulties or lost his ardour in the struggle.
Other leading members of the Miners' Federation might in
those early days have Socialist leanings or hold Socialist
convictions: but Smillie was outstanding in his advocacy of
Socialism.

At Conferences he had many a brush with Pickard, who
saw him as the representative and successor of Keir Hardie
in trade union heresies. When, on the election of Enoch
Edwards as President in 1904, the Scots put up Smillie for
the vice-presidency, the delegates preferred to keep as
Vice-President Sam Woods, whose state of health had made
it necessary for him to resign that year from the secretaryship
of the Trades Union Congress, and who therefore could not
take any active part in Federation work. It was not until
several years later (1909) that the delegates were prepared to
accept Smillie, the outspoken Socialist, as the Federation
Vice-President. By this time Smillie had, through five years'
work on the Royal Commission on Mines, gained a detailed
knowledge of both British and some continental coal-fields,
and had proved himself a skilful and shrewd negotiator. In
this way he had gained the respect of his older Liberal
colleagues, who came to know that his dour mien was the
result of an Ulster upbringing and early struggles rather than
the Socialist equivalent of Pickard's austere and aloof manner;
while amongst the mass of the miners the sincerity and
restrained passion of his eloquence won him thousands of
supporters. And if in mining matters of acute controversy he

often seemed at Conferences to adopt a cautious attitude and on occasion to hold a balance between left and right, this brought him no Laodicean reproach[1] but an increased influence as one to whom each side looked for aid against its opponents. For some half a dozen years before he became President he had steadily been gaining an ascendancy: and this had become more marked in the stormy period of the movement on abnormal places and the minimum wage. His succession to the acting-presidency in the summer of 1912 enabled him to push forward the causes that were nearest to his heart. No sooner were District Board decisions under the Minimum Wage Act published than Smillie obtained the agreement of the Executive Committee for the drafting of a coal-mines nationalisation Bill.

2. NATIONALISATION OF MINES RESOLUTIONS

It was not until the fifth year of the M.F.G.B. that a mines nationalisation item appeared on its agenda. But two years earlier at the Trades Union Congress of 1892 William Small of Blantyre, seconded by Robert Smillie representing the Larkhall Miners' Association, had got unanimous acceptance of two motions, one for the resumption of State ownership of minerals, the other for nationalisation of mines. The distinction between these two has to be borne in mind: for not only were they ultimately to be dealt with by separate legislation but they were separately regarded from an early period. The demand for nationalisation of coal-mining royalties was supported throughout by many opponents of Socialism: and brought about the appointment of a Royal Commission on Mining Royalties in 1891. Indeed, as was argued by Marxian Socialists, a consistent capitalist regime would nationalise land—and with it, of course, the minerals in the sub-soil. This argument had been put forward in so many words by a resolution of the Swansea Trades Union Congress in 1886, which ran:

That, in the opinion of this Congress, the royalty rents and other charges demanded by the landlords of this country are iniquitous

[1] The Revelation of St. John the Divine, iii, 15.

and injurious; iniquitous because they form a monopoly of our mineral resources, where they should be used for the good of all; injurious because they place a tax upon our staple industries, interfering with, and hindering our commercial prosperity, restricting the profits of the capitalists, and limiting the already too small wages of the workmen.

It was not, however, the teaching of Marx so much as the influence of Henry George's book *Progress and Poverty* which lay behind these sentiments of T.U.C. delegates in 1886: nor had anyone the illusion that the success obtained by Small and Smillie in 1892 represented a Socialist vote. It had little effect on the Royal Commission which, in 1893, reported against any fundamental change in the system of royalties.

When the matter came up for the first time before the Miners' Federation (at their Fifth Annual Conference) it was cast in a cautious wording: "That in the opinion of this Conference the best interests of the nation will be served by the nationalisation of the mines of the country" (January 19, 1894). Pickard who, as was noted in the earlier volume, was of a strong Liberal opinion, in his presidential address had said: "Everyone of you knows my opinion on this question. I am not a mines nationaliser. I don't think that if the mines were nationalised the miners would be a penny better off than they are today. The crux of the whole question affecting miners is not as to whom the mines belong, but as to how the coal should be sold which is produced in the mines and brought to the surface for public use." Nevertheless after "a long and animated debate" (of which no particulars are recorded except that it was moved by Tom Greenall of Lancashire and seconded by J. Wilson of Scotland) the resolution was carried by 158 votes to 50. This remained an isolated expression of opinion: and three years later a comprehensive socialistic resolution was defeated but at the same time a resolution for public ownership of land, mines and railways was carried. Thereafter the question, because it was felt to be academic, was transferred to the annual Trades Union Congress or to the annual conferences of the International Federation of Miners. There, from 1898 onwards, the desirability of mines nationalisation was regularly reaffirmed, with a number of the British delegates voting

MINERS' FEDERATION OF GREAT BRITAIN EXECUTIVE COMMITTEE AT SCARBOROUGH, OCTOBER 1913

J. McGurk, W. Straker, S. Roebuck, J. G. Hancock, V. Hartshorn, J. Robson, H. Murnin, G. Barker, A. Sharp, J. Robertson

Bottom row: S. H. Whitehouse, A. Stanley, T. Ashton, R. Smillie, W. E. Harvey, J. Wilson, W. Brace

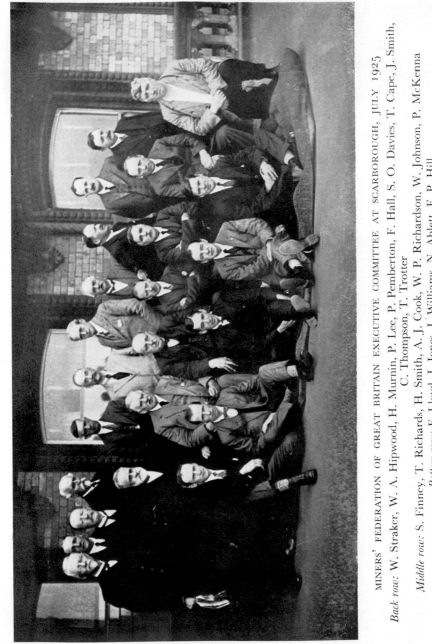

MINERS' FEDERATION OF GREAT BRITAIN EXECUTIVE COMMITTEE AT SCARBOROUGH, JULY 1925

Back row: W. Straker, W. A. Hipwood, H. Murnin, P. Lee, P. Pemberton, F. Hall, S. O. Davies, T. Cape, J. Smith, C. Thompson, T. Trotter

Middle row: S. Finney, T. Richards, H. Smith, A. J. Cook, W. P. Richardson, W. Johnson, P. McKenna

Bottom row: F. Lloyd, J. Jones, J. Williams, N. Ablett, F. P. Hill

against in a minority which diminished from year to year. In the Federation Annual or Special Conferences, loaded with immediate industrial or political business, the question seldom came up: and when it did it was usually as part of the wider demand for public ownership of land, railways and mines. For example, at the Fourteenth Annual Conference the proposition was put forward "That this Conference approves of and agrees to urge that the land, mines, minerals, and railways be nationalised" (October 10, 1902). Pickard stated he was always opposed to nationalisation, but ended by saying:

If you are going to look at this question as an ideal, then it is a very pleasant thing. I like to talk about ideals, I have made hundreds of speeches on ideals. . . . I have really no objection to the resolution as an expression of opinion.

After this peculiar confession of what may seem a curiously muddled outlook, the resolution was carried unanimously.

The complaisance which the older leaders thus adopted towards these resolutions emboldened the Scots to bring forward and get carried (without discussion) a resolution for general nationalisation of production, distribution and exchange at the 1904 Annual Conference,[1] and to have it repeated with a slight variation[2] in 1905. By 1906 there was a big change. Yorkshire had now been won over and it was a Yorkshire delegate, J. Walsh, who proposed:

That believing that the nationalisation of the mines and the minerals of this country will conduce to the benefit of the workers, we hereby reaffirm our previous resolution on the matter.

Smillie, speaking in support of this resolution, said:

I take it that if the mines are nationalised and held by the State and managed by the State the minerals could be produced at the lowest possible coast and [work] carried on under the least dangerous conditions. I recognise that the present Government will not be the best possible management. We must establish a Labour Government

[1] "That we hereby reaffirm our belief in the principle of the Nationalisation of the land, minerals, mines, railways and all means of industrial production, distribution and exchange, as only by this means can the workers obtain the full benefits of their labour and the miserable conditions resulting from capitalism in its present form be abolished" (October 4, 1904).

[2] The clause was altered to read as follows: "as only by these reforms can the workers obtain the full value of their labour, and the ruinous losses and suffering of strikes be avoided" (October 3, 1905).

in Great Britain before our interests will be safeguarded as they ought to be. I believe that the present Government is not a Government to have the mines in their hands. They ought to be worked for the public good and safety of the men, but so long as we continue to send mine-owners and landlords to the House of Commons, in their own interests they will prevent that measure being taken.

At that moment the Labour Party in Parliament and the Federation Members of Parliament amounted to little more than one-twentieth of the House of Commons. The next year, 1907, there were two resolutions carried: and each asked for a Bill to be prepared. One from Yorkshire declared that:

Seeing the enormous profits made by Colliery Companies, the exorbitant price of coal to consumers, the small wages obtained by miners generally, together with the large amount of unrest at most collieries regarding conditions of work, introduction of machinery, indirect reductions, that this Conference urges the Miners' Federation to draft a Bill and introduce it into the House of Commons at an early date for the Nationalisation of the Mines and Mineral Royalties; also that meetings be organised throughout the British coalfield in support of the proposal, believing that it is by the diminution of private ownership and the establishment of public ownership of Mines and Minerals that the just rights of producers and consumers will be obtained. (October 9, 1907.)

The Derbyshire resolution, simple and sanguine, instructed the M.F.G.B. Members of Parliament "to direct the attention of the Government to bring in a Bill for the Nationalisation of Land, Mines and Mining Royalties." In 1908 the Scots put forward a comprehensive resolution, declaring again that:

In the opinion of this Federation the workers cannot obtain the full value of their labour, and disputes be avoided, until the land, minerals, mines, railways and whole means of production, distribution, and exchange are owned and managed by the State for the people, and that workers should only send such representatives to Parliament and other public bodies as have a direct interest in working for this change and no vested interests biassing them against it. (October 8, 1908.)

As the greater includes the less, there was that year no separate resolution on mines. By 1909 Somerset put forward a resolution (moved by S. H. Whitehouse) chiding the Executive Committee for not having prepared a Bill, while

Yorkshire (on the motion of Herbert Smith) demanded that land and railways be also nationalised. In the combined discussion R. Brown declared: "We from Scotland felt yesterday that we had a little grievance against Yorkshire, that they were masquerading in a Scottish suit; but our feelings were a bit elated to think that what was put forward by Scotland some years ago was now being taken up by Yorkshire, and also likely to be taken up by this Conference." The emphasis in the speeches from every District, including the "new boys" from Durham and Northumberland, was laid upon the land nationalisation—"It is no use," said Brown, "talking about nationalisation of mines or railways or anything else until the land is nationalised"—for this was the year of the "land-tax" budget behind which Lloyd George had rallied a great volume of enthusiastic popular support, including the support of the miners. From Lancashire, however, there came a critical note; Harry Twist complaining that the Federation had been passing resolutions of this kind for a good number of years, "pious resolutions" which were "a string of hardy annuals which mean nothing and which we mean nothing by." He demanded that if they were to pass "fundamentally Socialistic resolutions," they should go out into the country and "set up a campaign for the realisation of the principles which our resolutions contain." In the end the Conference carried the two resolutions unanimously, the one from Somerset instructing the incoming Executive Committee to draft a Nationalisation Bill for mines and mining royalties and organise meetings in the British coal-fields in support of the proposals "forthwith"; and the other from Yorkshire stating that "the time has arrived when the land, minerals, mines, and railways should be owned and managed by the State, for the people, to avoid a stoppage of the principal industries of the country."

Six months later, when the Conference decisions came up for review, the Executive Committee set up a sub-committee for drafting a Bill "with full power to get information from any source they deem necessary," and at the same time decided that the Bill be drafted on the lines "that the Government take over the mines and minerals at a fair marketable value" (April 21, 1910). This decision had considerable significance. Hitherto resolutions had omitted all question of ways and means. In so far as the demand for nationalisation of mines had been put forward in the early days as part and parcel of the general Socialist programme, and not on the ground that mining was in a special position in relation to British economy, its sponsors would in many cases have refused to consider compensation. Left-wing Socialists saw the nationalisation of the means of production, distribution and exchange as the result of a social revolution—which was expected to be more or less simultaneous throughout Europe. But even the most right-wing socialists had been definitely opposed to compensation for expropriated capitalists. The Fabian Basis[1] for over a quarter of a century had been quite explicit: the "emancipation of land and industrial capital from individual and class ownership, and the vesting of them in the community for the general benefit" was to be carried out "*without compensation* (though not without such relief to expropriated individuals as may seem fit to the community)." Thus "no compensation" was the standpoint of all Socialists whatsoever. Yet when Keir Hardie in 1893 introduced a parliamentary Bill for the nationalisation of mines and minerals (see Appendix to this chapter) it was on a basis of State purchase of mining properties at their current values. The various resolutions dealt with above had paid scant attention to this matter. But when a Bill had to be drafted the sub-committee as we have seen reached the conclusion that Parliament would insist on compensation for the owners of the capital.

Nothing further however appears to have been done by this sub-committee: and some eighteen months later the Executive Committee had to apologise to the M.F.G.B. Annual Conference for their inaction in this matter. So soon, however, as Smillie became Acting-President there was a change of attitude. In the first week of July 1912 a sub-committee was set up to draft a parliamentary Bill. Its members were William Adamson, M.P., Vernon Hartshorn and William Straker. They got to work rapidly and secured the help of Mr. H. H. Slesser[2] who was then draftsman

---

[1] The Fabian Basis was the title of the statement of aims of the Fabian Society.
[2] Afterwards Solicitor-General and then Lord Justice of Appeal.

to the Labour Party in Parliament. The draft Bill was considered on September 24th by the Executive Committee, which made amendments. At the Annual Conference the delegates considered the Bill clause by clause, and resolved unanimously: "That the principles contained in the Mines Nationalisation Bill as drafted by the Committee be and are hereby approved" and instructed the Executive "to carry on the agitation" (October 3, 1912).

At its first meeting on October 15, 1912, the Executive Committee decided that copies of the Bill be sent to the Labour Party, and

that they be asked to give it first place on their list of Bills to be balloted for, and to be introduced in the House of Commons under the ten minutes rule.

The Labour Party had the draft Bill for some months and by April 1913 sent it back with suggested amendments. A sub-committee (Smillie, Ashton, Harvey, Hartshorn and Straker) went over the eleven amendments suggested by the Labour Party. They found that the Labour Party proposed compensation for royalties, which the M.F.G.B. Bill excluded. This amendment they refused to accept, and the refusal was confirmed by the Executive Committee at its meeting of May 21st–23rd. The Bill in its final shape was presented to the House of Commons and ordered to be printed on July 9, 1913, but it did not secure discussion. It was then reprinted as a Fabian tract and used at meetings in favour of mines nationalisation. Its preparation and provisions[1] marked an advance in the conception of what a Mines Nationalisation Bill should be. Some of its clauses will appear in altered form when we come to examine a still more important advance in the Bill of 1918.

3. THE FIVE-DAY WEEK

This question was considered at several conferences, and the Annual Conference, 1911, after full discussion, passed the following resolution:

That this conference is in favour of a uniform working policy over the whole British coal-field of five days per week, and instructs the

[1] Summarised in an Appendix to this chapter.

Executive Committee to at once take the necessary steps to bring it into operation. (October 4, 1911.)

The Committee, at a meeting held July 5, 1912, again considered this question. They were not prepared to draft a scheme until the Annual Conference could decide on the main points of it, for which purpose they requested the Districts to come fully prepared. Accordingly, another full discussion took place at the Annual Conference, which decided:

That the Miners' Federation of Great Britain adopt a five days working week for all mines in the country. (October 1912.)

For the resolution 71 delegates voted, and 50 against. A card vote was demanded, and the result of that vote was: 306,000 for the resolution, and 283,000 against. Chairman Robert Smillie advised that in view of the closeness of the vote, a ballot of the miners be taken. To this the Conference agreed, and the Executive Committee arranged for the ballot to be taken on January 29–30, 1913. When the result of the ballot vote was reported to the Committee, on February 5, 1913, the figures showed a majority in favour, but not an overwhelming majority. In the opinion of the Executive Committee, no action could be taken on the adoption of a general five days per week policy on the figures shown and so they decided that "the whole matter be reported to a Special Conference to be called at an early date."

There was, however, more to it than that. The Executive Committee realised that the matter bore upon their conception of democratic procedure. Hitherto the assumption in most things had been that of majority rule, even a bare majority of 51 per cent. Indeed, the radical outlook of the miners rejected with scorn the stipulation of a two-thirds majority for change of constitutional law in certain countries as mere devices for frustrating the will of the people and for bolstering up the *status quo ante*. Therefore "simple majority rule" was inscribed on their political banners. But more than one of the County Associations had special rules for strike action: and, in deference to these, the strike of 1912 had been made dependent on a two-thirds majority and had indeed been ended because there was no longer a two-thirds majority for its continuance. This decision of April 1912 had not been taken without much heart-searching: and some even of those who agreed with it considered it to be an infringement of democratic principles. The Executive, having first asked each District to supply a copy of its rule, resolved on getting a firm decision for the future.

The Special Conference had before it the complete returns of the ballot vote. There were in favour 253,541, against 209,826. On these figures the Chairman asked: Was it wise to try to carry out the five days policy? With the exception of a single delegate, the Conference was of the opinion that no action could be taken. Then came the larger question, and the following resolution was carried unanimously:

That before a national strike is entered upon as the result of any finding of a conference, a ballot vote of the members shall be taken, and a strike shall not be declared unless two-thirds of those voting vote in favour of such a strike. If a ballot vote be taken during the time a strike is in progress a vote of two-thirds of those taking part in the ballot shall be necessary to continue the strike. (March 27, 1913.)

4. TRADE UNION ACT, 1913

The Osborne Judgment[1] had resulted in a series of lawsuits against one or other section of the Federation. It was clear that unless new legislation were passed, it would only be a matter of time until the right exercised by the miners' unions since the early 'seventies of promoting parliamentary candidatures was swept away. The M.F.G.B., in conjunction with the Labour Party, had pressed for this new legislation: but the Asquith administration was by no means willing to yield to their demands. The Liberal Party had too many coal-owners and ship-owners amongst its prominent supporters to be in favour of promoting legislation which would restore the situation of the law as it was generally understood to be before the Osborne Judgment was delivered. On the other hand, the Government's parliamentary majority, after the December 1910 General Election, depended on the support of the Labour Party. Accordingly they brought in a Bill, but

[1] See *The Miners*, Chapter X.

its provisions were so unsatisfactory that after the opposition expressed at a Special Conference in 1911 of the Labour Movement, the project was dropped. Asquith, however, gave a pledge that a better Bill would be introduced in 1912. This Bill turned out to be only a partial reversal of the Osborne Judgment. It introduced new restrictions upon the political activity of trade unions, and contained provisions by which any member of the union might "contract out" from payment of any political levy. In the Grand Committee of the House of Commons the provisions were worsened from the Labour Party standpoint.

Meantime the situation was rendered more acute, so far as the miners were concerned, by yet another lawsuit, this time directed not only against one of the constituent unions but also against the Miners' Federation of Great Britain. In the course of this suit, the Parr case, it became abundantly clear that these lawsuits, if not examples of champerty,[1] were at any rate being promoted by political and industrial opponents of the Federation. In this case, heard in the Chancery Division on January 28 and 29, 1913, Thomas Ashton, the Secretary, had been served with a writ requiring him to produce books of the Miners' Federation of Great Britain showing what amounts had been received over a period from the Lancashire and Cheshire Miners' Federation for contributions to the Parliamentary Fund and what payments had been made to the Labour Party for affiliation fees, Parliamentary Fund, and salaries of eighteen Members of Parliament. The plaintiff was one Joseph Parr. Just how the action came to be brought was elicited from Parr's solicitor, Charles Thomas Wilkinson, by the skilful cross-examination of the M.F.G.B.'s counsel, Mr. Jenkins, as will appear from this excerpt of the verbatim report:

Were you solicitor for the Plaintiff in the original action of Osborne?—Yes.

[1] Champerty is defined in Halsbury's *Laws of England*: "Champerty" is a particular kind of *maintenance*, namely, maintenance of an action in consideration of a promise to give to the maintainer a share in the subject-matter or proceeds therefor. "Maintenance," in turn, may be defined as the giving of assistance or encouragement to any one of the parties to an action by a person who has neither an interest in the action nor any other motive recognised by the law justifying his interference. A person who was a common mover, exciter or maintainer of suits or quarrels was called a common barrator, and was guilty of the offence of barratry. This was an indictable offence and punishable by fine and imprisonment; it is now practically obsolete.

Since the decision of that case in the House of Lords you have had a number of actions against different Trade Unions?—Yes, I have.

How did Mr. Joseph Parr of St. Helens come to you?—He was introduced to me in connection with the Trade Unions Defence League.

Are you looking to anybody else but the Plaintiff for your costs in the action?—No, I am not, but I have assistance if I require it in the way of money.

That is a roundabout way of saying it—if the Plaintiff does not pay you somebody else will?—Well, I expect to be paid.

I thought so!—But I have no engagement to that effect.

No doubt you not only expect to be paid, but there is no reasonable doubt that you will be paid?—Well, there is some reason to doubt that I shall be paid. I do not expect I shall be paid in full.

No solicitor ever gets paid in full; you must not be too sanguine. You must take a bit off or have a bit taken off for you. What has Mr. Woodward got to do with this action?—Mr. Woodward is the local secretary of the Constitutional Labour Union and of the Trade Unions Defence League.

And it is part of their regular business to bring actions against trade unions who they think are infringing the Osborne Judgment? —No, it is not; they introduce to me the case, and if I consider it is a case which is infringing the Osborne Judgment I make arrangements with the party whom I consider injured and I go on with the case.

How do you find out the party injured; do you advertise for him?—No, I do not.

How do you get hold of him?—I am introduced to him by those who entertain the same feelings that I do myself in this matter.

They produce an injured party?—They do.

Was Mr. Parr produced as the injured party in this case?—By Mr. Woodward, yes.

Had he become caretaker at this club of Mr. Woodward's, before he was injured, or afterwards?—After.

What was the injury that led up to his having been made caretaker?—That he could not exercise his political opinions, whilst he was bound to contribute money to his society or trade union which made a compulsory levy for a party antagonistic to his own views.

Then this was given him as a sort of compensation for belonging to this trade union, was it?—Well——

Or for leaving the trade union,—which was it?—It was a case where the miners—we have had several cases against miners in Durham, North Wales, Warwickshire——

Do not go through it, I know you have had actions all over the country?—Yes.

You need not go through it all. I want to know how this injured person was produced?—He is produced by Mr. Woodward.

Is there a sort of menagerie for the supply of injured people; can he always produce an injured person when he is wanted?—I do not say that at all; he is interested.

There are enough of them to be able to support your action you have brought?—There are a great many more than would support this action in the country, a good many free men in the country; they do not consider they are free if they are under the slave principles of the Labour Party.

You tell us you have no sort of agreement with the Plaintiff that he should not pay your costs?—I told you I have an agreement with the Plaintiff that he should pay the costs.

I put it quite straight to you. Suppose for the sake of argument, the action failed, that is the time when it becomes most material. Do you mean to tell me now that the Plaintiff is going to pay your costs?—I mean to tell you now that the Plaintiff is liable to me for my costs, but if the action fails you know he is a poor man——

I am sure you will give me a straight answer. Although the Plaintiff, I agree, after what you have said, is legally liable for your costs, or may be, did you ever mean to look to him or do you?

MR. SPENCER BOWER: Is that a fair question? Does that matter?

MR. JUSTICE NEVILLE: Yes, I do not think it is an unfair question.

MR. JENKINS: Would you answer that?—It is no use my looking to him; therefore I have to look to others if it fails.

The judgment, given against the defendants on January 29, 1913, included various injunctions and ended with the words:

Rule 2, Sub-rule 8 in the Miners' Federation of Great Britain Rules, and Rule 30 (B) in the Lancashire and Cheshire Miners' Federation, are *ultra vires* Rules.

Meantime, lest there should be an adverse judgment, the Miners' Federation had refrained from transfer of affiliation fees to the Labour Party for those sections of the Federation who were already enjoined from paying or who, as in this case, might be so enjoined. This was fully understood by the Labour Party, whose Assistant Secretary wrote on December 7, 1912, to Thomas Ashton:

Mr. Walsh reported the proceedings for an injunction against you at our meeting this week, and we see the desirability of giving no occasion for your opponents to secure any direct evidence against you. Under these circumstances we are agreeable to accept payment on the uninjuncted section of your membership (viz. 128,000 at 1d. per member—£534 3s. 4d.).

The difficult position in which the trade unions composing the Labour Party had been placed was scarcely solved by the Government Bill. In the Grand Committee, William Brace had proposed a motion for the complete reversal of the Osborne Judgment: but by a two to one majority his amendment had been defeated. The Joint Board, a committee then composed of three representatives each of the Labour Party Executive, the Trades Union Congress Parliamentary Committee, and the Management Committee of the General Federation of Trade Unions decided to call a national conference of unions to decide upon a course of action. To a Special Conference of the M.F.G.B. called on January 2, 1913, to instruct its delegates to the National Conference, the Executive Committee submitted a resolution that "no measure or Bill can be accepted as satisfactory that does not completely reverse the Osborne decision," but accepting "the present Bill for the time being, subject to any further improvements or amendments that can be obtained during the further passage of the Bill." Only Yorkshire opposed this resolution, and it was carried and later adopted in substance by all the other trade unions. This enabled the Asquith administration to pass their Bill into law as the Trade Union Act of 1913.

This Act gave power generally to a trade union to spend money on any lawful purpose authorised by its constitution so long as its principal objects were those of a trade union, that is, the objects defined in the 1876 Act. A further provision excluded from this general power the financing of certain defined political purposes; in such cases, before these purposes could be added to the constitution of the union, a secret ballot of the members must be taken in a prescribed form. A special right of individual exemption from this particular activity was prescribed, and the Act laid down that the money to be spent on such political objects must come out of a special fund. Following upon the Act, it was decided at a Special Conference (March 27, 1913) that for political purposes the Federation should become one unit under the Trade Union Act; two months later this was accepted by the Registrar of Friendly Societies, to whom this power had been given under the Act. He was also empowered to approve new (political) rules. These, which were in a common form, ran as follows:

RULES FOR POLITICAL FUND

1. The objects of the Miners' Federation of Great Britain shall include the furtherance of the political objects to which Section 3 of the Trade Union Act 1913 applies, that is to say, the expenditure of money—

    (a) on the payment of any expenses incurred, either directly or indirectly, by a candidate or prospective candidate for election to Parliament or to any public office before, during or after the election in connection with his candidature or election; or

    (b) on the holding of any meeting or the distribution of any literature or documents in support of any such candidate or prospective candidate; or

    (c) on the maintenance of any person who is a member of Parliament or who holds a public office; or

    (d) in connection with the registration of electors or the selection of a candidate for Parliament or any public office: or

    (e) on the holding of political meetings of any kind, or on the distribution of political literature or political documents of any kind, unless the main purposes of the meetings or of the distribution of the literature or documents is the furtherance of statutory objects within the meaning of the Act, that is to say, the regulation of the relations between workmen and masters, or between workmen and workmen, or between masters and masters, or the imposing of restrictive conditions on the conduct of any trade or business, and also the provision of benefits to members.

The expression "public office" in this rule means the office of member of any county, borough, district, or parish council, or board of guardians, or of any public body who have power to raise money, either directly or indirectly, by means of a rate.

Further rules dealt with the prescribed form in which a member could claim exemption from contributing to the political fund and the rights of such members not to be "either directly or indirectly under any disability or disadvantage as compared with other members of the union (except in relation to the control or management of the political funds of the union)." A ballot vote on the adoption of these rules resulted in a poll of 71 per cent of the membership (standing at 619,000 in July 1912), or, with boys deducted, 81 per cent. It expressed a majority of 66,843 in favour of furtherance of political objects, with 261,643 voting for and 194,800 against. This ballot determined the future course of the M.F.G.B. But neither the Labour Party nor the Miners' Federation were able in the years that followed to obtain such an improvement in the law as would completely reverse the Osborne Judgment. Instead, the Act of 1927, introduced by the Baldwin-Churchill administration, considerably worsened the law; but by its repeal in 1946 the provisions of the 1913 Act came into force again.

5. THE PRESS AND EDUCATION

The miners, living in their separate villages in a score of coal-fields each cut off from the other, had long felt the need of a newspaper which would voice their common aims and in so doing bind them more closely together. As early as the 'seventies the matter was brought up and at more than one Conference resolutions were passed in favour of having a miners' paper. For example, the Central Board of the Miners' National Union, in Minutes of September 25, 1877, stated:

Newspaper.—This matter was transmitted from the Conference to the Board and so far we have found the matter a most difficult one. Forty papers were written to, asking them the cost of printing, etc., but not more than three or four have answered.

The Board thereupon took the decision "that the President (Alexander McDonald, M.P.), Secretary (William Crawford), and Mr. Ben Pickard make arrangements to have a paper issued as soon as possible." But this again was as far as it got. It was easier said than done.

Private ventures such as *The Miner and Workman's Advocate* of 1863, or the *Labour Tribune* (the organ of the miners and ironworkers of Great Britain) of 1886, had been made and

had each lasted for but a short while. With the memory of
the famous Chartist *Northern Star* and of its successors edited
by Ernest Jones still vivid in the minds of the next generation,
attempts were made from time to time to carry on workmen's
papers that covered all trades. But the inspiration was seldom
strong enough, in the absence of such an independent
political outlook as Chartism, to fill their sails for more than
a short trip.

The rebirth of Socialist propaganda in the 'eighties at last
gave the necessary impetus; and most of the Socialist weeklies
then begun lasted on for another generation and more. But
there was no daily paper as yet.

With the remarkable development of the newspaper Press
in the first years of this century, with the hostility shown by
most of that Press to strike struggles and to the Labour
Party, there arose in the unions, and not least in the miners'
associations, a growing repugnance towards the daily newspapers, which came to be described as "the capitalist press."
No sooner was this phrase current than it generated a demand
for "a Labour press," that is for a Labour or Socialist daily
newspaper. The outcome of this demand was the creation,
in 1912, of two newspapers, each claiming to be the heir to
all the aspirations of the Labour movement.

In mid-November 1911 the M.F.G.B. Executive Committee
Minute tells that "Messrs. J. R. MacDonald and A.
Henderson attended as a deputation from the Labour Party
and explained the proposed scheme for establishing a Daily
Labour Newspaper." It appeared that the lowest sum
required would be £100,000 but that it would be safer to
have a capital of £150,000: that the management would be
in the hands of the Labour Party: that of nine directors,
three would be from the Labour Party, three from the I.L.P.,
and three from the trade unions. The three directors from
the trade unions were to be appointed as follows: one from
the Trades Union Congress, one from the General Federation
of Trade Unions, and one from the Miners' Federation of
Great Britain. The M.F.G.B. Executive agreed to consider
this. No decision was taken by them immediately. The
scheme, however, went ahead: and early in 1912 Keir
Hardie's *Labour Leader* was joyfully announcing that before

many months were gone Labour would have its daily press.

Meantime, however, another seed had been sown in the course of 1911 (by a printers' strike bulletin) and was ripened during the winter of 1911–12 by some foreknowledge of what sort of paper Ramsay MacDonald was likely to sponsor. Thus suddenly, in the spring of 1912, there appeared the *Daily Herald*, first in the field. Presently George Lansbury, already an opponent of MacDonald within the I.L.P., had become the editor of the rival paper and was to remain at that post for another ten years.[1] But the main feature of the *Daily Herald* from the beginning was a full-page cartoon each day by the Australian artist Will Dyson, who for some two years blazed in the firmament as the creator of a new epoch in Socialist journalism.

The *Daily Citizen*, when eventually it appeared in the autumn of 1912, was bound to suffer by comparison with its left-wing rival, which seemed to have gathered behind it all the enthusiasm of the Socialist vanguard. Nevertheless, a number of trade unions dutifully invested funds in the *Daily Citizen*, which was edited by Frank Dilmot, a Fleet Street journalist trained in the Northcliffe school, and controlled by a Board headed by Ramsay MacDonald. Not until the *Daily Citizen* had come out did the Miners' Federation invest money in it: and it is in their balance sheet for the twelve months ending September 1913 that there appears the item "Investment in *Daily Citizen*—£10,000." That same autumn of 1913 the *Daily Citizen* began to get into low water, and urgent appeals were made by MacDonald to trade unions to come to its aid. The Miners' Federation responded by calling levies in varying number from its Districts which brought in a total up to September 1914 of £22,244 10s. 0d.

---

[1] George Lansbury (1859–1940) became a Socialist in 1890, was Chairman of the Social-Democratic Federation in the late 'nineties, but later became a prominent member of the Independent Labour Party. He was a member of the Royal Commission on the Poor Law, 1905–9, and a signatory of its famous Minority Report, drafted mainly by Beatrice Webb. From 1895 onwards he was a frequent candidate for Parliament, which he entered as a Labour member for the Bow and Bromley division of Poplar in 1910. In 1912 he resigned, to fight the parliamentary seat as an Independent and a supporter of suffrage for women. He was defeated and was not re-elected till 1922. MacDonald did not include Lansbury in his 1924 administration but made him First Commissioner of Works in the Labour Cabinet of 1929–31. On the defection of MacDonald, Lansbury became the Leader of the Labour Party from 1931 to 1935 when he was succeeded by C. R. Attlee. Lansbury's brief autobiography in *Who's Who* concludes with "Member of Church of England: teetotaller; non-smoker; twice in prison."

Their shares in this venture now stood at £31,000. In the first nine months of the 1914–18 war further M.F.G.B. levies brought in nearly £11,000 from which further shares to the amount of £10,500 were taken up. But these efforts, as well as the efforts of other trade unions, were made in vain. The *Daily Citizen* ceased publication in the first week of June 1915. Despite all efforts to keep it afloat it sank and carried down with it some £200,000 of trade union funds. Of this the Miners' Federation had contributed £41,500. The Executive Committee, extremely dissatisfied with this, sought for years to get from the liquidators some scraps from the wreckage. Therefore, when Lansbury at a later stage asked for trade union assistance for the *Daily Herald*, the Executive Committee were unwilling to help. They looked on it as "throwing good money after bad," and kept their purse-strings tight.

Another matter on which it was hard to get a common view within the M.F.G.B. Executive Committee was working-class education or, as it was often then called, adult education. Here District differed from District. For example, the Midland Federation looked on benevolently when R. H. Tawney organised a class of Staffordshire miners, the germ of what afterwards developed into the State-aided Workers' Educational Association, founded in 1903. Then after Ruskin College in Oxford, founded in 1899, had gathered way, a certain number of miners found their way thither, particularly from the more socialistic Districts. From the students of this college there came a new development which involved one M.F.G.B. District and was in later years to spread widely throughout the coal-fields. In 1908 the governing body of Ruskin College took some exception to the Darwinian and Marxist teachings of the principal, Dennis Hird. Thereupon the majority of the students came out on a strike, which resulted in a secession and the formation of a new college to which the South Wales Miners' Federation together with the National Union of Railwaymen gave the necessary support in money. Presently this became the Central Labour College, which, from its premises in London, radiated a new outlook on working-class education. The demand was put forward that State aid, with consequent State control of curricula and teachers, should be rejected and that the miners should themselves be responsible for the education of their members through central and local colleges and classes. The slogan was "independent working-class education."

By 1910 a monthly journal, partly devoted to a running controversy with the supporters of State-aided education, was being published under the name of *The Plebs* and presently there was formed the Plebs League to carry on propaganda for "independent working-class education," with its own badge proudly worn by its members who were never backward at trade union branches in raising this subject which was nearest to their hearts. From an early period *The Plebs* had the services as editor of J. F. Horrabin, a map-maker and diagrammatist of original trend. At first the scope of the movement "for independent working-class education" did not go far beyond the Central Labour College (later called The Labour College), the organisation of regular classes in South Wales and here and there in other coal-fields—for example in Durham. Elsewhere, apart from this, educational classes had been run by each of the existing Socialist societies, particularly in Scotland, where first James Connolly and then John McLean had been among the pioneers.

It was after 1918 that many of these local efforts were brought together in the National Council of Labour Colleges. The outlook at this stage is shown in a pamphlet[1] which criticises the "social science" taught in the universities:

The Universities are the storehouses of ruling-class ideas. They can soak the worker in ruling-class culture, but they *cannot explain to him how to raise his class out of its material and mental poverty*. There was a time when the workers thought that in industrial disputes the State was always impartial. The recent coal and railway disputes have killed that idea stone dead. It must be as clearly realised that the Universities are equally partial, partial to the present capitalist system of which they are a part.

. . . Independence of capitalist control, independence of capitalist ideas has been the watchword all along. It must be the watchword today, not merely in Trade Unionism and in Politics, but also in Education.

The question of independent working-class education is a very simple one. It can be put in this way:—Can a Trade Union expect

---

[1] *More Production—and More Poverty* by J. P. M. Millar with a preface by Robert Smillie written in 1922.

to have an understanding rank and file if it provides no antidote to the anti-working class sentiments absorbed in the schools, and later, from the capitalist Press?

Merely to present a man or woman with a trade union card does not make him or her a good trade unionist. The trade unionist must be educated—must understand the history of the working class and the problems that confront it. A Trade Union that fails to educate its members fails in its duty. It fails to recognise that *a Trade Union is only powerful to the extent that its members know what to do with it.*

The author, afterwards for many years (and up to the present) Secretary of the National Council of Labour Colleges, represented in this the current standpoint of what was as yet a minority in the M.F.G.B. Executive Committee. But the young miners who took part in this educational movement and its classes were within a generation to become prominent leaders both of the Miners' Federation and of the Parliamentary Labour Party.

6. THE PILOT'S DAUGHTER

What in these years was the home life of the mining family? In most coal-fields they still dwelt in the miners' rows put up by the colliery companies: and this housing of the miners, as exemplified in one particular coal-field, will be dealt with in detail in another volume. Their villages were still to be reached only by occasional trains on the same railway that served the pit: for passenger road transport was only in its beginning. Electric lighting was still infrequent: and the gas cooker was seldom then in use. In its place was the big kitchen fire, which also heated the water for the pitman to cleanse himself from the stains of his trade: for, despite the provisions in the 1911 Act, few collieries as yet had pithead baths.

Nearly every convenience which the nature of the miners' occupation demanded had to be furnished and maintained by the drudgery of the womenfolk. For of the mining community as a whole there was one half unorganised, unsafeguarded, unrepresented in Parliament—the wives and mothers of the working miners. How did they fare in this period? No Government reports measured from year to year the changes in their conditions of life: nor do they figure in statistical columns beyond their place in the tables of births, deaths and marriages. Their song, or their dirge, remained unsung or at any rate unheard. Here, to give some picture of their lives, is a sketch of the mother of a family on the north-east coast.

It was a typical mining family of those days. The grandfather, a winding engineman, had been Secretary of a local Chartist body in Northumberland and led a twenty-mile march to a great Chartist demonstration at White Mare Pool, Heworth. His seventh son, who was born nearly a century ago, had to the end of his life the most vivid memory of the terrible disaster at Hartley Colliery (in 1862). When he was nearly thirty he married the only child of a pilot on the River Tyne. The pilot's daughter became the mother of a large family, most of whom went down the pit. Conditions were very grim in the Northumberland coal-field when she was wed in the 'eighties of last century, so much so that soon her husband emigrated: and after spending two years as a miner in the United States returned to his young wife. Then she reared to manhood and womanhood nine sons and two daughters. The family had a very hard upbringing. In those days the pits worked an eleven-day fortnight, with fortnightly pays. Most of the coal was exported to the Baltic; a precarious trade, especially when the Baltic was frozen. One memory was of the pits being idle the first ten days and working only the last day, known as the Baff Saturday. One day's pay for a fortnight and at that time seven children to provide for!

Shortly before the father sought work across the Tyne in county Durham, the eldest son had to leave school and go to work in the pit when he was only twelve years of age. At the age of thirteen the next son began work at the colliery and so with the third son. Each successive son at work in the pits meant more toil for the mother at home. When I met her, nearly a third of a century ago, I got a picture of her working day, since confirmed by one of her sons, as follows:

The day began at 3 a.m. when the eldest son, a hewer, made his breakfast, took his "bait" put up the night before and went on shift at 4. Mother, if awake, would try and snatch an hour's sleep before preparing a younger son, a datal worker, whose shift started at 6 a.m. He would no sooner be off than Father would be coming in for breakfast and "bath," his shift ending at 6 a.m. He had started his shift at 10 p.m. the previous night. The repair shift worked a full eight-hour shift plus winding while the hewers worked 6½ to 7 hours per shift. In spite of the longer hours the repair workers had a smaller basic wage than the hewers.

By the time Father had had his breakfast and bathed in a tin in front of the fire it would be time for three children to get up and prepare for school. Even with this task performed, Mother had no time to rest. She had now to prepare a dinner for the eldest returning between 11 and 11.30 a.m. He would not have finished washing in front of the fire before the children returned from school for their mid-day meal. In all probability Father would get up and have something with the children at mid-day, go to the local for a pint, return at tea time and go to bed for a couple of hours.

With the children off to school for the afternoon Mother had to prepare for three more sons going on shift at 2 p.m. By the time she had got them off she had to prepare meal and bathing water for the son who went on shift at 6 a.m. and would be returning to house just after 2 p.m. By the time he was off the kitchen floor it was nearly time for the school children returning. On top of this continual round all the washing "laundry" was done at home as well as baking. There was no bought bread in northern mining villages in those days. The bread was all baked at home. This took sacks and sacks of flour.

Then she had to prepare for Father going on shift at 10 p.m.

The next preparation was the biggest of the day. After 10 p.m. the three sons who had gone on shift at 2 p.m. would be home. Not only had Mother to prepare their meals on the kitchen fire, but she had also to boil the water for their bath in pan and kettle. Altogether it would take anything up to two hours before they were all bathed, which they took successively in a tin on the hearth in front of the fire. It was always after midnight before they were all off to bed. This was the end of a normal day and the alarm clock would ring again at 3 a.m. for another day.

That was the life of a mother of a family in the great Durham coal-field with its system of multiple shifts. In the period covered by this history all the sons became active in their trade union: several of them suffered for their activities: and some played a national leading part. But in all the struggles of their lives, the hardest burden fell upon their mother, the pilot's daughter. There were scores of thousands of mining families in county Durham at that time: there were a million miners in the British coal-fields: and behind each man who had to go down the pit there was a wife and mother toiling to feed them and clothe them and keep them clean.

Appendix A

KEIR HARDIE'S BILL

A BILL to nationalise the Mines and Minerals of Great Britain and Ireland, and to provide for the working of the same.

(Prepared and brought in by Mr. Keir Hardie, Dr. Clark, Mr. Murray Macdonald, Mr. David Randell, Mr. John Burns, Mr. William Allen, Mr. Michael McCarton.)

Ordered, by the House of Commons, to be Printed
17th November 1893

WHEREAS coal having become an essential factor in the manufacturing industries and transport service of the nation, any interference with a regular and continuous supply is fraught with gravest dangers to our commercial supremacy:

And whereas the supply of coal is limited, and when exhausted can never be replaced:

And whereas the present system of working mines as private concerns leads to great waste of our mineral supplies, and to strikes and lock-outs thereby imposing great hardship on the mining community and trades dependent on a mineral supply for their continuance:

And whereas the nationalisation of the minerals and the mines would secure the economical working of the same, the just treatment and consequent contentment of the mining population, and a continuous and cheap supply of coal and other minerals:

Be it therefore enacted by the Queen's most Excellent Majesty by and with the advice and consent of the Lords Spiritual and Temporal, and Commons, in this present Parliament assembled, and by the authority of the same, as follows:

1. On and after the *first day of January one thousand eight hundred and ninety-five* all mines and minerals within the United Kingdom of Great Britain and Ireland shall be transferred, in fee simple, to the Crown, and shall thereupon become the property of the nation. *Transfer of mines and minerals to the Crown.*

2. All persons who are owners in whole or in part of the said mines or minerals shall on or before the *first day of May one thousand eight hundred and ninety-four* make a full and complete return to the Secretary of State for the Home Department showing the extent and nature of their pecuniary interest in the said mines or minerals. *Claims of ownership.*

3. (1) The Secretary of State for the Home Department shall appoint duly qualified valuers, who shall assess the present value of the said mines or minerals without regard either to the amount of capital invested or prospect of profits on the working of the same.

Value, how to be assessed.

(2) The said valuers shall carefully inquire into the present value as above defined of the mines and minerals of Great Britain and Ireland, and report to the Home Secretary, who shall thereupon issue an order upon the Treasury for the amount of the value so ascertained.

(3) *The Lords of the Treasury shall, on receipt of the said order, issue to the persons who have established their claim to be reckoned owners in whole or in part of said mines or minerals, bonds to the amount of their interests as found to exist at the date of the transfer to the Crown. The said bonds shall bear interest at the current rates, plus three per centum on the capital amount to form a sinking fund for the redemption of the capital sum.*

Payments, how to be made.

(4) The interest on the mining bonds together with the sinking fund shall form a first charge upon the working of the mines.

4. (1) *Previous to the first day of January one thousand eight hundred and ninety-five*, the Government shall create a special Mining Department with a President, who must be a member of the House of Commons, invested with full powers for the direct working and conducting of the mining industry of Great Britain and Ireland, without the intervention of any contractor or lessee, in such a way as will supply the legitimate demands for coal and other minerals, and ensure the safety and comfort of the persons employed.

Mining Department.

(2) The said Mining Department shall also pay such wages to persons employed in and about the mines as will ensure a healthy and comfortable existence to the said persons and their dependants.

Wages of workers.

(3) No women, nor any young person under *fifteen years* of age, shall be employed underground, nor shall any person be allowed to work alone in a mine until he has first served an apprenticeship of *three years'* duration.

Women and young persons not to be employed underground.

(4) No person shall be employed in a mine for a longer period than *eight hours* in any twenty-four hours, the time to be reckoned from the hour of descent to the hour of ascent from the mine.

Limitation of hours of employment.

(5) In the case of accident, fatal or otherwise, to any person employed in or about a mine, and sustained

Compensation, etc.

while in the performance of his duty as a workman, or any person unable to follow his occupation from old age, sickness, or other cause, over which he has no control, compensation or provision shall be made in terms of Schedule I of this Act.

(6) The cost of such compensation or provision shall be a charge upon the working of the mines.

5. On the establishment of a local parliament for any part of the United Kingdom of Great Britain or Ireland, the powers conferred upon the Mining Department under this Act shall, in so far as they relate to the country over which such local parliament has control, be transferred to and vested in the executive Government responsible to such local parliament.

Saving clause.

SCHEDULE

(1) During the continuance of incapacity, the result of an accident sustained while at work or of sickness, the workman shall receive his full weekly wages, and free medical and other attendance.

(2) In the case of fatal accidents the average wage for the time being prevailing shall be paid to the legal personal representative of the person killed for a period equal to the actuarial anticipation of the life of the person deceased.

(3) Persons retiring from work in the mines shall receive for each year of completed service a superannuation allowance equivalent to *one-sixtieth* of their average yearly earnings during the period of *five years* immediately preceding the date of retirement.

(4) In the event of the decease of a person receiving a superannuation allowance, *seventy-five* per cent of the said allowance shall be continued to the widow or other dependent relatives of the person deceased.

(5) Superannuation or other allowances to which any persons may be entitled under this Act shall not be forfeited by dismissal or any other cause.

Appendix B

NATIONALISATION OF COAL MINES AND MINERALS

A Bill to nationalise the Coal Mines and Minerals of the United Kingdom and to provide for the National Distribution and Sale of Coal.

Ordered to be brought in by Mr. Stephen Walsh, Mr. Tyson Wilson, Mr. William Edwin Harvey, Mr. James Parker, Mr. Pointer, Mr. Keir Hardie, Mr. George Roberts, Mr. Thomas Richardson, Mr. Sutton, Mr. John Taylor, Mr. Goldstone, and Mr. Hancock.

Ordered, by the House of Commons, to be Printed, 9 July 1913.

MEMORANDUM[1]

This Bill, which has been drafted for the Miners' Federation of Great Britain, has for its purpose the nationalisation of the coal-mines and minerals of the United Kingdom.

Clause 1 contains the usual formal provisions for the establishment of a new ministerial office. Clause 2 enables the Minister for Mines to enter into possession on the appointed day without waiting to obtain separate conveyances from all the owners of various interests. By clause 3 the owners of minerals, mineral rights, and mineral wayleaves are precluded from receiving the compensation which is awarded to the proprietors of the coal-mine itself. The powers given to the Commissioners under clauses 4 and 5 resemble those which are now possessed by the valuers under the Finance Acts. By clause 6 the purchase price is to be based in the main on the annual output of each colliery, and 10s. or 12s. per ton of such output[2] is named as the maximum price. The average annual output for the years 1906–10 was 261,726,945 tons, so that the maximum purchase price would be about £135,000,000. Under clause 7 payment is to be made in three per cent Government coal stock at par. Clause 8 provides for the Minister of Mines working the mines with his own staff. The power to purchase land compulsorily is also given him. Clauses 9 to 13 are financial. Under clause 14 the various Acts regulating labour in mines at present in force remain in operation. Clause 15 specifically preserves the right of the State coal-mine officials to form trade unions, strike and generally to join in industrial and political activities. By clause 16 a system of voluntary arbitration concerning industrial disputes in the mines is set up, and clause 17 places on the Minister for Mines the duty of ensuring that there shall be a sufficient supply of coal at reasonable prices throughout the country. The obligations of the railway companies to enable him to carry out his duty are also defined. Clauses 18 and 19 provide the necessary machinery for bringing the measure into operation.

[1] Explanatory Memorandum only is printed here. For full text see Bill 244 of 1913.
[2] Twelve shillings for those under, and 10s. for those over 100,000 tons annual output.

CHAPTER VI

THE MINERS IN WAR-TIME

I. ATTITUDE TO THE WAR

THE war of 1914–18 came as a terrible shock to the British miners as to the other sections of the working class. Thus, though the miners' unions through their international affiliations, had a better chance than many of anticipating events, their reaction to the outbreak of war was the same as that of the overwhelming majority of the British people. The attitude of the Miners' Federation of Great Britain had been determined beforehand, both as part of the Labour Party and as part of the International Federation of Miners. The trade union and Labour view on the question of a European war had been very clearly set forth in the 1907 resolution of the International Socialist Congress, to which the Labour Party, the British Socialist Party, the Fabian Society and the Independent Labour Party were affiliated. A second resolution was passed at the Copenhagen International Socialist Congress in 1910 and to this second resolution the Miners' Federation, having in the meantime joined the Labour Party, was committed as well as to the third resolution passed at the Basel Congress in 1912 to deal with the imminent danger of war. In each of these three resolutions the operative section ran as follows:

If war threatens to break out it is the duty of the working class in the countries concerned and of their Parliamentary representatives, with the help of the International Socialist Bureau as a means of co-ordinating their action, to use every effort to prevent war by all the means which seem to them most appropriate, having regard to the sharpness of the class war and to the general political situation.

Should war none the less break out, their duty is to intervene to bring it promptly to an end, and with all their energies to use the political and economic crisis created by the war to rouse the populace from its slumbers and to hasten the fall of capitalist domination.

It will be seen that this was a threefold policy: first for the prevention of war on the basis of class struggle, second (if war nevertheless broke out), to seek to stop the war, third to utilise the crisis arising from war to end the rule of the capitalist class. In July 1914 this threefold policy was put to the test, first by the threat of war and then by its actual outbreak. Austria-Hungary declared war on Servia on Saturday, July 25, 1914. The International Socialist Bureau met immediately in Brussels, called for the International Congress to meet in Paris ten days later and declared:

In assembly of July 29th the International Socialist Bureau has heard declarations from representatives of all nations threatened by a world war, describing the political situation in their respective countries.

With unanimous vote, the Bureau considers it an obligation for the workers of all concerned nations not only to continue but even to strengthen their demonstrations against war in favour of peace, and of a settlement of the Austro-Servian conflict by arbitration.

Things moved rapidly, and this statement proved to be the last expression of the united voice of the International. The Congress of Paris was not held.

It now remained for the national sections individually to carry out the first clause of the 1907–10–12 Resolution, which dealt with the prevention of war. In Great Britain the Labour Members of Parliament unanimously passed the following resolution on July 30th:

That the Labour Party is gratified that Sir Edward Grey has taken steps to secure mediation in the dispute between Austria and Servia, and regrets that his proposal has not been accepted by the Powers concerned; it hopes, however, that on no account will this country be dragged into the European conflict, in which, as the Prime Minister has stated, we have no direct or indirect interest, and the Party calls upon all Labour organisations in the country to watch events vigilantly so as to oppose, if need be, in the most effective way any action which may involve us in war.

On August 1st the British Section of the International Socialist Bureau issued its Manifesto to the British People which began with the words:

The long-threatened European War is now upon us. For more than 100 years no such danger has confronted civilisation. It is for you to take full account of the desperate situation and to act promptly and vigorously in the interest of peace. *You have never been consulted about the war.*

After calling for demonstrations ("everywhere vehement protests are made against the greed and intrigues of militarists and armament-mongers. We call upon you to do the same here in Great Britain upon an even more impressive scale. Hold vast demonstrations against war in every in-dustrial centre") the manifesto, which was signed by Arthur Henderson (the Secretary of the Labour Party) and Keir Hardie in their capacity of members of the International Socialist Bureau, ended with a strongly worded summons to oppose the war-mongers and the ruling class:

Workers, stand together, therefore, for peace! Combine and conquer the militarist enemy and the self-seeking Imperialists today, once and for all.

Men and women of Britain, you have now an unexampled opportunity of rendering a magnificent service to humanity, and to the world!

Proclaim that for you the days of plunder and butchery have gone by. Send messages of peace and fraternity to your fellows who have less liberty than you. Down with class rule! Down with the rule of brute force! Down with war! Up with the peaceful rule of the people!

On Sunday, August 2nd, a great demonstration representative of all sections of the working class held in Trafalgar Square, under the auspices of the British Section of the Socialist International, carried a resolution which began: "That this demonstration, representing the organised workers and citizens of London, views with serious alarm the prospects of a European War" and then went on to declare:

We stand by the efforts of the international working-class move-ment to unite the workers of the nations concerned in their efforts to prevent their Governments from entering upon war, as expressed in the resolution passed by the International Socialist Bureau.

Thus all sections of the British Labour Movement were united in their desire and their efforts for the prevention of war. In this they were carrying out the first clause of the 1907 resolution. But the attempt failed. Two days later (August 4th) Britain declared war on Germany.

The British declaration of war at once altered the situation and brought into prominence the second part of the 1907–10–12 resolution. What was to be done? Lloyd George and others who had been for neutrality now swung over, on the issue of the violation of international treaties by the German invasion of Belgium, to the side of Asquith and Grey; and, on this same issue, many Labour leaders rapidly reached a conviction that it was now a just war. In striking contrast to these was the case of John Morley, the old hench-man of Gladstone and author of his biography; and John Burns, one-time Labour leader who had succumbed to Liberal blandishments and accepted a Cabinet position. These two unhesitatingly gave up their ministerial portfolio and their place in the Cabinet in protest against the secret agreements that led this country into the war. With them went the junior ministers Ponsonby and Trevelyan. Some leaders were affected by the decision of the German Social-Democratic Party (the largest in the Reichstag) to cast its 111 votes for the war credits. Still for a few days matters hung in the balance. The Miners' Federation of Great Britain received a letter from the Chairman and Secretary of the Labour Party, informing them of the resolutions which were passed at a special meeting of the National Executive of the Labour Party on August 5th and 6th. These, after criticising the policy of the balance of power and of support to the Triple Entente, stated:

That the Labour movement reiterates the fact that it has opposed the policy which has produced the war, and that its duty is now to secure peace at the earliest possible moment on such conditions as will provide the best opportunities for the re-establishment of amicable feelings between the workers of Europe.

This letter, which ended with advice to concentrate on relief work "to mitigate the destitution which will inevitably overtake our working people while the state of war lasts," clearly showed that the Labour Party had receded quite a way from its earlier pronouncements in support of the 1907 resolution of the International.

By the end of the first week a division began to show itself between those who thought that Labour should sink all differences before the national danger and those who, while not opposing the war, still thought that Labour should maintain complete aloofness from the other parties. Needless to say, this view of entire independence was supported by the further section which was against the war itself. This last section is best represented in the manifesto published by the Independent Labour Party on August 13th. It began with an indictment of British foreign policy, of the armament race, and of secret diplomacy; it dwelt on the horror of war, and ended with the words:

We are told that International Socialism is dead; that all our hopes and ideals are wrecked by the fire and pestilence of European war. It is not true.

Out of the darkness and the depth we hail our working-class comrades of every land. Across the roar of guns, we send sympathy and greeting to the German Socialists. They have laboured unceasingly to promote good relations with Britain, as we with Germany. They are no enemies of ours, but faithful friends.

In forcing this appalling crime upon the nations, it is the rulers, the diplomats, the militarists who have sealed their doom. In tears of blood and bitterness the greater democracy will be born. With steadfast faith we greet the future; our cause is holy and imperishable, and the labour of our hands has not been in vain.

Long live Freedom and Fraternity! Long live International Socialism!

Thus by the middle of August the lines of distinction had been drawn on the political side of Labour. On August 29th the question of taking part in a parliamentary recruiting campaign came before the National Executive of the Labour Party: the Parliamentary Labour Party had already met and agreed to join in the campaign. It was decided:

That, in view of the serious situation created by the European war, the Executive Committee of the Labour Party agrees with the policy of the Parliamentary Party, in joining the campaign to strengthen the British Army, and agrees to place the Central Office organisation at the disposal of the campaign, and further recommends the affiliated bodies to give all possible local support.

The pronouncements of the trade unions came in September by which time the war policy of the Liberal Government was now whole-heartedly supported, e.g. in the manifesto of the

Trades Union Congress Parliamentary Committee, signed by all its members.

In these decisions of the bodies to which they were affiliated the Miners' Federation of Great Britain were naturally involved. They took no separate decisions, apart from an agreement to note the formation of the "War Emergency: Workers' National Committee" and the appointment of Robert Smillie, M.F.G.B. President, to be its Chairman. This body had been called together on August 5th by the Labour Party to comprise all the most important organisations of the Labour movement. Whatever their attitude might be towards the war, it was urged that on immediate social and industrial problems they could act together. Since neither majority nor minority were anxious to bring matters to a sharp issue, this compromise organisation met for a time with general acceptance.

The spirit of "agreement to differ" was manifest inside the Executive Committee of the Miners' Federation. The President, Robert Smillie, was a devoted friend of Keir Hardie and a leading member of the anti-war majority of the I.L.P. But in his speeches to the Conferences of the Miners' Federation this was not made obvious: and his anti-war activity was carried out in other spheres. Similarly with his colleagues, who were at least equally pro-war, the same rule held good. Nevertheless between the two sides there was a bitter feeling which, though it did not express itself openly for or against the war, often found expression in other quite petty questions. Thus the issue was never fought out within the M.F.G.B. There was throughout an uneasy truce, which remained till the war ended.

It makes an interesting footnote to these controversies of 1914 that a third of a century later the Secretary of State of the U.S.A., after twelve years' experience of office, should give the following definition:

The First World War was a culmination of years of intense, bitter rivalry among a number of daring and desperate Powers seeking territory, trade advantage, raw materials, control of trade routes, and political, economic or military domination of small and helpless peoples (*The Memoirs of Cordell Hull*, vol. 1, p. 75, 1948).

2. MAN-POWER AND OUTPUT

The year that followed from the first blast of war proved to be an eventful one for the miners of the United Kingdom. For some months, however, the normal tenor of the industry seemed but little disturbed. In several Districts the owners withdrew demands for reductions, but in Durham and Northumberland about 200,000 miners suffered decreases during the winter; while in the West Yorkshire coal-field a dispute over the refusal of certain mine-owners to carry out an award under the Minimum Wage Act dragged on for six months.[1] But soon after Christmas 1914 entirely new problems arose, of man-power and of prices, for which there was no guidance in past experience.

In the first months of the war, several Districts were working short time and unemployment was prevalent. As the winter advanced, there was an amount of enlistment among the miners so large as seriously to affect coal output. Taken in relation to recruitment from other industries this was in itself a terrible commentary on wages and conditions in the mining industry. As soon as this was realised, the coal-owners began to press for a suspension of the Eight Hours Act which had come into force five years earlier: they averred that production could not be brought up to the normal level unless this was done. An agitation on these lines was run in the Press and in Parliament. The miners, on their part, held meetings strenuously protesting and insisting that the shortage in supplies (with the corresponding high prices of coal) was due to causes other than the operation of the Eight Hours Act. By mid-February, 1915, the matter had become urgent. A Home Office Departmental Committee was appointed on February 23rd "to enquire into the conditions prevailing in the coal-mining industry with a view to promoting such organisation of work and such co-operation between employers and workmen as, having regard to the large number of miners who are enlisting for naval and military service, will secure the necessary production of coal

[1] In the first week of the New Year a Yorkshire strike ballot was taken and sanctioned on January 7, 1915, by an M.F.G.B. Special Conference. On February 9th, the owners conceded the men's demands.

during the war." Its members were: Sir Richard Redmayne, Chief Inspector of Mines (Chairman), Earl of Crawford and Balcarres, Vernon Hartshorn, A. F. Pease, Charles E. Rhodes, Robert Smillie and Stephen Walsh, M.P. Their report,[1] produced on May 27th, set out first to discover how far enlistment had depleted the collieries of labour.

The number of workers in coal-mines prior to the war was 1,116,648. After seven months of war 191,170 had enlisted. After nine months it was estimated that the number of miners in the forces was over 220,000 (a figure which rose to well over a quarter of a million by August 1915). The percentages in February 1915 were, for Scotland: 21·3 per cent; for Wales: 18·7 per cent; for England: 18·0 per cent.

Output in seven months had fallen by the same proportions as the net decrease in man-power. The probable fall for the first twelve months of war was put at thirty-six million tons and the net shortage (since many export markets had gone) at twelve million tons.

In the course of the enquiry proposals were made for counteracting the effect of shortage of labour due to re-cruiting by such measures as the curtailment of holidays, the reduction of avoidable absenteeism, the suspension of the Eight Hours Act, the introduction of labour from abroad, the employment of women on lighter work at the surface, and the lowering of the age limit for boys. The conclusions of the Committee did not fall in with these suggestions as put to them. Indeed, if any member of the Committee put an unwilling signature to the report, it was neither Smillie nor Walsh nor Hartshorn. The Committee uttered a warning against further recruiting of miners for the armed forces; suggested that questions of voluntary absenteeism or curtail-ment of holidays lay solely within the province of the Miners' Federation of Great Britain; ruled out any greater employ-ment of women or children; asked for a thriftier use of coal by the public; and laid most stress on solving the new problems of the industry (including the suspension, if any, of the Eight Hours Act) through the joint activity of the miners' unions and the employers' associations and stated in their concluding paragraph:

[1] Report of Departmental Committee to enquire into conditions prevailing in the Coal-mining Industry due to the War (Cd. 7939).

The basis of all the proposals and suggestions made by the Committee is harmonious co-operation between employers and employed through the medium of the organisations on both sides thoroughly representative of the parties.

Unless the organisations possess this power, and are able to act with authority for both owners and workmen, friction may arise and stoppages of work take place which ought to be avoided at the present time to the utmost extent possible.

In the highest interests of the nation, it is especially desirable that during the period of the war the employers should co-operate with the representatives of the workmen on such questions as non-unionism, or other questions likely to lead to any friction or stoppage during the present unprecedented circumstances.

During the spring and summer of 1915, efforts were put forth by the miners for more output. On July 29th a conference of employers and men met in London, with Sir John Simon, then Home Secretary, in the chair. He pointed out that they were short of three million tons of coal a month (which, for a solution, obviously called for men to be returned from the army) despite the sacrifices the men had made in curtailing their Easter and summer holidays and said that, if necessary, the Government might at a later date consult the industry as to the suspension of the Eight Hours Act. Lloyd George then made a general appeal, and finally Robert Smillie, as President of the M.F.G.B., urged an increase on the additional grounds that the grates of the poor should not be empty in the coming winter: every effort should be made and every means should be tried before recourse was had to a suspension of the Eight Hours Act. Thus matters stood at the end of twelve months of war. There was every indication then that unless production was immensely increased, hours of labour and the employment of women and children would shortly become issues of extreme urgency.

3. LIVING STANDARDS AND NEW AGREEMENTS

Prices, not only of coal but of all commodities, rose steeply during the winter of 1914–15 with the result that in the New Year wages demands were put forward in several industries. In the mining industry changes in wages had hitherto been regulated in Conciliation Boards where the sole factors taken into account, at any rate by the Independent Chairman, were the selling price of coal and the volume of output. Prices of other commodities, which made up the cost of living, had been left out of the reckoning. In this respect the living standards of the miners had been considerably worsened in the twenty years of rising prices since the English Conciliation Board had been set up in 1894. "In the first ten years of the century the purchasing power of the pound dropped to only 17s.," writes Francis Williams,[1] who also estimates that wages in the five principal industries including mining had risen by only one-thirtieth of the rise in London retail prices of food. Small wonder that so many miners were impatient with the trammels of the Conciliation Board and were seeking some means of keeping up their diminishing standard of living. But what the subtle thief of rising prices had stolen unperceived through so many years could no longer be hidden in the onset of war. Food prices rose in ten months by more than they had risen in twenty years. In the middle of March 1915—by which time the cost of food alone had risen by 24 per cent—the miners in conference decided that a national demand be made for a special advance in wages to meet the high cost of living. The demand was for an immediate increase of 20 per cent on earnings; and the owners' organisation, the Mining Association of Great Britain, was asked to hold a joint national meeting with the Miners' Federation of Great Britain. As on previous occasions, the Mining Association refused this request on the ground that it could not touch a question of wages, which must be dealt with in the Districts. An M.F.G.B. Special Conference on April 21, 1915, after rejecting a motion by South Wales to tender strike notices, decided to ask for Government intervention to bring the coal-owners' and miners' representatives together. After long delay and much negotiation a meeting was secured through the instrumentality and under the chairmanship of the Prime Minister—on the express understanding that it was not to be regarded as a precedent for national conferences on wages questions. The employers then offered an immediate national advance of 10 per cent, to

[1] *Fifty Years' March: The Rise of the Labour Party* with Foreword by the Rt. Hon. C. R. Attlee (Odhams), 1949.

be followed by local negotiations for further advances. This the miners rejected out of hand, and decided to leave the 20 per cent demand in the hands of the Prime Minister to be settled by arbitration. Asquith's decision was that a case had been made out for an immediate advance, but that, owing to the variety of local conditions, the actual amounts should be decided locally.

The results of the local negotiations, as might have been expected, were that some Districts were fairly satisfied while others did very badly. Northumberland and Durham, for instance, got only 15 per cent *on the standard* (less than half of what had been demanded). The Federated Districts gained $15\frac{1}{2}$ per cent *on earnings*. On their standard the Scottish miners got $18\frac{1}{2}$ per cent, and South Wales $17\frac{1}{2}$ per cent on theirs. Nowhere, however, did the miners obtain the full 20 per cent on earnings. The demand of the M.F.G.B. for national negotiations to meet a national rise in the cost of living was part of the centralising policy of the M.F.G.B., to make itself the unit for collective bargaining with the employers. The accession of strength which would come from this was fully realised by the employers, and this knowledge stiffened their opposition to national negotiations. Asquith's award was calculated to meet the desires of the coal-owners, in so far as it remitted negotiations to the Districts, and was immediately recognised to be a set-back to M.F.G.B. policy.

April 1, 1915, had been fixed by the M.F.G.B. as the date on which notice was to be given to terminate all existing Conciliation Board agreements. At their annual conference two years earlier in Scarborough, a resolution had been carried which provided that all new agreements entered into by Conciliation Boards must terminate at one and the same time; that in place of the obsolete standards of 1877, 1879 and 1888, a new standard rate of wages should be created, "by merging into the new standard all bonuses and percentages not less than the existing minimum percentages and bonuses recognised by the Boards." It had also been agreed to demand for all adult surface workers a minimum wage of not less than 5s. a day. In furtherance of these resolutions, as the time for giving notice approached, the Executive Committee carried a resolution (on February 4,

1915) that no District agreement be considered settled until after confirmation by the M.F.G.B. The employers and miners forthwith began to negotiate the terms of the new agreements. In the English Federated Area, in Scotland, Cumberland and Durham, a new agreement was drawn up more or less in accordance with the terms of the Scarborough resolutions; but in South Wales a protracted struggle took place between the owners and the men.

4. THE SOUTH WALES STRIKE

The history of the demand for a new wages agreement in South Wales presented special features and was of general importance, as it involved, among other things, the attitude of the miners to compulsory arbitration and the Munitions Act. On March 3, 1915, the South Wales Miners' Federation put forward proposals for a revision of the Conciliation Board agreement which had run for the five years from 1910. The main heads of their proposals were:

1. That the existing standard rate (1879) be abolished and a new standard established which shall have merged therein 50 per cent on the 1879 standard.[1]
2. That surface workers should have not less than 5s. a day.
3. That workers on the afternoon and night shifts should be paid upon the new standard at the rate of a turn and a fifth for each shift worked.
4. That the agreement should apply to all grades of workmen employed in or about the collieries.

There were other important provisions, on which the miners eventually yielded, without their becoming a bone of contention. The reply of the South Wales coal-owners to these proposals was that they felt it undesirable to begin a new agreement in the midst of war. They urged the miners to continue working under the old agreement, and in return for this surrender on the part of the men they were prepared to offer a 10 per cent war bonus. (It should be noted that the demand for a new agreement had taken place just at

---

[1] Certain collieries worked under a standard of 1877, to which 35 per cent was to be added to make the new standard of 1915.

the same time as the national demand for a 20 per cent war bonus.)

The miners, naturally, refused to agree. They pointed out that the owners had cleverly confused the issues, that the new agreement demand was quite separate from the war bonus demand, and that the withdrawal of the one could not be made a condition for the granting of part of the other. They pointed out, too, that the 10 per cent offered was much less than the miners were prepared to accept nationally, quite apart from considerations of standard rates. The reply of the owners to this was a curt refusal even to meet the miners to negotiate upon the proposed new agreement. April 1st marked the end of the 1910 agreement. The necessary three months' notice was given by the S.W.M.F. for a new agreement. During this period negotiations were supposed to go on, but the attitude of the owners made such a course impossible. During the three months from April to the end of June they persistently refused to negotiate; while the Government, which was afterwards to play a prominent part in the dispute, took no heed of the situation.

The Government had been having troubles of its own that summer. The vainglorious vaunts of a short campaign (with War Secretary Kitchener of Khartoum alone in his perspective of a four years' war) had faded early, leaving behind them a misplaced confidence in a victorious campaign in the New Year. But the year 1915 brought the disaster of Neuve Chapelle, the Gallipoli fiasco, which cost Churchill his seat in the Cabinet, the discovery of shell shortages and other shortages, and was to end in the Mesopotamian expedition where the main British force surrendered to the Turks. Its initial disasters were enough to cause the downfall of the Liberal Government and the formation by Asquith on May 26, 1915, of a Coalition Government made up of all parties in Parliament, except the four score Irish Nationalists. Three places were given to the Parliamentary Labour Party, then numbering two score out of 670 members of the House of Commons. Arthur Henderson became President of the Board of Education, William Brace Under-Secretary at the Home Office, and G. H. Roberts a junior Lord of the Treasury.

In the Coalition Government Lloyd George, till now Chancellor of the Exchequer, had carved out a new ministry, with himself at the head as Minister of Munitions. Some few weeks earlier, on March 17, 1915, there had begun a Treasury Conference between the Treasury and the Board of Trade on the one hand and the main trade union bodies on the other, which resulted in the Treasury Agreement of March 19th, which suspended trade union rules and regulations in munitions industries for the duration of the war. To this agreement neither the Amalgamated Society of Engineers nor the Miners' Federation were parties. The miners had attended on the first day of the conferences, but withdrew as they were unwilling to accept compulsory arbitration. Again, when the Munitions of War Act was being passed through the Commons in June 1915 and at the same time discussed with the unions concerned, the Miners' Federation was not one of these. It was opposed to the industrial conscription of the Munitions of War Act and to its prohibition of strikes. Thus, from the beginning of March till nearly the end of June the Government and its most dynamic personality stayed sedulously unconcerned with the situation in South Wales. Lloyd George was out for bigger game. Thus it was not until the end of June, when the three months' notices were running out, that the Government seemed to realise that, in default of a new agreement, there would be a stoppage in the Welsh coal-field. The President of the Board of Trade then intervened. This was Walter Runciman, son of a millionaire ship-owner and always regarded in his family as marked out for political place and power. He was believed to possess the capacity of preserving an impartial manner in matters where his whole training and outlook had already committed him to the standpoint of one side.[1] He initiated a series of conferences in the last week of June, but with little apparent result: for the representatives of the South Wales Miners' Federation felt that the solutions he proposed would not be accepted by their delegate Conference.

Eventually, on June 30th, when a stoppage seemed inevitable, the three Labour Members of the Government arrived in

---

[1] It was perhaps this reputation which led him to be chosen by Prime Minister Chamberlain, twenty-three years later, as "mediator" at Prague in the summer negotiations which led to "Munich" in the autumn of 1938.

Cardiff as Government emissaries. That evening, the South Wales Executive agreed to recommend that the last set of proposals put by Runciman should be accepted but only as a basis for future negotiations; and that, pending a settlement, the pits should continue working for a fortnight on day-to-day contracts. The delegate meeting accepted this recommendation of the Executive by a majority of eleven out of 235 delegates. Runciman's proposals for a new agreement were:

1. The rates of surface men which are below 3s. 4d. a day to be advanced to 3s. 4d.
2. Night men to receive six turns for five.
3. Hauliers employed on afternoon and night shifts to be paid the same rate as those employed on the day shift.
4. A new standard of 50 per cent on the 1879 standard to be established. Any standards in operation other than the 1879 standard to be correspondingly adjusted. (It is not intended that the alteration of the standard shall in itself affect an immediate change in wages.)
5. The maximum and minimum provided for in the 1910 agreement not to be operative.
6. Any question of interpretation of these terms to be submitted in writing.

During the first week of July the Executive Council of the S.W.M.F. pressed Runciman for such an interpretation of these unfavourable terms as might make them more palatable even considered merely as a basis for negotiations. On Friday, July 9th, three days before the assembling of the delegate meeting called for the Monday, July 12th, Runciman gave his interpretations. These were extremely unfavourable to the miners. He made it clear that men on afternoon and night shifts should be paid at the rate of six turns for five, and not, as demanded, at the rate of one turn and a fifth for each turn worked. The rates paid to underground day-wage men were left to the consideration of the Joint Conciliation Board instead of being raised to a uniform 5s. minimum. The question as to what classes of workmen were covered by the terms of July 1st was left to the decision of the Independent Chairman of the Joint Conciliation Board. The miners had demanded that the agreement should apply merely to those workers who were or might become members of the S.W.M.F. In other words, non-unionists and members of "sectional" societies were not to benefit. The reason for shelving a decision on this point was that, "as this may affect other Trade Unions, it requires more investigation and inquiry into local circumstances than Mr. Runciman can at present undertake." Runciman's failure to grapple with this point was, perhaps, more fruitful of dissension than anything else. Finally, the note that ran throughout his interpretations was that of reference to the Independent Chairman of the Conciliation Board. This did not satisfy the miners, who were demanding an immediate decision, and who knew that a question shelved was frequently a question lost.

Immediately the nature of these Runciman interpretations was made public, the South Wales Executive realised that it would be well-nigh impossible to prevent a stoppage of the coal-field. Runciman had given a decision which practically invited a strike. Nevertheless, the Executive put forward to the delegate Conference on July 12th, a resolution which endeavoured to secure the further continuance of work. By this time, however, the miners had had enough. For five years they had been bound down by an agreement in many ways unfavourable to themselves; notice had run for three months after the termination of that agreement; for fourteen days they had extended the period of working, but despite this extended notice, they were as far off a decision as ever. Indeed, the interpretation by Runciman of his own document only strengthened the opposition to the document itself. Thus they resolved to wait no longer but at once to bring matters to a head. The delegate Conference declared:

We do not accept anything less than our original proposals, and . . . we stop the collieries on Thursday next until these terms are conceded. (July 12, 1915.)

The resolution was carried by 1,894 to 1,037 votes, representing a Federation membership majority of 42,850.

To this decision the reply of the Government was to "proclaim" the South Wales coal-field under the Munitions of War Act. Consistently opposed to compulsory arbitration, and unfettered by any Treasury conferences, the Miners' Federation had negotiated[1] with Mr. Lloyd George to be

[1] "That our attitude be one of uncompromising opposition to the inclusion of the miners in the Bill."—M.F.G.B. Executive Committee resolution, June 23, 1915.

left out of the scope of the Bill. Eventually Lloyd George had agreed to insert, after the section in which it was stated that the penal clauses of the Act might be applied by Royal Proclamation to *any difference*, the following provision:

If, in the case of any industry, the Minister of Munitions is satisfied that effective means exist to secure a settlement without a stoppage of any difference arising on work other than munitions work, no proclamation shall be made under this section with respect to such difference.

In spite of this meagre concession, the proclamation was made in the case of South Wales. This attempt at coercion had absolutely no effect, and the 200,000 workers in South Wales struck despite, and perhaps partly because of, the Act. It was borne in upon the Government that it was impossible, especially when the machinery of the Munitions Act was as yet imperfect, to fine 200,000 strikers. Negotiations were resumed, but with no result. Eventually, after the strike had run for five days—during which time it had taken the chief place in public interest (the most violent Press campaign was conducted against the miners and their leaders)—Lloyd George, accompanied by Runciman and Arthur Henderson, arrived in Cardiff. After twenty-fours hours' negotiation, an agreement was reached, which conceded those points on which the miners had laid most stress, with the promise that His Majesty's Government would see that it was agreed to by the coal-owners. On this the miners returned to work.

A month later, further disagreement was caused by Runciman's interpretation of a point in the agreement in a sense other than the apparent meaning of the words. He excluded enginemen, pumpmen, stokers, etc., in spite of the clause that the agreement would apply to "all the workers who may be members of the South Wales Miners' Federation." A strike immediately threatened, but was averted by Runciman's hasty reversal of his decision; and the new Conciliation Board agreement of 1915 was then signed. But the miners retained an impression that the heir to Sir Walter Runciman's ships thought most readily as the coal-owners would have him do.

The troubles in the South Wales coal-field continued through the greater part of 1916. Not only the selling price of coal but the general level of all prices kept rising rapidly. Applications for rises in wages were met by counter-claims for reductions by the South Wales coal-owners. The machinery of the new Conciliation Board worked badly. There were difficulties with the "Independent Chairman." Viscount St. Aldwyn, now stricken in years, had resigned at the end of 1915. Lord Muir Mackenzie, an eminent lawyer who was chosen as his successor, failed to understand his function and was compelled to resign after eleven weeks in that office. His successor, Lord Justice Pickford, also proved unequal to his task. The two main wages claims (each for 15 per cent advance) had eventually to be settled directly by the Government, which conceded both in full; and on each occasion a coal-field strike was only narrowly averted. At last, on November 29, 1916, the Government, by order under the Defence of the Realm Act, brought the whole South Wales coal-field under State control. On December 5th Mr. Asquith resigned, and Lloyd George, the new Prime Minister, immediately let it be known that State control would be extended to the whole industry.

5. STATE CONTROL

The State control of the coal industry, announced by Lloyd George in terms which seemed to suggest nationalisation, was set up at the end of February 1917, with a Coal Controller heading a new department of the Board of Trade. Actually it amounted to State control over output and distribution: but in this case as in all others, efforts to reorganise the industry, whatever the control over output or distribution, were rendered futile through the fact that the first charge on the industry was always the profits of the coal-owners. There was a complex financial arrangement by which the coal-owners were to be guaranteed their profits from a profits pool to which the Government would contribute three-quarters of the excess profits tax proceeds. The coal-owners, who succeeded in getting all by-product works, coke-ovens and other ancillary undertakings (often the most lucrative part of their business) excluded from the accounting, were well enough satisfied with State control of this kind. But the miners also found that it worked to their own advantage. The setting up of a national pool at once destroyed the old contention of the owners, accepted by Mr. Asquith in 1915, that wages could not be settled nationally. Moreover, since the still rapidly rising cost of living, affecting all Districts, was the main basis of any further wage claims, there was another valid reason for settling on a national basis. The Government, however, when the M.F.G.B. Annual Conference in July 1917 demanded a 25 per cent war bonus on earnings, at first endeavoured to avoid giving an advance on a national basis. Eventually they yielded on this point, but proffered a flat rate advance of 1s. a day (and, later in the negotiations, 1s. 3d.) to all adult miners. This new principle of the "flat rate" instead of the normal "percentage" variation in wages (it helped the lower-paid men), was accepted by a Special Conference in September 1917: and after considerable haggling the actual figure was fixed at 1s. 6d. per day.

As the war went on, its events and its hardships began to have an effect upon the miners. Of these "external" events, the first with an appreciable effect in the coal-fields was the Easter Rising (1916) of Sinn Fein in Ireland, or rather the consequences of that rising. The protracted series of courts-martial upon prisoners and the shootings after the rapid suppression of the rising had a horrifying effect, which was voiced by liberal organs of opinion. In the coal-fields, where there were so many of Irish descent, the effect was to cause a revulsion of feeling. This for many centred upon the shooting of James Connolly, who had spent years in Scotland and was sufficiently well known throughout the Socialist movement. To this sentiment, which even led some miners[1] to cross into Ireland to help the Sinn Feiners, there was presently to be added the tremendous impact of the Russian Revolution. The subsequent publication by the Bolsheviks of the secret treaties between the Allies had the most disturbing effect in the factories and mines, where men and women were already sickened and weary of the ceaseless slaughter on the Somme and at Passchendaele. Throughout

---

[1] Including a future General Secretary of the N.U.M. (A. L. Horner).

the winter of 1917–18 a wave of war-weariness swept over the working population: and amongst the miners was voiced in a by-election struggle at Wansbeck in Northumberland. The candidate was Ebby Edwards, aged thirty-four, already prominent in his own county both as a leading trade unionist and as a staunch supporter of Smillie in his anti-war standpoint. The Labour Party refused to endorse the candidature which, however, received the full endorsement and financial backing of the Miners' Federation. Edwards was defeated, but the by-election struggle was significant of the mood that was growing amongst the miners.

Though the Labour Party continued its support of the war policy of the Lloyd George coalition, the events of 1917 were leading rapidly towards a more independent electoral attitude. It was felt that the time was ripe for a step in advance, for the formulation of a programme and a change in the Labour Party's constitution. These steps were worked out mainly by Arthur Henderson and Sidney Webb, who carried with them the Miners' Federation representatives on the Executive Committee of the Labour Party and in its Conferences of the spring of 1918.

The federal constitution of the Labour Party was altered so as to include individual members in the local Labour parties, and a programme entitled *Labour and the New Social Order* for the first time committed the Labour Party to a Socialist outlook—a commitment phrased by Sidney Webb in careful Fabian language.

By midsummer 1918 the cost of living had again risen. The Government had failed to check the rise. The following table shows the percentage increase over the level of July 1914 for each January and July until the armistice with Germany in November 1918.

COST OF LIVING

Month (beginning)	1915	1916	1917	1918
January	10–15	35	65	85–90
July	25	45–50	80	100–105

After wage increases through the Conciliation Boards or, in

the case of South Wales, direct from the Government in the autumn of 1916 (when the prices of food, rent, clothing, etc., were half as high again as at the beginning of the war), the M.F.G.B. did not make its national demand until the cost of living index had risen by another twenty-five points. Some twelve months later, by the end of May 1918, it had gone up yet another twenty-five points, making the cost of living just double what it had been in July 1914. A Special Conference on June 5, 1918, then demanded another 1s. 6d. flat rate addition to the "war wage" as it was called. By June 25th the Coal Controller offered 6d. This precipitated a critical situation. Within three days the Prime Minister hastily invited the M.F.G.B. Executive to a Conference, after which the 1s. 6d. a day was conceded as from June 30th. To this concession there was appended an agreement on Joint Pit Committees between the Controller of Coal Mines and the Miners' Federation of Great Britain. These were to be set up at all collieries and to be "charged with the duty of decreasing voluntary absenteeism and increasing output." They gave no say to the workers in the management of the industry.

By the armistice of November 1918 the cost of living index had again mounted by twenty-five points: and at the end of that month the Executive Committee decided, in accordance with a resolution of the Annual Conference, to ask for a further advance. This took the form of a claim for a 30 per cent increase on earnings, apart from the existing "war wage" of 3s. a day. This demand, however, owing to the General Election of December 1918, could not be presented to the Coal Controller till the New Year. When the New Year came, it had to be negotiated together with other demands of a very different kind. The negotiations were also to be of a nature hitherto unknown.

6. THE TRIPLE INDUSTRIAL ALLIANCE

As the end of the war approached, a new and seemingly powerful organisation, embracing three of the most potent trade union bodies in the country—miners, railwaymen and transport workers—came into prominence. This was the

Triple Industrial Alliance. This grouping of large industrial units had arisen from possibilities afforded on the one hand by the strike movement amongst the miners in 1912 and on the other hand by the formation in 1913 of the National Union of Railwaymen through the fusion of three out of the five previously existing trade unions on the railways. From the same period (1910) there dated the linking up into a single federation of the numerous unions of dockers and other transport workers that had sprung from the famous dock strike of 1889. The way in which these were brought into a wider alliance is best told in the words of Robert Smillie, in an article which he wrote for the *Labour Year Book* in the summer of 1915.

"One definite concrete result of the industrial unrest of recent years is the formation of the Triple Alliance proposed at a conference of the Miners' Federation of Great Britain, the National Union of Railwaymen and the National Transport Workers' Federation, held on April 23, 1914. The idea of such a conference was first brought into prominence at the Miners' Annual Conference in 1913, when a resolution was passed

That the Executive Committee of the Miners' Federation be requested to approach the Executive Committees of other big Trade Unions with a view to co-operative action and the support of each others' demands. (October 9, 1913.)

"The miners contented themselves in the first place with securing a joint meeting with the representatives of the two industries most comparable to their own—railways and transport. It was felt that if a working arrangement could first be concluded with a few of the larger sections, afterwards extensions to other groups could be made.

"The three bodies have much in common. Their membership is considerable, the miners numbering 800,000, the railwaymen 270,000 and the transport workers 250,000. The miners have done much fighting in the past, sectionally and generally; the railwaymen on more than one occasion have come through struggles similar to our own; and the transport workers are famed for their fighting spirit and fighting qualities. But while we achieved a great deal by our industrial struggles, and while we can hardly calculate the benefit conferred upon our people by these three bodies, it must be admitted that a great deal of suffering and privation has been caused. A strike on the railway system immediately affects the miners and the transport workers, as well as the others. Though these for the moment may not have any quarrel with their respective employers, yet within a few days they are placed in the same position as though they had. They are idle and are thrown upon the funds of their unions. The same result follows if the miners or the transport workers are on strike. When the miners struck in 1912 the cost to the railwaymen alone was about £94,000. Whenever any one of these three great sections have struck the others have had to stand by and suffer in silence.

"The meeting of the three Executives, held in April 1914, to consider ways and means of working in common and so avoiding the evils of disjointed action, was enthusiastic and unanimous. It resolved that a working agreement should be drawn up, and appointed a committee, consisting of the presidents and secretaries of the three organisations, for the purpose. The idea behind this agreement is not in any way the formation of a federation. The new body is not to be a rival to any other. Nor is it to be sectional in any sense. There is no suggestion, for instance, that if one section of the miners determines to strike they will receive the assistance of the new alliance. Action is to be confined to joint national action. Further, no action will be taken until all three partners have met in conference and have agreed upon the course to be adopted. Sympathetic action, in fact, is no longer to be left to the uncontrolled emotions of a strike period, but is to be the calculated result of mature consideration and careful planning. The predominant idea of the alliance is that each of these great fighting organisations, before embarking upon any big movement, either defensive or aggressive, should formulate its programme, submit it to the others, and that upon joint proposals joint action should then be taken.

"It is clear to everyone acquainted with industrial development that capital is now organised for the purpose of attacking trade unionism and for defence against trade union advance. Should the occasion arise, each section of the alliance must be ready to render sympathetic action, deliberately thought out and agreed upon, should any one of the partners in the scheme be the object of attack.

"While the scheme at the moment is not intended to include more than the three trades referred to, it may well be found advisable later on to extend the scope of the alliance in the general interests of Labour as a whole. Even now, indeed, it has already been discussed whether the Triple Alliance might not be in a position to assist our fellow workers in the textile industry if, at an adverse moment, they were threatened with a lock-out. Under such circumstances there is every probability that a stoppage of production would cause an immediate settlement. In every case the results of joint action on a large scale should be rapid and decisive and all the suffering and loss inseparable from trade troubles of the past could be prevented in the future.

"The mere calling of our conference caused somewhat of a sensation among the capitalists on the one hand, while on the other, it created a new hope in the ranks of the industrial forces throughout the country. With the coming of the war, however, the scheme had to be laid aside for a time, but already the annual meeting of the Railwaymen and the Transport Workers have signified their approval, and it now remains to be considered by the Miners' Conference at Nottingham in October 1915. If the approval of the miners is forthcoming, and, in view of the scheme being their original suggestion, there is little likelihood of any other decision, the committee will then be at liberty to go ahead with the details. It will be wise, indeed essential, to have the working agreement ready for the days of peace after the war. It is then that we may expect an attack on Labour by the employers; it is now, in the midst of war, that we must prepare for the industrial conflicts that the military peace will bring."

Smillie, stimulated perhaps by his own article, pushed matters rapidly forward. The railwaymen and the transport workers at their annual conferences agreed on the proposals that had been awaiting ratification when war broke out. The Miners' Federation Conference at Nottingham in November 1915 was also in general agreement with the scheme, of which it had been the originator. But on one point they were not agreed; the rules of the miners' unions and indeed their whole conception of democratic procedure laid it down that before a strike was called there must be a ballot vote of all union members. They wished to make this stipulation as part of the constitution of the new Triple Alliance, which otherwise they felt might appear to be empowered to call a nationwide strike simply by the decision of the three Executive Committees. This new stipulation, however, did not suit the railwaymen, for whom the delay caused by a ballot would have endangered the success of a strike, and who, in any case, had no such provision in their union rules. On this there was much discussion. Eventually an agreement was reached. In December 1915 the new Alliance was formally brought into being, with Robert Smillie as Chairman, Harry Gosling of a Thames watermen's union as Vice-Chairman, J. H. Thomas, M.P., as Treasurer and Thomas Ashton as Secretary. The scheme accepted on December 9th was as follows:

THE TRIPLE INDUSTRIAL ALLIANCE

1. That matters submitted to this joint body, and upon which action may be taken, should be those of a national character or vitally affecting a principle which in the opinion of the Executive making the request necessitates combined action.

2. The co-operation of the joint organisation shall not be called upon nor expected unless and until the matter in dispute has been considered by and received the endorsement of the National Executive of the organisation primarily concerned, and each organisation instituting a movement which is likely to involve the other affiliated organisations shall, before any definite steps are taken, submit the whole matter to the joint body for consideration.

3. For the purposes of increasing the efficiency of the movement for combined action periodical meetings of the three full Executives shall be held at least half-yearly.

4. There shall be appointed a Consultative Committee of six, composed of two members chosen from the Executive Committee of each of the three bodies, whose duty it shall be to meet from time to time, and who shall be empowered to call at any time a special conference of the Executives of the three bodies if in their opinion such conference be necessary. That a meeting be called on application made by any one of the three bodies.

5. With a view to meeting all management expenses incurred, each affiliated body shall contribute a sum of 10s. per 1,000 members per annum, or such sum as may be decided upon from time to time.

6. Simultaneously with these arrangements for united action between the three organisations in question every effort shall proceed among the three sections to create effective and complete control of their respective bodies.
7. Complete autonomy shall be reserved to any one of the three bodies affiliated to take action on their own behalf.
8. That joint action can only be taken when the question at issue has been before the members of the three organisations and decided by such methods as the constitution of each organisation provides, and the conference shall then be called without delay to consider and decide the question of taking action.
9. No obligation shall devolve upon any one of the three bodies to take joint action unless the foregoing conditions have been complied with.

Clause six of the above agreement, with its aim "to create effective and complete control of their respective bodies," was greeted with joy by those in the Labour movement who had striven for amalgamation along the line of industrial unionism. The propaganda of amalgamation had been going on since King's *Clarion* pamphlet in the 'nineties, but had received a fresh impetus from the influence of Syndicalist ideas and a new direction towards union by industry. The creation of the National Union of Railwaymen in 1913 was hailed as the "new model" as once the Amalgamated Society of Engineers had been hailed sixty years earlier. It was known that many members of the National Union of Railwaymen now held to this principle. The insertion of this clause in the agreement was taken to be their work and to have a purely ideological origin. However that may be, it had also a practical significance. At the June 1914 Conference of the three bodies, one of the transport workers' delegates had raised the question. He wanted to have the colliery enginemen and the railway enginemen operating with them in any strike, especially in view of their key position. These craft unions, on the other hand, much offended at their exclusion from the initial Conferences leading to the Triple Alliance, had taken up an aloof attitude. At the 1914 Annual Conference of the National Federation of Enginemen, comprising unions both in the railway service and in the collieries, angry speeches were made and the following resolution was carried:

This Federation fails to see why the joint conference of miners, railway workers, and transport workers cannot see their way clear to agree that the railway interests and mining interests represented by this Federation will have direct representation and recognition in the counsels and objects of that joint body. It resolves that under no circumstances can it agree that we should seek representation through the National Union of Railwaymen or through the Miners' Federation, and it reserves to itself the right to determine its own course in the event of any position arising which requires action being taken by the men represented by this Federation.

The matter was not, however, further thrashed out at the time, as the outbreak of war deferred all discussion. In December 1915 the sub-committee of the three main organisations stuck to the formula set out in clause six.

Ten months later the Southport M.F.G.B. Conference resolved that in future all mineworkers of whatever grade must belong to the Miners' Federation of Great Britain. By some this was taken as a declaration of war on the small unions of the mining industry, but it did not come to that. Diplomacy prevailed. Within two months the Executive Committee of the Federation agreed to the acceptance as constituent bodies of the various unions of colliery enginemen. They were against, however, acceptance into the Miners' Federation of any union with members in various industries. With such unions there remained a certain amount of friction which led throughout the rest of the history of the Miners' Federation to repeated discussions and numerous arrangements and treaties. The number of constituent Districts of the M.F.G.B. rose from eighteen to twenty (cokemen and enginemen being now reckoned as "Districts"), and total membership was increased by some 30,000.

In the case of the railwaymen the Associated Society of Locomotive Engineers and Firemen refused to hear the voice of the charmer, charming never so wisely. They remained outside and are outside to this day. In practice, however, when it came to the question, in the years after the 1914–18 war, of a strike on the railways, the members of the A.S.L.E. and F. stood in with their fellow railwaymen.

The first full meeting of the Triple Alliance held in April 1916 took up a series of post-war problems. They demanded full restoration of trade union rules and regulations, demobilisation by industry and not by military unit, full maintenance for discharged members of the armed forces and munition workers. A deputation was to be sent to the Prime Minister, to the Secretary of State for War, Lord Kitchener of Khartoum, and Walter Runciman, then President of the Board of Trade. On the day the deputation was received, much later that year, *The Times* wrote an editorial strongly attacking the Triple Alliance, which it said was "introducing an entirely new factor into public life." It went on:

This body of trade unionists is formally attempting to supersede constitutional government, and to frighten the appointed Ministers of the Crown into doing their will. The Triple Alliance was formed for this purpose, as we pointed out at the time. The present is its first essay . . . and it remains to be seen whether the Government will abdicate or not. (August 3, 1916.)

The Prime Minister, in his reply to the deputation, was suave, but he gave the Government's pledge of complete restoration of trade union rules and regulations.

The next meeting of the Triple Alliance in December 1916 passed a series of resolutions demanding, in view of the steep rise in the cost of living, that amounts due under the Workmen's Compensation Act should be increased and that the farm labourers' wages should be raised to a minimum of 30s. a week. They also protested against the proposed use of Chinese labour, in which they saw the danger of undercutting wage rates. That proposal had been much canvassed by Government circles who had appeared fascinated by the thought of China's huge population, at a time when there was a shortage of man-power in Britain. After this protest by the Triple Alliance, the proposal was heard of no more.

With this record of initial successes, not only *The Times* but the Labour movement as a whole were suitably impressed. This new powerful grouping seemed likely, even on general questions affecting the interests of labour, to achieve greater success than the Parliamentary Committee of the Trades Union Congress, which at that time had little more responsibility than to put forward by deputation or otherwise resolutions passed at an Annual Congress. It had no authority of any kind over the unions which were annually gathered together in the T.U.C. The big stick wielded by the Triple Alliance, which did possess the power of strike action, obtained it a respectful hearing from Ministers and roused hopes amongst both civilians and conscripts that this organisation might be their saviour in the troubled times ahead. With these sentiments widely spread there was renewed enthusiasm when, in June 1917, a Joint Conference of the three bodies formally ratified the constitution of the Triple Industrial Alliance.

CHAPTER VII

THE SANKEY COMMISSION

I. THE ARMISTICE AND AFTER

THE armies of the Central Empires began to retreat in the late summer of 1918, within a few months after their last offensive in the West. Before autumn the German Government sued for peace. Cease fire on the western front was sounded with the armistice of November 11, 1918. Within a few days thereafter a dissolution of Parliament was announced by the Lloyd George Coalition Government of which the Labour Party formed part. Hostilities over, should the Labour Party continue in the coalition? This was the big question that had now to be settled. On the decision would depend the future of the Labour Party. Those who had been opposed to the war or to the policy of Labour's participation in the Lloyd George coalition hitherto were naturally against: would this minority become a majority? There was little time for preliminary discussion in the affiliated units. The Labour Members of Parliament were in favour of continuing—by a majority which included most of the M.F.G.B. representatives. How would the votes go in the Labour Party Conference? On the very eve of this Conference the M.F.G.B. decided not to support continuance within the Lloyd George coalition on the ground that they would then be unable to contest mining constituencies that were already held by Conservatives or Liberals supporting Lloyd George. Arguments of a more political and less purely electoral nature were heard next day (November 14, 1918) in the Central Hall, Westminster, where the Labour Party delegates assembled for one of the most momentous gatherings in their history. It was known that Arthur Henderson was in favour of leaving the coalition, but that the majority of the Labour Members of Parliament (up to the M.F.G.B. decision a little before) were in favour of remaining. The delegates heard the voice of the shop steward movement when William

Gallacher, delegate from the Paisley Trades Council, urged that the overthrow of capitalism should now come on the order of the day. They also heard old Socialist and trade union leaders like Will Thorne, M.P., and J. R. Clynes, M.P. (then Food Controller) urge the need of securing "Labour claims" by continuing in the all-party coalition.

Many delegates were wavering. But the matter was clinched when Bernard Shaw stepped forward. Shaw, making his last speech as a delegate of the Fabian Society at a Labour Party Conference, said he always liked to hear his old friend Will Thorne hammering away, for if he hammered away long enough he was bound to hit the nail on the head sometimes; and Thorne had hit the nail on the head when he said "If you go into Parliament you must be prepared to play the parliamentary game." He (Bernard Shaw) agreed and said it was a matter of haggling and bargaining: "But where is the bargain here? What does the Prime Minister offer us in return for entering his Government? Mr. Clynes has just told us that Mr. Lloyd George has promised 'utmost sympathy and consideration for the claims of Labour.' I have heard that often before. In my recollection it has varied from a tip to a railway porter up to a post in the Board of Trade." When the prolonged laughter subsided Shaw said it was not a fair bargain and that Mr. Clynes should go back to Lloyd George and tell him "Nothing doing!"

After that there was no doubt of the results and by an overwhelming majority the Labour Party decided to leave the coalition and to fight the General Election as an independent party.[1]

The General Election followed a month later, on December 14th. The Lloyd George coalition won sweeping successes against its Labour and dissentient Liberal opponents. But this result was transient. The permanent result of the 1918 election was that it marked the decline of the Liberal Party and the rise of the Labour Party, hitherto only forty strong, to become the second party and the official opposition in Parliament. Had the M.F.G.B. fallen under the influence of the Lloyd George caucus at the one-day November Conference, the whole subsequent history might well have taken a different course. Fortunately for the working class, the Miners' Federation stood firm.

[1] Defections from its ranks (G. N. Barnes, C. T. Campion, J. Burgess, etc.) were formed into the National Workers' Party—which soon faded away.

2. THE MINERS' PROGRAMME

In the opening month of 1919 the Miners' Federation put forward a series of demands on wages, hours and mines nationalisation which were the fruit of long experience and mature deliberation at successive Conferences. In the previous summer the M.F.G.B. Annual Conference had decided on a wage demand, and on a reduction of the working day from a nominal eight hours to a nominal six; the demand for State ownership of mines they had reaffirmed with the new proviso that there should be "joint control and administration by the workmen and the State." The form of joint control had been worked out that winter in great detail and embodied in a draft Bill, the text of parts of which, for comparison with the earlier draft Bill of 1913, will be found in an appendix to Chapter VIII. They had waited till after the November armistice before taking any steps; and then had to wait till after the General Election of December 1918. Consequently their first demand, for 30 per cent upon total earnings (exclusive of the war wage) was not put forward to the Coal Controller until January 9th.

In January the disbandment of the vast war-time armies was the preoccupation not only of the soldiers but of the whole country. There were that month some fifty mutinies in the army—what Churchill a quarter of a century later reminiscently termed "a convulsion of indiscipline." The possible plight of the ex-soldiers was in the thoughts of every family in the coal-fields. Consequently, when the M.F.G.B. Special Conference met on January 14th at Southport, the delegates put in the forefront a series of demobilisation demands;[1] and coupled with these their programme of a Six Hours Act and mines nationalisation, saying: "In order to make easier the realisation of these demands we press the Government to amend the Mines Eight Hours Act." At this Conference the feeling was strongly entertained that not a 30 but a 50 per cent wage advance should have been asked for. Eventually, after an extra day's discussion, the Executive Committee's action was accepted by a majority.

[1] Subsequently condensed to a comprehensive demand for "full maintenance at trade union rates of wages for mineworkers unemployed through demobilisation."

So the wages demand was confirmed at the figure of 30 per cent on earnings (exclusive of the 3s. a day war wage).

On Friday, January 31st, all these demands were discussed between representatives of the Miners' Federation and the Minister of Labour, the Home Secretary and the President of the Board of Trade, together with the Coal Controller. The President of the Miners' Federation pointed out that no reply whatever had yet been given to the wages demand put forward on January 9th. The Minister of Labour, Sir Robert Horne, stated that the questions at issue would be put before the Cabinet for the decision of the Government.

At a further conference on February 10th, Sir Robert Horne read the reply of the Government to the miners' proposals. This was cast in the form of a memorandum. It dealt with (a) wages and hours; (b) demobilisation. Under the first heading it stated that so far as an increase to meet the cost of living was concerned, the Government would offer an additional war wage of 1s. to make it up to 4s. per day. With regard to the general claim for a wages increase irrespective of cost of living, and the demand for reduction of hours and nationalisation of the mines, they intended to set up a Committee of Inquiry into these matters and the position of the coal trade generally. The demobilisation demands were refused, with the exception of a minor concession to enable miners to obtain their out-of-work benefit through machinery to be set up between the employers and the workmen. Thus the considered reply of the Government amounted to an offer of 1s. per day, and the promise of a Committee of Inquiry.

Robert Smillie, remarking that the Government's reply did not come within measurable distance of the miners' demands, stated it would be submitted to the Federation Conference.

A Miners' Special Conference met two days later at Southport, on February 12th and 13th, to receive the report of the negotiations. Meantime, on the evening of the 11th, the Prime Minister delivered a threatening speech in the House of Commons, the purpose of which appeared to be to intimidate the Conference. If so, it had the reverse effect. For it was unanimously carried "That this Conference rejects the terms offered by the Government as being no answer to our claims." It was further decided to take a ballot vote of the membership on the question of a stoppage of work, and the Conference strongly urged the members to vote in favour of a stoppage.

The ballot paper, which was to be returned by February 22nd, ran as follows:

1. Application for 30 per cent increase in wages.
2. Six-hour day.
3. Full maintenance at Trade Union rates of wages for mine-workers unemployed through demobilisation.
4. Nationalisation of mines.
5. The Government having failed to grant any of the above proposals, *are you in favour of a National Strike to secure them?*

Yes................................ No................................

To this ballot paper Sir Robert Horne objected in a letter addressed to Robert Smillie, but published in the Press before Smillie had even received it. This made it appear as though the Government were catching at any pretext to discredit the Miners' Federation. This intention became perfectly plain a few days later, when the Government, at the cost of thousands of pounds of public money, inserted advertisements in most of the newspapers urging the miners to vote against the advice of the Conference. A fortnight later, Smillie elicited the information that Government Departments had supplied newspapers with alleged "facts" as to the effect on industry of the miners' proposals.

The Prime Minister, when he had a fair notion that these means had failed, invited the Federation Executive to meet him at 10, Downing Street. There he asked that the miners should delay for a fortnight the expiry of the strike notices (dated for March 15th), and should participate in a Commission which would be bound to present an interim report by March 31st. Smillie, in a moderate but strongly reasoned reply, reminded the Government that the miners' wages claim had been lodged as far back as January 9th. He held that the claim, having been reduced to the lowest possible, was just and fair from every point of view. He dwelt on the miner's housing conditions and the other conditions of his working life; and then said:

The mine-owners have always told us, and you tell us now, if you hand the mines back to them for free competition amongst each other, that we have no right to a voice in the working conditions in the mines—no voice on the commercial side at all. They say: "We invested our money in those mines and they are ours; you are merely our hands." Now, I say we invest our lives in those mines, which is of greater importance than the capital of the employer; and to that extent I have a right to have a say as to what the conditions shall be, not merely the working conditions, but we are entitled to have some information on the commercial side of the industry also. I believe, sir, that you have the data at hand, if you cared to use it, to be able to give us a reply on the wages question as to whether or not the claim which we put forward is unreasonable. (February 21, 1919.)

Finally, he said that the wages and hours claims, on which the information for decision was already in the hands of the Government, could be dealt with immediately, and need not stand over until a Commission reported. The Prime Minister refused this, and again said that those matters must be remitted to the Commission: the miners might serve on it.

The Executive Committee then agreed to call a Conference to consider whether or not the miners should participate. Meantime, the result of the ballot vote had become known. It showed a majority in favour of a stoppage of over half a million, the actual figures[1] being (February 25th):

For stoppage ..	..	..	..	615,164
Against stoppage	..	..	..	105,082
Majority for ..	..	..	..	510,082

[1] RESULT OF BALLOT VOTE

February 1919

District	For Stoppage	Against Stoppage	District	For Stoppage	Against Stoppage
Yorkshire	98,752	9,118	Scotland	77,130	14,601
Lancashire and Cheshire	60,668	5,219	South Wales	117,302	38,261
			Northumberland	24,316	6,909
Midland Federation	52,599	3,021	Durham	76,024	16,248
Derbyshire	31,070	2,403	Cleveland	5,282	1,450
Nottinghamshire	25,949	1,944	Forest of Dean	4,260	160
Leicestershire	5,167	457	Kent	845	106
South Derbyshire	5,656	293	National Union of		
North Wales	9,174	1,382	Cokemen	4,755	2,105
Cumberland	10,579	913			
Bristol	1,311	121	Total	615,164	105,082
Somerset	4,325	371			

Majority for stoppage, 510,082.

On February 24th the Coal Industry Commission Bill, statutorily establishing a Royal Commission, came before the House of Commons: as finally passed into law, with the changes resulting from a week's negotiations and parliamentary debates, it gave wide powers as may be seen from the first section of the Act. The Commissioners were to enquire:

into the position of, and conditions prevailing in, the coal industry, and in particular as to:
the wages and hours of work in the various grades of colliery workers, and whether and, if so, to what extent, and by what method, such wages should be increased and hours reduced, regard being had to a reasonable standard of living amongst the colliery workers, and to the effect of such changes on the economic life of the country;
any inequalities between different grades of colliery workers;
any scheme that may be submitted to or formulated by the Commissioners for the future organisation of the coal industry, whether on the present basis, or on the basis of joint control, nationalisation, or any other basis....

Other heads were the cost of production and distribution; selling prices and profits; social conditions of the miners; mining royalties; and

the effect of proposals under the above heads upon the development of the coal industry and the economic life of the country.

The Conference of the M.F.G.B. met on February 26th in London, and after a day's discussion adjourned. Strong arguments had been presented against participation, on the ground that if the report was adverse, the miners' case would be prejudiced. The next day, however, it was decided to participate, but only on strict conditions as to the miners' representation. It was also agreed to postpone strike notices till March 22nd, Lloyd George having promised that an interim report should be ready by March 20th. Eventually an understanding was reached that the miners should appoint four representatives directly, and that the other two representatives on the workers' side should be agreed upon between the miners and the Government, but formally nominated by the latter. Accordingly, about March 1st, the Commission was made up as follows:

Hon. Mr. Justice Sankey (*Chairman*)

Mr. Robert Smillie		Mr. Arthur Balfour	Government
Mr. Herbert Smith	Appointed by	Sir Arthur Duckham	nominees
Mr. Frank Hodges	M.F.G.B.	Sir Thomas Royden	
Sir Leo Chiozza			
Money			
Mr. R. H. Tawney	Agreed upon	Mr. Evan Williams	Representatives
Mr. Sidney Webb	between Govt.	Mr. R. W. Cooper	of coal-owners
	and M.F.G.B.	Mr. J. T. Forgie	

3. THE SANKEY COMMISSION HEARS THE EVIDENCE

The Coal Industry Commission held its first meeting on March 3rd, when it settled the method of procedure. By what can almost certainly be ascribed to the sound strategy of the Labour side of the Commission, it was decided to call Government witnesses first, thereafter representatives of industries immediately dependent on the coal industry, then coal-owners' witnesses and finally miners' witnesses. The public examination of witnesses began on Tuesday, March 4th, and concluded on Monday, March 17th. The Commission sat every day except Sunday and met several times in private, and after March 17th, deliberated entirely *in camera* until the report was ready.

The first witness called was the Financial Adviser to the Coal Controller. The revelations disclosed by him of the profiteering in coal during the war caused an immediate revulsion of public feeling in favour of the miners and against the coal-owners. By the evidence of the witnesses who followed, it became clear that the private ownership and distribution of coal had not merely meant swollen profits wrung out of the low wages paid to the miner and high prices paid by the public, but had also seriously hampered the national effort during the war by its inefficiency and wastefulness.

The evidence which was given on these points startled the public at the time. It became familiar throughout the coal-fields through the two pamphlets sponsored by the Miners' Federation, and compiled by R. Page Arnot, *Facts from the Coal Commission* and *Further Facts from the Coal Commission*, from which the following extracts are quoted.

PROFITS[1]

The total of profits and royalties of the coal-mining industry (not including the total profits from coke-ovens and by-product works) in the five years 1914–18 amounted to £160,000,000 which is 25 million pounds more than the total pre-war capital of the industry

Diagram showing Pre-war Wages, Prices and Profits compared with 1918.

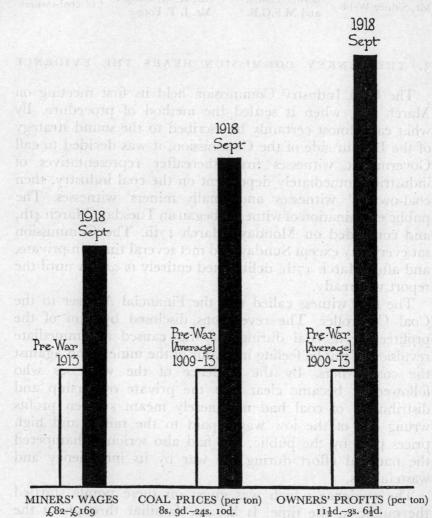

MINERS' WAGES	COAL PRICES (per ton)	OWNERS' PROFITS (per ton)
£82–£169	8s. 9d.–24s. 10d.	11½d.–3s. 6½d.

(£135,000,000). (Evidence of Dr. J. C. Stamp, Assistant Secretary to the Board of Inland Revenue.)

[1] When not otherwise indicated, figures are taken from the evidence of Mr. A. Lowes Dickinson, Financial Adviser to the Coal Controller.

TABLE A

	Tonnage Raised (Millions)	Pithead Price (per ton) s. d.	Profits and royalties Amount (Millions) £	Profits and royalties Per ton s. d.	Persons employed	Yearly Earnings per Person Employed £
Average of 5 years to 1913	270	8 9	19·1	1 5½	1,048,956	82 (1913)
Year 1914	265	10 0	21·5	1 7½	1,034,105	79
Year 1915	253	12 6	27·4	2 2	939,604	105
Year 1916	256	15 7	43·8	3 5	984,796	127
Year 1917	248	16 9	33·7	2 8½	1,006,299	129
January to June 1918 (on annual basis)	235	20 0	26·0	2 4½	966,355	149
July to September 1918 (on annual basis)	213	24 10	45·0	4 0½	929,524	169

TABLE B

	Average 1909–1913		1914		1915		1916		1917		1918 Jan. to June (on Annual Basis)		1918 July to Sept. (on Annual Basis)	
	Amount	Per cent	Amount s. d.	Per cent	Amount s. d.	Per cent	Amount s. d.	Per cent	Amount s. d.	Per cent	Amount s. d.	Per cent	Amount s. d.	Per cent
Profits per ton (excluding royalties) … 11½d. = 100	11½d. = 100	100	1 1½	117	1 8	174	2 11	304	2 2	230	1 8½	178	3 6½	369
Pithead prices per ton 8s. 9d. = 100	8s. 9d. = 100	100	9 11½	114	12 5½	142½	15 7¼	174	16 8½	191	20 0	238	24 10	283
Yearly wages (1913) £82 = 100	£79	96½	£105	128	£127	154	£129	157	£149	181	£169	206		

These profits increased enormously during the war, as is seen by Table A [on p. 191], which also shows the tonnage raised, the pit-head price, and other figures, both for the pre-war period and for each year during the war. In this most important table, of which some of the figures were only disclosed under the exceptional powers given to the Commission, the following points should be noticed:

(i) The pithead price represents the value at the pithead. The price to the ordinary consumer is very much greater (in London nearly double). This is due to middlemen and their costs and charges.

(ii) Profits from coke-ovens and by-product works, which were not under the Coal Control, are not included in the 1918 figures, though during the war they increased "very considerably" (Mr. Dickinson, Q. 56). They are estimated at 6d. a ton additional profit.

(iii) In the same period in which total profits were trebled, wages only doubled. Profits rose by 200 per cent, wages per person from £82 in 1913 to £169 (in each case subject to the reduction of a small sum for employers' deductions) or 106 per cent.

The total capital of the mining industry was estimated by Dr. J. C. Stamp (Q. 771) at £135,000,000. On the pre-war output of 270 million tons this works out at about 10s. per ton, while the pre-war profit (less royalties) of £13,000,000 is between 9 and 10 per cent, or nearly 1s. a ton (1s. 6d. a ton if royalties are included). Table B [on p. 191] gives detailed figures. The pre-war standard of profit, price and wages is taken as the basis line of 100. The initial figures of miners' incomes represent not the five years' average, but the year 1913.

The Excess Profits Tax took a certain percentage of profits over and above the pre-war standard of profits. Under the Finance Acts it was open for any firm, if it could show by taking four years out of six, or in some other way, that its profits were not very high for those years, to claim instead that a statutory rate of interest should be substituted for the profits standard. In the case of coal-mines *this statutory rate of interest was 9 per cent on capital.*

How profits were immensely increased during the war by price guarantees being fixed to ensure profits to even the least paying collieries also emerged.

Owing to the differences between collieries "it was perfectly clear that the price of coal that is a fortune for some collieries still spells bankruptcy for a large number of others" (Q. 103). When Mr. Sidney Webb asked "Is not that because the collieries are in different ownership?" the answer was "Of course, it is." Thus there might be a pithead price of coal which represented a loss of 6s. to one colliery and to another a profit of 6s.

This difference of 12s. a ton means that the consumer and the

WARWICKSHIRE MINERS' ASSOCIATION

From left to right, standing: W. Johnson (Junior), assistant-secretary,
C. Jacques, president;

Sitting: W. Spare, treasurer; W. Johnson (Senior), M.P., secretary.

WILLIAM JOHNSON, M.P. (1849–1919)
Secretary from 1885 of Warwickshire Miners' Association

miner both suffer. The price to the consumer (when there is no control) tended to be that which would keep the least efficient colliery going (and incidentally give a huge margin of profit to the more efficient or better equipped collieries). Either that or, where the price was not high enough for some, the mines were shut down and valuable coal was lost to the community (Q. 650 *et seq.*). Wages, too, depended on the ability of the worst mine to continue working.

Partly because of a Debate in Parliament over the Coal Control Agreement (Confirmation) Bill in February 1919, in the course of which the Government gave a pledge that the Coal Control should be made self-supporting, and partly because a large number of collieries were anxious to be in a more favourable position should the Coal Control cease, it was decided in June 1918, to add 2s. 6d. per ton to the price of coal.

Sir L. Chiozza Money: You had to be very tender to the colliery owners in the country? Mr. A. Lowes Dickinson: Yes. And we all had to pay for that tenderness?—Yes. Mr. Sidney Webb: If there had been one great coal trust there would not be that? If the profits had been pooled you could not put the price up? In short, if they belonged to the nation you would not put the price up?—That is my opinion. I do not know that I ought to give opinions. Further, even under private ownership, it would not have been granted had the Coal Control possessed the necessary information? If you had known what you know now probably the Coal Controller would not have recommended the 2s. 6d. in the face of the extraordinary profits?—That, again, is a matter of opinion. Sir L. Chiozza Money: You did not know, and therefore could not tell His Majesty's Government?—No. The War Cabinet did not know?—No. The Prime Minister did not know?—No. (Q. 203-9).

Particularly deadly was evidence given showing how huge profits were concealed by the capitalisation of reserves or other readjustments of capital.

Mr. Emil Davies said:

It will be seen that the most successful companies are able by these methods and by dividends, which are in reality much larger than they appear, to return to their shareholders every few years the whole of the share capital originally subscribed by them; and that the undistributed reserves are still so considerable that the present market price of the shares is several times their nominal value.

It is submitted that if the coal reserves of the country were pooled, the enormous profits made—and partially concealed—by the large companies would be available to meet part, at least, of any additional working costs that may be necessary; and the incentive to build up reserves for subsequent distribution, which obscures the enormous profits actually being made, would disappear.

The Powell-Duffryn Steam Coal Company

A company with an ordinary share capital in 1913 of £541,000 odd and £115,000 odd in preference shares disclosed profits, after deducting depreciation, Income Tax, Excess Profits Duty, and coal-mines excess payments for the fifteen years ending last year, of about five-and-a-quarter millions sterling, of which over three millions have been paid out in cash dividends, in addition to which £1,000,000 of bonus shares, which are now worth three times that amount, have been distributed as a free bonus. I have worked out that £1,000 invested in 1903 in those shares would have received dividends since that time equal to £3,800, and would, in addition, with the bonus shares received, now be saleable for about £5,500. The company has just recently offered another bonus to its shareholders by allowing them to take up new shares for 35s. at the rate of one for five, and the existing shares are quoted at 61s.

By the end of the first week, under the cross-examination of the Labour side, it had become obvious that the case for private ownership was labouring heavily. This applied not merely to the ownership of mines and minerals, but to the private control of distribution, both wholesale and retail. With a certain surprise the public, and also perhaps some of the miners, learned that nationalisation provided the only really adequate method by which to preserve and raise the miners' standard of life, besides being the only effective safeguard for the consumer.

SIR RICHARD REDMAYNE[1] gave, as his considered opinion: "that the present system of individual ownership of collieries is *extravagant and wasteful*, whether viewed from the point of view of the coal-mining industry as a whole or from the national point of view is I think generally accepted." The advantages which would result from a system of collective production he gave under heads of: (*a*) Enhanced Production; (*b*) Diminished Cost of Production; (*c*) Prevention of Waste.

The evidence presented by representatives of various capitalist interests purported to show that the effect of the miners' claims would be ruinous to industry. These arguments, however, weakened under cross-examination, and particularly when the witnesses were confronted with the broadly human aspect of the miners' claim for a higher standard of life.

[1] H.M. Chief Inspector of Mines, head of the Production Department of the Coal Controller.

Some very interesting hypotheses were put by Sir Leo Chiozza Money as to how the deficit of 5s. 4d. a ton could be covered by economies resulting from fall in costs, abolition of royalties, economies in distribution, railway costs, etc., quite apart from the saving to be achieved by nationalisation and improved methods of production. The 7s. 6d. a ton saved by these economies was more than the cost of 5s. 4d. a ton estimated by Mr. Dickinson.

The witnesses for the Miners' Federation were examined on Friday and Saturday, March 14th and 15th. These were:

	Subject
W. Straker (Northumberland)	Nationalisation
J. Robertson (Scotland)	Standard of life (Housing, Health, Education, Accidents, etc.)
J. Potts (Yorkshire)	Hours and Output
Vernon Hartshorn, M.P. (South Wales)	Wages

In each case the miners' point of view was ably stated and sustained under severe cross-examination from the coal-owners' side of the Commission. Mr. Straker, in particular, who had submitted draft provisions indicating the sort of control of the industry which the miners desired as part of any nationalisation scheme, was kept in the witness box all day, while Mr. Robertson's evidence on the abominable housing conditions in mining villages undoubtedly made a very deep impression both on the Commission and on the public. For example, not untypical was the evidence that

Even in England and Wales, where the housing conditions were acknowledged to be better than in Scotland, roughly one in every ten persons was living under conditions of overcrowding: *but in certain mining villages of Durham this was true of four out of every ten persons.*

The subjects of wages and hours had already been dealt with partially by previous witnesses, but here, too, the evidence of Mr. Potts and Mr. Hartshorn was of marked utility to the enquiry. John Potts, Treasurer of the Yorkshire Miners' Association, said:

With a working day from bank to bank reduced by 28 per cent it may be anticipated that the underground worker will go without an accident, on an average more nearly eight years than six. It must be counted, indeed, a distinct social advantage of a shorter working day in trades exposed to exceptional risk of accident, that it permits on an average to every worker (and therefore to every father of a family) a longer uncrippled life.

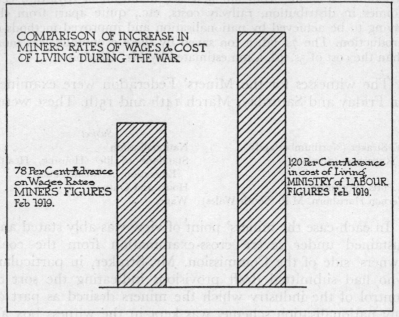

COMPARISON OF INCREASE IN MINERS' RATES OF WAGES & COST OF LIVING DURING THE WAR.

78 Per Cent Advance on Wages Rates MINERS' FIGURES Feb 1919.

120 Per Cent Advance in cost of Living MINISTRY of LABOUR FIGURES Feb 1919.

From *Facts from the Coal Commission*, page 29.

In regard to wages, Vernon Hartshorn, M.P., gave evidence, which the diagram illustrates.

"The necessity of meeting the rise in the cost of living (which the Ministry of Labour now puts, February 1919, at 120 per cent above the level of July 1914) enters into the demand. The total increase of wages since the beginning of the war averaged over all the districts of the Miners' Federation of Great Britain now stands at 78 per cent. This means that an advance of 42 per cent on pre-war wages is necessary in order to restore the miners to the position of 1914.

"But even suppose the miners' wages had risen further, or the cost of living had not risen so high, supposing the Government offer of 1s. (roughly equivalent to 10 per cent) had restored the miners to their pre-war position, this would leave 20 per cent as the miners' demand, which would be a very moderate rise when the whole conditions of the miners' life are taken into consideration. Further, if Mr. Lowes Dickinson's figures be taken, it would show that the profits of the coal industry had risen from a pre-war average of £13,000,000 to a rate of £39,000,000 for the quarter ended September 1918 while the miner's average income had risen from £82 to £169 in the same period.

"This would mean that profits had been trebled, while wages had little more than doubled. *But the Federation figures show 78 per cent advance during the war, and not 105 per cent.*"

The public sessions closed on Monday, March 17th, with evidence from co-operative societies and others, the effect of which was to reinforce the impression of the opening sessions, that private ownership in the production and distribution of coal was characterised by wastefulness and extravagance. On this important subject interesting points were made.

MR. TAWNEY pointed out that the existence of a coal ring in London together with the acceptance of the pre-war standards meant the handing over to distributors of a considerable share in monopoly profits (Q. 1,230).

The actual sum allowed to be charged by the dealers on each ton of coal after it had been brought to London, with the railway rate, wagon hire, and any factor's charge all paid, that is after it was lying in a London depot ready to be carried off, was no less than twelve shillings and sixpence (12s. 6d.). This singularly wide "margin," as it was called, of 12s. 6d., was taken by the 680 merchants and 1,600 coal dealers in the London area. It is no wonder that it could be stated at the Commission that "the men's demands in respect of wages, as far as London is concerned, comes to only a few pence more than the establishment charges of the retail agents, plus one more factor (Q. 1,650). . . .

The following facts from the Wholesale Co-operative Societies, into whose methods the Coal Control did not think it worth while to inquire, show that after all expenses have been paid and a margin allowed that is really fair (not "fair" as interpreted by the Coal Controller after his inspection of coal merchants' books) *the member of a co-operative society gets his coal from 2s. 6d. to 5s. a ton cheaper than the non-co-operator.*

Particularly striking were examples given of waste on railways:

In the autumn of 1917 the Coal Control divided the country into 23 areas of coal production and coal consumption. It was then found that North Wales, for example, did not produce enough for its own consumption. Its total production of rail-borne coal for inland consumption was 150,000 tons a month; its total consumption 220,000 tons. Yet it exported 40,000 tons, and so had to import 110,000 tons, whereas 70,000 tons should have sufficed. . . . Thus, while under private control of distribution men were literally carrying coals to Newcastle, the cost of this exploit to the community amounted to a sum (6d. a ton) which would have met half the cost of the Government's first offer to the miners. . . .

One of the difficulties of transport in the United Kingdom, both in the past and more particularly during the war, had been the system of privately owned coal wagons. These had to be returned empty to the collieries to which they belonged and one of the witnesses (Mr. Frank Tatlow, one of the Railway Executive Committee) stated that *half the mobile life of a privately owned wagon was taken up in empty running.*

When it is realised that the number of privately owned wagons (about 700,000) was nearly one-half of the total number running on our railways, and that each wagon has to be sorted out by complicated shunting operations, it can be seen how great a loss this represents.

One witness (Mr. E. H. Davies) reckoned that owing to this system we were using 35 per cent (over a third) more wagons than were necessary (Q. 2,052). It was found impossible to state a figure indicating what would be the approximate saving in money. An attempt was made by the Railway Executive to get these wagons pooled, but in face of the strong opposition of the private owners, representing separate interests, it broke down.

4. THE COMMISSION PRESENTS THE INTERIM REPORTS

It was found impossible to present a unanimous report, and eventually, on March 20th, three Reports were announced. First, the Majority Report; second, a Report signed by the Chairman and three other members; third, a Report signed by the three coal-owners. The Majority Report was signed by Messrs. R. Smillie, Frank Hodges and Herbert Smith, Sir Leo Chiozza Money, Messrs. R. H. Tawney and Sidney Webb.

The following is the summary of their conclusions:

1. We find that the miners' claim to an advance in their standard of life is justified; and that the percentage of rise of wages asked for, namely, 30 per cent (on earnings apart from war wage), is not excessive.

2. We find justified the claim to a substitution in the Coal Mines Regulation Act of 1908 of six for eight (making the future maximum working day underground vary from about six-and-a-half hours in some mines to eight-and-a-half hours in others, and averaging nearly seven hours). A corresponding shortening of the working day should apply to the surface workers.

3. We find justified the miners' claim for a more efficient organisation of their industry—the individual ownership of collieries being officially declared to be "wasteful and extravagant," while the method of retail distribution is unnecessarily costly; and in view of

the impossibility of tolerating any unification of all the mines in the hands of a capitalist trust we think that, *in the interest of the consumers as much as in that of the miners, nationalisation ought to be, in principle, at once determined on.*

4. As to the claims in respect of miners demobilised from the Army, we think that it would be better for these to be dealt with along with the cases of men in other industries.

In answer to the owners' attitude about the reduction of hours, the official pamphlet explains:

Some apprehension, said the Majority Report, has been caused by the phrase six-hour day. It was not true that the miners already had an eight-hour day, secured to them by Act of Parliament. The statute of 1908, not as introduced by the Government and passed by the House of Commons, but as altered at the very end of the session by the House of Lords, made the eight hours date from the moment the *last* man of each shift entered the cage to descend the shaft, until the *first* man of the shift reached the surface. This excluded all the "winding time," which normally consumes on the average something like an hour, and in the most extreme cases officially reported to us by the inspectors takes as much as two-and-a-half hours per day. *The underground worker is thus actually below ground exposed to a special risk of accident, not for eight, but, as we are informed officially, for between eight-and-a-half and ten-and-a-half hours per day.*

These conclusions were buttressed by several pages of closely-reasoned argument, illustrated by facts brought out in evidence.

The Sankey Report was signed by the Honourable Mr. Justice Sankey (Chairman) and by the three Government nominees, Mr. Arthur Balfour, Sir Arthur Duckham and Sir Thomas Royden, Bart. Its main recommendations as to wages and hours were as follows:

1. We recommend that the Coal Mines Regulation Act, 1908, commonly called the Eight Hours Act, be amended by the substitution, in the clauses limiting the hours of work underground, of the word "seven" for the word "eight" as and from July 16, 1919, and, subject to the economic position of the industry at the end of 1920, by the substitution of the word "six" for the word "eight" as and from July 13, 1921. Certain adjustments must be made in the hours of the classes of underground workers specifically mentioned in the Act.

2. We recommend that as from July 16, 1919, the hours of work of persons employed on the surface at or about collieries shall be 46½ working hours per week, exclusive of meal times, the details to be settled locally.

3. We recommend an increase of wages of 2s. per shift worked or per day worked in the case of the classes of colliery workers, employed in coal-mines, or at the pitheads of coal-mines, whose wages have in the past been regulated by colliery sliding scales. In the case of workers under 16 years of age, the advance is to be 1s.

4. We recommend the continuation of the Coal Mines Control Agreement (Confirmation) Act, 1918, subject to certain suggestions indicated in our report.

The Sankey Report had sharp things to say in recommending careful consideration for the collection of 1d. per ton (which would amount at that time to £1,000,000 a year) to be "applied to improve the housing and amenities of each particular colliery district." Evidence had been given, it continued, showing that

There are houses in some districts which are a reproach to our civilisation. No judicial language is sufficiently strong or sufficiently severe to apply to their condemnation.

But their recommendation which was to prove of greatest importance and to have tremendous repercussions dealt with nationalisation and control of industry by the workers. The famous passage from this interim report ran:

Even upon the evidence already given, the present system of owner-ship and working in the coal industry stands condemned, and some other system must be substituted for it, either nationalisation or a method of unification by national purchase and/or by joint control.

The Coal-owners' Report, signed by Messrs. R. W. Cooper, J. T. Forgie and Evan Williams, was confined solely to wages and hours, and its recommendations were:

1. One and sixpence per day for persons 16 years of age and upwards, 9d. for persons under 16.

2. A substitution of "seven" for "eight" hours in the Eight Hours Act.

3. Eight hours per day for surface workers.

The composition of this Coal Industry Commission had some unforeseen consequences. Never before was there a Commission on which Labour had half the representation. In this Commission it had really something more than half in effect, for it is no discourtesy to the employers' side to say that they were over-matched by the personalities on the Labour side. Against this team the owners' side could do but little. The result was that as the Commission proceeded it became less and less of a cold enquiry, and took on the aspect of an open trial of private capitalism in the coal-mining industry.

On Thursday, March 20th, these three Reports were presented to Parliament. The same evening Mr. Bonar Law who, as Leader of the Conservative Party, spoke for the Cabinet in the absence of the Prime Minister, announced that the Government had adopted the Sankey Report "in spirit and in letter." He also saw fit to say that if a strike took place "the Government would use all the resources of the State without hesitating," a threat which was at once resented by the Labour Members.

The meeting of the Miners' Conference, held in London on March 21st, after considerable discussion decided to recommend the Districts (whose strike notices expired the following day) to continue working on day to day contracts until Wednesday, March 26th, and meantime that the Executive should negotiate with the Government with a view to securing a modification of the Sankey proposals.

On Saturday, March 22nd, various points were urged before Mr. Bonar Law, who promised that he would give a reply by Tuesday, March 25th. On Tuesday, the representatives of the miners again met Mr. Bonar Law and Sir Robert Horne. Mr. Law announced, on the points put before him, that the Government could make no substantial change in the terms of the Sankey Report, which they had adopted as a whole. His general attitude, however, was conciliatory. Mr. Smillie restated the arguments of the miners, and while agreeing that the continuation of the work of the Coal Commission might mean the beginning of a new era, said that the Federation Conference must decide on the proposals.

At the Conference of March 26th, it was decided to take a ballot of the members as to acceptance of the Government proposals, the form and the other arrangements of the ballot to be drawn up by the Executive, and the Districts meantime to continue on day to day notices, and to recommend acceptance of the Government's proposals. The Executive Committee afterwards met and decided that the dates on which the ballot should be taken would be April

9th and 10th, the results to be in the hands of the Secretary by the 14th.

When the result of the M.F.G.B. ballot was declared on April 15th, it showed 693,084 votes for acceptance of the Government's terms and only 76,992 against.[1] So the M.F.G.B. Special Conference meeting the next day, ordered the withdrawal of the strike notices. The miners and the whole trade union movement were clear upon the point, that the Government had pledged itself to the ending of the private ownership of mines. The tension was loosened. The Government had weathered the crisis.

[1] The following is the form of the ballot paper:

MINERS' FEDERATION OF GREAT BRITAIN

BALLOT

The Government, as the result of the Coal Industry Commission, having offered:

HOURS

1. A reduction of one hour per day in the hours of underground workers from July 16, 1919, and "subject to the economic position of the industry at the end of 1920," a further reduction of one hour from July 13, 1921.

SURFACE WORKERS' HOURS

2. Forty-six-and-a-half working hours per week, exclusive of meal times, from July 16, 1919.

WAGES

3. An increase of 2s. per day worked to adult colliery workers and 1s. per day worked for colliery workers under 16 years of age employed in coal-mines or at the pitheads of coal-mines.

(The above to apply as and from January 9, 1919.)

NATIONALISATION

In view of the statement in the report of the Chairman of the Commission that "the present system of ownership stands condemned" and that "the colliery worker shall in future have an effective voice in the direction of the mine," the Government have decided that the Commission must report on the question of nationalisation of the mining industry on May 20, 1919.

RESULT OF BALLOT VOTE, APRIL 1919

The votes by District were as follows:

District	For Acceptance	Against Acceptance	District	For Acceptance	Against Acceptance
Yorkshire	107,362	12,254	Scotland	77,432	13,106
Lancashire and			South Wales	142,558	19,429
Cheshire	56,154	12,090	Northumberland	30,489	2,855
Midland Federation	58,060	2,319	Durham	95,648	6,845
Nottinghamshire	30,385	1,764	Cleveland	6,886	338
Derbyshire	36,559	3,020	Forest of Dean	5,431	393
Leicestershire	6,283	173	Kent	1,109	116
South Derbyshire	5,595	474	National Union of		
North Wales	11,874	872	Cokemen	8,376	103
Cumberland	5,925	702			
Bristol	1,644	75	Total	693,084	76,992
Somerset	5,314	64			

Majority for acceptance, 616,092.

CHAPTER VIII

THE SANKEY REPORT AND AFTER

I. EVIDENCE ON NATIONALISATION

WITH the acceptance of the Government terms the Commission, which had suspended its sessions for a month, was able to meet again and entered on its second stage which lasted from April 24th to June 23rd. These public sessions aroused widespread interest. It appeared as if private ownership of coal-mines had been put in the dock, while the conditions of life of the miners (together with the effect of the miners' claims) as revealed in the evidence were sufficiently startling. Lastly, the argument for transformation of existing ownership and control, whether by nationalisation or other means, received for the first time the full light of public enquiry. Now the Sankey Commission was to begin on the second stage, taking up a comprehensive investigation into schemes for "nationalisation or a method of unification by national purchase and/or by joint control." The interim Sankey Report, which the Government had accepted "in spirit and in letter," had already shown the lines on which approach was to be made to the problem of ending the condemned system of private ownership, declaring:

XIII.—No sufficient evidence has as yet been tendered, and no sufficient criticism has as yet been made, to show whether nationalisation or a method of unification by national purchase and/or by joint control is best in the interests of the country and its export trade, the workers, and the owners.

XIV.—We are not prepared to report one way or the other upon evidence which is at present insufficient and after a time which is wholly inadequate, nor are we prepared to give now a momentous decision upon a point which affects every citizen in this country; nor, as appears from the report in Hansard above referred to, did our Chairman ever pledge himself to do so.

XV.—We are prepared, however, to report now that it is in the interests of the country that the colliery worker shall in the future have an effective voice in the direction of the mine. For a generation the colliery worker has been educated socially and technically. The result is a great national asset. Why not use it?

In the interval between the two stages of the enquiry Sir Thomas Royden resigned owing to ill-health, and Sir Allan Smith (Chairman of the Engineering Employers' Federation) was appointed a Commissioner in his stead. A few days after the second stage had begun, Mr. J. T. Forgie was compelled to resign for reasons of health, and his place was taken by Sir Adam Nimmo (who had resigned his official post as adviser to the Coal Controller). These changes brought a considerable accession of strength to the owners' side of the Commission.

The second stage began on Wednesday, April 23rd, and lasted for nearly two months. Evidence was taken on twenty-eight days of this period and 116 witnesses were examined. Of these the expert economists were taken first, then royalty owners (including peers and representatives of boring companies), Home Office witnesses, witnesses as to the working of nationalisation abroad or in the Colonies, technicians, coal-owners, miners, miners' wives, industrial consumers, managers, expert administrators and sundry other witnesses who escape classification. There was, perhaps, no evidence submitted of so startling a kind as that given at the first stage of the enquiry. Considerable consternation, however, was caused by Mr. Smillie, who asked that various members of the nobility who were royalty owners be summoned before the Commission. This had, perhaps, a lesser effect on the Commission than it exerted in the country, where Mr. Smillie was much applauded by one section of public opinion, while on the other hand the Duke of Northumberland, who had vigorously answered his cross-examiners, became a hero in the columns of the *Morning Post*.

The evidence for the Miners' Federation of Great Britain was presented on May 23rd, 27th, 28th and 30th. Mr. Henry H. Slesser, Standing Counsel to the Miners' Federation, submitted a draft parliamentary Bill, embodying the miners' scheme for the nationalisation of mines and minerals. This was supported by Mr. Straker and Mr. Winstone, of the M.F.G.B., while evidence on the conditions of the miners' life was given by Mrs. Hart, Mrs. Andrews and Mrs. Brown, miners' wives from Lancashire, South Wales and Scotland respectively. In addition, in accordance with the precedent set by several previous Commissions, notably the Poor Law Commission of 1906–9, and the Commission on Ecclesiastical Discipline, 1904–6, two members of the Commission, Mr. Sidney Webb and Sir Leo Chiozza Money, went into the witness box and submitted plans for systems of ownership and management in substitution for the existing system.

The miners' own scheme was submitted by Mr. W. Straker (as part of the draft parliamentary Bill of the Miners' Federation, extracts from which are printed as Appendix A to this chapter). It was based on vesting all powers in a National Mining Council, consisting of the Minister of Mines for the time being and twenty whole-time members, ten appointed by the Government and ten by the Miners' Federation. The members were to hold office for five years, at the end of which time they were to be eligible for reconsideration. The composition of this body was intended to avoid a bureaucratic running of the mines, and this object was also sought in the institution of District Councils (with three years' tenure of office) and Pit Councils (one year) with powers delegated from the Mining Council. In each case half the members were to be representatives of the working miners. In addition there was to be a Mining Conference and a Fuel Consumers' Council. The Mining Council itself —the Minister of Mines being a member—was the supreme authority. The Straker scheme expressly contended that there be no restriction of the miners' right to strike. These provisions for control very greatly interested, one might say excited, the employers' side of the Commission. Mr. Straker, when he first indicated the miners' attitude on nationalisation in the earlier stages of the Commission, was subjected to a whole-day cross-examination entirely from the employers' side, and mostly on the question of control by the workers. It was quite clear that the employers were more upset by the idea of workers' control than by the proposal to abolish private ownership. His evidence had been an open expression of conflict between the opposing principles of autocracy in industry and industrial democracy. On that day it seemed as though the miners were speaking not for themselves only, but for the cause of all their fellow-workers, when through Mr. Straker they declared:

Any administration of the mines under nationalisation must not leave the mine-worker in the position of a mere wage-earner whose whole energies are directed by the will of another.

He must have a share in the management of the industry in which he is engaged, and understand all about the purpose and destination of the product he is producing; he must know both the productive and the commercial side of the industry. He must feel that the industry is being run by him in order to produce coal for the use of the community, instead of profit for a few people. He would thus feel the responsibility which would rest upon him, as a citizen, and direct his energies for the common good.

This ideal cannot be reached all at once owing to the way in which private ownership has deliberately kept the worker in ignorance regarding the industry; but as that knowledge, which has been denied him, grows, as it will do under nationalisation, he will take his rightful place as a man. Only then will Labour unrest, which is the present hope of the world, disappear.

The mere granting of the 30 per cent, and the shorter hours demanded, will not prevent unrest, neither will nationalisation with bureaucratic administration. Just as we are making political democracy world-wide, so must we have industrial democracy, in order that men may be free.

2. THE FOUR REPORTS

By June 20th four Reports were presented. The Report of the Chairman, Mr. Justice Sankey, was supported in the main by six Commissioners (Sir Leo Chiozza Money, Messrs. Robert Smillie, Herbert Smith, Frank Hodges, R. H. Tawney and Sidney Webb) who, however, presented their conclusions separately. A third Report was that of Sir Adam Nimmo, K.B.E., Sir Allan M. Smith, K.B.E., and Messrs. Arthur Balfour, R. W. Cooper and Evan Williams. Sir Arthur Duckham, K.C.B., M.I.C.E., was the only signatory to the fourth Report.

On two points all four Reports were agreed: first, on recommending the State ownership of all seams of coal, and hence of all royalties; and, secondly, in recommending, in view of the overwhelming evidence of the extreme wastefulness of the system by which coal is distributed to the household consumer, that the machinery of local authorities and the Co-operative Movement should be utilised for the purpose of distribution.

On the question of royalties, a special reservation was made by Frank Hodges, Robert Smillie and Herbert Smith, who "do not agree that any compensation whatever should be paid to the present mineral owners for the mineral rights to be acquired by the State." This did not rule out compassionate allowances in cases of small royalty owners expropriated in such a way as to deprive them of their means of livelihood.

The Chairman's Report recommended that the principle of State ownership of the coal-mines be accepted. It further recommended that some scheme for local administration be immediately set up with the aid of the Coal Controller's department, and legislation passed to acquire the coal-mines for the State, after the scheme had been worked three years from the date of the Report (during which time coal control would be continued), fair and just compensation being paid to the owners.

After dealing with the method of purchase and carrying on of the coal-mines, the Chairman's Report proceeded to outline a scheme of administration which the time at his disposal allowed him to put forward only as suggestions for the use of Parliament, not as recommendations. While following rather similar lines to Mr. Straker's scheme it failed to include his safeguards against bureaucracy. The main points of difference were that supreme authority was to be vested in the Minister of Mines, with the National Mining Council merely an advisory council to him; workers' representation on councils at all levels was less, the composition in the Sankey scheme being tripartite, with the miners having only a third (or less) instead of half the places; and it provided a form of binding contract for individual miners to which the Report signed by the six miners' and workers' side representatives took exception. Their Report, however, was in substantial agreement with that of the Chairman, and it was not thought necessary to set out any separate statement of their whole views. But they emphasised several points such as:

fuller representation on all councils on the lines of Mr. Straker's scheme, "with a view to securing the cordial co-operation of the workers in the success of the industry"; and that all coke and by-product plants should be acquired with the coal-mines.

The Coal-owners' Report is summed up in the sentence:

We have carefully weighed the whole of the evidence, and have come to the conclusion that the nationalisation of the coal industry in any form would be detrimental to the development of the industry and to the economic life of the country.

Not only was this Report against nationalisation, but it did not appear to be in favour of any substantial change in the then existing system of private ownership. It allowed only for the setting up of consultative Pit Committees. Their views were perhaps best expressed, not in their own words, but in those of one of the coal-owners, Lord Gainford, who, speaking as a witness, said:

I am authorised to say on behalf of the Mining Association that, if owners are not to be left complete executive control, they will decline to accept the responsibility of carrying on the industry, and, though they regard nationalisation as disastrous to the country, they feel they would in such event be driven to the only alternative— nationalisation on fair terms.

Sir Arthur Duckham's Report pronounced against nationalisation, but submitted instead a scheme of "district unification." It was suggested that the existing system of private ownership should be replaced by a system of publicly controlled corporations, with State guarantees of substantial minimum rates of interest. Out of all profits above a certain level, two-thirds were to be applied to reduce the price of coal. Further, he proposed that a Commission should be set up to decide the areas into which the country should be divided, where all separate colliery companies were to be amalgamated into statutory companies. It was clear that this was a scheme for setting up a dozen or more coal trusts, each monopolist within its area. There was no guarantee that such a statutory company or trust would be compelled to improve the life of the workers, or that it would be effectually disabled from utilising the various financial devices by which men skilled in the art could evade the proposed restriction of profits.

Thus, to sum up, all four Reports were agreed on the abolition of royalties and the State ownership of the coal seams. All were agreed as to the desirability of the distribution of coal being in the hands of public bodies. Secondly, eight of the thirteen Commissioners propounded schemes in place of the existing system of private ownership, already condemned in the first Sankey Report which had been accepted by the Government. Of the five Commissioners who refused to follow the accepted policy of the first Report, two had not signed it in the first instance, two had been appointed later, while the fifth, Mr. Arthur Balfour, gave no explanation of his change of view. Thirdly, of the eight Commissioners whose reports were based on the policy accepted by the Government, all but Sir Arthur Duckham were in substantial agreement as to nationalisation of the mines as the best method of unification.

How much of these proposals, whether unanimously agreed upon or supported by the majority of the Commission, was the Government to put into operation?

3. THE GOVERNMENT'S POLICY

It appeared clear that the Government, who received these reports on June 20th, were bound by their previous adoption of the first Sankey Report, "in letter and in spirit," to rule out any report which did not accept this principle of "nationalisation or a method of unification by national purchase and/or by joint control." As far as constitutional theory goes they were not bound to accept the reports of Royal Commissions. But in this case, when a specific pledge had been given, it was certain that the refusal to accept either the Chairman's Report or the Report of the six members would be regarded as a breach of faith. Further, the fact that seven of the Commissioners, including the Chairman, were agreed on nationalisation made a strong presumption in favour of the adoption of that principle; so strong, indeed, that in the absence of any political obstacles, its adoption was assured.

Apparently, however, political obstacles were not absent.

Before the end of June a formidable number of Members of the House of Commons had sent in a cartel to the Premier, in which they strongly deprecated any acceptance of the principle of nationalisation, and announced that they would fight against it. The signatures to this manifesto were, presumably, not collected without a certain amount of canvassing. There is, indeed, considerable evidence that during the second stage of the coal enquiry a strong campaign was being engineered by various coal-owning interests (the Chambers of Commerce with one accord began to send in anti-nationalisation resolutions to Sir John Sankey), and that this campaign, both publicly and behind the scenes, was intensified from the middle of June onwards. Meetings were held, addressed by Lord Inchcape, Lord Leverhulme and other heads of big monopolies. The Government received unmistakable warning of the deep hostility of the greater capitalists to any scheme of public ownership. Thus menaced, the Government adopted a waiting policy—or, as Mr. Bonar Law phrased it in his reply to a parliamentary question, the "matter remained under consideration."

Meantime the miners' organisations and the other trade unionists of the country (who had time and again in the Trades Union Congress declared for nationalisation) undertook no counter-agitation. At this critical stage they made the tactical error, which they tried to correct later (but when it was already too late), of simply awaiting the decision of the Government. But nationalisation of coal-mines became an issue in the July by-elections at Swansea and Bothwell where the Labour vote greatly increased, the Welsh seat being won by a substantial majority.

Week after week went past. The miners were drawing their wage increase of two shillings a shift, always referred to thereafter as "the Sankey wage." The Bill amending the Eight Hours Act to establish "Seven Hours" was passed through all its stages in Parliament. Suddenly, on July 9th, the Government decided to raise the price of coal by no less than six shillings a ton—a step which the miners regarded as unnecessary and caused only by the desire of the Government to turn public opinion against the miners' claims.

The attitude of the Yorkshire mine-owners caused a dispute

over the change in piece-rates consequent on the reduction of the working day by one hour. This led by July 17th to a District strike of the Yorkshire Miners' Association which lasted for over four weeks before it was settled.

All this while the Government refused to disclose its policy. The period of "lyin' low and saying nuffin'" was spun out till the third week of August 1919. Not till then did the Prime Minister announce his intentions.

The Government policy was to reject nationalisation.

Industrial harmony, said Lloyd George, would not come through nationalisation: and he called to witness the recent "strike against the Government" in Yorkshire, which he chose to treat as evidence that enabled him to throw overboard the recommendations of Mr. Justice Sankey. What did the Prime Minister propose should be done instead of nationalisation? He put forward the following:

That the minerals are to be purchased by the State; that a fund should be raised for the purpose of promoting schemes for the social improvement and the amelioration of the conditions and the amenities of life in the mining villages; that the State should not purchase the business of the mines, and certainly not run them; that unification should be promoted by amalgamation in defined areas. (August 18, 1919.)

In giving details of his proposals, the Prime Minister said:

That the industry should be so organised as to reduce to a minimum the expenses of management and working charges, and that with this end in view the country should be divided into convenient areas, in each of which an amalgamation of neighbouring mines should be undertaken within a limited period, say, two years. That the workers in and about the mines should have directors representing them on the body controlling the policy of the area groups to which they belong.

The scheme of amalgamation should be subject to the approval of the Government, and must conform to any conditions laid down by the Government for the protection of the general body of coal consumers. (August 18, 1919.)

There was a certain resemblance in this scheme to the recommendations of Sir Arthur Duckham; but, unlike Sir Arthur, the Premier made no mention of any provision (other than a vague generality that the Government would have power to oversee schemes in the interests of the consumer) by which dividends would be restricted. In fine, the Prime Minister's plan was not even for one national coal trust, but for a dozen or so gigantic combines which would benefit neither the nation nor the consumer, nor yet the miner. For it may be pointed out that the proposal to give the miners an effective voice in the control of the mines was in direct conflict with the position laid down by the mine-owners, to whose other demands Mr. Lloyd George had completely surrendered. Their position was "if owners are not to be left complete executive control they will decline to accept the responsibility of carrying on the industry." Thus, if the miners were given an effective control, the coal-owners would decline to co-operate. Either that or the proposed miners' share in control would be ineffective and a mere sham.

How strongly the miners felt about the Government's rejection of Mr. Justice Sankey's recommendation may be gauged from the words of Mr. Vernon Hartshorn in the same debate of August 18th. He said:

We did not ask for a Commission. We accepted it. We gave evidence before it.

Why was the Commission set up? Was it a huge game of bluff? Was it never intended that if the reports favoured nationalisation we were to get it? Why was the question sent at all to the Commission? That is the kind of question the miners of the country will ask, and they will say: "We have been deceived, betrayed, duped."

4. THE TRADE UNION POLICY

The Miners' Federation called a special conference which was held at the Westminster Hall on Wednesday, September 3, 1919. Before them was the fuller outline of the Government's proposals as set forth by the Prime Minister in his House of Commons speech on August 18th.

In his opening statement from the Chair, Smillie surveyed the situation and explained why the Executive Committee had rejected the Government's scheme. He ended with a reference to the Duke of Northumberland who, in a speech at the Liverpool Chamber of Commerce, had said that behind the Miners' Federation there must be "Bolshevik influence and Bolshevik gold." Said Smillie:

The Duke believes I am an honourable man . . . but I cannot be an honourable man if behind us, knowingly, there is Bolshevik gold or Bolshevik influence. I am not now speaking against Bolshevism; the Bolshevists are merely a majority of the people of the Socialist movement in Russia. As to the rightness or wrongness of their movement, I am not dealing with this point. I have considerable sympathy with them in their struggle to free their country from Capitalism. . . . I would like to ask the Duke of Northumberland either to prove his charge of Bolshevik influence or Bolshevik money, or to have the courage to withdraw it.

The resolution was then moved by William Brace, M.P., seconded by William Adamson, M.P. A telling speech in support was made by George Barker of South Wales who said:

I am certain that if the Conference that met at the Holborn Restaurant in February could have foreseen that the Government would have abjured the findings of the Commission they would never have agreed to the Commission being set up. I hold, personally, that the Government has broken faith with the miners of this country. I have in my hand several documents that would strongly support this very serious accusation that I have made. A speech by the Prime Minister in the House of Commons on February 24, 1919:

"They will find as a result of this inquiry they will get a Miners' Charter, which will be the beginning of greater and better things for them, and if they do so, and throw themselves into this inquiry and present their case—in some respects as I know, irresistible, in others requiring undoubtedly some greater proof than I have seen up to the present; but I am not prejudiced—they will achieve great things for their industry and for the men they so ably lead. And they will have the satisfaction when they have got these things of knowing that they obtained them without inflicting any hurt upon hundreds of thousands of other men and women engaged in honest toil like themselves."

One may ask, why this reference to a Miners' Charter if it did not specifically refer to the main principle of such a charter, namely, nationalisation of the mines with joint control by the workmen? If it did not mean that it was a deception.

A speech by Mr. Bonar Law, March 25th, 1919:

"If this Commission is allowed to continue, interim reports will be issued dealing with subject after subject in which you are all vitally interested; and not merely will these interim reports be issued, which in ordinary circumstances might be put into the waste-paper basket, but it is the part of the Government to deal with these reports in the spirit as well as in the letter, and steps will be taken to enable these recommendations to be carried into effect."

Though nationalisation is not here expressed, it is implied, or language has no meaning,

Finally, after quoting also the pledge given in Parliament a scant seven months earlier by the Home Secretary ("if on enquiry it is found to be the best thing for the community, then I unhesitatingly say, of course, I accept the principle of nationalisation") Barker concluded:

Therefore it is abundantly proved, it is on the records of the House of Commons, that the principle of nationalisation has been conceded to the industry providing the Commission found in favour of nationalisation, and the Government have taken the responsibility upon themselves of breaking faith with the greatest Trade Union in this or any other country, and by doing that they have administered a deadly blow to the principle of conciliation and negotiation so far as it affects the industries of this country in the future.

Vernon Hartshorn, M.P., spoke on the reasons which induced the Government to go back on their pledge to the miners. He reaffirmed "the clear understanding in Parliament" that if the Royal Commission reported in favour of nationalisation there "would be no alternative for the Government but to put that into effect." What had changed the situation? What had happened after the coal-owners "failed to make good" their case?

The coal-owners practically purchased the Press of the country. Look at every meeting of directors that is held in the mining industry today. What do you find? You find what has never appeared before —whole pages of the daily papers are devoted to the advertisement of speeches of directors of colliery companies, and in every speech that has been delivered they are making nationalisation their one and sole topic. They have been passing resolutions, issuing circulars, and sending them to the Members in the House of Commons, practically amounting to a threat that if they wanted in the future the support of these shareholders in the mining industry they must vote against nationalisation. Then the Prime Minister was informed that he must not introduce a scheme of nationalisation. What has happened is simply this, that the Prime Minister and his Government have surrendered to the mass of shareholders.

After these speeches in support the following resolution was carried unanimously:

Being convinced that the Government's scheme is wholly impracticable for the future working of the mines, the Executive Committee recommends the Conference to reject the Government's scheme, and records its regret that the Government have no better scheme than the creation of great trusts to secure the well-being of the industry.

We are convinced that the only way to place the industry upon a scientific basis for the purpose of giving the advantage of maximum production to the community consistent with the maximum economic and social well-being of the miners is to at once introduce the scheme of nationalisation recommended by the majority of the Coal Industry Commission.

We do not at this stage recommend the miners to take industrial action to secure the adoption of the report of the Coal Industry Commission, but we invite the Trades Union Congress to declare that the fullest and most effective action be taken to secure that the Government shall adopt the majority report of the Commission as to the future governance of the industry. (September 3, 1919.)

Earlier in the summer there had been strained relations with the Trades Union Congress Parliamentary Committee which had twice refused a request to call a special Congress on urgent questions such as conscription and military intervention in Russia. A special Conference of the Triple Industrial Alliance (as recounted elsewhere) had been called on July 23rd and a decision taken to issue a strike ballot on these urgent questions.[1] Now the Trades Union Congress Parliamentary Committee had agreed to take up the question of nationalisation. So on the day following the Miners' Conference of September 3rd, the Triple Alliance met in conference and confirmed the decision of their Executives to postpone the strike ballot. Accordingly, at the session of the Trades Union Congress in Glasgow on September 10th, Robert Smillie moved and J. H. Thomas, M.P., seconded a resolution. It

[1] The resolution, passed by 217 votes to 11, ran as follows:
"That this Conference of the Triple Alliance, having noted that the Parliamentary Committee have again refused to convene a Special Conference of the trade union movement, to enable the movement to decide whether it was prepared to take action to compel the Government to abolish conscription, to discontinue military intervention in Russia, and military intervention in trade union disputes at home, the Alliance decides to recommend its constituent parts to take such action, in accordance with their respective constitutions, to ascertain whether their members are prepared to take industrial action to enforce their demands. Where a ballot is required to accomplish this in more than one of the constituent bodies, a uniform ballot paper be prepared by the Sub-Committee to submit to the members" (July 23, 1919).

was opposed by J. Havelock Wilson, M.P., of the Sailors'
and Firemen's Union. The result was a fifty-five to one
majority, thus:

For the resolution	4,478,000
Against the resolution	77,000
Majority	4,401,000

The resolution ran as follows:

(*a*) This Congress having received the request of the Miners'
Federation to consider the Government rejection of the Majority
Report of the Coal Industry Commission, and the adoption in its
place of a scheme of District Trustification of the industry, hereby
declares that, in conjunction with the miners, it rejects the Government scheme for the governance of the industry as a scheme contrary
to the best interests of the nation, and it expresses its resolve to
co-operate with the Miners' Federation of Great Britain to the fullest
extent, with a view to compelling the Government to adopt the
scheme of national ownership and joint control recommended by
the majority of the Commission in their Report.

(*b*) To this end the Congress instructs the Parliamentary Committee, in conjunction with the Miners' Federation, to immediately
interview the Prime Minister on the matter, in the name of the
entire Labour Movement, to insist upon the Government adopting
the Majority Report.

(*c*) In the event of the Government still refusing to accept this
position, a Special Congress shall be convened for the purpose of
deciding the form of action to be taken to compel the Government
to accept the Majority Report of the Commission.

5. "THE MINES FOR THE NATION"

When the leaders of the Miners' Federation decided to put
their trust in the constitutional devices suggested by their
opponents, they did so whole-heartedly. It had been difficult,
with strike notices running, to persuade the miners in the spring
of 1919 to accept the Royal Commission; or again to accept its
findings. But once this was done, the Executive felt themselves committed against strike action for the time being,
indeed against any activity which might rouse the miners,
still very much in the mood for strike action, as was shown
by the July 1920 Yorkshire strike.

Thus they refrained from counter-propaganda when the

property owners had launched their anti-Sankey campaign in the summer of 1919, on the ground that they must first await the Government's decision. When that decision had been given against them (and against the Government's own previous pledges) they were for deferring strike action, and succeeded in getting the matter referred to the Trades Union Congress on the ground that this would broaden the basis of support. The procedure of the Trades Union Congress has never been hasty, and with the Government playing for delay it was not until after October 9th (when the crisis of the national railway strike was safely past) that the Prime Minister repeated his refusal to nationalise and so made it possible to call a Special Trades Union Congress in December. That special Trades Union Congress launched "The Mines for the Nation" campaign with the miners' leaders believing that public opinion would be so ripened by this propaganda as to support any strike action that might be necessary later. The reverse proved to be the case.

The mass of the people, for whom a railway strike and renewed anxieties on foreign and Empire affairs had acted as a buffer, were no longer so deeply interested. Memories of the Sankey Commission were fading: and the campaign launched with such massive and prolonged preparation was unable to make much stir outside the mining areas.

The campaign had been running for four weeks when the M.F.G.B. Executive Committee asked for the second Special Trades Union Congress to be held in the third week of February and decided the moment was approaching to consider the use of a general strike to enforce the people's will against the Government. So on January 9, 1920, they resolved:

That we ask our delegates to come to our Preliminary Conference instructed to say whether or not we should propose at the Special Trades Union Congress a general Trade Union Strike in the event of the Government continuing to refuse to nationalise the mines.

In case the Congress agrees to this proposal each Trade Union represented to be instructed to at once take the necessary steps to ascertain the views of their members for or against a strike.

The Special Congress, however, was not to be held as soon as they had planned. At the next meeting of the Executive Committee on January 27th they considered a letter from the Rt. Hon. Charles W. Bowerman, M.P., Secretary of the Trades Union Congress Parliamentary Committee, who questioned the advisability or political wisdom of holding the Special Congress so early. Eventually it was agreed between the Miners' Federation and the Trades Union Congress to hold it in the second week of March.

At the Miners' Federation Preliminary Conference on March 10th, the delegates came mandated for or against "industrial action," as a result of discussions within each District. The decision was for industrial action—but by a small majority. The result was 524 in favour and 344 against. The minority was made up from the votes of nine Districts, including Yorkshire and Durham. Thus the January tactics of the Executive Committee to consider the use of strike action for nationalisation found the miners themselves *divided*.

The next day at the Special Congress there was no doubt as to the lack of enthusiasm for strike action. By an overwhelming vote of 3,732,000 against 1,050,000, the Special Trades Union Congress decided against a general strike and in favour of political action in the form of intensive political propaganda in preparation for the General Election.

The miners were indignant. They knew what the decision meant. Nationalisation of mines, as an immediate aim, had been shelved for the time being. A General Election was not in sight. And "intensive political propaganda" could not be as intense over a long period as the previous months of propaganda, which had brought them nothing. So they drew the necessary conclusions. With nationalisation postponed to an indefinite future, they would now bend their activities to the questions of wages and prices.

For the enthusiasts for nationalisation, for the convinced Socialists within the Miners' Federation, it was a hard blow. But for Bob Smillie it was the defeat of the hopes and activities of a life-time. Smillie, who had been undergoing a severe strain for over a twelvemonth, took it to heart. By mid-February it was clear that "The Mines for the Nation" campaign was a fiasco. He announced by letter that he could go on no longer. The Conference refused to accept his resignation and sent messages pleading with him to come back as soon as his health would allow. Weeks passed by without any move on the part of the sick President. From March till June 1920, Smillie was absent. When eventually he came back it was to push through a policy of demanding on behalf of the domestic consumer a reduction of coal prices.

Though the miners realised that their cherished plans for nationalisation could not now be carried through for some time to come—and could not even be run as a campaign along with the wages and prices campaigns—they set it down as a measure to be won in the future. At their Annual Conference held at Royal Leamington Spa on July 6, 1920, and days following, a resolution on nationalisation of the mining industry, moved by J. Robson of Durham and seconded by George Spencer, M.P., of Nottinghamshire, was carried unanimously in these terms:

This Conference views with regret the failure of the Government to introduce legislation for the purpose of nationalising the mining industry, and reiterates its conviction that this industry will never be placed upon a satisfactory basis in the interests of the community until it is publicly owned and worked between representatives of the State and the technical and manual workers engaged in it, and resolves to continue to educate and organise working-class opinion until the Government are compelled to bring about this fundamental change in the ownership and management of the industry.

The Miners' Federation had been defeated in their immediate aim of mines nationalisation. Yet, just as in the struggle of a generation earlier for eight hours underground, it could not be defeated in the long run. But a quarter of a century was to pass by before they were once again within measurable reach of their goal.

Appendix A

THE NATIONALISATION OF MINES AND MINERALS BILL, 1919

(Summarised)

Sections 1, 2 and 3 establish a Mining Council of a President, who should be the Minister of Mines at a salary of £2,000, and twenty full-time members, "ten of whom shall be appointed by His Majesty and ten by the Association known as the Miners' Federation of Great Britain," for the purpose of "winning, distributing, selling and searching for coal and other minerals." The twenty members are to be appointed for five years, but eligible for re-appointment; with power for the Crown and the Miners' Federation respectively to remove members appointed by them and appoint others to fill vacancies for the unexpired term of office. The Crown will appoint a Parliamentary Secretary at a salary of £1,500; the Minister of Mines, and he to be responsible to Parliament: the Mining Council to appoint a Permanent Secretary and other officers at salaries to be fixed from time to time by the Treasury. Subsection (4) of Section 3 declares:

(4) Notwithstanding anything in any Act, order, or regulation, any society of workers, all or some of whose members are wholly or partly employed in or about mines, or in any other manner employed by the Minister of Mines, or the Mining Council or a District Mining Council, or Pit Council, or otherwise under this Act, may be registered or constitute themselves to be a Trade Union, and may do anything individually or in combination which the members of a Trade Union or a Trade Union may lawfully do. Provided further that notwithstanding any Act, order, or regulation to the contrary, it shall be lawful for any person employed under this Act to participate in any civil or political action in like manner as if such person were not employed by His Majesty, or by any authority on his behalf.

Provided, further, that no such person shall suffer dismissal or any deprivation of any kind as a consequence of any political or industrial action, not directly forbidden by the terms of his employment, or as a consequence of participation in a strike or trade dispute.

After Section 4 has conferred all normal powers to act as a corporation on the Mining Council, Section 5 provides for the transfer of ownership of "all coal, anthracite, lignite, ironstone, shale, fireclay, limestone or other mineral" (except certain minerals used in building); and of

Every colliery and mine (including all mines, quarries, and open workings of ironstone, shale, fireclay, and limestone, and every other mine regulated under the Metalliferous Mines Regulation Acts, 1872 and 1875) . . . and all associated properties (including vessels, lighters, railway rolling stock), and all works, including works for the manufacture of bye-products, in the opinion of the Mining Council belonging to any mine undertaking or connected with any colliery or mine, and every house belonging to the owners of any such colliery or mine, which, in the opinion of the Mining Council, is usually occupied by workmen employed at such a colliery or mine.

Together with all rights and easements, way-leaves and "other royalties, lordships or rights in connection therewith whether above or below the ground"; all these

shall be transferred to, vested in and held by the Mining Council in their corporate capacity in perpetuity, and shall for all purposes be deemed royal mines.

The Mining Council shall purchase the mines at the price and in the way later provided, but the value of easements, way-leaves and royalties "shall not be taken into account in computing such price, for all of which no compensation shall be paid." (Section 6.)

Sections 7, 8, 9 and 10 deal with the method of assessing the purchase price, by ten Commissioners, three each appointed by the Miners' Federation and the Mining Association, with a twelve-month time limit after which, if there is no agreement, the Chairman may fix the price; a valuation of all mines and associated properties and rights, the owners being required to give a return of all rent, interest, profits, etc.; and the issue of "Guaranteed State Mines Stock" in which the purchase price shall be paid. The purchase price is to be computed

by ascertaining the average annual number of tons of minerals actually raised during the five years preceding August 4, 1914:

Provided that as regards coal-mines in no case shall the maximum purchase price, exclusive of associated properties, be taken to be more than the following:

	s.	d.
When 100,000 tons or less have been raised per annum on the average during such five preceding years, a capital sum equal to one such year's output at	12	0 per ton
When more than 100,000 tons have been raised per annum on the average during such five preceding years, a capital sum equal to one such year's output at	10	0 per ton

The powers of the Mining Council are defined in Section 11; they are expressly forbidden to "lease or sell any mine or minerals or rights to any person, association, or corporation." But included is the power to "sell, supply and deliver fuel, coal and other products, the result of mining operations, either within or without the realm" and also to

employ any local authorities for any purpose they may think necessary.

The machinery to be set up is covered in Sections 12 and 13:

12. (1) The Mining Council shall, for the purpose of the carrying on and development of the mining industry, divide Great Britain into districts, and shall in each district constitute a District Mining Council of ten members, half of which shall be appointed by the Miners' Federation of Great Britain.

District Mining Councils and Pit Councils.

(2) The Mining Council may delegate to any District Mining Council or Pit Council, such of their powers under this Act as may conveniently be exercised locally, and the District Mining Council shall upon such delegation have and exercise within their district all the powers and duties of the Mining Council as may be delegated to them.

(3) A District Mining Council shall, subject to the approval of the Mining Council, have power within their area to appoint Pit Councils for each mine or group of mines, composed of ten members, half of which shall be members of the Miners' Federation of Great Britain, and nominated by the workers of the mine or groups of mines aforesaid, and the District Mining Council may delegate to such Pit Council such of their powers concerning the immediate working or management of a particular mine or group of mines as the District Mining Council may, subject to the approval of the Mining Council, think fit.

(4) The members of the District Mining Councils shall be appointed for three years, but shall be eligible for re-appointment, and the members of Pit Councils shall be appointed for one year, but shall be eligible for re-appointment.

13. (1) For the purpose of advising the Mining Council it shall be lawful for His Majesty to appoint persons, to represent the interests of consumers, to be known as the Fuel Consumers' Council.

Fuel Consumers' Council and Advisory Conference.

(2) The Mining Council shall have power to convoke at such time as they think fit and under such regulations and conditions as they may prescribe advisory conferences of representatives of District Mining Councils, and the District Mining Councils shall have power in like manner to convoke advisory conferences of Pit Councils within their area.

(3) The expenses of the Fuel Consumers' Council, National and District Mining Conferences shall, subject to the approval of the Treasury, be paid by the Mining Council.

Sections 14, 15, 16, 17 and 18 provide for the payment of members of the Mining Council, District and Pit Councils; how accounts are to be kept; the transference of existing assets and liabilities and so on.

By Section 19 the Mining Council is empowered to make regulations affecting the management of the mines, defining the functions of the District Councils, Pit Councils and other bodies. The concluding sub-sections provide that

(2) The Mining Council, before making or altering any regulations or conditions of employment, including wages, as affect workmen engaged in the mining industry, shall consult with the association known as the Miners' Federation of Great Britain, and, in the event of such representatives and the Mining Council failing to agree, the matter in dispute may be referred to arbitration on such terms as may be mutually agreed.

(3) Provided that nothing in this section shall be deemed to interfere with the right of any employed person, subject to his contractual obligations, to dispose of his labour as he wills.

Formalities concerned with earlier Acts of Parliament are dealt with in Sections 20 and 22; while Section 21 declares it to

be the duty of the Mining Council to ensure that there is a sufficient supply of fuel at reasonable prices throughout Great Britain.

To that end, therefore, it should be lawful

for the Mining Council, or for any local authority or Government Department acting on their behalf, to establish stores and depots and to employ vehicles and to use all other necessary means for the selling of fuel and to sell fuel within the area of every local authority, and, further, for this purpose it shall be the duty of the railway companies or authorities of Great Britain to provide such facilities for the conveyance of fuel as the Mining Council may deem necessary to enable them to carry out the duties imposed upon them by this section at rates not greater than such railway companies or authorities are now entitled to charge for the conveyance of fuel.

Appendix B

THE MINERS' INTERNATIONAL

THE last pronouncement of the miners on mines nationalisation in this immediate post-war period was at the Twenty-fifth Miners' International Congress in August 1920. On various occasions after the war old Thomas Ashton, who had temporarily retained the post of International Secretary which he had held since the beginning of 1890, had raised with the Miners' Federation of Great Britain Executive the question of reconstituting the Miners' International, suspended, if not shattered, by the 1914–18 war. The matter was several times considered by the Executive Committee. Eventually the Twenty-fifth

Miners' International Congress was held at the Maison du Faubourg, Geneva, from August 2 to 6, 1920. Assembled there were 65 delegates from Great Britain, 37 from Germany, 23 from France, 10 from Belgium and 6 from Czecho-Slovakia, together with one delegate each from seven other countries, making 148 in all, representing no less than 2,614,215 miners as compared with 1,434,300 in 1913. The membership of the countries represented was given by the Credentials Committee as follows:

America	..	..	.. 500,000	Great Britain	.. ..	.. 900,000
Austria	..	..	.. 22,000	Holland	.. ..	.. 4,000
Belgium	..	..	.. 123,540	Hungary	.. ..	.. 25,000
Czecho-Slovakia	..	.. 123,000	Jugo-Slavia	.. ..	.. 10,000
France	..	..	.. 130,000	Poland	.. ..	.. 4,000
Germany	..	..	.. 768,675	Luxemburg	.. ..	.. 4,000

Amongst the delegates were two present at the opening Congresses of the Miners' International thirty years earlier, the Rt. Hon. Thomas Ashton and P. Cingr of Czecho-Slovakia.

The Congress reconstituted the International Miners' Federation with a new set of rules, which on the stipulation of the British miners included a demand for nationalisation on the main lines of the Miners' Federation of Great Britain Parliamentary Bill.

Of the resolutions the most remarkable were one for an international miners' strike in case of war[1] and one on nationalisation which also included provision for an international miners' strike to attain their object.

The British delegation early in the Congress had secured the passage of the following resolution:

> This Congress is of opinion that each country should now definitely strive for the nationalisation or socialisation of mines in every country; the overthrow of capitalist ownership and the establishment of the control and administration of the industry by representations of the State and the workers engaged in the

[1] The text of this resolution was as follows:

"The delegates to the International Miners' Conference held at Geneva on the 2nd August 1920 and following days in connection with the reconstitution of the Miners' International upon a more real and active basis than ever before, are of the opinion that the International Miners' Federation can assure the peace of the world, this being the lesson from the events of the past. In view of the importance of the question of war and peace, which subject has been debated from time to time by the International Miners' Conference, and which question the German delegates have always evaded when it came to the question of an international miners' strike in the event of war, and, further, seeing that if this proposal had been put into force the terrible war of 1914 would have been avoided, for this reason and to avoid the repetition of such a crime, which was a disgrace to humanity, this Conference declares in favour of the principle that an international miners' general strike should be declared in the event of war, regardless of the Government which is responsible for the war, or proceed by way of a boycott of those countries, calling upon other organisations for their assistance if necessary."

This resolution was carried unanimously amid a scene of great enthusiasm, the delegates rising from their seats with cries of 'Down with war' and the French singing the *Internationale*.

industry, jointly with representatives of the consuming public. Each National Secretary to report to the International Office every quarter as to the progress made in each country towards this goal.

But on the last day, the French delegates submitted the following more elaborate resolution which was also carried unanimously:

The International Congress of Miners assembled at Geneva on the 2nd August, 1920, and following days;

Considering that the nationalisation or socialisation of the mines is the only way to obtain the practical reorganisation and regulation of the conditions of work, as well as the equitable remuneration for the efforts of the producer; that on this new reorganisation and regulation of work depends the increase in production which is indispensable in order to satisfy the needs of the peoples; that by these means alone it will be possible to recommence the economic life of all countries under normal conditions, through granting to each of them, by means of an international organism, the distribution and exchange of the products of the nationalised or socialised mines, which is necessary for their free development;

Considering that it is also the only way to put the peoples on an equal footing and to allow the producer and consumer in every country to obtain proper recognition and respect for their reciprocal rights;

The Congress declares that the International Committee of Miners shall meet within two months after the closing of this Conference to re-examine the claims of every country in this matter;

The Congress entrusts the International Committee with the duty of continuing from this time and with full powers and by all possible means, including international general strikes, if it becomes necessary, the prompt realisation of this demand in every country.

By means of reports from each country information will be distributed concerning the general situation, and will be used as a guide as to future conduct. If it be considered indispensable, in order to attain the end desired, to have recourse to extreme measures it will be necessary to make sure beforehand, by means of clearly worded engagements, of the co-operation of the different federated countries whose duty it will be to carry out fully the decisions come to. The different countries must henceforth prepare their members for all possibilities, so that they may be ready at any time whatever to carry out the decisions of the International Committee.

CHAPTER IX

WAGES FOLLOWING PRICES

I. THE TROUBLED BACKGROUND

FROM the end of the "Mines for the Nation" campaign in the spring of 1920 to the spring of 1921 a series of events and activities of a truly dramatic character were experienced not only by the miners but by the organised working class as a whole and by the nation itself. Unrecognised at first either by the Government or by the organised workers, the shadow of economic paralysis was creeping across the scene. The Government was encompassed with difficulties at home and abroad: and now the external difficulties were greater than in 1919. In India, Egypt and Ireland they were carrying on military operations on a large scale against national uprisings. With the United States, which had withdrawn from the League of Nations and the system of the Versailles Treaties, there was a coolness which, by the spring of 1920, had passed into an acrimonious exchange of diplomatic notes and into assurances by the Secretary of State for War (Lord Derby) that "war with America is unthinkable"—a sure indication that the thought had entered his mind. In Europe they were at loggerheads with their partners of the French Republic, though each Government was still full of plans and activities for crushing "the first Workers' Republic" in Russia. At home the redoubtable strength of the trade unions had already been shown by the strikes of 1919, while in numbers they were eight millions by 1920 as compared with four millions in 1913. The threat of a general strike on political issues had come up more than once in 1919 and 1920, an indication of the mood of the workers arising from the war and the conditions that followed.

Moreover, several of the issues which deeply stirred the organised Labour Movement bore upon the external policy of the Government, such as the attempt at violent suppression of the Irish struggle for independence through the use of auxiliary forces, the notorious Black-and-Tans.[1] At the same time repeated attempts were made in concert with the most reactionary circles in Europe to destroy "the first Workers' Republic," now the Soviet Union. These latter attempts had been opposed by the Federation throughout 1919. The M.F.G.B. Conference of March 26, 1919, had before it an Executive resolution against "the attempt to fasten conscription on this country" preceded by the words: "That this Conference calls upon the Government to immediately withdraw all British troops from Russia, and to take the necessary steps to induce the Allied Powers to do likewise." The first part of the resolution was inserted because there were armies of no less than fourteen Allied Powers operating on Russian soil after the war with Germany. Vice-President Herbert Smith (of the Yorkshire Miners' Association, which in this matter had taken the initiative), moved the resolution and said:

I want to submit to this Conference, that if we had no capitalistic money invested in Russia we should have no troops in Russia. It is a betrayal of the lads who have been called up to take on Military Service in that direction. They ought to manage their own affairs; they ought to be left alone, and it is not for us to interfere and land troops there to protect capitalist interests.

James Winstone of South Wales, in seconding, said:

This Government of ours are controlling the Press of this country, and not allowing the truth about Russia to come out; if they did, possibly there would be almost, if not quite, a revolution against the treatment that has been meted out to the men who have been fighting for liberty, and for justice, and democracy. I think it is one of the greatest scandals, and one of the greatest reflections upon what we sometimes call this free British country of ours, that our troops should be sent there in order to prevent these men and these women, who, like ourselves, are endeavouring to work out their own social salvation.

The resolution, carried unanimously, was afterwards adopted by the Triple Industrial Alliance on April 16, 1919, and the pressure exerted by it compelled the Government

[1] These Black-and-Tans, though preceding Italian or German Fascism, exhibited many of the characteristics of the Storm Troopers or the Black S.S., as was recorded by the Labour Party deputation which went to Ireland in 1920, some of whose members (e.g. Rt. Hon. Arthur Greenwood) were threatened in London with assassination.

to announce that British troops would be withdrawn from Russia, though Winston Churchill as War Minister and chief war-monger strove for the sending of further reinforcements to Archangel on the pretext that they would be required to assist the withdrawal. Meantime the Red Army was going from victory to victory over the "White" Russian invaders whom Churchill supplied with munitions and equipment to the tune of £100,000,000. After Kolchak, Denikin, Yudenitch and other Tsarist protégés of Churchill had been ignominiously defeated in the autumn and winter, there had appeared the possibility of peace by the early spring of 1920.

But the defeat of the Tsarist generals was the signal for the Polish Marshal Pilsudski to begin an invasion of Soviet Russia; and his drive into the Ukraine in April 1920 had curiously coincided with a congratulatory telegram[1] to him from King George V on the first anniversary of the Polish State. This time the initiative was taken by the Durham Miners' Association, whose letter "protesting against the help given to the Poles by the British and Allied Governments" for their war on Russia convinced the M.F.G.B. Executive Committee, on May 21st, that they should send a strong protest to the Prime Minister. Ten days later the matter was taken up at a meeting of the Triple Alliance sub-committee, which "in view of the extreme urgency of the question," took on themselves the responsibility of pressing for a special Trades Union Congress to deal not only with the Polish war upon Russia but also the military operations in Ireland. The M.F.G.B. Executive on June 9, 1920, not only agreed with this but took the unusual step of signifying its approval of the resolutions of another union. This was the Amalgamated Society of Carpenters, Cabinet Makers and Joiners whose resolutions on "Munitions for Ireland and Poland" and on "Amritsar" were approved and recorded in the M.F.G.B. Executive Minutes as follows:

MUNITIONS FOR IRELAND AND POLAND

That the British Government, in refusing to allow Ireland the form of Government chosen by the Irish people, and in assisting Poland in her attack on the Russian Republic, is betraying all the principles for which our nation fought, and that the most effective

---

[1] "Then there was the message which His Majesty was unfortunately advised to send to Marshal Pilsudski"—Lord Robert Cecil in the House of Commons, August 16, 1920.

way in which a protest can be made is for the organised workers to refuse to manufacture or transport munitions of war for Ireland or Poland.

AMRITSAR

That the action of the British General at Amritsar in causing his troops to surround and massacre a helpless and unarmed crowd of Hindu men and women assembled in orderly meeting is Prussianism of the type which our young men died to abolish. It will seriously impair the prestige of the British nation, and calls for immediate drastic punishment of all implicated, and stern repudiation of their action by the British Government.[1]

A resolution of similar content on Ireland and Russia was passed the next day at the M.F.G.B. Special Conference. On June 10, 1920, it protested against "the military domination of Ireland," condemned the "ruthless attack" on the liberties and independence of the Irish people, demanded immediate withdrawal of the troops, and urged the Parliamentary Committee to expedite the calling of a Special Trades Union Congress "to determine the attitude of organised labour towards the production and handling of munitions of war for Ireland and Poland."

Within two months, however, of their sudden invasion of Soviet territory the Polish armies had been driven back from Kiev by the Red Army and pursued to their own borders. Alarmed at the disaster which had befallen their latest protégé in the anti-Bolshevik war, the Governments of Britain and France threatened open war upon Soviet Russia. The Chiefs of Staff were called together, munitions were despatched in large quantities and military action on a full scale was in course of preparation. At the time of the American Civil War Marx had paid tribute to the British working class for the rapidity with which (in 1862) they responded to political events.[2] On this new occasion in 1920 they gave an immediate and striking demonstration of their political awareness. A movement spreading from one end of the country to the other condemned the action being taken

[1] The news of this 1919 atrocity (accompanied by an order that Indians must go on all fours when passing through the British quarter) was officially suppressed and for nearly eight months withheld from Parliament and the British public. General Dyer, however, so far from receiving "immediate drastic punishment," was given a purse of £20,000 and obtained a vote of approval by the House of Lords. He had killed 379 and left 1,200 wounded without means of attention.

[2] Marx, article in *Die Presse* (February 1862).

by the Government. Arthur Henderson, then leader of the Labour Party and later to become Labour Foreign Secretary, from his sick-bed sent telegrams to every locality calling for action to stop the war. The Labour Party and the Trades Union Congress together formed a National Council of Action, on August 9, 1920, while local Councils of Action were springing up all over the country—also under the direction of the Labour Party and Trades Union Congress. The anti-war feeling rose very high and even found expression and backing in the Press. On May 10th, there had occurred an event which will always have a place in the story of these stormy days. The London dockers called a strike and refused to load the *s.s. Jolly George* with munitions for Poland. The news of this went through the country like wildfire and anti-war activities of all kinds, demonstrations, marches, protest resolutions and telegrams were frequent and were encouraged from national Labour and trade union head-quarters. Attempts were made to co-ordinate the Councils of Action with similar movements expected in France and other countries. The ruling circles in more than one country recognised these Councils of Action as a startling revolutionary development. Even more so was this felt by many members or supporters of the Councils of Action, which in many places had taken over a measure of control and continued in being for months after the Polish war crisis was past, while everywhere the memory of these spontaneously formed bodies became strongly lodged in the consciousness of the trade union members. Actually within a few days the Government saw the red light and Mr. Lloyd George announced that the open war (but only the *open* war) against Soviet Russia was off. In this episode the Miners' Federation, by far the largest and most potent affiliation of the Trades Union Congress and the Labour Party, played a prominent part. The miners' leaders were not backward in agreeing to give the Council of Action power to call a general strike against war and to raise money directly from all trade unions by special levy.

Indeed during the summer and autumn of 1920 the miners were in an angry mood. The fiasco of "The Mines for the Nation" campaign had coincided with further steep rises both in the price of coal and in the general price level. In 1920, therefore, the M.F.G.B. submitted demands for a reduction of coal prices together with a rise in colliers' wages. This double demand was a far cry from the days when in the Conciliation Boards it had been assumed that wages were linked with coal prices in more or less direct ratio. The coal-owners, the miners now claimed, were making such large profits that both demands could easily be met. The Government, being in control of the mines and at that time engaged in lengthy negotiations over a Coal Mines Bill (which was to be still-born) at once rejected this double claim: if successful it would have torpedoed their propaganda that the high coal prices were due to "the greed of the miners." Upon this double demand in the summer of 1920 a strike ballot was taken and resulted in a large majority for a stoppage. Notices were issued to run out on September 25th and the Triple Industrial Alliance was asked for aid. The other unions of the Alliance, however, were unwilling at this point to be drawn into a strike and sought to effect a compromise. This led to the suspension of the strike notices for one week and to resumed negotiations with the Government and the coal-owners. New proposals, this time on wages only, were worked out and submitted to a ballot of the men. The proposals were overwhelmingly rejected. Accordingly on October 16, 1920, there began a national strike of miners which lasted for a little over a fortnight and ended on November 3rd, when yet another ballot yielded too small a majority against the terms to warrant continuance of the strike. This was the Datum Line strike, so called because under the temporary terms of settlement the wage advance granted was made to depend upon output reaching a given point—the Datum Line. The settlement was to last only five months, in which period the mine-owners and miners were jointly to work out a permanent settlement. In other words it was a truce. By this truce the issue was postponed to the summer season, a season in which the coal-owners were to be in an enormously advantageous position as against the miners. The Datum Line strike, it would have been agreed afterwards by many if not most of those who participated in it, was a mistaken effort. For it drained the accumulated strike funds of the miners without yielding any lasting gain and created the precedent that an appeal to their partners in the Triple Alliance could be made without result. The Government, however, took advantage of the strike situation to put into effect a long-cherished project— the passage through Parliament of a measure of strike repression, the Emergency Powers Act.

The Emergency Powers Act, becoming law on October 29th, 1920, altered the British constitution in a way that has received relatively small comment from political theorists. It enabled the Government, under certain widely defined conditions, to proclaim "a state of emergency" and thereupon to arm itself with such powers as had hitherto only been at its disposal in the Napoleonic wars and in the 1914–18 war. It endowed the Privy Council with recurrent overriding dictatorial powers such as it had not in practice possessed since the time of Tudor and Stuart monarchs. Moreover, these powers in their repressive aspects were to be exercised through the instrumentality of armed forces and a modernised police. From 1920 onwards it was possible for Britain to be converted into what it was later the fashion to call "a police State."

With the details of these events we deal in the sections that follow.

2. WAGES AND PRICES—THE FIRST APPROACH

On March 12, 1920, the day after a general strike for nationalisation of mines had been rejected by the Special Trades Union Congress, the Miners' Federation Conference passed a resolution "that the Executive Committee be instructed to make application for an advance of 3s. per day for those over sixteen, and 1s. 6d. for those under sixteen years of age, such advance to date from March 1st, 1920." The Federation hitherto had concentrated its energies on its demand for nationalisation and had held up the demand for more wages. Now that nationalisation was in effect shelved, the delegates, in their realistic way, turned immediately to the pent-up demand for higher wages. The Executive

Committee, keenly aware of the situation of wages and prices in relation to the cost of living and the profits of the coal trade, had, as early as January 8, 1920, asked the Prime Minister to meet them "at the earliest possible date" in order that the following points might be brought to his notice:

1. The enormous increase in the price of exported coal, resulting in enhanced profits to the colliery owners who are engaged in the export trade.
2. The continued high price of industrial coal for home consumers.
3. The failure of domestic consumers to obtain supplies since the reduction in the price of domestic coal by 10s. per ton, which took place on December 1st, 1919.
4. The effect of the continued high price of coal on the cost of living of the people.
5. An application by this Federation that there should be an immediate and considerable reduction in the price of industrial coal, followed by Government action to reduce the price of commodities now produced in factories, etc., into which the cost of coal largely enters; or, alternatively, the consideration by the Government of an application by this Federation for an advance in wages consequent upon the high cost of living.

These points suggest an entirely new development of policy by the Executive Committee. Throughout their lifetime the miners' leaders had been accustomed to regard the price of coal as one of the main factors affecting the level of wages. If the price of coal were high, there was a case for a rise in wages. Contrariwise if the price of coal fell, the owners, for generations back, could be expected to claim a reduction in wages. Now the Federation was making the entirely novel proposal that the cost of living should be brought down by lowering the price of coal; and, if this were done, were ready to forgo the rise in wages which otherwise they would be entitled to demand.

What was the reason for this startlingly new attitude? Why should there be this reversal of roles with the Government? The reason was political. The Miners' Federation, under the leadership of Robert Smillie, were offering an alternative policy to that of the Lloyd George coalition. The Government, usually regarded as protecting the consumers' interests against the danger of high prices, had taken the step in July 1919 of adding 6s. a ton to the price of coal. The miners and the Labour Party regarded this step as unwarranted by the situation in the industry, and as a political manœuvre designed to persuade the householders against the miners' claims for higher wages, shorter hours and nationalisation. The miners took their stand both out of regard for the needs of the people and also as a political counter to the Government's policy of high prices. High prices meant swollen profits. High prices were a Government preparation not only to defeat nationalisation but for a speedy decontrol of the industry, for handing it back to uncontrolled mastery by the coal-owners. As against this the Miners' Federation now stood out as the champion of the householders against profiteering coal-owners, as upholding the interests of the whole people suffering under the high cost of living against a Government which fostered and cherished the profiteers.[1]

On January 28, 1920, the Prime Minister (Lloyd George) accompanied by the Leader of the Conservative Party (Bonar Law) and other Conservative members of his Administration, met the Executive Committee of the Miners' Federation. No agreement was reached. A second meeting on February 19th was equally barren. Accordingly, the Special Conference of March 12th, in view of the Government's refusal to lower the price of coal, launched their demand for a wage increase.

The negotiations were resumed on March 25th and went on day after day until March 29th when Lloyd George made his "final offer." On this the M.F.G.B. Conference the same day decided to take a ballot vote, as follows:

BALLOT

Are you in favour of a stoppage of work to   FOR A STRIKE enforce the claim put forward by the Miners' Federation of Great Britain on behalf of all their members for an advance in wages of 3s. per shift flat rate for all persons over 16 years of age, and 1s. 6d. per shift flat rate for all persons below 16, to commence as and from Monday, 1st March, 1920?

[1] The Government, of course, was dependent for its majority in the House of Commons on the profiteers' representatives, the "hardfaced men who look as if they had done very well out of the war" as a Conservative unflatteringly described them in a remark quoted by Keynes (*Economic Consequences of the Peace*, p. 133).

Are you in favour of accepting the Government's offer of a 20 per cent advance on gross wages, excluding War wage and Sankey wage, with guaranteed flat rate of 2s. per shift advance for persons of 18 years and upwards, 1s. per shift for persons between 16 and 18, and 9d. per shift for persons below 16, to commence as and from the 12th March, 1920?

FOR THE OFFER OF THE GOVERNMENT

Please put your X in the space provided for the purpose, opposite the one which you favour.

Within a fortnight the result of the ballot[1] was available showing out of a total poll of 820,273 a small majority (65,135) for acceptance. Accordingly on April 15, 1920, the M.F.G.B. Conference, not without some protest from Lancashire, decided to accept the Government's offer, subject to certain matters of interpretation. These were cleared up

RESULT OF BALLOT VOTE
(April 1920)

District	Votes Recorded			Majorities		Percentage of Votes Recorded	
	Total	For Acceptance	For Strike	For Acceptance	For Strike	For Acceptance	For Strike
Scotland	106,272	54,708	51,564	3,144	—	51·48	48·52
Northumberland	33,684	24,651	9,033	15,618	—	73·18	26·82
Durham	112,038	72,600	39,438	33,162	—	64·80	35·20
Yorkshire	120,943	91,555	29,388	62,167	—	75·70	24·30
Lancashire	79,975	17,509	62,466	—	44,957	21·89	78·11
Derbyshire	37,482	25,051	14,431	12,620	—	66·83	33·17
Nottinghamshire	30,901	19,179	11,722	7,457	—	62·66	37·34
Midlands	54,593	32,654	21,939	10,715	—	59·81	40·19
South Wales	164,117	47,496	116,621	—	69,125	28·94	71·06
Cumberland	10,499	6,939	3,560	3,379	—	66·09	33·91
Cleveland	7,038	5,994	1,044	4,950	—	85·17	14·83
North Wales	12,673	7,375	5,298	2,077	—	58·19	41·81
Leicestershire	5,210	3,261	1,949	1,312	—	62·59	37·41
South Derby	5,841	4,102	1,739	2,363	—	70·23	29·77
Forest of Dean	5,224	1,716	3,508	—	1,792	32·85	67·15
Bristol	1,863	1,362	501	861	—	73·10	26·90
Somerset	5,613	4,557	1,056	3,501	—	81·19	18·81
Kent	922	582	340	242	—	63·12	36·88
Cokemen	8,717	7,128	1,589	5,539	—	81·77	18·23
Enginemen	16,668	14,285	2,383	11,902	—	85·70	14·30
Total	820,273	442,704	377,569	181,009	115,874	—	—
Majority for	—	65,135	—	65,135	—	53·97	—

in the course of the next two weeks and an Agreement beginning with the formal phrase

Whereas, by virtue of Regulations and Orders issued under the Defence of the Realm Act, all coal-mines in the United Kingdom are for the time being in the possession of the Board of Trade

and taking effect as from March 12, 1920, was signed on April 29th by the Controller of Coal Mines (A. R. Duncan) and by the M.F.G.B. Executive Members.

3. WAGES AND PRICES—"THE INDIVISIBLE DEMAND"
(May to August 1920)

Within a fortnight of the signing of the April Agreement, the Government again suddenly raised the price of coal. The rise in the case of industrial coal was 4s. 2d. a ton. In the case of household coal the rise was far greater. For the decrease of 10s. made in December turned out to be temporary and was now cancelled. Thus the consumers of household coal learned on May 12, 1920, that the price was raised to them by 14s. 2d. a ton at one fell stroke. Some amongst the miners held that this rise was unnecessary; and that once again, as in the previous July, the Government were manipulating coal prices in the hope that many of the consumers would trace the rise to the April increase in wages and would blame the miners; this they wanted to counter by demanding in June what they had failed to get in January: they would ask that coal prices be lowered.

It is clear, however, that the Government aimed at something beyond the creation of prejudice against the miners. There was, of course, no deficit or prospective deficit in the industry as a whole; on the contrary a huge surplus was being piled up and had been growing since the summer of 1919. The Government's intention, as was made abundantly clear by subsequent events, was to place each District and each pit on a profit-making basis. For this, no matter what swollen profits were drawn by the better pits and Districts, would enable the Government to meet the wishes of the coal-owners and revert to a completely uncontrolled industry.

This was clear to Robert Smillie, who was determined to frustrate a Government which had broken its pledge to nationalise and which now wished to decontrol the mines. When at a Special Conference of the Miners' Federation of Great Britain called to "determine the attitude of the Federation in connection with the recent increase in the price of inland coal, and to consider whether a demand should be formulated for an increase in wages," delegates were getting at sixes and sevens as to whether an advance should be flat rate or percentage and on other issues, Smillie intervened from the Chair with a statement of strategy:

We cannot burk discussion on this question. I am not sure if we grasp fully the significance of this question we are discussing here this morning. The claim by the miners at the present time for a substantial increase in wages cuts right at the root of the policy of the Government. We must put in a claim for an advance in wages— a substantial advance in wages—or we must force the Government to take off the 14s. 2d. a ton on coal; either the one or the other.

Either of these cuts fundamentally into the Government's policy. The Government cannot decontrol if we get an increase in wages. They would have to materially increase the selling price of domestic coal or else their policy could not be carried out.

—June 10, 1920 at the Farringdon Street Memorial Hall.

Then, after pointing out that they had shortened the working day ("The shortening of our hours of labour was equal to an advance in wages to our people"), he said that they ought to be pressing the Government "in every direction as well as in the wages direction":

We ought to be pressing the Government to endeavour to improve the home life of our people in addition to their wages. The proceedings at the Royal Commission, the evidence that we ourselves read as to the conditions of the families in many parts of the country, ought to have aroused the Government up to doing something in the interest of the health and happiness of our people.

Smillie particularised pithead baths and an improvement in housing conditions ("promised long ago"), as examples of a higher standard of living; and while disclaiming any preference by the Executive for one or other method ("Your Executive is as anxious as the rank and file are to ask for an increase in wages"), he ended on his basic theme of linking immediate demands with the strategic aim to prevent the pits being handed back to uncontrolled private ownership.

I want the miners to prove to Lloyd George that we are not prepared to allow the coal trade to be decontrolled and each colliery standing on its own legs, this would ruin every step forward for a good many months.

The delegates had thus laid before them what their President put as alternative means towards the fulfilment of a political strategy: either coal price reduction or wages advance. The discussion was brief. They decided unanimously "That the Executive be instructed to formulate a claim for a substantial advance in wages, and submit same to a Conference at an early date." (June 10, 1920.)

For the working miner, whether or not he agreed with the strategy of the Federation leaders, there was no question of the need felt for more wages. Hence whatever policy might be pursued to lower the price of inland coal, it must be joined with a policy of wage demand to meet the rise in general prices and the consequent high cost of living. However substantial or however frequent the wage increases of miners or other workers from the summer of 1919, they could not keep pace with the leaps and upward bounds of the cost of living. Wages were lagging behind. After four years of war, from 1914 to 1918, the average increase of all items of a working-class budget—such as food, rent, clothing, fuel and light, etc., was 100 per cent. From July 1914 to July 1918, the cost of living had doubled. Thereafter it had gone higher, but by mid-1919 the average increase stood at 105 per cent over 1914. Then prices began to leap upwards. By December 1920 the percentage increase was 125.

The miners strongly held that the 30 per cent Sankey wage increase of the summer of 1919 had been conceded not to meet a rise in the cost of living but to effect a permanent lifting of the standard of life in the coal-fields. So when the figure of 125 was reached, they claimed the wage advance which was put forward on March 12th and finally settled by the compromise agreement of April 29, 1920.

The ink was hardly dry on that agreement when the cost of living figure leapt nine points, from 132 per cent to 141 per cent in a single month. By the time the Federation

Conference met on June 10th to consider the Government's addition of 14s. 2d. to the price of household coal, the general retail price level had gone up again. In three months the increase was from 130 per cent to 150 per cent. What the miners had gained in the spring of 1920 after four months of consideration, conferences, prolonged negotiations and ballot votes, had been wiped out by the summer. Therefore they had to enter upon the same process once more. This time the figure for the wage increase was fixed when the cost of living stood at 152 per cent above July 1914. The miners reckoned that their wages by the April agreement stood at 124 per cent above the 1914 level. The Government, by adding in the Sankey 30 per cent increase of 1919, made it 154 per cent. This reckoning, the miners, as we have seen, would not accept, considering it to be fraudulent misinterpretation of Sankey. But in any case the cost of living was expected to rise—and did rise. During the negotiations of the summer and autumn of 1920 the cost of living kept mounting.

With all these considerations in mind the Executive Committee on June 21st proposed to ask for a reduction in the price of household coal coupled with a wage advance. Their proposals had first to be debated in the Districts; and then, after a fortnight's discussion, would come before the Annual Conference for further debate and decision.

4. DEBATE, DECISION AND REFUSAL

The Annual Conference of the Miners' Federation, meeting on Tuesday, July 6, 1920, at Leamington Town Hall, had to decide on the Executive's proposal to put forward as an indivisible demand the reduction of household coal prices by 14s. 2d. coupled with a 2s. a shift wages increase.[1] On the prices point as well as on the precise figure of wages claim there was a keen difference of opinion. Aware of opposition from some Districts, Robert Smillie from the Chair several times intervened in the discussion. First of all in his President's Address he said:

[1] i.e. for M.F.G.B. members over 18 years of age. For members over 16 the claim was 1s. per shift, and for boys under 16 the claim was 9d. per shift.

We have done many things which we believe to be in the interests of the nation as a whole. We have offered on many occasions to come out on strike if necessary with the rest of organised Labour, not for anything we ourselves sought or desired for ourselves, but in the interests of the nation as a whole. So that what your Executive will ask you to discuss this week is the question of whether or not the Government should be asked to reduce the price of coal to the householders of this country to the extent of 14s. 2d. per ton, and at the same time to give an increase in wages to the mine-workers of the country. . . .

If they refuse for some reason to reduce the price of domestic coal, then the miners will have to claim the full surplus from the coal trade, because it must be remembered that the employers have their profits—princely profits, profits never previously dreamed of in the coal trade—guaranteed to them by Act of Parliament.

Again, when the wages question came up on the agenda in private session, Smillie stated that the Executive Committee had gone into the question very fully, had realised the difficulties and were aware of a strong feeling in the Districts, but

they thought that if we ultimately have to fight, that we would fight with a far stronger public backing if a part of our claim was for a reduction in the cost of living. . . .

After the Secretary had given a clear exposition of the figures of prices, District coal profits, wages, cost of living, etc., on which the proposal of the Executive Committee was based Smillie rose to announce that the question was now open for discussion, but then once again, and this time in the fullest manner, he set forth his whole political strategy which may be summarised as follows:

The problem was difficult, like a game of chess, "or a game of dice, in which to a great extent the dice is loaded against us." The Labour Members in the House of Commons were in a difficult position, because "never in the history of this country has capital been more strongly entrenched in the country and in Parliament than it is at the present time." Therefore they could not play off the old political parties against one another, for in the Lloyd George Coalition there was a deliberate attempt on the part of capitalism to throw aside political differences.

Lloyd George, as Prime Minister, has not behind him an enormous coalition majority for the purpose of governing this country fairly for all people nor for the purpose of establishing a just and lasting peace amongst nations. That is not the main issue in the minds of the majority of the men in the House of Commons at the present time. The main issue is, how can we get most advantage for capital? How can we fight Labour, and discredit Labour, and ultimately succeed? That is what is keeping the present Government together more than anything else. . . .

Sometimes we say that public opinion is neither here nor there, that we are sufficiently strong to ignore public opinion. I believe as soon as our campaign, whatever form it takes, for this advance in wages is set on foot, you will perhaps have 99 per cent of the capitalist Press ranged against you, lying like troopers; and no troopers lie like some parts of the Press. There will be a campaign, particularly in the Sunday Press, as there already is, to mislead the public.

Now we do want ranged with us if possible the rank and file of the workers in this country, if we are ultimately faced with a fight. . . .

Do you not realise that probably 80 per cent of your fellow workers, especially the womenfolk, that 80 per cent believed when the campaign went on in the Press, that 14s. 2d. was essential because the miners forced their wages high? The newspapers have dinned that into their ears, and many believe the newspapers far more implicitly than they believe the people whom it is far more important they should believe. They are saying that all the evils that beset the worker, the high prices in almost every direction, may be laid at the door of the mining community.

Let me say that I know of no body of people in the country who, during these six terrible years, have been more unselfish and look more to the national interests and general working class interests than the men you represent.

On behalf of the Nottinghamshire Miners' Association, who were against the double-barrelled proposal, Frank Varley moved an amendment to omit any reference to household coal and to put in the figure of 4s., thus doubling the wages demand. The amendment was seconded by a very impassioned speaker, a delegate from South Wales, A. J. Cook, who later on became one of the greatest figures in the history of the Miners' Federation. He said:

I feel that we have been considering this question from a political point of view. We have been thinking from the House of Commons point of view and not from a Trade Union point of view, whilst the other Trade Unions have been going forward. Look at the action taken by the cotton people, the railwaymen, and printers. Despite the fact that there is no surplus to be considered they demanded an advance in wages based on the increased cost of living, and have raised their standard of living. . . . We, as miners, ought to have done the same. . . .

We were able to convince the men to agree to a flat rate advance commensurate with the rest of the coal-fields, but we cannot convince the men on a question of idealism or to try and practise altruism whilst the rest of the Trades Union Congress is using their organisation to increase their wages and increase their standard of living.

After the Executive Committee had received the backing of speakers from Durham, Yorkshire, Scotland and smaller counties, the Northumbrian standpoint in opposition to the Executive was put by George Warne. The debate went on, with George Spencer, M.P., speaking as a member of the Executive and against his own shire of Nottingham, and ended with D. R. Grenfell[1] of South Wales arguing against "this altruistic demand," urging the delegates "not to be influenced by sentiment" and finally asking:

Now, if we fail to get this 14s. 2d. off, what is the next step? Are we going to ask our men to come out on strike? I really cannot see myself asking men to come out on strike to reduce household coal, to reduce the selling price by 14s. 2d. If I were a workman myself I would not be willing to strike for that. I think if that is the position, let us go in for absorbing all the surplus, let us deflate values and lessen the spoils of the rich classes, and go in for reducing values to the utmost degree, and leave very little in the way of profits.

Once again Smillie intervened and closed the discussion with an eloquent appeal, in which he said:

The question turned largely on the fact that the recommendation of the Executive Committee was altruistic, idealistic, that is, that we were calling upon the miners to sacrifice something that might be of immediate benefit to themselves in the interest of the larger body of the working classes of the country.

We are advised by our Welsh friends who are about the first people in the world whom we would have looked upon as the idealists of the Labour movement, we are advised to drop idealism and let the bottom dog fight for himself. May I say to my Welsh friends and any others that when we drop idealism we stop reform.

I was considered in the earlier days of the movement a Socialist and a propagandist; I was told by some active people in the movement that it was foolish to ask for piecemeal reforms and that we

[1] David Rhys Grenfell, born at Penrheol in 1881, son of a miner, appointed agent in 1916, became M.P. for Gower in 1922 and was Minister of Mines 1940–42.

ought to allow things to remain as they were in order to bring the community to the sense of their position, and then they would rise in revolt, but just as we secured little reform after reform we lessened the desire of the working class for such a revolution; if we allowed things to go on without asking for immediate little pettifogging reforms we would bring about the social revolution all the sooner. I reasoned that with myself night after night—whether it was wise for me as a Socialist and a propagandist and a Trade Union leader to drop all idea of working for little reforms. Would it be wise to ask for an eight-hour day, would it not be far better to allow the miner to go on working ten hours? . . . Now these questions have arisen again and again and they were idealistic at the time, but we have succeeded in obtaining some of these reforms not by a revolution, and I do hope we will not require a revolution to obtain what we are out for.

Then a card vote was taken with the following result: out of 905 votes (each unit representing one thousand members), 545 supported the Executive Committee. The 360 votes against were made up of South Wales, 180; Lancashire, 80; Northumberland, 42; Nottinghamshire, 35; North Wales, 15; and Leicestershire, 8.

Smillie's policy had won over the Executive members ("I must say," said William Brace, M.P., "that I was a convert to this policy, because my own mind for a great time in the Executive was in favour of taking out of the industry by way of wages the entire balance of profit"), and now it had won over the Annual Conference. How would it fare with Lloyd George and the Government?

The reply of the Government, given on Monday, July 26th, by the President of the Board of Trade at his offices, was an uncompromising negative. There was no misunderstanding. Sir Robert Horne concluded that no case had been made out for the wage increase. On the lowering of domestic coal prices, in spite of the miners' estimate that export coal would produce in the next year £66,000,000 surplus profit (a figure not objected to by Sir Robert) he said that it was "not a question which can be decided upon mere figures. It has got to be decided upon principle." The principle of the Government was not to allow any of the surplus profit to be frittered away in reduced prices for household consumers or upon higher standards for the producers: the principle was to take it into the Exchequer. As Sir Robert Horne said explicitly:

The view of the Government is that whatever surplus profits are derived from the sale of coal during the next twelve months should go into the Exchequer. We do not know what they will amount to. Various estimates may be formed, but whatever they are, our view is that the Exchequer should get them.

Smillie immediately countered the arguments on which the Government based its refusal of the miners' claim. But the Government representatives would not budge from their blank refusal. Under these circumstances the M.F.G.B. representatives could only decide to summon a Special Conference. This done, they set off for Geneva to the Twenty-fifth Miners' International Congress, which business occupied them for over ten days. Meantime the Government was busy with a thoroughly misleading Press campaign which, owing to the absence abroad of sixty-five leading miners, had the field of propaganda pretty well to itself and met with no adequate rebuttal.

The Special Conference, held on Thursday, August 12th, was called to receive the report of the Executive Committee on the application of the Federation to the Government for the claims and "in view of the refusal of the Government" delegates were asked to come "instructed as to whether a ballot vote shall be taken of the members to ascertain their views as to whether or not strike action should be taken to enforce the claims." The Conference did not take long to decide. A strike ballot in a form adopted by the Conference[1]— to be carried through in a fortnight—was carried by 168 votes to 3: followed by an almost unanimous resolution "That this Conference recommends the members of the Miners' Federation of Great Britain to vote in favour of a stoppage in order to secure the demands which have been put forward."

Thereafter Smillie spoke on the Council of Action Con-

---

[1] The form was:

"In view of the refusal of the Government to concede the claims of the Miners' Federation of Great Britain for a reduction in the price of domestic coal by 14s. 2d. per ton, and an advance in wages of 2s. per shift for members of 18 years and upwards, 1s. for members from 16 to 18 years, and 9d. per shift for boys below 16 years of age, are you in favour of strike action to secure those claims?

For strike action.

Against strike action.

Please place your cross according to your choice in the space provided for the purpose."

ference to be held on the morrow to consider how to stop war against Soviet Russia. The delegates decided to be present in a body—a striking demonstration—and further decided in advance that if the Action Committee's report was "in favour of action being taken, that the Miners' Federation of Great Britain vote in favour of such action."

The result of the ballot, declared on August 31st, showed a majority of over two-thirds for strike action. Accordingly the M.F.G.B. Special Conference on Thursday, September 2nd, having accepted the ballot vote as submitted to them in its details,[1] agreed that all members of the Federation hand in notices "in accordance with the customs in the various districts, so that all members will cease work on September 25th, 1920."

[1] RESULT OF BALLOT VOTE
(September 2, 1920)

District	Votes Recorded			Majorities		Percentage of Votes	
	Total	For Strike	Against Strike	For Strike	Against Strike	For Strike	Against Strike
Scotland	112,421	85,520	29,901	52,619	—	72·40	26·60
Northumberland	36,318	24,955	11,363	13,592	—	68·71	31·29
Durham	109,652	76,869	32,783	44,086	—	70·10	29·90
Yorkshire	114,509	58,530	55,979	2,551	—	51·11	48·89
Lancashire	83,379	74,832	8,547	66,285	—	89·75	10·25
Derbyshire	34,491	28,352	11,139	17,213	—	71·79	28·21
Nottinghamshire	30,897	17,010	13,887	3,123	—	55·05	44·95
Midlands	58,735	48,044	10,691	37,353	—	81·80	18·20
South Wales	181,768	141,721	40,047	101,674	—	77·96	22·04
Cumberland	8,479	6,677	1,802	4,875	—	78·75	21·25
Cleveland	7,492	4,851	2,641	2,210	—	64·75	35·25
North Wales	11,781	9,195	2,586	6,609	—	78·05	21·95
Leicester	5,715	3,957	1,758	2,199	—	69·20	30·80
South Derby	6,302	4,569	1,733	2,836	—	72·50	27·50
Forest of Dean	5,520	5,132	388	4,744	—	92·97	7·03
Bristol	1,949	1,732	217	1,515	—	88·86	11·14
Somerset	5,872	4,837	1,035	3,802	—	82·37	17·63
Kent	1,625	956	669	287	—	58·83	41·17
Cokemen	8,022	3,928	4,094	—	166	48·96	51·04
Enginemen	15,720	8,115	7,605	510	—	51·62	48·38
Totals	845,647	606,782	238,865	368,083	166	—	—
Majority for Strike	367,917			367,917		71·75	28·25

5. PUBLICITY, AND THE TRIPLE ALLIANCE

Meantime in the last week of August the Executive Committee had held meetings where they had considered the need of a publicity campaign in order to put the miners' case before the public. The *Daily Herald*, then edited by George Lansbury, had offered its help. The officials were empowered to take the necessary steps for publicity: and at the Executive Committee on August 31st the Secretary reported that he had asked the Labour Research Department to give its aid.

This body, founded in 1912 as the Fabian Research Department with Beatrice Webb as Chairman, had begun with several important researches into the control of industry. After 1914 it also conducted numerous activities on behalf of trade unions and co-operative societies: and issued many publications. Prominently associated in its work at this time were Bernard Shaw (Chairman), Beatrice Webb, Sidney Webb, G. D. H. Cole, Mrs. Cole, William Mellor, W. H. Thompson, Eva Reckitt and R. Palme Dutt. From 1917 onwards the Labour Research Department, as an independent body whose object was "to carry on research into questions of interest to Labour" had the backing of the Miners' Federation of Great Britain and received also the support of other principal trade unions as affiliated bodies. Together with the Miners' Federation the Labour Research Department prepared a full statement, which was submitted to a Press Conference and published under the title *Facts About the Coal Dispute*. It began by giving the history of coal prices since 1914 when the average pithead price was 10s. a ton. This was mainly a record of increases, beginning with an increase in 1915 of 4s. a ton; of 2s. 6d. a ton in 1917; of 4s. in the summer of 1918; so that by the end of the war the Government had sanctioned or imposed an addition of 10s. 6d.

Then came the sudden imposition on July 21, 1919, of 6s. a ton, and, after a temporary lowering by 10s., the spectacular increase in household coal of 14s. 2d. a ton on May 12, 1920, together with 4s. 2d. added to the price of industrial coal. Thus in less than a post-war twelvemonth the Government had added 10s. 2d. a ton. The Government had never attempted to justify any of these charges by any figures of costing that would enable the public to form a judgment. The accumulation of surplus profits by the Government had gone on very rapidly. Their balance at the end of the financial year was £5,700,000. In May of 1920 the surplus was £3,800,000; in June £5,600,000; in the first two weeks of July (i.e. up to the date of the Miners' Federation of Great Britain's application) it was £2,800,000. With these figures, making in all £17,800,000, the Federation estimated future surplus profits of the order of £6,000,000 a month. If their claim for lowering coal price and raising wages were met it would still leave a *surplus* profit of over £8,000,000 per annum. This was their reckoning which, as we have seen, the Government spokesmen did not challenge. The pamphlet went on to state:

It is now clear that under the law nine-tenths of this would go to the Exchequer and the remaining one-tenth, subject to the ordinary Excess Profits Duty, would be added to the owners' guaranteed profits. It should be noted that these minimum profits of £26,000,000 received by the coal-owners are not subject to Excess Profits Tax, which is levied only on the excess over that amount. Thus while the average profits of the coal industry for the five years before the war amounted to £13,000,000 and over a period of 25 years before the war the average was only about £9,000,000, the coal-owners are now receiving twice as much as the five years' average before a penny of Excess Profits Duty begins to be levied. This is owing to the fact that the peculiar method of calculating standard profits under the Finance Acts works out extraordinarily favourably for the coal-owners, who are allowed to choose for this purpose the most favourable of the pre-war years. In the years immediately preceding the war, wages in the coal industry were subject in many cases to a maximum figure under the various Conciliation Board agreements then in operation. This meant that the big increase in prices in the years 1912 and 1913 went almost entirely to the coal-owners and was not shared in by the miners in the form of increased wages. The standard profits allowed to the coal-owners under the Finance Acts are thus far more favourable than the average of those allowed to other industries, with the result that an altogether disproportionate amount of profit, free of tax, is now being secured by them. Royalties, which amount to about £6,000,000 per annum, are not included in the above figures.

This statement was buttressed by a table of coal-owners' profits. The grounds were then given for the demand that household coal prices should be lowered by 14s. 2d. per ton, the Government arguments for refusal were countered and it was said of the May increase that "this increase was imposed directly with a view to the removal of control." The conclusion was drawn that such a removal of control would immediately lead to famine prices: and that it was therefore of vital importance "for the whole body of consumers to create a situation in which, while the coal industry as a whole pays for itself handsomely, prices cannot be raised, and the control which alone prevents them from rising towards the export price level cannot be removed." By supporting the miners the public would secure an immediate benefit in reduced cost of living; as well as prevent a still further rise.

The pamphlet then gave the arguments on the increase of wages as put forward in the negotiations, and after touching on the miners' coal and on output (both topics much handled in the newspapers) it ended with the following statement: "There can be no question, at the present time, so important as that of bringing about a reduction in the cost of living, and the miners feel that their attempt to take action for this purpose deserves a public sympathy and support which the majority of the Press has not yet seen fit to accord to it."

This appeal had little effect upon the Press Lords who continued to conduct their papers in the way Smillie had predicted.

But this all-important question of publicity was brought up at several Conferences of the Triple Industrial Alliance. The first of these, called as soon as a decision for strike action seemed likely, was held on August 31, 1920. To the assembled Executive Committees of the Miners' Federation, Transport Workers' Federation and National Union of Railwaymen, Robert Smillie as Chairman gave an explanation. After many questions had been put, the railwaymen and the transport workers each retired for two hours. J. H. Thomas, M.P., General Secretary of the National Union of Railwaymen, who earlier had said: "Based upon the cost of living, the miners' position is 125 per cent as compared with the dockers' 200 per cent, with our 185 per cent and with the seamen's 240 per cent—about," then reported the following unanimous decision of their full Executive Committee:

That, having considered the statement by the miners' representatives on their negotiations with the Government, and having considered the merits of the claim they have submitted, this Executive decides that the claim is reasonable and just. But, having regard to the grave circumstances that must ensue from a strike, this Alliance decides to inform the Government that, in the event of their being willing further to discuss the whole question with representatives of this body, we empower the sub-committee to act on our behalf, and report the result of their deliberations to a further meeting of this body. In the meantime the miners to take their own action to deal with the case.

The upshot of the Conference, which concluded on September 1st, was first a resolution moved by Ben Tillett: "That this Conference declares that it is satisfied that the miners' claim is based on justice and equity," and second, an agreement that the sub-committee of the Alliance should "act as a Press or Publicity Committee." Thereafter the materials prepared by the Labour Research Department were to be issued under the authority not of the Miners' Federation only but of the whole Triple Industrial Alliance.

6. A CHANGE OF CLAIM

The first part of the month of September the parties to the dispute were making public statements. The day after the strike was called at the M.F.G.B. Special Conference of September 2nd, Sir Robert Horne gave out the suggestion that the miners' claim (wages part only) should be sent to arbitration. The Trades Union Congress at Portsmouth passed on September 8th an emergency resolution that "This Congress, having heard the statement of the miners' case . . . is of the opinion that the claims are both reasonable and just, and should be conceded forthwith." As soon as this resolution was carried, Sir Robert Horne telegraphed a request to the miners' leaders to come to London. But Sir Robert had little new to offer. As Smillie said in his reply: "I wonder really if it was worth while to invite us to come from Portsmouth to practically reiterate in other words what you have said to us previously, which, put plainly, means the Government cannot see their way to recognise or concede the claims put forward by us." Actually, however, the President of the Board of Trade had thrown out a suggestion, of an extraordinarily vague nature, that coal-owners and miners should get together to work out a consolidated wage scheme on the basis of greater output. This was to become more definite at a later stage.

Within a few days after this reaffirmation of deadlock there was a change made in the Federation policy. So far the miners had based their claim on certain estimates which had not been substantially challenged by the Government spokesmen. The Board of Trade now published its summary of the financial and other statistics of the coal industry.[1] These figures suggested that the surplus would be £33,000,000 against the miners' previous estimate of £66,000,000. Secretary Frank Hodges carefully analysed and examined the Government statistics and reported in detail to the Executive Committee on Wednesday, September 15th, concluding that they were "not an acceptable guide for amount of surplus in the industry." But however just the criticism of this Government publication, there was no gainsaying that the outlook had been considerably altered by the facts as given and as accepted at their face value by the newspaper Press and the public generally. Consequently the miners' leaders decided to make a change in policy, which is recorded in the minutes in the following words: "The Committee after full deliberation undertook the responsibility of modifying the form of the claims now before the Government, and to decide that, provided the Government accepted such modifications, they would recommend the adoption of the change to a Special Conference to be called for the purpose." The modifications were:

1. The Government to concede forthwith the advance in wages as per our own proposals.

2. The Government to agree that the cost of such advance shall not be added to the price of home-consumed coal.

3. A competent and representative tribunal be appointed to inquire into and determine whether in view of the financial position

[1] Summary of Coal Output, Costs of Production, etc., for three months to June 30, 1920, Cd. 949.

of the industry a reduction in the price of domestic coal should take place, and, if so, to what extent.

4. The tribunal referred to above to report not later than October 31st, 1920.

5. The Government to adopt the recommendations of a majority of the tribunal.

6. The Government to accept a proposal for the establishment of a competent committee to be appointed to inquire into the cause of declining output and to make recommendations with a view to rectifying same.

7. The Miners' Federation of Great Britain accept the proposal of the Government for a full inquiry into the present wage system now prevailing in the industry with a view to creating up-to-date standards of wages for both piece-workers and time or day-wage workers.

On the two following days, September 16th and 17th, the Miners' Federation Executive Committee had prolonged conferences with Sir Robert Horne and his entourage but without result. The modified terms they put forward were rejected. While refusing the wage claim, the Government offered to submit the matter to an arbitration tribunal. On the other hand the Government refused to submit the question of prices to an independent tribunal. Once more Sir Robert Horne raised the question of output, saying: "I for one am prepared to take a totally different view of any wage claim which is based upon output." The Executive Committee, having met Sir Robert Horne on Monday, September 20th, to reaffirm their refusal to accept an arbitration tribunal on the wages claim, in the later afternoon took a decision "That we report to the Conference as to all the facts and negotiations up to date, and the reason for our action in changing the form of our claim and recommend the Conference to declare that nothing has emerged in the negotiations which will prevent a stoppage of work after Saturday next."

7. THE DELEGATE CONFERENCES

After the third meeting with Sir Robert Horne on Monday, September 20th, there followed a crowded week of Conferences. The M.F.G.B. Special Conference began on

Tuesday, the 21st, and went on till Friday, September 24th. The railwaymen and transport workers held Delegate Conferences on the Tuesday. A full delegate meeting of the Miners' Federation, the National Union of Railwaymen and Transport Workers' Federation (the Triple Industrial Alliance) began on Wednesday, the 22nd, and continued till Friday, September 24th. In addition, at 10 Downing Street there were conferences with the Prime Minister and leading members of his Cabinet; on Wednesday, September 22nd, at 5.30 p.m. the Prime Minister met the representatives of the Triple Alliance; on Friday, September 24th, at 11.15 a.m. he met the M.F.G.B. Executive. Finally, on Saturday, September 25th, the miners' representatives met representatives of the coal-owners. To get clear the course of the negotiations the sequence of events is given day by day.

Tuesday, September 21st

The M.F.G.B. Special Conference heard with a sense of shock the report of the Executive Committee. There was some sharp criticism and condemnation of the change of policy on the hitherto generally accepted claim. Eventually the report was accepted. But the cleavage was manifest in the debate on what was now to be done. A resolution for strike action by the end of that week was put forward by Tom Greenall of Lancashire as follows:

That unless the 2s., 1s., and 9d. is conceded by the Government by the end of this week, the miners be advised to bring out their tools: 73 delegates voted.

This was defeated and the resolution submitted by the Executive was carried:

That in the opinion of this Conference nothing has emerged during the negotiations between the Executive Committee and the Government to justify them in advising the miners to continue work: 105 delegates voted.

The same day there were the Delegate Conferences of the National Union of Railwaymen and of the Transport Workers' Federation. Each reaffirmed its standpoint that the miners' claim was just; and each resolved to abide by the meeting of the Triple Alliance on the following day.

Wednesday, September 22nd

The full Delegate Conference of the Triple Alliance met in the morning, Robert Smillie presiding. Smillie, to this larger gathering, explained the situation up to date. J. H. Thomas set forth the standpoint of the railwaymen in support of the miners but ended by claiming that the Triple Alliance should control policy in the event of a Triple Alliance fight. He said:

If it is to be a Triple Alliance fight the railwaymen are as entitled to share in all the deliberations as the miners. Up to now, in accordance with the constitution, it has been the miners' case; the miners have conducted their own case, as the Chairman says, in accordance with their constitution, and it has been a miners' fight. If, on the other hand, it is going to be a Triple Alliance fight it immediately comes out of the hands of the Miners' Federation in that sense. Therefore, the railwaymen have debated it from that point of view, they have decided to remain in session, not only after today's meeting, but to any time that negotiations or anything transpire. Immediately the last word is said they will, as a full executive and governing body, determine what action they ought to take.

In the discussion that followed some of the possible weaknesses of the Triple Alliance peeped out from valiant speeches. But Havelock Wilson for the Sailors' and Firemen's Union came out into the open. Beginning as a wordy agitator in the late 'eighties, he had for many years distinguished himself by an increasingly reactionary attitude on all questions affecting the working class, including the members of his own union. On this occasion he opposed any resolution for practical support to the miners and said a strike would not have the backing of the mass of the people. He recommended postponement of the strike notices for two weeks, while a ballot was taken of other organisations involved. Eventually a resolution was passed to send a deputation of the Triple Alliance "to interview the Government to urge further the acceptance by the Government of the miners' claim."

The Miners' Federation of Great Britain Special Conference met in the early afternoon. Leading delegates feared that the Triple Alliance might want to take the conduct of negotiations out of the hands of the Miners' Federation. In the end it was agreed to "accept the suggestion of sending a deputation of the Triple Alliance to the Government." Late that afternoon at 10 Downing Street, the deputation from the Triple Alliance met the Prime Minister accompanied by Bonar Law, Sir Robert Horne and others of his ministry. The Prime Minister took up the same standpoint as Sir Robert Horne. He offered two alternatives: either a reference of the dispute to arbitration or an advance in wages conditional upon higher output as might be arranged between coal-owners' and miners' representatives. Thereupon the deputation withdrew, to report to the full Congress of the Triple Alliance, reassembled at 6.30 that evening, that the Government had not moved from its previous attitude.

Thursday, September 23rd

The full Delegate Conference of the Triple Alliance met in the morning at 10 a.m., heard from Smillie that the Government's attitude was unchanged and adjourned till 6 p.m. to enable each of the three sections to meet separately and take their decisions.

To the M.F.G.B. Special Conference in the afternoon the Executive Committee, being divided in opinion, brought no recommendation. Then Smillie, who had not been able to win a majority in the Executive, pleaded with the Conference for the acceptance of arbitration or rather for taking a ballot vote of the men on this proposition. This, of course, would have suspended the strike notices. Smillie argued powerfully. When he sat down he was assailed at once by old Tom Greenall who said: "I was at the formation of the Miners' Federation of Great Britain as an official of the Lancashire and Cheshire Miners' Federation, and therefore I don't think anyone can call me young." He had been, he said, "depressed" by Smillie's speech, particularly by the suggestion made by Smillie that the men should be balloted as to whether or not they should go before a tribunal, which was "arbitration." He said:

I want to remind this Conference—you, Mr. President—that this Federation has consistently ever since its formation—I want the delegates to know this—consistently, ever since it was formed, opposed arbitration in connection with wages questions.

THE CHAIRMAN: May I correct Mr. Greenall. The main thing that I and others have fought on the floor of the Trades Union Congress and in all our own Conferences has been against compulsory arbitration. This is voluntary arbitration. May I say, Mr. Greenall, your district has had their wages regulated for years by arbitration of this kind by your Conciliation Board.

MR. GREENALL: I repeat again that the records of the Federation will prove—I defy contradiction—from the records of this Federation, that we never would agree to submit a case of wages to arbitration, never since it was formed. . . . The Chairman talks about the future of the Miners' Federation. You may depend upon it if this Federation decides to submit this question to a ballot of our men whether we shall go to arbitration or not it will be the first step in the downward direction to the splitting up of this Federation.

I would plead with you delegates. I would plead with you to look back at the history of the Miners' Federation of Great Britain. You have told us what it has done, but the reason for what it has done is because the leaders have shown fight on the occasions when it was absolutely necessary. Our friend from Yorkshire said he could go back, he said to 1912. Well, my mind goes back much longer than 1912, and I have been wondering what the great stalwarts of Yorkshire would think about the attitude we are taking up, the stalwarts of Yorkshire in the past—what would Ben Pickard think if he could be in this Conference and hear our leaders talking in the way we are talking. He would have said something if he had been there. No, Mr. Chairman, it is by the work of men like Ben Pickard, Cowey, and others that this Federation was built up, and if this Conference decides today that this question shall be submitted to our men with a view to a ballot in connection with arbitration, I repeat, that will undermine the great work that these men did in the past.

Backing Greenall against Smillie were other speakers, notably A. J. Cook and Noah Ablett, both young men from South Wales, and, fiercest of all, George Barker. Robson of Durham also argued against taking a ballot. When the matter came to a vote Smillie's standpoint was defeated by 545 to 360.[1] There was to be no question of arbitration.

To the adjourned meeting of the full Triple Alliance reassembling late that afternoon of September 23rd the miners' President briefly announced the decision just taken. In response, the leaders of the railwaymen and of the transport workers had no actual decisions to communicate from their

---

[1] How the twenty Districts were divided is shown by the voting. The majority against "referring the principle of a tribunal back to the men" was made up of: South Wales (180), Durham (126), Scotland (90), Lancashire (80), Derbyshire (49) and South Derbyshire (6), Somerset (6), Forest of Dean (6) and Kent (2).

respective meetings, but their statements made it clear that having themselves accepted arbitration methods that year, they were not enthusiastic about the strike prospects. The district committees of the transport workers were asking for explanations, said Ernest Bevin. "Why, seeing we had to use considerable influence to get our people to accept a Court of Enquiry, we have to use our influence now to get them to strike because you will not accept the Court of Enquiry." It looked as though the Prime Minister's proposal for arbitration might be the thin end of a wedge. Of this Lloyd George was fully aware: and he now exerted a further effort in the shape of letters directed to Robert Smillie—and communicated to the Press. These letters, dealing with his alternative proposal of wages being tied up with output, were read to the Triple Alliance delegates just before an adjournment interval.

It was a very astute move by Lloyd George. Seldom, since Eris set the gods a-quarrelling, had the apple of discord been cast with such deftness and skill. As will be seen from their wording, the letters were closely calculated to sow dissension among the Triple Alliance leaders and between the miners' leaders and their rank-and-file. The effect of their carefully-timed publication in the Press was to have repercussions some three weeks later at a Federation Conference. The first letter was sent in the early morning of September 23rd and ran as follows:

Dear Mr. Smillie,
On perusing the report of yesterday's interview I gather the impression that, while the miners' Executive are not averse in principle to basing an increase of wages on output, they have some difficulty in presenting to their delegates a proposal which is at present only in outline. The Government have great hesitation in attempting to make a detailed scheme for the reasons so well stated by Mr. Smillie—that increased production depends not merely on the miners, but on the co-operation of the owners with those who work in the mines. On this ground, the Government were and are of opinion that the only satisfactory method of procedure is for the representatives of the owners and miners and the Coal Department to sit down together and work out the details. At the same time I recognise the anxiety of your delegates to know more than at present has been stated, and I add to what I said yesterday the following explanations of what is in the mind of the Government. There will

be fixed certain datum lines on which rates of wages will be calculated in the following way. If output reaches:

x tons, wages will be increased by 1s. per shift.
x plus y tons, wages will be increased by 2s. per shift.
x plus y plus z tons, wages will be increased by 3s. per shift.

If after increases have been obtained there are subsequent diminutions of output, the increases will come off. It is impossible for us now to say what figures would be represented by these letters. These must obviously be arranged in conference between representatives of the owners, miners and the Mines Department, but I think it will be apparent, looking to recent figures of output, that there is so much room for improvement that the miners can make a certainty of increased pay. To give the scheme a beginning, the figures of output for October will be taken, and any increase in output will be remunerated according to the arrangements set out above as from October 1st, payment being made retrospectively.

These, as you will understand, are only the general outlines of a scheme which might come into effect for the next quarter. There are many other factors which will require further determination for the purposes of a permanent scheme, but these can be adjusted by yourselves and the owners in consultation with the Mines Department. The results of a coal strike would be so serious, both for the miners themselves and the whole country, that I am anxious to make sure that it will not occur on any misunderstanding and if there is anything in this communication of which you desire an explanation, the Government will be glad to give it.

Yours faithfully, D. LLOYD GEORGE.

To this letter the M.F.G.B. Executive Committee, then deep in discussion of Smillie's proposal to ballot the coalfields for acceptance of the Prime Minister's first proposal for an arbitration tribunal, paid the courtesy of immediate discussion and swift reply. In their answer, signed by Smillie and Hodges, they thanked Lloyd George for his explanation and then somewhat drily observed that "Our Committee fully understood from their interviews with both yourself and Sir Robert Horne the nature of your proposals for the future regulation of wages in our industry."

We must state, however, that the creation of a scheme for the permanent regulation of wages is a question of such magnitude as demands much thought and attention. Many meetings of the interests concerned would be necessary, and the consent of our membership secured before any scheme could be adopted. Our Executive repeat their assurance to the Government that when the present wage claim is disposed of, they will be prepared to undertake an inquiry into the whole wage system prevailing in the industry with the view of putting it upon a modern basis, and which will have to receive the approval of the men as a whole.

To this the Prime Minister immediately replied on that same morning of September 23rd, once more addressing his letter to the President only.

Dear Mr. Smillie,

I have to acknowledge the receipt of your letter in reply to the communication which I sent you this morning. Although a scheme for the permanent regulation of wages in the coal industry might take a little time to arrange, the proposal of the Government involved a plan which could be made immediately operative, and would give to the miners an increased rate of wages in return for an enlarged output which, as you yourself are confident, can be readily obtained. The plan proposed would meet your "present wage claim," and, in our belief, would give to the miners great and permanent advantages, whilst contributing to the prosperity of the community as a whole.

If, however, you still reject this suggestion, I would remind you that a peaceful method of settling the wage claim is still open to you by a means similar to that which is adopted by the railwaymen and the majority of your colleagues of the Triple Alliance.

Yours faithfully, D. LLOYD GEORGE.

The sting of the second letter was in its tail (as well as in a postscript saying the correspondence was being sent "to the Press this morning") and it was with this last sentence still in their ears that the delegates at the Triple Alliance Conference went off to their separate meetings.

That night at the adjourned meeting of the full Triple Alliance there was a fierce debate. During the adjournment of two hours the allies had met separately. The full Triple Conference now heard the announcement by J. H. Thomas that the National Union of Railwaymen delegates had decided against a proposal to come out on strike on Saturday midnight of September 25th in support of the miners. Harry Gosling, Chairman of the Transport Workers' Federation, announced no actual decision but a decided opinion in support of Thomas that a further effort be made to avoid a strike. Several of the miners' delegates were angry and gave full vent to their feelings. Vernon Hartshorn abruptly proposed the immediate dissolution of the Conference: and this was seconded by Frank Hodges in a few bitter words. Then the delegates heard the oratory of Ben Tillett, as he pleaded with them not to pass that resolution. Frank Hodges he spoke of as "a brilliant young man[1] who, however much he may exult in his virility, his intellectual powers and his genius" must nevertheless realise the position caused by the miners' refusal to meet the proposal of a tribunal. Tillett said:

That places them in a very serious position indeed, not merely in the public eye, but in the eyes of the experienced trade unionists of the country. Worse than that, it left in the hands of Mr. Lloyd George and his Government a weapon that, however eloquent and powerful your speeches may be and however enthusiastic your followers may be, will be used to the bitter end against you.

Tillett ended by suggesting that as a Triple Alliance, "as a united body with firm courage and strong decision," they should now approach the Government "to ask them what they mean by a tribunal." This was a bit too much for the miners' delegates: there was an indignant interruption; and then Smillie from the Chair, after saying "Mr. Tillett, this full Conference will not send a delegation" went on quietly

We do not think your going to the Prime Minister will be of any service to us. We have waited to hear what decision you would come to. We have your decision. We have heard the best and worst of it, and the position now is that if the miners stop work they will stop alone.

Smillie then urged "do not let us begin recriminations" and after repeating the words "The miners are going to fight," he said:

We will have at least the consolation of knowing that the railway people and the transport people feel that we are right in the claim we are making. They may doubt whether we are right in refusing to submit our claims to a tribunal, but at least they believe that our claims are just. From the beginning we have not misled them. Every point in our case has been put before them. We are sufficiently long in this movement to know that recriminations or fault-finding will not do any good. It is solidarity in our fight, as far as we can get it, that we want. It ought to be remembered that down to the present

[1] In the same speech Tillett was cheered when he said "I want that brilliant young man to be in the future a great leader of this movement, not merely of trade unionism, but of a great political movement, and to take his place in the ranks of the Government when Labour, as it must inevitably, comes into its own."

time the miners have not asked their colleagues in the Triple Alliance to come out on strike with them; we have left that entirely to them, knowing the whole of the circumstances.

After this it was possible for the debate to go on. Vernon Hartshorn, after saying "I should like to explain to my friend Tillett, however, that if he or any one else harbours the delusion that this is a Frank Hodges' movement he makes a very great mistake," went on to give the argument for the miners' decision to reject a tribunal:

Now, Sir, in regard to the suggested tribunal. We have already been before a tribunal—the Sankey Commission. The other side put all the brains and wealth they had at the disposal of those who represented them before their tribunal in order to defeat us in a contest on evidence, and they got beaten. What did they do with us? They spent hundreds of thousands of pounds in a Press Campaign, by means of which they created an atmosphere in this country against the miners.

They have called in the Press on this occasion, and with the same end in view. A greater campaign of villainy and perjury has never been inaugurated, even in the Press, against us. If we allow the Press to defeat us in this campaign, then good-bye to Trade Unionism.

More and more of the transport workers' leaders (J. H. Thomas was the sole spokesman for the railwaymen) took the floor to plead against the dissolution of the Conference: and, at length, close on midnight it was agreed to reassemble on the morrow.

Friday, September 24th

When the Triple Alliance Conference reassembled the next morning, its first business was to adjourn to enable the miners to hold a separate meeting. What happened thereafter is best told in the words of Robert Smillie when he reported some hours later to the joint meeting of railwaymen and transport workers in another room of the Holborn Hall:

"We are sorry," he said, "to have kept you waiting so long but it was quite impossible that we could, until now, put the information before you which I am going to give you. We decided to ask the Prime Minister to meet us in order that we might let him and the Government know that the miners were going to stop work tomorrow morning. We thought that it was courteous to go personally to him and tell him instead of sending him a brief note. We went down there and let him know that our men were stopping tomorrow, that they had decided by a vote to turn down the proposal to go before a tribunal, and that we thought it right to tell him in person.

"He expressed his deep regret because of the serious effect a strike would have, not only on the miners themselves, but on the nation. He began to discuss, as he had previously discussed it more than once, the question of output and other things. We said we were only there to let him know that we were stopping work.

"He asked could we not suspend the notices for a week and in the meantime meet the mine-owners and endeavour to discuss with them and evolve some scheme that might tend to increase output. Of course we pointed out that we were not prepared to say our present claim ought to depend on a future increase of output but that we were quite willing to meet the owners. We suggested to him that we should meet the owners, and try to come to some arrangement whereby we felt that working mutually together output might be increased, and if the owners felt that it was possible to increase output by their efforts and by our efforts.

"Frankly we desire to increase output if it can be done. I mean that it is absolutely untrue to say that any member of our Executive of the Miners' Federation or any authorised official, so far as I know, is desirous of deliberately reducing output. We desire in the national interest to increase output; we are desirous for the sake of Europe to increase output. But we told him that we were not prepared to go back to our people and ask them to endeavour to increase output at a further risk to the lives of the men. We said that any man who was doing an honest day's work at any kind of mining was doing sufficient, and we were not prepared to increase output at the risk of increasing loss of life, neither were we prepared to try to increase output if the money from that increased output was to go into the Exchequer or into the pockets of the mine-owners of this country. Otherwise we were quite anxious to endeavour to increase output.

"We asked this: If the owners were convinced, and we were, that they were going to make an honest effort to increase output, would the Government be prepared to give the increase in wages if the owners themselves said it ought to be given? The Government would not pledge themselves to that, but said that it would carry great weight with them if both sides could be convinced that the increase in wages should be given. We could not get them to go any further than that, and I do not think we could expect them to go any further than that.

"We were not anxious to plunge the nation and our own men into a strike with all its effects. We came back and our Executive considered the matter. Some people feel their dignity so keenly that in no circumstances will they allow it to drop. Our Executive found that dignity was all right but that there were times when you must set it aside. We decided practically unanimously to advise our Conference to suspend notices for a week.

"The Conference agreed to suspend notices for a week and we
are going to meet the owners next week. There would be no further
good at the present time in our asking you to hold another joint
Conference. I believe it will have relieved your minds considerably
that there is to be even a week's truce during which we may be able
to settle up the dispute altogether, but I have pledged myself to
our Conference that we will ask the leaders of the National Union
of Railwaymen and the leaders of the Transport Workers' Federation to be prepared to meet at any time, and if we feel it necessary
to call on them to assist us, that they would place themselves at our
disposal."

It had indeed been decided by 134 votes to 31 at the
M.F.G.B. Conference earlier that afternoon:

That this Conference accept the recommendation of the Executive
Committee to suspend notices for one week to give the Executive an
opportunity of meeting the coal-owners. (September 24, 1920.)

The great relief felt by the miners' allies at the suspension
of the strike was voiced by J. H. Thomas and Harry Gosling,
each of whom made congratulatory speeches. But before the
close a few minutes later of the Conference Ernest Bevin
struck another note. He said:

The men in the country believe that since this Triple Alliance
was formed constructive organising work has been going on to make
it a workable machine, and my charge is that the six men who are
at the head of affairs have not constructed an organisation that is
capable of working when the test comes. It has not been capable of
working during the present test. I have appealed at meeting after
meeting of my own Executive and others when the Triple Alliance
question has come up, for that to be done. I have said over and over:
"When the test comes, if you do not make it a real organisation it
will be found to be a paper alliance." By God, it has revealed itself
to be a paper alliance this week.

The delegates cheered when Smillie suggested that the
three bodies should hold a Conference to try to improve the
constitution of the alliance.

8. THE OWNERS' DATUM LINE REJECTED

When the miners' leaders met the owners' representatives
on Saturday, September 25th, they asked them to agree to
the 2s. advance on the basis of the existing output, further

advances to depend on increased output. The owners refused on the ground that they were bound by the Government's refusal and that they could negotiate on an advance only to the extent that output was increased. Negotiations then went on for several days. After some days, the owners put forward a definite proposal of an output bonus of 1s. a day (with 6d. for youths and 4½d. for boys) if the output in the first fortnight of October were to be at the rate of 242 million tons a year; 2s. a day if at the rate of 250 million tons; and higher bonuses if the annual rate were still higher than this. In the M.F.G.B. counter-proposal the current output for the third quarter was to be taken as "the datum line"; on this the claim of 2s. a shift, etc., was to be granted as from July 14th, and if the output rose in October to the annual rate of 244 million tons an additional advance of 6d. a shift was to be paid as from November; and a rise in any succeeding month to the rate of 248 million tons would yield an additional 6d.

On this difference there was deadlock. On Wednesday, September 29th, owners and miners reported to the Government their failure to reach an agreement. The Government suggested that they try again. The matter was then placed before an M.F.G.B. Special Conference on September 30th, which after full discussion adjourned to October 1st to enable the Executive Committee to bring forward proposals. On October 1st, there was a joint meeting of the Executive with the coal-owners and the Prime Minister at which each side made some concessions, but not enough to close the gap between the two sets of proposals. Lloyd George then suggested that there were four ways out of the impasse: (i) a ballot vote on the owners' terms; (ii) a tribunal; (iii) continued negotiations with the owners with further suspension of notices; (iv) strike. The M.F.G.B. Executive considered the suggestions and decided to recommend to the Conference the taking of a ballot on the terms suggested by the owners.

It was the largest Conference held that year, with 212 delegates from the coal-fields, but on the matters before it, decisions were taken by card votes. They accepted the Executive recommendation by a majority,[1] and accordingly,

---

[1] Out of 931 card votes, 530 were cast for reference back to the men in the Districts and 401 against, the minority being made up of South Wales with 180, Durham with 127, Lancashire with 80, Leicester with 8 and Forest of Dean with 6. On the question

notices were "suspended for a fortnight until Saturday, October 16, 1920." The ballot was to be taken on October 11th and 12th and the Conference was to be held on October 14th. On the ballot paper itself it was agreed "That no recommendation be made, but everyone to be left free."

On the back of the ballot paper there was printed the "Owners' Offer" signed by their Chairman, Evan Williams. The main clause of this offer was now for an advance in wages of 1s., etc., a day if output in the first fortnight of October were at the rate of 240 million tons per annum; if at the rate of 244 million tons, 1s. 6d., etc., a day; and 6d. a day more for each additional 4 million tons. That week in the coal-fields of Britain nearly a million miners were making up their minds. At the end of that time they gave their verdict by a more than three to one majority against the offer.[1]

whether the ballot vote should deal only with the employers' final offer or also with submission of the dispute to a tribunal, the vote was 619 for the former proposition against 226 for the latter, the minority being made up of Scotland's 110, Nottingham's 35 and half a dozen smaller Districts: Lancashire with 80 and Forest of Dean with 6 remained neutral.

[1] RESULT OF BALLOT VOTE ON OWNERS' OFFER
(October 14, 1920)

District	Votes Recorded			Majorities		Percentage of Votes	
	Total	For Offer	Against Offer	For Offer	Against Offer	For Offer	Against Offer
Bristol	1,970	530	1,440	—	910	26·90	73·10
Cleveland	7,327	2,673	4,654	—	1,981	36·48	63·52
Cokemen	7,079	3,778	3,301	477	—	53·37	46·63
Cumberland	8,889	2,171	6,718	—	4,547	24·42	75·56
Derbyshire	36,169	10,250	25,919	—	15,669	28·34	71·66
Durham	95,935	17,185	78,750	—	61,565	17·91	82·09
Enginemen	16,103	10,421	5,682	4,739	—	64·72	35·28
Forest of Dean	5,232	718	4,514	—	3,796	13·72	86·28
Kent	1,519	518	1,001	—	483	34·10	65·90
Lancashire	87,641	9,467	78,174	—	68,707	10·80	89·20
Leicestershire	5,626	830	4,796	—	3,966	14·76	85·24
Midlands	54,247	13,061	41,186	—	28,125	24·07	75·93
Northumberland	31,760	9,986	21,774	—	11,788	31·44	68·56
North Wales	13,053	2,231	10,822	—	8,591	17·09	82·91
Nottingham	28,157	6,541	21,616	—	15,075	23·23	76·77
Somerset	5,414	2,156	3,258	—	1,102	39·82	60·18
South Derby	5,673	1,374	4,999	—	2,925	24·22	75·78
South Wales	180,438	22,006	158,432	—	136,426	12·20	87·80
Yorkshire	116,312	39,295	77,017	—	37,722	33·79	66·21
Scotland	107,982	26,237	81,745	—	55,508	24·30	75·70
Totals	816,526	181,428	635,098	5,216	458,886	—	—
Majority against offer	453,670			453,670		22·22	77·78

When the Special Conference assembled on Thursday, October 14th, there was a tense atmosphere. Feeling in the coal-fields was very strong and the delegates brought this feeling into the Conference where they had before them the Executive Committee's recommendation "That in view of the ballot vote the men be advised to allow the notices to expire, and that a cessation of work take place after Saturday, October 16, 1920." This was accepted by 154 votes against 27 for a motion put forward by W. Hogg of Northumberland to suspend notices further and accept a tribunal. After much discussion it was agreed "That an intimation should be sent to the Prime Minister in writing giving the decision arrived at by this Conference." The Conference then discussed other business and agreed to wait in London till the morning in case a reply from the Government had to be considered.

The proceedings on Friday, October 15th, began with the Chairman reading a letter from Lloyd George which had arrived the previous evening:

Dear Mr. Smillie,

It is impossible to conceive of any action more likely to bring about a serious disaster to the trade of this country, especially when it is recollected that at the present time industry is confronted with great and increasing difficulties, and the prospect of unemployment amongst the masses of our people is causing grave anxiety. Nor is it only in these isles that the injurious effect of your action will be felt. Many struggling peoples on the Continent of Europe are today dependent upon the supply of coal which this country gives them.

The Government has exhausted every effort to prevent this calamity. We have suggested to your Federation two possible remedies. In the first place we proposed that your claim to an increase of wages should be referred to a tribunal peculiarly fitted to deal with the matter with complete impartiality, and experience and knowledge of similar questions. It is the means of decision which would most readily recommend itself to civilised communities. Many other of the great Trade Unions of this country have their wages questions settled in this way, and the majority of your brethren of the Triple Alliance resort to such an arrangement for the decision of similar questions which affect them. It is significant in connection with the present difficulty that some of the most prominent leaders of your Federation favoured this method of settlement, and that their proposals were supported by a very large body of opinion in your delegates' Conference.

In the second place, we put before you a means by which your members could be assured of the increased wage which they ask by giving the country once more the measure of output which the mines yielded in the first quarter of this year. You will readily understand the position of the Government in this matter, because you yourself have acknowledged, on behalf of your Federation, the anxiety which you feel over the declining output of coal. It is very unfortunate that recent increases in wages have been followed almost automatically by a reduced production.

If this plan had been approved by your members it would at once have benefited them and the great mass of our people. It would have increased the revenue of the country and lowered the cost of living; it would have provided cargo for our out-going ships and helped to pay for the commodities which, as an island people, we must import. I take note of the fact that our suggestion was supported by you and other leaders of great prominence in the Miners' Federation, and the whole country must deplore the fact that your advice has not been followed.

In facing the trials which the decision of your Conference has imposed upon our people, the country will no doubt be fortified in its determination to endure by the fact that the proposals made by its elected Government have received the support of the most responsible and experienced minds within your Federation. Upon our part we have explored, and are still ready to explore, every avenue that might lead to a peaceful solution of this difficulty. I can only express my profound regret that proposals which all must regard as supremely reasonable have received a final rejection at the hands of your Conference.

Yours faithfully, D. LLOYD GEORGE.

Smillie remarked that no answer had been sent, since the letter must in the first place be submitted to the Conference: and then said

I don't think that letter gets you any further forward than you were yesterday. As you can see, it is very cleverly written. It is the amazing ability of the Prime Minister, who has put the letter in such a way as is likely to secure the greatest possible amount of support outside amongst the general public. So far as I can see, it does not in any way alter the decision which you came to yesterday. There is nothing in it, so far as I can gather from the context, there is nothing in it, no reply to your statement sent yesterday that you had decided that notices were to run out at the end of this week. Now, is there any comment?

The delegates recognised all too well the nature of this "very cleverly written" letter. They realised clearly how the

Prime Minister had been playing his hand in such a manner as to break away wherever possible public support for the miners' case. It was in this knowledge that they passed the two following resolutions:

(i) That this Conference do not agree to revert back to the previous claim, including the 14s. 2d.
(ii) That in view of the unsatisfactory reply of the Government to the letter sent yesterday in connection with the claim for 2s., 1s., and 9d. per day increase in wages, this Conference do now adjourn and that notices finish tomorrow afternoon.

After these resolutions were passed the real danger created by the Prime Minister's letters was thrown right into the faces of the delegates. Just as they were about to leave, the Chairman rose and said "Before any of the delegates leave I would like to put my position before this meeting. I hope you will bear with me." He then made a statement which created a sense of shock never before experienced in a miners' Conference. Smillie recalled the fact that leaflets, pamphlets, and newspaper articles had been "spread over the whole country," stating that output was declining, that every increase in wages that the miners received meant less output, and that the fault for this lay with the miners. He, on the contrary, had felt all along that the chief reason for diminished output "lay at the door of the mine-owners of this country." An opportunity of proving that the mine-owners were responsible "and, I believe, criminally responsible for the declining output," could have been secured had they gone before a tribunal. Then he said:

I recommended that as strongly as I was capable of. . . . I felt the seriousness of the crisis justified me in asking the men to accept the datum line as a temporary measure in order to enable us to secure the information that I believed we could get to prove to the nation who was to blame for loss of output. Well now, the men have turned that down and, personally, I feel that I must accept that as a vote of no confidence in myself.

At this the delegates shouted out "No." But their Chairman maintained that it was so: and that for this reason he had not taken part in the debates of these two days of Conference or in the Executive. He then recalled a day when he had been spokesman for the miners at a meeting in 1912 when Asquith was Prime Minister:

I was pointing out to Mr. Asquith that unless recognition of the minimum wage for miners of this country was accepted by the employers or by the Government, there would be a strike. The Prime Minister turned to me and said: "Do you think there ought to be a strike?"

I said: "My opinion is, unless the miners' position is accepted, there will be a strike."

He turned again, and said: "Do you think there ought to be a strike?" I said: "Yes, I think there ought to be a strike."

If the present Prime Minister had put similar questions to him, had asked whether he thought a tribunal ought to be accepted or that a datum line ought to have been accepted, he would have had to say "Yes." That was still his opinion. Consequently, the vote of the men, and the vote of the Conference must be taken as a vote of want of confidence in his own views:

In this dispute you will have enough to face without carrying about with you a Jonah in the shape of your President. . . . I don't think I can be of service to the Federation any longer. I have reluctantly come to that conclusion. The recommendations I have made have been turned down by the men, which they have a right to turn down; that is their business. But I feel now as strongly as I have done at any time that was the way out of the difficulty, either one method or the other; and holding that view, as I do, I don't think that the Federation can afford to carry me with them in this dispute —this life and death struggle that we are about to enter.

In conclusion the Chairman said that Hodges and himself were in a special position as whole-time paid permanent officials of the whole Federation. "Mr. Hodges and myself," he said, "have had an honest difference of opinion on this question. He believed the tribunal was wrong, because he thought we would not get an honest and fair decision. I believed our case was so strong we would make out a case for an advance in wages at least, so that we honestly differed in that." He ended by saying "Therefore, gentlemen, I sincerely hope you will relieve me from the position of President of the Miners' Federation." This resignation proffered by their Chairman, at the very moment of this "life and death struggle that we are about to enter," astonished and dismayed the Conference. Their feelings were voiced by Herbert Smith of Yorkshire, the Vice-President, who rose and said:

Well, gentlemen, this is a thunderbolt to everybody here. . . . I want Bob Smillie to be in his place here. We want him to be in this fight with us. We have got to fight, and we shall want all the brains and all the help we can get to come through successfully. I have been in plenty of scraps, and have come through them. I was opposed to this strike, but I shall be in it with the rest of you. I appeal here on behalf of this Conference, and on behalf of the men in the districts for you to withdraw and say: Herbert, I will join hands with you and stick to you through this fight and fight it through.

After Levi Lovett, of Leicester, had made a similar appeal, Secretary Hodges got up. In a not very gracious speech, he dealt with the principle of the minority abiding by the judgment of the majority and made a reference to black-legging ("If Mr. Smillie should resign now, at this stage, you would find a parallel in the 181,000 men who voted against a strike continuing to work, whilst the others were on strike"), but ended by joining in the appeal for withdrawal. G. H. Jones, of the Midland miners, rose and said:

I must say, from a boy, I have looked upon Robert Smillie as a kind of hero, and there is a great deal of hero worship in our coal-field, even though our men were opposed to this datum line. . . . I think it will be a disaster if he goes out of the movement at this time. The Press would make a great deal of it, and therefore I trust you will reconsider your position.

He was followed in similar vein by Tom Richards of South Wales ("there is no coal-field where there are severer critics to be found of Mr. Smillie"); and then the Treasurer, James Robson of Durham, clinched it with some unsentimental remarks, saying:

If we are to win now it will only be by unity, and set aside all opinions, or else the consequences will be disastrous to the whole body of men. This is not the time for differences amongst either officials or local men. The Press is waiting for this; they have tried to create divisions amongst us. Why, this morning I believe that the letter from the Prime Minister was intentionally written to create division in our ranks, in seeking to apportion blame. . . .

What will be the effect on thousands of people in the North of England and Scotland when they read in the Press that the President has resigned? That, I think, makes the thing hopeless at the start. I do not think it ought to be raised at this stage, at this crisis, and I do hope he will not at this stage take this step, because, when this thing is over, there will be plenty of time to consider the position, and if he then feels it is wise for him to take this course, that is a matter for himself, and at a time when he will be better able to judge the whole situation than he can at the present time.

Smillie was dour. But he was not proof against these appeals. He rose and said:

I am sure you feel that I don't desire to injure this movement. . . . I am more convinced than ever of the justice of the men's claim. I wanted an opportunity of being able to prove it by other means. Evidently these other means are impossible. I recognised when I read this letter the Prime Minister was again making capital out of the advice some of us conscientiously gave to the men.

Now, I am not so strong as I was in the last big fight we had, but I hope I have still some energy left. Well, for what it is worth that energy will be given to our movement. We as individuals are of very little account side by side with the great movement. My dream has been to endeavour, slowly as it may be, but surely, to improve the conditions of the men, women, and children connected with the mining industry, to improve their home life and raise them especially in their own estimation rather than in the estimation of other people. We are only at the beginning even now, and whether we are defeated or successful in this fight, that will have to go on.

Thus the resignation was withdrawn.

The Conference delegates, having first agreed that their previous resolutions still stood with regard to men necessary to keep the pits safe, dispersed to their Districts to carry the word for action. For next day the strike would begin.

9. THE DATUM LINE STRIKE

The strike, which came to be known as the Datum Line strike, began on Saturday, October 16th. A million miners withheld their labour. The pits were left naked, deserted and useless: without the miners, the pit property below ground or above ground stood worthless.[1] The Government, in conjunction with the coal-owners, had made very extensive

---

[1] The compensation payment former mine-owners receive today is made possible not by a hole in the ground or by machinery above the ground, but by the fact that miners are prepared to go down and dig coal.

preparations, including the building up throughout the whole of the summer months of great stocks of coal. Many other arrangements had been made in advance of a kind never contemplated before the 1914–18 war. The enormous powers conceded to the Government during the war by the Defence of the Realm Act had not been forgotten. Moreover, whereas in 1912 the Government had been compelled to intervene in a quarrel between masters and men, this time the Government was the master-authority for all the coal-mines of the country. It was the Government which had refused the 2s. advance claimed. Thus the miners were in a more difficult position than in 1912. But on the other hand the existence of the Triple Industrial Alliance was a possible source of strength, and a weapon of unpredictable power. Against the possibility of Triple Alliance action the Government planned their measures.

For five days the strike went on. A debate in the House of Commons stimulated general demand for mediation without the Government showing any willingness to make a concession. Then on Wednesday, October 20th, a delegate Conference of the National Union of Railwaymen met to consider what should be their attitude to the miners' strike. The Transport Workers met the same day. On Thursday, October 21st, the National Union of Railwaymen took a decision of first importance, a decision which shook the confidence of the Government and brought about a change in the whole situation. When the Miners' Federation Executive met in London on the morning of Saturday, October 23rd, they found letters awaiting them from two sources, from their allies and from their opponents.

The first letter, signed by C. T. Cramp on behalf of the N.U.R., conveyed the following resolution carried at a Special Delegate Meeting at Unity House on October 21st:

That this Special General Meeting having carefully considered the position created by the Miners' Strike, and being satisfied that their claims are reasonable and just and should be conceded forthwith, decides to instruct the General Secretary to intimate to the Prime Minister that unless the miners' claims are granted or negotiations resumed by Saturday, October 23rd, which result in a settlement, we shall be compelled to take the necessary steps to instruct our members in England, Scotland and Wales to cease work.

A further and urgent letter from "the delegates to the Special General Meeting now sitting in connection with the Miners' Dispute" asked the M.F.G.B. Executive Committee to meet the N.U.R. "not later than 4 p.m. tomorrow (Saturday)."

The following letter from the Prime Minister to Frank Hodges, delivered by hand, and received a short while previous to the sitting of the Committee was also read:

I learn that the members of your Executive Council have returned to London.

As you are aware, the Government both before and since the discussion in the House of Commons on Tuesday evening has been examining the possibilities of finding a peaceful solution of the present unhappy controversy. We are, as I have already stated, ready to meet your Executive at any time to discuss proposals which hold out any hope of a settlement of the strike, but before any such formal meeting is held I should be glad to meet your office bearers or such representatives of your Executive as they might select, for the purpose of making an attempt to arrive at a basis of settlement. Such a meeting could take place over the week-end at short notice, if that is convenient to you.

Yours faithfully, D. LLOYD GEORGE.

The Executive Committee at once realised that this conciliatory letter was a direct consequence of the railwaymen's threat to strike in support of the miners. After discussing the whole situation they agreed to appoint the officials to meet the Prime Minister the following day (Sunday) at ten o'clock. They also accepted the invitation of the National Union of Railwaymen to meet them at 4 p.m. that afternoon, and decided to ask them to postpone the operation of their resolution to take strike action on Sunday night, the 24th, until further notice, in view of the resumption of negotiations with the Government. At four o'clock the Executive Committee left for Unity House and stated the position at the Special General Meeting of the National Union of Railwaymen. The application of the Executive Committee was agreed to by that body.

At the same time as Lloyd George hurriedly thrust his olive branch at the Miners' Federation's Executive, he also hurriedly introduced, on Friday, October 22nd, into the House of Commons, the repressive measure already prepared. This was the Emergency Powers Bill. Thereupon the Parliamentary

COAL LOCK-OUT, APRIL 1921
Will Latham and Sam Finney, M.P.

SMILLIE, ROBSON AND H. SMITH LEAVING NO. 10 DOWNING STREET

JAMES HASLAM M.P. (1842–1913)
Founder of Derbyshire Miners' Association

Committee of the Trades Union Congress met and at once summoned an emergency conference of all the trade union Executives.

Meantime the Miners' Federation officials met the Prime Minister on Sunday morning, October 24th. That day and for the next four days negotiations went on; draft after draft was discussed at 10, Downing Street.

On the other side of Whitehall, the Government were simultaneously pushing their repressive measure through all its steps in Parliament. On Wednesday, October 27th, the Royal Assent was given and the Emergency Powers Act became law. It was a measure which gave such drastic powers of suppression and arrest to the King's Ministers and police as had never been known in time of peace. The T.U.C. conference of Executives passed a strong protest.

The next day, Thursday, October 28th, the M.F.G.B. Executive Committee meeting is minuted thus:

At 10, Downing Street, S.W.

After considering the final terms of the Government offer as now drawn up, the following motions were moved:

(a) That the terms be referred for acceptance or otherwise to a Special Delegate Conference instructed to vote thereon.

(b) That the terms be referred for acceptance or otherwise to a ballot vote of the workmen.

It was decided by the Chairman's casting vote that the latter course be adopted.

The Committee also decided by vote that the workmen be recommended to accept the terms as a temporary settlement, pending the setting up of the permanent scheme.

That evening the form of the ballot paper was passed, the vote to be taken on Tuesday, November 2nd, as to whether or not they were in favour of the Government terms.

The terms, which involved many detailed calculations, can be summed up as follows. First the advance of 2s. a shift was conceded immediately and was equated to a figure of output. Secondly, additional increases of wages were set out on a scale corresponding to further increases of output. Thirdly, the scheme was to continue only till the setting up of a National Wage Board, to be negotiated upon between owners and workmen, who were bound to report on a permanent scheme not later than March 31, 1921. Fourthly, the Government were to guarantee the 2s. a shift advance to the end of December, in any event: and were to guarantee export prices at 72s. a ton.[1]

At the M.F.G.B. Special Conference on Tuesday, November 3rd, the ballot showed the small majority of 8,459 against the Government's terms.[2] The Chairman began by citing the Rules of the Federation:

That before a national strike is entered upon as the result of any finding of a Conference a ballot vote of the members shall be taken and a strike shall not be declared unless two-thirds of those voting vote in favour of such a strike. If a ballot vote be taken during the time a strike is in progress a vote of two-thirds of those taking part in the ballot shall be necessary to continue the strike.

At this there was murmuring. Considerable discussion

[1] See Appendix to this chapter.

[2] RESULT OF BALLOT VOTE ON GOVERNMENT'S OFFER
November 3, 1920

| District | Votes recorded | | | Majorities | | Percentage of Votes | |
	Total	For offer	Against Offer	For Offer	Against Offer	For Offer	Against Offer
Bristol	1,612	953	659	294	—	59·12	40·88
Cleveland	5,805	4,217	1,588	2,629	—	72·64	27·36
Cokemen	6,680	5,430	1,250	4,180	—	81·29	18·71
Cumberland	6,400	3,547	2,853	694	—	55·42	44·58
Derbyshire	28,586	15,917	12,669	3,248	—	55·69	44·31
Durham	91,408	51,589	39,819	11,770	—	56·44	43·66
Enginemen	16,781	14,427	2,354	12,073	—	86·00	14·00
Forest of Dean	3,726	1,765	1,961	—	196	47·37	52·63
Kent	1,088	666	422	244	—	61·21	38·79
Lancashire	84,709	14,600	70,109	—	55,509	17·23	82·77
Leicestershire	6,804	3,913	2,891	1,022	—	57·51	42·49
Midlands	56,280	33,587	22,693	10,894	—	59·68	40·32
Northumberland	27,376	16,993	10,383	6,610	—	62·07	37·93
North Wales	9,684	6,966	2,718	4,248	—	71·93	28·07
Nottingham	28,097	13,591	14,506	—	915	48·37	51·63
Somerset	4,635	3,548	1,087	2,461	—	76·55	23·45
South Derby	3,940	2,235	1,705	530	—	56·67	43·33
South Wales	149,699	51,647	98,052	—	46,405	34·51	65·49
Yorkshire	73,690	51,059	22,631	28,428	—	69·29	30·71
Scotland	77,549	41,395	36,154	5,241	—	43·38	46·62
Totals	684,549	338,045	346,504	94,566	103,025	—	—
Majority against offer		8,459		8,459		49·38	50·62

followed. A vote was taken. The result, and the subsequent resolution, were minuted thus:

For rule being carried out: 121 delegates voted.
Against rule being carried out: 46 delegates voted.

That, having regard to the small majority cast in favour of a continuance of strike, this Conference agrees to declare the strike at an end in accordance with the rules of the Federation.

It was then decided that the men be instructed to return to work the next day. The Datum Line Strike was ended.

APPENDIX TO CHAPTER IX
(Back of Ballot Paper)
October 28, 1920

SUMMARY OF GOVERNMENT'S OFFER
Temporary Scheme

AN advance of wages of 2s. per shift for persons over 18 years of age, 1s. per shift for persons between 16 and 18 years, and 9d. per shift for persons below 16 years of age, be paid as and from the date of resumption of work. The advance to be guaranteed by the Government until December 31, 1920, in any event.

The January wage to be the same as the December wage if values from export sales exceed the values of the average export proceeds for the September quarter by a sum sufficient to cover the full wage advance. The period to be taken to ascertain the increased values for regulating the January wages is the five weeks ending December 18, 1920.

If the increased values during the above period are less than the amount required to continue the advance in January, then for every £288,000 less than the full amount required, a reduction of 6d., 3d., and 2¼d. for adults, youths, and young persons respectively, will take place on January 3rd, 1921.

The following table shows the increases of wages payable under this temporary scheme, as and from January 3rd, 1921, in accordance with output and increased values arising therefrom.

WAGES SCALE AND VALUES

Output Rate per Annum		Increased Values per Week	Increase of Wages Payable per Day
When Not Less than Million Tons	And Not Exceeding Million Tons	£	s. d.
238	242	Zero	1 0
242	246	288,000	1 6
246	250	576,000	2 0
250	254	864,000	2 6
254	258	1,152,000	3 0
258	262	1,440,000	3 6
262	266	1,728,000	4 0

For every 6d. reduction in wages the owners will lose a quarter of their profits above the guaranteed profits. Similarly, for every advance of 6d. per shift in wages the owners' profits in excess of their guaranteed standard will be increased by a quarter. The

Government guarantee export prices at the figure of 72s. per ton whether they rise or fall below this figure.

The scheme is temporary in character, and will continue only until a NATIONAL WAGE BOARD is established. OWNERS AND WORKMEN to report to the Government on the permanent scheme not later than March 31, 1921.

FINAL GOVERNMENT PROPOSALS

1. Recognising that on the increased production of coal there depend not only the prosperity of all who are engaged in the coal industry, but also the welfare of the nation and the cost of life of the people; and having in view that this urgent need can only be met if the miners and mine-owners throughout the country work together cordially for this common purpose; and, further, having regard to the necessity of setting up machinery for regulating wages in the coal trade so as to get rid of present anomalies and provide against future difficulties; the Mining Association and the Miners' Federation solemnly pledge themselves to make every effort to achieve these objects.

To that end they shall:

(a) Co-operate to the fullest extent to obtain increased output, and for this purpose will arrange to set up District Committees and a National Committee;

(b) Proceed forthwith to prepare a scheme for submission to the Government at the earliest possible moment, and not later than the 31st March, for the regulation of wages in the industry, having regard, among other considerations, to the profits of the industry and to the principles upon which any surplus profits are to be dealt with.

2. Pending the preparation of the scheme referred to in 1 (b), wages shall be regulated on the following basis without prejudice to the ultimate scheme above mentioned:

(a) An advance of 2s. a shift to persons of 18 years of age and over, 1s. to persons of 16 and 17, and 9d. to persons under 16 will be paid from the date of resumption of work to the classes of colliery workers entitled to Sankey Wage, and subject to the conditions under which Sankey Wage is payable.

(b) For the purposes of this temporary arrangement the advance referred to shall be automatically adjusted on the basis set out below from the 3rd January, 1921, in the light of the results of the five weeks ending 18th December, 1920, and similarly from 31st January and thereafter every four weeks on the results of the four weeks immediately following the last preceding test period—but the Christmas holiday week shall not be counted in any such period. And an adjustment will be made in those cases where the holiday period falls wholly or partly within the New Year week.

The basis on which the advance shall be adjusted is as follows: If the weekly average of the proceeds of export coal during the test period are maintained at the weekly average of the proceeds of export coal during the September quarter the advance shall be 1s., 6d., and 4½d. respectively. If (after deduction of the cost of extra output) they exceed the September figure an additional 6d., 3d., and 2¼d. respectively will be paid for every complete £288,000 of the excess.

(c) For this purpose the amount of export coal in each period shall be assumed to be the excess of the tonnage produced over the rate of 219,000,000 tons annually; the proceeds shall be calculated by multiplying that excess tonnage by the average f.o.b. price as shown in the Trade and Navigation Accounts for the quarter ended 30th September, 1920; and the cost of extra output shall be taken as 15s. per ton for each ton produced in excess of the rate of output for the quarter ended 30th September, 1920.

(d) As part of the settlement hereby concluded the Government undertake to make an Order under Section (3) of the Mining Industry Act which shall provide for the variation of the one-tenth share of the Excess Profits of the industry payable to the owners under the Coal Mines (Emergency) Act by the deduction therefrom, or addition thereto, of one quarter of the said tenth part for each 6d. by which the men's advance is reduced or increased.

(e) The certificate of the Secretary for Mines as to the amount of the proceeds and the advances payable shall be accepted as final.

CHAPTER X

THE GREAT LOCK-OUT OF 1921

1. THE TRADE SLUMP

NINETEEN-TWENTY saw the end of the short-lived boom in trade which had followed upon the first world war. By the end of that year a slump hit the economy of Britain and of other countries, and was registered in ever-increasing figures of unemployment. This economic crisis, beginning in Japan in the late spring of 1920 and spreading therefrom to other countries, differed from previous cyclical crises in Britain. For, while it was overcome more or less rapidly in other countries, in Britain it passed into a chronic depression of trade which year after year remained below the pre-1914 level. The course of the crisis, already signalled by a fall of wholesale prices in the early summer of 1920, became clear in the winter of 1920–21 with the shrinkage of trade and the rapid growth of unemployment. The numbers of unemployed were revealed by December 1920 to be 691,103 out of approximately twelve million workers covered by the extended Unemployment Insurance Act of 1920, or nearly 6 per cent, i.e. almost three times the figure of the year 1913. For the total wage-earning population, the figure was considerably higher. Thereafter the number of unemployed mounted until by March 1921 the total stood at over one-and-a-third million or more than a ninth of the total of insured persons.

As the figure rose week after week alarm spread throughout the Labour Movement. There were insistent demands from almost every locality that measures must be taken to cope with this peril to the livelihood of so many. Partly on the initiative of the newly-formed London District Council of Unemployed the matter was dealt with at a special Labour Conference on December 29, 1920, when it was decided to call another conference four weeks later. An M.F.G.B. Special Conference held on January 26th had this unemployment problem as the first item on its agenda; and the miners' delegates decided to give their support at the Labour Conference on the next day to a very comprehensive resolution which in its beginning declared that the growing volume of unemployment was "largely due to the failure of the Government to secure the resumption of trade with Russia and Central Europe," called for work or maintenance ("at not less than 40s. per week for each householder") and went on:

The Conference, moreover, calls upon the Government immediately to reverse its policy with regard to expenditure: by bringing promptly to an end its military adventures in Mesopotamia and elsewhere in the East; by terminating its military oppression and lawless reprisals in Ireland, which are stopping productive industry and lessening the economic resources of the country.

The Government was asked also to reverse its recent policy of (a) postponing or slowing down the carrying into effect of the Education Act of 1918, (b) "slowing down, and in many cases actually obstructing, the building of the urgently required houses," and (c) forbidding Local Authorities to carry out local works of improvement. The next section of the resolution bore upon it the stamp of Beatrice and Sidney Webb (the latter of whom, as member of the Labour Party Executive Committee, may very well have been responsible for the actual drafting), and expressed their policy set forth in the 1909 Minority Report of the Royal Commission on the Poor Law:

The Conference declares that, in a period of unemployment, the policy of the Government should be one of expansion, not of contraction, of rightful and economical public expenditure; and that the necessary public works and services which must certainly be executed within each decade, ought to be, as far as possible, concentrated on the years of industrial depression, so as to avoid the waste of keeping workers in one year in idleness upon unemployment benefit, and in another year on excessive hours of labour at over-time rates.

A declaration on the "vast amount of necessary work waiting to be undertaken" was followed by a list which covered road, rail and waterways: electrical power, school buildings, afforestation, agriculture, harbour improvement and land reclamation, and "the prohibition of all overtime in order to minimise the number of workers to be discharged." The concluding paragraphs of the resolution, after demanding shorter hours and maintenance, "both for the unemployed and the under-employed," protested against wage-cutting and ended with a call to trade unions "to resist to the utmost any effort to destroy the workers' standard of life" and to report any movements in this direction "so that the two National Executives may give their united assistance to the Unions whose wages standards are threatened."

The Labour Conference of January 27, 1921, passed this resolution and then adjourned for a month, "to enable the Executives of the Trade Unions to take the opinion of their members in order to decide on any further steps that may be necessary to secure the adoption of its recommendations." What sanctions, to use a term of diplomacy, was the Labour Movement prepared to use in order to enforce this policy? Naturally the policy would be put forward in Parliament— indeed, was put forward in a two-day Commons debate and was there defeated by 262 votes to 84. But was a debate in Parliament the sole method of bringing forward this policy? On this there turned out to be a variety of opinions in the Miners' Federation of Great Britain. In South Wales a Delegate Conference on February 19th unanimously decided:

That we recommend, as the Government have refused to put into operation the policy of the Labour Party for dealing with unemployment, measures to be taken to get the whole Labour Movement to take drastic action within fourteen days to enforce its policy.

When, on February 22nd, the M.F.G.B. Special Conference opened with unemployment as the first item on its agenda, George Barker, M.P. (for ten years a member of the M.F.G.B. Executive Committee, a position he had relinquished only at the beginning of January 1921 after his election to Parliament), gave a harrowing picture of the ravages of unemployment already showing in South Wales, an exporting District; over half the miners in Monmouthshire were under notice: and therefore he moved the South Wales resolution. His successor on the M.F.G.B. Executive Committee, A. J. Cook, said he was coming to the conclusion after the last two

months "that all the virtue has gone out of this Federation";
he said:

It seems to me, looking back and seeing the growth of Trade
Unions, that with that growth and power there seems to be a lack
of fighting spirit. . . . I am amazed at what I have heard from
leaders of the Labour Party in this country. You know that Mr.
Thomas, in discussing the merits or demerits of strike action, gave
the Government to understand, before Parliament opened, that he
was not going in favour of drastic action at all. I have been trying
to analyse this matter, and have come to the conclusion that we
cannot solve this problem under the present system. It is impossible.
Now, so far as we are concerned, we have started to levy our men in
South Wales, the men who are working, in order to keep the men
who are unemployed.

But the other Districts were not prepared to subscribe to the
South Wales resolution. Smillie, from the Chair, stated that it
was inopportune, especially when their own organisation had
been weakened "very largely by the recent strike" and said:

There was a time during the agitation by the Miners' Federation
to bring about a change in your own position when we might have
had a general strike; that was immediately after the sitting of the
Coal Commission, when we roused this nation to the state of matters.
That was the time when action should have been taken. The whole
of that propaganda carried on by Hodges, Smith, and myself, and
our three colleagues on that Commission, is practically lost. In my
opinion the whole of the Trade Unions of this country would be
against you attempting to carry through a general strike, and more
than that, all our own, the vast majority of our own, poor, unfortunate, half-starving men and women, would be against you. . . .
My heart is sad for the unemployed and their families, and I feel
sure every man in this room feels the same. We would make any
personal sacrifice, we would be prepared to make it in order to help
the unemployed in any industry or in our own industry, but I do
not think we can help along the lines of general action.

After this the motion for "drastic action" was rejected by
106 to 51 votes. What was the alternative? The Conference
asked the Business Committee to draft a resolution. But when
that afternoon the requested resolution was put forward by
W. Straker:

That we recommend, as the Government has refused to put into
operation the policy of the Labour Party for dealing with unem-

ployment, measures be taken to get the whole Labour movement to adopt a four-day working week policy

it failed to find a seconder: the question of putting it forward to the Labour Conference on the next day was summarily rejected. With the action or inaction of other unions this narrative is not concerned: but the upshot of it all, at the Labour Conference the next day, was nothing eventful. The miners' delegates were somewhat perturbed at such a minimal result from so much conferring ("most of us came away from that Conference sad at heart," said Robert Smillie. "It did seem a sad spectacle that organised Labour had to leave that Conference practically admitting so far as they were concerned they were powerless to take any action"), and they devoted the main part of their continued Special Conference on February 24th to unemployment. The practical question was whether they should have a voluntary or a compulsory levy in aid of miners out of work. Finally it was agreed that the Executive Committee should "send out a recommendation and ask districts to reply within a reasonable time." Events, however, moved too fast in the coal-fields and unemployment spread too rapidly for the Districts to be able to undertake the raising of levies to help maintain those who were out of work.

From the end of 1920 onward the number unemployed out of the twelve million insured persons mounted as follows:

	Number Unemployed	Percentage of Insured Persons
December 1920 ..	691,103	5·8
March 1921	1,355,206	11·3
June 1921	2,171,288	17·8
September 1921..	1,484,829	12·2
December 1921 ..	1,934,030	16·2

In 1922 the figure gradually declined to a million and a half and thereafter for seven years never fell below the million mark. It was a chronic condition of crisis. In addition the number in England and Wales alone who came on the Poor Law rose from under half a million in March 1921 to one-and-three-quarter millions in June 1922. These figures of unemployment and Poor Law relief reflect the appalling widespread misery which fell upon more than a sixth of the whole population, and tended to depress the standards of most of the remainder. It was the manifest sign at home of a new epoch of general crisis of capitalism. It was the beginning of the "between-the-war" period which, with its dreadful consequences, was to last for nearly twenty years. It is against this background that the miners' history moved in the next twenty years; and the memory of that background was to persist still longer.

The trade slump had immediate consequences in the actions of Governments and employers. A great capitalist offensive was launched early in 1921 and continued for several years. It fell upon the miners to bear the brunt of that offensive in their 1921 struggle.

2. SCHEMES FOR THE FUTURE

Amid this gathering crisis the Federation leaders were quietly going ahead with plans on wages and output. They were negotiating with the coal-owners in order to present to the Government by March 31, 1921, an agreed scheme for the future of the industry, as had been laid down on November 3rd in the terms of the strike settlement. The two sides met on November 12, 1920; and thereafter joint committees which should elaborate proposals were set up. The miners were greatly interested in a scheme for consolidation of wages and with the factors that should affect alteration of wage rates. They had some hope of reaching agreement with the owners, who were also prepared to have wages consolidation, to adopt a new standard as the basis for wage alterations and to work out new factors that would govern advances or reductions. There, as it turned out, preliminary agreement ended.

There was for some weeks, as Smillie explained later, a certain amount of "fishing," waiting for a bite as it were, on the part of the owners—and also on the part of the miners. Nevertheless, the range of proposals on the workmen's side had been settled by the M.F.G.B. Executive Committee by the middle of January 1921. As finally formulated these proposals comprised (1) a national board to regulate wages and profits, (2) a new 1921 standard wage, (3) changes in wages to be by flat rate (and not by percentage), (4) the proceeds or surplus income of the whole industry to be shared between owners and workmen in an agreed proportion, (5) a National Profits Pool.[1]

To some of these proposals the coal-owners took objection, and to others they were inflexibly opposed. For example, they objected to national settlement of wages and insisted on a return to the old arrangements of wages settlement by Districts. The old arrangements were that each District had its own basis of rates of wages, fixed some thirty or forty years earlier and in some cases revised from 1911 onwards. Changes in wages were carried through by means of Conciliation Boards,[2] the five chief Boards being those for the Federated Area,[3] South Wales, Durham, Northumberland, Scotland. Wages moved up or down by percentages reckoned on the basis year. The chief factor taken into account in the negotiation of these changes was the selling price of coal. The sudden steep rise in the cost of living in the 1914–18 war was a new factor which along with Government control of coal-mines and coal prices threw the old machinery of conciliation out of gear. To meet this high cost of living all grades of miners received first a war bonus and then successive national flat rate advances, amounting by the end of 1918 to 3s. a day and called the "war wages." To this in 1919 was added 2s. a day flat rate (the "Sankey wage") regarded by the Miners' Federation not as an increase to meet the rise in the cost of living, but as a substantial improvement in the miners' standard of life.[4] Then, with the cost of living still rising, the Government, as from March 1920, granted 20 per cent with the proviso that if this did not yield 2s. a shift, the 2s. must be given: this 20 per cent was reckoned upon the basis rate plus the percentage additions plus the piece-rates adjustment; but not upon the war wage or the

[1] See Appendix to this chapter.   [2] See *The Miners*, Chapters IX and X.
[3] Lancashire and Cheshire, Yorkshire, Derbyshire, Nottingham, Leicester, North Wales, and in the main, the unions of the Midland Miners' Federation.
[4] As a result of another of the Sankey recommendations, the change from an Eight Hours' Act to a Seven Hours' Act, there was, in the case of piece-workers, an adjustment made to piece-rates which, on the average, could be reckoned as a little over 14 per cent.

Sankey wage. Finally, another new factor was brought in by the stipulation in November 1920 that a further advance in wages would depend upon total volume of output from all pits—which yielded an addition of 3s. 6d. a day in January 1921,[1] 1s. 6d. a day in February 1921 and nothing at all in March 1921.

Both sides were agreed that there should be consolidation of these highly involved arrangements in a new standard wage which would be made up of a minimum plus a floating margin. The miners wanted the new standard wage to be 16s. 5d. with 5s. flat rate additions. An alternative was to divide the total into 70 per cent which would become the new standard or basis, while the 30 per cent would become the new percentage on this standard. These came to pretty much the same in the opening of 1921: but there would be a difference if and when wage changes took place, the flat rate being more favourable to the lower-paid man when wages were rising and less favourable for him in a time of falling wages. The Miners' Federation decided by a District vote for flat-rate changes in future. The mine-owners, however, preferred percentage changes. The employers were also opposed to a new 1921 standard with a minimum at over two-thirds of the then existing wage rates and proposed instead a modified 1914 standard, with a minimum at about half the existing wage rates.

But what factors were in future to determine the shifting level of wages? For generations up till 1915 it had been chiefly the variable selling price of coal, but this had not been effective for some years past. This was much discussed on the Joint Committee: and by January 12, 1921, the

[1] How this worked out in practice was shown in an M.F.G.B. circular which gave the following example of a highly-paid Welsh coal-hewer, working on piece:

	s.	d.
1. Price-list earnings (equivalent to basis wage of time-worker)	8	0
2. District percentage (50 per cent)	4	0
3. Piece-work adjustment for shorter hours (14·2 per cent)	1	8·4
4. March 1920 advance (20 per cent with 2s. minimum)	2	8·8
5. War wage	3	0
6. Sankey wage	2	0
	21	5·2
If we add output wage (January 1921)	3	6
then the total daily in January would be	24	11·2

M.F.G.B. Executive Committee had reached a decision to adopt an entirely new principle for settling both the amount of wages and the amount of any extra wages. This was the principle of "profit-sharing." Instead of selling price or cost of living or output, they took the view "that the principle of a minimum wage with a corresponding minimum profit as first and second charges respectively upon the industry be adopted." Then, as corollary to this, they agreed that "the principle of the division of surplus income accruing to the industry on the basis of a share to owners and a share to workmen be adopted." The owners also were in favour of this principle.

Within the M.F.G.B. Delegate Conference the policy of "a minimum profit standard in relation to a minimum wage standard" was not to be accepted without some questioning. A. J. Cook raised the matter on January 28th, saying that while for a long time the miners would have nothing to do with any general industrial co-operation or co-partnership scheme, yet "the suggestion put forward has for its object co-partnership or joint working to stabilise the industry, minimum wages and minimum profits." Smillie immediately answered that "We have always been against co-partnership" and went on to say:

Capitalism could not go on unless it gets its profit on coal, unless it gets a certain amount of interest paid on invested capital. Our point in our negotiations ought to be to get that interest or profit down to the very lowest possible point. The employers want the highest possible point.[1] Our duty is to try to reduce it to the lowest possible point and then have some clause in the agreement dividing the surplus squarely between the producers, the consumers, and capital invested in the mines.

Frank Hodges waited till the end of that day's debate, and in summing up said that "no purely political consideration" should disturb their judgment on the economical value of any particular proposal.

[1] The division of proceeds suggested by the miners was ten-elevenths to be wages and one-eleventh to be profits. The owners for their part wanted 2s. a ton which was just about double average profits before war-time: and they were inclined to claim a proportion of proceeds that would be nearer two-elevenths. The owners also wanted a quarter (in January the proposition was one-third) of any surplus in excess of standard wages and standard profits, while the miners considered one-tenth would be enough for the owners. In the scheme as formulated, however, no figures were set down and it was left to be settled at a later date.

We are entering a system by which we share the profits of the industry with the owners, and if it does appear to assume the name of co-partnership don't let us, because of any name, give a lesser and graver consideration to its value. Have we not always protested, ever since our forefathers set up the Conciliation Boards, have we not protested against the system of making prices determine wages? Has it not been propagated for long years, and this is the first opportunity we have had to fully share on proportions agreed upon, the prosperity of this industry?

This was the first general presentation and acceptance of the principle of sharing the proceeds and of determining how much should go to wages through the method of coal-field quarterly ascertainments—though ascertainments of relevant figures by chartered accountants had begun in the days of Ben Pickard's presidency.

As the Executive Committee worked upon this further, they added the proviso that the wages must be distributed nationally by a National Wages Board and that the profits must be distributed out of a National Profits Pool. The owners were against this proviso; and it was on this rock that all possibility of an agreement foundered.

The meetings with the sub-committee of the coal-owners had gone on during January and February: and in the last week of February, after each side had consulted its members, deadlock was reached. Evan Williams, on behalf of the owners, stated that they had been influenced to a very considerable extent by the decision of the Government to decontrol the trade financially on March 31st as against August 31st as prescribed in the Coal Industry Act, and that "such decontrol would seriously embarrass the owners and make it impossible for certain districts and collieries to maintain themselves in production." The owners, therefore, had concluded that they could not agree to the establishment of a National Wages Board and "under no consideration could they agree to the establishment of a National Profits Pool as in the absence of financial control the good collieries would have to provide out of their natural profits the means for maintaining the poor collieries in production." They considered:

It would be bad for the trade as a whole. The general efficiency of the industry would decline because the incentive to remain efficient or to improve efficiency would disappear once it were established that the skill and energy of the good concerns were to be used to subsidise the inefficiency and indifference of the poor concerns. They, therefore, could only agree to a proposal to establish District Wages Boards on the lines of the Conciliation Boards in existence before the outbreak of war, with this difference, that whereas under the old Conciliation Boards wages were determined nearly exclusively by the price of coal, wages would now be determined by the capacity of the district to pay. They, therefore, suggested that each district should at once proceed to ascertain the existing financial position so that it would be known what wages were payable to the workmen after the 31st March.

There seemed little likelihood of bridging the gulf between the two sides that had been cleft by the action of the Government. Nevertheless the M.F.G.B. Special Conference, in endorsing the scheme prepared by the Executive Committee for the future regulation of wages and profits in the trade, instructed the Committee:

To present the scheme to the coal-owners with a view to it being adopted by them and put into operation as soon as possible after March 31st, and, failing agreement with the owners thereon, the Committee be requested to bring the scheme before the Government in accordance with the terms of the agreement of November 3rd, 1920. (March 10, 1921.)

The scheme, as endorsed, was sent out the next day to the Districts, and as agreement with the owners failed, was sent in to the Government which at the same time received a counter-document from the owners. These conflicting documents[1] were the outcome of four months' deliberation, research and negotiation. They were now before the Government. The M.F.G.B. representatives had presented their scheme to the President of the Board of Trade, on Friday, March 11th. What the attitude of the Government was likely to be was not fully revealed except on one point, which emerges from Sir Robert Horne's reply letter of March 15th, when he wrote that it was unwise for him "to pronounce on some matters," but that on "your proposal that the less profitable collieries should be subsidised out of the earnings of those which—whether from better management or greater

[1] See General Appendices.

natural advantages—succeed in realising better results," he had come to the conclusion that:

it would be impossible for the Government to introduce legislation to put it into effect. It would not only be contrary to the principles upon which we believe the commercial success of this country to be based, but it would be disastrous to the coal industry itself.

Not only on this matter but on wider questions of industry the position of the Government was abundantly clear. They were intent on throwing off all the controls built up in the previous period. The definite announcement of this policy by the Government affected all previous plans, to which the Government itself had been party. This was explicitly stated by the representative of the coal-owners on February 25th, when he mentioned the embarrassing effect of the Government's decision "to financially decontrol the trade on 31st March as against 31st August as prescribed in the Coal Industry Act." To this decontrol we must now turn.

3. OFF WITH CONTROLS

New Year's Day, 1921, could not be considered a holiday for the Executive Committee, for on that day a letter came to them asking them to make preparations for a meeting on January 5th at the Board of Trade, whose President wanted "an informal discussion of certain questions affecting the coal-mining industry." Ostensibly the discussions were on lesser questions such as the removal of restrictions upon distribution of supplies, but they learned that a wider decontrol was in the offing. In reply to a request for a further meeting a week later, they agreed to go but wrote a letter of protest, saying: "we cannot acquiesce in any proposal for the decontrol of the coal trade until the coal-owners and ourselves are able to present to the Government a jointly agreed plan for the national control of the industry which will effectively substitute the present arrangements."

At that meeting, on January 13, 1921, the President of the Board of Trade stated that he had read their letter "very carefully"; but that in the temporary agreement [due to expire on March 31], the Government took the big risk of guaranteeing prices, and they had been hopelessly wrong in their conclusions. As a result of the big decrease in export prices, the industry was now losing money rapidly, and their anticipations were that the surplus pool of profits already accumulated, would, as a result of the wage advances awarded, be exhausted in ten weeks. . . . The Government therefore proposed to decontrol prices and distribution entirely on the 1st March, but to keep on with the pooling of profits for some time longer, say, to take a date at random, until the 30th June, 1921. By that time it was hoped the two parties in the industry would have come to their conclusions on the point.

When, a fortnight later, the Executive Committee had before it an invitation to meet the President of the Board of Trade for what he intimated would be "the last day available for discussion" before he took necessary steps, they reaffirmed their previous decision that they could not acquiesce in his proposals and wrote to Sir Robert Horne saying that in these circumstances "no useful purpose would be served in meeting you today."

So far the Government had spoken in terms of decontrol gradually over a period of months. Now on Wednesday, February 23rd, Sir Robert Horne invited the miners' representatives to meet him and there he said:

I have to announce to you in private conference, because we have held all these conferences privately, that the Government has decided—I again say, subject to anything you have to submit to me today—to decontrol the coal trade absolutely as at the 31st March.

So what the Miners' Federation had so strenuously fought against was now to become an accomplished fact. Decontrol would mean an appalling cut in the miners' wages. The war wage of 3s. a shift, the Sankey wage of 2s., the 20 per cent granted eleven months earlier (not to speak of any increases following on November 1920)—all these would be swept away through decontrol. For these had all been given under the authority of the Coal Controller and would not in the circumstances be in any way the responsibility of any coalowner. As was stated by the President of the Board of Trade: "Their only efficacy or authority sprang from the fact of the control. As soon as the control ceases they cease to have any authority." He therefore hoped that they would reach some agreement with the coal-owners to cover these and other matters. Smillie began his reply by saying the M.F.G.B. was "very much surprised" at the intimation that March 31st would see final decontrol, which neither employers nor workmen had expected till the end of August, and there followed a dialogue recorded in the Minutes of Proceedings thus:

MR. ROBERT SMILLIE: I suppose we may take it that the passing of the control, if it passes at the 31st March, means that the Government have no further responsibility in connection with wages or in connection with the profits of the employers.

SIR ROBERT HORNE: That would be so.

MR. SMILLIE: I think you are aware that the employers' view of the matter is that that would be a breach of a pledge given to them when the Act was passed.

SIR ROBERT HORNE: So they have informed me; but I have done my best to disabuse them of that view.

MR. SMILLIE: Well, we are of opinion that it is a breach of an understanding so far as we understood the position. We recognised that you could give up control of prices, but we felt that you could not give up control of the industry so far as the national pool was concerned until the end of August. . . . We were strongly against that. I do not see how the Government can wipe their hands of the responsibility for the position in which the trade is now. They took upon themselves, rightly or wrongly—I think rightly—to regulate the prices of coal, the distribution of coal, and indeed largely the output of coal. They felt that it was necessary in the interests of the nation that that should be done. During the war it could not be left in the hands of private individuals who might put their own interests before the national interest. Consequently the Government took the responsibility of directing the coal trade in every direction. Well, I do not think the Government can fairly merely wash their hands of that now and hand back the coal trade into the old channels that it was prior to the war.

I notice that you are urged by the employers, before you rid the Government of the pool and of the control of the mines—a request has been made to you publicly, if not privately—to reduce wages and to bring wages down to the point which would make the coal trade on an economic footing—that economic footing meaning that the rate of wages would be reduced down to the point that would enable any colliery that continued to meet its liabilities in wages and cost of production.

You have instanced a colliery to us that was going on at a loss of 53s. per ton.

Sir Robert Horne : Yes.

Mr. Robert Smillie : It is perfectly plain that supposing they had been paying no wages at all, they could not go on.

Sir Robert Horne : No.

Mr. Smillie : So that we are in the position that wages might be taken away altogether if the coal trade is to be carried on and the colliery is to continue, but that perhaps is an extreme case.

Sir Robert Horne : A very extreme case; a very exceptional case, of course. I gave it as the most extreme example I could think of. It was a pit which was resuscitated during the war because of lack of coal. A pit like that cannot continue it is quite obvious under present circumstances.

Bob Smillie was familiar enough with this old trick of the politician to bring forward exceptional cases; and he gave an effective answer when he said:

The coal trade should be treated as a whole. Very often collieries are carried on under these conditions: that certain districts of a mine are clearly not paying, and cannot pay, their way, and other districts of that mine have to make up for the poor districts in the mine. That is an everyday occurrence in collieries in every part of the country. It cannot be conceived that every district of every mine is at all times paying, neither is it possible to conceive that at all times every colliery shall be paying.

Your remedy, if decontrol takes place, is that all collieries which are not paying would have to shut down because, after all, behind all this is the reducing of wages. I have never heard yet of any attempt being made to bring down the cost of stores or the hundred and one things that go to make up the price of a ton of coal.

All this is aiming at very substantial reductions in wages.

If the miners are to go on producing coal, the miners will have to get a livelihood.

Sir Robert Horne : That is so.

Mr. Smillie : I think you have admitted more than once that the first claim on the price of a ton of coal ought to be reasonable wages to the person who produces that coal.

He pointed out that for a very considerable period the home consumer, whether in industry or the domestic consumer, had been getting coal considerably under its real value. Because we were getting very high prices from people who were buying our coal abroad, many of our industries benefited by cheap coal.

Then he went on:

I know that in your inmost souls you and your colleagues are aiming at either getting rid of this industry or the responsibility for this industry in order that the colliery owners may begin to reduce wages so that you yourselves would not be forced to take that line. We cannot agree with you that the coal industry should be decontrolled and that the national pool should be abolished. We will not, if we can avoid it, I assure you, see the wages of the miners in one district of this country being reduced down to the starvation point or below starvation, while miners in other parts of the country more favourably situated are receiving fair remuneration for their labour.

The Conference with the President of the Board of Trade was reported the next day to the M.F.G.B. Special Conference, which unanimously resolved:

That this Conference confirms the attitude of the Executive Committee in protesting against the proposal of the Government to decontrol the coal trade, and declares that the Federation will oppose by every means in its power any such proposal of the Government which is prejudicial to the interests both of the coal trade and the nation generally. (February 24, 1921.)

The owners for their part had also been dissatisfied with the Government, but on different grounds. Looking after their own interests and conscious that members of the Government were their friends, they felt that the huge surplus profits (wrung from the European consumer by fabulously high export prices and taken over by the Chancellor of the Exchequer) ought to have been used, in part at any rate, to provide more and better profits to the coal-owners. They were not wrong in their belief that the Government were their friends. Their complaint was met and satisfied. The Government "compensated" the coal-owners by paying the full standard profit up to the end of 1920 and nine-tenths of that up to the end of the first quarter of 1921. With this the owners, but not without some grumbling, withdrew their opposition. There was no question raised by them of "compensation" for the miners.

The Government, having reached agreement with the owners, could now go full speed ahead, or rather full speed astern. The legislative measure for decontrol, mentioned in the King's Speech in mid-February, took shape three weeks later as a Bill which passed through all its stages in the House of Commons in the second week of March. The Royal Assent was given on March 24th and it became the Coal Mines (Decontrol) Act. Chaos was let loose in the mining industry.

The mining community was burdened with all the evil consequences.

In this critical month of March 1921 the Miners' Federation were deprived of the guidance of their President, Robert Smillie. The argument with Sir Robert Horne on February 23rd was the last occasion on which he put forward the case for the miners as advocate-in-chief. His Conference speech the next day on unemployment, which the much-impressed Executive Committee issued as a pamphlet, was his last utterance as President. In the first week of March his letter of resignation was sent in with the words "please take this as final" and the entreaties of his closest colleagues could not move him. Many rumours were current at the time as to the real reasons for his resignation; and it was widely believed that an intrigue by the ambitious Hodges was at the bottom of it. But when the letter came to the Special Conference the Acting Chairman, Herbert Smith, put the matter simply as one where entreaties would be of no avail. The tribute then uttered by George Barker, M.P., came all the more effectively from one who had most strongly opposed Smillie's policies of 1920:

We have come evidently to the end of the career of one of the greatest men that this Federation has ever produced. This letter of Mr. Smillie's will not only have significance for this Federation, but it will have significance for the whole of the Labour world. I have differed with Smillie many times, but there is no man living that has a greater admiration for his character and for his pugnacity than what I have. I shall always remember him as one of the greatest workers who has ever fought the cause of the down-trodden and oppressed. I shall always remember Smillie fighting election after election in the great interests of the workers of this country. After being counted out in one, two, three, four, five, six and seven times, he still came up to fight for the workers.

I shall always remember him in the Sankey Commission when he was voicing the needs, and the distress, and the lack of houses for the workers of the country. It is in that light that I shall always remember Bob Smillie. I look upon him as a man who gave of his best to the movement, and now he recognises that the time has come when his physical powers are waning; he thinks he can render greater service by vacating the position and giving way for some younger man. I think that this Conference will be cruel to attempt to lash Smillie into any further effort after resigning, which we have had one, two, or three times from his hands. I shall always look upon him with the greatest reverence and regard, and I hope that this Federation will pay some tribute of a substantial character on his leaving the movement.

The Delegate Conference accepted the resignation and unanimously passed the following resolution:

That we accept Mr. Smillie's resignation with regret, and thank him for his long and valuable services to the Miners' Federation of Great Britain, and trust that he will be spared for many years to serve as best he can and as his health will permit the great Labour movement in general and the miners' cause in particular.

Smillie went back to Scotland, to his miner's cottage in a miners' row in Larkhall, the colliery village where he had founded a local miners' union in the eighteen-eighties. Thereafter, though he occasionally in the next five years came to Conferences and once or twice spoke as a delegate, the man who had been the most sage and far-sighted leader of the British miners was their leader no more.

4. THE OWNERS AND THE CONTRACTS

The coal-owners lost no time, once they had reached an understanding with the Government on the terms of decontrol, in putting into operation their declared policy of cutting wages. From the beginning of March 1921 onwards notices were posted throughout the coal-fields that all contracts of service (including those of the pumpmen and other "safety-men") would end on March 31st. The new terms on which the pits would be open to employment were not immediately stated. Each District Association of coal-owners put forward its separate terms, which in most cases meant a huge cut in wages. The colliers had expected demands for a reduction of wages because of the trade slump, and the fall in the cost of living from mid-winter onwards. But the reductions demanded, in some Districts halving the wages of certain grades, went far beyond their worst expectation. Never in the recorded history of coal-mining had there been a cut so drastic as this. The M.F.G.B. Executive Committee met on March 17th to consider what figures were then available on the way the Mining Association's scheme would operate without temporary subsidy from the Exchequer. Should they abandon all their grand schemes and, for the time being, drop back into District agreements? If so, they must the next day ask the delegates from the County Associations to empower them to do this. Accordingly they decided:

That we recommend the Conference to secure the opinion of their respective districts by Conference decision as to whether or not they are prepared to temporarily abandon the policy of a National Wages Board and a national pool, and empowering the National Executive to proceed with the negotiations with a view to establishing a temporary agreement on a district basis for the period of the present abnormal state of trade and prices, and that the Executive Committee proceed to secure principles for the future guidance of districts for application in a more normal period of trade. (March 18, 1921.)

After much discussion this was agreed upon by the Conference, which then adjourned for six days to await the result. When the Special Conference reassembled on March 24th the delegates voted immediately as they had been mandated in the Districts. Of the larger Districts only Yorkshire and Northumberland had been in favour. The voting was 627 to 241 against the Committee's resolution to abandon temporarily the National Wages Board and National Pool. It was, as Herbert Smith said from the Chair, a declaration of war. Everyone realised this; and without much more said, the Conference dissolved, after empowering the Executive Committee to do whatever might be necessary. They had to call together the Triple Alliance and to consider what other bodies might be approached: they had also to communicate the decisions of the Conference to the coal-owners and to the Government.

At the Board of Trade on Wednesday, March 30th, the matter was argued out with Sir Robert Horne. The Federation representatives put a very strong case for a subvention (or subsidy as it was called later) in order to maintain the wages of the miners, but this was rejected out of hand. Then later in the meeting this led to the following exchanges between Sir Robert Horne and the Scottish and Welsh members of the Federation. Duncan Graham, M.P., began by asking, "Is it the intention of the Government to support the employers?" and when Sir Robert Horne hurriedly disclaimed any such intention, Graham went on:

MR. GRAHAM: During the period of control did the Government fix prices?

SIR ROBERT HORNE: Yes, it was in a position to do it.

MR. GRAHAM: Which, in other words, means that the Government considered they were perfectly entitled to call upon the miners to subsidise the nation.

SIR ROBERT HORNE: I do not think that is a correct way of putting it.

MR. GRAHAM: I want to know. Can you tell me?

SIR ROBERT HORNE: The basis on which these prices were fixed was always regarded as a fair one.

MR. GRAHAM: Not as far as the miners' wages were concerned relatively to other wages.

SIR ROBERT HORNE: Relatively to other wages, I think the miners' wages stood high.

MR. GRAHAM: I think you will find that the iron and steel workers' wages are 240 per cent over their 1914 wages.

SIR ROBERT HORNE: I do not think the iron and steel wages will be able to stand at that.

MR. GRAHAM: But that is what they are with the present reduction.

SIR ROBERT HORNE: How many steel works are running today?

MR. GRAHAM: How many collieries have closed down?

SIR ROBERT HORNE: I should think the proportion of steel works closed down is very much greater than anything that has taken place amongst the collieries.

MR. GRAHAM: I venture to suggest that is not quite so.

SIR ROBERT HORNE: I am talking from a good deal of knowledge.

MR. GRAHAM: In any case, I want to submit to you that the Government took control and regulated prices; in other words, they compelled the miners to subsidise the nation during the period of control, and if you pay us back what we have given to you there will be no subsidy, not by a long way. (Hear, hear.)

This rapid cut-and-thrust roused Tom Richards, M.P., who indicated his approval of Graham's statements and then said:

We ought to tell you in this room, what I want to tell you without offence, what we have already told our men and our owners. Our men in South Wales, getting on for 300,000 of them, are in a desperate condition. There is no doubt about that. They are asked to meet the owners. The owners say, "We are prepared to give every penny we have; what have you to say against that?" We asked why they were in that position. Mr. Graham has put the position. We are in that position because we did not think about the economic profits during the war; you made us subsidise the nation. We say that the Government has scuttled the ship. (Hear, hear.)

It is necessary that we should tell you what we feel. Under ordinary conditions, I am not a fighting man; all my life I have been considered to be much too peaceful; but this situation is desperate— there is no doubt about it—and I want to impress it upon you. Having every penny there is in the industry at the present moment in South Wales means a reduction of from 45 per cent to 50 per cent.

James Winstone, also of South Wales, then took the matter up and in a few words showed what a calamitous fall in wages was coming:

From every indication which came from the Welsh owners yesterday, after next month there is a possibility—I think the probability—of our highest paid men having to work for £2 1s. 3d. per week, and the labourers for 30s. per week.

Sir Robert Horne took up Tom Richards' adjective "desperate" saying, first that it was "not nearly so desperate in the coal trade" as in most other industries, second that it was because "the position of the world is desperate that the coal trade is in trouble" and then descanting at some length on the economic crisis, this "great world convulsion." In conclusion he repeated the Government's refusal to consider a subsidy which he described as "an absolutely impossible proposal."

The miners were angered at what they felt to be a callous attitude. The miners' wives, it is known, were even more insistent than the men themselves on making a firm stand. The M.F.G.B. Executive Committee, well aware of the mood in the coal-fields, had by a majority decided that same day (March 30th) to send instructions "that all notices should be allowed to expire regardless of occupation." This meant that the enginemen, pumpmen and others concerned with keeping the pit in working order, who had received notices like everybody else, would cease work with everybody else: and this in turn meant that a certain deterioration of the coal-owners' property would set in. The coal-owners, in declaring their universal lock-out, had not assumed that this loss of property through inflow of water would be one of

the consequences. They were furious: and when, at the close
of the interview at the Board of Trade on March 30th, Herbert
Smith had bluntly put the position, Sir Robert Horne, whose
professional experience had largely been that of protecting
property interests, stood completely aghast. Within a few days
this decision on the enginemen, pumpmen and others was
assailed in Press and Parliament and used for an unscrupulous
campaign of abuse against the miners.

5. THE GOVERNMENT AND THE EMERGENCY
POWERS ACT

On March 31, 1921, the Government gave up control of
the mines. The next day over one million miners were idle,
locked out, standing in the village streets, gazing at the gaunt
and silent machinery on their pithead. Immediately the
Emergency Powers Act passed just five months earlier was
brought into operation, so that on the very day of the lock-out
a Proclamation was issued in the name of the King, "signed
by his own hand" as is the usual formula, declaring the
country to be in a "state of emergency." The Government,
on Monday, April 4th, issued Emergency Regulations under
the Act. Troops were moved into the coal-fields, a measure
which caused intense anger amongst the miners. "Machine-
guns in our pit!" was an indignant comment repeated in
scores of places.

On Tuesday, April 5th, the War Office cancelled all leave
and it was announced that troops were being brought back
from Ireland, where civil war was being waged against the
Sinn Fein headed by Eamon De Valera. On April 6th the
parks in London and elsewhere began to be used as armed
camps. On Friday, April 8th, the tension was mounting.
There were four new Royal Proclamations. In the House of
Commons Lloyd George announced that these measures
meant: (1) Army and Navy reservists had been called up;
(2) Officers and men had been re-enrolled in the Air Force;
(3) a new volunteer "Defence Force" would be enrolled for
ninety days. All these measures were taken in view not only
of the mining lock-out but of the possible wider strike move-

ment of the Triple Alliance and other unions, as dealt with below in the next section.

But at the same time Lloyd George did not neglect the uses of publicity. He had the means to hand in the liaison he had built up with the chief newspaper proprietors, amongst them Lord Northcliffe (formerly Alfred Harmsworth) who had control of the *Daily Mail, The Times* and other organs. With such a champion on his side, the Prime Minister might have said, paraphrasing Shakespeare:

> Sweet are the uses of publicity;
> Which, like the toad, ugly and venomous
> Wears yet a precious jewel in his head.

Of this "publicity" especial use was made in the matter of the enginemen, pumpmen, etc., the withdrawal of whose labour might lead to flooding of certain pits. The loss of mine-owners' property was suddenly transformed into a humanitarian concern for the underground pit ponies whose lives were declared to be endangered by the callous strikers and their still more callous leaders.

In this atmosphere the next shots were fired in the House of Commons on Monday, April 5th. The stage was set at Question Time, with a series of questions on the sufferings of pit ponies, inspired by the Press scare stories. Next came the reading of the King's Proclamation under the Emergency Powers Act, and a resolution of Humble Address of Thanks to His Majesty for the Proclamation, standing in the name of Mr. Austen Chamberlain. In the gallery the mine-owners, Sir Adam Nimmo and Mr. Evan Williams, heard emotional appeals, largely from high-ranking military and naval officers, on behalf of their property, or at least one part of it, the "dumb beasts." To Colonel C. Lowther, for example, it was "a terrible thing to think that at this moment there may be ponies in the mines, and I believe they are none too rare, either drowning bit by bit or gradually starving to death." In the same speech he drew a picture of the miner "told by Bolshevik agitators paid by German gold" that the mine-owners desired only "to ruin him, to profiteer and to get everything possible out of him." The Secretary of Mines had at last the grace to admit that the miners' Secretary had promised "that he will send a telegram to any place which

I know of if ponies are still below to assist in getting them brought up" (the next day he was to state that no pit ponies had been lost in the mines). But the Prime Minister, in his speech, passed over that inconvenient admission. He assured the House that the Government would be willing to promote further discussions between owners and miners. Given two conditions, the Government would itself enter the negotiations; these were that there should not be any expectation of maintaining the industry out of general taxation, nor of re-control. At the end of his speech he remarked that it was essential that the Miners' Federation should help to prevent the pits from being destroyed and to save the lives of "these poor dumb animals." He added: "I only want to make that condition, and I think it is worthy of the House to protect these poor animals. I am perfectly certain that everybody in every section of the House will sympathise with that object." (Lieut.-Commander Kenworthy: "What about the miners' children?")

Next morning the Miners' Federation received the following letter:

6th April, 1921.

Dear Mr. Hodges,

I would direct the attention of your Executive to the statement which I made in the House of Commons last night on behalf of the Government with regard to the desirability of negotiations being resumed between your Federation and the Mining Association. I desire to repeat that the Government tenders the use of its good offices for the purpose of bringing the parties together, and I shall be glad to know whether your Federation is willing to reopen negotiations. I am sending a similar communication to the Mining Association.

Yours faithfully, D. LLOYD GEORGE.

Immediately the reply was sent that the Executive Committee were "in a position to meet the coal-owners with representatives of the Government present at any time or place convenient to all parties." The Chairman of the Mining Association also replied, agreeing to meet the miners, and adding:

but I assume that if the latter agree to meet the owners they will ensure that the collieries are kept free of water and in a safe condition for a resumption of work.

No mention here of pit ponies. The "poor dumb animals" had served their turn.

Lloyd George reacted instantly to the stimulus. He intervened in the afternoon's debate on the Emergency Regulations to read the correspondence to the House, while a further letter was on its way from him to the Federation. This time he laid down a condition which must be complied with by the miners before negotiations would be reopened.

6th April, 1921.

Dear Mr. Hodges,

I have to thank you for your letter stating that your Federation is willing to resume negotiations with the coal-owners; and as they also intimated their readiness to reopen discussion I shall be obliged if you will meet them in the Council Room of the Board of Trade tomorrow morning at 11 a.m.

You will remember that in my speech last night in the House of Commons, which set forth the conditions upon which such resumption of negotiations should take place, I stated that:

"It is essential that the Miners' Federation should give every facility and assistance to prevent the pits from being destroyed and also to save the lives of those poor dumb animals which, I am sorry to say, in a few instances, at the present moment are living under horrible conditions, and have been allowed to remain down the pits."

I accordingly assume that your Executive will tonight give instructions for the resumption of work by men who are necessary for the pumping and preservation of the mines, and for rescuing any animals which are in danger.

Yours faithfully, D. LLOYD GEORGE.

Immediately they replied:

6th April, 1921.

Dear Prime Minister,

Your letter of this afternoon to hand suggesting a joint meeting of representatives of owners and workmen at the Board of Trade at 11 o'clock tomorrow morning. To this proposal the Federation readily gives its assent, but it should be made clear that the condition and expressed assumption that the "Executive Committee will give instructions tonight for the resumption of work by the men who are necessary for the pumping and preservation of the mines and rescuing any animals which are in danger," are unnecessary for the resumption of discussion with the Government and the owners.

It is not part of the Federation policy to allow any pit ponies to be left to their fate in the mines. In fact, the Federation have already made it known that the workmen will co-operate with the managements to bring up every pit pony to the surface. If, at this stage, any pit ponies still remain underground, they are there with the approval of the managers in every case, and, in several instances, against the expressed wishes of the men.

The Executive Committee do not propose to issue tonight the instructions as to pumping suggested by you, but this is no bar to any further negotiations with a view to arriving at an honourable settlement.

Yours faithfully, FRANK HODGES.

At this Lloyd George wrote yet again, dropping any further reference to pit ponies, but saying that he regretted they would not agree "to send the necessary instructions for keeping the pumps and engines going for the preservation of the mines pending negotiations." His letter went on:

I feel that there must be some misunderstanding on the matter and shall be very glad if your Executive Committee will meet me tomorrow as early as possible. Until this question is cleared up, I cannot take the responsibility of convening the proposed conference.

Before 8 p.m. that night he rose and dramatically announced it to the House. It would be, he said,

quite impossible to have negotiations whilst the mines are gradually crumbling owing to the difficulties of keeping them from being flooded.

MR. DUNCAN GRAHAM: Am I to understand from what the Prime Minister has said that this is to be taken by the Miners' Executive and the mine-owners as a refusal on the part of the employers to meet the Miners' Executive tomorrow?

PRIME MINISTER: It is not a condition of the owners. It is a condition that the Government laid down last night before the owners ever wrote their letter.

Next morning, on Thursday, April 7th, at 10 Downing Street the Prime Minister with Austen Chamberlain (who had a physical resemblance to his famous father), Sir Robert Horne (now become Chancellor of the Exchequer) and other members of the Government met the Executive Committee of the Miners' Federation. Lloyd George began the Conference in an ingratiating humour. As a member of the Executive Committee was to describe it a few hours later in the House of

Commons, "he was then very well disposed to us, and I think he could have cracked jokes with us." The Prime Minister asked that there should be "a truce" in this industrial warfare, and that the pumpmen should go back to their work. To this Acting President Herbert Smith replied that the owners had given every workman notice to leave his employment, including the safety men. "If we are to have any truce," he said, "why do not we all go back to work on the conditions on which we came out on March 31st? That is a truce." He added:

We are equally as anxious for peace as anyone else. But our first charge is against the Government for removing the responsibility, for tricking us into an agreement in November last with their eyes open, knowing what they were going to do directly afterwards to us. Our second position is that the owners are backed up strongly by you in taking the action they have taken.

Smith showed that he regarded the talk of truce applied to the return of the safety men as a specious attempt to help the employers: and he ended by saying:

We are anxious to save the mines, but we are equally anxious to save women and children, and that appeals more to us than the mines, which are the property of the owners. The Prime Minister told us in the war with Germany to put sentiment on one side. We have against us today a force as bad as Germany—we have two of you against us—the Government and the employers, and if there is to be a truce it is going to be on those lines I have indicated as far as the Federation is concerned, namely, that everyone goes back to work on the terms on which they left at the 31st March.

Other members of the Executive Committee took up the arguments. The miners' leaders were angry at the refusal to have any negotiations until a preliminary condition was fulfilled, to the advantage, as they believed, of the owners.

MR. STRAKER: You are asking us to go into negotiation with some of the men helping to fight against us.

THE PRIME MINISTER: No.

MR. STRAKER: You are laying it down as an absolute condition before the negotiations are opened up that some of the men should go back to work. I think that is an absolute mistake. I am not the most hot-headed of men in the world, but personally, I would rather capitulate absolutely than enter into negotiation with a condition of that kind laid down beforehand.

THE PRIME MINISTER: But why do not you yourselves take action? All we are asking is, that whilst the negotiations are going on firing shall cease, and the armies shall stand to arms.

MR. HERBERT SMITH: Without being fed; that is what your conditions are. It is no good our bargaining about this Mr. Prime Minister. We have got to get those two fundamental principles agreed to—the National Wage Board and the national pool—and then we can talk about the safety men.

MR. RICHARDS: You are not only asking that firing shall cease——

THE PRIME MINISTER: If that is your view, Mr. Herbert Smith——

MR. HERBERT SMITH: That is it, sir.

THE PRIME MINISTER: As far as we are concerned, if you insist upon that, and say that the safety of the mines will not be conceded, that you will not permit our taking the necessary steps to ensure the safety of the mines until we have conceded beforehand the two things which, amongst others, will have to be discussed, then it is an impossible position. That is an ultimatum of a much more serious character.

MR. FRANK HODGES: To be perfectly frank, that is the decision of the Federation.

THE PRIME MINISTER: I am very sorry.

The members of the Cabinet then retired for some twelve minutes. When they came back Lloyd George said that he had invited them because he had thought it was only some misunderstanding which could be cleared up but now he realised there was "a much graver divergence of opinion" than he had anticipated:

What I understand is this, that the threat to destroy the mines by the deliberate action which has been taken to achieve that end is to be utilised as a means to force the owners, who have got their interest in the mines, and to force the nation, which has a still greater interest in the mines, to a capitulation upon the two main claims which are put forward by the Miners' Federation. Mr. Richards very frankly stated that position.

The challenge which has been put forward by the Miners' Federation is of a much graver, a much deeper, a much more fundamental character than even I had realised.

This last remark was very much in line with Lloyd George's attitude eighteen months earlier, when he had described the strike of railwaymen for higher wages as an "anarchist conspiracy," but on this occasion he conveyed a similar impression without the same violence of language.

That night of April 7th there was a debate in Parliament on

the crisis. The Prime Minister had to display all his customary agility when hard pressed by Arthur Henderson and others to justify "the bar that has been put up by the Government and the employers before a meeting could be held." Duncan Graham, who was "stating not his personal opinion, but the opinion of the British Miners' Executive, that they are prepared to go into a conference unconditionally," said:

The statement of the Prime Minister is very clever, but that is all that can be said for it. . . . We were anxious to find out whether the Prime Minister was prepared to remove that ban and allow us to meet the employers, but he rather cleverly converted the discussion into one whereby he got an opinion of the position the miners would adopt when they met the employers. He immediately makes that a cause of trouble, and now takes the side of the employer, I suppose quite naturally. . . . If you are anxious to look at this matter from the standpoint of national interest, let it be remembered that the employers do not consider the national interest at all. If it were possible for you to get the facts as to what happened during the last few months, you would find that millions of pounds' worth of material have been put into the mines and hidden. That is in preparation for the passing of control.

The next day there was a further rapid interchange of letters.

8th April, 1921.

Dear Mr. Hodges,
In the course of the discussion in the House of Commons last night, certain suggestions were made by leaders of the Labour Party which have led me to make to you the further proposal for a meeting with the coal-owners in order to make a start towards a solution of the present dispute.
A suggestion was made to the effect that a conference might be summoned by the Government which should deal in the first instance with the question of pumping and preservation of the mines, and that that matter should be disposed of before any other question was entered upon.
The Government has considered this suggestion, and I have now to invite your Federation to send representatives at 12 o'clock noon today to a conference to be held at the Board of Trade on these terms.

Yours faithfully, D. LLOYD GEORGE.

The miners replied immediately that they had already

stated to you in clear terms that we are willing and ready to meet the owners and the Government at any time and place convenient to all parties, and are willing to meet as soon as we hear from you that the conference is to be held entirely freed from any preliminary conditions as to what is to be or is not to be discussed. We desire to be free to fully discuss every aspect of the present situation with a view to arriving at a speedy and honourable settlement.

The Prime Minister answered that the Government had

never suggested that any limitation should be imposed upon discussion, but as regards the order in which matters are to be discussed, the national interest in the preservation of the mines is paramount, and it must take first place. While the mines are hourly being flooded and ruined, and one of the most valuable national assets being destroyed, it is impossible to expect other questions to be debated. Accordingly the question of the safety of the mines must first be discussed and disposed of before other matters are taken up.

To this the miners noted

your clearly stated condition that the question of the safety of the mines must first be discussed and disposed of before other matters are taken up.

As previously stated, we are willing to meet the owners and the Government in conference at once, if we are allowed to meet unconditionally. We trust that the Government will raise no obstacle to ensure this end.

Lloyd George had begun the correspondence when he knew of the imminence of a Triple Alliance strike. It is not known whether in the meantime he had had an opportunity to consult his military and other advisers as to whether they were fully prepared to cope with and crush (or attempt to crush) a widespread strike movement of many industries. On the other hand he almost certainly had the means of knowing that J. H. Thomas and a leader of the transport workers would be approaching him to mediate, which would give him the opportunity of playing upon them. He now closed the correspondence with a letter pre-eminently suitable, from his point of view, for subsequent publication.

8th April, 1921.

Dear Mr. Hodges,

I have received your letter, and I note with the greatest regret the decision at which your Committee has arrived.

In view of the grave consequence involved it is difficult to understand how any discussion designed to promote a settlement could usefully proceed, unless we were all agreed that the first task should be to secure the preservation and safety of the mines, without which there must be widespread and continued unemployment and distress, not only for those whose occupation is in the mines, but for the whole industrial population.

So far from placing any obstacle whatever in the way of negotiation, the action of the Government has been dictated solely by a desire to remove the main obstacle that stood in the way of fruitful negotiation. The mines are vital to the life of the community; their destruction is as fatal to the nation as would have been defeat in war, and to secure their preservation must be the paramount duty of Government.

Yours faithfully, D. LLOYD GEORGE.

6. THE TRIPLE ALLIANCE

Where, during all these happenings, was the Triple Alliance? Before the lock-out and as the day of decision came nearer, as negotiations with the coal-owners and with the Government yielded no result, the miners' leaders got into touch with the other leaders of the Triple Alliance. Everyone realised that this occasion was much more serious than anything hitherto. Consequently, after the discussion with Sir Robert Horne on March 30th, the M.F.G.B. Executive Committee, about to enter a meeting the next morning of the Triple Alliance Executives at Unity House, decided beforehand "that we ask the other organisations in the Triple Alliance to take strike action in order to assist the miners in the present crisis." After this Triple Alliance Conference, the railwaymen and transport workers met separately. The N.U.R. Executive, in a Press statement, said they were "deeply impressed with the gravity of the situation, and they regard the position as being the prelude to a general attempt to destroy national negotiations and reduce wages." They had decided to inform all branches and to call a special delegate meeting for April 6th "in order to decide what action shall be taken." The Transport Workers' Federation stated it was not only a miners' question, "but an attempt to get back to the old days of district negotiations rather than national negotiations, which would affect us in the same way as the miners." They had decided to call together on April 5th the Executives of all the unions in the Federation for the purpose of dealing with the matter.

Thus on April 1st the public learned that the Government in dropping the controls and the coal-owners in locking out over a million miners[1]. had precipitated something that would lead to an industrial upheaval on a much vaster scale. Within less than a week, the Conference of all the Executive Committees of the unions that made up the Transport Workers' Federation and also the special delegate meeting of that National Union of Railwaymen had met and taken their decisions. Each declared for action in support of the miners. On Friday, April 8th, the full Conference of the whole Triple Industrial Alliance assembled. That day the miners' partners issued strike orders.

The decision was made. The other members of the Triple Alliance would take strike action as from Tuesday midnight, April 12th, in support of the miners.

But once this decision was taken, the other members of the Triple Alliance claimed an interest in negotiations. Accordingly the two partners of the miners met the Government early on Saturday, April 9th, and urged that by mediation an endeavour should be made to prevent a widespread dislocation of trade and industry. They were told that the Government could not take up the olive branch, so long as the Miners' Federation held to its decision about the pumpmen. So they consented to use their influence with the miners to get them to abandon their standpoint. The miners' leaders, having the experience of the previous autumn fresh in their minds, were anything but pleased when the first action of their allies was a demand that would weaken their own strike tactics. But they had no option. If they did not yield to their allies, that non-yielding might become the grounds for their allies leaving them. So on Saturday, April 9th, unwillingly enough, they yielded: and the following telegram was sent to all Districts:

A conference with the owners being opened unconditionally, we

[1] All the members of the Miners' Federation (including the great majority of the pumpmen and safety men) were out. Some mineworkers were members of unions such as the Amalgamated Engineering Union, the Electrical Trades Union, the National Union of Enginemen, etc. These unions, together with a number of small unions of colliery deputies and firemen, instructed their members not to work when the miners were locked out.

urge upon all our members to abstain from all action which will interfere with the measures necessary for securing the safety of the mines, or will necessitate the use of force by the Government.

Negotiations began on Monday, April 11th, at 11 a.m. in the Conference Room of the Board of Trade. There were present representatives of the Government, headed by the Prime Minister, the Central Committee of the Mining Association of Great Britain and the Executive Committee of the Miners' Federation of Great Britain. Among the other Government representatives were the Chancellor of the Exchequer, Sir Robert Horne, and Stanley Baldwin, the new President of the Board of Trade. These negotiations, in which many hopes were reposed, were to be fruitless. Each side restated its case on the Monday afternoon and evening. The spokesman for the Federation was Frank Hodges; his exposition roused the admiration of his colleagues on the Executive, which that evening passed a minute,[1] signed by all of them, recording their appreciation of his skill. Later on the "skill" of the Federation Secretary was to be used as a pretext for the desertion of the miners by their allies.

The only concession in the Conference so far was that made by the M.F.G.B. Executive who offered, in view of the recent fall in the cost of living, to forgo 2s. a shift, equivalent to 30 per cent of their pre-war standard. Negotiations were continued into Tuesday, April 12th, when to begin with the Government representatives met the miners' representatives at Downing Street at 1 p.m. Since these negotiations were still continuing, the N.U.R. and the T.W.F. issued orders postponing the strike due that midnight. In the later afternoon, back at the Board of Trade, the three parties met again and discussed "terms of settlement" which Lloyd George put forward with his customary eloquence. Apart from an offer

[1] "That this Executive places on record its high appreciation of the splendid service rendered by the Secretary (Mr. Frank Hodges) to the miners in their struggle for a National Wages Board with a National Profits Pool. The masterly way in which he has put and defended the miners' case before the Government and the coal-owners commands and most richly deserves the respect and admiration of all his colleagues." Signed:

HERBERT SMITH (Acting President)	GORDON MACDONALD	J. WINSTONE
JAMES ROBSON (Treasurer)	WILLIAM WHITELEY	THOMAS RICHARDS
FRANK B. VARLEY	W. P. RICHARDSON	SAMUEL ROEBUCK
FRANK HALL	ROBERT SHIRKIE	W. STRAKER
JOHN POTTS	SAMUEL FINNEY	W. WHITEFIELD
NOAH ABLETT	JOHN McGURK	A. J. COOK
	LEVI LOVETT	DUNCAN GRAHAM
	W. LATHAM	

of a subsidy (which less than two weeks earlier the Government had ruled out completely), these terms made no substantial change from the terms offered by the owners. The first four clauses were a propagandist argument against the National Pool of Profits; the fifth clause proposed District settlement of wages, as did the coal-owners; the sixth and seventh clauses were subsidiary to the fifth. Only the eighth and last clause contained something new, namely that:

8. If and when an arrangement has been arrived at between the coal-owners and the miners as to the rate of wages to be paid in the industry, fixed upon an economic basis, the Government will be willing to give assistance, either by loan or otherwise, during a short period, in order to mitigate the rapid reduction in wages in the districts most severely affected.

The M.F.G.B. Executive Committee had still to consider at their office, but Herbert Smith gave Lloyd George the Federation view immediately, without mincing his words:

This scheme that you have put before us, with the exception of Clause 8, is absolutely the owners' scheme. If you had copied the words from their scheme it could not be put in more explicit language than theirs. I do not see that they have any scruples at all; they will be glad to accept Clause 8. We are not able to accept it. . . .

It may be that you have it in your minds that it will be possible to starve us into submission. If you do it will not bring peace to the coal trade. I want to put it again, Mr. Prime Minister, that the men are going to be the biggest contributors in areas where they are earning good wages now or at the 31st March, and they are prepared to make their sacrifice, realising that they have something to do to help their weaker brothers in those districts. If the owners are determined that they are going to carry on nearly like they carried on before the war we will be starved to submission before we accept it. . . .

A moment of anger came over Smith as he said that "It is a bad thing when a case has to be won through women's and children's stomachs," and when after recalling an example of equivocation by one of the owners, he burst out "That is the way you people have been dealing with us for years. We have been too honest to mix amongst you." And again when he came to what he clearly held to be "thieves' cant"—the talk of co-operation:

We know the practical side of the thing, but you people never did. When Lord Gainford talks about co-operation—it is a myth. I dismiss it like that. (Snapping his fingers.) There is nothing in it.

Mr. Prime Minister, before we leave let me say this. This is a serious thing for this country and we realise it. Would to God we could avoid it. (Hear, hear.) But we cannot make the settlement you have indicated here today. We are bound to face the consequences whatever they are, and we go into it with the understanding that we have failed here to arrive at a sensible settlement which would be a benefit to the industry.

After Lloyd George had protested against Herbert Smith's statement that the Government proposals were practically the owners' proposals, the Miners' Executive withdrew. That evening they resolved "That, having fully considered the terms set forth in writing by the Government, we reject such terms, as they offer no solution to the present dispute." The negotiations had been a complete failure. From the Government point of view, however, the failure was not complete. The two days spent in fruitless negotiations had effected a postponement of the railway and transport strike notices: and a strike postponed is often half-way to no strike at all.

On Wednesday, April 13th, the full Triple Alliance met again. Faced by a complete deadlock, the N.U.R. and transport workers re-issued the call for a strike and fixed the date for two days later, at 10 p.m. on Friday, April 15th. The two partners of the Triple Alliance were now joined by others. The Associated Society of Locomotive Engineers and Firemen had decided to help the miners with strike action: and their representatives now attended the Triple Alliance Conferences. The Executive Committee of the Electrical Trades Union (whose London District Council had decided on strike action) came to consult with the Triple Alliance. So did the Executive of the Union of Post Office Workers, which had already secured a pledge from the Postmaster General that none of its members would be asked to do "black" work. The Executive of the Railway Clerks' Association recommended strike action to its members. In preparation for the strike the Co-operative Wholesale Society offered its powerful aid. On the next day, Thursday, April 14th, the National Joint Council of Labour, made up of the Committees of the Labour Party, the Parliamentary Labour Party and the Trades Union Congress, met at the House of Commons and resolved to support the miners. The issue was widening from a Triple Alliance strike to a strike that would involve hundreds of thousands of other workers, from a dispute over wages to a gigantic head-on collision between the embattled forces of the owners of property, with the Government using on their behalf all the resources of the State, and the combined forces of the trade union, Co-operative and Labour Movement. For two weeks the miners had been locked out. Now the mighty Triple Alliance was coming up with powerful reinforcements. Behind the Triple Alliance were the vast reserves, the responsible bodies of the entire Labour Movement. These, too, had now given their pledge of support. With such backing, the miners' cause was bound to win. Lloyd George and his Coalition Government would have to yield. Nay, it was even openly canvassed that the Government of "hard-faced men" might have to resign and make way for one of a better and more progressive character.

7. "BLACK FRIDAY"

Thursday, April 14th was the eve of the day set for the great demonstration of solidarity which would be expressed in the action to be taken by the other members of the Triple Alliance. That Thursday night private meetings of Members of Parliament were held in the Committee rooms of the House of Commons. The first of these meetings was addressed by the Chairman of the Mining Association, Evan Williams. His replies to questions, especially on the exact size of the wage-cut demanded, left many Members dissatisfied. The second meeting was addressed by the Secretary of the Miners' Federation, Frank Hodges, whose replies to questions, expecially on the possibilities of a temporary settlement, had momentous consequences. No one knows exactly what Frank Hodges said in these replies. His own version of it, cited below, was given a week later, after the damage was done. The version given next day by the newspapers, none of whose reporters were present, was that Hodges was prepared for a temporary settlement on a District basis. The effect of his reply, whatever its wording, was such that a group of Government supporters rushed round to see the Prime Minister that night and urged him to bring about a temporary settlement on these lines.

The next morning, Friday April 15, 1921, when the Executive Committee of the Miners' Federation met at their offices, they had before them a letter from the Prime Minister:

15th April, 1921.

Dear Mr. Hodges,

Several members who were present at your House of Commons meeting last night have conveyed to me the purport of your concluding offer. They had not taken down the actual words you used, but the general impression made on their minds was that you were now prepared to discuss with the owners the question of wages without raising the controversial issue of the pool, provided the arrangements to be made were of a temporary character and without prejudice to a further discussion of proposals for a National Pool when a permanent settlement comes to be dealt with.

If this is a fair representation of your suggestion I invite you and your fellow delegates to meet the owners at the Board of Trade at 11 this morning to consider the best method of examining the question of wages.

Yours sincerely, D. LLOYD GEORGE.

After consideration of the above letter, the Committee decided that the following reply be sent:

Dear Prime Minister,

My Executive Committee have fully considered your letter and ask me to state that the only condition upon which a temporary settlement can be arrived at is one that must follow the concession of the two principles already made known to you, viz. a National Wages Board and a National Pool. In those circumstances my Committee feel that no good purpose would be served in meeting the owners today on the basis suggested in your letter.

Yours faithfully, FRANK HODGES.

They had considered it, and rejected it. It would have meant, in their view, surrendering the principles for which they were contending and which had been reaffirmed by their National Conference. If they gave away these principles for a temporary settlement, what hope was there of winning them back in later discussions for a permanent settlement? Thereupon Hodges resigned: but was later prevailed upon by the

Executive to withhold his resignation. The minute, drawn up by Hodges, runs as follows:

In view of the fact that the Committee had not agreed to see the Government and the owners on the question of wages, Mr. Hodges informed the Committee he felt he had no alternative now, in view of the statement he had made in the House of Commons, but to resign his position as Secretary of the Federation.

The Committee considered the written resignation of Mr. Hodges, and later Mr. Hodges was called in, and was informed by the Chairman that the Committee had unanimously agreed to ask him to reconsider his decision in the interest of the movement, whereupon Mr. Hodges stated that in view of this unanimous request he was prepared to continue in office for the sake of the mining community.

The miners' representatives duly reported their decision to their partners in the Triple Alliance, who, after discussing the matter amongst themselves, sent their leaders to ask the M.F.G.B. Executive to reverse its decision, and to accept the Prime Minister's invitation. This the miners indignantly refused to do and made it clear that they expected their allies to come out on strike that evening as already fixed. When J. H. Thomas indicated that the strike might not take place, if the miners persisted in their previous decision, the miners knew they were in danger of being abandoned by their allies; and showed that they knew: it was not a harmonious hour.

Then their allies went back to Unity House, the headquarters of the N.U.R. There the atmosphere was now near to hysteria. Fear that they might wreck their organisations, fear of Lloyd George's cleverness, fear of the forces that would be opposed to them, all these fears oppressed the delegates. In such a mood panic was possible. Those who had been utterly opposed to the strike, and who wanted the strike to be cancelled more than they wanted to help the miners or to act up to their obligations triumphed in that atmosphere. One or two speeches stampeded the Conference: and within a few minutes, J. H. Thomas, unable to disguise his relief, was out speaking to the Pressmen who waited at the doors and telling them that the strike was cancelled.

It was true. The unbelievable step had been taken. Only a day or two before, at the meeting of these allies with the Prime Minister, Harry Gosling had said to Lloyd George,

"We should be rotters if we deserted the miners." But they deserted them.

The news caused such a revulsion of feeling within the Labour Movement as no one could remember in earlier days. Indeed, in earlier days it would not have been possible. It took all the circumstances of the twentieth century, all the frenzied atmosphere of the Coalition Parliament, of snap decisions, of million-sale newspapers with their millionaire owners, of unstable and aspiring politicians, all the previous history of the Triple Alliance itself and all the records of the leaders to make possible this desertion on the field. Indignation was well-nigh universal in the Labour Movement that evening when the strike was so abruptly cancelled. But indignation is not a mood that lasts long. True, the London District officials of the Dockers' Union resigned as a protest against "betrayal of the miners by the Transport Workers' Federation and the National Union of Railwaymen." True, too, that for many a one the hopes of a life-time in the valour and the advance of the Labour Movement seemed to be shattered. Bitter anger was felt throughout the trade union movement and in all parts of the country. They wanted to do something to help the miners. But their desires could find no practical outlet. Then a mood of discouragement became plainly observable following abortive attempts to retrieve a position that had been given away.

The miners took it in a stoic mood.

They had had the experience of the previous autumn; on the top of that they had had in the past few days more than one indication of how their allies were likely to behave; lastly, they had spent the later part of the morning with J. H. Thomas and anxious and nervous men. So the Executive Committee minute with grim brevity recorded the news as follows:

The following decision, arrived at by the other two sections of the Triple Industrial Alliance, was received by telephonic communication from the National Union of Railwaymen, and later confirmed in writing, as follows:

Copy of communication received from Unity House on Friday, April 15, 1921:

Dear Mr. Hodges,

The Sub-Committee which waited upon the Miners' Federation Executive this afternoon reported the result of their interview to the Executive of the National Union of Railwaymen, the Associated Society of Locomotive Engineers and Firemen, and the Transport Workers' Federation. After serious consideration of the whole position, they passed the following resolution:

"This joint meeting of the N.U.R., the A.S.L.E. & F. and T.W.F., having very carefully considered the latest situation in connection with the miners' dispute, decides to call off the strike."

Yours faithfully,
C. T. Cramp.

The Committee agreed to return to districts and report fully to the men upon the situation as at present existing.

A week elapsed. Amongst the miners, now left alone to face the struggle, there had been little recrimination. But when their former allies began to justify themselves, the Executive Committee decided on Thursday, April 21st, to put forward to the National Delegate Conference of the following day this resolution:

That this Conference, having fully considered the circumstances surrounding the failure of the other two sections of the Triple Alliance to put into operation their decision to strike in our support on Friday last, and a full report having been given of what transpired at the meeting of Members of Parliament addressed by Mr. Hodges at the House of Commons, the delegates emphatically protest against the official explanation of the other two sections attributing their defection to the refusal of the Miners' Executive to meet the coal-owners again at the invitation of the Prime Minister.

Over and over again, before and after the Triple Alliance had arrived at their decision to strike, it had been quite clear that it was impossible for the Miners' Executive to accept a settlement except on the terms of the concession of the National Wages Board and Pool. The real cause for the sudden unexpected and unjustifiable withdrawal of the other two sections of the Alliance must be looked for in the character and structure of the Triple Alliance itself.

At the Conference the following day, the first business was for the Districts to report on how the position stood. Each District spokesman stood up and reported no change: everyone was for a National Wages Board and a National Pool. Then the Chairman called on the Secretary to give a report on behalf of the Executive Committee. Frank Hodges began by first making a report "more or less of a personal character, because of the peculiar circumstances associated with my name" and in the course of it gave his recollection of what replies he had given in the now notorious meeting eight days earlier. He began by saying he had no bitterness of feeling, no rancour

although many unpleasant things have been said about me in one section of the coal-field—I believe the only section—even towards the men who have felt disposed to unduly criticise, I want to assure them I feel exactly towards them as I feel towards the rest. The greatest man that ever lived, who carried the Cross up the hill to Calvary, He never murmured; He was crucified without a murmur; and while I am a very insignificant individual as compared with Him, I think when the destinies of a million men, with their four million dependants, are at stake, you cannot afford to sit by the wayside and argue with your traducers. You must continue to carry your burden, if you feel in doing so you are doing right.

He then told about the meetings at the House of Commons and referred to the belief that the demand for the National Pool was political in character. Then he dealt with his speech to the private meeting of Members of Parliament and with his answers to questions, of which he regarded the following as the most significant:

Then came what I regard as the effective questions of the evening, questions which probably were designed by some of the questioners, who put them to put us in an embarrassing situation. Thank God I had the wit to see that there were such possibilities, that there were questioners who desired to put questions in a manner as would put us in an embarrassing situation. There were people who, I have no doubt, had held the view that they were going to get the miners to say, we will not consider wages under any circumstances, and it would then be apparent and clear at once all we were out for was a political manœuvre to get a form of bastard nationalisation through the medium of the pool.

The first question asked was on this point—Are you prepared to consider a temporary settlement of the wages question, leaving the question of the National Board and Pool to be later determined? My reply was—There was no such proposition had ever been put forward by the owners or the Government. The only settlement suggested to us during the whole of the discussions being one of a permanent settlement on a district basis.

I was then asked—Suppose such a proposition was made, what attitude would we take? My answer was, that the Executive were prepared, were always prepared, to hear and consider any proposal as to wages, but it must be clearly understood that any such consideration was not dependent on giving up the fundamental principles for which we stood.

I was then asked—Suppose an offer was made to effect a temporary settlement on the basis that wages shall not fall below the cost of living, what would be our attitude? I replied, any such offer coming from an authoritative source would receive very serious consideration at our hands, and I repeated that we had only had one proposal from the Government, that is, a permanent settlement on a district basis; they refused any temporary national settlement.

I answered the question the more eagerly because these inspirations come to you sometimes at critical moments, because I knew, as you must know, that any temporary settlement of a national character which brings wages down to the level of the cost of living implies a continuance of the control, it implies financial control of the industry by the Government during the temporary period, because you cannot have a uniform reduction at one time where you have such a tremendous variation in the case of districts without the Government assuming or re-assuming control.

Later in his speech Hodges said that he felt on the morning of Friday, April 15th, that the Executive had made a mistake in not going to meet the Prime Minister. This brought up Tom Richards, M.P., of South Wales, who said, "Suppose, however, we accept what the Secretary has said, that he is right: then the Committee is wrong. That is a situation which must be cleared up in this room." When a vote of confidence in the Secretary was moved, some thought it might reflect on the Committee. A. J. Cook of South Wales said:

So far as I am concerned, there is something more to me than Mr. Hodges or myself and that is the unity of this Federation. I want to put this. That Mr. Hodges, as Secretary of this Federation, is not going to defy majority rule of this Federation. I don't care whether it is him or Jesus Christ, he is not going to do it. We don't want any Jimmy Thomases in our Federation. I went back as an honourable man together with the rest of the South Wales representatives, as honourable men, and acted accordingly. I defended Mr. Hodges and asked that the whole thing should be left where it was. Mr. Hodges went into the Press and Mr. Hodges still says he is right in the Press, and he still says he is right and the majority of the Executive is wrong. He says, had we thought the matter out as he did, perhaps we should have arrived at a different conclusion. I say I think it would have been an impossibility, we should never have arrived at a different conclusion.

JOHN WADSWORTH, M.P. (1850–1921)
Secretary Yorkshire Miners' Association

SAMUEL ROEBUCK (1871–1924)
Secretary Yorkshire Miners' Association

FRANK HALL, J.P. (1860–1927)
Secretary, Derbyshire Miners' Association

HENRY HICKEN
Secretary Derbyshire Miners' Association 1927–42

The Chairman then intervened to cast oil upon the troubled waters and put to the Conference the following double-barrelled vote of confidence:

That this Conference expresses its complete confidence in the Secretary and the Executive for the way we have and are conducting the miners' case,

which was carried unanimously, as was the Executive resolution (given above) on the Triple Alliance partners.

8. THE GOVERNMENT'S TERMS OF THE END OF APRIL

Following "Black Friday," a day never to be forgotten by the miner or by the whole working class, it was clear that a contest of endurance lay ahead. The miners had nailed their colours to the mast—National Wages Board and National Pool. The coal-owners insisted on District settlements. The Government backed the coal-owners in this: and in addition gave them the powerful backing of the Emergency Powers Act, under which the Royal Proclamation of Emergency was reissued each month. Many arrests were made, both of strikers and of workers taking sympathetic action. Speakers were arrested: and the struggle had to be conducted under such conditions of governmental repression as had scarcely been known since well-nigh a century earlier.

Successive sets of negotiations, with intervals between, marked the varying endeavours of the parties to end the dispute. The first of these, after the collapse of "Black Friday," was in the last week of April. The Conference which met on Friday, April 22nd to hear Frank Hodges' statement had to adjourn to await the result of a Conference that same afternoon with the mine-owners and the Government. The negotiations were spun out because the mine-owners were unable at first to table precise figures: and so the Miners' Delegate Conference, receiving from time to time reports on progress, remained in session day after day from April 22nd to 28th. On that day Sir Robert Horne, for the Government, made his previous suggestion of a possible subsidy (which on March 30th he had ruled out as "absolutely impossible") into a definite offer in the following terms:

The Miners   X

The Government is prepared to come to the assistance of the mining industry at the present time with a grant of £10,000,000. We propose that in the month of May no greater reduction should take place in the wage of the miner in any district than 3s. a shift, and in the month of June no greater reduction should take place than 3s. 6d. a shift. The remainder of the sum of £10,000,000 to which I have referred should thereafter be divided between the months of July and August, two-thirds in the month of July and one-third in the month of August. The money supplied by the Government will in each of those months go to increase the wages in the districts which require it, where the district wage is not sufficient to meet the point of reduction.

Then, after telling the miners' representatives it was in their option to choose whether the reductions would be uniform, he made it clear that it was given on the basis not of a temporary but a durable settlement as from the end of August; which settlement would last for at least twelve months and thereafter be terminable upon three months' notice. It would go on, that is, until November 30, 1922. He referred to the National Pool of profits and once more turned it down, saying:

Now we regard that issue as really a political issue, upon which, as a Government, we had to make up our minds. It would, in the circumstances, have involved legislation, because it was apparent that no voluntary agreement could be arrived at. We are not prepared to introduce legislation for this purpose. Even if we believed that such a scheme could be successful and permanently useful to the industry—which we do not believe—we do not think it would be possible to carry it into effect at the present time, and under present conditions.

The door thus locked, Sir Robert barred and bolted it by saying that under these circumstances there must be "systems of district settlements." When these terms were submitted to the National Delegate Conference in the afternoon, they were rejected by a vote of all Districts, unanimous except for Northumberland. By 890,000 to 42,000 the delegate card vote carried the resolution:

That this Conference rejects the Government's proposals, as they do not concede the fundamental principles for which we stand; accordingly, the Conference terminates, and delegates report to the men in their own districts. (April 28, 1921.)

Then the delegates went back to the coal-fields, where they found the miners and their wives, despite all the set-back they had experienced, undismayed and resolute to carry on the struggle.

9. GOVERNMENT'S OFFER AT THE END OF MAY

In the last week of May the Prime Minister invited the M.F.G.B. Executive to confer "with the mine-owners and the Government" at the Conference Room, Board of Trade, on Friday, May 27th. The Executive Committee accepted. There were present: The Prime Minister, Sir Robert Horne (Chancellor of the Exchequer), Mr. Stanley Baldwin (President of the Board of Trade), Mr. W. Clive Bridgeman (Secretary for Mines), Mr. E. A. Gowers (Permanent Under-Secretary, Mines Department), Mr. W. Brace (Chief Labour Adviser, Mines Department), Sir David Shackleton (Ministry of Labour), the Central Committee of the Mining Association of Great Britain, and the Executive Committee of the Miners' Federation of Great Britain.

The Government's "new offer" could be described as "*Verballhornung*," [1] since it scarcely differed from that of April except in adding the suggestion that if coal-owners and miners could not agree on a durable scheme there should be arbitration to settle it. Herbert Smith used the occasion, not to comment on the new offer, but to raise a complaint about proceedings under the Emergency Powers Act and unnecessary police interference in the Districts. The Executive Committee took the proposals and resolved:

That the latest Government proposals as submitted to them on the 27th inst. be sent out to districts, who be asked to report their views thereon in writing to the Secretary by Friday, the 3rd June, and the Executive Committee meet again on that date to receive and consider the replies of districts. (May 28, 1921.)

These proposals were for a temporary arrangement leading up to a permanent scheme. During the temporary arrange-

[1] The story goes that a certain Herr Ballhorn of Munich once brought out a book with a crowing cock on the title page. A few years later on he advertised widely the publication of a "new and improved edition." Careful scrutiny showed no change whatever from the first edition except that wattles had been added to the cock; and ever since then this sort of thing has been called "*Verballhornung*."

ment there would be a step by step cutting of wages "until they reach the economic level which the industry is capable of sustaining."

By June 3rd the reports had come back, showing that the proposals had been rejected by every District. The Prime Minister, informed of this, wrote a letter on Saturday, June 4th, as follows:

Dear Mr. Hodges,

I have received your letter and greatly regret to learn the decision at which your Executive have arrived.

The Government have nothing further to propose. I feel bound, however, to make it clear to you that the grant of ten millions which the Government are prepared to make to ease the difficulties of the men in the districts most hardly hit by the great fall in coal prices cannot be regarded as available indefinitely. We made this offer with considerable misgiving, having regard to the very serious burdens which are being sustained at the present time by all the other industries and citizens who make up the taxpayers of the country. Every week during which the strike has lasted has depleted the resources of the nation, and has lessened its capacity to afford this assistance to a particular industry.

We have, therefore, come to the conclusion that we cannot prolong the offer for more than another fortnight—which should give you sufficient time to take a ballot of your members on the Government suggestions; if you should think that course advisable— or to reach a settlement in some other way.

Yours faithfully, D. LLOYD GEORGE.

Behind this endeavour on the part of the Government to bring pressure to bear on the miners there was apparently a belief that the men and women in the coal-fields had by this time been so reduced by their privations that a direct ballot vote would show signs of yielding. Those who held this belief were presently to be undeceived.

10. OWNERS' OFFER GOES TO BALLOT VOTE

On the Monday after the Lloyd George letter on withdrawing the offer of a subsidy, which by his usual practice had been given to be published by the Sunday papers, the Miners' Executive got the following letter from Evan Williams:

Pall Mall, S.W.1,
June 5th, 1921.

Dear Mr. Hodges,

The letter of the Prime Minister to you, which is published in this morning's papers, by putting a time limit upon the Government's proposal of a grant, introduces a factor into the situation which, in my opinion, the coal-owners cannot ignore.

The offer of the Government to provide a sum of £10,000,000 as a subvention to wages, to tide over a difficult period, while it does not financially affect the coal-owners in any way, is to the workers in the industry of immense value, which we are most desirous they should not lose; and I feel that if any elucidation of the position can be brought about by a conference between your Executive and our Central Committee, we, on our side, should not allow any formal considerations to stand in the way of our taking a step which may perhaps be easier for us than for you.

I have therefore called a meeting of the Central Committee of the Mining Association for 10.30 tomorrow (Monday) morning, at which I shall propose that an invitation be sent to your Executive Committee to meet us to talk the matter over.

I remain, yours sincerely, EVAN WILLIAMS.

The Executive accepted the invitation. That day and the following days they spent with the Central Committee of the Mining Association. On Tuesday the 7th, they resolved to call for three days later a National Delegate Conference which they would recommend to decide on a ballot vote of the men upon the owners' proposals. These proposals they scrutinised; they drew up a series of written questions to which by the Friday they had received written answers. The Conference, meeting on Friday, June 10th, accepted the Executive Committee's recommendation.

The ballot paper was as follows:

MINERS' FEDERATION OF GREAT BRITAIN
BALLOT PAPER

Are you in favour of fighting on for the principles of the National Wages Board and National Pool, with loss of Government subsidy of ten million pounds for wages if no settlement by June 18th, 1921? ....

Are you in favour of accepting the Government and owners' terms as set forth on the back of this ballot paper? ....

Please place your "X" in the space provided for the purpose.
June 10th, 1921.   FRANK HODGES, General Secretary.

BACK OF BALLOT PAPER

NOTE.—The Government and owners having definitely rejected the principles of the National Wages Board and the National Pool now offer the terms fully set out below. You are now asked to say whether you will continue the fight for the National Wages Board and the National Pool, or accept the terms offered by the Government and owners. The Government offer of ten million pounds grant in aid of wages referred to below is to be withdrawn on June 18th unless an agreement is arrived at by that date.

TEMPORARY PERIOD

Government offers ten million pounds to prevent large reductions in wages where reductions are necessary.

First reductions not to exceed 2s. per shift for all workers of 16 years and upwards, and 1s. per shift for workers below 16 years.

No further reductions until August 1st.

Further reduction after August 1st to be agreed mutually until Government grant is exhausted.

The temporary agreement will come to an end as soon as Government grant is used up.

PERMANENT SCHEME
Owners' Proposals

National Board to fix principles for guidance of districts. Board to be comprised of equal number of representatives of both sides with independent chairman.

The parties have already agreed the principle that profits shall only be a fixed percentage of wages paid.

The Board to fix the amount of the percentage of profits to wages.

The Board to fix the amount of the new standard wage.

In this connection the owners have offered as a standard wage the total wages paid in July, 1914, plus district additions to standards, plus the percentage for piece-workers caused by the reduction of hours from 8 to 7, and a minimum percentage of 20 per cent added thereto. This minimum percentage to continue until June 30th, 1922.

The Board will also fix the items of cost, which must be taken into account by the district auditors when ascertaining the district revenue.

Wages during permanent scheme to be based upon the capacity of each district to pay.

In the event of a low paid day-worker receiving a wage which does not provide him with a subsistence wage, the District Board will fix a wage which will secure it for that workman.

The decision of the National Board as to the permanent scheme to be binding upon both parties for a period of twelve months and thereafter subject to three months' notice on either side.

When the Conference of June 10th had agreed by a majority to take a ballot vote, and also by a majority, 105 to 46, to accept the Executive's view that no recommendation at all be made, the minority had wanted a recommendation to the men to reject the terms. No such recommendation was needed. The Government and owners' terms were rejected by an overwhelming majority[1] of 434,614 to 180,724. This was after ten weeks of the lock-out when for many a day the miners' wives and families had not had enough to eat, and were able to keep going in many cases only by the soup from the communal kitchens set up by the Lodge Committees.

11. LAST DAYS OF THE STRUGGLE

On Friday and Saturday (June 17th–18th), after the announcement that the miners had rejected the terms, a serious

[1] RESULT OF BALLOT

(June 17, 1921)

District	Total	Votes Recorded for Continuing Fight for Principle	For Government and Owners' Terms	Majorities	
				For Fight for Principle	For Government and Owners' Terms
Bristol	1,562	1,338	224	1,114	—
Cokemen	5,005	1,593	3,412	—	1,819
Cumberland	6,716	5,168	1,548	3,620	—
Derbyshire	20,998	10,050	9,948	1,102	—
Durham	90,735	69,991	20,744	49,247	—
Enginemen	14,287	3,876	10,411	—	6,535
Forest of Dean	5,881	5,222	659	4,563	—
Kent	1,480	1,208	272	936	—
Lancashire	71,501	64,084	7,417	56,667	—
Leicestershire	4,589	2,537	2,052	485	—
Midlands	35,896	20,030	15,866	4,164	—
Northumberland	27,453	14,695	12,758	1,937	—
North Wales	9,556	6,474	3,082	3,382	—
Nottinghamshire	15,069	8,099	6,970	1,129	—
Somerset	4,583	3,843	740	3,103	—
South Derbyshire	3,444	1,832	1,612	220	—
South Wales	151,525	110,616	40,909	69,707	—
Yorkshire	80,873	52,829	28,004	24,785	—
Scotland	65,185	51,129	14,056	37,073	—
TOTALS	616,338	434,614	180,724	263,244	8,354
Majority for continuing fight for principle		254,890		254,890	

Footnote continued overleaf

problem confronted the Executive Committee, which comprised in its two dozen members many varieties of age and experience from all over the coal-fields. There were, for example, old Whitefield of Bristol, who had first been a member over a quarter of a century earlier, and Sam Finney, M.P., of the Midlands with nearly as long an experience in the coal-fields and in the Federation. Sitting side by side were younger men in their thirties, Noah Ablett and Arthur Cook. Before them was laid a letter from the Prime Minister:

10 Downing Street, Whitehall, S.W.1.
18th June, 1921.

Dear Mr. Hodges,

I very much regret to receive the information conveyed to me by your letter of last night.

It is a very grave step for the Miners' Federation to continue a stoppage which is bringing untold loss upon the country.

I previously indicated to you that the longer the stoppage continues the greater is the loss to the resources of the Exchequer, and consequently the less able are we to give assistance to tide the mining industry over its present troubles. We were, therefore, compelled to announce a fortnight ago that our offer of ten millions would terminate this week-end.

Footnote continued from previous page

	Percentage of Votes		Membership	
	For Continuing Fight for Principle	For Government and Owners' Terms	Total	Votes Recorded. Per cent of Total
Bristol	85·66	14·34	2,200	71·00
Cokemen	31·83	68·17	9,800	51·07
Cumberland ..	76·95	23·05	13,500	49·75
Derbyshire ..	52·63	47·37	49,000	42·85
Durham	77·14	22·86	126,240	71·87
Enginemen ..	27·13	72·87	20,200	70·70
Forest of Dean ..	88·79	11·22	6,000	98·02
Kent	81·62	18·38	2,000	74·00
Lancashire ..	89·63	10·37	90,000	79·45
Leicestershire ..	55·28	44·72	7,900	58·09
Midlands	56·33	43·67	64,000	56·08
Northumberland ..	53·53	46·47	41,500	66·15
North Wales ..	67·75	32·25	16,300	58·62
Nottinghamshire ..	53·74	46·26	35,000	43·05
Somerset	16·15	83·85	5,620	81·54
South Derbyshire..	53·19	46·81	6,400	53·81
South Wales ..	73·00	27·00	200,000	75·76
Yorkshire	65·32	34·68	142,500	56·76
Scotland	78·44	21·56	110,000	59·17
TOTALS	70·67	29·83	957,610	64·36

The difficulties of the financial position can only be emphasised if the result of the ballot now communicated to me is to receive effect. Under these circumstances the Government have no option but to make final their decision that their offer of assistance cannot remain open after tomorrow night.

Yours faithfully, D. LLOYD GEORGE.

The Executive Committee decided "that the letter be received": and went on to think out what new steps they could take. Notice of motion for the next Executive meeting was given "That the Executive Committee decide to withdraw the safety men." Were there any possible allies? Other unions were being threatened with demands for wage reductions. So they resolved:

That we ask various Executive Committees of unions affected by wage disputes to meet the Executive Committee of the Federation with the object in view of taking national action with the miners to secure their mutual demands.

It turned out to be a vain hope. None of the unions affected were prepared at that moment to take action.

Therefore, the Executive Committee, after a further week had gone by, had once more to face the situation that confronted the miners, but with the knowledge that no succour would come from outside. Eventually, says the minute, "After a long and protracted discussion on the position in districts and the whole of circumstances in connection with the stoppage," the Committee resolved:

That we ask the Government and the owners for a meeting with a view to negotiating a satisfactory wages agreement, which we can recommend our members to accept.

They had been driven to sue for peace: and, when they were about to enter the meeting with their opponents on Monday, June 27th, they resolved that:

(a) We attend the Conference with the owners and Government as suggested.
(b) The Government be informed that, providing satisfactory terms are agreed on wages, we recommend our members to accept.

At the Board of Trade offices, after long consideration of the proposals and arguments submitted by the owners, the Committee passed the following resolution:

That we accept the owners' proposition of the profits ratio to wages, providing the owners agree that the 20 per cent to be added to the standard wage shall be continued to the end of the proposed agreement.

Finally, back at Russell Square, the Committee passed the following resolution :

That, in the event of the ten million pounds being granted by the Government, districts be consulted on the terms, which the Executive Committee recommend be accepted; returns to be at Central Office, Russell Square, by Friday, 1st July, 1921.

TO THE MEMBERS OF THE MINERS' FEDERATION

Your Executive Committee have today provisionally agreed to terms of a wages settlement with the Government and the owners. These terms are brought to your notice herewith with the object of getting them ratified, so that a general resumption of work may take place on Monday next. The important and responsible step of taking power as a Committee to negotiate a wages settlement, even after the last ballot vote, was the result of our certain knowledge that the National Wages Board, with the National Profits Pool, could not be secured by a continuation of this struggle. Every economic and political factor is dead against us. In order that no more suffering should be endured by a continuation of this struggle, we took upon ourselves the freedom to negotiate a wages settlement. This wages settlement which is now before you represents the maximum which can be secured in the present circumstances. It is an improvement upon the wage terms which were submitted by the owners, and upon which you voted in the last ballot. The Government grant has been restored; the maximum wage reductions in districts where reductions must take place are now known up to the 1st October. A minimum of 20 per cent will be added to the new standard wage, which will operate during the lifetime of the agreement, and not end on the 30th June, 1922, as originally proposed by the owners. This principle is of the greatest possible value in the mining industry. The remaining principles which are to govern wages and profits during the lifetime of the agreement have also been established. These mark an entirely new departure in the mining industry, and it is our sure belief that when anything like normal trade returns these principles will provide a more just method of fixing profits than we have ever had before in the industry.

Up to now the unity of the men has been magnificent: whole districts which had nothing to gain in the form of wages have stood loyally by the other districts whose wage reductions would have been of the most drastic character. This loyalty and unity will have been maintained to the end of the dispute, despite the great odds against us, if a general resumption of work takes place on Monday next.

We, therefore, strongly urge you, with the knowledge of the seriousness of the situation, to accept this agreement, which we have provisionally agreed to today, and authorise your Committee to sign the terms by Friday next.

Yours, on behalf of the Executive Committee,

HERBERT SMITH, Acting President.

JAMES ROBSON, Treasurer.

FRANK HODGES, Secretary.

June 28th, 1921.

Four days later the reports came back from the Districts. Lancashire and the four smallest Districts (Bristol, Forest of Dean, Somerset and Kent) were opposed, totalling, all told, 105,820. All the other Districts (except Cumberland which reached no decision) were for acceptance to a total of 832,840. The Committee thereupon, on Friday, July 1, 1921, authorised the following:

Overwhelming vote in favour of resumption of work. Workmen to return without delay.

SMITH, Acting President.

HODGES, Secretary.

The lock-out was ended.

The miners were defeated. They had come through great tribulation and the end of it was not in sight. But they were not dismayed, for they had in them the knowledge that they would live to fight another day.

Appendix A

WAGES OF COAL-HEWERS*

PERCENTAGE CHANGES† FROM 1910

At End of Year	Percentage Above Basis Wage-Rates of 1888		Percentage Above Basis Wage-Rates of 1879		
	Federated Area	Scotland	Northumberland	Durham	South Wales
1910	50	50	31¾	43¾	51¼
1911	50	50	27½	38¾	50
1912	55	68¾	• 38¾	46¼	57½
1913	65	87½	52½	60	60
1914	65	75	50	53¾	60
1915	98	118¾	83	75	88¾
1916	110½	150	131	107½	133¾
1917	118½	150	• 120	107½	133¾

* For earlier years see *The Miners*, p. 303.   † *Ministry of Labour Gazette.*

Flat Rate Changes[1]
(applied nationally from the dates given below)

1917 *17th September*: 1s. 6d. per day to all colliery workers of 16 years of age and over, and 9d. per day to those under 16 years. To be paid for every day on which a worker works, and for every day on which a worker is ready and able to work, but is prevented owing to the work of the pit, seam or place being stopped by causes other than strikes, excluding recognised holidays, Sundays, stop-days, etc., but including days on which the work of the pit, seam or place is temporarily stopped through lack of trade (first "War wage").

1918 *1st July*: The same (second "War wage").

1919 *9th January*: 2s. per shift worked, or per day worked. 1s. in the case of workers under 16 years of age (Sankey wage).

1920 *12th March*: 20 per cent increase on gross wages, excluding War wage and Sankey wage, subject to a minimum increase of 2s. per day for adults, 1s. per day for persons of 16 years and under 18 years of age, and 9d. per day for those under 16 years of age.

4th November: 2s. per day for workers over 18 years of age, 1s. for those of 16 years and under 18 years of age, and 9d. for workers under 16 years of age together with Bonus on Output resulting in:

[1] *Colliery Year Book*, 1926.

1921 *3rd January*: An addition of 1s. 6d. per day for adults, 9d. per day for youths and 6¾d. per day for boys.

1st February: A reduction of 2s. per day for adults, 1s. per day for youths and 9d. per day for boys.

1st March: A reduction of 1s. 6d. per day for adults, 9d. per day for youths, and 6¾d. per day for boys.

NOTE.—The War bonus granted in May 1915, was reckoned on Basis wage-rates in some Districts, and as a percentage upon current wage-rates in others. In all Districts the bonus has been calculated above on the Basis wage-rates. In 1917 the bonus was increased and has been dealt with similarly. In the Cumberland, South Wales and Monmouthshire, Somerset and the Federated Districts, the earlier Basis wage-rates have been revised at various dates since 1911. The percentage changes shown in *italics* above represent the corresponding changes based upon the earlier Basis wage-rates. The actual changes upon the revised Basis wage-rates are shown below:

| Year | Percentage above Basis Wage-Rates at the end of each Year in | | | |
	Cumberland (1915 Basis Wage-Rate)	South Wales and Monmouthshire (1915 Basis Wage-Rate)	Federated Districts (1911 Basis Wage-Rate)	Somerset (1917 Basis Wage-Rate)
	Per cent	Per cent	Per cent	Per cent
1915	32	25¾	32	—
1916	40½	55¾	40½	—
1917	45½	55¾	45½	33⅓

Appendix B

THE COAL-MINING INDUSTRY DISPUTE
1921

TERMS OF SETTLEMENT

1. A National Board shall be constituted forthwith, consisting in equal numbers of persons chosen by the Mining Association of Great Britain and persons chosen by the Miners' Federation of Great Britain.

There shall also be established District Boards, consisting in equal numbers of persons representing owners and workmen in each district.

The National and District Boards shall draw up their own rules of procedure, which shall include a provision for the appointment of an Independent Chairman for each Board.

2. The wages payable in each district shall be expressed in the form of a percentage upon the basis rates prevailing in the district,

and shall be periodically adjusted in accordance with the proceeds of the industry as ascertained in such district.

3. The amount of the percentage to be paid in each district during any period shall be determined by the proceeds of the industry in that district during a previous period, as ascertained by returns to be made by the owners, checked by joint test audit of the owners' books carried out by independent accountants appointed by each side.

4. The sum to be applied in each district to the payment of wages above the standard wages as hereinafter defined shall be a sum equal to 83 per cent of the surplus of such proceeds remaining after deduction therefrom of the amounts of the following items during the period of ascertainment:

(a) the cost of the standard wages;

(b) the costs of production other than wages;

(c) standard profits equivalent to 17 per cent of the cost of the standard wages;

and the share of the surplus applicable to wages shall be expressed as a percentage upon the basis rates prevailing in the district.

Provided that if in any period the ascertained proceeds, after deduction of costs other than wages and the cost of the standard wages, prove to have been insufficient to meet the standard profits, the deficiency shall be carried forward as a first charge to be met out of any surplus, ascertained as above, in subsequent periods.

5. If the rates of wages thus determined in any district do not provide a subsistence wage to low paid day-wage workers, such additions in the form of allowances per shift worked shall be made for that period to the daily wages of these workers as, in the opinion of the District Board, or in the event of failure to agree by the parties, in the opinion of the Independent Chairman, may be necessary for the purpose. Such allowances shall be treated as items of cost in the district ascertainments.

6. For the purpose of these periodical adjustments the units shall be the districts set out in the Schedule hereto, and shall only be varied by the decision of the District Board or Boards concerned, provided that no variation shall take place prior to 1st February, 1922, in the grouping of any district unless it is mutually agreed by the representatives of both sides in the district or districts concerned.

7. The standard wages shall be the district basis rates existing on the 21st March, 1921, plus the district percentages payable in July, 1914 (or the equivalents in any district in which there has been a subsequent merging into new standards), plus in the case of piece-workers, the percentage additions which were made consequent upon the reduction of hours from eight to seven.

8. In no district shall wages be paid at lower rates than standard wages plus 20 per cent thereof.

9. The National Board shall forthwith consider what items of

cost are to be included for the purpose of paragraph 4 (*b*) above, and in the event of agreement not being arrived at by the 31st July, the matter shall be referred to the Independent Chairman for decision.

10. The wages payable by the owners up to the 31st August inclusive shall be based upon the ascertained results of the month of March, and the wages payable during September shall be based upon the ascertained results of the month of July. The periods of ascertainment thereafter shall be decided by the National Board.

11. During the "temporary period," as hereinafter defined, the following special arrangements shall apply in modification of the general scheme set out above:

(*a*) In calculating the proceeds for March the deduction to be made in respect of costs other than wages shall be the average of such costs during January, February, and March.

(*b*) In any district in which reductions in wages continue to be made after the first ascertainment, no part of the surplus proceeds shall be assigned to profits if and in so far as this would have the effect of reducing the wages below the level in the preceding month.

When in any district there is a break in the continuity of reductions in wages upon the periodical ascertainments, at that point and thereafter the general scheme shall apply fully in regard to owners' surplus profits.

(*c*) The proviso to paragraph 4 regarding the carrying forward of deficiencies in standard profits shall not apply, but any net losses shall be so carried forward.

(*d*) The Government will give a grant not exceeding £10,000,000 in subvention of wages.

(*e*) The subvention shall be available for making such increases to the wages otherwise payable in any district as may be necessary to prevent the reductions below the March rates of wages being greater than the following amounts:

During July, 2s. a shift for persons of 16 years of age and upwards, and 1s. a shift for persons under 16.

During August, 2s. 6d. and 1s. 3d. respectively.

During September, 3s. and 1s. 6d. respectively, provided that the balance of the subvention is sufficient for this purpose.

(*f*) If any district in which in any month the proceeds available for wages, calculated in accordance with the terms of this settlement, are sufficient to admit of a rate of wages equal to or higher than the rate payable under the maximum reduction for that month, the wages payable by the owners shall be calculated not in terms of basis plus percentage, but on the same basis as during March, less flat rate reductions uniform throughout the district for persons of 16 years of age and upwards, and persons under 16 years of age respectively.

(g) In any district in which the wages calculated in accordance with the terms of this settlement are less than the wages payable under the maximum reductions aforesaid, the difference shall be met by the owners in that district during September to the extent of the aggregate net profits realised by them on the district ascertainment for July, and during October to the extent of the aggregate net profits realised by them on the district ascertainments for July and August.

(h) The expression "temporary period" means the period from the date of the resumption of work to the 30th September, 1921.

12. The period of duration of this agreement shall be from the date of resumption of work until the 30th September, 1922, and thereafter until terminated by three months' notice on either side.

13. It is agreed as a principle that every man shall be entitled to return to his place when that place is available for him, and that men temporarily occupying places during the stoppage shall give way to men working in those places before the stoppage.

It is agreed that, on the other hand, there shall be no victimisation of men who have been keeping the collieries open, not in the sense that they are to remain at the jobs they filled during the stoppage, but that they shall not be prevented from going back to their own jobs or from working subsequently at the colliery.

For and on behalf of each member of the Central Committee of the Mining Association of Great Britain and for the Mining Association.

EVAN WILLIAMS, President.
THOMAS R. RATCLIFFE-ELLIS, Secretary.

For and on behalf of each member of the Executive Committee of the Miners' Federation of Great Britain and for the Miners' Federation.

HERBERT SMITH, Acting President.
JAMES ROBSON, Treasurer.
FRANK HODGES, Secretary.

For and on behalf of His Majesty's Government.

WILLIAM C. BRIDGEMAN, Secretary for Mines.
E. A. GOWERS, Under-Secretary for Mines.

Mines Department, July 1st, 1921.

SCHEDULE REFERRED TO

Scotland

Northumberland

Durham

South Wales and Monmouth

Yorkshire, Nottinghamshire, Derbyshire, Leicestershire, Cannock Chase and Warwickshire

Lancashire, North Staffordshire and Cheshire

North Wales

South Staffordshire and Salop

Cumberland

Bristol

Forest of Dean

Somerset

Kent

Appendix C

POST-WAR LEGISLATIVE CHANGES

APART from special war-time and post-war enactments affecting the coal industry there were several Acts of Parliament that closely concerned the Miners' Federation, namely:

   (i) Coal Mines Act, 1919;
  (ii) Coal Mines (Emergency) Act, 1920;
 (iii) Mining Industry Act, 1920;
 (iv) Coal Mines (Decontrol) Act, 1921;

Of these the first instituted the nominal seven hours working day from mid-July 1919, as one of the Sankey Commission recommendations accepted by the Government. The second dealt with state control over coal mines (distribution of profits, provisions as to wages, etc.), while the fourth dealt with the ending of it. The third, the Mining Industry Act, had a chequered career. While it was under discussion as a Bill, the M.F.G.B. Annual Conference had resolved that it

> hereby decides to refuse to operate the Bill should it become law, and urges the Labour Party to use every means at its disposal to prevent its passage through the House (July 7, 1920).

The Act was in three parts. The miners' objection was not to Part I, which established a Department of Mines with a Secretary for Mines under the Board of Trade and transferred to it most mining matters from other Ministries: nor was it to Part III, under which a levy of a penny per ton on coal output was to form a Welfare Fund (another of the Sankey recommendations) which would be managed by a Welfare Commission. They objected to Part II, which set up committees (pit and District) and boards (area and national) provided that both coal-owners and workmen elected their representatives to them. The miners, as Smillie mentioned on January 28, 1921, rejected Part II because of the six area boards which they regarded as a division of their ranks at the moment when their aim was to have all wages questions dealt with nationally. From the other side the statement was "we all intend as coal-owners to do our part and work these provisions honourably."

  After the 1921 lock-out the M.F.G.B. notified the Secretary for Mines that they were prepared to operate Part II of the Mining Industry Act; whereupon the coal-owners announced that they, too, had changed their policy and were no longer prepared to operate the Act. This was too much for W. C. Bridgeman, the old Tory aristocrat who was then Secretary for Mines. An acrimonious correspondence between him and Evan Williams (copies subsequently were laid before Parliament)[1] was followed by the publication of

[1] Cmd. 1551 of 1921.

draft statutory rules and orders (1922) under Part II. But then the Prime Minister intervened. Lloyd George, expert in tergiversation, blandly explained in February 1922 that the Government would now let Part II fall to the ground. The Miners' Federation protested, got the Labour Party to vote against this in the House of Commons, and finally thanked Lord Haldane for his attempt in the House of Lords in March 1922 to get the Government's decision reversed. The coal-owners, satisfied with the settlement of July 1921, wanted to put an end to governmental "interference" as well as to the fragment of "Sankey" embedded in Part II of the Mining Industry Act.

CHAPTER XI

THE REVIVAL OF 1924–25

I. THE BACKGROUND

THE effect of the National Wages Agreement of July 1921 was that coal-mining, from being for a short time one of the best-paid trades, fell to being one of the worst paid. After the autumn of 1921 the decline set in. "The decline has been swift and well-nigh universal," stated the M.F.G.B. Executive Committee in the spring of 1923, for by July 1922 "nine districts out of thirteen scheduled to the Agreement had fallen down to the minimum." The average wage per shift worked had gone down to less than half what it was in the winter months of 1920–21. In June 1914 it had been nearly 6s. 6d.; in November–December 1922, with subsistence allowance added, it stood just over 9s. 6d. That is, while the cost of living stood at 80 per cent over the 1914 level, wages stood at 47 per cent. The miners were now much worse off than they had been before the war. There was unemployment, too, though less than in most insured trades: and there was victimisation. The further effect of all this was a drop in trade union membership, ranging in the larger Districts from a fall of 41 per cent in two years in South Wales to a fall of 2 per cent in Yorkshire. The M.F.G.B. total fell by 22 per cent from 957,610 in March 1921 to 744,464 in March 1923.

The situation was very hard for the miners and their delegates. The M.F.G.B. Conferences and Executive Committee were in an intolerable situation, for the great majority felt they were not in a position to give notice to end the agreement. So they tried one thing after another from the summer of 1922 onwards, but always their spokesman might say:

Came out by the same door as in I went.

They tried the owners: no result. They tried the Prime

Minister: no result.[1] They tried parliamentary activity, urging that the Minimum Wage Act of 1912 be brought up to date: no result. After many weary months they went back to the owners, who so far from agreeing to a wages increase, told them (on April 26, 1923) that the only way to secure a higher wage was to go back to a longer working day.

The winters of 1921 and 1922 were indeed bleak with hardship and poverty common throughout the coal-fields. The year 1923, which found most industries in a condition of depression following on the 1921 slump, actually found a short-lived boom in coal exports. It almost appeared as though once again the road to prosperity was open. But conditions were never again to repeat the simple rhythms of nineteenth-century capitalism. Then the miners did not need to look far beyond the ups and downs of the coal trade. Now there was rapid change and transformation in the whole background, not only of trade but of politics—and not only in the United Kingdom but in world economics and politics. In this new epoch the miners were to learn how closely their own livelihood was bound up with international affairs. From 1919 onwards the aloofness of the United States, the hostility towards the U.S.S.R. and Franco-British quarrelling over Germany wrecked the pathetic hopes that had been lodged in the ill-starred League of Nations. The danger of war remained: and with the first advent of fascism, in Italy in 1922, the danger increased. Where fascism was not lodged, as in Italy and Spain, a melancholy retrogression from democracy afflicted, one after another, several countries in the continent of Europe.

At home the changes were no less sudden and unexpected. In October 1922 the Lloyd George coalition Cabinet broke up and was succeeded by the first purely Conservative Government since 1905. Bonar Law, taking over from Lloyd George, died six months later, being succeeded by Stanley

---

[1] "The Executive Committee proceeded to Downing Street to present the miners' case for an advance in wages to the Prime Minister, and was informed by Mr. Lloyd George, M.P., that he was no longer Prime Minister, having a few minutes previously handed in his resignation to the King, and that the King had accepted his resignation. He therefore could not discuss with the Executive the case they were prepared to submit, because he would only be able to consider it, in any case, as an individual, and not as representing the Government."—E.C. Minute of October 19, 1922. A subsequent interview with Bonar Law on December 2nd got from him an admission that the miners' conditions were "horribly bad" but no other result.

Baldwin, a former iron-master. In his book on *The Truth about Reparations and War Debts*, ten years later, Lloyd George was to characterise Baldwin in scarcely flattering terms. Describing how Baldwin had gone to negotiate in the United States about the British debt, together with the Governor of the Bank of England ("a dangerous counsellor for a man of Mr. Baldwin's equipment"), Lloyd George comments on the two leading negotiators, British and American:

Mr. Mellon was keen, experienced, hard, ruthless; Mr. Baldwin casual, soft, easy-going, and at that time quite raw. Mr. Baldwin admits that since then he has learnt a great deal. At that time he merited his constant boast that he was only a "simple countryman." A business transaction at that date between Mr. Mellon and Mr. Baldwin was in the nature of a negotiation between a weasel and its quarry. The result was a bargain which has brought international debt collection into disrepute.

Only seven months after he had become Prime Minister, Mr. Baldwin proposed a general measure of protectionist customs tariffs and sought support for this by a dissolution of Parliament and a General Election. The Liberal Party, whether Asquithite or Lloyd George Liberals, were united in opposition to this proposal, as was also the Labour Party, now once more led by Ramsay MacDonald. The General Election of December 1923 brought an increase in Labour and Liberal and a decrease in Conservative representation. The figures of parties in Parliament were: Conservative 258; Labour 191; Liberal 158; others 8. The Miners' Members, whose numbers had risen from 28 in the Parliament of 1918–22 to 42 at the General Election of 1922 now rose further to 43.

At the end of January 1924, after an adverse Liberal and Labour vote in the House of Commons, Mr. Baldwin resigned and advised the King to send for Ramsay MacDonald. The first Labour Government took office. Amongst its members were Stephen Walsh, who resigned his post as M.F.G.B. Vice-President to take charge of the War Office, William Adamson, Secretary of State for Scotland, Vernon Hartshorn, Postmaster-General, and six other mining representatives in junior posts. Emanuel Shinwell was Minister for Mines.

The advent of the first Labour Government in Great

Britain astonished or delighted the peoples both at home and abroad. High hopes were raised. But the new Government was to be even more short-lived than its predecessor. After nine months, following an adverse vote in the Commons on the question of the arrest of J. R. Campbell, editor of the Communist *Workers' Weekly*, Ramsay MacDonald handed in his resignation and appealed to the country. In the General Election of 1924 the Red Letter forgery had a big effect in returning a Conservative majority. Mr. Baldwin again took office, with Winston Churchill as Chancellor of the Exchequer: and this Conservative Government lasted till June 1929, when a second Labour Government came and held office for two years. Thereafter a series of coalitions, narrow or broad, were in office for another fourteen years.

Amid these changing political currents and whirlpools the Miners' Federation had to steer their course for a quarter of a century after the end of the first world war.

The effect of the existence of the Labour Government on trade unionism was immediate. The revival already visible gathered strength. The miners had already after the General Election in December 1923 given three months' notice to terminate the wages agreement. They now hoped for bigger things as well. The new hopes were partly symbolised in their choice of a new Secretary. For Mr. Frank Hodges, Secretary since January 1919, had stood successfully as a parliamentary candidate: and as the M.F.G.B. rules laid it down that their Secretary must give his full time and therefore could not sit in Parliament, he could no longer hold the office. Frank Hodges had been outstanding for his cleverness, his accomplishments and his oratorical abilities. He was polished, quick-witted and resourceful. For the first couple of years of his secretaryship he had figured as a spokesman of the more advanced miners, while he had the benefit for some three months of daily close association with veteran leaders and Socialists in the work of the Sankey Commission. But in the winter of 1920–21 he also came into close association with the most sharp-witted of the coal-owners: and with them he found a way of working in considerable harmony after the overwhelming defeat in 1921. He ceased to voice radical views and won golden opinion amongst the coal-masters and other industrialists. In these circumstances, elevated to a high position in the world of labour, Hodges came to be possessed of an overweening view of his own abilities and indeed of his own destiny. He was intensely ambitious. The secretaryship of the largest trade union body in the world he saw as a mere stepping stone to a political career that would end—who knows—in his becoming Prime Minister. His abilities were recognised. Before the election Arthur Henderson, as Secretary of the Labour Party, came personally to ask that the rules of the Federation might be relaxed. The M.F.G.B. Annual Conference, however, refused to alter the rules. Hodges remained convinced that the rules would yet be suspended in his favour. He made up his mind to this and also, according to the testimony of his near acquaintances, that if there was a Labour Government he would be taken straight into the Cabinet. But after the election there were other claimants for Cabinet posts—and he had to be content for the time being with a post as Junior Minister. To his chagrin, the Federation Rules as to the secretaryship were not suspended (in this case, too, there were other claimants for the post), and the M.F.G.B. Conference of December 14, 1923, decided to uphold the rule, which meant there would soon be a new Secretary. If ever there was a case of

> Vaulting ambition, which o'erleaps itself,
> And falls on the other.

it was Frank Hodges: for within nine months he was neither a Minister nor a Member of Parliament, and he was no longer Secretary of the miners.

His successor, A. J. Cook of South Wales, was cast in a different mould; and the choice of him by the miners was eloquent of their sufferings for the past three years. It was a token of spirit undismayed by hardship. It was a choice which meant a renewal of struggle.

2. THE REVISED AGREEMENT

A boom in coal exports throughout 1923, due to the French armed occupation in that year of the German Ruhr coal-field and the cessation of production there, led to a renewed demand for the ending of the 1921 wages agreement. After an unfruitful joint committee of owners and men, a ballot vote taken in December 1923 resulted in acceptance by the very heavy majority of 510,303 to 114,558 of the M.F.G.B. Executive's recommendation to end the agreement. From the detailed figures[1] it can be seen that all Districts, including those which at the moment had an advantage from the agreement, followed the lead of the Executive—even Nottinghamshire, where some of the county officials had advised rejection of the Executive's advice.

Accordingly the Executive on January 17th gave three months' notice to end the agreement. It was not till March 12th that the coal-owners put forward their alternative proposals. The next day these were considered by the M.F.G.B. Conference and then a fortnight later by the adjourned Conference, which recommended their rejection as not good enough. The ballot vote of the men confirmed the Conference view, but with so small a majority as to make strike action unlikely.

[1] RESULT OF BALLOT VOTE ON NATIONAL WAGES AGREEMENT

(December 1923)

District	Total Valid Votes	For Termination	Against Termination	Per Cent For	Per Cent Against	Majorities for Termination
Bristol	1,555	1,295	260	83·28	16·72	1,035
Cumberland	6,465	5,610	855	86·77	13·23	4,755
Durham	95,479	73,210	22,269	76·67	23·33	50,941
Derbyshire	24,493	18,747	5,746	76·54	23·46	13,001
Enginemen	10,403	5,684	4,719	54·64	45·36	965
Forest of Dean	4,055	3,429	626	84·56	15·44	2,803
Kent	1,053	820	233	87·37	22·63	587
Lancashire	59,221	55,875	3,346	94·35	5·65	52,529
Leicestershire	3,714	2,319	1,395	62·44	37·56	924
Midlands	28,058	21,913	6,145	78·09	21·91	15,768
Northumberland	31,643	23,263	8,380	73·51	26·49	14,883
North Wales	7,657	6,773	884	88·45	11·55	5,889
Nottinghamshire	16,451	11,392	5,059	69·25	30·75	6,333
Scotland	82,038	69,590	12,448	84·82	15·18	57,142
Somerset	3,760	2,210	1,550	58·77	41·23	660
South Wales	144,390	129,591	14,799	89·75	10·25	114,792
South Derbyshire	3,517	2,777	740	78·96	21·04	2,037
Yorkshire	100,909	75,805	25,104	75·12	24·88	50,701
Totals	624,861	510,303	114,558	81·66	18·34	395,745

NOTE.—Excludes juveniles and half members. Excludes spoilt papers.

The figures[1] were 322,392 for acceptance and 338,650 against.

On April 11th the M.F.G.B. officials reported both the result of the ballot and the desirability of a wages enquiry to Mr. Emanuel Shinwell, Secretary of the Mines Department. Accordingly, on April 15th the Minister of Labour, under the Industrial Courts Act of 1919, appointed a Court of Enquiry consisting of Lord Buckmaster (a Liberal ex-Lord Chancellor) as Chairman, Roscoe Brunner, J.P. (of the firm Brunner, Mond and Co.) and A. G. Cameron (Secretary of the Amalgamated Society of Woodworkers). The terms of reference were strictly limited:

to enquire into and report upon the question of wages in the coal-mining industry and the matters in issue between the Mining Association of Great Britain and the Miners' Federation of Great Britain relating thereto.

The Court of Enquiry began on April 24th and lasted for five days, much of which time was taken up in explanations to the Court of how mining wages were calculated. In their Report[2] the Court succeeded in giving a fairly clear summary

[1] RESULT OF BALLOT VOTE ON OWNERS' PROPOSALS

(April 1924)

District	For Acceptance	Against Acceptance
Bristol	221	1,406
Cumberland	4,053	3,853
Durham	79,619	24,505
Derbyshire	11,215	16,275
Enginemen	9,299	1,974
Forest of Dean	1,991	2,511
Kent	809	387
Lancashire	16,158	50,448
Leicestershire	2,788	1,610
Midlands	17,005	13,527
Northumberland	26,943	7,169
North Wales	5,655	3,902
Nottinghamshire	7,909	7,506
Scotland	13,022	42,280
Somerset	1,266	2,846
South Wales	58,490	101,613
South Derbyshire	1,626	2,053
Yorkshire	64,323	54,785
Totals	322,392	338,650

[2] Cmd. 2129 of 1924.

of the agreement dated July 1, 1921, which had provided a new principle for the determination of District percentages upon the basis rates in each District. Under this agreement the industry was divided into thirteen new Districts. Many of these corresponded to the Districts covered by the constituents of the M.F.G.B. The chief exception was the new "Eastern Division" comprising Yorkshire, Nottinghamshire, Derbyshire, Leicestershire, Cannock Chase and Warwickshire with an average employment figure in 1923 of 354,600. South Wales and Monmouth came next with 239,600. Then came Durham with 170,000; then Lancashire, North Staffordshire and Cheshire with 139,500; then Scotland with 137,800 and Northumberland with 62,400. The numbers in these six Districts amounted to more than 95 per cent of the total employed. The other seven were mainly the old outlying smaller Districts where conditions had often been harder to maintain, viz. North Wales with 17,800, Cumberland with 11,800 and Salop with 9,600, followed by Forest of Dean, Somerset, Bristol and Kent—the whole seven comprising less than 5 per cent of the total number employed. In each of the thirteen Districts thus constituted the percentage additions to the basis rate were reached on the following principle:

From the total aggregate proceeds of the sale of coal in each district over an agreed period, certain deductions were made, viz. (i) the cost of wages at a certain national level, called "standard wages," representing current basis rates plus the district percentage in force in 1914; (ii) a sum equal to 17 per cent of the sum of "standard wages" called "standard profits"; and (iii) the costs of production exclusive of wages. Of any surplus then remaining 83 per cent was added to "standard wages," and the total was then expressed in terms of basis rates plus a percentage addition.

To illustrate the application of this formula, if the proceeds in any district are taken at £868,000, of which £400,000 are regarded as "standard wages" and £300,000 the other costs of production, there would then fall to be deducted £68,000, representing 17 per cent of the £400,000. This would leave a balance of £100,000, of which £83,000 would be added to the "standard wages" of £400,000, making a total of £483,000 as the "wages fund" for the district. This amount would then be ascertained arithmetically to be a certain percentage of the basis rates, and the figure would be applicable to every pit in the district. This arrangement was subject to the provision that in no district should wages be paid at lower rates than the equivalent of 20 per cent over "standard wages," whilst a further safeguard for the low paid day-wage worker was made by a provision that, if the rates of wages thus determined in any district did not provide a subsistence wage to low paid day-wage workers, additions in the form of allowances per shift worked should be made, the amount of the additions being determined separately for each district. There was also a provision that if the proceeds in any ascertainment period, after deduction of costs other than wages and the costs of "standard wages" were insufficient to meet "standard profits" the deficiency should be carried forward as a first charge against any surplus in a subsequent ascertainment. The owners stated that, for reasons which it is not necessary to explain, this clause had proved ineffective. (Cmd. 2129, §12 and §13.)

The operation of this "profits-sharing" agreement was such that, as shown by figures put forward by the owners themselves to the Court of Enquiry, 14 per cent of the pieceworkers in Lancashire, North Staffs and Cheshire earned less than 40s.: 37 per cent of them between 30s. and 50s. As to the day-wage workers the position was worse. As the Report states:

If 1914 were taken as a measure of the proper wage to be paid in the mining industry, practically every class of day-wage worker is, in terms of real wages, worse off today than he was then. In some cases this deficiency is most marked.

In dealing with the question of miners' wages compared with wages in other industries, the owners made a great point of the fact that mining is an "unsheltered trade," and that, therefore, the miners must expect a low wage, owing to the competition from other countries. In support of this they produced a comparative wages table, which was immediately challenged by A. G. Cameron, and which, on examination, proved to be calculated in such a way that it was not possible to check the figures. In the one case where this checking was possible, the figure was found to be incorrect. The contention that mining was an unsheltered trade could also be challenged, for there was no competition in the home market, which constituted two-thirds of the trade.

The general impression of the sessions of the Court of Enquiry was that the owners' case was utterly weak and untenable. The miners, on the other hand, had furnished the Court with complete and voluminous tables of statistics and other information (much of it prepared by the Labour Research Department), no item of which was challenged; and this information was backed up by their presentation of the Federation case.

The Report of the Enquiry, published on May 8th, gave a survey of the various proposals worded, on the whole, in favour of the miners, and concluded with the recommendation that negotiations should continue with a view to a modification of the terms of the agreement of 1921.

Negotiations were resumed accordingly between the two parties. On May 15th the following main terms of settlement were arranged, to be submitted to a Delegate Conference on May 29th, and possibly to a ballot vote thereafter:

1. Standard profits shall consist of a sum equal to 15 per cent of standard wages instead of 17 per cent as at present.

2. The surplus remaining after the deduction from proceeds of the cost of standard wages, costs other than wages, and standard profits, shall be divided between wages and profits in the proportions of 88 per cent to wages and 12 per cent to profits instead of the present proposal of 83 per cent to wages and 17 per cent to profits.

3. The general minimum percentage on standard wages shall be increased from 20 to $33\frac{1}{3}$.

4. In no district shall the wages of any adult able-bodied day-wage workman fall below a figure 40 per cent above the standard wages (as defined in clause 7 of the wages agreement dated July 1, 1921) of the lowest-paid class of day-wage workmen in the district.

Other clauses provided for more subsistence wages and an increase of one-eighth on those already existing, while owners agreed to deal with anomalies in border-line cases among the lowest paid. An important point was that when standard profits were not reached, only one-third of any available surplus in the next ascertainment should be used to make them up; the remaining two-thirds should be divided between wages and profits, and the deficiency carried forward again.

The M.F.G.B. Conference on May 29th accepted the terms by 473,000 to 311,000, with South Wales, Scotland and Lancashire voting against. Amongst the miners the new agreement was soon generally accepted. Amongst the mine-owners there were sections in the smaller coal-fields who stood out for some time, but these in the end accepted.

3. COOK'S CAMPAIGN

At the M.F.G.B. Annual Conference that summer of 1924 the miners could look back with satisfaction on the new agreement as giving some alleviation of the hard conditions endured for nearly three years past. It was not all they had hoped for. But it was enough to bring them out of the slough of despond and to rally their spirits. To this other circumstances contributed. The year 1924 registered a very noticeable revival of trade union activity. Brisk discussion began in various industrial bodies on the need for greater unity and on the ways and means of achieving it; and was focused in the proceedings of the Hull Trades Union Congress. The urgent need for unity on an international scale was apparent in view of the fact that at this period there were two international trade union organisations. There was the International Federation of Trade Unions (of which the dominant organisations were the Germans, the West Europeans and the British) and the Red International of Labour Unions on which were represented the Soviet trade unions and various others, some European and some Asiatic. A strong demand for international trade union unity was voiced in the address of the Chairman, A. A. Purcell, and in a resolution empowering the General Council to raise the matter within the International Federation of Trade Unions. To this the German, Dutch and other continental trade union leaders raised strongest objections. Meantime, however, seven members of the T.U.C. General Council, including Herbert Smith, went on a T.U.C. delegation to the Soviet Union in November and December 1924. The Report of these delegates, published in a massive illustrated volume by the Trades Union Congress[1] was subjected to an intense scrutiny both at home and abroad. The presence of Herbert Smith alone, nineteen years President of the Yorkshire Miners' Association and now for several years President of the M.F.G.B., made the Report of particular interest to the colliers. The Report and the discussions around it predisposed many British trade unionists to a close friendship with Russian trade unionists and a greater

[1] *Russia: the official report of the British Trades Union Delegation to Russia and Caucasia, November and December 1924.*

interest in Soviet achievements. The upshot was the formation, in the spring of 1925, of an official Anglo-Russian Trade
Union Committee. This was to have consequences affecting
the miners in days ahead.

At home the concern in the trade unions was for unity of
action. At the M.F.G.B. Annual Conference a resolution for
the formation of an industrial alliance had been remitted to
the Executive Committee. Some of them had doubts of the
wisdom of any such step. But all these doubts were soon to
be dispelled as a result of the agitation in the coal-fields
carried on by the new Secretary, A. J. Cook.

Arthur James Cook, whose father was a soldier for twenty-
one years in the 21st Lancashire Fusiliers, was born in
Wookey, Somerset, in 1885. From his elementary school, he
entered the pits in South Wales, where he worked underground for twenty-one years. In his early days a local
preacher, by 1910 he had become one of the group in the
Rhondda Valley responsible for the bitterly fought-out
Cambrian Combine strike. In 1911 he won a two years'
scholarship at the Central Labour College, then maintained
largely by grants from the South Wales Miners' Federation.
He was one of the writers of the famous pamphlet *The
Miners' Next Step* and of another called *One Union for
the Mining Industry*. He became a miners' agent in the
Rhondda District: and was imprisoned in 1918 for his share
in strike activities. He was elected to the M.F.G.B. Executive
Committee in 1918, again in 1921 and finally in January
1924. For the part he played in the 1921 lock-out he had
suffered a further term of imprisonment. With this background, he was the favourite candidate for the M.F.G.B.
secretaryship not only in the South Wales Miners' Federation,
which put him forward, but in many other Districts as well,
especially amongst the younger miners and those who
belonged to the recently-formed Miners' Minority Movement.
Consequently the election of this agitator was regarded as a
triumph of the more advanced elements in the coal-fields.

There were some who comforted themselves with the
reflexion that the cares of this high office would restrain his
exuberance and tame his spirit. But Cook disappointed any
such expectations. He was unlike any other trade union

General Secretary, who has to learn the technique of administration, the minute detail of office work, the habit of cautious speech in negotiations with employers or Government departments. When a highly placed Government official visited Cook on some delicate or intricate problem, he would harangue for a whole hour on the grievances of the miners and simply ignore the particular problem or any matter that was beyond his compass: and the Cabinet emissary would have to retire, baffled.

Cook made several innovations in the conduct of his office, but none was more significant than his practice of week-end agitation amongst the pitmen. His speeches were not so much programmatic as revivalist. He put forward not so much a policy as a recital of grievances. He could tell of the hard lot of the colliers, for he himself had suffered it, and suffered the more because of his protests: and in the telling of it he roused the miners to mend it or end it. He came to be a mirror of the coal-fields, to reflect the mood of the colliers, to voice what had been brooded over underground for a couple of generations. The effect was that soon a greater trust was reposed in him than had ever before been confided in any miners' leader. Audiences greater than ever gathered to listen to Keir Hardie came to hear A. J. Cook. They hung upon his words: and when what they had obscurely felt was so openly spoken, they ceased to trouble over niceties of policy. Throughout the coal-fields the desire to end their hard lot grew strong and was expressed in successive District and national Conferences.

On one question of principle, the necessity of unity within all working-class bodies, Cook hammered untiringly. He had accepted it as a principle in the Miners' Minority Movement, of which he had been an ardent supporter. On this matter of unity, a strength of emotion was roused which provided the drive to overcome all obstacles. By the end of 1924 the M.F.G.B. was officially sounding other unions with a view to the formation of an industrial alliance. Thus for nearly two years onwards from the summer of 1924 there was proceeding a drive for "international trade union unity" while at the same time, on M.F.G.B. initiative, both within and without the framework of the T.U.C. General Council, measures for effective unity of action were being discussed or worked out. The dismissal of the Labour Government in the autumn of 1924 did nothing to damp these two campaigns. On the contrary, so strongly was it felt that the voting at the General Election had been swayed by a forgery (the "Red Letter"), comparable to the famous Piggott forgeries[1] of the 'eighties, that the Baldwin Government were regarded as having gained office on false pretences. If this was the general feeling in the Labour Movement, it was to be expected that some of the trade union leaders would be ready to use their industrial strength to maintain the standard of living of the working class. Thus the Conservative victory gave an impetus to the campaign for unity in the struggle against the employers.

That a struggle was approaching was common knowledge. For a big change had come over the international situation, which in 1923 had been so favourable to the British coal trade. Other substantial changes were now impending. Of these the most important in 1924 was the Dawes Plan for German reparations, and in 1925, the restoration of the Gold Standard. To these we must now turn.

4. THE DAWES PLAN

Dark days were looming up for the coal industry in the United Kingdom. After ten years of ups and downs it was now face to face with a real crisis, partly due to the failure to modernise the industry and partly to external causes. The Treaty of Versailles in 1919 obliged Germany to pay reparations which, by April 1921, were fixed at an annual amount of some £150,000,000. *Coal reparations*, in addition, were due each year for a decade to France, Belgium and Italy. By 1924 Germany's maximum annual liability for coal deliveries was $31\frac{1}{2}$ million metric tons, or nearly half the pre-1914 export of coal from the United Kingdom.

By the end of 1922 the Allies were at loggerheads over the policy towards Germany. The French Government stood strictly by the terms of the Treaty. On January 18, 1923, the Reparations Commission, by a majority, declared "a volun-

---

[1] *History of The Times*, Vol. III.

tary default" of Germany in its coal deliveries. Five days later Belgian and French troops occupied the Ruhr. The British Government disassociated itself from this step. The immediate effect was a highly disturbed condition of the Ruhr area: Ruhr miners and other workers went on strike, with the full support of the German Government, which at once ceased reparations payments and met all expenses by a recourse to the printing press. Marks were printed in such huge quantities as to cause a vast inflation of currency. By November 1923 the mark, nominally worth a shilling, had depreciated to such an extent, had fallen into such an abyss, that it took over a million marks to buy a box of matches. All wages had to be spent on the day they were received: for by the next day they were almost worthless. This produced a revolutionary situation in Germany. This in turn made all the Governments and bankers concerned anxious to reach an agreement to stop the inflation and to make new provisions for German economy and war reparations. A committee of bankers, headed by the American Charles Dawes, was appointed and the conclusions of this committee, submitted to the Allied Governments early in 1924, were known as the Dawes Plan for German reparations.

Meantime, throughout 1923 the British coal trade had enjoyed an export boom, shipping coal to markets which normally looked to the Ruhr mines for their supply. The export figure was 79,000,000 tons, the highest on record. It was this situation which had emboldened the M.F.G.B. to ask for a revision of the wages agreement, while it was the existence for the first time of a Labour Government, with all its dread potentialities in the minds of coal-owners, which had helped to secure that revision. The end of the revolutionary situation in Germany and the resumption of work in the Ruhr sobered up the coal trade. The Dawes Plan was successful in strengthening reaction in Germany, and in bringing to an end the revolutionary situation, with the result that a new great drive was made for output in the German coal industry. This also put an end to the high hopes of the British coal trade and foreshadowed a slump to follow the short-lived boom. Consider the effects of reparations coal.

What were these effects? The example of Italy, where there

was no complication such as the French problem of war-devastated pits, shows a contrast between 1913 and the year of the Dawes Plan discussions:

IMPORTS OF COAL AND COKE INTO ITALY
(in metric tons)

Country of Origin	1913	1924
United Kingdom	9,394,000	5,905,000
Yugoslavia	—	36,000
Austria-Hungary	134,000	—
Belgium	4,000	1,000
France	165,000	292,000
Germany	967,000	4,411,000*
Holland	73,000	—
U.S.A.	94,000	537,000
Other countries	—	38,000
	10,831,000	11,220,000

* Including 3,652,000 on account of reparations.

British export of coal to Italy had shrunk from 9,400,000 pre-war (in round figures) to 5,900,000 in 1924. German coal exports to Italy had jumped from less than 1,000,000 metric tons to a figure of 4,400,000. In this last figure no less than 3,600,000 was reparations coal. For the British coal trade this was indeed a serious problem, which might well have made the owners cry aloud in Whitehall. But the coal-owners were clay in the hands of the American, British and allied financiers. They sang dumb. Therefore the question of reparations and of the adverse effect of the Dawes Plan upon the coal industry fell to be handled by the other side of the industry, the Miners' Federation of Great Britain.

The miners, however, did not view this question of reparations simply from the standpoint of how it affected the British coal trade. A nobler rage possessed them than that of hucksters cheated of their market. Reparations in general they considered to be bad in principle, since they believed that these would bring ill to the workers of the country that paid them as well as to the workers of the country that received them. In the report of the Executive Committee to the Annual Conference in 1925, it was stated that "the question of reparation coal deliveries is one in which the liveliest interest has been evinced by our members"; and a brief account of coal reparations and the Dawes Plan was followed by the declaration:

Now, the Federation, in common with the Labour Movement, has always strenuously opposed the general principle of Reparations; their imposition places a great burden upon the shoulders of the working classes of the paying country, resulting in lower wage standards and longer hours of labour, with an inevitable reaction upon the conditions of the workers of other countries. Moreover, they upset the normal channels of trade and thus further tend to inflict hardship and suffering upon the working classes of both the paying and receiving countries.

The Executive Committee, examining the Dawes Plan, as set forth finally in the London Agreement of 1924, concluded that it was "undoubtedly detrimental to the interests of our members"—a conclusion "reached only after the most careful examination and investigation into the whole matter." Their report goes on:

We interviewed the Prime Minister of the day, Mr. Ramsay MacDonald, M.P., and expressed our views to him. Mr. MacDonald assured us that the effects of the Dawes Plan would be watched by his Government with the greatest care, and everything possible would be done to safeguard the interests of our membership during the operation of the scheme.

In point of fact, as a matter of strict historical accuracy, it was not true that the Labour Movement, or the Federation, as part of it, had "always strenuously opposed the general principle of reparations." The Labour Party in Parliament in 1919 had supported the ratification of the Treaty of Versailles. Moreover, no member from any party had objected to the demand for reparations—as Lloyd George was careful to recall some twenty years later. The representatives of the Miners' Federation had formed the largest single section of the Labour Party, which, indeed, at that moment was led in Parliament by one of the miners. Nevertheless, the miners were correct in believing that they had objected to reparations in principle for as long as they could recall. What circumstance was it that had led them to take up this attitude so definitely that they had afterwards come to believe that they had always held it? Undoubtedly the answer must be in the writings of the Cambridge economist, J. M. Keynes, and in particular his book *The Economic Consequences of the Peace*, published at the end of 1919 six months after the Treaty was signed.

The Cambridge school of Liberals was then at its highest point of literary achievement and its writings, like the glow of sunset, captivated habitual opponents in the short period before the sun of Liberalism fell below the horizon. Their mastery of literary expression overthrew the Victorian idol and idyll and dazzled all the young with its ruthlessness. For here at last, it seemed, was the naked truth. Well, it was certainly a new fashion in truth. It was not Socialism: but it almost seemed to be Socialism worn with a grace that robbed that turbulent doctrine of all its grossness. And so it imposed itself on many of the new Labour Party as something better than the old. Actually it was the last leap of the Whigs. Oxford might continue to be the "Lethe wharf" of lost causes, but Cambridge in those days was to gleam with an enlightenment, to furnish a Utopia and to supply the mirage. And so, just as a Lytton Strachey could win an historical battle by literary skill, or a Bertrand Russell could adorn the old Whiggery with epigram and pointed wit, so, too, J. M. Keynes could turn the "dismal science" of political economy into something at once entertaining and instructive. By sheer literary skill, *The Economic Consequences of the Peace* not only convinced its readers that reparations were bad in principle, but persuaded them that they had always thought so. The result was that within the Labour Movement, two tendencies joined to reject reparations: those like Lansbury who held that Versailles was an imperialist peace and therefore bad, and those like Thomas who held, with Keynes, that it was not a good enough imperialist peace in that it might cause revolution in Europe.

5. THE GOLD STANDARD

The Dawes Plan shift in the economic climate of Europe had causes beyond the direct needs of the German situation or of the baffled victors of Versailles. A wind was blowing

across the Atlantic Ocean, a wind laden with gold dust. To
the Bank of England it was a refreshing breeze. That institution, under Lord Cunliffe and perhaps even more under his
successor Mr. Montagu Norman,[1] was all for gold. The
pound sterling, like other currencies of Europe, had been
forced off its golden pedestal by the outbreak of war in 1914:
and from the end of that war, though exporters did well
enough under a managed currency (the Federation of British
Industries protesting in 1923 against any return to the Gold
Standard) in Threadneedle Street there was mourning for
seven years. Meanwhile nearly all the gold of the world had
been drained away year after year into the United States,
until by the winter of 1924–25 they were beginning to talk
in Wall Street of "the danger of gold inflation." Wall Street
feared that so much gold within the United States might
cheapen the value of gold in relation to goods, so that internal
prices would rise. If prices rose they might go so high that
their native merchants would be unable to export, while from
Europe imports would flood over the high tariff dykes of
American protectionism. It was partly to avoid this "danger"
that United States finance-capital was now once more taking
a keen interest in the economic and financial affairs of Europe
and showing readiness to take up large investments abroad.
To this new attitude the magnates of the City were highly
responsive. It seemed the occasion to regain at one leap the
position lost in 1914. A Committee (mainly of bankers)
appointed in 1924 by the previous Chancellor of the
Exchequer to examine whether Treasury notes should give
place to Bank of England notes now was found to be demanding as a prerequisite the return to the Gold Standard. This
demand was not resisted by the new Chancellor of the
Exchequer, Mr. Winston Churchill, whose versatility had
never been shown in economics or finance. On the other hand
Mr. Churchill was fully capable of viewing this complex
currency problem as a matter where national prestige was
at stake. Accordingly in the spring of 1925 he announced the
departure from a managed currency in tones which suggested

[1] "Mr. Montagu Norman is the high priest of the golden calf and his main pre-
occupation was to keep his idol burnished and supreme in the Pantheon of Commerce.
In his honest view it was the only god to lead the nation out of the wilderness."—D. Lloyd
George, *The Truth About Reparations and War Debts*, 1932.

that he was nailing the Union Jack to the Gold Standard. The public were told that this measure would "enable the pound sterling to look the dollar in the face."

The return to the Gold Standard, however patriotically presented, was certain to result in an upheaval of British economy, especially in the export trades. These inevitable results (for which some twenty years later Ernest Bevin scornfully twitted Mr. Churchill with his past as a "financial wizard") were set forth by J. M. Keynes, in the guise of the Treasury advisers (whose acknowledged pontiff he was not as yet) saying that the fall in the export trades would "produce an atmosphere favourable to the reduction of wages." But Churchill, it was explained, would "have to see to it that there is unemployment in the sheltered industries also." The way to this was through credit restriction:

By means of the restriction of credit by the Bank of England you can deliberately intensify unemployment to any required degree, until wages *do* fall.[1]

Indeed, the decision to restore the Gold Standard, to force up the exchange from $4.40 to $4.86, had results that could be foreseen. It was bound to mean a lowering of the standard of life, or, as it was to be phrased later, that "the wages of all workers must come down."

6. JOINT INVESTIGATIONS

Before all these major economic and financial changes had been carried through, the coal-owners took the initiative, on November 28, 1924, to invite a joint meeting "in view of the extremely serious condition of the coal industry at the present time." Was it their hearts' desire to get back the longer working day? This the miners' leaders suspected, but nevertheless felt that when the owners offered to investigate, the offer should be taken at its face value and accepted.

The meetings of the full Executives of each body went on throughout the first half of 1925. Each side put forward its separate programme of investigation, and each side supplied

[1] J. M. Keynes, *The Economic Consequences of Mr. Churchill* (1925).

numerous facts and statistics[1] for their subjects. These, on the owners' side, were limited to export markets for coal, inland markets and production. The workmen's side proposed that the whole basis of the quarterly ascertainments should be widened so as to bring in selling agencies or coking and by-product plants; that not merely production but the organisation of production by the owners should be examined; and further that distribution be brought under review. They bluntly raised the question of "multiple ownership," by which was meant a vertical combination wherein colliery owners in some cases were the possessors also of steel works, shipping properties or similar interests abroad. Finally they challenged the efficiency and economy of the administration of collieries and stated their wish to examine, jointly with the owners, such matters as "the amount of directors' fees" and "multiplicity of directorships and consequently of the fees taken."

With this difference in emphasis upon the subjects put forward for joint enquiry, the factual materials found and furnished by each side were correspondingly different. What purported to be a dispassionate enquiry into the economic position of the coal industry early took on the appearance of preliminary manœuvring for position between two antagonistic sets of interests. If it was not as yet the close encounter of wages negotiations, it certainly presented the spectacle of mutual long-range shelling with statistics. By the beginning of May it seemed abundantly clear to the workmen's side that the owners had for the time being abandoned any plans of seeking an agreement to increase hours and were bent on proving the case for a reduction of wages. By this time there was some restiveness in the coal-fields as to what might emerge from this unprecedented joint enquiry, and accordingly in the month of May the M.F.G.B. submitted a statement covering some of the subjects under discussion and also circulated it privately to its constituents. The introductory paragraphs of the statement were a clear declaration of policy and ran as follows:[2]

The coal-mining industry of Great Britain, under its present

[1] For the Miners' Federation the Labour Research Department was called on to furnish statistical materials.
[2] The Economic Position of the Coal Industry, May 1925. M.F.G.B. *Privately printed.*

ownership and management, is faced, we are told, with a position of crisis. Various causes are assigned for this, both by the owners and by independent economists. These causes may be summed up under three headings:

(1) The continued crisis in capitalist production resulting from the war, varying in intensity from country to country, and having as one of its effects a general shrinkage in world consumption of coal, to which shrinkage the general level of the purchasing power of the working class is contributory;

(2) The increased industrialisation and development of other countries such as America, South Africa, India and France, thus raising new and formidable competitors to British capitalism.

(3) The progressive development of sources of power alternative to black coal, particularly oil (either in the form of oil bunkers or Diesel engines) and hydro-electric power.

As far as the British coal trade is concerned all these causes, besides others that may be adduced, are being focussed by the owners on the question of PRICE. No matter what the degree of under-consumption is, no matter how much the facilities for oil burning, etc., are developed, it is, they say, the present high price of British coal to the consumer which is the root of the matter. Viewed simply from the standpoint of the coal trade, the problem according to them is one of cutting prices.

The owners, we understand, have in mind the facile solution of cutting miners' wages, either by direct lowering of wages or lengthening of the working day, or both, and thereby reaching "a competitive level."

To this outlook on the part of the owners the reply of the miners' representatives is threefold:

First.—That the crisis in the world's coal trade is greater than can be solved by any facile lowering of price.

Second.—That, in any case, whether the price of coal to the consumer is lowered or not, the living wage of the miners (together with hours and conditions) must be *untouchable*; that the present wage is not a living wage; and no question other than that of raising the present wage to meet the rise in the cost of living can be entertained.

Third.—That, if the owners pin their faith to a lowering of price, the miners are prepared to examine where and how the present organisation of the industry, both in finance, production and distribution, is placing a burden on the price of coal which could be and ought to be shifted, and that the waste and parasitic growth of profits in recent years are choking the industry.

The first portion of the statement under the heading "The European Coal Situation," dealt with such matters as the shrinkage in world consumption, the effect of the Versailles Treaty, the position of Germany, the means to recover the lost Russian market, etc., and reached the following three conclusions:

1. The present economic position of the British coal trade is part of a general world problem, a problem of under-consumption coupled with Reparations. It cannot be solved by any automatic scheme of price cutting. To reduce costs means an elaborate and ruthless reorganisation of the capitalist side of the coal-mining industry. This is dealt with in Part II.

2. The problem of under-consumption is due to the general crisis in the capitalist world, to the growth of new forms of power and substitutes for coal, and to the development of coal-fields on other continents which restrict imports into the countries in which they are found. The remedies for these causes of under-consumption lie beyond the bounds of what it is possible for either the coal-owners alone or the coal-miners alone to undertake. They have their roots in economic and political conditions of a general nature, which can only be solved by a general policy of the world working-class. Towards the making of such a general policy the present move to international Trade Union unity is a first step.

3. The other main cause of the difficulties confronting the British export trade is the scheme of Reparations now being operated under the Dawes Plan. This scheme of Reparations, this Dawes Plan, requires political action in order to be abrogated. This political action the Miners' Federation have already adopted. They have protested against Reparations, and they can now state with more conviction than ever that until steps are taken to cancel the Dawes plan and the whole scheme of Reparations there will not even be a lightening of the horizon for the coal-mining industry on its export side.

Part II of the statement followed up the subjects or "propositions by the workmen's side" as submitted on February 20, 1925, relating particularly to the high range of coal prices. It stated:

This examination shows that not only are the prices referred to in a large degree attributable to the present wasteful and inefficient methods of producing and distributing coal, coupled with general maladministration of the collieries, but also that the figure of profits earned (based upon the pithead price of raw coal alone) is by no means a true reflex of the position of the industry in its wider sense.

Further, these figures, both in the aggregate and in respect of individual colliery concerns, are misleading when considered in relationship to the nominal and inflated figure of capital employed arrived at by the methods described hereunder.

Modern development of industry is making it more and more impossible to treat of coal-mining as something completely separate and with only accidental connections with other industries. Recent developments are making what are sometimes called subsidiary and ancillary industries an essential part of modern coal-mining as carried on on a large scale. It appears that the typical coal-mining concern is becoming more and more a complex unit. In some cases it is becoming a unit which so far transcends ordinary industrial divisions that it can only be described as a heavy industry unit. It does not apply to all the pits, it is true, but in measuring an industry the workmen feel that *it is the modern and most developed form of the industry which must be taken as the type*. The workmen's side feel that the time is come when this modern type with all its additional sources of profit must be taken into account in the tasks of the settlement of wages. In their view, therefore, the inclusion of the activities of coke ovens, by-product plants, smokeless fuel, patent fuel, merchanting depots, etc., is essential to an appreciation of the true financial position of the industry, and for an equitable adjustment of their wages.

These contentions were supported by a number of appendices containing detailed figures and specific examples. On the employers' side, as shown by the minutes of the Joint Enquiry, there was an even more extensive array of figures.

There was no telling what might come out of such a confrontation of figures; and no obvious reason why the successive echelons of computators might not stretch to the crack of doom. Where both sides seemed equally sure of their rights, the decision must rest with the more powerful. Force must decide. Actually it was the mine-owners who realised this clearly enough, broke up the joint enquiry and in the latter part of June 1925 made it clear that the time had come "to have it out" with the miners.

7. THE OWNERS' PROPOSALS

The wages crisis in the coal industry occupied the whole of July 1925. Every day of that month passed amid increasing tension. All the consequences of the precedent economic and political events, of the manœuvring and diplomatic exchanges within the industry since the previous November, of the carrying through on the foreign field of the Dawes Plan and of a policy more hostile to the U.S.S.R., of the return, above all, to the Gold Standard now suddenly came to a head. The central problem was declared to be the lowering of prices, in the first place of coal prices. The corollary was seen as the lowering of wages, in the first place of miners' wages. Coal had been the staple export for generations. Once again, as in 1921, the miners were to bear the brunt of the attack.

It was on the last day of June that the M.F.G.B. received notice from the owners of the termination of the National Wages Agreement which had been in force since June 18, 1924. The notice was to run for the month of July and "to terminate at midnight of Friday, 31st July, 1925." In an accompanying letter the Chairman and Secretary of the Mining Association of Great Britain referred to "the unwillingness of the Miners' Federation to consider an extension of the seven-hour day" (which had been made evident at the last meeting of the joint enquiry on June 23rd) for, as they said "the terms which can be offered under a seven-hour day are necessarily much less favourable than those which could be offered under an eight-hour day." This letter was immediately made public, against the wishes of the Miners' Federation of Great Britain, and was thus clearly intended as a manifesto of policy. It was the first shot. The next day, on July 1st, they sent to the Miners' Federation their proposals for a new wages agreement.

These wage proposals were startling enough. They not only meant an immediate reduction in wages but there was more to follow; the guarantee of a minimum wage was to disappear and a guarantee of profits to take its place. Such was the effect of the operative clause 4.

These terms and the exact effect of them for each grade and in each District were the subject of wide discussion and bitter comment. One of the clearest statements of their implication was given by the M.F.G.B. to the Trades Union Congress in the course of the month. It was pointed out that the existing agreement provided for a general National Minimum Wage of $33\frac{1}{3}$ per cent upon standard wages, with a further proviso that the wage of no able-bodied adult day-wage workman should fall below a figure of 40 per cent upon the standard rates of the lowest paid classes of labour in the various Districts. The new proposals altered all that. It was now proposed that minimum wages should be abolished. This meant both that the principle of a national minimum percentage would be lost and also that there would be no limit to the extent to which the wages of the general body of mine-workers could be reduced.

The difference as regards profits was this: whereas, under the 1924 agreement, if in any period of ascertainment the proceeds, after all other costs of production were met, should be insufficient to provide minimum wages, then such deficiency had to be made good by the owners who might recoup themselves in subsequent periods provided that a surplus was available in sufficient quantity for that purpose. Under the July 1925 proposals, inasmuch as the provision of minimum wages was to be abolished, the owners would not have to make up wages in any way. On the contrary, they would secure in the aggregate a guaranteed profit of £13 out of every £100 of the proceeds after the full costs of production, other than wages, had been met. Thus, according to the M.F.G.B. statement, "it is proposed that a definite portion of the proceeds should be allotted to profits in each ascertainment period, irrespective of the amount of the proceeds and irrespective of the position of wages. Wages would thus no longer be a first charge on the industry."

Whereas the 1924 agreement provided for the lowest paid classes of workmen receiving a subsistence allowance, which in the normal way was met by the mine-owners and the higher paid workers in the respective proportions in which they shared the proceeds, the owners now proposed that subsistence allowances, if any, should be paid entirely by the other workmen.

In figures, the effect of the owners' proposals could be shown and were shown in various ways. Thus, for example, the actual figures of the proceeds for the nine months up to March 31, 1925, had, according to the Mines Department Quarterly Summaries, been £159,607,477 or 17s. 4·12d. per ton raised, which after other costs (less guaranteed and subsistence allowances) had been deducted to the amount of

£45,077,327, left a balance of £114,530,150 or per ton raised 12s. 5·34d.

Out of this balance £3,323,441 had gone to profits and £111,206,709 had gone to wages. If, however, the owners' first July proposals had been in operation they would have received £14,888,919 in profits as against £99,641,231 going to wages or an increase on the one hand (and a decrease on the other) of £11,565,478. Worked out per ton raised it meant that whereas the owners did receive 4·33d. they would, under their new proposals, have received for the same period no less than 1s. 7·41d. in profits per ton.

Another way of reckoning the effect of the owners' proposals was to take the average earnings per man-shift in May 1925 as compared with 1914 and then to show what the effect would be under the first July proposals and also what it would be if earnings had been based on the cost of living index. The cost of living index in the summer of 1925 stood at a level of 73 per cent above the level of 1914. Therefore, in tabular form, the results were as follows:

	Average Earnings per Man-Shift	Percentage Increase Over 1914
	s. d.	
1914	6 5·91	
May 1925	10 8·13	64·46
August 1925, under owners' offer	8 10·61	37·84
May 1925, on cost of living index (1914 plus 73 per cent)	11 2·78	73

In summing up the effect of the proposed new wages agreement, the M.F.G.B., in the statement they submitted later in the month to a special Trades Union Congress, put it as follows:

These proposals, if put into operation, would, in effect, transfer all the economic ills of the industry to the already overburdened shoulders of the mine-workers, and the mine-owners would assure to themselves a good profit under all conceivable circumstances. There would be very little incentive to efficiency on their part, and they would be able to automatically rid themselves of all their troubles by progressive reductions in wages.

Experience teaches us that the awful state to which the mine-workers would be eventually reduced, if these proposals were operated, is too terrible to contemplate. It must be borne in mind that the mine-owners have consistently refused to allow us to have any share of the control of the industry, yet we are asked to allow our wages to be entirely at their mercy, and the burden of bad management, inefficient methods of production, administration and distribution, could all be automatically transferred to our shoulders without any let or hindrance whatsoever.

Even the newspaper Press, though quick to assume that the miners were in the wrong, found it hard to stomach these terms when they were published on July 1, 1925.

On July 2nd the M.F.G.B. Executive Committee met and, as the minute tells us, "received the notice by the colliery owners to terminate the general wages agreement at the end of July with a view to a further attack upon the already inadequate wages of the mine-workers and of securing guaranteed profits to the owners." They recommended their rejection. The next day, on Friday, July 3rd, the delegates at the Special Conference at the Kingsway Hall, London, in turn unanimously decided that "for the following and other reasons these proposals cannot be accepted":

1. The removal of the guaranteed minimum wages, which are already below the level of the present cost of living.
2. The provision of guaranteed profits to the colliery owners irrespective of the rate of wages.
3. The immediate great reduction in wages, varying from 13·14 per cent to 47·91 per cent on basis rates.
4. The continued separation of the mining operations from the profitable undertakings in connection with the coking and by-product departments, etc.

This Conference decision, duly communicated the same day to the Mining Association of Great Britain, disquieted the owners, not so much for what it said as for what it omitted to say. There were no counter-proposals (though it was known that some Districts had been pressing for an improvement) and, more significant still, there was complete silence as to any negotiations between the parties. The miners were "abiding in their tents."

8. ATTITUDE OF OWNERS AND GOVERNMENT

The next move of the coal-owners and of the Government was to persuade the miners' leaders to accept discussion on the basis of the situation created by the ultimatum issued by the owners, which meant an acceptance of a serious reduction in wages. When the Chairman of the Mining Association had failed in this endeavour, the Goverment took two successive steps. The first was to nominate the First Lord of the Admiralty (then Mr. W. C. Bridgeman) to act as mediator; the second was to appoint a Court of Enquiry under the Industrial Courts Act of 1919. Neither step produced any result and by the last week of the month the Prime Minister was compelled to enter into open conference with the M.F.G.B. By the end of July the issue was clearly between the Cabinet and the owners on the one hand, and the M.F.G.B. (with the backing of the Trades Union Congress) on the other.

For in the meantime, since that first week-end in July, the M.F.G.B. had not only reached a further stage in their plans for an Industrial Alliance but had also got the backing of the General Council of the Trades Union Congress, and so came to feel itself in an unexpectedly strong position. In that same month of July, when various members of the Cabinet undertook "to bring the parties together," it was for some of them the first occasion of encountering the blunt and unyielding personality of Herbert Smith. It can hardly have been a surprise to the coal-owners' Chairman, who knew Herbert, that his request on July 7th for "an interchange of views" should have met with a refusal ("there is no room for negotiations in those proposals") and curt intimation that future letters should be addressed to the Secretary of the committee. But W. C. Bridgeman, First Lord of the Admiralty, was probably rather taken aback by what must have seemed to him the brusque behaviour of the miners' President. The First Lord of the Admiralty had met the mine-owners on the 9th, and the Federation on the 10th: the mine-owners were willing to do anything—except withdraw the notices: whereas the Federation wanted the owners' proposals withdrawn before they could enter into negotiations. It was a deadlock which was not eased by the way in which pleasantly worded letters from the First Lord were passed on by Herbert Smith, to be curtly answered in single-sentence replies from A. J. Cook. When, later in the month, the First Lord with other members of the Cabinet met the Executive, he hopefully induced them to enter the same room with the owners and himself, only to find Herbert Smith insisting that the Cabinet's responsibility, so far from ending, had now only begun. In the Special Conference held a month later (August 19, 1925), the Chairman told the story:

Mr. Bridgeman put this question to your Executive. He said: "Supposing I ask you and the owners to meet me, will you refuse to meet?"

We thought there was more in that question than what really appeared on the surface. We said to Mr. Bridgeman: "When you invite us to attend a meeting with you together we shall be there."

So of course, he ultimately called us and invited the owners. When he got us together he said: "Well now, gentlemen, my services nearly look at an end now. I have got you together."

We said: "Look here, Mr. Bridgeman, make no mistake about it as to your services; if they are ended then ours will be ended. There have got to be three in this piece this time. You are responsible for the position we are in—your Government. An inquiry was held in 1919, and certain findings were the result of that inquiry. A Coalition Government was in power at that time, and both pledged themselves: yet you have refused to accept it; or in other words, you believe in private enterprise; although private enterprise has failed to function. It is your baby, which you must supply with milk."

He didn't think it was a fair position to put him in. We said: "That is our position."

We made it perfectly clear that we were not prepared to meet the owners to discuss their proposals, because we could accept no reduction; not a cent, nor work a minute's extension of time. Anything beyond that we are prepared to talk, to meet them to discuss, but we are not prepared to go beyond that.

This same attitude was adopted by the M.F.G.B. when the Government took its second step and set up the Court of Enquiry. The announcement of this came at the beginning of the second week-end of July. Under the Industrial Courts Act, 1919, the Minister of Labour was empowered to refer any

A. J. COOK (1885–1931)
Secretary M.F.G.B. 1924–1931

HERBERT SMITH (1862–1938)
President M.F.G.B. 1922–1929

matters which seemed to him relevant to a trade dispute, "whether existing or apprehended," to a Court of Enquiry. On this occasion, following on the joint enquiry of the Mining Association and the M.F.G.B. the former had given notice to terminate the National Wages Agreement, and a deadlock had arisen in the industry. Giving as his motive the "very grave effect on trade and industry" that would result from a "stoppage of work" (the correct expression "lock-out" was not used), the Minister on July 13th appointed the Rt. Hon. H. P. Macmillan, K.C. (Chairman), W. Sherwood, Esq. (a trade union official) and Sir Josiah Stamp, G.B.E., to constitute the Court of Enquiry with directions "to enquire into the causes and circumstances of the dispute in the coal-mining industry and to report thereon" and with powers to request any person to attend as a witness and give evidence, produce documents, furnish particulars or to require a witness to give evidence on oath.

All this panoply of juridical ceremonial failed to impress the miners. The Thirty-seventh Annual General Conference of the Miners' Federation was in session at Scarborough when formal intimation that the Court was set up reached the Executive. On Wednesday, July 15th, the Conference took its decision, which reached the Minister of Labour (Sir Arthur Steel-Maitland) in the shape of a telegram signed "Cook, Secretary" announcing that the M.F.G.B. "can accept no Court of Enquiry that has for its object the ascertainment of whether mine-workers' wages can be reduced or their hours extended—but it repeats its willingness to meet the coal-owners in open conference as soon as they have withdrawn their proposals." In a letter the same day to the Minister, Cook explained the reasons for this decision. After saying that Steel-Maitland's letters of the 11th and 13th had been fully considered by the Conference and repeating this decision, Cook went on:

A Royal Commission made an exhaustive inquiry into all phases of the coal-mining industry in 1919, but the majority findings of the Commission were not given effect to by the Government of the day.

An inquiry under the Industrial Courts Act was held in April of last year, and the findings of the Court have special significance in relation to the present position. The Court found:

"That the wages paid to the day-wage workers in the coal-mining industry were substantially less than the equivalent of their pre-war earnings, and that this was also true of the piece-workers in certain collieries, but not in all.

"That the provision of a minimum wage should have precedence over the distribution of profits."

The present position of wages in the industry has not materially changed since the report of the Court was issued; the proposals of the coal-owners, however, if put into operation, would not only effect further large and immediate reductions in wages, but would abolish the payment of a minimum wage, in respect of which principle a Court of Inquiry has already reported in the terms stated above.

In view of these facts, and also the fact that the great public inquiries referred to dealt exhaustively with the wages and hours questions, the position of the industry is well known to the Government and the public, and the Federation feels that no good purpose would be served by yet another inquiry.

In regard to the particular inquiry now set up, I have to say that it certainly can take no part in proceedings, which, from the terms of reference and the constitution of the Court, are so obviously designed to justify the present attack upon the mine-workers' standard of living, and in respect of which it was in no way consulted. The Federation, however, is perfectly willing to meet the mine-owners again, in open Conference, if and when the present proposals are withdrawn.

Yours faithfully,

July 15, 1925. A. J. COOK, Secretary.

In response to this came a telegram (Thursday, July 16th) from the Minister of Labour, claiming that the Conference decision was based on a misapprehension as to the objects of the Court of Enquiry and trusting that the miners' representatives would attend on the Friday morning. This was followed by a succession of requests, formal and informal, to Herbert Smith and A. J. Cook (and invitations to "any other representatives of your Federation whom you may desire") to attend the Court, which hopefully adjourned till the Monday. Their hopes were in vain. Neither Smith nor Cook would attend, nor any other miner. The Court thereupon entered on its enquiry, in which they heard the case put by only one party to the dispute: and though for this reason, as they protested in their subsequent report, the Mining Association's case may have been the more severely examined, the effect was nonetheless unfortunate. It certainly was not what the Ministry of Labour or the Cabinet had intended. Indeed, as the repeated biddings, official and unofficial, brought not a single miner before the Court, Sir Arthur Steel-Maitland might have felt as though Hotspur's gibe[1] applied also to himself and his high office. Under these circumstances the three members of the Court were left with little more than walking-on parts in this national drama. They duly went through their paces: but no one was waiting with bated breath to hear their utterance. The Trades Union Congress agreed with the miners. The Government had to bestir itself in other ways to deal with the deadlock. In the midst of these more important discussions on which public attention was concentrated, the Report of the Court of Enquiry issued on July 28th received little notice. True, *The Times* paid it the compliment of an editorial in which its criticism of the owners was approved and the next day the Mining Association of Great Britain paid it the further compliment of a furious attack. But otherwise oblivion rolled over it. Nothing more was heard of it, then or later.

9. THE FEDERATION STRATEGY

The Federation strategy was to obtain the widest backing of the organised workers. For this purpose they had been moving for the Industrial Alliance of heavy industry and transport unions and had reached the stage on June 14th of setting up a sub-committee to elaborate its constitution. While awaiting the report of the sub-committee the Federation had decided to lay its case before the General Council of the Trades Union Congress, which accordingly met the full Executive Council of the M.F.G.B. on Friday, July 10th. The impending coal dispute was exhaustively reviewed, and a very detailed and explicit statement of the causes of the deadlock was made on behalf of the Miners' Federation. After the miners' representatives had left the meeting, the

[1] GLENDOWER: I can call spirits from the vasty deep.
HOTSPUR: Why, so can I, or so can any man;
But will they come when you do call for them?
King Henry IV, Part One.

General Council conferred further and passed a resolution recording their "complete support" of the miners and undertook to co-operate wholeheartedly with them "in their resistance to the degradation of the standard of life of their members." The next day this attitude of the General Council was further expressed in a statement issued to the Press, which declared that the Mining Association's terms would eventually "cause chaos within the industry."

The General Council appreciate to the full the fact that no self-respecting body of organised workers could negotiate on such terms, and they completely endorse the refusal of the Miners' Federation to meet the owners until the proposals have been withdrawn.

The General Council particularly approve of the steadfast opposition of the Miners' Federation to any proposals for a lengthened working day, and deplore the misrepresentation which has led the public to assume that the seven-hour day represents the actual length of the miners' time underground.

They ended by declaring that they placed "themselves without qualification and unreservedly at the disposal of the Miners' Federation."

It was also announced that a committee of nine had been appointed "to maintain continuous contact with the negotiations now taking place," and with power to summon the full General Council "in event of the necessity arising." Thereafter the M.F.G.B. kept this Special Committee, as it was called, fully informed of each stage in negotiations: and letters to it were sent from Scarborough, from the five-day Annual Conference of the Federation.

When it concluded on July 17th there was held the second plenary meeting of the unions[1] concerned in the proposed Industrial Alliance to receive the report of the sub-committee appointed on June 4th. The June meeting had been very cool to the miners' proposals: but the atmosphere had greatly altered in the six weeks that followed, owing to the fact that there was not only the mining crisis but that trouble was looming ahead in other industries. The meeting heard a complete statement by Ernest Bevin, who had acted as

[1] These, apart from the M.F.G.B., included the three railway unions, the transport and dock workers' unions, the Iron and Steel Trades Confederation, the Engineering and Shipbuilding Trades Federation, the Amalgamated Engineering Union, the Electrical Trades Union and the unions of boilermakers and foundry workers.

Secretary of the sub-committee; and they unanimously accepted the draft constitution for consideration by the unions concerned. This meant that the Constitution had to wait for ratification and that nothing in its provisions would be immediately operative; but the temper of the assembly and the occasion of its meeting constituted a powerful moral support for the miners. This impression was strengthened by the uncompromising wording of the more important provisions of the Constitution as then made public, namely that their objects were:

To create by means of an alliance of the specified organisations, a means of mutual support, to assist any or all of the allied organisations, in defending the hours of labour and wage standards, and securing advancement of the standard of living, or to take action to secure acceptance of, or to defend, any principle of an industrial character which may be deemed vital by the allied organisations.

The conditions of membership of this Alliance shall involve the allied organisations in definitely undertaking, notwithstanding anything in their agreements or constitutions to the contrary, to act as directed by the General Conference of the Alliance.

All this was bound to have an immediate effect on the General Council of the T.U.C. "Through the Industrial Alliance," reported Herbert Smith to the M.F.G.B. Special Conference a month later, "we got such an atmosphere created in the Trade Union world as we have not had before."

Still more explicit pledges of help now came from particular unions. On Monday, July 20th, the first Delegate Conference of the three-year-old Transport and General Workers' Union opened with a speech by the Chairman, Harry Gosling, largely devoted to the question of aiding the miners: and on the next day, after hearing a report from Ernest Bevin, the Conference empowered the Executive, acting in consultation with the General Council, to call a strike if that were rendered necessary by the course of the coal dispute.

Two days later the M.F.G.B. Executive, having been informed in the meantime that the Associated Society of Locomotive Engineers and Firemen (John Bromley, Secretary) would also accord the fullest support, reiterated its refusal to meet the coal-owners unless and until the owners' proposals were withdrawn. They then turned to the Trades

Union Congress, not only for continued backing of the kind already given, but in the hope of support by action if that were needed. In this hope they were not to be disappointed. They had convinced the other unions of the justice of their case, they had advanced a stage in the creation of machinery that would enable help in action to be given speedily; but they had to face the fact that the General Council had not as yet the formal powers that would enable it to issue mandatory instructions and they were all aware of how often in labour history "the native hue of resolution" had been "sicklied o'er with the pale cast of thought." The miners had reason for some anxiety. Therefore when they met the Special Committee on the morning of Thursday, July 23rd, though they had every confidence in most of the members, they realised that fateful days had now come: and so they made a statement which concluded with the words "they placed their case unreservedly in the hands of the General Council of the Trades Union Congress as the supreme trade union committee." Thereupon it was decided to approach the Prime Minister to bring about an unconditional conference between the miners and the mine-owners. The full General Council met the M.F.G.B. Executive that same afternoon and agreed to all that had been proposed. The next day, Friday, July 24th, a special Trades Union Congress, called to deal with the subject of unemployment, was being held: to this a document (given in an appendix) setting forth the whole situation was submitted by the Federation, while Herbert Smith and A. J. Cook delivered speeches which were reported to have made a deep impression on the assembled delegates.

The M.F.G.B. document, after dealing with the economic position of the coal industry, the owners' wage proposals and the Court of Enquiry, put the issue in such a way as to bring home to the whole trade union movement how necessary it was they should concern themselves in the impending struggle and become an active part of it. The conclusion ran:

We may say that the mine-workers most earnestly desire a peaceful settlement of the present dispute. They realise fully the disastrous consequences, not only to themselves but to their fellow Trade Unionists, of a stoppage of work in the mines at the present time. At the same time they are confident that their fellow workers will not expect them to accept degrading conditions of employment, or to assent to the retrograde step of reverting to the eight-hour day.

It is possible that the lock-out notices may be postponed: they may even be withdrawn indefinitely. If so, so much the better. We feel bound to say, however, that the mine-owners are perhaps the most obstinate set of employers in this country, and present indications seem to point to their having made up their minds to force the lock-out irrespective of the consequences.

We hope our worst fears may not be realised, but we must make our calculations, and we must ask our fellow Trade Unionists to make theirs on the basis of a million-and-a-quarter mine-workers being locked out in ten days' time.

It is not for the Miners' Federation to lay down what action it considers Congress should take. As one of the constituent bodies of the Trades Union Congress, it considers it sufficient to set the facts before the Congress and to indicate the probability of the miners requiring its early and substantial help. It feels assured that such assistance will be readily forthcoming, and on this occasion, if a lock-out matures, it will not be left to a section to fight alone, but the struggle will be taken up, and the issue joined, by the whole Trade Union Movement.

With the favourable reception by the Special Trades Union Congress of this document, and of the speeches by Smith and Cook, the climax drew nearer. The next day the T.U.C., having got agreement for practical measures of support from the railway and transport unions, took the last remaining step. The agreement thus reached—to put an embargo on all movement of coal in case of a mine-owners' lock-out—altered the situation and took it right out of the realm of pious resolutions or of displays of moral force unaccompanied by any means of enforcing moral superiority. In this necessary stage of bringing the other unions on to the field, the climax was now reached. The Federation strategy in avoiding complicated issues and centring all attention in defence of the miners' wages had proved successful. The final stage could now begin.

From this moment onwards, the General Council of the T.U.C., equipped with the necessary sanctions as provided by the transport and railway unions, kept up regular contact with the M.F.G.B.

10. THE T.U.C. CONDUCTS THE STRUGGLE

The whole of the last week of July 1925 was occupied by discussions and negotiations, all of them conducted in the light of the transport and railway unions' resolutions not to handle coal. Though this was fully in line with the traditional doctrines of trade unionism not to handle "black work" (i.e. blackleg work), it was nevertheless something that had never happened before on a national scale in a mining dispute. Still, resolutions do not always mean action, and until the last moment of the week the Government, if not the mine-owners, appeared to hope for a break in the trade union ranks.

On Monday, July 27th, the Prime Minister, who now took charge, heard a T.U.C. deputation urge that notices be postponed and wage proposals withdrawn: this marked the entrance of the Trades Union Congress into the arena.

On Tuesday, July 28th, the Prime Minister met the mine-owners and found them obdurate. The Cabinet discussed the now critical situation. As for the miners' representatives, they were in Paris seeing the representatives of the International Miners' Federation and the International Transport Workers' Federation and arranging an embargo on coal movements.

On Wednesday, July 29th, the Prime Minister was meeting the mine-owners, the miners, the representatives of the General Council and the Secretary of the International Federation of Trade Unions. In the morning the Prime Minister told the M.F.G.B. definitely "that the Government would not grant any subsidy" and that the coal industry "must stand on its own economic foundations." Thus up to this point, while the mine-owners maintained their refusal to postpone notices and withdraw the unacceptable wage proposals, the Government were equally determined not to assume any responsibility for a situation to which their own policy had materially contributed. There was no easing of the tension. That same morning the details of the practical application of the embargo decision were considered.

Thursday, July 30th, was the crucial day. Morning, afternoon and evening the meetings went on: meetings of the Prime Minister with the owners and the miners, meetings of the Cabinet, meetings of the trade union bodies. Of these last by far the most important was the Special Conference of Trade Union Executives, who met in the Central Hall, Westminster, to receive the statement of the miners and the report of the T.U.C. Committee which had now ratified the embargo decisions.

The miners reported to the thousand delegates that they had heard that morning from the lips of Mr. Baldwin that not only must the miners accept a reduction but all the workers in the country must take a reduction in wages to help put industry on its feet.[1]

This put the fat in the fire. If there had been any doubts before, this swept them away. The Conference of Trade Union Executives not only approved the T.U.C. report, but *empowered it to give financial support* and to issue strike orders.

That day the Prime Minister had put the utmost pressure on the miners' representatives to give way either on wages or hours. He came to them saying he had secured from the mine-owners a concession on Districts, followed reluctantly by the concession of a minimum wage. "What have you to give?" he asked the miners. "Nowt," was the sturdy reply of the unyielding Herbert Smith, "we have nowt to give." Mr. Baldwin had to be content with stressing the importance of a full enquiry, to which the M.F.G.B. had conceded it would agree. This perhaps showed how the wind was blowing: the Cabinet was already concerned with securing the path of its retreat, should retreat prove unavoidable.

By that same evening retreat was manifestly the only course left to the Prime Minister. For that evening instructions were issued for the embargo on coal movements to be put into force. The first of the operative clauses began: "wagons

---

[1] In the *Daily Herald* of July 31st this significant passage in the conversations between the Prime Minister and the miners (after the former had urged the miners to make a contribution toward meeting the difficult situation of the industry) was reported as follows:

MINERS: "But what you propose means a reduction of wages."

PRIME MINISTER: "Yes. All the workers in this country have got to face a reduction of wages."

MINERS: "What do you mean?"

PRIME MINISTER: "I mean all the workers of this country have got to take reductions in wages to help put industry on its feet."

Several months afterwards a somewhat belated denial that this statement had in fact been made was issued from Downing Street.

containing coal must not be attached to any train after midnight on Friday, July 31st, and after this time wagons of coal must not be supplied to any industrial or commercial concern, or be put on the tip roads at docks for the coaling of ships."

This document deserves to be given in full: for hitherto no such powers had been taken by or yielded to the Trades Union Congress. Signed by the Chairman of the Transport Sub-Committee of the General Council and by the Secretaries and Presidents of the unions involved (including J. H. Thomas and Harry Gosling, each of them Privy Councillors) and countersigned by the unions and by all the Special Committee of the General Council, the document ran as follows:

Official Instructions to all Railway and Transport Workers, as agreed unanimously by a Joint Conference of the National Union of Railwaymen, Associated Society of Locomotive Engineers and Firemen, Railway Clerks' Association, and the Transport and General Workers' Union Executives, and approved by the General Council of the Trades Union Congress.

RAILWAYS

1. Wagons containing coal must not be attached to any train after midnight on Friday, July 31st, and after this time wagons of coal must not be supplied to any industrial or commercial concerns, or be put on the tip roads at docks for the coaling of ships.

2. All coal en route at midnight on Friday to be worked forward to the next siding suitable for storing it.

3. Any coal, either in wagons or stock at a depot, may be utilised at that depot for the purpose of coaling engines for passenger and goods trains, but must not be moved from that depot to another.

DOCKS, WHARVES, ETC.

Coal Exports.—All Tippers and Trimmers will cease work at the end of the second shift on July 31st.

Coal Imports.—On no account may import coal be handled from July 31st.

General.—A general stoppage of men handling coal on other classes of tonnage on Friday midnight.

WATERWAYS AND LOCKS

All men on canals, waterways, etc., engaged in carrying coal will cease Friday midnight, with the exception of men who have coal en route, who will be allowed to take it to destination and tie up. Safety men for pumping, etc., will be permitted to work for safety purposes only.

ROAD TRANSPORT

All men engaged in delivering coal to commercial and industrial concerns will cease Friday night, July 31st. Men delivering for domestic purposes will cease at 12 noon, Saturday, August 1st.

LOCAL COMMITTEES

For the purpose of carrying out these instructions the members of the organisation herein concerned shall, from each district, establish small sub-committees so as to co-ordinate policy in giving effect to same.

GEORGE HICKS (Chairman, Transport Sub-Committee).

Associated Society of Locomotive Engineers and Firemen—

B. H. JENKINS	D. S. HUMPHREYS (President)
O. W. SKINNER	JOHN BROMLEY (General Secretary)

National Union of Railwaymen—

F. FOWLER	J. H. THOMAS (General Secretary)
ARTHUR LAW	C. T. CRAMP (Industrial Gen. Secretary)
W. DOBBIE (President)	J. MARCHBANK (Assistant Secretary)

Railway Clerks' Association—

GEORGE LATHAN	T. GILL (President)
	A. G. WALKDEN (General Secretary)

Transport and General Workers' Union—

HARRY GOSLING (President)
ERNEST BEVIN (General Secretary)

General Council Special Committee—

A. B. SWALES (Chairman)	G. HICKS	B. TILLETT
J. BROMLEY	J. MARCHBANK	A. G. WALKDEN
A. HAYDAY	E. L. POULTON	W. M. CITRINE (Assistant Secretary).

The effect was immediate. Another Cabinet meeting was called. Then came discussions up to midnight and beyond. Within a few hours of the issue of these instructions for an embargo (i.e. a refusal to handle blackleg work or materials) the Prime Minister, who had been "whispering 'I will ne'er consent,' consented." He had previously been very firm that there would be no subsidy and had declared his intention, as against the embargo, to maintain all vital services. Now he was willing to offer a nine months' subsidy in return for which the owners would be willing to withdraw their notices, while during the nine months a full enquiry would be held. The actual notification of this took place at 3.45 in the afternoon of Friday, July 31st, when the Prime Minister met the Special Committee of the Trades Union Congress General Council, together with the Executive of the Miners' Federation, and explained that the owners had agreed to suspend notices, that an enquiry would take place and that in the meantime the Government would guarantee financial assistance up to May 1, 1926.

At 4 p.m. on the last day of July the following wire was sent to General Secretaries of District organisations in the coal industry:

Notices suspended. Work as usual.—COOK, Secretary.

The same day the General Council of the Trades Union Congress sent a letter to all its affiliated trade unions and to all Trades Councils. The concluding sentences ran:

The Miners' Federation have conveyed their most sincere thanks to the General Council, the Special Committee, and to the whole of the members of the Trade Union movement, for their ready and complete promises of support.

The enforcement of the reductions which the owners have tried to effect in the existing agreement would have meant a loss in the wages of miners of many hundreds of thousands of pounds. The loyal co-operation of the railway and transport unions has been an immense stimulus to every trade unionist.

The manifestation of solidarity which has been exhibited by all sections of the Trade Union movement is a striking portent for the future and marks an epoch in the history of the Movement.

The notices are suspended for a fortnight and, while there is little doubt that the conflict has been avoided, the Trade Union movement must be alert and vigilant in case the necessity should again arise for it to act in defence of its standards.

Yours sincerely,
A. B. SWALES, Chairman.
W. M. CITRINE, Assistant Secretary.

Thus at the last moment the Government, upon whom the coal-owners had reckoned as on a firm fortress, had given way and yielded to the threat of an embargo on movements of coal. It was a red-letter day in the Labour calendar: indeed it was well named Red Friday.

11. SIGNIFICANCE OF RED FRIDAY

What was the significance of Red Friday? What were its lessons? These were vital questions which, for the first two weeks after Red Friday, were smothered behind the furious newspaper discussion of the Government's withdrawal and the angry questioning of "Who lost?" and "Who won?"

Whoever lost, it was certainly not the mine-owners. They were granted a subsidy to make up the difference between their extravagant claims and the extent to which any pit fell short of these claims. On July 29th, 1925, *The Times* had written that in view of the findings of the Court of Enquiry it was "impossible for the mine-owners to maintain the ground on which they have hitherto taken their stand" and that the proposals of the mine-owners had been "rejected by an impartial and competent tribunal after a searching examination." Nevertheless it was in the main the "rejected" claims which became the corner-stone of the subsidy arrangements with the Treasury, much to the dismay of the miners as expressed in their August Delegate Conference.

There was, however, no doubt in the editorial columns of many newspapers that Labour had won and that the Government had lost. As the Trades Union Congress General Council said in its report, written early in August,

The Settlement was regarded by the Capitalist Press as a humiliating defeat of the Government by the organised workers.

It is indeed difficult to convey without a most extensive series of quotations the concentrated fury with which the newspapers greeted the Government announcement. In both the national and provincial Press and in the smaller sheets the event was analysed day after day. In the course of the discussion which thus raged in the newspapers, the controversy began to be narrowed down to the issue of whether Mr. Baldwin and the Cabinet had been pusillanimous or whether they had merely been prudent. But this meant an unmistakable warning to Mr. Baldwin and his colleagues that if a second occasion came, discretion would not be held the better part of valour. When the subsidy period came to an end, he would be expected to take a firm stand against the miners and the trade union movement generally. The final effect of all this discussion was to alarm, warn and prepare the anti-Labour forces for a future struggle—an effect made clear in the last stages of the discussion when the question was raised of how the Government, if faced with a similar situation next year, would be fully equipped and ready to meet it. "Was nine months enough?" some asked. Others thought that full preparedness could be reached in a shorter time. The discussion which began with criticism of the Cabinet ended with calling attention to the need of preparedness for a decisive conflict that lay ahead.

This, in turn, was the keynote struck by the Cabinet in answer to its critics. The first into the fray was the Home Secretary, Sir William Joynson-Hicks, who had already won sufficient notoriety by his brutal utterance on India.[1] Now this same man as Home Secretary, hot from the Cabinet discussions of their "humiliating defeat" and their burning sense of injury, made clear the Government outlook:

He said to them, coming straight from the Cabinet Councils, the thing was not finished. The danger was not over. Sooner or later this question had got to be fought out by the people of the land. Was England to be governed by Parliament and by the Cabinet or by a handful of trade union leaders? If a Soviet were established here . . . a grave position would arise. On the other hand, if people were prepared to support the Government . . . then he said quite frankly, quite seriously, there would be for a time grave trouble in the land, but if the heart of the people were sound, they could stand it.

(Speech at Northampton, as reported in *The Times*, August 3, 1925.)

It will be noticed from this speech that, after Red Friday, a new issue, not raised in the discussions between the Prime Minister and the T.U.C. representatives (nor raised afterwards in sundry discussions the next month, September, between the Prime Minister and the M.F.G.B. representatives), was now suddenly brought forward. The organised application by the unions engaged in transport of the all-important trade union principle "not to handle black work," albeit on a national scale, could not be, and was not,

---

[1] "We did not conquer India for the benefit of the Indians. I know that it is said at missionary meetings that we have conquered India to raise the level of the Indians. That is cant. We conquered India by the sword and by the sword we shall hold it. We hold it as the finest outlet for British goods."

objected to in any public statement in July. It was the carrying out in practice of this principle and on so large a scale that had made the difference for the Cabinet, and decided them not only to make a temporary retreat but to do it with the conscious purpose of getting all ready for a successful conflict with organised labour in the future. But to do this effectively it was necessary to rouse the activities of their supporters and also to present the question in a new fashion. The new ground of a future struggle was no longer to be the need to reduce wages. The matter was to be put as a constitutional issue. This was made quite clear in the debate in Parliament on August 6th, after the Government had been taunted by their opponents with cowardice ("afraid of facing cold steel," said Lloyd George), both by the Prime Minister and by the Chancellor of the Exchequer, Winston Churchill, who said:

In the event of a struggle, whatever its character might be, however ugly the episodes which would mark it, I have no doubt that the State, the national State would emerge victorious in spite of all the rough and awkward corners it might have to turn. But if you are going to embark on a struggle of this kind, be quite sure that decisive public opinion is behind you. . . . As the struggle widened, as it became a test whether the country was to be ruled by Parliament or by some other organisation not responsible by our elective processes to the people as a whole—as that issue emerged more and more, and with every increase in the gravity of the struggle, new sources of strength would have to come to the State or some action, which in ordinary circumstances we should consider quite impossible, would, just as in the case of the Great War, be taken with general assent and as a matter of course. (*Hansard*, August 6, 1925.)

Meantime, on the Labour side there had been a natural enough tendency to stress the "victory" of Red Friday. This exultation was not shared by the miners, at whose Delegate Conference on Wednesday, August 19th, in the Kingsway Hall, London, the Chairman in his opening speech said:

We have no need to glorify about a victory. *It is only an armistice*, and it will depend largely how we stand between now and May 1st next year as an organisation in respect of unity as to what will be the ultimate results. All I can say is, that it is one of the finest things ever done by an organisation. I know some people are saying we have forced the hands of the Government and that we are

Bolshevists and all that sort of thing. If it means by Bolshevism the spreading of brotherly love for each other, and not seeking to put the country into a chaotic position, without going back to slavery, then I do not mind being called a Bolshevist, as I do not intend going back there.

John McGurk, of Lancashire, a District which like several others had been concerned to get an advance, asked of Cook: "Did you yourself, on behalf of the Committee, ask the Prime Minister to give us the cost of living wages during the negotiations so that we could have a good price list? I don't know much about a glorious victory." And after Cook had given in some detail an affirmative answer John McGurk interjected, "You did ask for the cost of living; then for God's sake give over talking about a glorious victory." Again, when the provisions of the subsidy·or "subvention" were mentioned there was the following exchange:

Mr. D. R. Grenfell (South Wales): After succeeding in getting the 13 per cent of the amount at disposal after other costs have been met, does not the agreement itself suggest that the owners have got what they asked for, 13 per cent of the profits of the industry after other costs have been met? I think it is quite clear that the owners have succeeded in getting all they asked for. Have they not got from the Government everything they asked for? They have got it from the Government instead of the workmen.

The Chairman:·I want to submit to this Conference if the owners have got everything they have asked for they have not got it out of the miners' wages. That is a question outside of us. But they have not got all they asked for. They have got all they asked for in profits, that is quite true, but they are not exploiting the miners' wages or local conditions.

I am not putting this as a glorious victory, *it is only an armistice*, but so far as the Trade Union Movement is concerned it has been a glorious victory for unity of purpose.

So far were some of the delegates from regarding it as a victory (unless the gain of the mine-owners were to be taken as a victory for the Mining Association), that a motion was moved to express "profound disappointment with the settlement" and to protest against its being made without having been "endorsed by a delegate Conference." At this stage James Robson, of Durham, made a speech which influenced the delegates to accept the report and actions of the Executive Committee. He said:

In 1921, we came out of that as we did still suffering, because there was not unity amongst ourselves. . . .

I can realise the difficulty the Committee must have had in securing unity amongst the other sections which had been secured on this occasion, and I want to suggest that it is owing to the solid front the Labour Movement has presented we are able to come here in the position we do at this moment.

In 1921, I would like to deal with that aspect in regard to the great hole we got into. We said to the other sections: Will you please come into it? Before you have a voice in the matter of determining our policy. Please get into it. We got into a struggle before we allowed them to have a voice in it. . . . Now how could we expect these people or anybody else to get into a struggle before they had had any voice in it?

Now on this occasion we said: Whilst this is our trouble today, it may be yours tomorrow, and we put the matter in your hands to form a policy along with us in order that we may obtain your assistance. You know that was the right plan to adopt. In my judgment, the secret of the whole of our success was the unity of the rank and file, due to the tremendous effort and the appeal our Chairman and Secretary made to that body, which was responded to in the way it was. . . .

The Sankey Commission covered a wide field. I was there and so was Mr. Smith. It covered a wide range of subjects and I want to suggest that if those findings had been embodied in legislation it would have gone a considerable way to help. We had an extended inquiry—the Buckmaster inquiry, then this one at which we were not present. We have got—in my judgment it will not be a question of the Sankey Commission—we have got on this occasion to substantiate whether it is possible to organise or reorganise the industry in such a form that a reduction in the cost of production can be secured at a moment which will maintain our wages. . . .

We have got to remember the families in our districts, the men, women, and children, who are looking to us, in facing this problem; therefore, we have to sit down and help to prove to the general public that what we have been saying is correct—that organisation can be so altered as to give to them a cheaper article, and also secure to us not only our present wages but an improved wage for the future.

There had been more than one cross-current in the Conference. For example, at one point, Mr. G. A. Spencer, M.P., of Nottinghamshire created a little eddy of excitement which is recorded in the minutes as follows:

MR. G. A. SPENCER, M.P. (Notts): I would like to ask the platform whether they endorse what Mr. Cook has been saying Sunday after

Sunday with regard to a revolution. The language which has been used is going to break this Federation. I shall myself protest against it outside. It does not make for unity.

MR. COOK: I am coming to Mansfield, you can do it there.

MR. SPENCER, M.P.: Is the platform in favour of the statements which have been made?

MR. RICHARDSON: I want to raise a point of order. This matter which has been raised has nothing to do with the resolution.

THE CHAIRMAN: I will manage this meeting, if you will allow me.

MR. McANULTY: A point of order——

THE CHAIRMAN: This Federation is only responsible for what appears in this Federation's name and not for any individual whether it is Herbert Smith or anybody else.

But after Robson's speech there was no doubt as to the issue and with practical unanimity the decision was taken:

That this Conference accepts the report of the Committee upon the terms on which the employers' notices were withdrawn, and instructs the Committee to take such steps as it may be deemed necessary to present the Federation's case before the proposed inquiry. (August 19, 1925.)

At the Scarborough Trades Union Congress some three weeks later the same unanimity was manifest. Throughout the whole of the six weeks that followed Red Friday the whole Labour Movement appeared to be completely agreed on the steps taken and the lessons learned.

There was, however, one discordant note. Mr. Ramsay MacDonald, speaking immediately after the event to an I.L.P. summer school, said:

The Government has simply handed over the appearance, at any rate, of victory to the very forces that sane, well-considered, thoroughly well-examined Socialism feels to be probably its greatest enemy. (*Manchester Guardian*, August 4, 1925.)

Actually the Government had handed over "the appearance of victory" to the General Council of the Trades Union Congress. The next morning MacDonald, realising his blunder, issued an "explanation" to the effect first that the speech had never been intended for a wider audience—and that he had never intended to refer to anybody but "the Communists." As there were no Communists at that time either on the General Council or on the M.F.G.B. Executive, this was felt to be a somewhat lame apology. Exactly six years later, in August 1931, the remarkable coincidence of MacDonald's views on Red Friday with those of Right-Wing Conservatives could be recalled. But no further account of it was taken at the time: and MacDonald, to save his face, hastened to utter praise for the trade unions on several occasions during the next nine months.

STATEMENT SUBMITTED TO SPECIAL TRADES UNION CONGRESS AT CENTRAL HALL, WESTMINSTER, S.W.
(JULY 24, 1925)

THE JOINT INVESTIGATION INTO THE ECONOMIC POSITION OF THE MINING INDUSTRY

FELLOW TRADE UNIONISTS,

The Inquiry conducted by the representatives of the mine-owners and ourselves into the economic position of the mining industry was abruptly concluded by the mine-owners as a consequence of our refusal to agree with them upon the necessary remedial measures for lifting the industry out of its present deplorable position. Our own views as to the causes of the present position of the industry have been set forth in a separate document, entitled, "The Economic Position of the Coal Industry," which contains a clear summary of the economic position, and copies of which are available to the Trade Union Movement.

It may be said at once that a world coal crisis exists, and the position of the mine-workers in other coal-producing countries is almost entirely similar to our own. The following facts are, however, fundamental, and should be clearly borne in mind when considering the solution suggested by the mine-owners:

(1) The output per person employed in Great Britain is greater than any other coal-producing country, excepting America. (2) In America where the geological position and superior technique allow of a greater output per person employed, and consequently of a very much lower cost of production, a similar situation exists to that obtaining in this country; unemployment is rife, and there is a larger under-consumption of coal. (3) The hours of labour underground in this country are, in reality, only about 20 minutes per day less than the general eight-hour bank to bank day of European and American miners.[1] (4) Immense stocks of coal exist in all countries and all have equal difficulty in disposing of them. This is peculiarly true of Germany, our supposedly principal competitor. (5) Real wages are higher in all other countries than in the exporting districts of this country.

The situation with which we are confronted is thus one of a world

---

[1] NOTE.—This is explained by the fact that the seven hours' day operating in this country is exclusive of winding times; but the eight hours' day of other countries includes winding times.

shrinkage in the consumption of coal, and this is due to a variety of causes, the chief of which are:

(a) The extensive use of black coal substitutes, particularly brown coal or lignite. (b) The increasing growth of other sources of power, such as oil and hydro-electricity. (c) The increase and improvement of scientific processes for the general conservation of black coal. (d) The failure of capitalist production to scientifically organise and develop on new lines, and in a way which would counteract the new developments and take advantage of the processes which science is constantly developing for the use of coal. (e) The unsatisfactory political international relationships which are preventing the full operation of all coal consuming industries.

The situation in this country has been further aggravated by the interference with our normal markets by German Reparation coals, the loss of the Russian market, and the premature return to the gold standard.

It will be clear from this that the mine-owners' solution for this crisis, namely the cutting of wages and the lengthening of hours, is no solution at all, and must simply lead to a repetition of the same process a few months later. The enormous sacrifices which the mine-workers are asked to make would thus be in vain.

THE OWNERS' WAGE PROPOSALS

The proposals which have been submitted by the mine-owners have already been condemned by the General Council of the Trades Union Congress, who have endorsed our refusal to negotiate those terms. The terms have been widely commented upon, but we think we should re-state in some detail for the benefit of the Trade Union Movement their precise meaning and implication.

The present Wages Agreement provides for a general National Minimum Wage of $33\frac{1}{3}$ per cent upon standard wages, with a further proviso that the wage of no able-bodied adult day-wage workman shall fall below a figure of 40 per cent upon the standard rates of the lowest paid classes of labour in the various districts. It is now proposed that minimum wages should be abolished. The principle of a national minimum percentage would thus be lost, and there would be no limit to the extent to which the wages of the general body of mine-workers could be reduced.

The position of profits under the present Agreement is, that if in any period of ascertainment the proceeds, after meeting all other costs of production, are insufficient to provide minimum wages, such deficiency must be made good by the mine-owners, who may recoup themselves in subsequent periods, providing the surplus proceeds are sufficient for that purpose. Under the present proposals, inasmuch as the provision of minimum wages is to be abolished, the mine-owners would not have to make up wages in any way, but, on the contrary, would secure in the aggregate a guaranteed profit of £13 out of every £100 of the proceeds after the full costs of production other than wages had been met. In short, it is proposed that a definite portion of the proceeds should be allotted to profits in each ascertainment period, irrespective of the amount of the proceeds and irrespective of the position of wages. Wages would thus no longer be a first charge on the industry, but would rank equally with profits, each taking a definite share of the proceeds whatever they may be.

In regard to the lowest paid classes of workmen, the present Agreement provides for a subsistence allowance being paid to these, which, in the normal way, is met by the mine-owners and the higher paid workmen in the respective proportions in which they share the proceeds. The mine-owners now propose that subsistence allowances, if any, should be paid entirely by the workmen who are in receipt of wages above those of the lowest paid class in each district.

These proposals, if put into operation, would, in effect, transfer all the economic ills of the industry to the already overburdened shoulders of the mine-workers, and the mine-owners would assure to themselves a good profit under all conceivable circumstances. There would be very little incentive to efficiency on their part, and they would be able to automatically rid themselves of all their troubles by progressive reductions in wages. Experience teaches us that the awful state to which the mine-workers would be eventually reduced, if these proposals were operated, is too terrible to contemplate. It must be borne in mind that the mine-owners have consistently refused to allow us to have any share of the control of the industry, yet we are asked to allow our wages to be entirely at their mercy, and the burden of bad management, inefficient methods of production, administration, and distribution, could all be automatically transferred to our shoulders without any let or hindrance whatsoever.

It is impossible to seriously consider such a position.

We attach to this report a series of statistical tables which show the extent of the reductions in wages in August if the proposals were put into operation. The accuracy of these figures cannot be questioned, and they may be accepted by the Trade Union Movement with entire confidence. It should, however, be clearly realised that these figures only show the immediate effect of the proposals. The position which would eventually be reached is not one which we care to seriously contemplate.

THE COURT OF INQUIRY

In view of the strength of our case, and the character of the proposals which have been made to us, it is natural that our fellow trade unionists should ask us why we refuse to take part in the present Government Inquiry. The reasons for this refusal are many and varied, and, though the decision of our Conference on this point was unanimous, it was made only after the most careful thought and discussion.

The terms of reference of the Court are limited. At best it can make only a partial inquiry. The object of the Court is obviously to issue its report before the 31st of July. With all respect to the persons who constitute the Court, we venture to suggest that, in view of the magnitude and complexity of the subject, it is impossible for it to adequately consider in the time available all those wider aspects of the case which we would desire to bring forward. In our view, therefore, it is inevitable that its consideration of the subject would, in the main, be limited to the questions of hours and wages, and, indeed, the terms of reference of the Court entirely justify that view. Further, these questions would be considered mainly in the light of the figures supplied in respect of the financial position of the collieries. In other words, the Court would judge of the capacity of the industry from the narrow standpoint of the financial position of the industry as indicated by the returns made in respect of the pithead sale of raw coal, and it would be impossible to give proper consideration to all those wider aspects of the subject which are essential to a proper judgment upon our case.

If our view as to the scope of this Inquiry is a correct one, then we may at once point out that a partial inquiry of this character was held only a little over twelve months ago, and we feel we are justified in quoting the findings of that Court as being reasons which entirely obviate the necessity of another inquiry of the same character. The Court found:

That the wages paid to the day-wage workers in the coal-mining industry were substantially less than the equivalent of their pre-war earnings, and this was also true of piece-workers in certain collieries, but not in all.

That the provision of a minimum wage should have precedence over the distribution of profits.

The position of wages has not materially changed since the above findings were issued. The proposals of the coal-owners would, however, at once reduce wages to a point where the average increase over pre-war earnings would be approximately only 37 per cent, and would abolish the payment of a minimum wage in respect of which principle a Court of Inquiry has already reported in the terms stated above.

In regard to a fuller inquiry, such as that held in 1919, that would be a very different matter. We feel, however, that we are quite justified in referring to our bitter experience following that inquiry, when, after we had proved our case, the Government refused to give legislative effect to the majority findings of the Commission, as, in itself, sufficient justification for our refusal to participate in the present inquiry. In view of all these circumstances, we feel confident that our fellow trade unionists will endorse our action in this matter.

CONCLUSION

[*THE FOUR PARAGRAPHS OF THE CONCLUSION HAVE BEEN QUOTED ON PAGES* 374–5.]

Yours fraternally,
On behalf of the Executive Committee of the Miners' Federation of Great Britain.

HERBERT SMITH, President; THOMAS RICHARDS, Vice-President; W. P. RICHARDSON, Treasurer; A. J. COOK, Secretary.

July 22nd, 1925.

CHAPTER XII

THE NINE MONTHS

I. PREPAREDNESS—SCENE ONE

THERE were some who thought that the Cabinet in their parliamentary defence on August 6, 1925, were meeting their critics by brave words but that no real preparations for action against organised labour were intended. When the promised enquiry was announced in the shape of the Royal Commission on the Coal Industry some five weeks after Red Friday there were some who saw in this new body the mainstay on which to tie their wishes for a peaceful outcome. Yet the Cabinet had made it plain in their statements that for the purposes of any future conflict there would have to be both moral and material preparation. The first public move for the moral preparation was precisely the careful choice and appointment of the Royal Commission.

The first public announcement of the other kind of preparedness came not from the Government but from a body of private persons. On September 25, 1925, the newspapers announced the formation of a body called the "Organisation for the Maintenance of Supplies," thereafter known under the initials O.M.S. The announcement ran:

For many months past it has been evident that a movement is being organised to take advantage of a trade dispute, exceptionally difficult to solve, in order to promote a general strike. . . . Numerous suggestions have since been made from various quarters for organising those citizens who would be prepared to volunteer to maintain supplies and vital services in the event of a general strike.

It seems, therefore, that the moment has come to announce publicly that such an organisation has already been constituted and is at work in many metropolitan boroughs, while steps are being taken to create corresponding organisations in all the principal centres of the Kingdom.

After giving the Council, the officers, etc., the statement proceeded:

The object it has in view is to register and classify those citizens of all classes and of either sex who are prepared to render voluntary assistance in maintaining the supply of food, water, and fuel and the efficiency of public services indispensable to the normal life of the community.

It has no aggressive or provocative aims. It is not formed with any idea of opposing the legitimate efforts of trade unions to better the status and conditions of employment of their members, and it is in complete sympathy with any constitutional action to bring about a more equitable adjustment of social and economic conditions.

If, however, in order to secure a particular end, an attempt is made to inflict severe privation on the great mass of the people who have no direct part in the actual dispute, this Organisation of Citizens, serving the interests of the general community, will place its entire resources at the disposal of the constitutional authorities.

There followed further details with regard to the funds ("Certain funds . . . have been placed by a few patriotic citizens at the disposal of the Council"), details as to local organisation, an enumeration of the five categories of volunteers wanted (the first category to be of military age).

This organisation was of a kind entirely new in the annals of strike-breaking societies. It was not so much its careful phrasing, as the names and standing of its originators, that marked it off from all previous class-conscious efforts with similar objects. Its titular head was Lord Hardinge of Penshurst, an ex-Viceroy of India, and on its Council were Admiral of the Fleet Lord Jellicoe, General Sir Francis Lloyd, etc., etc. These gentlemen were not of the type usually described as die-hards: the peers were not, to use a well-known phrase, "backwoodsmen"; the commoners had not suddenly emerged from obscurity. They were, all of them, trusted public servants, carrying the highest reputation for faithful service in their respective professions. They were all of them on half-pay; their participation did not involve the Government directly; any one of them might conceivably have acted for once in his life in an irresponsible manner; but by all the canons of common sense the participation of such a group was something more than the irresponsibility of single individuals and as a consequence did involve the Government.

While the *Manchester Guardian* deplored this step, the *Daily Herald* affected to treat it not as a blow at the Labour Movement but as an insult to Mr. Baldwin ("this insulting intimation that he is unfit for his job") and a day later quoted from other newspapers passages to show that the O.M.S. "had met with a very chilly reception." However, if the newspapers were cool, it was the more necessary to warm them up. It might mean premature disclosures: but that was a risk at which Joynson-Hicks had never been known to blench. Accordingly, within a week, in reply to an anonymous correspondent enquiring about the O.M.S., the Home Secretary issued the following statement:

I will be perfectly frank with you. I have known of the inauguration of this body for many weeks past; in fact, the promoters consulted me as to their desire to form some such organisation. . . . I told the promoters of the O.M.S. that there was no objection on the part of the Government to their desire to inaugurate the body to which you refer; that, if and when an emergency arose, the Government would discharge the responsibility which is theirs and theirs alone, but that it would be a very great assistance to us to receive from the O.M.S., or from any other body of well-disposed citizens, classified lists of men in different parts of the country who would be willing to place their services at the disposal of the Government.

From this statement you will see that not only is there no reason why you should object to the O.M.S., but that you, or any other citizen who would desire the maintenance of peace, order, and good government in times of difficulty, would be performing a patriotic act by allying yourselves with this or any other similar body, formed for the sole purpose of helping the public authorities in the way I have suggested.

During these same weeks a series of parallel events was taking place. The Labour Party met in conference during the last week of September at Liverpool, where the main business was the drive made by Ramsay MacDonald for the expulsion of the Communists. This was followed a week later by the Conservative Conference held at Brighton. Here the attack was opened by passing a resolution calling on the Government to pass laws to cripple the trade unions. Their next step was a violent attack on the Communist Party which the Conservatives now felt had become isolated by the Labour Party Conference decision. The Communists had exposed themselves to the wrath of the Conservative Associations by energetically advocating counter-measures of preparation by the working class against the plans laid by Lord Hardinge and his O.M.S. and by the Government itself. Speaking on

October 8th, Baldwin promised the Conservative Conference that the Communist Party would be prosecuted. Within the shortest possible time after the two Conferences, twelve of the leaders of the Communist Party were arrested and charged with seditious libel. After five with previous convictions had been sentenced to a year's imprisonment, the other seven were offered their freedom if they would renounce their membership of the Communist Party. On their refusing all were sentenced to six months. When their trial reached what appeared to have been a foregone conclusion, the following resolution was passed by the Executive of the Miners' Federation, on November 27, 1925:

This Committee unanimously protests against the altogether unwarrantable and severe sentences inflicted upon the officials of the Communist Party, considering that the whole proceedings were influenced at every stage by political bias.

We unite with the other Trade Unions in demanding their immediate release and the prevention of this attempt to interfere with the freedom of the Press, free speech and personal liberty of opinion.

During the third week of November the preparations for each locality in the event of "an emergency" were disclosed. Circular 636 from the Ministry of Health to local authorities dated November 20, 1925, set out the relevant plans for the administering of the Emergency Powers Act. It announced that, "should such an emergency occur," England and Wales were to be divided into ten divisions, each under a Minister acting as Civil Commissioner on behalf of the Government, under whom the Local Authorities were to operate, to administer essential services and control road transport and food and fuel supplies, getting volunteers where necessary; and to organise "the maintenance of law and order," and to recruit "able-bodied citizens of good character to serve as Special Constables." Similar arrangements were made for Scotland.

This circular, taken in conjunction with the previous Ministry of Health circular of 1922 (and before that the plans and schemes set afoot in 1919, as revealed by Mr. Lloyd George in his Mansion House speech after the railway strike of September–October 1919), was really concerned to build up an extra-constitutional body in each locality, something which, however much it might be consonant with recent Acts of Parliament, was designed to supersede or subordinate the whole traditional structure of local government in Great Britain. The local governing bodies, either generally or in particular places, may have a different political complexion from that of the national Government. They might even, in places, have a Labour majority. The object of these elaborate preparations was clearly to provide machinery which the Government could regard as politically reliable. The Mayor of an English borough, the Provost of a Scottish burgh, is not, and never has been, an official of the central Government. The new array of officials to be set up would take their orders from Whitehall.

Again, this circular was another occasion upon which previously secret preparations were brought into the open and made as public as possible. When Mr. Taylor, M.P., in the House of Commons, had asked the Home Secretary "if he is aware that Town Clerks are receiving letters marked 'secret,' stating that it has been decided that the organisation for maintaining essential services during a national emergency should be set up by H.M. Government, and that Town Clerks are being interviewed," Sir William Joynson-Hicks, replying to this and other questions, said that the Government had

prepared plans for carrying out this duty. If, however, any unofficial organisation is in a position to prepare classified lists of persons willing to render help in an emergency, and if such organisation is prepared to place such lists at the disposal of the public authorities when required, the Government welcome such assistance. (November 19, 1925.)

Needless to say, it was only a small portion of these preparations that was made public; but that preparations were going on, and on the most extensive scale, was something which few people doubted.

Whatever doubts there might have been as to the intentions of the Government were swept away by Winston Churchill's speech on December 10, 1925. Speaking on the Coal Mining Industry Subvention, the Chancellor of the Exchequer made a programmatic speech, making it clear that half-way through the crucial nine months the Government were well on the way to being fully prepared. He said that they were impressed with the fact that "the country as a whole was not sufficiently informed about the character and immense consequences of such a struggle as that with which it was confronted." He said :

It is quite clear that a conflict of this kind, launched in this way, might easily cease to be a mere ordinary industrial dispute about wages and conditions and might assume a character altogether different from such industrial disputes. If that were to ensue, then it is quite clear that such a conflict between the community on the one hand, with the Government at its head, and many of the great trade unions on the other, could only end in one way, namely, by the community, at whatever cost, emerging victorious over an organised section of its citizens, however valuable, important, and even numerous that section was.

We considered, therefore, that should such a struggle be found to be inevitable at the very last moment, it was of supreme importance that it should only be undertaken under conditions which would not expose the nation needlessly or wantonly to perils the gravity of which cannot possibly be over-estimated.

We therefore decided to postpone the crisis in the hope of averting it, or, if not of averting it, of coping effectually with it when the time came.

2. PREPAREDNESS—SCENE TWO

On the side of organised labour the letter sent out on Red Friday from the General Council had stressed that "the Trade Union Movement must be alert and vigilant in case the necessity should again arise for it to act in defence of its standards." Moreover, the M.F.G.B. Conference on August 20th had been clear that it was not a victory but a truce for a limited period. A similar attitude was taken in the report of the General Council to the Scarborough Trades Union Congress (September 5th–10th) at which the President, Mr. A. B. Swales, delivered an address in a resolute and confident key. Recalling Red Friday, the "demonstration of Trade Union solidarity, connected with the miners' struggle, a month ago," he went on :

Those of us who were privileged to share in the victory and who helped to rally the forces of Trade Unionism behind the miners, lived a glorious week—one that will ever be remembered. It was historical.

As we marshalled our forces, day by day, to meet the pending attack of the representatives of capitalism, the response of all sections to defend the standard of wages and hours was most gratifying. It must be our work to harness that spirit to our organising work, and weave it into the fabric and structure of the Trade Union Movement of the future. The capitalist class will learn lessons from this skirmish, and will use their great influences in present-day society to compel a retreat.

The Congress passed a series of "left" resolutions which strengthened the impression already created throughout the ranks of organised labour by the events of Red Friday. For example, this Trades Union Congress passed strongly-worded resolutions on foreign policy; including one of support to "our working-class Chinese comrades," and for "the right of all peoples in the British Empire to self-determination, including the right to choose complete separation from the Empire." In similar tone they were also to pass a resolution which displayed a new attitude to the Dawes Plan. For this Plan, signed the previous autumn by J. Ramsay MacDonald as Prime Minister and unopposed at the time even by the miners (despite reparations coal), there was now a strong and explicit condemnation:

That this Trades Union Congress condemns the enslavement of the German workers by the Dawes Plan. It declares that the low wages and long hours existing in that country are directly due to the successful attempt of the employers to place the burden of the plan on the German workers.

Further, we pledge ourselves to assist the German workers in every possible way to improve their standard of life and resolve to support the General Council in its efforts to obtain International Trade Union unity which will enable the workers to fight on an international scale for the repudiation of the Dawes Plan.

The drive for international trade union unity was also the subject of a separate resolution which recorded "appreciation of the General Council's efforts" to promote this and urged the incoming General Council "to do everything in their power towards securing world-wide unity" of the trade union movement. It was preceding this resolution that Fred Bramley, the Secretary of the T.U.C.—then ill and within a few months of his death—made a moving appeal in favour of international solidarity with the Russian workers.

Resolutions of this kind raised high hopes of solidarity nationally and internationally in the ranks of organised labour, including the miners. But there was another side to the Scarborough Congress. First, a resolution to give greater powers to the General Council was referred back for later decision: second, in the elections to the General Council J. H. Thomas, once more General Secretary of the National Union of Railwaymen, was chosen. From his previous record it was unlikely that Thomas would operate a militant policy or anything like it. This change in the T.U.C. leading body, on the conduct of which the outcome might depend, was to be followed, as we have seen, by the Labour Party's Liverpool Conference when a counter-offensive had been conducted against all Left-Wing resolutions with the expulsion of the Communist advocates of vigorous counter-preparations. A month after the State trial of the Communist leaders came wholesale arrests and severe sentences upon anthracite miners who had come out on strike at Ammanford, in South Wales.

What was to be the strategy on the side of Labour? How far were preparations being made for defence?

Apart from these demonstrations and counter-demonstrations at Scarborough and Liverpool, there was no visible sign of steps taken by the General Council towards that preparedness which had been called for in August and early September. Instead of preparedness, there was visible reliance on the activities of the new Royal Commission, as though the advent of that body had relieved the T.U.C. General Council of its responsibilities.

3. THE MINERS AND PREPAREDNESS

Meanwhile the Miners' Federation, while reposing in the General Council a degree of confidence apparently warranted by the events of Red Friday, had gone ahead with its earlier project of a broad-based alliance of unions in heavy industry and transport. On September 5th an M.F.G.B. Delegate Conference adhered to the Industrial Alliance as adopted by the unions concerned at the meeting of July 17th. On September 9th the National Union of Foundry Workers also adhered to the constitution, to be followed within a week by the Associated Society of Locomotive Engineers and Firemen and by the Electrical Trades Union. By November 5th a Delegate Conference of all the unions concerned, meeting in Essex Hall, London, accepted the draft constitution. Before it could come into force, however, it was necessary in several cases to take ballot votes of the union members, which meant considerable delay. For example, it was not till the second week of January that the proposals were submitted for ballot vote of the Amalgamated Engineering Union; and not until March 23rd that the ballot resulted in a favourable decision by 70,695 to 31,423 votes. A day later the Foundry Workers' Union also decided in favour. Towards the end of February the Iron and Steel Trades Confederation had also voted in favour by a large majority. But in mid-March the Boiler-makers had voted against it.

To these delays and tardy ballots there was added another difficulty. At the meeting of November 5, 1925, the repre-sentatives of the National Union of Railwaymen had proposed as an amendment that a condition of membership should be the preparation of a scheme for fusion between the unions in any given industry. Apparently laudable, this amendment was aimed at the Associated Society of Locomotive Engineers and Firemen of which John Bromley was the Secretary. Mr. J. H. Thomas, Secretary of the N.U.R., must have been aware that such an amendment would make it difficult to have all the operative grades of railwaymen in the Alliance.

All the delays, however caused, could have but one result. The Industrial Alliance by the spring of 1926 was like an addled egg. This part of the miners' plan had "gaun a-gley." Nevertheless, the constitution of the Industrial Alliance, which existed but never functioned, is of considerable interest; adopted on November 25, 1925, it is to be found in the Appendix to this chapter.

4. THE ROYAL COMMISSION ON THE COAL INDUSTRY

The Government and O.M.S. had organised their weapons and furbished up their machinery; the miners were rallying their allies. Now Baldwin was to bring into play an important part of his moral preparations. From "Our Court at Balmoral, the fifth day of September, one thousand nine hundred and twenty-five, in the sixteenth year of Our Reign," came a Royal Warrant establishing yet another Commission on the Coal Industry. It was to be known as the Samuel Commission, after its Chairman, Sir Herbert Samuel: the three other Commissioners were General Sir Herbert Lawrence, Sir William Beveridge and Mr. Kenneth Lee. They were "to inquire into and report upon the economic position of the coal industry and the conditions affecting it and to make any recommendations for the improvement thereof."

This Royal Commission was very differently composed from Royal Commissions or Courts of Enquiry on this industry in the previous six years. Here were no representatives of organised labour, as on the Sankey Commission of 1919, or on the Buckmaster Court of Enquiry of 1924 or even the MacMillan Court of Enquiry of 1925. Sir Herbert Samuel, born in 1870, with extensive family connections in finance, had considerable experience of government both in Britain and Asia. In the Liberal Government of 1905 onwards he held successively the posts of Under-Secretary of State for Home Affairs, Chancellor of the Duchy of Lancaster, Postmaster-General, President of the Local Government Board and Secretary of State for Home Affairs. From 1919 onwards he ruled Palestine as British High Commissioner. From governing Arabs and Jews he returned in 1925 to head the Royal Commission. Sir William Beveridge began his public activities as a leader-writer to the *Morning Post* from 1906 to 1908, and developed in the Board of Trade, where he was mainly concerned in the establishment of Labour Exchanges. During the war of 1914–18 he was in the Ministry of Munitions; afterwards in the Ministry of Food. Later he resigned from the Civil Service to take up the Directorship of the London School of Economics. General Sir Herbert Lawrence was managing partner of Glyn, Mills and Co., the well-known banking house, and was also on the board in several other important companies. Mr. Kenneth Lee was Chairman of Tootal, Broadhurst, Lee and Co. (the great cotton firm) and Chairman of the District Bank. Some of the concerns on which General Lawrence and Mr. Lee sat belonged to the Federation of British Industries. Here we may quote a phrase used in *The Coal Crisis*:[1]

> The Government, of course, represented this Commission as an impartial body. It is true it is not directly representative of the Mining Association, but it is difficult to imagine any small body of persons more completely representative of Capitalist interests, and more completely trained in approaching matters from the Capitalist standpoint.

The Royal Commission, thus composed, took evidence in public between October 15, 1925, and January 14, 1926. The Report itself was completed on March 6, 1926, and published within a day or two. It contained a survey of the whole industry, in some 300 pages, buttressed by three volumes of evidence and statistical material, while dovetailed into the survey of the industry were a number of recommendations.

In the next section we deal with the reception of the Report and the progress of negotiations that took place from the date of its appearance. Here we are concerned only to consider the Report regarded as one of the means by which public opinion was "prepared" for the renewed attack on the miners' wages which was made in April 1926. Roughly speaking, the Report can be summed up as a proposal for reorganising the mining industry, to be put into effect at some future date, together with proposals for a reduction in wages, to take effect at once.

Concerning the immediate crisis, a wages struggle between the employers and the miners in the coal industry, the central feature of the Report was its recommendations that wages should be reduced. Everything in the Report tended to this end.

The same trend of no concession was found in economic policy. The Labour Government in 1924 had proposed resumption of full trade with Soviet Russia together with long credits or a loan of some £100 million for this purpose. The exports would have been in the main manufactured metal goods, while into the maw of these furnaces would have been poured anything from ten to fifteen million tons of coal.

---

[1] *The Coal Crisis: Facts from the Samuel Commission, 1925–26.* Foreword by Herbert Smith, Labour Research Department, 1926.

But for the Commissioners to make such a recommendation would have been to run counter to the policy of the Baldwin Government which set them up as a Commission. They remained discreetly silent. Government economic policy was treated as being of the same order as the geological formations.

It was an artificial picture of the coal industry, while of the possible remedies nationalisation was dismissed ("we perceive in it grave economic dangers") and it was argued that private enterprise (under a future reorganisation) would provide all the advantages claimed for nationalisation. But one remedy was brought to the forefront—to reduce wages. The parties to the Report wished to divide the Labour Movement, to convince those who were ready to be convinced, as well as those who were less ready, that the miners should suffer a reduction in wages and that the other trade unions would not be justified in repeating their action of the previous July. As well as recommending immediate wage reductions ("the revision of the minimum percentage addition to standard rates of wages"), the Commissioners came out strongly against the subsidy, saying:

> We express no opinion whether the grant of a subsidy last July was unavoidable or not, but we think its continuance indefensible. The subsidy should stop at the end of its authorised term, and should never be repeated.

However, they were "strongly of opinion that national wage agreements should continue." Their other proposals can be conveniently described by quoting from a summary which was to form part of a statement prepared later for a Conference of Executives of trade unions. It runs:

(1) Amalgamation of existing mines where units are at present too small.
(2) A closer connection of mining with allied industries.
(3) More extensive research.
(4) State purchase of Royalties.
(5) The formation of co-operative selling agencies, especially for the export trade.
(6) The establishment of an official system of sampling and analysis of coal.
(7) The retail sale of coal by local authorities.
(8) The use of larger wagons, and concentration of the ownership of wagons.

(9) The official declaration of transfer prices and the inclusion of the profits of selling agencies in the ascertainments.

(10) The extension of multiple shifts and possibly the redistribution of the existing total hours over the working week.

(11) Revision of the minimum percentages.

(12) The establishment of joint pit committees.

(13) The extension of payment by results.

(14) The introduction of the family allowance system.

(15) Profit-sharing schemes to be set up.

(16) General establishment of pithead baths and proper provision of houses.

(17) National negotiations and agreements to continue.

5. HOPES AND FEARS FOR SOLIDARITY

The Industrial Committee of the Trades Union Congress General Council, reappointed after the Scarborough Congress with slight but significant alterations (J. H. Thomas became a member and also Arthur Pugh, as T.U.C. Chairman) was charged with the duty of keeping in touch with the situation and of taking such steps as might seem necessary. Up till the end of the year and beyond it, it did not seem necessary to them to take any decisive steps. When, however, the nationalisation evidence had been very coolly received by the Royal Commission the M.F.G.B. Executive Committee decided (on January 15, 1926) to ask for a joint meeting: and to this the Industrial Committee agreed. A month later they heard a statement from Herbert Smith in which he set forth the most important principles for which the M.F.G.B. stood: and it was thereupon arranged that joint meetings should be held of the nine members of the Industrial Committee with an equal number from the M.F.G.B. Executive Committee. After the first of these joint meetings held on February 19th (that is, three-quarters of the way through the subsidy period of nine months) the following official statement was issued:

The two Committees gave full consideration to the possibility of a crisis arising in connection with the Mining situation. From the Trade Union point of view the question is entirely one of wages and conditions of employment in the coal-fields.

The circumstances which led the Trade Union Movement, last

July, to pledge the united support of the miners will constitute, in the opinion of the Joint Meeting, a menace to the miners' standard of life. The Committees particularly desire to urge the Trade Union Movement not to allow itself to be influenced by unauthorised and unofficial suggestions which are being made in many quarters regarding the Mining problem.

The attitude of the Trade Union Movement was made perfectly clear last July, namely, that it would stand firmly and unitedly against any attempt further to degrade the standard of life in the coal-fields. There was to be no reduction in wages, no increase in working hours, and no interference with the principle of National Agreements. This is the position of the Trade Union Movement today.

This declaration of policy was confirmed in a statement from the second meeting held a week later, on February 26th.

Another fortnight went past: and the Report of the Coal Commission was published on March 10th and sold at the artificially cheap price of 3d. for nearly 300 pages, to ensure the widest possible circulation. In contrast to the contempt meted out to the Macmillan Enquiry of the previous July, this Samuel Commission Report was greeted with the utmost respect, almost with worshipfulness. On March 11th the M.F.G.B. not only accepted the proposal of the Prime Minister that no pronouncement should be made until after due examination of the document, but at a joint meeting with the T.U.C. Industrial Committee requested them to take a similar line. The official statement ran "In view of the fact that the Miners' Federation is consulting its members, and examining thoroughly the report of the proposals therein, at the miners' request, the Meeting unanimously decided that in the best interests of all parties, adequate time should be given to all concerned before coming to any decision." The miners' Conference of the next day accordingly dispersed to the coal-fields without making any pronouncement, while that week Arthur Cook advised all miners and miners' wives to read the Samuel Report.

Four weeks elapsed, weeks filled with rumours of one kind and another. On the day before the adjourned miners' Conference, the representatives of the Federation approached the General Council for an assurance that the declaration of February 19th still held good. The Industrial Committee, after full discussion, composed the following resolution:

That having discussed with the representatives of the Miners' Federation the present position in the Mining Industry, with special reference to the views of the miners on the Coal-owners' statements of their attitude in regard to the Report of the Coal Commission, this Committee re-confirms its previous declarations in support of the miners' efforts to obtain an equitable settlement of outstanding difficulties.

This Committee is of opinion that negotiations betwen the Mining Association and the Miners' Federation of Great Britain should be continued without delay, in order to obtain a clear understanding with regard to the report of the Coal Commission, and to reduce points of difference to the smallest possible dimensions.

That this Committee holds itself available to assist in any way possible to reach a satisfactory settlement.

In sending this resolution to the M.F.G.B. on April 8th, the Acting Secretary described how they had "carefully considered" the miners' statement, and went on:

The Committee fully realise the seriousness of the present position, but they are of the opinion that matters have not yet reached the stage when any final declaration of the General Council's policy can be made.

It appears to them that negotiations are yet in a very early stage, and that efforts should be made to explore to the fullest extent the possibility of reducing the points of difference between your Federation and the Coal-owners, and for that purpose they advise the immediate continuance of negotiations as suggested in the accompanying Resolution.

It would be an advantage to the Committee if you could furnish them, after your conference tomorrow, with a detailed statement of the views of your Federation in respect of the various recommendations put forward by the Commission.

The Committee wish to assure you that they are extremely desirous of doing anything they possibly can to facilitate settlement, and they will hold themselves in readiness in case your Federation should desire to utilise their services.

Yours sincerely, WALTER M. CITRINE, Acting Secretary.

Meantime there had been, on March 24th, a meeting between representatives of the Mining Association and of the Miners' Federation and the Prime Minister, who read to them the following Cabinet decision:

The Government have considered with great care the Report of the Royal Commission. The conclusions reached by the Commission do not in all respects accord with views held by the Government and some of the recommendations contain proposals to which, taken by themselves, the Government are known to be opposed. Nevertheless, in face of the unanimous report of the Commission and for the sake of a general settlement the Government for their part will be prepared to undertake such measures as may be required of the State to give the recommendations effect, provided that those engaged in this industry—with whom the decision primarily rests— agree to accept the Report and to carry on the industry on the basis of its recommendations. It is our hope that in that event, by the co-operation of all parties, it may be possible to find in the Report a lasting solution of the problem.

This left it to the owners and the miners to reach some agreement. At joint meetings of owners' and miners' representatives on March 25th and 31st and on April 1st it became clear that the owners were in favour of the longer working day and District agreements as well as a reduction in wages. No agreement was reached between the parties.

When the miners' Conference, attended by 156 delegates representing 804,000 members, met and received the report of the negotiations with the owners and of the discussions with the Trades Union Congress Industrial Committee, they passed the following resolution unanimously:

That this Conference, having considered the Report of the Royal Commission and the proposals of the colliery owners thereon, recommends the districts as follows:

(*a*) That no assent be given for any proposal for increasing the working day.

(*b*) That the principles of a National Wage Agreement with a national minimum be firmly adhered to.

(*c*) That inasmuch as wages are already too low we cannot assent to any proposals for reducing wages.

These recommendations to be remitted to the districts for their immediate consideration and decision, after which a further Conference be called as speedily as possible for the purpose of arriving at a final decision. (April 9, 1926.)

Once more, on April 13th, the owners' and miners' representatives came together: the owners said they would meet District representatives to consider in each case the District minimum: the miners were opposed: it was full deadlock. The owners thereafter in most Districts posted notices in the pits to end existing contracts: employment on existing terms would cease on April 30th. It was a lock-out: the owners had delivered their ultimatum.

The T.U.C. Industrial Committee, informed of this the next day by the M.F.G.B. representatives, passed the following resolution:

This Committee protests against the action of the mine-owners in abandoning national negotiations and in attempting to open negotiations with the districts. This, in the opinion of the Committee, is calculated to create ill-feeling and suspicion at a critical time, and is a course of action contrary to the spirit of conciliation and the expressed views of the Royal Commission, and prejudicial to the prospect of an amicable settlement.

The Committee reiterates its previous declaration to render the miners the fullest support in resisting the degradation of their standard of life, and in obtaining an equitable settlement of the case with regard to wages, hours, and national agreements. (April 14, 1926.)

This resolution was immediately brought by the Special Committee to the Prime Minister, who invited the M.F.G.B. representatives to meet him the next day; at the meeting Mr. Baldwin undertook to try to get the mine-owners to resume negotiations on a national basis. It was a week before the miners' and mine-owners' representatives came together. This meeting of April 22nd confirmed the deadlock. The owners were not willing to discuss any minimum percentage to be applied nationally over the coal-fields, or even to discuss nationally the District rates of wages and conditions that they had framed. As a matter of information they supplied copies of the terms which had been prepared in each county by the District Owners' Association. According to the estimates made by the M.F.G.B. officials, these terms would have meant wages reductions in the main Districts of from 2s. 8d. to 5s. 11d. per shift in South Wales and Monmouth; 2s. 10d. in Durham; 2s. in Scotland; and from 1s. to 1s. 6d. in Yorkshire, Nottinghamshire, Leicestershire, Cannock Chase, South Derby, Lancashire, and North Staffordshire.

Once again the Industrial Committee went to the Prime Minister, who next day, April 23rd, met both miners and mine-owners: a committee from each was appointed, but without any result. Matters were at a complete standstill. Thereupon the Industrial Committee appointed J. Ramsay

MacDonald and Arthur Henderson to be present at all meetings. This had no immediate result beyond making the closest contact with the two leading figures of the Labour Party.

In face of the deadlock and with the lock-out notices due to run out on April 30th, a Special M.F.G.B. Delegate Conference was summoned for April 28th, and a Special Conference of Trade Union Executives for Thursday April 29th. Each Conference was to be in session till the afternoon of May 1st. But in each case there were frequent adjournments, as most of the time was taken up in negotiations. The multitudinous details of those negotiations amid feverish anxiety in the Press and throughout the country need not be here recounted. The general situation reached up to this point was described in the May issue of the monthly circular of the Labour Research Department (which had been working closely with the M.F.G.B.) in the following terms:

So far as the coal industry is concerned, April, 1926, has seen an almost exact repetition of July, 1925. On the one hand, the miners and the whole trade union movement, on the other the mine-owners and the Baldwin Government; negotiations, known in advance to be fruitless; and, in the end, the posting of notices by the mine-owners; advertising to the whole working class the futility of the Samuel Commission, and calling their attention once more to the immediate vital issue—wages. And, as last July, every merchant, every consumer of coal is piling up stocks; and every possible strike-breaker is being organised directly, or indirectly, by the Government.

6. THE CONFERENCE OF EXECUTIVES

When, in July 1925, the Government had retracted, to seek a nine months' breathing space, a Conference of Executives of trade unions had been in session. Now, with the subsidy period fast running out, a similar Conference of "Labour's general staff" met together, called by the T.U.C. General Council.

The Conference of Executive Committees of trade unions affiliated to the Trades Union Congress was a relatively new expedient. It had been devised to overcome the limitations of the Trades Union Congress. That body, from its origin in the late 'sixties, had failed to develop into an annual Parliament of Labour (however much newspapers might use such phrases to describe it) in its first twenty-five years; and accordingly its limitations had been pointed out and to a certain extent criticised by the Webbs in the early 'nineties. With the expulsion of the Trades Councils in 1895 the possibility of structural development of the T.U.C. came to an end. Nevertheless, attention was fastened after 1910 upon the Parliamentary Committee (annually elected by the T.U.C.) as insufficient. The agitation to have "a general staff of Labour" did not lead to the creation of such a general staff, but it did lead to the setting up of the General Council of the T.U.C. in 1921; concentration on this agitation had hidden from the movement the weakness of the parent body. When, however, questions of immediate action came up it was immediately clear that assent must be obtained from the most immediately responsible bodies, the Executive Committees of the trade unions, for delegates chosen several months in advance might not carry the union with them in decisions about action. On the other hand a Conference of Executives, through the growth of the trade union movement and the enlargement of its committees, had become a somewhat unwieldy body, very expensive to call together and keep in London for more than a short time, and having no regular continuity with any predecessor or successor. It seemed, however, the only way in which any surrender of the autonomy of each union for a special occasion could be effected. Consequently this assembly, unknown in the first fifty years of the T.U.C., came to supersede that body on questions of decision for action in the troublous years from 1916 onwards.

The Conference on its first day, Thursday, April 29th, heard a full report from Mr. Arthur Pugh, Chairman for that year of the T.U.C. He gave a broad picture of the situation as compared with that of the previous July, made a recital of events and activities in the period immediately preceding the Conference and ended with a statement of the General Council's proposals on the coal question. This statement summarised the Commission's recommendations, and analysed them in detail. It continued:

We are satisfied, after careful investigation, that these cannot provide a solution for the immediate difficulties which arise on the 1st May. In the negotiations which have ensued between the Government, Mining Association, and the Miners' Federation, attention has been concentrated almost exclusively upon questions relating to the wages, hours, and working conditions of the mine-workers. Far more consideration needs to be given to the drastic reorganisation which both the Commission and the mine-workers consider is required. In our view the wages and working conditions of mine-workers are already so depressed as to render it imperative to seek for remedies other than a further degradation in their standards of life, or the abrogation of the present standard hours, a course which the Commission declared would not provide a remedy. . . .

The present position has been aggravated by the method by which the subsidy has been granted by the Government and used by the coal-owners to lower artificially the price of coal. The present price is unquestionably an uneconomic one, and does not reflect the real position of the industry. . . .

We regard the maintenance of national negotiations as imperative, and the continuance of a National Wages Board. Throughout the negotiations the Miners' Executive have repeatedly expressed their willingness to consider any proposals which the Government or the Mine-owners are prepared to submit for securing the speedy and effective reorganisation of the mining industry.

After having heard this statement, the Conference accepted a resolution moved by the Right Hon. J. H. Thomas, M.P., who chiefly laid stress on the need for the withdrawal of lock-out notices now due to run out in less than forty hours. Ernest Bevin, in his speech as seconder, was more definite as to the future: he said:

You are moving to an extraordinary position. In twenty-four hours from now you may have to cease being separate Unions for this purpose. For this purpose you will become one union with no autonomy. The miners will have to throw their lot and cause into the cause of the general movement, and the general movement will have to take the responsibility for seeing it through. But at the moment we feel that to begin wielding any sort of a threat in connection with the negotiations, in the stage they are now in, would be to place a weapon in the hands of our opponents.

We are asking you to stay in London. You are to be our Parliament, you are to be our Assembly, our consituent assembly, an assembly where we will place the facts and figures and the proposals and the problems that have to be submitted for calm judgment, and at the end take your instructions. . . .

The resolution was carried by a show of hands with only one or two dissentients and ran as follows:

That this Conference of Executives of Unions affiliated to the Trades Union Congress endorses the efforts of the General Council to secure an honourable settlement of the differences in the coal-mining industry. It further instructs the Industrial Committee of the General Council to continue its efforts, and declares its readiness for the negotiations to continue providing that the impending lock-out of the mine-workers is not enforced.

That this Conference hereby adjourns until tomorrow, and agrees to remain in London to enable the General Council to consult, report and take instructions. (Thursday, April 29, 1926.)

All the next day the Conference kept meeting and adjourning, while waiting anxiously for news from their Special Negotiating Committee. Late that Friday evening, at 11.25 p.m., Pugh reported on negotiations since Thursday evening. When they met the Prime Minister, said he, they had pointed out that no definite proposals had been received either from the Government or from the employers on which negotiations could be conducted. All that had appeared was a notice, posted at the pit-heads, with regard to reductions in wages, "which the Government itself and public opinion would declare the miners were entitled definitely to refuse." Consequently there was nothing to go upon. These discussions went on till about 1.30 a.m. of Friday, April 30th (less than twenty-three hours left!), and ended with the understanding that the Prime Minister was in touch with the mine-owners and that definite proposals would be made that same day. That afternoon came a letter from the Prime Minister to Herbert Smith:

10 Downing Street, S.W.1.
30th April, 1926.

Dear Mr. Smith,

I am communicating with you by letter because it is important to save time.

I have now received from the coal-owners the offer which, as I told you last night, they have been considering in conjunction with their district representatives. The offer is as follows, namely:

A uniform national minimum of 20 per cent over 1914 standard on a uniform 8-hour basis, with corresponding hours for surface men. (The representatives of North Wales do not wish to stand out of the national agreement, but feel that the pits in that area would be unable to work on this minimum.)

In putting before you this proposal from the coal-owners, I would remind you that, as I explained to you yesterday, it is contemplated that the 1919 (Seven Hours') Act should remain on the Statute Book, and that there should be legislation providing temporarily for the working of the additional hours.

The Government would set up a Commission not later than December 31st, 1929, to advise whether as a result of reorganisation or better trade or both, the condition of the coal industry has improved to an extent that makes a reversion to the standard hours justifiable.

There would, of course, be a national agreement on the lines of the owners' draft, which has already been submitted to you, amended, however, to provide for a national minimum. I should like to hear from you what is your considered view upon this proposal.

It will be seen that a uniform national minimum is possible if there is for the time being a modification of the present hours. If, however, a temporary modification of hours is ruled out, the owners do not feel able to put forward proposals which differ from those which they have already submitted. They are, however, prepared to negotiate the matter with you, in the first place nationally, in accordance with the report.

There would, of course, be the national agreement as already indicated. The Government has already intimated its general acceptance of the report of the Royal Commission, provided it was accepted also by the mine-owners and the miners, and although unfortunately there has not been on the part of the mine-owners and the miners the same unqualified acceptance, the Government desire, nevertheless, to reaffirm their willingness to give effect to such of the proposals in the Report as we believe will be of benefit to the industry.

In particular, the Government propose in any case at once to arrange an authoritative inquiry into the best method of following up the recommendations of the Commission with regard to selling organisation and amalgamations.

If the proposals now before you are not acceptable, I should be glad to receive from you any counter-proposal and I am holding myself available to meet you again as soon as you let me know that you are ready for further discussion.

I am sending a copy of this letter to Mr. Pugh.

Yours very truly, STANLEY BALDWIN.

The miners' Executive and the Conference considered the owners' proposals, and instructed the officers to reply to the Prime Minister:

30th April, 1926.

Dear Mr. Prime Minister,

The proposals of the coal-owners, delivered by messenger this afternoon (April 30th), have been considered by our Executive Committee, and also by the Conference which, as you are aware, has been in London since Wednesday, to which we are empowered to send the following reply:

The miners note with regret that, although the report of the Coal Commission was issued on 6th March, 1926, the mine-owners have only submitted a proposal for a national wage agreement and a national uniform minimum percentage so late as April 30th, at 1.15 p.m., when at least two-thirds of the mine-workers in the coal-field are already locked out by the coal-owners.

The proposals, stated briefly, provide for a reversion to the minimum percentage of 1921, i.e. 20 per cent on 1914 standard wages, which means a uniform reduction of $13\frac{1}{3}$ per cent of the standard wages of the miners, and, further, is conditional upon the extension of the working day for over three years, such an adjustment to be reviewed after December, 1929.

The reply of the miners, after considering the proposals in the light of the present situation, is therefore as follows:—They are unanimously of the opinion that the proposals cannot be accepted, but, on the other hand, feel that the statement of proposals submitted (as enclosed) of the Trades Union Congress affords a reasonable basis of negotiations and settlement.

Our views on the question of extended hours are well known to you, and it is only necessary to say that the present hours

(a) Are long enough to supply all the coal for which a market can be found;

(b) Are as long as men should be expected to pursue such a dangerous and arduous calling; and

(c) That to extend hours in present circumstances is simply to swell the ranks of the unemployed;

(d) That to increase hours is to invite similar measures on the part of our foreign competitors;

(e) That such a proposal is contrary to the findings of the Royal Commission.

As to counter-proposals, we can only say that we will co-operate to the fullest extent with the Government and the owners in instituting such reorganisation as is recommended by the Commission. Until such reorganisation brings greater prosperity to the industry, the miners should not be called upon to surrender any of their present inadequate wages and conditions.

On behalf of the Miners' Federation. Yours faithfully,

HERBERT SMITH (President); T. RICHARDS (Vice-President)
W. P. RICHARDSON (Treasurer); A. J. COOK (Secretary).

After Arthur Pugh had read these letters to the Conference the Press was admitted. J. H. Thomas then gave a descriptive account of the negotiations, in which a most telling passage ran as follows:

My friends, when the verbatim reports are written, I suppose my usual critics will say that Thomas was almost grovelling, and it is true. In all my long experience—and I have conducted many negotiations—I say to you, and all my colleagues will bear testimony to it, I never begged and pleaded like I begged and pleaded all day today, and I pleaded not alone because I believed in the case of the miners, but because in my bones I believed that my duty to the country involved it. Therefore, I shall be content for our case to be judged on the verbatim reports that will be produced. But we failed. The Cabinet was summoned—such additional members as had not previously been in the negotiations, a number of whom had heard nothing of what had taken place, were called in to give their final decision, and their final decision was a refusal to accede to your request. Please observe, not to effect a settlement, but a refusal to accede to your request for a suspension of the notices so that negotiations could continue.

Before this rejection of the plea to suspend notices the Cabinet had already set in motion the vast and ramifying machinery of the Emergency Powers Act. The situation thus created by the Cabinet's refusal and its other overt activities left the Conference of Executives with no option. Therefore, when it reassembled at 12.30 p.m. on Saturday, May 1st, the Conference had placed before it, for the first time in the history of the British working class, a proposal for a General Strike. This was to take effect at midnight on Monday.

The proposal was overwhelmingly accepted. Only Havelock Wilson cast the 49,911 votes of his union against, while for the General Strike there were cast the votes of 3,653,527 trade unionists.

Thus the greatest dramatic event since the days of the Chartist Movement was presented before the world with all the United Kingdom as the stage.

Here attention may be drawn to the opening remarks of Ernest Bevin as an indication of the feeling that pervaded the Conference:

I desire to point out that, with a view to doing nothing at all which would aggravate the position, these proposals were not ready to hand to the General Secretaries, or rather the documents in the form in which you received it, until after we had received in our room the news that the Emergency Powers Act had been signed, and after the O.M.S. had already placed upon the printing press their preparatory literature. We looked upon that, and I think rightly, while our people were down there and we did not know what was really happening, as indicating that the Government, behind the scenes, was mobilising the forces of war. I think it was a right deduction in view of subsequent happenings. Sometimes it is said, that he who draws the sword perishes by the sword, and we all looked upon the action of the Government last night as equal in stupidity to the actions of the well-remembered Lord North and George III combined, and the result may be fraught with as serious consequences as the action of George III in the history of this country. . . .

We look upon your "yes" as meaning that you have placed your all upon the altar of this great movement, and, having placed it there, even if every penny goes, if every asset goes, history will ultimately write up that it was a magnificent generation that was prepared to do it rather than see the miners driven down like slaves. . . . I rely, in the name of the General Council, on every man and every woman in that grade to fight for the soul of Labour and the salvation of the miners.

Inspiring speeches such as this were soon to be put to the test of action.

CONSTITUTION OF INDUSTRIAL ALLIANCE (NOVEMBER 1925)

1. *Objects.*—To create through a Trade Union Alliance a means of mutual support and to assist any or all of the allied organisations: (*a*) to defend hours of labour and wages standards; (*b*) to promote or to defend any vital principle of an industrial character. To take such steps for mutual co-operation on economic and industrial matters as may from time to time be decided upon.

2. *Constitution.*—The Alliance shall consist of organisations representing workpeople engaged in all forms of transport (Railway, Docks, Waterways, Road, Sea, Air), Engineering, Shipbuilding, Iron and Steel production, Mining and all forms of Power production and distribution.

3. *Government of the Alliance (General Conference).*—For the government of the Alliance there shall be a General Conference. Those eligible to attend must be either officers and/or members of the Executive Council of an allied organisation. Such Conference shall meet at least once per year in London; also at such times as may be called by the Executive Council as hereinafter provided. Voting at such Conference shall be: (*a*) By Societies; (*b*) First by show of hands; (*c*) If challenged, then by proportional voting, as follows:

(1) For each allied organisation with a membership up to 50,000 . . . ONE VOTE; (2) For each allied organisation with over 50,000 members up to 200,000 . . . TWO VOTES; (3) For each allied organisation with over 200,000 members up to 500,000 . . . THREE VOTES; (4) For each allied organisation with over 500,000 members . . . FOUR VOTES.

4. *Executive Council.*—The Executive Council shall consist of appointed persons as follows:

(*a*) For each allied organisation with a membership up to 50,000 . . . ONE MEMBER; (*b*) For each allied organisation with over 50,000 up to 200,000 members . . . TWO MEMBERS; (*c*) For each allied organisation with over 200,000 members up to 500,000 members . . . THREE MEMBERS; (*d*) For each allied organisation with over 500,000 members . . . FOUR MEMBERS.

Each allied organisation shall pay the expenses of its own representatives upon the Executive Council. Each of the Allied Executive Councils shall have power to appoint or change its representative or representatives upon the Executive Council.

5. *Duties of the Executive Council.*—The Executive Council shall circulate all its minutes to the allied organisations. They shall, as herein-

after provided, call meetings of the General Conference, and shall be the only recognised authority for carrying out the decisions of the Conference. They shall keep the General Council of Trades Union Congress informed of all developments, and where necessity arises endeavour to secure their co-operation in the co-ordination of the whole trade union movement.

6. *Procedure for Securing Assistance of the Alliance.*—(a) Any allied organisation being involved in an official dispute in respect of which the assistance of the Alliance may be required under the provision of Clause 1—"Objects" of this Constitution—shall, before committing themselves to a national or general stoppage, communicate the whole of the facts and circumstances to the Executive of the Alliance through the Secretary, and shall also at each stage of the dispute keep the Executive informed. The Executive shall equally keep the allied organisations informed with regard to the dispute. (b) On receipt of a definite request for assistance, the Secretary shall immediately call the Executive Council, who shall examine all the facts and circumstances, and if in their judgment the circumstances warrant action, they shall, within fourteen days, call the General Conference, and shall submit a report definitely setting forth the nature of the dispute and the proposed form of the assistance to be given. The Executive Council shall not have power to take action without the authority of the General Conference. The General Conference shall not be empowered to grant assistance unless satisfied that the allied organisation making application has observed its own constitution and procedure. (c) Upon the General Conference sanctioning assistance, the conduct of the movement shall then pass into the control of the Executive Council, who shall work in consultation with the union or unions involved, and shall keep the allied organisations fully informed, and shall, as necessity arises, call together the General Conference and report.

7. *Forms in which assistance may be given.*—(a) Negotiation. (b) Financial. (c) Partial Sympathetic Action. (d) Sympathetic Action by stages. (e) Complete Sympathetic Action. In each case the Executive Council shall clearly set forth in their report to the General Conference the form and extent of the assistance proposed by them.

8. *Settlement of Disputes.*—If, as a result of the intervention of the Alliance, terms are obtained which may be regarded as acceptable, the Executive Council, after the fullest consultation with the society on whose behalf assistance has been rendered, shall report same to the General Conference for ratification. The General Conference shall have full power to order or terminate assistance.

9. *Conditions of Membership of the Alliance.*—The conditions of membership of this Alliance shall involve the allied organisations in definitely undertaking, notwithstanding anything in their agreements or constitutions to the contrary, to act as directed by the

General Conference of this Alliance, and each shall periodically (as may be determined by the Executive Council) supply a full return of their membership and the industries in which they enter. Nothing in this constitution shall interfere with the right of the allied organisations promoting movements on their own behalf, but in such cases they shall not be entitled to the assistance of the Alliance.

10. *Officers.*—There shall be a Chairman and a Secretary, both of whom shall be elected by the General Conference.

11. *Finance.*—In order to meet administrative costs, each allied organisation shall contribute 5s. per thousand members per annum, or such other sum as the General Conference may, from time to time, determine.

12. *Financial Assistance.*—In order to render financial assistance, the General Conference shall be empowered to call upon the allied organisations to subscribe such sums per thousand members as may be deemed necessary by the General Conference.

13. *Observance of Constitution.*—The procedure under this constitution must be strictly conformed to by any allied organisation desiring assistance from the Alliance.

14. *Withdrawal.*—Any allied organisation desiring to withdraw from the Alliance shall give one year's notice in writing, and during the currency of such notice they shall observe the constitution of the Alliance.

CHAPTER XIII

THE GENERAL STRIKE

I. MOBILISATION

THE coal-owners' notices imposing a lock-out on the million miners of Great Britain were posted in mid-April. They were due to run out on the last days of the month and in all cases by midnight on April 30th. For nine months events had moved slowly to this climax, and for the last nine weeks with the apparent inevitability of a geologic process.

For this foreseen climax a whole series of steps directed against the miners had already been taken by the Government and its various agencies. The knowledge that few, if any, corresponding steps had been taken on the other side strengthened the confidence of Cabinet Ministers in their capacity to handle the situation. In every "War-Book" of the European Powers before 1914 there was a crucial moment when the order for "mobilisation" was given. From that crucial moment onwards events hurry after one another with increasing speed and almost total irrevocableness: a vast and growingly uncontrollable machinery is set in motion: war is not yet declared, but the mobilisation order makes war all but inevitable. The counterpart of all this in the civil life of Britain was not known until 1920, when the Emergency Powers Act was passed. Thereafter the declaration by royal proclamation of "a state of emergency" has the same effect in civil strife as a "mobilisation" order on the brink of war. This momentous step was now taken by the Cabinet: on April 30th at Buckingham Palace the King signed a proclamation.[1]

[1] BY THE KING
A PROCLAMATION

George R.I.

Whereas by the Emergency Powers Act, 1920, it is enacted that if it appears to Us that any action has been taken or is immediately threatened by any persons or body of persons of such a nature and on so extensive a scale as to be calculated, by interfering with the supply and distribution of food, water, fuel, or light, or with the means of locomotion, to deprive the community, or any substantial portion of the community,

With the issue of this proclamation it became lawful for the Government, by Orders in Council, to take any steps it wished without resort to Parliament. Powers and duties could be given to the various Government departments to make regulations, to create new classes of offences and to prescribe penalties therefor. These regulations, though subject later to periodic review by Parliament, came into force immediately they were issued. In short they gave to the Government, and under them to the armed forces and the police, the powers exercised in the world wars beginning in 1914 and in 1939 —with this difference only, that the Royal Proclamation had to be renewed from month to month. How drastic these regulations could be, and how sweeping their abolition of customary civil liberties, may be judged from one example out of many:

Regulation 21.—(1) If any person attempts or does any act calculated or likely to cause mutiny, sedition, or disaffection among any of His Majesty's forces, or among the members of any police force, or any fire brigade, or among the civilian population, or to impede, delay, or restrict any measures taken for securing and regulating the supply or distribution of food, water, fuel, light or other necessities, or for maintaining the means of transit or of locomotion, or for any other purposes essential to the public safety or the life of the community, he shall be guilty of an offence against these regulations:

provided that a person shall not be guilty of an offence under this regulation by reason only of his taking part in a strike or peacefully persuading any other person to take part in a strike.

(2) If any person, without lawful authority or excuse, has in his possession, or on premises in his occupation or under his control, any document containing any report or statement, the publication of which would be a contravention of the foregoing provisions of this regulation, he shall be guilty of an offence against these regulations unless he proves that he did not know and had no reason to suspect that the document contained any such report or statement, or that he had no intention of transmitting or circulating the document, or distributing copies thereof to or amongst other persons.

of the essentials of life, We may, by Proclamation, declare that a state of emergency exists:

And whereas the present immediate threat of cessation of work in Coal Mines does, in Our opinion, constitute a state of emergency within the meaning of the said Act:

Now, therefore, in pursuance of the said Act, We do, by and with the advice of Our Privy Council, hereby declare that a state of emergency exists.

Given at Our Court at Buckingham Palace, this Thirtieth day of April, in the year of our Lord One thousand nine hundred and twenty-six, and in the Sixteenth year of Our Reign.

GOD SAVE THE KING

On the same April 30th Government departments were sending out detailed instructions, e.g. the Ministry of Health sent out to local authorities a reminder of its November 20th circular to put them on the alert: the names of the Civil Commissioners were published together with lists of their staffs and headquarters in the dozen Divisions of Great Britain: official announcement was made of troop movements: and a placard of the strike-breaking body (the O.M.S.) calling for recruits was posted throughout the country.

It was to the accompaniment of these "mobilisation" orders, which were given the fullest publicity, that the Friday, April 30th negotiations were carried on to their final breakdown. At noon of the next day, several hours after the miners had been locked out, the "counter-mobilisation" of organised labour began with the vote of the Conference of Executives, approving the General Council's proposal for a General Strike as from midnight on Monday, May 3rd–4th.

The lock-out had applied to all miners. The strike was to apply for the time being to a limited number of trades, viz., all transport; printing; heavy industry (iron and steel, metal, heavy chemicals); building (except housing and hospitals). Sanitary services were to be continued. As regards health and food services the trade unions were recommended *to organise the distribution of milk and food to the whole of the population*, while everything from hospitals to schools was to be safeguarded. Strong adjurations to maintain discipline, to preserve peace and order, to watch out for spies and *agents provocateurs* were added. The actual strike call was left to the unions, who were, however, to place their powers in the hands of the General Council and carry out its instructions. The General Strike order began as follows:

The Trades Union Congress General Council and the Miners' Federation of Great Britain, having been unable to obtain a satisfactory settlement of the matters in dispute in the coal-mining industry, and the Government and the mine-owners having forced a lock-out, the General Council, in view of the need for co-ordinated action on the part of affiliated Unions, in defence of the policy laid down by the General Council of the Trades Union Congress, directs as follows:

Except as hereinafter provided, the following trades and undertakings shall cease work, as and when required by the General Council.

Then, after listing in detail the trades and undertakings that were to cease work, the General Council amongst other instructions directed that:

the trade unions concerned shall take steps to keep a daily register to account for every one of their members:

Point 3 was headed "Trades Councils" and ran as follows:

The work of the Trades Councils, in conjunction with the local officers of the Trade Unions actually participating in the dispute, shall be to assist in carrying out the foregoing provisions, and they shall be charged with the responsibility of organising the Trade Unionists in dispute in the most effective manner for the preservation of peace and order.[1]

Further, in Point 5, the General Council directed that:

the Executives of the unions concerned shall definitely declare that in the event of any action being taken and Trade Union agreements being placed in jeopardy, it be definitely agreed that there will be no general resumption of work until those agreements are fully recognised.

The General Strike order was signed by Arthur Pugh as Chairman and Walter Citrine as Acting Secretary.

It may be noted that the only measure relating to resumption of work was Point 5, the object of which was to commit the union Executives not to stop the strike until existing agreements were fully recognised.

In the later hours of May 1st, the unions began to issue strike orders.

Meantime the Government gave it to be understood that it would commandeer the British Broadcasting Company.[2] On hearing of this the General Council, who were busy on the Saturday evening making preparations, issued a protest and stated they would arrange for direct communications with the trade union head offices and branch officers.

The second day of the Government's mobilisation for internal war ended with a message from Mr. Baldwin:

Keep steady. Remember that peace on earth comes to men of goodwill.

---

[1] The carrying out of this directive is described in detail in *The General Strike, May 1926: Trades Councils in Action*, by Emile Burns.

[2] In point of fact Churchill wanted to commandeer the B.B.C. Sir John Reith objected. Baldwin, satisfied after a conversation with Reith as to what was likely to be the behaviour of the B.B.C., turned down Churchill—who appears never to have forgotten this rebuff. See Lord Reith's *Into the Wind*.

2. PEACEMAKERS GET THE COUNTER-CHECK
QUARRELSOME

All day and all night long on Saturday, May 1st and Sunday, May 2nd, the Government mobilisation unfolded; over the network of Britain's railways trains sped loaded with coal and general goods traffic; army and navy staffs were busy in conjunction with the dozen Civil Commissioners; each section of the Government was humming with activity. On the Labour side, the full preparatory work on a nation-wide scale could not begin till after the General Strike counter-mobilisation order at 2.30 a.m. on May 1st. But thereafter the most urgent part of the activities of Labour headquarters was concentrated on a further process of negotiations.

Despite the deadlock reached on the Friday the members of the Industrial Committee unweariedly took up the task again of persuading the Government into a more yielding frame of mind. As soon as the Conference ended, the General Council met and sent the following letter to the Prime Minister:

MINING LOCK-OUT

I have to advise you that the Executive Committees of the Trades Union Congress, including the Miners' Federation of Great Britain, have decided to hand over to the General Council of the T.U.C. the conduct of the dispute, and all the negotiations in connection therewith will be undertaken by the General Council. I am directed to say that the General Council will hold themselves available at any moment should the Government desire to discuss the matter further.

Yours faithfully,
WALTER M. CITRINE, Acting Secretary.

On receipt of this letter the Prime Minister invited the T.U.C. representatives to meet him at 8 p.m. that evening of May 1st at 10 Downing Street. Then a sub-committee of three from each side was appointed and were discussing forms of words till after midnight.

The M.F.G.B. representatives did not agree to these negotiations. The General Council, however, meeting on the Sunday, May 2nd, decided to accept what had been done so far but to raise further questions. Accordingly the sub-committee again met the Prime Minister and his two colleagues in the Cabinet room at Downing Street. From these discussions the following formula emerged:

We will urge the miners to authorise us to enter upon a decision with the understanding that they and we accept the Report[1] as the basis of a settlement, and we approach it with the knowledge that it may involve some reduction of wages.

This formula had to be taken back to the General Council and discussed with them. In turn the miners' representatives were called into discussion. To these midnight discussions there came a sudden interruption. The Government had sounded out how far some members of the T.U.C. General Council would go. Now it was ready to precipitate matters. Baldwin broke off the private negotiations he had been holding with the T.U.C.'s sub-committee.

The letter handed to the T.U.C. representatives declared that there could be no solution without "the sincere acceptance of the report of the Commission," including the immediate "adjustment of wages or hours." If the miners or the negotiating committee would "say plainly that they accept this proposal," the Government would have been ready to resume negotiations and to continue the subsidy for a fortnight. Getting down to its real business, the letter continued:

It has come to the knowledge of the Government, not only that specific instructions have been sent under the authority of the Executives of Trade Unions represented at the Conference, convened by the General Council of the Trades Union Congress, directing their members in several of the most vital industries and services of the country to carry out a general strike on Tuesday next, but that overt acts have already taken place, including gross interference with the freedom of the Press.[2] Such action involves a challenge to the constitutional rights and freedom of the nation.

---

[1] The Report of the (Samuel) Commission on the Coal Industry.

[2] The episode of the *Daily Mail* printers' strike is described in Allen Hutt's *The Post-War History of the British Working Class* as follows:

"In Carmelite Street the edition of the *Daily Mail* was ready to go to press. A blood-and-thunder leading article proclaimed that the General Strike was 'a revolutionary movement intended to inflict suffering upon the great mass of innocent persons in the community.... It must be dealt with by every resource at the disposal of the community.' 'For King and Country' blared the headline. Set, made up, moulded, plates cast and on the grey lines of rotaries—the paper had gone through its usual routine. But down in the vast machine-room angry men in blue overalls read that leading article as they glanced through trial copies. They gathered together and talked it over. The Natsopa

Before continuing negotiations, the Government required a repudiation of these actions and "an immediate and unconditional withdrawal of the instructions for a general strike."

To this curt message the General Council sent a reply at 3.30 a.m. on Monday, May 3rd, that

The trade union representatives were astounded to learn that, without any warning, the renewed conversations, which it was hoped might pave the way to the opening of full and unfettered negotiations, had been abruptly terminated by the Government for the reason stated in your communication.

The first reason given was that specific instructions have been sent under the authority of trade unions represented at the conference, convened by the General Council of the T.U.C., directing their members in several industries and services to cease work.

I am directed to remind you that there is nothing unusual for workmen to cease work in defence of their interests as wage-earners, and that the specific reason for the decision in this case is to secure for the mine-workers the same right from the employers as is insisted upon by employers from workers, namely, that negotiations shall be conducted free from the atmosphere of strike or lock-out. This is the principle which Governments have held to be cardinal in the conduct of industrial negotiations.

With regard to the second reason, that "overt acts have already taken place, including gross interference with the freedom of the Press," it is regretted that no information is contained in your letter. The General Council had no knowledge of any such acts having occurred, and the decision taken by them definitely forbade any such independent and unauthorised action. The Council are not aware of the circumstances under which the alleged acts have taken place. It cannot accept responsibility for them, and is taking prompt measures to prevent any acts of indiscipline. The Council regret that they were not given an opportunity to investigate and deal with the alleged incidents before the Government made them an excuse for breaking off the peace discussions which were proceeding.

The public will judge of the Government's intentions by its precipitous and calamitous decision in this matter, and we deplore with the General Council that the sincere work which the Council has been engaged in to obtain an honourable settlement has been wrecked by the Government's unprecedented ultimatum.

Yours faithfully,

ARTHUR PUGH, WALTER M. CITRINE.

Chapel met and after a brief discussion told the management that they could have their newspaper if the leader was deleted, but not otherwise. Other Chapels in machine-room, foundry, packing department, backed them. There was no *Daily Mail* that night. Perhaps no other single act of the whole General Strike evoked such universal delight throughout the whole working-class movement."

Thus the Government had faced the T.U.C. General Council with the harsh alternative either to submit, which would have meant defeat not for a section but for the whole trade union movement, or to enter into a class battle none of them had ever seriously contemplated or prepared for. Further, it had abruptly shifted the emphasis away from miners' wages and hours and had fallen back on "the challenge to the constitution" as the ground of the quarrel, exactly as had been forecast nine months earlier.

The General Council negotiators could find no way out of the impasse. In the grey dawn of that May morning, as they went to snatch a few hours' sleep, they were worried, uneasy men who might have said to themselves, "Verily, the way of the peacemakers is hard."

3. EVE OF THE GENERAL STRIKE

Monday, May 3rd opened with Mr. Baldwin's statement at 1.15 a.m. that negotiations had finally broken down; that the Government had learned that a General Strike had been called; that this was "a challenge to constitutional rights and freedom"; and that its "immediate and unconditional withdrawal" was demanded. In the debate in the House of Commons that afternoon appeals for resumption of negotiations were refused by the Cabinet. "It is not wages," said Mr. Baldwin, "that are imperilled; it is the freedom of our very constitution. No man who remains at work shall be prejudicially affected afterwards."

That day all army leave was stopped. The following statement was issued by the Council of the O.M.S:

The Council of the O.M.S. desires to make it clear that the whole organisation has now been handed over to the Government, and requests all O.M.S. Committees to place themselves and their registered personnel at the disposal of their local Volunteer Service Committee chairman forthwith. (May 3, 1926.)

On the side of organised Labour there was this advantage: that every trade unionist was fully aware of the strike call and of the time of stoppage; any attempt of the Government to use its powers to stop strike telegrams was thus discounted in advance. In point of fact the stoppage began on the Monday evening here and there as shifts ended. All later editions of London evening papers carrying anti-working-class editorials were stopped by strikes of workers against the character of the contents.

The General Council of the Trades Union Congress issued a manifesto on the evening of Sunday, May 2nd, which recounted the events and declared that

The Trade Unions disclaim all responsibility for the calamity that now threatens. Their action is not directed against the public. Responsibility for the consequences that must inevitably follow a general cessation of work lies with the mine-owners and the Government entirely.

No proposals for a national settlement of the mining problem were made by the mine-owners until within a few hours of the time fixed for the expiration of the lock-out notices, and after thousands of men had already left the mines under such notices. By their refusal to require a withdrawal of these notices to enable negotiations to continue, except upon the condition that the mine-workers agreed in advance to accept wage reductions, the Government made it impossible for the representatives of the Trade Unions to effect an honourable settlement. . . .

All attempts to reach an understanding based on acceptance of the Commission's proposals for the drastic reorganisation of the mining industry were frustrated by the Government's attitude as to free and unfettered discussion thereon. . . .

Having regard to the earnest efforts that have been made and the readiness of the workers' representatives to discuss the report in its entirety, there is no shadow of reason why the miners should be locked out or the grave decision of a general stoppage should be allowed to take effect. If it does, then it must be repeated emphatically that the responsibility will lie with the Government and the mine-owners.

Whatever wavering there might be was not to be heard from the trade unions. There was one curious statement of Ramsay MacDonald, leader of the Labour Party in Parliament. On Saturday, May 1st, speaking to the Conference of Executives after the crucial vote for a General Strike, MacDonald had said:

In that firmness of purpose—purpose you want, not words—in that firmness of purpose we will stand by you. . . . We are there in the battle with you, taking our share uncomplainingly until the end has come and until right and justice have been done.

These were brave words. But by Monday evening his tone had altered to something much less than a trumpet call, as may be seen from the following:

As far as we can see we shall go on. I don't like General Strikes. I haven't changed my opinion. I have said so in the House of Commons. I don't like it; honestly I don't like it; but honestly, what can be done?

But to offset this tepid send-off (and a still more remarkable utterance by the wife of his lieutenant, Mrs. Philip Snowden, who said "We must stand quietly behind the Government—any Government, for it would have been the same if a Labour Party had been in power—in all it does to maintain law and order"), there came from overseas, both from countries of the Empire and of Europe warm messages of solidarity and promises of support. But the messages from inside Britain that evening were more heartening still, for they made it clear that there would be a full response to the strike call and that few had been won over by the Prime Minister's guarantee to strike-breakers.

4. OPENING OF THE NINE DAYS' STRIKE

In his pamphlet *The Nine Days*, written hot after the event, the Miners' Secretary described what nearly everyone on the side of organised Labour felt at the time.

Tuesday, May 4th, started with the workers answering the call. What a wonderful response! What loyalty!! What solidarity!!! From John o' Groats to Land's End the workers answered the call to arms to defend us, to defend the brave miner in his fight for a living wage.

Hurriedly the General Council formed their Committees, made preparations to face this colossal task—the first in the history of this country. No one could over-estimate the greatness of the task that faced the General Council, and to the credit of many of the members —especially Ernest Bevin—they made every effort possible to bring into being machinery to cope with the requirements.

The difficulties of transport, of communication, of giving information, were enormous; but the foresight and energy of the officials in the country and of the rank and file rose to the occasion. Links were formed, bulletins were issued; officials, staff and voluntary workers of the T.U.C. and the Labour Party worked night and day to create the machinery necessary to link up the whole movement—machinery that would have been prepared by commonsense leadership months and months before.

It was a wonderful achievement, a wonderful accomplishment that proved conclusively that the Labour Movement has the men and women that are capable in an emergency of providing the means of carrying on the country. Who can forget the effect of motor conveyances with posters saying "By permission of the T.U.C."? The Government with its O.M.S. were absolutely demoralised. Confidence, calm, and order prevailed everywhere, despite the irritation caused by the volunteers, blacklegs, and special constables. The workers acted as one. Splendid discipline! Splendid loyalty!

A. J. Cook's picture was not overdrawn. The T.U.C.'s communiqué was emphatic on the completeness of the response to the strike call:

We have from all over the country, from Land's End to John o' Groats, reports that have surpassed all our expectations. Not only the railwaymen and transport men, but all other trades came out in a manner we did not expect immediately. The difficulty of the General Council has been to keep men in what we might call the second line of defence rather than call them off. There are also no reports other than those of a quiet, orderly and good-tempered desire to keep the peace of all sections of the community.

It was a different Britain that morning. There were no passenger trains, no coal or heavy goods traffic, no evening papers, no trams or omnibuses. Not only the organised workers in the trades affected, but in most cases the unorganised workers responded also to the call. The slogan popularised by Arthur Cook was taken up everywhere: "Not a penny off the pay; not a minute on the day."

On the other side the Government was busy enrolling volunteers through all its agencies to break the strike, while at the same time it began its repressive measures with the arrest of Shapurji Saklatvala, then the solitary Communist who was a Member of Parliament, for a speech delivered on May Day.

5. SECOND DAY OF THE GENERAL STRIKE

On Wednesday, May 5th, there appeared the *British Gazette*. The previous day Winston Churchill, Chancellor of the Exchequer, had marched at the head of a motley array of hand-picked followers into the offices of the *Morning Post*, and announced that the Government was commandeering their equipment in order to produce an official newspaper, under his super-editorship. Thus "The Great Dictator" was on the job. The first issue made it clear that the strike of printers had been a severe blow to the Government—despite their reliance upon the B.B.C.; and that by means of this official paper they hoped to keep up the morale of their supporters. On hearing of this the Trades Union Congress took over the *Daily Herald* equipment in order to produce an official strike news bulletin, called the *British Worker*. The first number of May 5th, issued after preliminary confiscation by the police, contained a message from the General Council, emphasising that the strike was an industrial dispute and calling for peaceful behaviour. It also contained the manifesto of the Miners' Federation.

Comrades.—The struggle has begun. Menaced with an onslaught on their standards of life by the mine-owners and the Government, the Miners' Federation of Great Britain submitted their case to the judgment of their fellow trade unionists. The General Council and Conference of Trade Union Executives considered it with a full sense of their grave responsibility and pronounced it just beyond all possibility of question.

Today the whole body of British workers stands united as one man in their unconquerable determination to resist demands which were a calculated and deliberate attack, not only upon the miners, but on every worker in the country and upon the very existence of the Trade Union Movement itself.

On behalf of the Miners' Federation we express our heartfelt thanks for the magnificent loyalty with which you, our fellow-workers, have responded to our appeal for aid.

We have laboured for a peaceful settlement, but the Government, not only by its words but by its actions, has shown only too plainly that peace is not what it desires. In insisting that the miners should pledge themselves to accept a reduction in wages before even entering negotiations, it advanced an unheard-of demand which no body of Trade Unionists could accept. In suddenly breaking off negotiations with the General Council and the Miners' Federation on Sunday night, it revealed its determination to force upon the Trade Union Movement a struggle for which the Government had long prepared.

It is on the Government, and the Government alone, that the responsibility for the present situation rests.

There is no need for us to call for your assistance, for you have already given it. With you we shall stand firm to the end in defending the rights of the organised workers. With you, we know that justice is on our side. With you, we are confident that the resolute action of a united movement will bring victory to the cause of the workers.

6. THIRD DAY OF GENERAL STRIKE AND UP TO SIXTH DAY

By Thursday, May 6th, the improvised arrangements for the conduct of the strike were functioning both nationally and locally. Local strike organisation was in touch with union and T.U.C. headquarters. The General Council established that day five sub-committees for guidance of the strike, dealing with transport and communications; information; food supply; control and instructions; finance. Thereafter it was a tug-of-war between the two sides, neither gaining any spectacular advantage. But in so far as the Government did not succeed in carrying on services which it had undertaken to do, it was bound to lose prestige; and correspondingly, whenever a strike organisation ensured food supplies to the people it was gaining prestige and authority. No estimate could be made at any stage of the exact position. For the Government alone had all sources of information and these it did not disclose. Instead such means of publicity as had been commandeered were used for propaganda purposes; and awkward facts were suppressed, as for example when the B.B.C. (under Government pressure) and the official *British Gazette* refused to let it be known that the Archbishop of Canterbury "after full conference with the leaders of the Christian Churches in England" had intervened with proposals for a settlement, which he desired "to make public."

Those proposals, printed in the *British Worker*, declared that

a real settlement will only be achieved in a spirit of fellowship and co-operation for the common good, and not as a result of war.

Realising that the longer the present struggle persists the greater will be the suffering and loss, they earnestly request that all the parties concerned in this dispute will agree to resume negotiations, undeterred by obstacles which have been created by the events of the last few days.

If it should seem to be incumbent on us to suggest a definite line of approach, we would submit as the basis of a possible concordat a return to the *status quo* of Friday last. We cannot but believe in the possibility of a successful issue. Our proposal should be interpreted as involving, simultaneously and concurrently:

1. The cancellation on the part of the T.U.C. of the General Strike.
2. Renewal by the Government of its offer of assistance to the coal industry for a short, indefinite period.
3. The withdrawal on the part of the mine-owners of the new wages scales recently issued.

Nevertheless the step taken by the Archbishop was very damaging to the Government's policy. An ecclesiastic had to be found prepared to condemn the strikers from a religious standpoint, as a counter-blast to the Archbishop. There was such an ecclesiastic: Cardinal Bourne was given full publicity for the following declaration at High Mass in Westminster Cathedral on Sunday, May 9th:

The time through which we are passing is of an exceptional character, and the present strike is of a nature quite unlike any others which have preceded it. It is necessary that Catholics should have before their minds the moral principles which are involved:

1. There is no moral justification for a general strike of this character. It is a direct challenge to lawfully constituted authority, and inflicts, without adequate reason, immense discomfort and injury on millions of our fellow-countrymen. It is therefore a sin against the obedience which we owe to God, who is the source of that authority, and against the charity and brotherly love which are due to our brethren.
2. All are bound to uphold and assist the Government, which is the lawfully constituted authority of the country, and represents, therefore, in its own appointed sphere the authority of God Himself.
3. As God alone can guide both rulers and ruled to wise and successful understanding, it is the duty of all to pray earnestly and constantly for His guidance that the day may be hastened when these unhappy conflicts shall terminate in a just and lasting peace.

No facilities were given to Mr. Lloyd George to make known his profound disagreement with the Conservative Government's policy; but the *British Gazette* printed immediately statements from those Liberal leaders (H. H. Asquith and Lord Grey of Fallodon) who agreed with the Tories and were prepared to join in the general chorus against the men on strike.

Sir John Simon in a speech in the House of Commons on Thursday, May 6th, declared that the strike was "illegal." Mr. Justice Astbury, described nearly twenty years later by the Attorney-General[1] as "an obscure Chancery Judge," took occasion in an *obiter dictum* on Tuesday, May 11th, to characterise the "so-called General Strike" as "illegal." These statements, presumed to carry great authority (though the Government subsequently was so little convinced of their validity that it passed an Act of Parliament to make illegal the General Strike), were also given the widest publicity.

In short, apart from the actual struggle carried out in thousands of localities and scores of trades between strikers and the Government as strike-breakers, there was a propaganda combat carried on during the whole of these days, in which the chief engine was the British Broadcasting Company (for neither the *British Gazette* nor the *British Worker* covered more than a tiny fraction of the circulation of the daily Press, which relies normally on a transport system which was then out of action), with its carefully selected news and statements from one side only. Of these the culmination for the first week was the Premier's broadcast on Saturday, May 8th, in which he appealed to the employers to "do all in their power to keep their works running." The Government position, he said, was that the General Strike must be called off "absolutely and without reserve. The mining industry dispute can then be settled." He ended by saying:

A solution is within the grasp of the nation the instant that the Trade Union leaders are willing to abandon the General Strike.

I am a man of peace. I am longing and working and praying for peace, but I will not surrender the safety and the security of the British Constitution. You placed me in power eighteen months ago by the largest majority accorded to any Party for many years. Have I done anything to forfeit that confidence? Cannot you trust me to ensure a square deal, to secure even justice between man and man?

---

[1] Sir Hartley Shawcross, taken to task for this description as reflecting on the judiciary, made amends in a further statement in Parliament. (See *Hansard*, April 1, 1946.) No judge is obscure, not even in Chancery.

The next day the Prime Minister spent some time visiting the zoo. This news, when broadcast, fetched ribald comment from miners. Was he there, asked some, to observe the crocodile, fabled to shed tears over its victims? Surely, said others, Baldwin had nothing to learn from that animal!

"The workers must not be misled," wrote the *British Worker* that day, "by Mr. Baldwin's renewed attempt last night to represent the present strike as a political issue. The trade unions are fighting for one thing, and one thing only— to protect the miners' standard of life."

7. THE STRIKE IN THE LOCALITIES

The best way to get a picture of how and whither the workers were moving in the towns and villages of Great Britain during the opening days is to set forth the plans and preparations of one particular locality. It may be taken as typical, at any rate, of most mining areas.

In this locality of the Northumberland–Durham division, the local Trades and Labour Council had called a meeting of all its delegates for the Sunday evening, May 2nd; and had invited thereto all other sections and representatives of all working-class organisations, including members of Co-operative Boards of Management, officers of the Women's Co-operative Guild and of the women's section of the Labour Party, representatives of the Communist Party and the Plebs League, Labour Guardians, Labour Councillors and County Councillors.

A plan of campaign was put before the meeting, which after brief discussion accepted the plans and constituted itself a Council of Action.

PLAN OF CAMPAIGN

Preamble.—No time to be spent tonight on discussion of *purpose* of strike (to aid the miners) or origin or possible ending or national aspect or international aspect. Not concerned for next few days with any wider horizons; concerned only with concentrating on our limited objective.

Objective.—To defeat the Civil Commissioner appointed for this Region. The Civil Commissioner is appointed by the Government and is armed with the Emergency Powers Act in order to break the strike. Our immediate aim is to prevent him doing that in this town. But in order to do that effectually we must offer a resistance throughout the whole region over which he has been given plenary powers. That is, we must defeat the Civil Commissioner and all his strike-breaking apparatus.

The E.P.A. Apparatus.—The apparatus of a regional Civil Commission comprises:

(1) The arrangements and organisation built up by the Ministry of Health during the last nine months.

(2) The arrangements and special organisation prepared by the Home Office.

(3) The plans and arrangements devised by the War Office, Admiralty and Air Force.

(4) Sundry other arrangements and organisations provided or prepared by Government Departments and placed under his jurisdiction.

That is to say, there will be concentrated against the strikers in this Region the whole of the Civil and Military institutions that are under central control; and also the civil institutions usually classed as Local Government.

With regard to the last of these it remains to be seen whether he would be able to make the full use of them that he would wish.

The Strike-Breakers' Man Power.—The actual bodies of men at the disposal of the Civil Commissioner are:

1. Local and national Government Officials.
2. The Organisation for the Maintenance of Supplies.
3. Various other strike-breaking bodies, composed mainly of middle-class persons.
4. The Fascisti, one of whose organisations has entered into an arrangement with the O.M.S.
5. The Special Constabulary, in which it is likely many of the Fascisti will enrol.
6. The Special Civil Constabulary, a body of armed men with steel helmets organised solely for the purpose of coping with the strike.
7. The regular County and Borough Police Forces.
8. The Army, Navy and the Air Force, equipped with tanks, machine guns, submarines, torpedo boats and aeroplanes.

Working-Class Machinery.—To meet all this we must improvise. The improvised machinery must be simple, easy to throw up, all inclusive. All activities in each locality should be centralised in a single body to be called Council of Action, Strike Committee, Trades Council or what you will; all such bodies should be linked up and centralised in the county capital town under a body responsible for the whole region.

Councils of Action.—The first task: Tonight's meeting should set up a Council of Action and plan out all the machinery and all the tasks for the locality.

The second task is to set up replicas of this Council of Action in every corresponding locality throughout the various counties, so as to make a network of Councils of Action linked up with a central directing body whose authority and scope on our side would exactly answer to the Civil Commissioner.

The Regional Authority.—The third task is to assemble the district officers of Trade Unions, men who by experience and routine are capable of thinking in terms of the counties as a single whole. In certain unions there will not exist any such divisional officers or regional committee. In such case recourse must be had to other units of the organisation until such time as formal arrangements can be entered into and a formal constitution drawn up. Meantime an assembling of district or divisional officers will in itself constitute a body of sufficient experience and make sufficient pooling of authority to do the work effectively.

Special Newspaper.—Task No. 1 can be solved tonight. The other two tasks, the building of district authority and a network of local bodies, must be solved mainly by the printing and scattering broad-cast of a special strike newspaper.

Strike Bulletin.—This strike bulletin should appear each day during the strike, but it will have two purposes; it will have one purpose up to the moment the general strike is declared and another purpose thereafter. Its purpose up to the moment of the declaring of the general strike is precisely this—to organise the whole of our counties in Councils of Action and to link up the organisation in a regional authority. It is impossible to send speakers all over the counties or to do anything else than to print this bulletin and spread it by despatch riders. In this way only can the necessary machinery be rapidly improvised.

Tasks of Councils of Action.—The Council of Action will have a number of tasks for which Sub-Committees should be set up. These will include:

Communications (Despatch Riders, etc.); Feeding Centres; Food and Transport; Co-operative Societies; Local Government; Sports (to serve a double purpose); Defence Corps; Picketing; Permits; Organisation of Women; Publicity (a) Local Stencils, (b) Other Publicity; Information.

Local Government.—The Urban District Councils, etc., are not necessarily to be handed over to the Civil Commission in their entirety. A struggle may take place for the possession of the machinery of such authority as is possessed by Boards of Guardians or Urban District Councils. It may be possible to impede the operations of the Civil Commissioner and his officers under the E.P.A.; perhaps even to transform part at any rate of the Urban District Council into strike machinery.

Food and Transport.—The T.U.C instructions for the general strike, if and when it should come off, include the provision of Food Transport and Health Services. Whatever the intention of the General Council in laying down this instruction, it is clear that on this point depends the success of the general strike. Whoever handles and transports food, that same person controls food: whoever controls food will find the "neutral" part of the population rallying to their side. Who feeds the people wins the strike! The problem of the general strike can be focused down to one thing—the struggle for food control.

Morale.—All these activities and all this machinery needed for these activities are designed for the purpose of defeating the Civil Commissioner's attempt to break the general strike. But they have another object. That is the building up of our own morale both locally and nationally. Every officer who reports that picketing has stopped his transport, every military officer who reports that he cannot trust his men to act against the strikers because of effective fraternisation, is a means by which when the report has filtered through to Whitehall the morale of the Chief Civil Commissioner, and thence of the Cabinet, is impaired and weakened.

Some localities may have been better prepared than others. But in the first days of May the working class in most parts of Britain were moving along lines broadly similar to those in the north-east of England.

It is of interest that in the particular case given above the aims of the plan of campaign were achieved in the main earlier than had been allowed for and in one respect (the negotiations opened up by the Civil Commissioner) very much earlier. The local Council of Action was set up that night to be followed in other localities throughout the region. The strike bulletin was printed (before Monday midnight) and circulated. The regional authority took shape, early on Tuesday, May 5th, as the Northumberland and Durham General Council, together with a Joint Strike Committee, which took over, and was given supreme authority subject only to the Trades Union Congress General Council. This authority was acknowledged in effect, if not in theory, by the Civil Commissioner, Sir Kingsley Wood, who, having found himself and his staff in serious difficulty, after forty hours of the general stoppage, came by night to negotiate personally with the Strike Committee. Sixty hours after the strike began Sir Kingsley Wood, accompanied by General Sir Kerr Montgomery, were once more at Burt Hall, making a plea for "dual control" of the transport of food. This proposal was immediately rejected by the Joint Strike Committee ("we cannot agree to our men working under any form of dual control"), which at the same time decided "that we now use the discretionary powers vested in us by the Trades Union Congress and withdraw all permits today."

The Minutes of the Joint Strike Committee (from which this narrative and quoted words have been taken) were set out in full on this matter within the official report[1] approved by the Northumberland and Durham General Council on May 20th, for the simple reason that the Cabinet was found to have deceived the House of Commons as to the facts. The passage in the report begins with the words:

As these interviews of Sir Kingsley Wood and his officers with the representatives of the Joint Strike Committee have received a certain amount of publicity, and since it has been officially denied in the House of Commons[2] that any such negotiations took place, it may be well to give in some detail the substance of the negotiations as reported to the Joint Strike Committee immediately after each conversation had take place. We quote from the minutes of the Joint Strike Committee:

Extract from Minutes of the Joint Strike Committee,
Wednesday, May 5, 1926

(9) At this juncture White, Flynn and Tarbit left to interview Kingsley Wood in Edwards' office.

(10) Subsequently the deputation reported as follows: Wood had stated that his duty was to see that food supplies are main-

---

[1] An Account of the Proceedings of the Northumberland and Durham General Council and Joint Strike Committee. (Presented May 20, 1926.)

[2] Mr. Connolly, the Member for Newcastle East, whose references on Thursday, May 6th to this matter had been met by an unblushing denial, formally asked a question in the House of Commons on Monday, May 10th, as follows:

Is it not a fact that the Commissioners, the Under-Secretary for Health and General Montgomery were in conference on Wednesday and Thursday with the Strike Committee; that the meeting on Thursday lasted two and a half hours; that the Minister offered the Strike Committee a system of dual control, which was refused; and further, has the hon. Gentleman's notice been drawn to the following statement issued by the Newcastle Trades Council. . . .

Sir H. Barnston: I am informed that all those statements are absolutely untrue, and I am a little bit surprised that the hon. Member is not ashamed to repeat them.

Mr. Connolly: Is the hon. Gentleman within his rights in telling me I ought to be ashamed of speaking what I know to be the truth?

Mr. Basil Peto: If such statements as that just made from the Opposition Benches were made outside the House, would it not be immaterial whether they were true or untrue? Would they not involve the arrest and imprisonment of the person making them under the Defence of the Realm Acts?

Events after Monday moved too fast for the Government to have the opportunity of denying the truth thrice. Enough however was said to show that in this strike the Government was not much troubled by any finer scruples.

tained. There would, he said, be no interference if the Trade Unionists would continue to do the work. Tarbit had explained why the men had withdrawn their labour, and Wood replied that he had no knowledge of the importation of the outside labour (O.M.S.), and it had certainly made its appearance on the quay without his knowledge or authority, and would not allow, so long as he got the food to the people of Newcastle and District, anyone, in any way, to interfere with the habitual occupations of people who usually do this, so long as they will do it. Tarbit raised the question of unloading ships, part of which only was foodstuffs, and stated that his men would equally object to working with the Emergency Organisation (formerly O.M.S.) if these people unloaded the other parts of the cargo. Wood asked what our proposal was in such cases. We made the suggestion to him that the ships could either go to anchorage in the river with their non-food cargoes on board, waiting the end of the dispute for complete discharge, or return to their port of origin. It was further represented by us to him with the utmost emphasis that he should take steps to have the naval contingent, which had been berthed alongside the quay, in a most provocative manner, moved back to the usual naval anchorage at Jarrow, as it was impossible for us to agree that our men should be forced to work under the shadow of their guns. Wood stated that he had no control over the Admiralty in this matter, but appeared to indicate that a suggestion from him to the Commanders of the vessels might have the desired effect. He repudiated the idea that the anchorage taken up by the naval contingent had reference to the quay workers, but that these boats were kept in their present position to deal with possible riots or attacks upon power stations. He expressed himself as being obliged to us for the statement of our position, and thanked us for the valuable information we had given relating to quay work, &c., and stated he would like an opportunity of talking the matter over with his officers. He asked if we would adjourn the conversations, and meet him and General Kerr Montgomery on the morrow at 12.30. We agreed. Report received and agreed that the same deputation continue the conversations tomorrow with the whole of the Strike Committee in session at 12.30 to consider any proposals which might come from Wood and colleagues.

Minutes of Strike Committee, Thursday, May 6

(1) Flynn, White and Tarbit met Kingsley Wood, Kerr Montgomery and Moon (Food Officer) in Edwards' room at 12.30, and subsequently reported as follows:

Wood stated they agreed to take steps to see that no outside people were brought in. He suggested that so far as the quay is concerned the Trade Unions appoint an officer to work in conjunction with an officer appointed by him (Wood) to deal with any trouble which might arise and to supervise the work. Generally, they (Wood and Co.) agreed to the definition of foodstuffs as outlined by the T.U.C. and felt no disagreement would arise on this head. We asked what would be the position regarding non-unionists and blacklegs, as our men would only acknowledge permits issued to the Trade Unionists by the Strike Committee. Wood replied, "they would welcome any suggestions which we can make inside the Government scheme, but any question of Trade Union labour loading and unloading vessels should be obviated by dual control." We suggested that this could only be met by him clearing off the quay altogether and leaving the men who usually did the work to carry on as usual. He replied that he could not abrogate his function or act contrary to the instructions he had received. Montgomery stated that the full extent to which they would go, and they were anxious that this should operate, was that "all men now doing their ordinary work should continue to do so." Wood concurred, and stated "he would take any steps in conjunction with the Executive here to see that this is carried out." The general discussion then took place in reference to non-union labour, and Montgomery stated that they would go as far as to see that any chauffeur whose normal work is not to drive the lorries would be put off. Wood concurred, and in saying the position was reasonable, stated he would take steps to stop anyone not normally doing the work of transport. We replied that we would have to make a report to our Executive and would convey our decision later, and Wood requested that his proposals should be put fairly before the Executive. In promising to do this Flynn stated that he would not be able personally to recommend the form of dual control proposed. It was agreed that Montgomery should come back again at 4 p.m. to receive our reply.

(2) It was agreed after hearing the foregoing report that the representatives of the Executive inform Montgomery that:

"Having heard this report and recognising that our men cannot, and will not, work in conjunction with O.M.S., we instruct that a reply be sent to the gentlemen named that we cannot agree to our men working under any form of dual control."

(3) It was further agreed that we strongly recommend to the Trades Union Congress General Council that they shall empower us to withdraw all permits for the transport of food and everything else for which permits have been issued.

(4) Agreed that we now use the discretionary powers vested in us by the T.U.C. and withdraw *all* permits today.

It is hardly surprising that the next section of this report (compiled from a shorthand note of daily proceedings) begins with an assurance of success:

On Friday the success of the general strike appeared completely assured. It was clear to everyone that the O.M.S. organisation was unable to cope with the task imposed upon it. The attitude of the population was favourable to the strikers and unfavourable to the Government. There were no disturbances, the Trade Unionists maintained an almost perfect discipline. There was no change from the ordinary except for the quietness in the streets and the absence of traffic.

In the session of Friday evening the Joint Strike Committee were able to discuss the situation with Mr. C. P. Trevelyan, M.P. (who had arrived from London as special emissary from the General Council) on a basis of the complete mastery of the difficulties that had so far confronted it. The situation as a whole was now well in hand.

The use of this authoritative phrase ("situation well in hand") reflected the passing of authority as far as strike permits for transport were concerned, and in other ways as well, from the hands of the Government and its agencies into the grasp of the Strike Committee and the Councils of Action. But in another respect the two sides were unevenly matched. The trade unions could not arrest policemen or strike-breakers, let alone coal-owners or governmental leaders; whereas the Commissioners and chief constables under the enormous powers confided to them by orders under the Royal Proclamation could and did arrest strike leaders. An example early on in Tyneside was the arrest and subsequent imprisonment of two initiators of the improvised organisation, Will Lawther, then a checkweighman and Harry Bolton, then Chairman of the Blaydon Urban District Council. Such arrests as these, and the extensive police batoning of strikers that followed, served only to stimulate anger amongst the trade unionists, whose machinery of control was daily growing stronger.

8. THE COMBAT THICKENS

Over the week-end and for the sixth, seventh, eighth and ninth days of the strike the struggle became more intense.

On the Sunday, May 9th, A. A. Purcell, leader of the Strike Organisation Committee of the General Council, stated that the Government had issued warrants for the arrest of himself and of Ernest Bevin. Later *Lansbury's Labour Weekly* (issue May 22nd) stated that the Government had decided to arrest the members of the General Council and of local strike committees, to call up the Army Reserves and to repeal the Trade Disputes Act of 1906. Meantime the number of arrests ran to many hundreds including that of Noah Ablett, a member of the Executive Committee of the M.F.G.B., and the Government, through the B.B.C., on the Monday announced many sentences of one to six months' imprisonment.

On this same Monday morning (May 10th) there appeared in the *British Worker* under the heading "ALL's WELL" a "General Council's message to Trade Union members":

We are entering upon the second week of the general stoppage in support of the mine-workers against the attack upon their standard of life by the coal-owners. Nothing could be more wonderful than the magnificent response of millions of workers to the call of their leaders. From every town and city in the country reports are pouring into the General Council headquarters stating that all ranks are solid, that the working men and women are resolute in their determination to resist the unjust attack upon the mining community.

The General Council desire to express their keen appreciation of the loyalty of the Trade Union members to whom the call was issued and by whom such a splendid response has been made. They are especially desirous of commending the workers on their strict obedience to the instruction to avoid all conflict and to conduct themselves in an orderly manner. Their behaviour during the first week of the stoppage is a great example to the whole world.

The General Council's message at the opening of the second week is:—"Stand Firm. Be Loyal to Instructions and Trust your Leaders."

Meantime the effect of the strike was beginning to be felt in trades that had not been called upon. In some cases the workers came out on strike (e.g. Paisley where 32,000 textile workers came out on Monday, May 10th) and in other areas (e.g. Lancashire and the Midlands) textile works and other undertakings closed down for lack of fuel. However occasioned, these stoppages added to the strength of the strike.

Then Sir Herbert Samuel put forward some proposals for a settlement, to be known as the Samuel Memorandum, the main points of which were that the General Strike should be called off; the subsidy to be renewed "for a reasonable time" while negotiations were reopened; a National Wages Board under an Independent Chairman to seek a settlement, with no revision of wage rates without assurances that the Commission's reorganising scheme would be adopted. By resolution the Miners' Executive rejected this on May 11th, whereupon Samuel submitted it to the General Council.

Meanwhile, the General Council had made its first call on reserves by issuing a strike order (to take effect from Tuesday midnight) to all engineering and shipbuilding workers not yet affected by the strike. On its side the Government were able to report nearly a quarter of a million registrations of police volunteers and were able, also, to make announcement of still more extensive arrests and sentences; in which care was taken to specify cases of arrest of Communists. Nevertheless the Government, through the B.B.C., could not report any major success. Typical B.B.C. bulletins ran:

Tuesday, May 11th—afternoon bulletin:
Still no sign of relaxation of the strike situation as a whole.
Tuesday, May 11th—evening bulletin:
There is as yet little sign of a general collapse of the strike.
Wednesday, May 12th—10 a.m. bulletin:
The position as a whole is still one of deadlock.

9. THE TERMINATION OF THE GENERAL STRIKE

Two short hours later came the noon bulletin on the B.B.C.: "General Strike ceases today."

Incredulous miners, workers, and general public clustered round the radio. Stunning confirmation reached them in the announcer's reading of a message from the King-Emperor in Buckingham Palace addressed "to my people":

The nation has just passed through a period of extreme anxiety.
It was today announced that the General Strike had been brought to an end.
At such a moment it is supremely important to bring together all my people to confront the difficult situation which still remains.
This task requires the co-operation of all able and well-disposed men in the country.

Even with such help it will be difficult, but it will not be impossible.

Let us forget whatever elements of bitterness the events of the past few days may have created, only remembering how steady and how orderly the country has remained, though severely tested, and forthwith address ourselves to the task of bringing into being a peace which will be lasting because, forgetting the past, it looks only to the future with the hopefulness of a united people.

What had happened to bring this about? Within twenty-four hours of their cheerful message, "All's well," and the exhortation to "stand firm; be loyal to instructions and trust your leaders," the T.U.C. General Council had decided to sue for peace and asked the Prime Minister to meet them. The official account of that meeting at Downing Street, where seven Ministers headed by Baldwin, Worthington-Evans and Birkenhead received the General Council including Arthur Pugh, J. H. Thomas, Ernest Bevin and Walter Citrine, runs as follows:

THE PRIME MINISTER: Mr. Pugh, will you be good enough to make a statement.

MR. PUGH: Well, sir, when we separated something over a week ago it was, of course, recognised and expressed on both sides that the ultimate end would be a settlement of this matter by negotiations, and although the conflict has been very much extended and developments have taken place since then, clearly both sides and all sides and all parties have had in view—they must have had—the ultimate arrangements that would have to be made to bring this trouble to a successful end. We, of course, like yourself, have had.

Despite whatever developments might have taken place, everybody has had to direct their thoughts in that channel, and to use such opportunities as presented themselves, and such public opinion as existed with a view to effecting a resumption of negotiations. In that respect, sir, your contribution was made in the statement delivered to the people of the country through the wireless stations. That was something which we on our side certainly could not ignore.

On the other hand, we had been exploring other possibilities with full knowledge that, whatever happened, and however long the present position lasted, or whatever might be its consequences, in the long run the process of negotiations would have to be gone through. Well, as a result of developments in that direction and the possibilities that we see in getting back to negotiations, and your assurance, speaking for the general community of citizens as a whole, that no stone should be left unturned to get back to negotiations, we are here today, sir, to say that this General Strike is to be terminated forthwith, in order that negotiations may proceed, and, we can only hope, may proceed in a manner which will bring about a satisfactory settlement. That is the announcement which my General Council is empowered to make.

THE PRIME MINISTER: That is, the General Strike is to be called off forthwith?

MR. PUGH: Forthwith. That means immediately. There is just a point about the actual arrangement, but that is in effect what it means. It is merely a matter of the best way to get it done with the least confusion.

THE PRIME MINISTER: I mean there would be a great deal of work for both of us to do. All I would say in answer to that is, I thank God for your decision, and I would only say now—I do not think it is a moment for lengthy discussion—I only say now I accept fully and confirm fully all I have said in the last two paragraphs of my broadcasted message. I shall call my Cabinet together forthwith, report to them what you have said, and I shall lose no time in using every endeavour to get the two contending parties together, and do all I can to ensure a just and lasting settlement. I hope it may be possible before long to make a statement of the lines on which we hope to accomplish that end.

MR. THOMAS: Only one or two of us wish to say anything to you, and it will be very brief. You answered us in the way we knew you would answer us—namely, that just as you recognise we have done a big thing in accepting the responsibility, we felt sure the big thing would be responded to in a big way. We are satisfied all too well that it will not be a day or two or a week in which the dislocation and difficulty can be put right, but whatever may be the view of the merits of the dispute now ending there is common agreement that assistance from those who were opposing parties ten minutes ago is essential to rectify and make good and start things on the right road again. Your assistance in that is necessary; our assistance is necessary. We intend to give it, and in doing that we believe you can help. We want you to help us in that direction—I never liked the word war, and I do not want to use it, but we want your help when the dispute is ended. We trust your word as Prime Minister. We ask you to assist us in the way you only can assist us—by asking employers and all others to make the position as easy and smooth as possible, because the one thing we must not have is guerilla warfare. That must be avoided, and in that both sides have to contribute immediately. Nothing could be worse than that this great decision which we have taken should be interpreted otherwise than as a general desire to do the right thing in a difficult moment for the industry of the nation.

MR. BEVIN: I think you will agree in the difficulties we have had before us, at least we have taken a great risk in calling the strike off.

I want to urge it must not be regarded as an act of weakness, but rather one of strength. I am not talking of muscle and brawn, but rather that it took a little courage to take the line we have done. I want to stress Mr. Thomas's point, and ask you if you could tell us whether you are prepared to make a general request, as head of the Government, that facilities, etc., ready facilities for reinstatement and that kind of thing, shall be given forthwith. The position is this. Some of the undertakings that are affected, of course, are affected by associations which are get-at-able; otherwise they are all over the country. When this goes out in the Press it may cause untold confusion, but if you could agree with us to make a declaration it would, I think, facilitate matters. Employers no doubt have been acting at least in carrying out the spirit of the Government during the fight, naturally, and they would no doubt respond to a statement of that character, and I would put it to you very strongly that that is one of the easiest ways of doing things. One of the reasons I want to put it to you is this. In a dislocation of this character it does affect production very much, especially in producing trades, and if there is a resumption with a sort of good feeling then the thing gets back on to its usual footing very rapidly. If there is not, then it does affect the restoration.

I remember after the 1912 strike, when we were beaten, Sir Joseph Broodbank went into it very carefully, and the loss in output of transport was something like 25 per cent for some time until the war. We do not want that kind of thing. We have had a row, and it does upset things, but we are quite willing to co-operate with our men to repair the damage just as much as the employers, but the employers are the people who can facilitate that kind of feeling, and I am sure they would respond to you if you issued that as a statement. It would be very helpful to us before we left the building if we could have some indication in that direction, because we shall have to send telegrams to Unions whose headquarters are not in London, with whom we cannot converse, and coupling with it a declaration from yourself would, in a way, give the lead as to how the thing is to be approached.

You said, sir, also you were going to call the parties together in order to effect a just settlement. Now, we have called our show off, and work will be resuming pretty quickly. I do not know whether I am overstepping the bounds, but I would like you to give me an idea of whether that means that there is to be a resumption of the mining negotiations with us, or whether all the negotiations have to be carried on while the miners still remain out.

MR. THOMAS: That implies that we interpret your speech to mean what I am sure it did mean.

MR. BEVIN. It helped us to rise to the occasion. I thought personally—of course, it is so difficult when you have to take it without conversing—I really felt in the event of our taking the lead in

GENERAL STRIKE CARTOON
from St. Pancras Bulletin No. 4, May 6

GENERAL STRIKE CARTOON
from St. Pancras Bulletin No. 9, May 10

assuring you we were going to play the game and put our people back, that it was going to be free and unfettered negotiations with the parties very speedily, because thousands of our people cannot go back if the colliers are still out, and if the colliers are still out it is going to make it extremely difficult to get a smooth running of the machine. Those are the two points I wish to put to you.

THE PRIME MINISTER: Well, Mr. Bevin, I cannot say more here at this meeting now. I did not know what points you were going to raise, or that anything would be said beyond the statement of Mr. Pugh. The point you have put is one I must consider, and I will consider it at once. I would only say, in my view the best thing to do is to get as quickly as possible into touch with the employers. I think that the quicker that is done the less friction there will be. You know my record. You know the object of my policy, and I think you may trust me to consider what has been said with a view to seeing how best we can get the country quickly back into the condition in which we all want to see it. You will want my co-operation, and I shall want yours to try to make good the damage done to the trade, and try to make this country a little better and a happier place than it has been in recent years. That will be my steady endeavour, and I look to all of you when we are through this for your co-operation in that. I shall do my part, and I have no doubt you will do yours.

In regard to the second point, there, again, I cannot say at this moment what will happen, because I shall have to see the parties. My object, of course, is to get the mines started the first moment possible, and get an agreement reached. I cannot say until I have seen them exactly what the lines will be upon which my object can best be attained, but you may rely on me and rely on the Cabinet that they will see no stone is left unturned to accomplish that end. Now, Mr. Pugh, as I said before, we have both of us got a great deal to do and a great deal of anxious and difficult work, and I think that the sooner you get to your work and the sooner I get to mine the better.

MR. PUGH: Yes; that sums up the position for the moment.

MR. BEVIN: I am a little persistent. I do not want to take up your time, but shall we be meeting on these two points soon?

THE PRIME MINISTER: I cannot say that, Mr. Bevin. I think it may be that whatever decision I come to the House of Commons may be the best place in which to say it. I cannot say at the moment whether the better thing would be to do it there or meet again; but we are going to consider right away what is best.

This verbatim report makes it clear that Mr. Baldwin had been expecting from the lips of Mr. Pugh an unconditional withdrawal, and was either unprepared or unwilling to let the meeting go beyond this ceremony of capitulation.

That, then, was what happened on the fatal May 12th. But why had it happened? To answer this we must turn to the statement of their reasons for calling off the strike which the General Council issued that evening to affiliated societies, Trades Councils and Strike Committees. It ran:

The General Council, through the magnificent support and solidarity of the Trade Union Movement, has obtained assurances that a settlement of the mining problem can be secured which justifies them in bringing the general stoppage to an end. Conversations have been proceeding between the General Council representatives and Sir Herbert Samuel, Chairman of the Coal Commission, who returned from Italy for the express purpose of offering his services to try to effect a settlement of the differences in the coal-mining industry.

The Government had declared that under no circumstances could negotiations take place until the General Strike had been terminated, but the General Council feel, as a result of the conversations with Sir Herbert Samuel and the proposals which are embodied in the correspondence and documents which are enclosed, that sufficient assurances had been obtained as to the lines upon which a settlement could be reached to justify them in terminating the General Strike. . . .

The General Council considered the practicability of securing a resumption of work by the members in dispute at a uniform time and date, but it was felt, having regard to the varied circumstances and practices in each industry, that it would be better for each Executive Council itself to make arrangements for the resumption of work of its own members. . . .

Throughout the negotiations and during the whole of the stoppage the General Council have declared that they have been fighting to protect the miners against an intolerable degradation of their standard of life and working conditions. . . . The Unions that have maintained so resolutely and unitedly their generous and ungrudging support of the miners can be satisfied that an honourable understanding has been reached.

But there were some points which this statement did not make clear. Only the day before, May 11th, the Miners' Federation of Great Britain had rejected Sir Herbert Samuel's proposals, both through the mouth of their Chairman, Herbert Smith, and also by explicit resolution of their Executive Committee.

Nor was it generally known on Wednesday, May 12th,

when the General Strike was called off by telegram, that a telegram of a very different nature had been sent that same day by A. J. Cook to all Districts of the Miners' Federation telling them that "miners must not resume work pending decision of national conference." Nor, finally, was any immediate Conference of Executives of trade unions called to decide on termination of the strike, or receive a recommendation for its termination from the General Council.

On the Wednesday afternoon and evening and on the next day (Thursday, May 13th) there was stunned bewilderment in the trade union movement. The question was everywhere asked, "Why has the strike been terminated?" To this question the answer provided in the General Council's circular of May 12th was no answer at all : and delegates were sent to London to ascertain the facts. Attached to the General Council's letter was the Pugh–Samuel correspondence as follows :

May 12th, 1926.
Dear Mr. Pugh,
As the outcome of the conversations which I had with your Committee, I attach a memorandum embodying the conclusions that have been reached. I have made it clear to your Committee from the outset that I have been acting entirely on my own initiative, have received no authority from the Government, and can give no assurances on their behalf. I am of opinion that the proposals embodied in the memorandum are suitable for adoption, and are likely to promote a settlement of the differences in the coal industry. I shall strongly recommend their acceptance by the Government when the negotiations are renewed.
Yours sincerely, HERBERT SAMUEL.

London, May 12th, 1926.
Dear Sir,
The General Council having carefully considered your letter of today, and the memorandum attached to it, concurred in your opinion that it offers a basis on which the negotiations upon the conditions in the coal industry can be renewed.
They are taking the necessary measures to terminate the General Strike, relying upon the public assurances of the Prime Minister as to the steps that would follow. They assume that during the resumed negotiations the subsidy will be renewed and that the lock-out notices to the miners will be immediately withdrawn.
Yours faithfully,
ARTHUR PUGH, Chairman.
WALTER M. CITRINE, Acting Secretary.

The Samuel Memorandum did not bind the Government. The General Council, nevertheless, in the wording of their reply to Herbert Samuel, seemed to have clutched at it as at an authoritative document. Any hopes thereby raised (though, as we have seen, they were not warranted in face of the M.F.G.B. rejection of Samuel) were presently to be dashed to the ground when two days later the Prime Minister put out his proposals for a settlement. *They differed from the proposals set out in the Samuel Memorandum.* Moreover, as though to underline this difference, on that same day (May 14th) the correspondence that had been carefully exchanged between Sir Arthur Steel-Maitland (one of the Cabinet) and Sir Herbert Samuel nearly a week earlier was now made public.

May 8, 1926.

My dear Samuel,

It has occurred to me since our conversation this afternoon that in dealing with a matter so delicate it would be better to place upon record in writing the attitude of the Government as I understand it.

We have repeatedly stated that we cannot negotiate until the General Strike has been withdrawn. This statement has a very particular meaning. It means that until the necessary orders have been given to withdraw the strike, or unless the strike has come to an end, we cannot, as a condition or inducement, take part in negotiations in relation to the mining issue. For if we did so, there would and could be no unconditional withdrawal of the strike notices. . . .

It is therefore plain that they cannot enter upon any negotiations unless the strike is so unreservedly concluded that there is not even an implication of such a bargain upon their side as would embarrass them in any legislation which they may conceive to be proper in the light of recent events.

In these circumstances, I am sure that the Government will take the view that, while they are bound most carefully and most sympathetically to consider the terms of any arrangement which a public man of your responsibility and experience may propose, it is imperative to make it plain that any discussion which you think proper to initiate is not clothed in even a vestige of official character.

Yours sincerely, ARTHUR STEEL-MAITLAND.

The ex-Governor of Palestine, thus disavowed beforehand, went on with his self-imposed task of volunteer go-between. His reply ran:

The Reform Club, May 9, 1926.

My dear Steel-Maitland,

I have duly received your letter of yesterday. Let me take this opportunity to put on record the assurance I gave you in conversation that in the discussions which I have had on the present situation I have made it perfectly clear that I have been acting entirely on my own initiative, and without any kind of authorisation from the Government.

I am quite satisfied that there has been no possibility of misunderstanding on that point.

In any further conversations that may take place I shall, of course, maintain the same attitude.

Yours sincerely, HERBERT SAMUEL.

Meanwhile on May 12th the millions of trade unionists who had been engaged for nine days in an unprecedented strike struggle had to make what they could out of the varied pronouncements which the wireless hurled at them from noon onwards. They were not reassured by the B.B.C. broadcast that "the Cardinal Archbishop of Westminster asks us to announce that a *Te Deum* will be sung in Westminster Cathedral after the High Mass at 10.30 tomorrow, Ascension Day": Cardinal Bourne, one of the bitterest opponents of the strikers, was now announcing a song of thanksgiving after victory. Still less reassuring was the Government official communiqué that they would not compel employers to take back workers who had participated in the strike and that the Government had not taken on itself any such obligation: in some cases, it went on, dismissals of workers would be inevitable in view of the decrease of production caused by the strike and in view of obligations incurred by employers in regard to volunteer labour. This meant that blacklegs were to be cherished and trade unionists victimised. It was obvious that the General Council had been duped, or had duped themselves, into making the claim that an honourable understanding had been reached. As darkness fell on the stricken field on that May 12th, amid all the confusion and bewilderment that so beset the workers the Cardinal's jubilation and the curt communiqué from the Government came like a bugle blown in the night. The strikers—the keenest of them—remained on the alert.

10. THE MORROW OF THE GENERAL STRIKE

With the noon tidings of the ending of the strike, there had been certain resumptions of work on the afternoon and evening of Wednesday, May 12th. This led many to think that work generally would be resumed on Thursday, the 13th. The reverse, however, proved to be the case. The miners were still locked out and were continuing the struggle. In many industries employers were endeavouring to impose new conditions of employment on humiliating terms. Railway companies, for example, posted notices that strikers, having broken their contracts, were considered as dismissed and would be later taken on only with individual contracts. So, in face of this threat to their conditions and to their unions, the men remained on strike.

Throughout Thursday, May 13th, the B.B.C. bulletins displayed surprise that work was not resumed.

The General Council, on the other hand, were complaining that employers were "trying to impose vindictive terms on the workers"; and actually called on the Government for aid against such employers:

The General Council called off the General Strike in the confidence that the Prime Minister meant what he said when he asked for a resumption of the negotiations towards an honourable peace. Peace depends upon the employers abstaining from attempts at victimisation. It depends upon their declining to follow the example some are setting of using their position to attack the position of Trade Unionism. The effect will be that the Unions for self-protection will be compelled to offer the most stubborn resistance. The whole purpose expressed by the Prime Minister will be made null and void if this occurs. The Government, if it means what the Prime Minister said, must stop this attack on Trade Unionism. It must demand that the employers abstain from victimisation. Unless this obligation is fulfilled, the Trade Unions will have no alternative but to resist to the uttermost. Their resistive capacity is unimpaired. They cannot tolerate the imposition of conditions which attempt their destruction.

The good faith of the Prime Minister is involved. Peace without vindictiveness is impossible unless this attack ceases. A vindictive peace only means a new struggle. We need acts and not words if work is to be resumed. The workers will not surrender their hard-won gains of many years. The Government has stated it does not desire this. Let it act firmly and quickly to that end.

Meantime the refusal of the vast majority of the strikers to return to work (Friday, the 14th, began with the B.B.C. announcing "as yet no general resumption of work") was having its effect in cooling down the hotheads in the Government and amongst the employers. The notion that possessed many employers in the flush of victory that they could now finish with trade unionism depended on the assumption that there would be an immediate and universal return to work. Whoever had thought it was a case of

> If I can catch him once upon the hip,
> I will feed fat the ancient grudge I bear him

were beginning to have second thoughts. Already on Thursday evening in the House of Commons Baldwin began in a less triumphant tone: "The supreme interest of this country today requires that the largest body of men possible should be brought back at the earliest possible moment" and ended on a note of anxiety: "Let us," he said, "get the workers calm as soon as we can."

So on the next day the employers' organisations met the trade union representatives and drew up agreements for resumption of work. Employers, baulked in their hopes of smashing trade unionism by the continuation on strike of the rank-and-file, were resolved to make the union leaders eat humble pie. Here, for example, are the terms of the railway agreement reached on Friday, May 14th:

1. Those employees of the Railway Companies who have gone out on strike to be taken back to work as soon as traffic offers and work can be found for them. The principle to be followed in reinstating to be seniority in each grade at each station, depot, or office.

2. The Trade Unions admit that, in calling a strike, they committed a wrongful act against the Companies, and agree that the Companies do not, by reinstatement, surrender their legal rights to claim damages arising out of the strike from strikers and others responsible.

3. The Unions undertake—(a) Not again to instruct their members to strike without previous negotiations with the Company. (b) To give no support of any kind to their members to take any unauthorised action. (c) Not to encourage supervisory employees in the special class to take part in any strike.

4. The Company intimate that, arising out of the strike, it may be necessary to remove certain persons to other positions, but no

such persons' salaries or wages will be reduced. Each Company will notify the Union within one week the names of men whom they propose to transfer, and will afford each man an opportunity of having an advocate to present his case to the general manager.

5. The settlement shall not extend to persons who have been guilty of violence or intimidation.

On behalf of the General Managers' Conference:

> FELIX J. C. POLE, H. A. WALKER, R. H. SELBIE, H. G. BURGESS, R. L. WEDGWOOD.

On behalf of the Railway Unions:

> J. H. THOMAS and C. T. CRAMP, National Union of Railwaymen; J. BROMLEY, Associated Society of Locomotive Engineers and Firemen; A. G. WALKDEN, Railway Clerks' Association.

In this agreement it will be seen that the railway companies registered a victory and had their right to victimise acknowledged. The victimisation was to be widespread—not only in industries where similarly worded terms were imposed on the trade unions, but even more in the less organised trades or sections. Meantime no amnesty was declared for the hundreds now undergoing prison sentences: indeed the arrests and sentences of imprisonment continued. The Labour M.P.s, however, protested against "unfounded, inaccurate and provocative statements that the General Council had unconditionally surrendered."

But an unconditional surrender events indeed proved it to be.

CHAPTER XIV

THE GREAT LOCK-OUT OF 1926

1. THE MINERS FIGHT ON

THE General Strike had come to a sudden end. The workers puzzled, uncertain, gloomy, went streaming back to the factories, leaving the miners alone on the field. Their position was desperate: unwillingly deserted by their allies, with the Government openly favouring the coal-owners, and the coal-owners, now confident of victory, ready to impose the full measure of their will upon the miners. No convincing reason had been given them for the abandonment of the struggle in face of the obvious fact that the Samuel Memorandum, which they had rejected, meant a cut in their already too low wages. Nevertheless they avoided reproach or recrimination. That morning of Wednesday, May 12th, after they had heard successively Bevin, Purcell and Ben Turner urging them to concur in the General Council's decision within that hour to call off the General Strike, the M.F.G.B. Executive Committee again considered the matter. They passed a resolution in which, after reaffirming their rejection of the Samuel Memorandum, they expressed "our profound admiration of the wonderful demonstration of loyalty as displayed by all workers who promptly withdrew labour in support of the miners' standards."

The next day they went further: amid the confusion and bewilderment that followed the termination of the strike they were ready to give any help they could to the other unions. The resolution put forward by them to the M.F.G.B. Special Conference, on Friday, May 14th, "expresses its profound appreciation of the self-sacrifice and loyalty displayed by their fellow trade-unionists and pledges itself to render every possible assistance to the organisations who at the termination of the stoppage are confronted with difficulties arising from the strike." In this attitude there was a magnanimity which stood them in good stead with the workers in other industries and which also boded ill to any hopes the owners or the Cabinet might have of easy victory. The delegates had come in haste from all the coal-fields where on the Thursday their fellow trade-unionists, ordered suddenly to resume work and faced with the danger of widespread victimisation, had in many cases remained on strike. The delegates were filled with concern for those who had stood by them; and they gave a sympathetic hearing to their President when he appealed to them to safeguard the unity of the movement and to think only of those who had been staunch and true. "There may," he said, "have been a few of what I might term market-men who had no stomach in this business, but there have been some genuine men in a regular place[1] that came out and had some stomach in them." Herbert Smith, though unable wholly to hide his own feelings,[2] was able to get the assent of the Conference not to utter reproaches.

A. J. Cook and Treasurer Richardson gave a report since "our last conference in this hall last Saturday week . . . in which we all were imbued with the highest hopes as to the ultimate outcome of our own people." Then Richardson told of his journey to Belgium to meet the International Miners' Federation, where he found that the miners' union in each country, having met with their own "Trades Union Congress," had "so arranged and organised their work that no coal might come from the Continent." At this point the announcement that the Government was preparing a document which the Executive Committee would have to consider caused the adjournment of the Conference. Next morning, Saturday, May 15th, the document was put in their

---

[1] His reference to these, a few minutes earlier, as "men who have got to consider their £2,000 a year salary, who have come out with you" indicates the strength of trade union traditions and discipline in the people of Britain.

[2] "Last Tuesday night we made a statement to them and I do not want to fill this meeting with excitement; we said: 'Are you people going to take this arrangement or suggestion from Samuel and report to the Prime Minister, when you make an unconditional surrender without remembering these men and women who have taken up the stand. Have you no consideration for their position, to secure them going back?'

"Because we always understand this as mine-workers, that one of the first things we do after getting into a row, we insist upon an agreement which includes a clause something like this, that every man and boy must go back to the position he left. When he left, that position ceased to exist, and not to be filled by somebody else, and before any new men are set on these men must be certain. We impressed it upon them before they took the step. We impressed it upon them, because probably we had more experience in such cases. They said, 'We are prepared to take the consequences.' The consequence has shown itself."

hands. It required careful examination and would need interpretation in many of its clauses. So, having instructed the Districts to send in particulars of any prosecutions and convictions, so as "to act jointly with the other unions if desired," the Conference adjourned for five days, during which time the Executive was instructed to consider the proposals and interpretations which had come with the following letter:

14th May, 1926.

Dear Mr. Herbert Smith,

Enclosed you will find an outline of proposals which, in the opinion of His Majesty's Government, should provide a reasonable basis for the settlement of the dispute in the Coal Mining Industry on the lines of the Royal Commission's Report. I trust both sides may see their way to accept them.

It is not necessary for me to urge your Federation in the present grave circumstances to give their most earnest consideration to these proposals, and I shall not expect a reply before Monday at earliest.

Yours very truly, STANLEY BALDWIN.

The enclosed outline included the introduction of a series of Bills and administrative proposals for giving effect to the Royal Commission's recommendation for improving "the organisation of the industry and increasing its efficiency." But none of this could be put in hand until fully considered by the Coal Advisory Committee of the Secretary for Mines, which was to review progress on the Commission's recommendations from time to time.

There was, however, to be no such breathing space when the Prime Minister got down to the miners' wages and hours. Promising "further financial assistance to the industry to the amount of approximately £3,000,000" Mr. Baldwin's proposals continued:

5. For a period not exceeding —— weeks—

(i) The miners will accept a reduction of —— per cent in minimum wages (other than subsistence rates) in all districts.

(ii) The owners will bear wages equivalent to 100 per cent of ascertained net proceeds (in January–March) so far as necessary to maintain those wages.

(iii) The Government will fill the gap with a subsidy to be debited against the £3,000,000 aforesaid.

6. In the meantime

(i) A Board shall be set up consisting of three representatives of the coal-owners and three representatives of the miners, with an independent chairman.

(ii) The Board shall frame a National Wages and Hours Agreement governing the principles on which the general wage rates should be ascertained in each district, and shall also decide the minimum percentage on basis, taking into consideration the state and prospects of the trade, the reorganisation proposals of the Commission and other relevant factors.

(iii) Subsistence wages shall not be reduced in any district where they at present yield 45s. per week or less for a full customary week.

(iv) The Board shall decide also what the districts shall be.

(v) The Board shall issue its decision within three weeks.

(vi) In the event of disagreement in respect of wages the decision shall rest with the independent chairman.

7. If the parties agree that it is advisable that some temporary modification should be made in the statutory hours of work, the Government will propose the necessary legislation forthwith and give facilities for its immediate passage.

Now from the outset the M.F.G.B. in that second week of May had opposed the decision of the General Council on two grounds, first that the terms of the Samuel Memorandum were unacceptable and second that there was no guarantee that the Government would take any account of them. The General Council, however, had taken its momentous decision "relying on the public assurances of the Prime Minister as to the steps that would follow," and had further explicitly set down their assumption that during resumed negotiations "the subsidy will be renewed and that the lock-out notices to miners will be immediately withdrawn." The Samuel Memorandum, certainly, had begun with the words "The negotiations upon the conditions of the coal industry should be resumed, the subsidy being renewed for such reasonable period as may be required for that purpose." But it was not the Samuel proposals that were now put forward by the Prime Minister: once the General Strike was called off, the Samuel proposals, having served their turn, were cast on one side. The M.F.G.B. Conference had to face entirely new proposals. The lock-out notices were not withdrawn; nor was there any provision for this in the Baldwin proposals. The offer of a subsidy was conditional on an immediate wage-cut of 10 per cent. Within three weeks this wage-cut was to be followed by a further reduction. The wages of the lowest paid men were no longer to be guaranteed if they were in any place above 45s. a week. The Baldwin proposals meant, in addition to wage-cuts, the abolition of the national minimum; the sapping of the seven-hour day; an increase of unemployment; the weakening and splitting of the Miners' Federation by the introduction of District settlements; the substitution of compulsory arbitration for collective bargaining. Since these proposals involved the defeat of the trade union principles which not only the miners but the whole organised Labour Movement was pledged to defend, it is not surprising that the following resolution was put forward by the Executive Committee at the adjourned M.F.G.B. Conference:

This Committee having given long and careful consideration to the terms submitted by the Prime Minister as a basis for a settlement, together with what transpired at the interview with him yesterday, comes to the following conclusions:

We are largely in agreement with the legislative and administrative proposals set forth and are prepared to render every assistance possible to ensure their success, but see no reason why such measures should be first reviewed by the Coal Advisory Committee.

We are unable to recommend the mine-workers to accept his proposal that a Board with an independent chairman shall be empowered to abolish the National Minimum and enforce varying minima throughout the districts.

We consider, that in making these proposals the Prime Minister is not honouring the pledge he gave to the country in the message broadcast on the 8th May as follows:

"I wish to make it as clear as I can that the Government is not fighting to lower the standard of living of the miners, or of any other section of the workers." (May 20, 1926.)

Two days later came the reply from Downing Street—though no longer signed by the Prime Minister in person—which, after a stiff acknowledgment, continued:

Among the most emphatic conclusions of the [Samuel] Commission was their conclusion that a disaster was impending over the industry which could only be averted by an immediate reduction in labour costs of production. It is clear from the resolution of your conference that your Federation, though they largely agree with the

Government's legislative and administrative proposals, still refuse to consider any alteration of wages or hours. So long as this is their attitude, and in the absence of any practical proposals from the Federation designed to meet the circumstances of the industry, the Prime Minister does not see that any useful purpose would be served by his meeting you, but he will hold himself available to arrange a further discussion the moment that he is informed that you find yourselves in a position to submit suggestions of the kind required.

The Government have never concealed the fact that there are recommendations in the Report that they only accepted with reluctance, and could not have accepted except in the hope of a general settlement. This hope has been disappointed. In these circumstances, it must be clearly understood that the Government regain their freedom for all purposes, and no longer hold themselves bound by the terms of an offer which has been rejected. In particular, in view of the great and growing burden imposed on the national finances by the general strike, and the present stoppage in the coal-mining industry, it would be impossible for the Government to hold over beyond the end of the present month the offer of any further subsidy.

I have only to add, with reference to the last paragraph of your letter, that you are mistaken in supposing that there is any discrepancy between that sentence in the Prime Minister's broadcasted speech, to which you refer, and the proposals put forward by him on behalf of the Government. No such discrepancy exists, and in the opinion of the Prime Minister the terms proposed, if accepted on both sides with good spirit, would by their results have fully justified those sentences of his speech to which you call attention.

I am, sir, yours faithfully, RONALD WATERHOUSE.

The Baldwin proposals had also been rejected by the mine-owners, who would have nothing to do with either the wages scheme or the reorganisation proposals. They proposed instead an eight-hour day and rather ungratefully demanded "freedom from political interference." Their conclusions (issued on Friday, May 21st) after insisting on the eight-hour day and wage reductions, which would "not exceed 10 per cent when wages are at the minimum in the worst placed districts," continued:

The proposals of May 14, calculated as they are to limit freedom of administration, will not be helpful in securing the increased efficiency of the industry. It will be impossible to continue the conduct of the industry under private enterprise unless it is accorded the same freedom from political interference as is enjoyed by other industries.

To this, on the next day, Mr. Baldwin issued a statement on the reception of his memorandum by miners and mine-owners, which put the blame on the miners, saying that he was

aware that the immediate cause of the present deadlock is the refusal of the Miners' Federation to consider any concession that would give such a reduction in costs of production as the Royal Commission pointed out was indispensable

and that

while the attitude of the Miners' Federation remains exactly what it was last July, the colliery owners have made some advances from their original position in order to try to reach a settlement.

Defending the Government's "political interference," he added to the owners that he deplored

your Association's apparent inability to recognise that it was quite impossible for a Government to have stood aside in matters where the national well-being is so vitally and disastrously affected.

With these exchanges all illusions that the mining lock-out might reach a speedy ending vanished. No man knew how long the struggle would last.

The Government immediately took three main measures. They prepared for the importing of foreign coal (according to the *Daily Herald* of May 25th). Two days later they began to prepare public opinion by issuing regulations restricting the allowance of coal for domestic purposes to one hundred-weight a fortnight. On the last day of May a state of emergency was once again proclaimed under the Emergency Powers Act.

On the other hand an earnest of support for the miners was given at the Co-operative Congress, which by a unanimous resolution expressed "its strong belief that the miners' standard of life should not be reduced" and further resolved:

that, as a practical means of giving assistance to the workers involved in the dispute, the Co-operative Union should organise within the movement a central fund for the purpose of helping societies and their members to meet the demands made on them in consequence of any dispute. (May 25, 1926.)

2. JUNE 1926

All hopes for an early settlement had now proved vain. From the last week of May onwards there opened out the prospect of a prolonged struggle, the greatest in the industrial annals of Britain. The whole population was affected: and the General Strike had visibly split the population into two contending portions. Beyond the shores of Britain there was an extension of this partisanship. The eyes of the world were bent on the struggle in this island. Foreign policy was affected, not only in Europe but as far away as the Pacific Ocean where the Chinese Revolution, now in its fifteenth year, was entering on a new phase. From the base established by Sun Yat-sen in Canton, the forces of the new China were sweeping northward to the Yangtze-kiang, abolishing the feudal overlords and affronting the vested interests of the British merchants, who found their far-away Government unready, by reason of the coal dispute, to give them aid and comfort. The locked-out British miners were for a time a shield to the Chinese Revolution.

From a score of countries gifts of money began to flow into the Miners' Relief Fund. The biggest sums came from the trade unionists of Soviet Russia. This, while it caused a wave of gratitude amongst the miners, was taken particularly ill by the Baldwin Cabinet, whose foreign policy for over a year had been increasingly hostile to the Union of Soviet Socialist Republics. Following on a Press campaign against Russia, the British Government on June 11th sent a note to the Soviet Government protesting against the transmission of money from trade unions there to trade unions here. Home Secretary Joynson-Hicks declared that "money had been sent from Russia, including some money from the Russian Government for the purpose of the General Strike." A fortnight later there was a debate arranged on "Russian gold" in the House of Commons (June 25, 1926). In the debate, which was conducted with a great deal of venom against the miners as well as against the Russian workers, George Lansbury, after reading a moving letter from his daughter, Violet, then in Russia, said:

AFTER THE GENERAL STRIKE
Herbert Smith and W. P. Richardson, May 14, 1926

COAL LOCK-OUT 1926

Smith, Cook and Richardson go to Downing Street, August 26, 1926

I do believe in the class war. I believe the class war is responsible for the starvation of my kith and kin, people who are bone of my bone and flesh of my flesh, down in the coal-fields of Britain. The only thing that is being asked today by the Government and the capitalists is that the workers should sacrifice. I hope to God that the workers will be able to stand out and with their women defeat the most nefarious campaign that has ever been waged against them. . . .

The Speaker did not call a single one of the nearly fifty miners in the House. This was felt to be unfair and *Hansard* records the end of the debate thus:

AN HON. MEMBER: We want a miner.

Mr. J. JONES: Sit down, sit down! (Continued interruption.)

Mr. DEPUTY SPEAKER: Grave disorder having arisen, I now Adjourn the House, without Question put.

Within Britain the Government had resumed its public professions of impartiality as between mine-owners and miners. On June 1st, Mr. Baldwin stated he was willing at any moment to help with negotiations; he agreed that though the subsidy offer had lapsed, a temporary subsidy in some form was essential. On June 10th he stated in Parliament that he was keeping the coal situation under review, but was not in a position to make any further statement. On June 15th he outlined a "scheme" for the settlement of the dispute; the kernel of this was new legislation to lengthen the working day in mines. A week later, on June 22nd, the general intentions of the Government were disclosed at a meeting of the Central Committee of the Government's party: Lord Chancellor Birkenhead put forward plans for restricting trade union rights; and that meeting responded with a resolution urging upon the Government the amendment of the Trade Disputes Act of 1906, the auditing of trade union accounts, balloting and "proper legal notice" before all strikes.

Meanwhile the Miners' Federation of Great Britain had been seeking means to strengthen their side. On June 3rd the national officials left for Brussels to discuss on the International Miners' Committee what measures might be taken to prevent foreign coal coming to Britain. The same day the President of the Mining Association of Great Britain wrote a personal letter to Herbert Smith suggesting an informal meeting of a few representatives to discuss the deadlock. On

June 8th the M.F.G.B. Executive Committee authorised the four national officials to meet the mine-owners that day; after three hours this joint meeting broke up in complete deadlock. "There is," stated A. J. Cook, "no change in the position. . . . The owners have not receded in the slightest from the demands they have made for longer hours and lower wages."

Two days later a Federation statement set forth "the only possible basis" for a settlement (maintenance of wages and hours, national wages agreement, immediate reorganisation of the industry), and on June 15th issued an appeal to all trade unions for financial help. In particular they asked the transport unions to refuse to handle coal.

The Federation had written on May 19th to John Bromley, of the A.S.L.E. and F.:

Dear Mr. Bromley,

My Committee have been discussing today the question of transporting and conveying of coal that is already stocked in sidings or at the docks. We feel sure that your members will not do anything detrimental to our interests and will still assist us as far as possible in the struggle which we are engaged in. I am sure you will realise that by handling coal it would affect us in our struggle.

Yours fraternally, A. J. Cook.

The same day a letter in the same terms was written to the National Union of Railwaymen. By return came a joint reply:

Dear Mr. Cook,

Your letter of the 19th instant was placed before our Joint Executive Committees at their meeting this afternoon, and the following resolution was adopted:

That in reply to the letter from the Secretary of the Miners' Federation re the transfer of coal on the railways, the Joint Executive Committees decide in view of the fact that the Railway Unions took common action on the instruction of the General Council of the Trades Union Congress, along with other unions, and declared the strike off on the instructions of that body, we consider that we have carried out our obligations in conjunction with the other unions.

We might add that by reason of the coal stoppage we are now engaged in a tremendous fight for the re-employment of all our members, very many of whom are stopped as a result of there being no coal to transport. You will gather from this how difficult our position is at the moment.

Yours faithfully,
C. T. Cramp, N.U.R.
J. Bromley, A.S.L.E. & F.

Something other than this reply had been hoped for, but the reply was not altogether unexpected. Throughout the organised Labour Movement a bitter controversy was raging over the General Council's termination of the strike. The attitude of the union officials was impugned. Accusations and counter-accusations were being bandied about in speeches and writings in the Labour Press. This controversy, begun in the second week of May, was reaching its height with the approach of the Conference of Trade Union Executives called for Friday, June 25th, to which the General Council would give its report and from which it would ask for a verdict.

Right in the midst of this came a Government announcement of legislation to lengthen the miners' working day. This was a real shock, not only to the miners, but to the others engaged in the controversy. As a consequence it was decided that in view of "the attacks which the Government and the employers are making to reduce the standard of life of the workpeople" the controversy should be called to a halt. The hatchet was to be buried, at any rate for the time being. Thus, in the eighth week of the lock-out, the General Council and the Miners' Federation issued a joint statement postponing the day of reckoning until after the mining dispute should be settled "so that a united policy may be adopted to resist to the fullest possible extent the Government's action." It continued:

It must be clearly understood that neither the General Council nor the Miners' Federation desire to postpone unduly the Conference but they regard the design of the Government and the owners to increase hours of labour as being of such fundamental importance to the working-class movement both nationally and internationally as to make it essential to concentrate upon the present position rather than to devote attention to past events.

The General Council and the Miners' Federation regard it as of the greatest importance at this juncture that all sections and parties should avoid statements, either in speech or writing, which create friction and misunderstanding, and which divert attention from the purpose in view.

The General Council and the Miners' Federation feel assured that the affiliated organisations and the rank and file of the movement generally will appreciate the importance of this declaration and in the circumstances with which the movement is now faced will accord the agreed policy their fullest approval and support. (June 23, 1926.)

This agreement was fairly widely accepted. The pamphlet *The Nine Days*, by A. J. Cook, was withdrawn from circulation. A protest, however, against the postponement came from the Executive of the Associated Society of Locomotive Engineers and Firemen, in whose journal the "not-to-be-published" report of the General Council had found publication. Nevertheless, the immediate meeting of the General Council (June 24th) to consider further measures in connection with the lock-out seemed to many to show that some closing of the ranks had followed on the Government's action to lengthen the hours of labour in the mines.

The effect of this Coal Mines Bill of 1926, which was passing through the House of Commons in the last week of June, and became the Coal Mines Act, 1926, with the Royal Assent on July 8th, was to suspend for five years the seven-hour day, secured in July 1919. The lengthening to eight hours was made permissible: wherever adopted it would make the average time spent underground about eight-and-a-half hours, since the eight hours covered only the time from last man down to first man up.

The suspension of the seven-hour working day marked a stage in the struggle. The Samuel Commission on the hours question had been explicit enough, when they examined the Mining Association's proposal to add one hour to the working day:

It would make the working day of every British miner longer by half an hour to an hour than that of miners in any European coalfield of importance except Upper Silesia. Subject to the same exception it would make his working week about as long as any to be found abroad, and, in many British districts, longer. The comparison with other countries, so far as it bears on the standard of life that we should seek to establish for miners here, tells against the proposal of the Mining Association rather than in its favour (pp. 170, 172).

The Samuel Commission had also adversely criticised the Mining Association's proposal because of its effect on production, markets and employment and concluded:

The gain through the lengthening of working hours is not a net gain, either to the country as a whole, or to the mining industry, if that be taken to include the miners themselves. There is a heavy loss, in unemployment and distress and expenditure to relieve distress, which must be set against the apparent gain (p. 174).

But the Samuel Commission was no longer to be cited as a justification of Cabinet policy: yet one more Royal Commission Report was jettisoned, now that it had served its turn. The Government were free to move to their next step. Mr. Baldwin had now adopted completely the Mining Association's proposal to lengthen the working day.

3. JULY 1926

The Government Bill to lengthen the hours of labour in coal-mines passed its Third Reading in the House of Commons on July 1st. The next day, when the Commons were debating the renewal, for yet another month, of the Emergency Powers Act regulations, the General Council of the Trades Union Congress issued a manifesto to its affiliated unions and Trades Councils denouncing the Eight Hours' Bill and the Government's attitude to the dispute; calling for financial support for the miners and for workers imprisoned or victimised; and urging the Trades Councils to strengthen and develop their organisation. But the effort of the Miners' Federation to get an embargo and their suggestion of a levy on the members of trade unions were both of them turned down.

The mine-owners did not wait until this Bill became law before they took advantage of its provisions to post new notices in the Districts, based on an eight-hour day. The Yorkshire owners went further. They posted notices involving an alteration in the former ratio of wages and profits. This, however, was to go faster than suited the Government, who induced the Yorkshire masters to abate their demands for the moment. Meantime the Government went further with their scheme to purchase foreign coal and sums for this purpose—to the tune of £3,000,000—were voted (on July 7th) by the obedient House of Commons.

In this hardening situation the Miners' Federation looked round for help. They made their request, as we have seen, to the General Council: but it soon became clear that the miners' request would not be granted.

They turned to friends abroad: A. J. Cook and Treasurer W. P. Richardson went to the President and Secretary of the Russian Miners' Union; a decision was reached to set up an Anglo-Russian Miners' Committee, which on July 10th published an appeal for help for the British miners. At the same time help was pouring in from the collections organised by the Labour Women's Fund and tens of thousands of miniature miners' lamps were bought and worn as a badge by contributors to that fund.

The strain of the lock-out was now beginning to tell on the whole population. The representatives of the Christian Churches, headed by the Archbishop of Canterbury, had been rebuffed by the Cabinet when they sought to interfere in the General Strike, and their appeal suppressed. Now that the strike was many weeks past it seemed to them there might be a better chance of mediation. Accordingly they approached the M.F.G.B. Executive Committee, which at its meeting on June 29th agreed to meet the churchmen, and on July 15th, having considered the proposals, decided to recommend them to the Delegate Conference.

These proposals were for an immediate resumption of work on the conditions prior to April 30th, 1926; the Government to grant temporary assistance under a scheme to be prepared by the Samuel Commissioners, pending a national settlement, which was to be reached within four months; the Commissioners to prepare Bills to incorporate the reorganisation scheme, and the Government to give assurances that the new legislation should go on the Statute Book at the earliest possible moment; and finally, if agreement were still not reached, a Joint Board to appoint an Independent Chairman whose award should be accepted.

The leaders of the Churches, armed with the M.F.G.B. Executive's assent to these proposals, asked for an interview with the Prime Minister. But when they met Mr. Baldwin on July 19th, it was only to find that he was firm in rejecting their mediation proposals, and that the main reason vouchsafed was that no subsidy could be given by the Government.

If, however, the proposals were brusquely rejected by the Government, they were by no means accepted by the whole of the miners. The Executive of the Durham Miners' Association, in this following the example of the South Wales Miners' Executive, protested on July 21st against the acceptance of the Church leaders' proposals by the M.F.G.B. Executive without the authority of a Federation Conference. When the Special Conference met on July 30th the matter was keenly debated. It became clear that there were two trends of opinion developing within the Federation. The Executive, sharply criticised, appealed for a District vote and this was agreed upon.

The opinion of the miners, thus ascertained by the District vote, showed a majority of 34,614 against the proposals.[1] When these figures were made public on August 16th, it was already four weeks since the Cabinet had rejected "the Bishops' Memorandum," as it was often called. The bishops and their Nonconformist friends were forced to retire from the field.

As the thirteenth week of the lock-out drew on, the miners with their families (counting something more than one tenth of the population of Britain and bigger than the total population of some of the lesser European States) were in a

[1] RESULT OF DISTRICT VOTE

District	No.	In Favour of Proposals	Against Proposals
Bristol	1,900	1,900	—
*Cleveland	5,000	—	—
Cokemen	4,200	4,200	—
Cumberland	8,500	—	8,500
Derbyshire	35,000	35,000	—
Durham	120,000	120,000	—
Group No. 1	19,600	19,600	—
Forest of Dean	5,000	—	5,000
Kent	2,000	2,000	—
Lancashire	75,000	—	75,000
Leicestershire	7,000	7,000	—
Midlands	60,000	60,000	—
Northumberland	37,836	37,836	—
North Wales	10,000	10,000	—
Nottinghamshire	25,000	25,000	—
*Scotland	80,000	—	—
Somerset	4,500	4,500	—
South Derbyshire	6,000	6,000	—
South Wales	129,150	—	129,150
Yorkshire	150,000	—	150,000
Totals	785,686	333,036	367,650

* No vote taken.

difficult position. They were being starved out, they felt, by coal-owners and Government in alliance. Their resources were less, as each day and each week of their endurance went by. Yet they stood firm as stood the defenders of their hearth and home in the *Song of the Fight at Maldon* well-nigh a thousand years ago:

> Mind shall be harder,
> Heart the keener,
> Mood shall be greater
> As our might lessens.

But though the mood of the miners as a whole was becoming keener, more indomitable, there were showing in parts of the Federation signs of weakening in this month of July. In Warwickshire, for example, a number of miners had yielded and had begun to work in the pits. The danger of a breakaway from trade union decisions was stemmed for the time being in that area through a prodigious week-end campaign by A. J. Cook on July 24th and 25th. But henceforth it was upon foreign coal and the prospect of a more extensive breakaway that the owners and the Government placed their reliance.

4. AUGUST 1926

In the fourteenth week of the lock-out, on August 4th, Parliament adjourned till August 30th. The mill-stones of the Emergency Powers Act went on grinding out their weekly grist of arrests and imprisonments. During the month delegations from the Miners' Federations arrived in the United States of America (four), Europe (three), and the Soviet Union (ten), to raise funds or to assist in the collection of monies for the relief fund. The funds were sorely needed; and, as the lock-out reached its fifteenth, sixteenth and seventeenth week, the strain on the miners and their families grew ever greater. Hitherto the Government had not interfered with the collection of relief funds (except in so far as the note to the Soviet Government might be so regarded); but now it went a step further. On Sunday, August 7th there was published a message to the United States from Mr. Baldwin, stating that there was no hardship or destitution amongst the miners.

This message, which aroused widespread indignation, led to the following resolution, passed at the M.F.G.B. Special Conference held in Kingsway Hall on August 16th–17th:

That this conference emphatically protests against the action of the Prime Minister in sending an untrue communication to the American Press, timed to reach America when the Miners' Federation delegation landed in that country. This was done obviously with the object of preventing so far as he possibly could the American trade unionist and general public from subscribing to the fund for the relief of the wives and children of the British miners who are the principal sufferers through the lock-out of the miners by the mine-owners.

This affords further evidence that the Government has definitely decided to assist the mine-owners to defeat the miners by starvation.

At the Conference there was a keen division of opinion as to the next step. Was the organisation to stand by the three principles laid down at the beginning of the stoppage (no change in wages, hours and national agreements) or were they to take a new course? After two days' debate it was decided by 428 to 360 votes (Yorkshire, Lancashire and South Wales with Forest of Dean making up the minority), to empower the Executive Committee to open negotiations with the coal-owners and the Government for a settlement of the dispute.

Two days later, on Thursday, August 19th, a meeting was held between the Central Committee of the Mining Association of Great Britain, thirty-six in number, and the twenty-two members of the Executive Committee of the Miners' Federation of Great Britain. The coal-owners' Chairman, Mr. Evan Williams, always inclined to be supercilious, opened the proceedings with a gibe:

Mr. Smith, I do not know whether, with your recent ecclesiastical associations, you have developed the habit of starting the proceedings with prayer and a hymn, and I hope you will not find it strange if we do away with that this afternoon and get straight on to business.

Ignoring this the Chairman of the Miners' Federation, Herbert Smith, explained that on the 111th day of the dispute he wished to see on what they agreed, on what they disagreed and whether there could be any approach to a settlement: the Federation was for a National Wages Agreement for the seven-hour day as before, while they were prepared to consider reorganisation of wages and the possibility of Government assistance during reorganisation. To this last suggestion Evan Williams at once replied in the negative: and loaded his negative with a sneering reference to the bishops who had tried to mediate and to one of the Royal Princes who was considered to be sympathetically disposed towards the miners.

We have never had any faith in princes or in Governments— whether they are princes of the Church or whether they are princes of another kind—as far as industrial questions are concerned; and no settlement can possibly be as good as a settlement which is made between the people who are engaged in the industry.

In the owners' view there must be a change in wages and hours, and further these changes must be carried out in the Districts: they were against national agreements as "deleterious and detrimental"; the District Associations of coal-owners had "indicated the terms upon which the collieries are open for work."

To this Herbert Smith replied:

If your answer from your people is that, first, we have got to work an eight-hour day, and second, we have got to have district agreements, and third, without any inquiry at all, we have to have a reduction in wages—I will say to you this afternoon, "Good afternoon. We have met you. We are parting again until you people think otherwise." That will be simply my reply, because if anything has been brutal this has been brutal—after all these days to meet here and then to be told we have to have this and the other. We cannot. We are not beaten yet—do not get it into your minds that we are. Some of us have made an offer—whether you believe it or not, a sincere offer—to be able to get together in this direction. Would to God I had not made it now, as far as I am concerned, because it is wrong.

The Chairman of the Mining Association then wound up the proceedings saying

While we differ in this way on these fundamental points it does not seem to me that any good purpose can be served by our prolonging this meeting, or meeting again as two national bodies.

The owners had thus served notice that they would no longer negotiate with the Miners' Federation. This brought Herbert Smith to his feet with a parting speech:

We said we did not intend to increase our working day; we made that clear to you. We said we were prepared to inquire into the particular point, utilise it to the best advantage, and do all we possibly can to save our faces if we have to have reductions, and ask the Government to play their part.

It is no good saying you are anxious to get a settlement; if you ask me to say the truth, I do not think you are. I intend putting a bit more fight into this than I have done; I have to do it whether I want to do it or not. I get no younger, but I will fight on while there is a bit left of me. If there is a feeling that you are the only persons on earth and we have to do this and that, I want to say I have not been bred that road. A fair deal I will put up with, but I will not have it crammed down me—that I will resist. Good afternoon.

A week later on Thursday, August 26th, came a meeting "between His Majesty's Ministers and the Miners' Federation at 10 Downing Street." Mr. Baldwin had left for the Continent on the previous Sunday and the four miners' officials found the Right Hon. Winston Churchill, M.P. (Chancellor of the Exchequer) waiting to meet them, together with Steel-Maitland (Minister of Labour) and Lane-Fox (Secretary of Mines). The Federation had already sent the verbatim report of the meeting with the owners to the Government; and Herbert Smith now said, "We are asking if there is any good service you can render to bring about negotiations to see if a settlement can be arrived at and as to what amount of help can be given by the Government not only in negotiations but financially for a period." To this Churchill, tough as Evan, at once replied that "the question of giving any financial help to the industry has long passed out of the sphere of practical politics"; he had hoped for new and definite suggestions. To him Herbert Smith answered:

After your statement I do not think we need detain you long. You seem to me to be of the same mind as the employers. I am not here to make a petition. If that is what you think I am here for you are mistaken. I am here to get an honourable settlement. I have never yet burked the position. I made a statement when we first met that I am prepared to take that book and examine it page by page and accept its findings, but I was not prepared to come into a conference and agree to a reduction in wages before that inquiry took place. You people have shammed to accept this Commission's Report.

First when you write to me on the 30th April and say the owners are prepared to come to a settlement on that Report with a reduction of 13⅓ per cent and an hour's extension. That is not in the Report. That is the first thing you do. If what you say represents the view of your colleagues I do not think we need go any further into the question. We can carry this fight on a bit further yet. We have got to do it if you can force us to do it. We have been trying to avoid it. We have been doing all we possibly could to avoid any pit flooding, but after that speech we have to fight on; we are forced to fight on; you force us to do it, because we are not prepared to extend the hours.

Steel-Maitland denied that the Government had "shammed in the acceptance of the Report"; they were prepared to carry it out. Churchill ended the discussion by intimating that if the miners would yield on this or that the Government would try to bring the parties together and "we see no reason why district settlements and a national settlement should not be combined."

It was clear that nothing was to be got in Downing Street. So at the week-end the M.F.G.B. Executive issued a manifesto refusing to agree to terms which would break up their national organisation or deprive them of the seven-hour day, but offering to negotiate on wages. Then they held conference with the mining Labour M.P.s and with the Executive Committee of the Labour Party; Parliament was sitting again on that August 30th, when the "stage of emergency" was once more extended.

The next day the House of Commons was due to rise for the long ten-week summer recess, the Government refusing an Opposition plea that the adjournment should be for a week only, during which determined efforts ought to be made to reach agreement. The debate on the Motion for the Adjournment was devoted to the mining situation, in which Churchill made it clear indeed that the Government would take no further steps. Spokesmen for the coal-owners, speaking in the bitterest terms of the miners' leaders, particularly Cook, Herbert Smith and Smillie, emphasised that the Mining Association would no longer negotiate nationally.

To quote the words of Mr. Austin Hopkinson (Lancaster, Mossley), the Mining Association "tell the public and I tell the public now from the Floor of this House, that there is no central negotiating body of the coal-owners of Great Britain at the present time, and I hope and firmly trust that there never again will be such a body." Throughout the debate, Government supporters kept returning to the all-important question of the national agreement, plainly indicating their hope of District breakaways. They were quick to seize upon the significant remarks of George Spencer, M.P., whose speech was greeted by the coal-owner, Mr. Herbert Wragg, in the following terms:

I should like to compliment the hon. Member for Broxtowe (Mr. Spencer) on the very moderate speech that he has delivered, and to assure him—I think all on this side of the House will agree with me—that had he been in control of the negotiations on behalf of the Miners' Federation from the beginning there would have been no stoppage, or if there had been a stoppage, it would have been over months ago.

Praise for him was expressed, too, by Lieut.-Colonel Headlam, in contrast to what the hon. and gallant Member thought of the Federation's leaders:

I would like to say in what agreement I am, in the main, with the hon. Member for Broxtowe (Mr. Spencer). I thought that his speech exactly touched the situation. He has proved that he has the courage to say exactly what he believes to be true.

But George Hardie cut across these hopes of disruption, and put it bluntly:

It is quite evident that the Government have made up their minds, apart altogether from the question as to whether British industry is to be prosperous or not, that they are going to risk smashing British industry and commerce in an effort to smash the Miners' Federation. They might just as well give it up at once because they will never do that. If the Government brought out all the military and all the Navy they could not smash the national combination of the miners.

Throughout the debate Government spokesmen—no doubt

somewhat embarrassed by the candour of their backbenchers —were at pains to deny "the not very worthy insinuation . . . that we have been a committee to do the owners' will," as Sir Arthur Steel-Maitland put it. "Whatever we have done," he declared, "we have done on our own judgment." To which there were cries of "His master's voice!" An unexpected flank attack, with the same insinuation, came from the Liberal benches. No longer in centre stage, Lloyd George gibed at Churchill's conduct of negotiations:

You will not get propositions from the mine-owners. They feel that they are on top, there is no doubt, and they mean to take full advantage of that. Their one idea is to get the men back to the eight-hours' day, and they are going to use every advantage. There are some of them who are not doing badly. They are selling their rubbish at 3s. 6d. a sack, and they are not doing so very badly, some of them. At any rate, they feel that they would prefer fighting it out, and I do hope the Government will not take up the attitude which the mine-owners have taken in that respect.

The Chancellor of the Exchequer rose to answer him, and showed unwonted sensitiveness to the charge, which he rebutted by saying:

Mr. Evan Williams is quoted by the Leader of the Opposition as saying:
"We have exerted all our influence on the Government to secure the Eight Hours Bill."
Mr. Evan Williams can say exactly what he likes, and I take no responsibility for what he says, but this I do know, that no influence except that of argument, and no influence except that which should be exerted through the legitimate status of one of the parties to a great dispute, has weighed in the least with the Government.

It was left to the stalwart old miner, Robert Smillie, to voice the feeling of the men and women in the coalfields:

In this fight we have everything against us. The fight is absolutely unequal. It is not of our seeking. There will be no hunger in the homes of any colliery owners, their children will be fed and clothed, housed and educated just as usual, no matter now long the stoppage continues. On our side, there is privation, there is hunger and there is untimely death caused by this dispute. Therefore, we are not on equal terms.

I want, even in face of the speech delivered by the Chancellor of the Exchequer, to say that there is another force against us besides the employers. The Government of the country is on the side of the mine-owners and against the miners in this dispute. I am loath to say anything that I feel to be untrue or unfair, even against such a thing as a Government, but I feel sure that the history of the past eighteen weeks is a clear proof, and the passing of the Eight Hours Act was a clear proof that the Government of the country are on the side of the mine-owners in this fight. Then, we have the Press practically unanimous against us. Nothing is too filthy for them to say, not merely about the leaders of the miners, but of the miners as such.

And so, it being "Five of the Clock," the House rose to enjoy a ten weeks' vacation: Churchill and other Ministers saw the Mining Association's President and Secretary, who declared that they had no power to negotiate nationally: the miners' leaders turned to meet the delegates of the hungry men and women in the coal-fields.

5. SEPTEMBER 1926

The Miners' Conference met on Thursday, September 2nd. It was the 125th day of the lock-out. Funds were running low. Treasurer Richardson reported the last money they had paid out was 3s. per head and that they had in hand that morning only 1s. 8d. per head. The total received up to August 30th was £879,578 11s. 8d.: of this £517,000 had come from the trade unionists of the Union of Soviet Socialist Republics, £112,000 from the Women's Committee, £38,000 from the Trades Union Congress, £25,000 from the International Miners' Federation, £16,000 from the National Society of Woodworkers, £15,000 from the Amalgamated Weavers' Association and £8,000 from the American Federation of Labour. Since August 30th another £7,000 had come, £6,000 of it from the European delegation working through the International Federation of Trade Unions.

The reports from Districts showed how many had gone to work in the mines. The following figures were given:

Bristol	..	..	Nil
Cleveland	..	..	Nil
Cokemen	..	..	Nil
Cumberland	..	..	None in pit; 500 to 600 outcropping
Derbyshire	..	..	3,400, about 1,600 to 2,000 outcropping
Durham	..	..	250
Forest of Dean	..	..	625
Kent	..	..	6
Lancashire	..	..	1,500
Leicestershire	..	..	480
Midlands	..	..	17,300
North Wales	..	..	754 at pits, including surface workers and deputies
Nottinghamshire	..	..	8,000, includes topmen and safety-men
Scotland	..	..	2,000
Somerset	..	..	Nil
South Derbyshire	..	..	400
South Wales	..	..	250
Northumberland	..	..	1,420, includes 450 outcroppers
Yorkshire	..	..	400
Total ..	..	..	36,785

This total of 36,785 was small in relation to the total number of miners. It was less than 5 per cent of the membership of the Federation. Had it been evenly spread, it would have been negligible. But in those counties where it was not a mere trickle (like Yorkshire's 400 out of 150,000) it was more serious. The Midlands, and in the Midlands Warwickshire, was the largest figure; but the position in Derbyshire, and still more in Nottinghamshire, was soon to cause real anxiety. At the moment, however, these figures caused reassurance amongst delegates who had been daily reading exaggerated reports in the Press.

The Conference, having read the report on the meetings with the owners and with the Ministers, had now to decide on future action. Again there was a difference of opinion, some wishing to concentrate on a campaign to reduce blacklegging and otherwise to stand fast. But when the vote was taken, Lancashire and South Wales alone made up the minority of 225,000 against 557,000 on the following resolution:

That this Conference having accepted the report upon the efforts made by the Committee to secure a resumption of negotiations with a view to settlement, resolves to authorise the Committee to take the necessary steps to submit proposals for the setting up of a National Agreement for the Mining Industry.

Further, that when they consider there are proposals for a settlement arrived at that the Committee are prepared to recommend the workmen to accept, a further Conference shall be called for their consideration. (September 2, 1926.)

Next day the Federation wrote to Winston Churchill, having first agreed the terms of the letter after consultation between him and Ramsay MacDonald:

September 3rd, 1926.

Dear Sir,

I beg to inform you that the Executive Committee and the Special Delegate Conference of the Miners' Federation, having again carefully considered the present deadlock in the mining dispute, have resolved to ask you to convene and attend a Conference of the Mining Association and the Federation. We are prepared to enter into negotiations for a new national agreement with a view to a reduction in labour costs to meet the immediate necessities of the industry.

Yours faithfully, A. J. COOK, Secretary.

The Government that same day, as soon as they received this letter and read the words "reduction of labour costs," issued a statement saying here was a basis sufficient to justify it in requesting the Mining Association to resume negotiations and that accordingly it was communicating with that Association. But the Association immediately responded with a declaration that it had no power to negotiate and that any suggestions would have to be put to the District Associations.

On the Monday, September 6th, there followed a meeting at 10 Downing Street between His Majesty's Ministers and the Mining Association. This time Churchill had with him the Secretary of State for War (Worthington-Evans), the First Lord of the Admiralty (Bridgeman), the Minister of Labour (Steel-Maitland), the Parliamentary Secretary for the Mines Department (Lane-Fox), as well as leading civil servants.

Twelve coal-owners, headed by Evan Williams, represented the Mining Association, which had already refused to take part in the proposed three-corner conference. The discussion was to be on one topic only, the relation between the allies in the dispute or, as Churchill in his opening remarks put it, "the basis of understanding which has subsisted between H.M. Government and the Mining Association during this long-

drawn and protracted dispute." He recalled that the owners
had come to the Government on May 14th and "pressed
strongly for the introduction of an Eight Hours' Bill." "As
you know," he went on, "it was a very serious thing for His
Majesty's Government to introduce a measure facilitating
the lengthening of hours in coal-mines. It undoubtedly is a
step which is greatly resented by large masses of the industrial
population, a step which was bound to be represented as part
of a regular scheme and a policy of lengthening hours." He
recalled further concessions to the coal-owners which also,
he argued, assumed that a settlement would finally include a
national agreement as well as District agreements; so that
"We, as Ministers of the Crown, were justified in our belief
that at the time we introduced the Eight Hours' Bill there was
no question of departing from the negotiation of a national
agreement." Now there was a change made by the coal-
owners, who were neither willing to have any national agreement nor to meet the men's representatives nationally, not
even with the Government present. "It is," he said, "on the
point of your relations with the Government that I earnestly
ask you to consider very carefully what your attitude should
be in regard to our formal, deliberate request that you should
come with us and meet the men in an open, unprejudiced
discussion."

In his reply to this Evan Williams traversed all the arguments put forward. He disclosed that the Government had
urged the owners to offer relatively high terms in certain
Districts in order to get what a national settlement could not
bring about, namely "a breakaway piecemeal, district by
district." This common strategy of the Government and the
owners, he held, ruled out any possible national agreement:
and there had not been on the part of the owners any departure from the understanding they had with the Government.
Apart from this he stated the general standpoint of the
owners as follows:

As I said, it was with the greatest reluctance that we had at any
time entered upon national agreements and national negotiations.
It is the experience which we in the country have had of those agreements that has strengthened us so much in the view that we put
forward, that we say quite definitely and emphatically that the

Mining Association will not enter into negotiations with the Miners' Federation on this point. . . .

We have been faced with crisis after crisis whenever an agreement has come to an end. In 1924 we were faced with a crisis through a national settlement, and it was only averted by the owners giving way to the representatives of the Labour Government of that day. In 1925 there was another crisis, and that was only settled by the Government giving way to the threats of the miners. In 1926 a similar position was brought about which was not averted because neither the Government nor the owners gave way. As certain as there is a national agreement which brings all the districts of the country under one arrangement, so certain will there be crises of that character, and looking not only at the interests of the coal-owners themselves, but the industry as a whole and the country as a whole, we feel that we entered into an arrangement which inevitably makes every industrial question in the mining industry a political issue. . . .

I say it is a political issue pure and simple, and the moment you have set up a national agreement with a national board you bring every question that is relevant to that board forward as a political issue, with debates in the House of Commons, and you get the Government involved on a different plane from every other industry. . . .

It may be thought that by entering into discussion with the Miners' Federation in some way we should solve this problem. We hold the contrary view absolutely. There are districts where the owners' offer has been accepted without reference in any way at all to national agreements. That movement is spreading rapidly.

The next day, Tuesday, September 7th, the Central Committee of the Mining Association of Great Britain upheld their opposition to national negotiations but agreed to refer the matter again to the District Colliery Owners' Associations. On the same day the miners' leaders, at the request of the Government, returned from the Bournemouth Trades Union Congress to London, where they met Mr. Churchill. Next day, Wednesday, September 8th, he wrote to the Mining Association:

8th September, 1926.
Dear Mr. Evan Williams,

I have to thank you on behalf of His Majesty's Government for having deferred to our earnestly expressed wish that the Mining Association should consult its constituents upon the question of resuming national negotiations for a settlement of the coal dispute. I take this opportunity of explaining the kind of three-party conference that the Government have in view and the scope of its work.

Hitherto, national settlements have prescribed the way in which the percentages payable from time to time in the districts shall be determined, viz. the ratio of division, the intervals of ascertainment, the principles of recoupment, the definition of "other costs," and the minimum percentage payable. They have set up a National Board of the industry. They have laid down the principle of subsistence wages to be determined in the districts. They have defined the various districts and made provision for their alteration by local agreement.

It is obviously quite impossible in the present circumstances for any conference sitting in London to do more in the first instance than lay down certain broad principles and recommend the practical steps necessary to secure an early and universal resumption of work.

We believe that with such national guidance the task of negotiating agreements on wages, hours and other conditions could be undertaken in each district with the assent of both parties under favourable conditions and without any further delay. We cannot afford any further delay or long ceremonial procedure. At least 1,700,000 families affected by the dispute are looking for the opportunity of regaining their weekly wages. Our procedure must be planned to bring this about as quickly as possible on fair and sound terms.

District settlements concluded in conformity with the agreed general principle should form a basis on which work would be immediately resumed. In so far as they dealt with matters which by custom are settled nationally they would require to be referred to the central body for confirmation or where necessary for reference back to the district. It ought not then to be difficult to conclude a national agreement governing many, if not all, of the points that have hitherto been dealt with on a national basis. One point of difficulty, no doubt, will be how the national character of the minimum can be reconciled with the inevitable allowance for district conditions. We ought not to assume that this is insoluble with goodwill once the parties are together.

After prolonged thought, His Majesty's Government believe that this is about the best and shortest path that can be found to reach the vital object in view, namely, a businesslike and honourable settlement for a good long time.

Yours sincerely, WINSTON S. CHURCHILL.

The reply did not come immediately: and by the time it came the Bournemouth Trades Union Congress was over and the position of the miners was worsened. The miners had continued to hold high hopes of the Congress, and that a spectacular change in the situation would come from its debates and decisions. But these hopes had been dashed to the ground. Yet if the prospect of a levy on all British trade unionists had receded, additional help now came from a quarter that had already helped much. The Chairman and Acting Secretary of the Soviet trade unions wrote to Herbert Smith and A. J. Cook:

The Presidium of the U.S.S.R. C.C.T.U. at the joint meeting with representatives of the Central Committees of the Trade Unions and all the present members of the Plenum of the U.S.S.R. C.C.T.U. on August 31st, proposed to all Trade Union organisations in the U.S.S.R. to place for consideration at all Trade Union assemblies the question of the regular contribution of 1 per cent of the wages during the entire course of your struggle.

Knowing the ardent sympathy of the workers of the U.S.S.R. toward your heroic struggle and the readiness to aid it, we are sure that our proposal will meet a most warm response on the part of the 8,500,000 of our Trade Union members.

Knowing your extreme need at the present moment, the Presidium of the U.S.S.R. C.C.T.U. on September 4th resolved to transfer to the Executive Committee of the British Miners the contributions on hand and an advance on account of future contributions, altogether 3,000,000 rubles.

We heartily wish you success in your struggle.

Moreover on Thursday, September 9th, at a meeting in London of the Committee of the Miners' International Federation, the following resolution had been tabled by the M.F.G.B.:

That, having regard to the reports received from the various countries upon the subject of importation of coal to Britain, the Committee resolves to submit to the whole International Miners' Organisation the consideration of taking international strike action in support of the British miners.

That a further meeting of the Committee take place on or before the 30th September, when, in the event of the proposed negotiations for a settlement proving abortive, the Committee shall adopt such action as will be warranted upon the reports of the affiliated countries.

On Tuesday, September 14th, the following reply of the Mining Association to Churchill was made public:

With the exception of one small inland district, the twenty-four district associations have replied clearly and emphatically declining to give the Mining Association power or authority to enter into agreements on their behalf in regard to terms of employment of the workmen in their respective districts.

You will accordingly see that the meeting which you propose in your letter could serve no useful purpose.

There is no person who would be entitled to speak or to listen on behalf of the coal-owners, and I am sure you will agree that no good, but harm, would result from a meeting held under conditions which would expose the parties to a charge of insincerity.

The district coal-owners' associations have been and are willing and anxious to meet the miners' associations in their districts at any time without ceremony or any preliminary procedure whatsoever.

There is no valid obstacle to this. There is no question of principle that need delay them.

None of the district associations raises any objection to the principle of wage regulation by reference to ascertained results, the principle of a minimum percentage below which wages cannot fall, or the principle of subsistence wages.

The quantitative determinations on these and all other points can only be made in the light of the circumstances of the districts by those who know them and have to face the results.

A realisation of these facts is imperative, and it is failure to recognise them that stands in the way of these negotiations being entered into at once, and is alone responsible for the prolongation of the stoppage.

I desire to add that the decisions of the districts, which reaffirm the declarations made to you last Monday, arise from a deep and earnest conviction that settlements on a national basis, by linking the industry with politics, inevitably take the consideration of purely industrial questions out of their proper economic sphere, have been destructive of peace and prosperity to those engaged in the industry, and, as experience of the immediate past has shown, are a menace to the community as a whole.

EVAN WILLIAMS.

At this the Miners' Federation unanimously resolved that:

This Committee, having assembled in readiness to attend a joint meeting with representatives of the coal-owners as proposed by the Government, regret to find that the coal-owners still consider themselves entitled to be the sole arbiters of the interest of this country in matters arising from the lock-out of the miners, having refused the advances made by the miners' representatives with a view to a settlement, and the invitation of the Government to a joint meeting.

The Committee are, therefore, left with no option but to request the miners in every area to resist the efforts of the coal-owners to secure their defeat, and await further instructions from the Committee pending the decision of the Government upon the refusal of the coal-owners to attend such Conference. (September 14, 1926.)

Three days were now taken up in Cabinet discussions. The Prime Minister, back from his holiday on Wednesday, September 15th, consulted with Churchill and Bridgeman. The Cabinet and the Cabinet Coal Committee met on the 16th and agreed on their policy. The next day the Prime Minister met Evan Williams and thereafter conferred with the four M.F.G.B. officials. From Baldwin's proposals they learned that the coal-owners had been successful: Churchill's policy had been abandoned.

Later in September Herbert Smith related to the miners' delegates how at one of the meetings with Churchill earlier in the month, the miners' Chairman had said "Now we have mounted the horse, let us see who is going to dismount first. We are prepared to ride exactly with you to that Conference and meet on these terms." On September 17th altogether different terms were presented: "and," related Smith, "we said to Churchill 'We understood you were a man of courage, but you have broken down at the first fence! You have dismounted. Have you been doing wrong while the masters have been away; and got reprimanded?' He did not like it."

These terms were set out in a letter from Baldwin, who recounted the Mining Association's attitude and continued:

It is evidently not within the power of His Majesty's Government to bring about a conference. However, the Mining Association have declared that the coal-owners in all districts are willing to observe the main principles that a national agreement would be designed to secure. A satisfactory settlement should combine district arrangements with national supervision. If the miners are at length ready to face the economic facts of the industry and restart work on provisional district settlements His Majesty's Government are prepared to secure by legislation that these principles are properly applied by means of a National Appeal Tribunal. We therefore lay before you in broad outline the enclosed memorandum, what we are prepared to do and the limits within which we find ourselves able to act. If your members are prepared to resume work on the basis of district settlements, subject to the security afforded by these conditions, and when work has been generally resumed we shall submit these proposals to Parliament in the form of a Bill.

We feel it necessary, however, to say that this offer has been made by us out of a sincere desire to arrive at an early settlement, and the Government will naturally expect to receive the views of your Executive without delay.

Yours faithfully, STANLEY BALDWIN.

MEMORANDUM

1. As soon as there has been a general resumption of work through provisional settlement arrived at by local negotiations the Government will pass an Act of Parliament setting up a National Arbitration Tribunal, unless the earlier conclusion of a National Agreement renders it unnecessary.

2. Either party to any provisional settlement which provides for working more than the old hours may refer to the Tribunal for review any matter dealt with by such settlement being a matter of a kind which up to July, 1925, was customarily dealt with by national settlements.

3. The Tribunal shall confirm or modify a provisional settlement in respect of the matter referred to it, and as from the date fixed by the Tribunal every man affected by the award and employed in any pit which works more than the old hours will be entitled by law to receive wages in accordance with the decision. (*Annexe*—September 17, 1926.)

All that week-end the miners' officers considered the implications of the new policy, now so coolly announced by the Government. It had created a new and grave situation calculated to prolong the dispute, as they pointed out in a statement sent to the Prime Minister on the Tuesday, September 21st. They recalled in detail their concessions and the course of their dealings with Churchill. Then the statement went on:

It would now appear, though the Federation is reluctant to believe it, that it was mistaken in taking the Chancellor's declaration seriously at all. On September 17th, the Government completely abandoned the policy which he announced on September 8th, and advanced proposals of a diametrically opposite character. Its latest announcement would involve, if it could be carried out, the entire surrender of the principle of national negotiations and agreements, a principle which the Commission stated (Report, pages 152–3) to be essential, and which was endorsed in the letter of the Chancellor of the Exchequer.

Thus, the Government now proposes, the miners are to resume work on such terms as the owners in each district may be in a position to dictate.

In those districts in which, in accordance with the Commission's recommendations, the hours worked prior to the stoppage are maintained, they are to receive no protection whatever from a national authority, however unreasonable the terms imposed by the owners may be. In the remainder, after the scales have already been weighted against them by district agreements, they are to have an appeal to a national tribunal, the construction of which the Government has not, as yet, thought fit to specify.

Two months ago, in response to representations from the Mining Association, and in defiance of the Commission's Report, the Government passed legislation depriving the mine-workers of their statutory right to a seven-hour day. Now, in response to representations from the same quarter, and contrary not only to the Commission's Report, but to the Government's own explicit declaration it is proposed to abandon national negotiations and national agreements. Such a proposal, in sharp contradiction as it is with the statement made by the Chancellor of the Exchequer, carries its condemnation on its face. The Miners' Federation is reluctant to believe that it can represent the considered judgment of the Government. It has no desire to enter into useless recriminations, but in the event of the stoppage being prolonged by the attempt to force the mine-workers back into district agreements the responsibility for its continuance should be placed upon the shoulders of the Government and the mine-owners.

Even now, however, the Federation hopes that wiser counsels may prevail. In spite of what has passed, it adheres to its statement of September 3rd that it is "prepared to enter into negotiations for a new national agreement with a view to a reduction in labour costs to meet the immediate necessities of the industry." It must maintain the principle of national negotiations and agreements, because experience has shown that, in the absence of such common agreements governing the industry as a whole, the effect must be, in the words of the Commission (page 152) "to expose the standards of the more efficient and prosperous areas, on which the future of the country rests, to undermining by the weaker areas." Further, it would point out that the suggestion that a settlement will be accelerated if negotiations are begun in the districts is devoid of foundation. The inevitable result of throwing the task of negotiating terms on to twenty-four districts without any guidance by a central body, must be to multiply points of friction, many of which would not have arisen had the principles to be embodied in any settlement been determined in advance by a national authority.

The mine-workers are desirous of an honourable settlement. But they will not be coerced into accepting terms which they hold to be unjust, and which the Commission declared to be injurious to the industry.

A dictated settlement, such as is desired by the mine-owners, will be precarious, insincere and short-lived. If a genuine and lasting peace is to be achieved, it must rest on a frank recognition of the fact that, whatever the difference between districts, the miners of Great Britain form a single body with common interests, and that they are entitled to insist that those interests shall continue to be protected by their national organisation. (September 21, 1926.)

At nine o'clock that night their representatives were summoned to meet the Prime Minister. Before they went the Executive Committee had debated anxiously and at length whether they should put forward definite proposals for a settlement. Finally they put to him that they would recommend an immediate resumption of work temporarily at wages prevailing under the 1921 agreement; the terms of a National Wages Agreement to be referred to an independent tribunal, which should also consider putting into effect the recommendations of the Samuel Commission.

Three days later came the cool intimation from Downing Street that

while recognising the advance which the proposals indicate, His Majesty's Government do not feel that they afford the means of reaching an early or a lasting settlement of the present dispute.

In these circumstances I am to say that the Government are not prepared to go beyond the maturely considered proposals conveyed to you in the Prime Minister's letter of the 17th instant. These proposals cannot of course remain open indefinitely, but your Federation are still free to avail themselves of them by taking the practical step of ordering district negotiations to be set on foot subject to the subsequent review of an independent tribunal, where any departure from the old hours is involved. (September 24, 1926.)

The day after this discouraging reply from the Government was made known, the Durham Miners' Association asked the M.F.G.B. Executive Committee to approach the T.U.C. General Council to call a special Trades Union Congress at the earliest possible moment.

On Monday, September 27th, the House reassembled, this time with the Premier speaking for the Government. Their summer vacation was interrupted: as the Royal Message read by the Speaker declared, "the continued cessation of work in coal-mines on the 22nd day of September, 1926, having constituted in the opinion of His Majesty, a state of emergency within the meaning of the Emergency Powers Act, 1920," their main task was once again to extend the operation of the Regulations, this time in the teeth of keen opposition. That done, for two days the debate continued on the coal dispute. This time the mood was different: Government supporters were convinced of ultimate victory; the mining M.P.s, among them Vernon Hartshorn, Robert

Smillie, the veteran R. Richardson, J. J. Lawson, G. H. Hall and W. Paling, fought a dour defensive battle for the miners' offer to be accepted. W. Paling, who had been touring the coal-fields, described the determination of the miners in face of attack from all sides:

I have had the opportunity during the last seven or eight weeks of going through the coal-fields almost from one end of the country to the other, and, in spite of the long struggle, in spite of the poverty, in spite of the attempts of the Ministry of Labour to cut down and to put people off unemployment benefit, in spite of all the restrictive attempts of the Ministry of Health and of Boards of Guardians to stop giving pay, in spite of the action of the police and the Emergency Powers Regulations—in spite of all this misery, I have found that the miners are so convinced of the justice of their cause, that even after twenty or twenty-one weeks they are determined to fight this issue to the bitter end.

Especially bitter was the feeling about the Government's action in forcing through the Eight Hours' Act. As J. J. Lawson put it:

I remember, when the Prime Minister told us he was going to put the Act through, and we asked him what had taken place between the Government and the coal-owners, how indignantly he and other Ministers on the Front Bench repudiated the idea that there had been any co-operation or any real, practical discussion between them and the coal-owners about it. Stage by stage, the whole of the proceedings have become public, and we are now getting to understand that there has been something like a deal with the Government and that the owners do not intend to keep to that deal.

This was powerfully supported in a hard-hitting speech by G. H. Hall:

The miners are the only people since April 30th last up to the present time who have made any real concessions, while the mine-owners are in the same position in this respect as they were at the time of the lock-out. The mine-owners have locked out the men and therefore they are more responsible for the stoppage than the miners, the only difference being that ever since the commencement of the stoppage the mine-owners have had the powerful backing of the Government. . . . I find in the mining areas at present—and I only left them this morning—the miners are as determined to fight this question of the eight hours as they have ever been. They will fight the Government because they feel the Government are responsible as merely being the pawn of the coal-owners in this matter.

But the Government was adamant, and once again the adjournment was carried, against eloquent appeals from the miners' M.P.:s, conscious of the Special Conference due to open the next day.

The M.F.G.B. Special Conference held on Wednesday and Thursday, September 29th and 30th, first of all reviewed how they stood in the various Districts and received the following figures of men working in the pits, exclusive of outcroppers:

Bristol	..	..	..	..	—
Cleveland	..	..	..	..	—
Cokemen	..	..	..	..	—
Cumberland	..	..	..	..	—
Derbyshire	..	..	..	..	10,600
Durham ..	..	..	..	..	250
Enginemen	..	..	..	..	1,400
Forest of Dean ..	..	..	..	2,200
Kent	..	..	..	..	..	250
Lancashire	..	..	..	..	1,600
Leicestershire	..	..	..	..	2,400
Midlands	..	..	..	..	34,000
North Wales	..	..	..	..	2,000
Nottinghamshire	..	..	..	16,000
Scotland	..	..	..	..	3,260
Somerset	..	..	..	..	—
South Derbyshire	..	..	..	900
South Wales	..	..	..	..	720
Northumberland	..	..	..	2,000
Yorkshire	..	..	..	..	3,598

	81,178
Previously reported September 2, 1926	36,785

Thereafter they heard the report of their Executive Committee's actions and the new proposals of the Government. It was clearly unnecessary to do more than report back what the Executive Committee had done; but it was necessary to get a vote of the Districts on the Government proposals. They therefore adjourned for a week to enable this District vote to be taken.

6. OCTOBER 1926

When the M.F.G.B. delegates reassembled on October 7th, there was an overwhelming majority against the Government proposals of 737,000 against 42,000, Derbyshire and Leicestershire being alone in favour of acceptance.[1] They had also before them a letter sent on the eve of the Conference from Downing Street about the "conditional offer of legislation," stating that the Government would not

consent to any further prolongation of the offer, which has now been before your Federation for nearly three weeks, but must ask the Conference to give a definite decision either to accept it or to refuse it. If the offer is accepted by the Miners' Federation, and an immediate and general resumption of work takes place in consequence of it, the Government will introduce the necessary legislation at the earliest possible opportunity. Otherwise, the offer, which will then have obviously failed in its primary purpose, must be regarded as withdrawn. (October 6, 1926.)

Not only the tone of the ultimatum read to the Conference but the "attenuated, very misty and altogether unsatisfactory Government proposal" steeled the delegates to make a big decision. The South Wales Miners' Federation were ready with a policy resolution. This time the difference of opinion came out very strongly. After a full discussion, the following resolution was put to the vote:

[1] RESULT OF DISTRICT VOTE
(in thousands)

	For the Government's Proposals	Against	Neutral
Bristol ..	—	2	—
Cleveland	—	—	4
Cokemen ..	—	5	—
Cumberland	—	9	—
Derbyshire	35	—	—
Durham ..	—	120	—
Group 1 ..	—	20	—
Forest of Dean	—	5	—
Kent	—	2	—
Lancashire	—	75	—
Leicestershire	7	—	—
Midlands	—	60	—
Northumberland	—	38	—
North Wales	—	10	—
Notts	—	25	—
Scotland ..	—	80	—
Somerset	—	—	5
South Derbyshire	—	6	—
South Wales	—	130	—
Yorkshire	—	150	—
Totals ..	42	737	9

That we revert to the *status quo* conditions. In order to obtain this the policy of the M.F.G.B. on the following items to be:

(1) Safety Men.—All such to be withdrawn from every colliery.
(2) Embargo.—That we urge this on all foreign-produced coal.
(3) Outcrops.—That the M.F.G.B. immediately order the cessation of this practice.
(4) Levy.—That a Special Congress of the Trade Unions be called specifically to deal with this matter.
(5) Propaganda.—(*a*) That we send speakers to all black areas.
   (*b*) That the Labour Members of Parliament be marshalled for a nation-wide campaign.

In the event of any or all of these proposals becoming the National policy, that central control of the operations be vested in the M.F.G.B. Executive Committee, who shall direct them to the supersession of all local barriers where necessary.

The resolution was carried by 589 to 199 (in units of a thousand), the minority being made up of Scotland, Derbyshire, Nottinghamshire, Leicestershire and the smaller counties and groups. But the Chairman ruled, in accordance with the views of the Executive Committee, that this far-reaching resolution, before it could be acted upon, had to be referred to a vote of the Districts.

Conference then turned to a different question—one which was to have repercussions for ten years to come. The question having been raised of a Press report on G. A. Spencer's actions in the Nottinghamshire District, it was agreed that he "be summoned to attend this Conference tomorrow morning to make a statement and then decide on the facts."

George Spencer, M.P., duly appeared and made his statement from which it was clear that he had negotiated with the employers on the terms of a return to work at the Digby Pit. He ended "I don't regret it, and I do not plead extenuating circumstances. I believe I did the best day's work in my life for these men, and you can pass your sentence."

From the Chair Herbert Smith replied:

If Mr. Spencer does not regret it, I am sorry for him, and I say that this Federation ought to deal exactly with Mr. Spencer as with anybody else. . . . Whether it is cowardice or not, I would rather be shot in the morning than do what you have done. You are a paid servant of this Federation.

MR. G. A. SPENCER, M.P.: There was no negotiating a settlement, I want you to understand that. The only negotiations there were was because the manager said he was only going to set on those he wanted, and all I wanted was fair treatment for everybody.

MR. COOK: I hope this Conference will treat Mr. Spencer as they would treat a blackleg. Mr. Spencer is a blackleg of the worst order. A conscious blackleg. I want to say here that Notts has been more responsible for the present position we are in, and Mr. Spencer is more responsible for Notts than any other district in the coal-field.

That is the opinion of Derbyshire, and the opinion of everyone else. While we are fighting, Mr. Spencer is prepared to accept a reduction, and advocated a district agreement in his own district.

MR. G. DAVIS (South Wales): Mr. Spencer has been helping people to get to work. He is a blackleg. He has admitted that he is guilty, and that he has done something contrary to the findings of this Federation. There should be no different treatment between him and anyone else, because he is a Member of Parliament. He should not have special treatment as against any other delegate.

It was suggested that the expulsion of G. A. Spencer and his suspension as a miners' Member of Parliament be referred to the Nottinghamshire Miners' Association and that he be requested to leave the M.F.G.B. Conference immediately.

Some 759,000 votes ordered him out.

The International Report, apart from dealing with the conduct of Frank Hodges,[1] was concerned with the failure of the American and other mining unions to come out on strike.

When it came to the finances, the Treasurer reported that out of the £1,275,077 received, £1,257,535 had been paid out, leaving a balance of £12,541. He warned the delegates:

We have this in hand at the present moment, and unless we get a big gift from Russia we are not likely to send anything out at present.

Russia has sent two-thirds of what has been sent out.

While a crucial policy vote was being taken that week in the coal-fields, the Twenty-sixth Annual Conference of the Labour Party was being held at Margate. The Chairman, Robert Williams, in his opening speech, said: "The miners' decision to continue the dispute is heroic. They may be likened to the sightless Samson feeling for a grip of the pillars of the temple, the crashing of which will engulf this thing we call British civilisation." At the close of this address, Harry

[1] See Appendix to this Chapter.

Pollitt (Boilermakers and Iron and Steel Shipbuilders) rose to move "That, in view of the insolent attack made from the Chair on the policy decided upon by the miners, this Conference takes the mining crisis as its first business," but the Chairman declined to accept the resolution. When on the next day an Executive resolution was put forward congratulating the miners on their "magnificent resistance," protesting against "the action of the Government in supporting the mine-owners" and declaring for nationalisation as a permanent solution, the reference back was moved by David Kirkwood, M.P., seconded by H. Pollitt. J. H. Thomas, M.P., and J. Ramsay MacDonald supported the resolution, which received 2,159,000 votes against 1,368,000 for the reference back.

On Friday, October 15th, the Labour Party Conference having yielded them little but fair words, the M.F.G.B. Executive Committee considered the steps to be taken to carry into effect the new policy. For the vote was in, and showed 460,150 for the South Wales policy of struggle and 284,336 against.[1] Among the minority were Yorkshire, the Midlands and Northumberland: Nottinghamshire and Leicestershire recorded no vote.

[1] RESULT OF DISTRICT VOTE

District	No.	For	Against
Bristol	1,900	—	1,900
Cleveland ..	4,000	—	—
Cokemen ..	4,200	—	—
Cumberland	8,500	—	8,500
Derbyshire	35,000	35,000	—
Durham	120,000	120,000	—
Group No. 1	19,600	—	19,600
Forest of Dean	5,000	5,000	—
Kent	2,000	—	2,000
Lancashire	75,000	75,000	—
Leicestershire	7,000	—	—
Midlands	60,000	—	60,000
Northumberland	37,836	—	37,836
North Wales	10,000	10,000	—
Nottinghamshire	25,000	—	—
Scotland	80,000	80,000	—
Somerset	4,500	—	4,500
South Derbyshire	6,000	6,000	—
South Wales	129,150	129,150	—
Yorkshire	150,000	—	150,000
Totals	784,686	460,150	284,336

DELEGATES LEAVING RUSSELL SQUARE FOR THE MINER'S CONFERENCE AT KINGSWAY HALL,
NOVEMBER 10, 1926

Left to right, back row: G. Blackledge, J. Smith, J. M. Gillians, W. Latham, F. Hall, N. Ablett
Left to right, front row: J. Doonan, P. McKenna, Alfred Smith, A. Flatley, J. W. Smith

A SOUTH WALES STRIKE (1929) IN THE GARW VALLEY
Non-unionists under heavy escort of police

The Executive Committee on October 15th decided on steps to put the policy into effect. On the withdrawal of the safety men, they were to consult with the National Federation of Colliery Enginemen and Boiler Firemen. They were to approach the T.U.C. General Council for a joint meeting to discuss "an embargo on imported coal and a levy upon the affiliated membership." They also decided:

That in order to bring the greatest possible influence upon the men to remain loyal to the Federation and to persuade those men who had returned to work to come out again:

The Committee hold future meetings in the coal-fields, and that the next meeting be held in the Nottinghamshire coal-field.

All Federation speakers were to be rallied and Members of Parliament were to be asked to "hold themselves at the disposal of the Committee until further notice."

The next day came the result of the ballot taken by the Nottinghamshire Miners' Association on the question:

Are you in favour of ceasing work and standing by the Miners' Federation of Great Britain and disfranchising all those who do not act accordingly?

There were 14,331 for; 2,875 against: a majority of 11,456. Thereupon the Council of the Nottinghamshire Miners' Association suspended twenty-five of its delegates who had resumed work; and also G. A. Spencer, M.P. On the same day the Warwickshire Miners' Association stated it had asked Frank Hodges to resign his membership but that he had not complied with the request.

The effect of the new policy was seen in the next week. On Monday, October 18th, the Ministry of Mines admitted a decrease of 20,351 in the number of men working: and two days later the Press admitted that there was a large decline in the number working in Lancashire and the Midlands. It was now the twenty-fifth week of the lock-out. The M.F.G.B. Executive Committee met on Tuesday, October 19th, at Old Basford in Nottinghamshire and there arranged for a campaign of meetings in the county by Executive members.

Back in London, on Friday, October 22nd, they met the T.U.C. General Council and urged upon it the need for a levy upon the membership affiliated to the Congress to support the miners in the struggle.

There was no doubt that the miners were in need of this. A remarkable total had been received by the Miners' Federation during the twenty-six weeks of struggle, amounting at this time to £1,618,745. How much the miners owed to the spirit of international solidarity was shown by the fact that over two-thirds of this had come from overseas : £986,000 from the Russian trade unions, £43,000 from miners in other countries, £21,500 from the International Federation of Trade Unions, and £13,945 from the American Federation of Labour being the main items. From all British sources the total received was £532,000, of which the Women's Committee Fund accounted for £249,000 and the T.U.C. for £68,000. Some forty-four trade union organisations individually had contributed from £500 upwards, the largest being the Union of Post Office Workers (£20,390), the Amalgamated Society of Woodworkers (£17,869) and the Amalgamated Weavers' Association (£15,000). But taking the membership of the trade union movement, as the miners' Treasurer, W. P. Richardson, pointed out, the contributions represented

just 3s. per member during the whole twenty-six weeks of the stoppage, or just over 1½d. per week per member. If we take the total Labour vote at the last election, which is the proper figure to take in assessing the assistance given by the movement, we find that it works out at 2s. per voter for the whole period of the stoppage or just under 1d. per voter per week. . . .

To these organisations and to all others who have helped us, the miners are deeply grateful, but when all is said and done, the hard fact remains that the total contribution received from the movement is less than 1d. per head per week. (October 22, 1926.)

The reaction of the Government to the new policy was two-fold. On the one hand they intensified immediately their measures of repression. Blacklegging was lessening through the campaign meetings held by the Federation. As we have seen, the Government strategy was to stimulate any breakaway tendency. On Sunday, October 24th, Cook's meetings in Staffordshire were prohibited: next day, Herbert Smith's meeting at Wombwell, on his own doorstep, was banned by the police. The occasion of a parliamentary debate on the same day was taken by the Lord Chancellor Birkenhead to utter a speech attacking A. J. Cook. Secondly, the Government was once more ready to meet a body of mediators. Such a body was available.

A letter from Arthur Pugh in *The Times* of October 21st had been endorsed by a letter six days later from the leaders of the Churches. On the same day, Tuesday, October 26th, representatives of the T.U.C. General Council met the Prime Minister, who told them that the Government was prepared to intervene, if the miners accepted District settlements with a national tribunal—substantially the Baldwin offer of September 17th. When the General Council Sub-Committee met the M.F.G.B. Executive Committee on Friday, October 29th, to report this, they explained that they had signed a statement as representing their present view which ran as follows:

The Miners are in our sincere belief prepared to negotiate with the Government for an immediate ending of the dispute by district settlements providing that satisfactory conditions can be arranged with the Government for the subsequent review and co-ordination of such district settlements in accordance with certain agreed national principles. Failing agreement with the Government all offers are withdrawn.

The Miners' Executive replied that there could be no departure from present policy until another Conference was held; one was fixed for November 4th.

7. NOVEMBER 1926

The seventh month of the struggle opened with the news that the suspended members of the Nottinghamshire Miners' Council, led by G. A. Spencer, M.P., had decided to meet the local owners in order to negotiate a District settlement. This blow was not wholly unexpected. But on the next day there was to be a heavier blow; the meeting with the transport unions, arranged through the T.U.C. General Council, proved barren of results.

The miners had explained to the representatives of transport workers' unions that the figures of imported coal had risen from 600,000 tons in June to 4,000,000 tons in October, the average normal production of coal being 5,000,000 tons a week. This imported coal was one of the main factors in breaking the unity of the men, 800,000 being still out, and of those who had gone back a considerable proportion were safety men and officials. An international decision to stop it had failed, because of the difficulty in discovering the destination of the coal. If only the transport unions would impose an embargo on handling foreign coal, it could be stopped.

The seamen's representative said their members would be liable to imprisonment, and a port ballot had shown 10,060 to 908 against any embargo. For the transport workers it was said that they already had 85,000 on dispute pay through the lock-out; what were the miners doing about "black coal" produced in Britain? Decisive was the statement by J. H. Thomas that all three railway unions unanimously were of the opinion that an embargo on coal was impossible; his union would not be able to protect members victimised or fined. They had been told that the London, Midland and Scottish Railway was carrying 67 per cent of the pre-strike loads of coal. The meeting was adjourned for the General Council representatives to report back. It was clear; there was little hope now left to the Federation of an embargo on foreign coal.

The next day, Wednesday, November 3rd, the Conference of Executives of Trade Unions, summoned to discuss a levy in aid of the miners, passed a resolution recommending "a special daily contribution of not less than one penny from every one of its members for every day such member is at work until the dispute is settled." This compared not unfavourably with the one per cent levy of the Soviet trade unionists, except, of course, that it came two months later. It was welcomed. As, however, it was a "voluntary levy" the regular receipts from it could not be reckoned ahead. The same day a joint deputation (Trades Union Congress, Labour Party and Miners' Federation) went to the Home Secretary to complain of prohibitions of meetings and to uphold the right of peaceful picketing under the Trade Disputes Act, 1906.

It was in this situation that the M.F.G.B. Special Conference assembled on Thursday, November 4th. There was a full and careful discussion. The "*status quo*" resolution, as decided by the Conference and by the District vote a month earlier, was put forward by a minority of the speakers. Arthur Horner, of South Wales, said:

. . . The question for us is as to what is the best slogan that can hold the vast majority of our men in loyalty to this Federation. . . . Now if it is argued that the strike is being continued not in order to resist district settlements or longer hours, but only to resist them in a certain degree, then from that angle I say stand by the *status quo* . . . to continue on the *status quo* is a better rallying slogan than one which the men cannot understand. . . .

We are face to face with this factor, that huge numbers of our men at the beginning of this struggle could have continued work on the *status quo* conditions, but they were prepared to sympathise with their comrades in the exporting districts, and once you reduce your demands below what they have been offered in these districts, you put these men in the position of fighting against their immediate interests, and more easily directed back to work, and thus we are weakening in consequence in this struggle.

This standpoint was opposed by Executive Committee spokesmen, by Straker of Northumberland, Robert Smillie for Scotland and also by Aneurin Bevan from South Wales. In the end it was decided that the Executive Committee should continue discussions with the General Council's mediation committee, A. Pugh, Ben Turner, J. H. Thomas, A. B. Swales and W. M. Citrine.

When they met on Friday, November 5th, the sub-committee told them that the Government were prepared to discuss with the Federation the principles to be agreed upon prior to the Miners' Executive ordering District negotiations. They gave the T.U.C. representatives authority to tell the Government that, subject to such principles being satisfactory, they were prepared to order immediate District negotiations.

The Sub-Committee of the General Council then left for a meeting with the Government. Later in the day a message was received that the Prime Minister now wanted to see the miners' Executive. They went off to Downing Street. When later Herbert Smith reported to the delegates the Conference adjourned. The Prime Minister kept in close touch with the coal-owners that day and the next, during which the talks with the General Council sub-committee and the M.F.G.B. Executive also continued. Then came a statement of the Cabinet of "the general principles which the Government understand the owners in each district are prepared to follow in negotiating district settlements." These were to be:

1. That wages should continue to be determined by the results of the industry in the district, ascertained jointly by accountants appointed by each side with provision as hitherto for joint test audits, and the reference of any question arising therefrom to the independent Chairman of the District Board; and that the owners in each district should discuss with the workmen's representatives any methods suggested for removing doubts about the fairness of transfer prices.

2. That the ratio for the division of net proceeds between workmen and owners should range between 87–13 and 85–15.

3. That the minimum percentage on basis should, subject to district settlements of hours and working conditions, be not less than the equivalent of 20 per cent on standard.[1]

4. That subsistence wages should be paid to low paid day wage men, the amount to be settled by arbitration in the district in the event of failure of the two sides to agree.

To the wording of these general principles, which contained no mention whatever of hours, the miners' Executive could not agree. Moreover, they put their finger on a significant point. To quote their minute, it would have to be pointed out

to the Government that the letter contained no reference to any national machinery for safeguarding national principles and co-ordinating district agreements, and that it was essential that provision be made for this. (November 8, 1926.)

The rest of Monday, November 8th, was spent at Downing Street with the Prime Minister and the Cabinet Coal Committee. After prolonged discussion, the General Council consulting the miners and the Government conferring with the coal-owners, and after the Executive Committee had

---

[1] NOTE.—"Standard" means the basis rates in force for the time being (in Scotland the 1888 basis) plus the percentage paid on basis in July 1914 (or the equivalent thereof where part of the 1914 District percentage has been merged in basis rates) plus any percentage that may be agreed to be paid to piece-workers in respect of an underground working day shorter than eight hours.

repeatedly retired to hold private meetings, midnight witnessed a complete deadlock. The minutes record it thus:

The Committee had explained to the Government, that it had understood, when agreeing to the memorandum submitted by the Trades Union Congress representatives, that the question of hours was not one which would be open to discussion and it had proceeded upon the assumption that both parties understood that the seven-hour day would remain; the Government had stated that such was not their understanding, but, on the contrary, it had understood and had proceeded on the assumption that no subject could be ruled out of the district negotiations.

The Committee considered the position in private, and after a long discussion passed the following resolution:

That the Chairman make it clear to the Cabinet that while ready to negotiate an honourable settlement, the Executive Committee are not prepared to authorise district negotiations which involve an extension of the working day.

The Committee later met the Sub-Committee of the Trades Union Congress, who informed the Committee that the Government had sent for them and asked them for their views of the understanding upon which the present discussions were opened and whether in their view it was understood that the question of hours would not be a subject of district discussion.

The Trades Union Congress had replied that while they had not discussed with the Miners' Executive any particular feature of the negotiations to be pursued in the districts, their interpretation of the word "negotiations" was negotiations with a view to settlement and which would exclude nothing from consideration. (November 8, 1926.)

Thereupon the Government told the miners that they would not discuss any question of national principles and safeguards until the Executive were "in a position to direct unfettered district negotiations."

An M.F.G.B. Special Conference was called at once. It met on Wednesday, November 10th, and sat for four days.

It was over six months since the beginning of the lock-out. For 194 days, the miners, with themselves, their wives and their children subsisting on a dwindling pittance, had withstood the might of the British Government and of all the other forces arrayed against them. The reports from the counties showed the majority still standing firm, but such a breakaway in a number of Districts that the total

working was now 237,547. This was well over a quarter
of the organised miners. On the other hand the Secretary
of Mines had stated the previous day that the total
coal produced in British mines since May 1st was only
10,500,000 tons, equal to some two weeks' normal output.
After full discussion it was agreed, on the second day, to
authorise the Executive Committee "to continue the negotiations with the Government unfettered." Negotiations went
on that evening and during the night.

In the early hours of Friday, November 12th, there came
a lengthy Memorandum of Settlement from the Government.
These proposals included an immediate resumption of work,
the hours not to be excluded from District negotiations; in
some Districts the owners would offer "to pay temporarily"
a District percentage not less than the rates prevailing on
April 30th. There was no guarantee against victimisation;
the "workmen shall be reinstated as opportunity offers
without prejudice to the men at present at work." For the
permanent "terms of employment," all agreements were to
be arrived at by Districts, through a District Board with an
independent chairman, and outlines were given of what the
terms of a "standard agreement" should be, the ratio of
division of net proceeds to vary between 87–13 and 85–15; and
District agreements were to last not less than three years. In
whatever Districts the hours were lengthened, there would be a
formal right of appeal to a national arbitral authority which
the Government would later set up for a period of six months
only.

When the delegates to the Special Conference heard these
grim terms, they decided to ask the Government for further
explanations. Arranged in question and answer form, they
show vividly the fears the miners entertained. Typical were
the following:

Q.—Will the Government give a guarantee that district customs
will not be interfered with?

A.—It is impossible for the Government to give any guarantee on
such a subject.

Q.—For how long a period does the offer of the Owners to pay
the general district percentage apply?

A.—For varying periods; the shortest to end of November, the
longest for one year.

Q.—Is the Owners' offer (of temporary payment) based on longer hours?

A.—Yes.

Q.—In the event of failure to agree upon the question of hours, who is to decide?

A.—This authority is not vested in anyone.

Q.—Can the Owners in the district be compelled to pay the subsistence wages prevailing in April last, up to the end of January?

A.—If they do not pay these rates the men can appeal to the National Tribunal who has power to award them.

Q.—In the event of failure to make an agreement in a district which conforms to the conditions of a standard agreement, how can either side secure access to the National Arbitral Authority?

A.—By making a provisional agreement under protest, resuming work, and lodging an appeal.

After studying these answers the Conference decided that the proposals should be remitted to the Districts for decision as to whether they be accepted as the basis of settlement, and by 432 to 352 recommended that they be so accepted.

Yet the men in the coal-fields still stood to their guns; they rejected the proposals by 460,806 to 313,200. Among the majority were South Wales, Durham, Scotland, Lancashire and Northumberland. After considering this the Conference finally decided by 502 to 286 to recommend all Districts to open negotiations. But it was still a fighting retreat, for the Conference instructed the Executive to draw up their own memorandum of what the general principles should be, to guide the Districts. Moreover, it was firmly laid down that:

No district shall enter into a final settlement until a further National Conference is held to receive reports of all the negotiations.

When the M.F.G.B. Special Conference met on Friday, November 26th, to hear the terms offered by the owners to the County Associations and Districts, they waxed indignant as the tale was told by one delegate after another. They knew also that in four Districts the owners had refused to meet the miners' representatives; while three days before a "non-political" union had been formed by George Spencer, M.P., the "Nottinghamshire and District Miners' Industrial Union." So they passed a resolution:

That this conference expresses its indignation at the terms offered by the coal-owners in the several districts, and invites the attention of the Cabinet to the action of the employers in Notts, Bristol, Leicester, Kent, in refusing to meet the accredited representatives of our members. (November 26, 1926.)

They would not give their assent to any District settlement that included longer hours or otherwise did not conform to the guiding principles laid down by the previous Delegate Conference. But, with the question of unemployment benefit becoming more urgent,[1] they left it that Districts would make agreements on their own responsibility.

By Monday, November 29th, work was resumed in all important coal-fields, except South Wales, Yorkshire and Durham, in which three the feeling of hatred against their opponents was exceptionally strong and bitter. The next day South Wales and Yorkshire went back. In Durham county a ballot was taken. It showed 49,217 for rejection of the owners' terms and 40,583 for acceptance: majority against 8,634. In view, however, of the two-thirds majority against the terms not being secured, Durham County Federation on the last day of November instructed the men to return to work. The lock-out struggle had lasted for over seven months. Never in the history of the British or other trade unions had there been such a struggle.

8. CONCLUSION

The Conference of Executives of all unions affiliated to the Trades Union Congress, postponed from the end of June 1926, was eventually held on Thursday and Friday, January 20 and 21, 1927. It was summoned "to consider the report of the General Council on the National Strike." This report, as originally prepared in the early summer of 1926, had been divulged at that time by publication in the journal of the Associated Society of Locomotive Engineers and Firemen. To this original report the General Council, not without protest from the miners, had decided to add a supplementary report giving an account of their work and policy in relation to the mining disputes from mid-May onwards.

[1] Not only was the benefit insufficient to meet the needs of an unemployed miner, but all sorts of difficulties were being put in the way of his receiving it.

The discussion at this Conference was animated enough; but it was in a very different atmosphere from that of June 1926; and while the magnitude and heroism of the struggle told on some of the delegates, for others it meant only that they were meeting under the shadow of a great defeat. Under these circumstances the result was a foregone conclusion. The figures in favour of the acceptance of the report of the General Council were 2,840,000; against acceptance 1,095,000.

Prior to the Conference the M.F.G.B. circulated to the delegates a statement which, though it failed to win over the delegates, deserved to be recorded. As will be seen, the document was signed not only by the members of the Executive Committee but by practically every county leader who could be considered to have taken an official part in the long-protracted struggle. It is truly an official document and can be accepted as the miners' epilogue to the great drama of 1926:

FELLOW TRADE UNIONISTS!

I.

After seven months of grim struggle, on a scale the like of which has not been known in Trade Union history in this or in any country of the world, the M.F.G.B., in common with the other Trade Unions, is called to give its judgment on the events of the first fortnight of that struggle.

II.

The population of these islands had never previously experienced anything resembling the situation created by the General Strike of May 4th to May 12th. Limited though it was both in number of workers affected, in the objective aimed at and in the time it lasted, the General Strike showed the working class to be possessed of qualities of courage, comradeship, and disciplined resource that had not hitherto been called forth and that gave a good omen for future solidarity.

III.

If we were deserted and forced to fight a lone fight, it was not by the workers that we were abandoned. Their hearts beat true to the end. From the workers of our country, and of the world, and especially from the Trade Unionists of Russia, we obtained unstinted aid. For the help given, whether from Union funds or from individual workers, we convey the gratitude of the miners' wives and children.

IV.—THE CAUSES OF THE STRIKE

The lock-out of May 1st, the General Strike of May 4th to 12th, were the climax of a struggle which had been preparing for months and years before. That struggle was on the widest possible scale. It was the concerted attempt of the employers of Great Britain to reach "stabilisation," to solve all their problems by cuts in wages. Towards this end the Dawes Plan, the return to the Gold Standard, etc., were so many stages which could only be carried out to their logical conclusion by an attack on the standard of living of the working class.

V.

For the moment, in 1925–26, the struggle narrowed down to one industry. Coal-mining exhibited in a special degree the difficulties which confronted the whole of British capitalist industry. Technically backward, carrying on its back the royalty owners, and robbed by the ancillary and distributing concerns, the coal-raising industry was faced with special difficulties from the competition of new fuels, new sources of power, new coal-fields, with the dwindling of markets from these causes and from the poverty of the peoples stricken by the world war. In these circumstances, the larger coal-owners, closely allied with the coal-using and coal-distributing concerns, and through their semi-monopoly position drawing substantial profits, determined to make use of the miserable position of the poorer collieries to stage a general attack on the miners' conditions.

VI.—THE CHALLENGE OF JULY, 1925

In the spring of 1925 the coal-owners endeavoured to beguile the miners, under the cloak of a "Joint Investigation" into a surrender of their standards. The investigation was suddenly dropped by the mine-owners, who abruptly terminated the existing agreement, and put forward impossible conditions for employment in the mines after August 1st, 1925. The new terms offered, with their revelation of the coal-owners' desire for longer hours and district agreements, as well as for lower wages and larger profits, were the cause of the July crisis of 1925.

VII.

The whole movement, under the strong and determined leadership which then marked the General Council, stood behind the miners in their resistance to the coal-owners. The Government, which had till then backed the coal-owners, was compelled by the threat of the united action of all Trade Unions to forgo this first example of general wages reduction and to stave off the conflict, in order to give themselves time to load their guns.

VIII.

A Royal Commission was appointed. The ostensible purpose of this Commission, on which the miners were refused representation, was to find a solution of the troubles of the industry. The miners pointed out that it was entirely unnecessary to hold a further Commission for this purpose, as the deficiencies of the industry, and the remedies therefor, had been clearly revealed by the Sankey Commission. The real purpose of the new Commission, however, was to find an argument that would divide the united front of the whole movement. It was part of the moral preparation of the Government.

IX.—THE QUESTION OF PREPAREDNESS

The Government had given themselves nine months, so that the conflict could be resumed at the moment most favourable for them. But their preparations for meeting united Trade Union action by strike breaking were well-nigh complete by Christmas, 1925.

X.

Did the General Council foresee the General Strike? If so, did it prepare? In August, 1925, the words were written that promised preparedness. Actually at the beginning of February, 1926, it was clear to the General Council that another crisis was inevitable. What preparations were made between August and January to meet the possible crisis? What after January, when the possible had become the inevitable? No one on the General Council can avoid these questions.

XI.—THE GENERAL COUNCIL CONFIRMS THE MINERS' PROGRAMME

From the crisis of July, 1925, one thing stood out clearly—that the whole movement was united behind the miners in their resistance to an attack on wages, hours, or national agreements. As for the miners, they have proven during their wonderful seven months' struggle that bad conditions could be imposed on them only by force. Did the General Council maintain this attitude?

At the end of January, 1926, they were aware that there must be either a renewed crisis, or a yielding. At the end of February they met us; and afterwards in the circular letter to all Affiliated Unions they said:

"The attitude of the Trade Union Movement was made perfectly clear last July, namely, that it would stand firmly and unitedly against any attempt further to degrade the standard of life in the coal-fields. There was to be no reduction in wages, no increase in working hours, and no interference with the principle of national agreements. This is the position of the Trade Union Movement today."

XII.—THE SAMUEL COMMISSION CONFIRMS THE MINE-OWNERS' WAGE
REDUCTION PROGRAMME

The Report of the Coal Commission was published in the second
week of March 1926. That the Report was critical of the existing
organisation of the industry could hardly have come as a welcome
surprise to anyone in the Labour Movement.

This certainly created no change in the situation, for every
Inquiry into the industry has shown the same result. That it focussed
its criticism on the smaller concerns and recommended amalgamations under the larger concerns could equally have surprised no one
in the Labour Movement who had studied capitalist tendencies and
the personnel of the Commission. This certainly created no change
in the situation, unless it be maintained that the greater concentration of industry under the Baldwin or the Aberconway groups is
so desirable that the workers must joyfully accept wages reductions
to achieve it. Finally, that the Government's interpretation of the
Commission's Report was insistent and urgent on one particular
point—immediate reductions in wages—certainly did not create a
change in the situation. If the Commission's Report created any
change at all, it was only to provide the Government and the
owners with the necessary argument for the contemplated attack
on the miners' wages. The Miners' Federation very carefully considered the Commission's Report, and tabled reasoned answers to
the recommendations, which answers we specially presented to the
General Council at their request.

XIII.—THE GENERAL COUNCIL AND THE MINERS

On the 12th March, the Miners' Conference met. At that Conference it was made clear that no change had been made in the
mandate determining their attitude in July, 1925. There was, however, no reaffirmation of the position at this particular Conference,
in view of the fact that there was no occasion to reaffirm a policy
which had already and recently been reaffirmed by the General
Council.

A month later (on the 9th April), the Miners' Federation Conference met again, and in view of the propaganda with which the
Press had been filled in the interval, in favour of the Commission's
Report and immediate wage reductions, it was felt essential that the
policy should again be explicitly stated, to remove any possible
doubt in the minds of the workers as to the miners' attitude. Before
meeting, we tried to find out if the General Council still stood for a
definite policy. But on 8th April we received a reply of which the
opening paragraphs ran:

"The Industrial Committee of the General Council have carefully considered the statement placed before them by your representatives at their meeting today, during which you asked for a
declaration from the Committee as to the support they would

accord to your Federation in respect of any attempt by the coal-owners to enforce:

(a) a reversion to District Agreements.
(b) a lengthening of hours.
(c) a reduction in wages.

The Committee fully realises the seriousness of the present position but they are of the opinion that matters have not yet reached the stage when any final declaration of the General Council policy can be made."

A significant hesitancy!

XIV.

On the following day, April 9th, the Miners' Conference passed the following resolution, in which they recommended the districts:

"(a) That no assent be given to any proposals for increasing the length of the working day.

"(b) That the principle of a national wages agreement with a national minimum percentage be firmly adhered to.

"(c) That inasmuch as wages are already too low, we cannot assent to any proposals for reduced wages."

XV.

On April 13th, the Central Committee of the Coal-owners' Association, at our meeting with them, informed us that they would proceed by means of district negotiations and had abandoned national negotiations with the M.F.G.B. On April 14th, the miners met the Industrial Committee of the T.U.C., and that body added to a protest against the action of the mine-owners the following significant statement:

"The Committee reiterates its previous declaration to render the miners the fullest support in resisting the degradation of their standard of life and in obtaining an equitable settlement of the case with regard to wages, hours, and National Agreements."

It appeared that the Committee had once more taken up the line of July, 1925, and was definitely supporting the decision of the Miners' Conference. This, at any rate, was an interpretation which all of us were confident should be put upon the resolution.

XVI.

It appeared the only interpretation which could be put on the paragraph in the statement submitted by the General Council to the Conference of Executives on April 29th, reading as follows:

"In our view the wages and working conditions of mine-workers are already so depressed as to render it imperative to seek for remedies other than a further degradation in their stan-dards of life, or the abrogation of the present standard hours, a course which the Commission declared would not provide a remedy."

It certainly was the interpretation of the whole movement, when the Conference of Executives passed its resolution, saying:

"That the Conference of Executives of unions affiliated to the Trades Union Congress endorses the efforts of the General Council to secure an honourable settlement of the differences in the coal-mining industry."

No one at that Conference took exception to the statement of the Miners' Secretary when he said: "The resolution, if I understand it aright, meant the confirmation of the statement sent out on 26th February."

XVII.

Summarising the foregoing it may be said: The Miners and the other Trade Unionists stood together in July, 1925. This position was reaffirmed by the General Council in February, 1926. Some six weeks later, after the publication of the Coal Commission Report, it was reaffirmed by the Miners but not at that moment by the General Council. The hesitation on the part of the General Council to reaffirm the position for which it had stood for seven months, and to which it had committed the movement, was not given special publicity to enable the movement to understand that the General Council had either changed its mind, or had not yet made up its mind.

XVIII.

What is quite certain is that the workers in the Trade Unions did not for a moment think that the General Council had changed its mind; and they entered into the General Strike on which they were called out in the belief that they were fighting for the policy which had been first enunciated in July, 1925, and then as recently as the end of February, 1926.

XIX.

Thus the General Council had failed to prepare for the General Strike—though they foresaw it, and promised to prepare for it. Secondly, they failed to maintain the standpoint of common resistance to a reduction in the miners' standards which had been established at "Red Friday." Lastly, they failed to warn the workers that they were thinking of yielding, that they contemplated receding from the position of July, 1925, and February, 1926. But now the second of these failures is acclaimed by the General Council as a triumph of common sense. Let us recount their claim.

XX.—THE GENERAL COUNCIL'S ARGUMENT FOR ABANDONING THE MINERS' PROGRAMME

The General Council contend:

1. That the Coal Commission Report had so altered the situation as to make it necessary to modify the attitude hitherto maintained by the Miners and by the General Council.

2. That the refusal of the miners to modify their attitude left the General Council with no option but to continue to render such help as they could towards effecting a settlement of the dispute, but without committing themselves to the programme of the miners (until recently their own programme as well).

3. That it was solely in order to effect a settlement (and not necessarily in order to back up the full demands of the miners) that the General Council during the last weeks of April approached the Prime Minister.

4. That it was only on the refusal to suspend the lock-out notices, and in order to enable negotiations to be resumed (but not in order to back up the miners' refusal to accept wage reductions) that the General Council invited the affiliated Trade Unions to declare the General Strike.

5. That the handing over of the issue of War or Peace to the General Council actually left it still possible (and in a sense made it more possible than before) for negotiations to be resumed—on a basis of wage reduction.[1]

XXI.

It will thus be seen that the hesitancy and failure of the General Council to give a clear definite lead, led to a provisional acceptance by the General Council of wages reductions on behalf of a million miners, and this at the moment when some millions of other workers as well as the miners confidently believed that the standpoint of 1925, and the early months of 1926, was still maintained by the General Council, and that "There was to be no reduction in wages, no increase in working hours, and no interference with the principle of national agreements."

XXII.

The acceptance of the Report of the Royal Commission meant not only lower wages, but, through lower wages, the ultimate acceptance of longer hours. The principle of the Royal Commission's Report—stripped of its flummery—was that the workers should pay for the inefficiency of the mine-owners. But there is a limit to the cutting of wages, a limit at which the pressure from the employers

[1] Witness the Birkenhead formula subscribed to by representatives of the General Council:

"We will urge the miners to authorise us to enter upon a discussion with the understanding that they and we accept the Report as a basis of a settlement, and we approach it with the knowledge that it may involve some reduction of wages."

is convertible into longer hours of labour. Once the principle of the workers paying for the inefficiency of the mine-owners was accepted, longer hours would become inevitable. Again, acceptance of lowered standards without a struggle would have meant not only ruin for the miners, but for all other workers as well. Everyone would have understood that the Trade Union Movement had yielded without a struggle in face of the propaganda and elaborate preparations of the Government and the employers. Every employer would have taken his cue. The principle of the living wage for which a generation of Trade Unionists had striven would have been finally thrown overboard. We miners, therefore, felt that the General Strike was in defence of the standards of the whole working class.

XXIII.—THE SAMUEL NEGOTIATIONS

After the decisions of May 1st, we consider that the General Council had no right whatever to negotiate in our absence, or to modify the decisions of the miners and the Trade Union Movement. On Saturday and Sunday, May 8th and 9th, it came to the knowledge of the miners' representatives that discussions had been opened between individuals of the General Council and some person or persons unknown, whom upon investigation we found to be Sir Herbert Samuel. On Monday, the 10th May, the officials of the Miners' Federation were invited to meet Sir Herbert, by, and in company with, the officials of the General Council. Sir Herbert then made certain proposals which were not committed to paper, but which represented a departure from the settled policy of the movement. The Miners' officials re-affirmed the position of their own constituents, and made it perfectly clear to Sir Herbert that they could not accept proposals which involved reductions in wages. Nevertheless, on Tuesday evening, the 11th May, the Miners' Executive were sent for by the General Council, and were informed that they (the Council) had agreed upon and accepted proposals as the outcome of conversations between their officials and Sir Herbert Samuel that day. The proposals were handed to us by the General Council, and we were asked to consider them and let the Council have our decision upon them that evening. It must be clearly pointed out that the proposals, when handed to the miners' representatives, had already been accepted by the Council, were not open to amendment in any way, and constituted a departure from the policy of the movement. Further, the General Council had already decided to call off the strike and had arranged a meeting with the Prime Minister to inform him of this decision.

The action of the General Council in accepting the proposals in advance of any decision by the miners was, in fact, an ultimatum by the Council to the miners; they were obviously determined to compel us to a decision which would mean a breaking of pledges to our own constituents.

XXIV.

The miners' representatives felt that whatever the consequences might be they must not break faith with their own people but must keep their own hands perfectly clean. They also felt very strongly, and their fears were afterwards amply justified, that there was no real guarantee behind the terms and no warrant that they would be accepted by the Government and the mine-owners.

The following resolution was therefore passed, which was at once handed over to the General Council:

"The Miners' Executive have given careful and patient consideration to the draft proposals prepared by the T.U.C. Negotiating Committee and endorsed by the General Council as representing the best terms which can be obtained to settle the present crisis in the coal industry.

"They regret the fact that no opportunity for consideration was afforded the accredited representatives of the Miners' Federation on the Negotiating Committee in the preparation of the draft or in the discussions of May 11th leading thereto.

"At best the proposals imply a reduction of the wages rates of a large number of mine-workers, which is contrary to the repeated declarations of the Miners' Federation, and which they believe their fellow Trade Unionists are assisting them to resist.

"They regret therefore, whilst having regard to the grave issues involved, that they must reject the proposals. Moreover, if such proposals are submitted as a means to call off the general strike such a step must be taken on the sole responsibility of the General Council."

XXV.

On Wednesday, May 12th, the Miners' Federation Executive Committee met again and re-affirmed its previous rejection of the Samuel memorandum, although the General Council used every effort of persuasion and intimidation to induce them to accept a change of policy. It must be made clear that when the General Council issued its circular letter on May 12th to the affiliated unions, stating that:

"The General Council accordingly decided at their meeting today to terminate the general stoppage *in order that negotiations could be resumed* to secure a settlement in the mining industry, *free and unfettered from either strike or lock-out.*"

it knew that the Miners' Federation had repudiated the suggested terms and that therefore there would be neither an end of the lock-out nor a resumption of negotiations. The circular letter was therefore entirely misleading, but it was the only way in which the General Council dared to tell the workers of its abandonment of the miners.

XXVI.—THE GENERAL COUNCIL'S CASE FOR ABANDONING THE MINERS

The concession policy of the General Council had been met by no corresponding concessions from the Government and the coal-owners, but by successive hardenings of attitude, until the moment when the pretext of the *Daily Mail* printers was used to hurl an ultimatum at the General Council, and through it at the whole Trade Union Movement. This, however, taught no lessons to the General Council. This must be said for them, that having once decided on a policy of yielding, they yielded consistently until the end. Their argument in the second week appears to have been:

1. That the declaration of the General Strike and the ultimatum of the Government had in no way altered their policy—which was to seek a way out by means of concessions.

2. That, therefore, the General Council were bound to seek some means for resuming negotiations on the basis of a wage reduction, the actual formula for which was provided by the Memorandum prepared by Sir Herbert Samuel.

3. That the alternative to a resumption on these lines was to go on fighting until (*a*) the Government was defeated; or (*b*) until the Trade Union funds were exhausted.

4. That this left them with no option but to surrender at discretion, but in possession of a guarantee.

5. That the guarantee was to be found in Sir Herbert Samuel's memorandum, or in the circumstances connected with it, or in premises or understandings about it.

6. That the Miners, if they would only have accepted this guarantee, would have seen how very good a guarantee it would have been; and that this would have been so, notwithstanding the Government's explicit repudiation of the memorandum, and the Prime Minister's subsequent denial of any guarantee in the House of Commons, and to the Miners when he met them on May 13th.

XXVII.

We have set forth the arguments of the General Council, as developed after the event, in such publications as have been accessible to us. There is no need to refute such arguments, which bear their own refutation. To put it bluntly, the General Council, whether they knew it or not, were leading the miners into a trap. But the Miners refused to be entrapped.

XXVIII.

It is said "The Miners made a mistake in not accepting the Samuel Memorandum. They would really have done better to accept the terms." Would it really have been better for the working class, once the General Council had surrendered, for us to surrender also? Let us examine the facts.

XXIX.

First of all these terms were illusory. They were merely a bait. They had no backing, no guarantee. That this was the case is proved conclusively by the following:

1. The letter from Sir Arthur Steel-Maitland, Minister of Labour, to Sir Herbert Samuel, dated May 8th, 1926. The concluding sentence of this letter was as follows:

"It is imperative to make it plain that any discussion which you think proper to initiate is not clothed in even a vestige of official character."

2. The letter from Sir Herbert Samuel to the General Council, dated May 12th, i.e. the day on which they called off the strike. The full text was as follows:

"Dear Mr. Pugh,

As the outcome of the conversations which I have had with your Committee, I attach a memorandum embodying the conclusions that have been reached.

"I have made it clear to your Committee from the outset that I have been acting entirely on my own initiative, have received no authority from the Government and can give no assurances on their behalf.

"I am of opinion that the proposals embodied in the memorandum are suitable for adoption, and are likely to promote a settlement of the differences in the Coal Industry.

"I shall strongly recommend their acceptance by the Government when the negotiations are renewed.
"Yours sincerely, (Signed) HERBERT SAMUEL."

3. The statement made to the Miners' Federation by the Permanent Under-Secretary for Mines, at an interview on May 17th. This statement was:

"The proposals of the Government should be read and treated as entirely independent of the proposals contained in the Samuel memorandum; the latter document has no official existence, and if the Miners had accepted it on the understanding that the Government had also done so, an impossible situation would have arisen for all concerned."

4. The following question and answer in the House of Commons on June 15th:

MR. WHEATLEY asked the Prime Minister whether at any time during the period of the General Strike he indicated that he was willing to accept the memorandum of Sir Herbert Samuel as a basis of settlement in the mining dispute. . . .

THE PRIME MINISTER (MR. BALDWIN): The answer is in the negative.

XXX.

What warrant, therefore, is there for imagining that the Samuel proposals would ever have been operated by either the Government or the owners? If the documents themselves were not sufficient proof, the subsequent history of our struggle shows quite clearly that no such warrant ever existed. If, therefore, we had accepted these proposals, what would have happened? The other workers would have been lured back to work—there to meet with an even worse victimisation than was in fact their lot. The Miners would have found themselves still locked out. The General Council would have been a laughing-stock, and an object of unmitigated contempt to all workers of this and other countries. The Miners saved them from this.

XXXI.—THE REAL ISSUES

The Owners (and the Government) from the very beginning stood for Eight-hours and District Agreements. This was their programme put forward in January; again on April 30th; again in June; again in November 1926. Throughout there was rigid adherence to this programme. Never were valid compromise proposals put forward.

XXXII.

Proposals, such as those named after Samuel, the Bishops, Churchill, were indeed put forward one after another. For every gesture we showed ourselves willing to make, the other side hardened their heart. Chancellors of the Exchequer might be thrown overboard, the leaders of the Churches might be treated with unusual disdain, but from the first to last there was never any possibility of the forces arrayed against the miners accepting anything but lower wages, longer hours and district agreements—UNLESS COMPELLED TO DO SO BY THE UNITED STRENGTH OF THE WORKING CLASS.

XXXIII.

This from the spring right on throughout the struggle the General Council failed to see. The point of difficulty, however, is not so much this error of judgment, as the fact that in 1925 they saw the necessity for a united front; in 1926, when to all others the need seemed a hundredfold clearer, they suddenly failed to see the necessity.

XXXIV.

The Miners are charged with lack of discipline because they refused to surrender, to abandon the policy laid down not only by repeated Miners' Delegate Conferences but by the General Council itself in July, 1925, and as recently as February, 1926. The claim of any leader or group of leaders to discipline, to loyalty, can only be accepted by the Trade Union Movement in so far as the leader or group accept the instructions of the men they represent, and remain loyal to the policy laid down. The Miners' Federation Executive showed, as was their duty, discipline and loyalty to the men they represented, and to the policy which had been accepted by the General Council itself. In carrying out this duty they were compelled to repudiate the claim of the General Council to change that policy, nor could they possibly have given the General Council absolute authority to sign away the settled policy of the whole movement.

XXXV.

The fight is not over. The conditions of the employers are imposed conditions and bring with them no goodwill or spirit of conciliation. Longer hours and lower wages cannot bring peace in the coal-fields; nor will we allow district agreements to shatter our strength and unity. Our organisation is still intact, and we are determined to recover the ground that has been lost. In this endeavour we look with confidence for the full support of the whole Trade Union Movement.

Yours, etc.,

On behalf of the Miners' Federation of Great Britain.

HERBERT SMITH, President.
T. RICHARDS, Vice-President.
W. P. RICHARDSON, Treasurer.

J. BAKER	H. HUGHES
J. BERRY	J. JONES
S. BLACKLEDGE	W. LATHAM
P. CHAMBERS	P. LEE
T. CAPE	W. MANSFIELD
S. O. DAVIES	P. McKENNA
J. DOONAN	J. A. PARKINSON
EBBY EDWARDS	G. PEART
S. EDWARDS	A. SMITH
J. ELKS	J. SMITH
T. FLATLEY	J. W. SMITH
C. GILL	W. K. SMITH
J. M. GILLIANS	W. STRAKER
J. GILLILAND	J. E. SWAN
FRANK HALL	C. THOMPSON
W. S. HALL	T. TROTTER
F. J. HANCOCK	F. B. VARLEY

A. J. COOK, Secretary.

January 12th, 1927.

Appendix A

MINERS' RELIEF FUND

STATEMENT OF ACCOUNTS FOR THE
14 MONTHS ENDING JUNE 30TH, 1927[1]

RECEIPTS[2]

	£	s.	d.
To Donations from sources in Great Britain and Ireland:—			
Trade Union Organisations (Central and Branches)	191,703	7	7
Independent Labour Party, local Labour Parties and Trades Councils, local Relief Organisations and Committees, National Unemployed Workers' Committee Movement, Labour Clubs and Institutes, Co-operative Societies	33,027	4	6
Women's Committee for Relief of Miners' Wives and Children	112,000	0	0
The Trades Union Congress General Council	164,039	4	6
Mining Members of Parliament	2,855	0	10
Shop and Work Collections, Collections at Meetings, etc., Donations from sundry organisations and from individual and anonymous donors	25,024	7	11
	528,649	5	4
„ Donations from other Countries	1,283,807	12	10
„ Bank Interest	1,223	16	4
Grand Total	£1,813,680	14	6

[1] In a note accompanying the statement the Treasurer and Secretary point out that it covers only the moneys received at the Headquarters of the Miners' Federation. In addition there was a Relief Fund of the National Committee of Labour Women; a number of local Relief Funds; and heavy contributions made by some trade unions to the National Strike Fund opened by the General Council, "a large portion of which was not forwarded by the Congress to our own fund, but was nevertheless contributed for the common cause." There were, in addition, large parcels of clothing, boots and other gifts in kind. Nor, adds the note, "must we forget the heavy financial sacrifices made by the Unions who directly participated in the stoppage, the extent of which would of course probably outweigh the total of the whole of the Relief Funds."

[2] Receipts only. Payments, not shown here, were simply the disbursements mainly through the county unions to the mine-workers and the mine-workers' wives and children.

Appendix B

MAIN PROVISIONS OF THE DISTRICT WAGES AGREEMENTS

IN OPERATION DURING THE YEAR 1929 (based on 9th Annual Report of the Secretary for Mines)

District	Period of Agreement (in years)	Ratio of Wages : Profits	Minimum Percentage Increase on Basis rates	Hours per shift Underground (Saturday figure in brackets)	Surface Hours per week	Remarks
Northumberland	2	87 : 13	40	{ 7½ hewers 8 others	49	Shifts on alternate Saturdays
Durham	1	87 : 13	65	{ 7½ hewers 8 others	49	At two-thirds of collieries 7¼ hours bank to bank for all underground on alternate Saturdays
Cumberland	3	85 : 15	30	8 (6½)	49	
Lancashire and Cheshire	3	87 : 13	32	8 (6)	49	
Yorkshire	3	85 : 15	32	7½ (7)	48–49	6.1% addition for pieceworkers
Nottinghamshire	5	85 : 15	38	7½ (5½)	46½	7% addition for pieceworkers
North Derbyshire	5	85 : 15	38	7½ (5½)	46½	7% addition for pieceworkers
South Derbyshire	3½	85 : 15	35	8 (6)	—	
North Staffordshire	3	86 : 14	35	8 (6)	48	
Cannock Chase	4	85 : 15	42	8 (5½)	46½	
South Staffordshire	4	85 : 15	40	8 (6)	48½	
Leicestershire	4	85 : 15	40	8 (5½)	48	
Warwickshire	4	85 : 15	43	8 (5½)	46½–49	At certain collieries lower percentages were payable
Salop	—	—	—	8 (6)	46–48	No agreement recorded
Forest of Dean*	3	85 : 15	68.75	8 (7)	49	The standard was 100 : 15, the surplus 85 : 15
Somerset	5	85 : 15	31.5	8 (7)	51½	
Kent	—	—	—	7½ (6½)	48	No agreement recorded
South Wales and Monmouth	3	85 : 15	28	8 (7)	48	
North Wales	3	84 : 16	22	8 (6½)	49	
Scotland	3	87 : 13	110	8 (8)	49	

Note.—The agreements were concluded at various dates between the end of the 1926 lock-out and April 1, 1927. The ascertainment periods also varied, but were in most cases from one to three months. Deficiencies were carried forward in every District, except in Derby, Nottingham, Leicester and Warwick where limitations were set.

* Bristol (not shown separately) was similar to Forest of Dean both in hours of labour and in ratio of wages to profits.

Appendix C

THE END OF FRANK HODGES

Frank Hodges, who lost his minor Government office in the autumn of 1924, was chosen as Secretary of the International Miners' Federation (not without some protests, voiced by Robson of Durham amongst others) in April 1925. Within a twelvemonth he aroused the keenest dissatisfaction in every District of the Miners' Federation by his public utterances. Both before and during the lock-out he supported the standpoint of the owners on lengthening of hours of labour. In addition, within the International Miners' Federation he used his position to operate against the miners' interests as represented by their elected officials which made it (as was stated at a Special M.F.G.B. Conference which dealt with this matter on June 2, 1927) "very painful for the British representatives to have an International Secretary as their opponent at every meeting when requests and appeals were made for action by the International." To such an extent did this go that, according to the same report,

> At a conference held on September 30, 1926, the Chairman made a statement that not only were we fighting the Government and the owners, but Mr. Hodges.

After the lock-out, the Executive Committee considered resolutions from the Districts on the activities of Frank Hodges and his statements "during the course of the lock-out which were calculated to seriously weaken the Federation and impair its chance of emerging successfully from the struggle," and resolved "That the British representatives to the Miners' International Committee be instructed to ask that body to request the resignation of Mr. Hodges as Secretary of the Miners' International Federation."

Meantime the Conservative Government, not unmindful of the capacity of Hodges, had made him a member of the National Electricity Board, described as a part-time post at £750 a year. Now the conditions under which Hodges became International Miners' Federation Secretary had been laid down very strictly. He was to devote "his whole time" to it: and his salary was to be "£500 per annum plus house rent, rates and taxes, coal and light." The M.F.G.B. Executive held that the agreement precluded Hodges from accepting this Government post: to this, according to the report of Treasurer Richardson, "Mr. Hodges claimed that the agreement . . . did not prevent him from taking this office, on the ground that the £750 was out of pocket expenses." It was found out later that the Electricity Board post was £750 plus expenses. In the discussion on an International Committee, so Mr. Cook reported to the M.F.G.B. Special Conference of June 1927, Mr. Hodges contended that "he had plenty of time to do the two jobs, and that really the position on the Electricity Board was an asset to us as he was representing Labour there." Eventually, however, Hodges at the end of April was compelled to resign as International Secretary as from the end of June 1927; and it was decided that the minutes written by him, in which he had omitted to refer to his attitude in the struggle, should be revised.

A month afterwards Hodges came out publicly in support of Spencer's "non-political" union. In July he spoke at a Newcastle meeting (to which free rail and bus tickets were issued by the coal-owners) called with the object of destroying the miners' county unions linked up in the M.F.G.B. Later Hodges was taken on as director of several companies (colliery, iron and steel, chemicals, finance, etc.) while he retained his post on the Electricity Board. At his death in 1947 he was possessed of £132,959.

CHAPTER XV

THE AFTERMATH

I. DECLINE OF THE COAL TRADE

FOR many years after the lock-out of 1926 there was a decline in the British coal trade even more than in the trade of the country in general. The policy of the Conservative Government, which played into the hands of the mine-owners, was to solve the problems of industry by longer hours and lower wages for the miners. This policy, however, failed to achieve its object. Though coal-cutting machinery was introduced in part—but not so extensively as to modernise the mines effectively—and though output per man-shift went up, total production fell year by year. Markets shrank and many pits were closed for ever. In every colliers' village there were miners idle. This decline in production, and the consequent decline in the number employed, is shown in the following tables. The first table begins with 1913, the zenith year of the British coal trade, and gives both the four years of the 1914–18 war and the three years after up to the three months' lock-out of 1921.

TABLE 1*

Year	Number Employed (Thousands)	Output (Millions of Tons)	Exports
1913	1,107	287	94
1914	1,038	266	78
1915	935	253	57
1916	981	256	51
1917	1,002	248	45
1918	990	228	41
1919	1,170	230	47
1920	1,227	230	39
1921	1,132	163	36

* Statistical Digest of the Ministry of Fuel and Power, 1913–22.

The second table shows the zenith in exports of 1923, mainly due to the French occupation of the Ruhr coal-field, which also affected 1924. Thereafter the decline from 1926 onwards is plainly seen; and the recovery from the slump of 1930 onwards is at a lower level than the recovery from the slump of 1920–21.

TABLE 2

Year	Number Employed (Thousands)	Output (Millions of Tons)	Exports
1922	1,094	250	82
1923	1,160	276	98
1924	1,172	267	79
1925	1,086	243	67
1926	*	126	28
1927	998	251	68
1928	922	237	67
1929	932	258	77
1930	917	244	70
1931	850	219	57
1932	803	209	53
1933	772	207	53
1934	774	221	53
1935	759	222	51
1936	756	228	46
1937	778	240	52
1938	782	227	46

* National dispute lasting approximately seven months from May 1st.

With this picture of decline in the coal trade of the United Kingdom, it is instructive to contrast the world figures, which show a slight over-all increase in the same twenty-five years with the output of some countries growing fast, especially towards the end of the period taken.

From the table overleaf it may be seen that the total world production, which had rushed upwards throughout the nineteenth century and till 1913, had now come to an end of its rapid upward course; in some years it fell below the 1913 level; and the net increase between 1913 and 1938 was but slight. Within this world total the development was uneven. Not only was the United Kingdom producing less but the United States, whose growth had been so spectacular in the three decades before 1913, suffered a still greater setback. On the other hand Germany, mainly through a greater output of lignite, had gone up from 1913 to more than half as much again. The same was true of India and China. Japan was producing two-and-a-half times as much as in 1913. But the greatest proportionate change was in the Soviet Union, whose coal output showed a fourfold increase.

The United Kingdom, which in 1870 had produced more than half of the world's total coal, in 1895 more than a third, in the five years prior to 1913 exactly a quarter, was yielding little more than a fifth by 1930 and considerably less than a

WORLD OUTPUT OF COAL AND LIGNITE

(Million Metric Tons)

Country	1913	1920	1930	1938
United Kingdom	292	233	248	231
United States	517	597	487	354
Germany	242	229	302	381
France	44	25	55	48
Soviet Union	33	13	54	132*
Belgium	23	22	27	30
Japan	22	31	34	55
India	16	18	24	26
Australia and New Zealand ..	14	15	14	17
China (including Manchuria) ..	15	23	27	27
Poland	41	30	37	38
Czechoslovakia	37	31	34	26
TOTAL (including all other chief producing countries)	1,253	1,212	1,275	1,271

* Lignite figures not available.

fifth by 1938. Apart from the change in Britain's relative position, the export market had also shrunk since 1913, when nearly one-tenth of all coal consumed abroad was exported from this island. By 1938 British exports had shrunk from a hundred million metric tons in 1913 to less than half that amount.

Contributory to this shrinkage were the increased use of alternative fuels such as oil or sources of power such as hydro-electricity. But of greater importance was the general world shrinkage of trade, and the special circumstances of British economy as a whole during the greater part of the period between the two world wars.

2. CONDITIONS IN THE COAL-FIELDS

For nearly ten years after 1926 conditions in the coal-fields steadily worsened. Longer hours, lower wages, harder toil combined with unemployment and widespread mal-nutrition to lower the miners' standard of living. Amongst the youth there was a general desire for something better than the prospects offered them in the mining industry—and an even greater desire to escape from what their parents had been for so long enduring, with the result that a constant drift away from this industry became evident, and showed itself a generation later in a very serious shortage of man-power. The immediate effect in the mining villages was an appalling condition of hunger and misery.

Wages fell rapidly from the 1925–26 level, which in turn had been well below the level of 1920–21, and remained depressed from 1927 to 1929. Thereafter they went lower still in the years of the great slump. The first stage is shown by figures of 1927–29.

EARNINGS

Year	Per Man-Shift		Weekly Average		Quarterly Average		
	s.	d.	s.	d.	£	s.	d.
1926 (January to April) ..	10	5	—		34	6	4
1927	10	0¾	47	0	30	13	1
1928	9	3½	44	0	28	9	2
1929	9	2½	45	0	29	11	7

These figures of earnings, averaged over the whole country, varied considerably from District to District. For example, earnings in 1929 were highest in South Wales (49s. 6d. a week) where unemployment was also highest, and in Scotland (50s. a week) ; and lowest (38s. 6d. a week) in Northumberland. But in all Districts they remained on the minimum basis wage rate, as fixed by the separate agreements imposed at the end of 1926.

These earnings were more and more drawn from mechanised working. The proportion of coal cut by machinery, which had risen from 7·7 per cent in 1913 to 20 per cent in 1925, now rose to 28 per cent in 1929, 42 per cent in 1933 and 59 per cent in 1938. The process is seen from the following table.

MECHANISATION OF MINES

	Per Cent of Coal Cut by Machinery	Tonnage—Machine Cut	No. of Conveyors in Use
1913	7·7	24,370,000	268
1925	20	48,133,000	1,513
1926	—		—
1927	23	58,472,000	2,185
1928	26	61,388,000	2,856
1929	28	71,950,000	3,218
1930	31	75,756,000	3,747
1931	35	76,864,000	3,953
1932	38	80,286,000	4,120
1933	42	87,226,000	4,756
1934	47	103,701,000	5,369
1935	51	113,265,000	6,140
1936	55	125,750,000	6,727
1937	57	137,118,000	7,300
1938	59	134,958,000	7,826

In this mechanisation, again, there was great variety between Fife (90 per cent), Northumberland (91 per cent), Derbyshire (92 per cent) on the one hand and on the other hand South Wales (26 per cent), Durham (42 per cent), Yorkshire (56 per cent).

The increased use of machinery underground, together with the closing down of pits (the number of pits working fell from 2,861 in 1927 to 2,120 in 1937), the eight-hour day, the practice of overtime, and "speeding-up" had as their outcome an increase in output per man-shift—and also in the number unemployed. There were two hundred thousand miners out of work in January 1927. This figure was at first presented as something that might have been expected following the bitter struggle of 1926 and was looked upon as a temporary dislocation, natural after a seven months' lock-out. But it proved to be anything but temporary. For the figures of unemployment did not decrease in the months that followed. By July 1927 the number of mine-workers insured under the Unemployment Insurance Act who were recorded as "unemployed" had risen to over a quarter of a million. From the

JOSEPH JONES (1891–1948)
President M.F.G.B. 1934–1938

W. E. HARVEY, M.P. (1852–1914)
Vice-president M.F.G.B. 1912–14

258,203 of July 1927 there was a fall in the autumn and in the winter months of 1927–28. But thereafter the figures rose until they reached a peak of nearly a third of a million in July 1928, at which point nearly one out of every three miners was idle.

UNEMPLOYMENT IN MINES

Month of 1928	Unemployed Miners
May	245,590
June	299,449
July	324,932
August	296,480
September	251,080
October	280,010
November	282,293
December	252,364

Thus from the peak of July the figures continued to be above a quarter of a million to the end of the year, by which time an increasing number of miners had exhausted their statutory benefits.

To the poverty caused by this mass of unemployment there was added the hardship suffered through the administration of the law. So many were the complaints that the Government set up the "Morris Committee," the purpose of which was:

To consider and report upon the constitution and procedure of statutory authorities performing the functions of insurance officers and Courts of Referees under the Unemployment Insurance Acts, and the nature of the evidence to be required as to the fulfilment of the conditions or the absence of the disqualifications for the receipt of Unemployment Benefit under the Acts.

In a memorandum to this "Morris Committee" the Miners' Federation in September 1929 submitted evidence of "the many hardships and injustices suffered by the mine-workers through the present administration of the Acts." Unemployment in coal-mining had special features: its magnitude; its long duration; and "the existence of large numbers of unemployed mine-workers who are segregated together in large groups in areas where coal-mining is the chief and in some cases the only industry and where consequently no alternative means of obtaining employment are available." The memorandum dealt at length with the fulfilment of the Fourth Statutory Condition, "genuinely seeking work but unable to obtain employment," the administration of which it treated as the most important of the features which were causing "an enormous burden of suffering" in the coal-fields. First and most important of these difficulties, the memorandum pointed out, was the responsibility which had been placed upon the unemployed mine-worker of proving that he had fulfilled the first part of the fourth Statutory Condition entitling him to benefit, namely, that of "genuinely seeking work." The memorandum proceeded:

9. The onus thus placed upon the unemployed applicant has caused more friction—more heart-burning and more suffering in the coal-field than anything else in the administration of Unemployment Benefit, and this can be readily understood in the special circumstances of the industry referred to above.

10. In the view of the Miners' Federation the practice which has grown up in connection with the fulfilment of this condition has entirely subverted the Employment Exchanges from the main function for which they were originally set up, namely, that of bringing unemployed applicants into touch with vacancies. This primary function has now been relegated to the background, and the responsibility for finding vacancies has been thrust upon the unemployed.

11. It is interesting to note how this system works out in actual practice. The applicant for Unemployment Benefit is in the first instance interviewed by Exchange officials. These officers act as judges of the individual's effort to obtain work. They interrogate the applicant, and in the vast majority of cases the success of the application depends on the answers given. The statement prepared on the basis of these questions is then placed before the applicant for his signature.

12. The statement forms the record to be sent, if necessary, to a Court of Referees. Nine times out of ten it determines the question as to whether benefit shall be allowed or not.

13. The average workman has no notion of the importance of these interviews, nor the slightest idea that he is on trial. Frequently he is cross-examined, and the slightest confusion or hesitation is noted and may be used to his prejudice. The statement may very often be quite unrepresentative of the applicant's real efforts. Whatever it is, and however prepared, it forms the record to be sent, if necessary, to the Court of Referees.

14. With the report of the interviewing officer and other information before them, the Referees (more often than not the Chairman alone) immediately begin to question the applicant upon his efforts.

"Where have you been outside the district?"

"Where have you been within the district?"

"Have you been to so-and-so? What kind of man is the manager?"

"How did you approach the place? Where were you on such and such a day?"

"Where did you say you were daily over the last week or two?"

"Where have you been since you were here before? Who owns the colliery?"

"Have you been to such and such a place?" (naming places where it is well known that there are thousands of a similar class of workmen unemployed).

If the workman, knowing the futility of visiting such a place, says "No," this is used against him by the Chairman of the Court of Referees. The slightest confusion, hesitation, or contradiction is once more noted and may, as often is the case, be regarded as evidence of his not being trustworthy. Variations of the above questions are put daily and deliberately at Courts of Referees in order to trap or attempt to trap them.

15. Here, too, comes the difficulty of deciding how far might the unemployed worker be expected to proceed, without resources, in search of employment. While in theory it is recognised that they cannot go far afield, yet in actual practice the unemployed worker, weakened by prolonged privation, under-nourished and ill-clad, is expected to walk daily a distance of anything from 10 to 50 miles. This may appear to be an exaggeration, but can be proved any day by attending the Court of Referees. In fact, these men are expected to maintain with regularity an exertion which athletes can only do for short periods of time. There is an almost entire failure to appreciate the heartbreaking effect of this continuous daily, weekly, monthly march vainly seeking that which does not exist. Let the worker but admit that he failed on one day to make a call, that during the last three months he missed some particular town, village, colliery, workshop, contractor, road, quarry, a house or a farm possibly named by the Chairman, and his fate is sealed.

16. The Umpire, and it might be held reasonably, assumes that the Referees understand fully the local circumstances and conditions and will give due consideration to any and every factor so that appeals against large numbers of decisions are in vain. In the ordinary way the procedure at Courts of Referees does not permit of the workman's representative acting in any real sense as an advocate. It must be admitted that if they did the whole machinery would break down. Large numbers of cases are turned down which

might have been saved had the advocate been permitted to open a case with a statement instead of the man being directly subjected to a process of examination and cross-examination. The representative is really put in the position of trying to extricate his client from a difficulty into which he has either been led or quite innocently landed himself.

17. The evils which follow from this system will be apparent to anyone possessed of any degree of imagination. It is obvious that the system tends to encourage the very abuses which it is supposed to check. In time, some of the applicants become aware that benefit will depend upon the answers given. Thus they prepare themselves for the ordeal; it becomes a duel of wits between the Chairman and the applicant; the applicant is compelled to adopt all sorts of subterfuges, mis-statements and untruths in order to save his Unemployment Benefit. Those who are best able to maintain their position are admitted to benefit, while on the other hand, large numbers of *bona fide* unemployed workers who are genuinely seeking work, but who have not prepared themselves for the ordeal, and would in any case refuse to resort to such methods, are turned down.

18. The Miners' Federation would also direct attention to the fallacy of the assumption which must underlie this practice, namely, that somewhere or other a job exists for every unemployed person. True this is not stated in so many words, but when assumed, as it is for all individuals appearing before the Court of Referees, it must be so assumed for the whole. On this basis it must be further assumed that on the basis of available work, all unemployment is avoidable. Such an assumption has only to be stated for its absurdity to be exposed.

In their conclusions the Miners' Federation stressed particularly that the Labour Exchanges should perform the function for which they were originally created (i.e. to bring all the vacant jobs available to the notice of suitable unemployed workmen); that the only test of "genuinely seeking work" should be the offer to the applicant of a definite job which should be "suitable employment"; and, finally that an unemployed workman whose benefit was being considered by the Local Committee should have the right to have his case presented by his trade union official.

Following on the recommendations made by the Morris Committee the Labour Government put forward, and Parliament passed, an amending Act early in 1930 by which the "genuinely seeking work" clause was repealed and the onus was put upon the authorities to prove that the applicant for benefit had refused a suitable offer of employment. Three years of harsh administration had gone by before this amending Act did something to lessen the hardships suffered by miners and other unemployed workers.

Meantime from the end of 1927 onwards an increasingly large army of mine-workers had exhausted their statutory benefits and with their families were become destitute. Indeed the figures of unemployment, in that they dealt only with those who were still insured, rapidly ceased to give anything like a true picture of this spreading morass of destitution. By 1928 the gap between the official figures of insured persons "unemployed" and the total numbers out of work was so significant that it engaged the main attention of the Miners' Federation. "Nineteen twenty-eight was perhaps the darkest year of the British coal trade," according to the Annual Report of the M.F.G.B. Executive Committee (June 1929), which went on to say, "the ordinary work of mining trade unionism had, to some extent, to take a secondary place to the work of relieving the victims." As the conditions in the coal-fields became known, a certain amount of relief action had begun, including the starting of a fund by the Lord Mayor of the City of London. But this Lord Mayor's Fund, despite repeated appeals, had, from its inception on April 2, 1928, up to the end of September, gathered only £88,770. A first direct appeal by the Miners' Federation had similar ill success: "The public remained apathetic and indifferent." A second appeal from the Miners' Federation, with every step taken to ensure wide publicity, including an approach to the daily newspapers and other periodicals, was launched on November 29, 1928. Signed by Smith, Richards, Richardson and Cook, it pointed out that the operation of the Eight Hours' Act and the reorganisation measures in the industry had resulted in huge numbers being unemployed, and said:

Of these 200,000 to 250,000 constitute a permanent unemployed surplus. With their wives and children, this means that over 1,000,000 souls are faced with starvation unless help is speedily rendered them.

The mining population, in short, is faced with a cataclysm comparable to the destruction wrought by some great earthquake or other giant disturbance of nature. In the words of Mr. John Galsworthy:

"Through forces utterly beyond their individual control . . . a heart-breaking process is going on among a million in one of the best classes of our people . . . idle, hopeless and increasingly destitute. . . ."

Unemployment has been of such long duration that large numbers of men have long exhausted the benefits to which they were entitled under the Unemployment Insurance Acts, and the machinery of the Poor Law is utterly inadequate to cope with the situation.

In course of time alternative avenues of employment may be opened up, and the transference of mine-workers to other areas has already begun on a small scale. *To bridge the transitionary period provides unlimited scope for private help on the part of all persons of goodwill.*

In these circumstances, we appeal to the nation to help the sufferers combat the rigours of the approaching winter and to provide some little cheer for them during this Christmastide.

Through its District organisations, the Miners' Federation of Great Britain is hourly in direct touch with the sufferers in every coal-field. Footwear, clothes, and blankets are urgently wanted for immediate needs. These may be sent to any of the addresses on the attached list. Contributions in cash should be sent to The Treasurer, Miners' National Distress Fund, 55 Russell Square, London, W.C.1.

This appeal to charity had much greater success. Within one week, the amount of money received was double that given in the previous six weeks, while an impetus was given both to the Lord Mayor's Fund and to the funds of other voluntary organisations. The Executive report records:

The indifference and apathy of the public had at last been banished. Thereafter the subject of miners' distress was of first importance. It became a topic of daily discussion and comment in the Press. The Government stepped in with its £1 for £1 grant. The interest and enthusiasm of the public was aroused in ever-increasing degree and the splendid appeal of the Prince of Wales, on Christmas Day, was received everywhere with manifestations of the utmost sympathy and goodwill towards the miners of the country.

WE HAD ACHIEVED OUR PURPOSE OF MAKING THE RELIEF OF DIS-TRESS IN THE COAL-FIELDS A MATTER OF NATIONAL CONCERN AND IMPORTANCE.

Apart from cash, the Miners' Federation received free gifts of clothing and foodstuffs, both from individuals and from large trading organisations, to a value far greater than the amount of cash received. These gifts in kind came partly from the multiple shops, chain stores and foodstuffs manufacturers in the United Kingdom and partly from a score of big packing companies in California. Their handling and distribution to unemployed mining families was carried out entirely by the Miners' Federation and its constituent unions.

The report of the Executive Committee singled out for special mention one amongst the donors. The *Daily Mail*, the newspaper which was the inveterate opponent of higher wages or improved conditions for the miners, was now, in response to the appeal, prepared to use its columns for this particular form of charity and had organised the sending of 114,000 hampers of food and cast-off clothing:

The work of allocating and arranging the despatch of these large consignments was performed by our Head Office in conjunction with the representatives of the *Daily Mail* and the representatives of the railway companies and the trading organisations. . . .

It was not to be expected that a work of such magnitude could be put through without a few complaints arising from individuals who considered themselves to have been harshly treated. On the whole, however, surprisingly few such complaints arose.

The Executive Committee then quoted a letter to A. J. Cook from the Manager's Department of Associated Newspapers Ltd. (the Rothermere combine) which, they said, showed "that the *Daily Mail* were perfectly satisfied with the arrangements and that we retained its entire confidence."

The Executive report concluded "Our very best thanks are due to the *Daily Mail* and its readers and to all the organisations concerned."

As this unusual report circulated in the stricken coal-fields the thankfulness for what had been received was mingled with memories of what had once been the proud and unyielding stand of their trade unions. Many mine-workers in their enforced idleness had been thronging the public libraries and reading there tales of other countries and other times. Maybe some of the miners took the opportunity to read the Iliad of Homer, which ends with the stricken Priam kissing the hands of Achilles, the terrible hands that had slain his sons and made his house desolate. Had all their epic struggle gone for this, that they must be suppliants and kiss the hands of the *Daily Mail*? Was this to be the end of their Iliad?

3. STRIFE WITHIN THE FEDERATION, AND WITHOUT

The great struggle of 1926, ending in defeat, led to two sets of conclusions. On the one hand there were those like Philip Snowden, who was prompt to conclude that the struggle itself had been a mistake, that never again should there be resort to a strike and that henceforth the aim should be "peace in industry." On the other hand there were those, headed for some two years by A. J. Cook, who acknowledged the defeat but sought to draw from it lessons which could be applied to strengthening the organisation and the policy of the trade unions. To them, Snowden was proposing a cowardly submission: Cook taunted Snowden[1] with having accepted the policy and action of the Government and the owners ("they make a desolation and call it peace"), by their plea for "peace in industry." Throughout the next few years in the mining industry, and in other industries too, there are these two warring outlooks.

In the first few months after the lock-out had ended in victory for the owners, the general outlook in the miners' lodges as in the Federation Executive Committee was not definite either way, although the younger miners and the younger leaders were ready to follow the lead of A. J. Cook. But the immediate concern of all was to resist the further attacks by the Government and by the mine-owners. The Government, as soon as the mining struggle was over, resumed the preparation of its anti-trade-union Bill, and brought it before Parliament in the spring of 1927. The provisions of what afterwards became the Trade Disputes and Trade Unions Act (1927) were to worsen the legal position of trade unions and thrust them back to the conditions in some ways of over fifty years earlier. The Miners' Federation and all its Members of Parliament took an active part together with the Trades Union Congress and the Labour Party in the agitation against the Bill and, though they carried their resistance no further after the Bill had become an Act, they recorded their demand for its repeal in subsequent Annual Conferences.

---

[1] A. J. Cook, *Is it Peace?* (1927).

The further attack by the owners took another form. Not content with having, in alliance with the Government, defeated the miners and imposed a type of District settlement which enfeebled the Federation, they now stimulated by every means in their power the formation of a "yellow" union in rivalry to the Federation and the County Associations. A beginning had been made in the Nottinghamshire coal-field when George Spencer, M.P., expelled from the Miners' Federation Conference (see page 495) had set up a rival organisation entitled the Miners' Industrial (non-political) Union. This body, usually called the Spencer Union, opened up branches in the course of 1927 and 1928 in Scotland, Durham, Northumberland, Yorkshire, Staffordshire, Derbyshire and South Wales. In the Welsh valleys it claimed 107 branches out of a national total of 273. The coal-owners gave it every encouragement by victimising active members of the County Associations and by giving preference to those who joined the Spencer Union. In Nottingham, for example, at the end of 1927 the New Hucknall Coal Company made the announcement that none but Spencer Union men would be employed in the Welbeck Pit. A vigorous campaign was opened there in the first week of March 1928 by Arthur Cook, S. O. Davies and Arthur Horner, while the General Council of the Trades Union Congress met specially at Nottingham in the same month and there decided to ask for a meeting with the Nottingham Coal Owners' Association. Similarly, in South Wales a sort of guerilla warfare was carried on, the owners in some places getting the Spencer Union started, and in other places what appeared to be a strongly established branch of the Spencer Union would suddenly disappear while its members sought to return to the ranks of the South Wales Miners' Federation.

By some inside the Federation it was felt that the fight against the Spencer Union was not being waged with requisite vigour and speed (it was not concluded till ten years later). It must be remembered that there was much talk at this time of Mussolini's Corporative State, into which conception the appearance and growth of yellow unions would easily fit, and the fears then prevalent of a swing in Britain towards this type of Fascism was given some substance by a speech of the

Chancellor of the Exchequer[1] in Italy where he had given provisional approval to the method of Fascism.

While these measures by the Government and the mine-owners were being put into operation, the weakness of the Federation was becoming visible, not only in the diminished functions in regard to wages and conditions but also in a sharp fall of total membership. At the Llandudno Annual Conference Herbert Smith, in his presidential address, laid stress on this:

When last we met in this town we called the roll with 131 delegates, representing 957,610. Last year at Southport that figure had shrunk to 784,986, whilst at the present moment we have 625,576 members. This should of necessity cause all of us seriously to think.[2] The year through which we have passed has proved a severe test of our people. We had many prophets in various walks of life prophesying all manner of gloomy forebodings as to what was likely to happen. Unfortunately, one has reluctantly to admit facts. Our membership has gone down. Why? There have been divers agencies at work, such as for example: unemployment; low wages; debts; internal differences. (July 17, 1928.)

Both in 1928 and 1929 the report of the Executive Committee ended with a plea for the composition of differences within the Federation. That the differences were widespread was notorious. The strategy of the owners in their insistence upon District settlements[3] had effectively torn the constituents of the Federation apart from one another. In the course of the first few years after 1926 this was made painfully evident more than once by Federation Conference decisions being ignored by this or that District. In November 1929 such a difference led to the abrupt resignation from the presidency of Herbert Smith, who felt he must stand by the Yorkshire Miners' Association then at loggerheads with the majority of the Federation. The continuity in the office-bearers which had marked the first thirty years of the M.F.G.B. was now effectively broken; both ex-President Robert Smillie and ex-President Herbert Smith were now present at Conferences only as delegates from their Districts; and there were rapid

---

[1] Winston Churchill.
[2] A year later at the Blackpool Annual Conference, in giving the still lower figure of 543,822, Herbert Smith referred to it as "a matter of the utmost concern."
[3] See Appendix to chapter xiv.

changes for some time in the tenure of the presidency. But while the aftermath of the defeat of 1926 witnessed many such dissensions within the Federation mingled with much personal quarrelling, there was at bottom one big difference of principle and policy. It was stated in a contemporary journal[1] in the following terms:

From the termination of the 1926 lock-out and the conclusion of separate district agreements there have been two main currents of policy within the miners' organisations. One, which can be said to be that of the District Executives generally, is in favour of maintaining the existing district organisations, and working within the limits imposed by the new agreements, while trying to modify the hardships resulting for the men. The second line of policy, associated with A. J. Cook and the "Left" elements in the lodges, is based on the view that the agreements were imposed by force and that their further working out can only bring continually worsening conditions; and that therefore the merging of the district associations in a single Miners' Union is essential, as this step would liquidate all district agreements and secure strength enough to fight on a national scale.

These conflicting policies are being discussed in the lodges and in the Press, and the results are emerging, on the one hand, in the election of "Left" officials, and on the other hand, in the attacks on the "Left" by the District Executives; while support of or hostility to the development of relations with the Russian miners is also involved.

The two conflicting policies within the Miners' Federation were not limited to the coal industry. In other industries as well the fight for the strengthening of the trade union movement and for the struggle against capitalism came up against an ever-growing support of "Mondism" on the part of the older leaders. The name derived from Sir Alfred Mond (afterwards Lord Melchett), a Liberal Member of Parliament who had helped to amalgamate the firm of Brunner Mond with Nobel's Explosives and two other giant firms in the complete monopoly of heavy chemicals thereafter known as Imperial Chemical Industries Ltd., or I.C.I. Sir Alfred Mond was the leader of a prominent group of employers who were initiating a drive for "rationalisation of industry," a drive which would be carried through more easily in harmony with the trade unions. In the day of their strength few trade union Executives

[1] *Labour Research.*

would have found it possible to accept such proposals. But the events of 1926 and the advantage sedulously taken of them by the Baldwin Cabinet and by the employers had left the trade union leaders only one choice, either for a series of rearguard actions while building up forces for a renewal of struggle, or a compact with their adversaries, which would mean submission to the employers' standpoint in the form of "Mondism." Some leaders advocated this compact, which they felt would help to make British industry more competitive, though at the cost of increasing the number of unemployed and breaking down many working conditions established by trade union action in the past.

In the Trades Union Congress of September 1927 the current was already setting in strongly for the latter choice. During 1928 the stream of "Mondism" was running still more strongly and by September 1928 the Swansea Trades Union Congress had gained a majority for a programme of "Mondism," which explicitly repudiated any revolutionary aspirations on the part of the unions. Within the various unions there was a minority rowing against the stream; but they had to labour hard on their oars.

Within the Miners' Federation this struggle took various forms, including the development of a sort of vendetta against Arthur Cook, who in the course of 1926 had made some mistakes of which his opponents now sought at this later date to take advantage. In the spring of 1928 Cook became associated with James Maxton, the Member of Parliament for Bridgeton, in what was known as the "Cook–Maxton campaign." This was an endeavour to bring about a broad general movement that would unite the progressive elements in the trade unions and the Labour Party. But then, while Cook in this, as in his efforts for the miners, put his whole heart into the business, the others associated with him allowed timidity to be their guide.

Latterly Cook had to struggle on alone, swimming against the stream. But he could make little headway against the current, and at length, in the spring or early summer of 1929, Cook himself was swept away by it. Sick in body and spirit, Arthur Cook for several months languished in the camp of Ramsay MacDonald, uttering speeches such as no audience had ever heard from his lips before and failing even to please his new-found allies. It was only a short period before his last illness set in. A few months more, and at the age of forty-six he was dead.

There never had been a British miners' leader like Arthur James Cook; never one so hated by the Government, so obnoxious to the mine-owners, so much a thorn in the flesh of other General Secretaries of unions; never one who during his three years' mission from 1924 to 1926 had so much unfeigned reverence and enthusiastic support from his fellow-miners. Neither to Tommy Hepburn nor Tom Halliday, neither to Alexander McDonald nor Ben Pickard, neither to the Socialists Keir Hardie nor Robert Smillie did the miners of Britain accord the same unbounded trust and admiration as they reposed for these three years and more in A. J. Cook. That support was his strength, and it was his only strength. When he lost it, he lost the ground on which he lived and moved and had his being. To-day his faults are forgotten or forgiven amongst the older miners who tell the younger men their recollections of past days; and still, in every colliery village, there abides the memory of a great name.

4. SEVEN-AND-A-HALF HOURS

As the M.F.G.B. came to realise, during the aftermath of 1926, that their forces had been dispersed and that from being in policy a single body, they had now become a federation not only in name but in function, the majority of the leaders sought to accommodate themselves to this new situation. They might be accused of making friends with the mammon of unrighteousness: they might be told they were abandoning the class struggle; but such accusations merely made them seek a theoretical justification for the course on which they were set. To a certain extent, though under greatly changed conditions, they were turning to the same type of activity as, forty and fifty years earlier, had been the main function of the defunct Miners' National Union. They were sending deputations to Ministers, asking for legislative enactments or keeping watch on how existing legislation was administered in an endeavour to get some amelioration of harsh conditions. They got little comfort from the Baldwin–Churchill Cabinet.

The less they were able to get in the field of industry, the more they turned their attention to politics. The presidential addresses of the first years of the aftermath express the longing for a change of Government. Baffled in all their efforts to soften the heart of the Conservative Government, all the more they placed their hopes in the return of a Labour Government. At the General Election of June 1929 they put forward their candidates, and out of the increased total of Labour Members the number sponsored by the M.F.G.B. was forty-three. The second Labour Government was formed, once more with Ramsay MacDonald as Prime Minister.

In the House of Commons the Parliamentary Labour Party was in a minority and had to rely on Liberal support, or at any rate Liberal tolerance, of its legislative programme. The miners had hoped for a Labour Government which would restore the seven-hour day, nationalise the mines, and repeal the Trade Disputes and Trade Unions Act of 1927. They had some promises from Ramsay MacDonald of what the Government would do for the miners: but what it did attempt was far less than this: and actual performance fell short of what was attempted. It could hardly have been otherwise, given the situation of the industry, the strong position held by the mine-owners, the weakness of the Miners' Federation and the composition of the Cabinet. Of the measures carried by the second Labour Government the miners benefited particularly from the amended Unemployment Insurance Act of 1930, by which the onus of proving that an applicant was "genuinely seeking work" no longer fell upon the out-of-work man, as already mentioned.

Of the measures concerned directly with the coal industry there was but one of importance, and the preparation for this took up much of the time of the Federation Executive and Conference from the autumn of 1929 onwards. The second reading of the Coal Mines Bill was carried in the House of Commons on December 15, 1929, by 283 votes to 275 (a majority of eight) and it did not finally become law as the Coal Mines Act, 1930, until eight months later, during which time there had been many modifications of the Bill in its original form. The Act provided for output quotas of coal by pit and by District; for District amalgamations of colliery companies under a Board of Trade committee; and for various other District and national committees, for the purpose of investigations and appeals. But its main provision was for a seven-and-a-half-hour day. This provision was to run "during the continuance of the Coal Mines Act, 1926" (i.e., until April 1931); provided that the "spread-over" system of the 45-hour week could be agreed upon by the M.F.G.B. and the Mining Association of Great Britain.

These provisions, a far cry from the Labour Party's 1918 programme of nationalisation as set forth in *Labour and the New Social Order* or in *Labour and the Nation*, and also very much less than had been hoped for by the Miners' Federation in 1929, proved difficult to work out in practice. In particular the hours of labour proved a thorny problem. It did result in a meeting of the officials of the Miners' Federation of Great Britain and of the Mining Association on March 27th (the first recognition since the 1926 lock-out) but no agreement was reached. Subsequently this forty-five-hour week and the vexed question of the "spread-over" were to lead to much dissension as between one District and another within the Federation. Nevertheless, the seven-and-a-half-hour day (as confirmed by subsequent legislation in 1931 and 1932) came to be looked back upon as the first significant step out of the slough of despond into which the miners had been cast by the concerted measures of the Conservative Government and the mine-owners in the summer of 1926.

From this time, though wages and conditions were to worsen in the early 'thirties, the move to the reconstitution of the Miners' Federation of Great Britain in its power as of old, and even greater than as of old, had definitely begun. How long would the process take to accomplish? Few in 1930 could have foreseen the immense changes that would be carried through in less than a generation. But the account of all that happened in the score of years from 1930 onward is a subject for separate study. It is outside the scope of this volume, which has told of the miners in the acute and bitter struggles in the second and third decades of the twentieth century.

APPENDIX TO CHAPTER XV

"THE MINER"

THE weekly penny paper, *The Miner*, having begun as an offshoot of the Independent Labour Party's *New Leader* during the great lock-out of 1926, was at first subsidised and then controlled by the Miners' Federation of Great Britain. The paper, which was edited at an early stage by John Strachey and later for a time by S. B. Potter (and continued to be published by the *New Leader*), was the subject of many, and often bitter, discussions[1] at Federation Conferences, where resolutions were passed repeatedly from 1927 to 1930 to make special efforts to maintain it in being. Eventually, and with much reluctance, it was decided "That the necessary powers be given to the officials to arrange for publication to cease and the paper be wound up in a manner least expensive to the Federation" (October 16, 1930). In the annual statements of accounts the following items appear under the heading of "Grants" (to June 30th):

	£	s.	d.
1927	690	0	0
1928	1,695	14	1
1929	2,345	7	4
1930	2,840	0	0
1931	1,468	19	2

[1] Some delegates compared the paper, and to its disadvantage, with the *Sunday Worker* which, under the editorship first of William Paul and then of Walter M. Holmes, ran from the spring of 1925 to the end of 1929, with A. J. Cook for most of the time as one of its principal regular contributors.

GENERAL APPENDICES

(i) TABLE OF MEMBERSHIP

From the General Fund Table showing the number of members returned to the Federation for each quarter of the year upon whom 1½d. (1d. up to 1922) per member was paid: with average number of wage-earners (including up to 1921 over 20,000 clerks and salaried persons) except in the dispute years 1921 and 1926.

Year	Average number of Wage-earners (in thousands)	M.F.G.B. Membership (end of year)
1910	1,028	597,154
1911	1,045	588,000
1912	1,069	586,500
1913	1,107	645,900
1914	1,038	761,184*
1915	935	720,804
1916	981	724,628
1917	1,002	738,311
1918	990	754,183
1919	1,170	805,939
1920	1,227	945,487
1921	—	889,460
1922	1,094	802,064
1923	1,160	756,368
1924	1,172	790,512
1925	1,086	804,236
1926	—	783,463
1927	998	750,700
1928	922	561,359
1929	932	521,345
1930	917	529,958

N.B.—No percentage rate of trade unionism can be shown, as many thousand wage-earners were in unions other than those comprising the Miners' Federation.

* Figures up to this year from the Seventeenth Abstract of Labour Statistics. Figure for 1914 as given in the International Miners' Federation report.

(ii) LIST OF EXECUTIVE COMMITTEE MEMBERS OF THE MINERS' FEDERATION OF GREAT BRITAIN, 1911–1930

OFFICIALS

President:	ENOCH EDWARDS 1911–1912
	ROBERT SMILLIE 1912–1921
	HERBERT SMITH 1922–1929
	THOMAS RICHARDS 1930–
Vice-President:	ROBERT SMILLIE 1911–1912
	W. E. HARVEY 1912–1914
	W. HOUSE 1914–1917
	HERBERT SMITH 1917–1922
	STEVE WALSH 1922–1924
	THOMAS RICHARDS 1924–1930
	EBBY EDWARDS 1930–
Treasurer:	W. ABRAHAM 1911–1918
	JAMES ROBSON 1918–1921
	W. P. RICHARDSON 1921–1930[1]
Secretary:	RT. HON. THOMAS ASHTON, 1910–1919
	FRANK HODGES, 1919–1924
	ARTHUR J. COOK 1924–1930

MEMBERS OF THE EXECUTIVE COMMITTEE

(in the order of their first election and arranged according to counties and groups)

LANCASHIRE

S. Blackledge	..	1911, 1926, 1930	J. E. Sutton ..	1918
			J. Tinker ..	1919, 1928
J. McGurk	..	1912, 1920, 1929	G. MacDonald..	1920
			T. Brown ..	1921
J. A. Parkinson..		1913, 1925	J. Hilton ..	1923
S. Walsh	..	1914, 1921	P. Pemberton ..	1924
T. Greenall	..	1915, 1922, 1924	F. Lloyd ..	1924
			J. Berry ..	1925
H. Roughley	..	1916	T. Flatley ..	1926
H. Twist	..	1917, 1927	G. Wood ..	1927

[1] Thereafter the treasurership was "held in abeyance."

YORKSHIRE

J. Wadsworth	1911	J. Potts ..	1920–1922
H. Smith ..	1911–1916, 1918, 1920, 1921	A. Smith ..	1923, 1924–1930
S. Roebuck ..	1912–1923	J. Jones ..	1924–1930
J. Hoskin ..	1917–1919	J. A. Hall ..	1930

MIDLAND FEDERATION

W. Johnson ..	1911, 1916	W. Johnson (Jr.)	1921, 1924
A. Stanley	1912	J. F. Dean	1922
S. Finney	1913–1915, 1918, 1920, 1921, 1923	H. Whitehouse ..	1923
		H. Leese	1923
		J. Cooper	1924
S. Edwards ..	1917, 1925	T. Richards ..	1925
J. Baker	1919, 1922, 1925	G. H. Jones ..	1927
		F. J. Hancock ..	1926, 1927
W. Latham ..	1920, 1926, 1930	J. Blakemore ..	1928
		W. Bagnall ..	1929

SCOTLAND

W. Adamson ..	1911, 1922	W. Webb ..	1919
T. M'Kerrell ..	1911	D. Graham ..	1920, 1929
H. Murnin ..	1912, 1924	J. Hood ..	1920, 1927
J. Robertson ..	1912, 1917	J. Sullivan ..	1921
J. Murdoch ..	1916	J. Clarke ..	1921
R. Brown ..	1915	W. B. Small ..	1922
H. Gallacher ..	1914	J. Welsh ..	1923
M. Lee	1914	R. Smith ..	1923, 1930
D. Gilmour ..	1915	P. McKenna ..	1924–1926
J. Brown ..	1916	P. Chambers ..	1925
J. Tonner ..	1913, 1918	J. Doonan ..	1913, 1926
S. Hynds ..	1918	J. Potter ..	1927
J. Cook	1919	A. Clarke ..	1928

SOUTH WALES

V. Hartshorn ..	1911–1917, 1919–1920, 1922–1923	J. Winstone ..	1915–1918, 1920
		E. Morrell ..	1921, 1924
		T. Richards ..	1921–1930
G. Barker ..	1911–1920	N. Ablett ..	1921–1926
C. B. Stanton ..	1911	A. J. Cook ..	1921
W. Brace ..	1912–1914, 1919–1920	S. O. Davies ..	1924–1930
		A. L. Horner ..	1927

NORTHUMBERLAND

W. Straker   1911–1925   J. M. Gillians[1]   ..   1926
E. Edwards   ..   1926–1930

DURHAM

T. H. Cann   ..   1911, 1913, 1916, 1918, 1921
S. Galbraith   ..   1911, 1914
J. Hobson   1912
Dr. J. Wilson   ..   1912, 1914
W. House   1913
J. Robson 1915, 1920
W. Whiteley   ..   1915, 1918, 1920
T. Trotter 1916, 1919, 1922, 1924, 1926, 1928, 1930
J. Batey 1917, 1919, 1922
W. P. Richardson   ..   1917, 1920–1921
P. Lee 1921, 1923–1924, 1926, 1928, 1930
J. E. Swan 1923, 1925, 1927, 1929
J. Gilliland 1925, 1927, 1929

NOTTINGHAMSHIRE

W. Carter 1911, 1914, 1917
J. G. Hancock   ..   1912, 1915, 1926
G. Bunfield 1913, 1916, 1918
G. A. Spencer   ..   1919, 1921
F. B. Varley   ..   1920, 1922–1926
H. Booth   1927

LEICESTERSHIRE

L. Lovett 1911, 1916

CLEVELAND

H. Dack   ..   1911, 1917   W. Stephens   ..   1914

DERBYSHIRE

J. Haslam   ..   1911   F. Hall   ..   1913–1921,
B. Kenyon   ..   1912   1923–1927
                                   H. Hicken   ..   1928–1930

SOUTH DERBYSHIRE

W. Buckley 1913, 1918

CUMBERLAND

A. Sharp   ..   1912   T. Cape   ..   1915, 1918,
                                               1926

[1] Mechanics. Also present at 1928 meetings.

SOMERSETSHIRE

S. H. Whitehouse 1912   F. Swift   .. 1917

BRISTOL

W. Whitefield   .. 1915

FOREST OF DEAN

G. H. Rowlinson 1914   H. W. Booth .. 1919

NORTH WALES

E. Hughes 1913, 1916, 1919

KENT

J. Elks   1926

GROUP 1 (ENGINEMEN)

R. Shirkie	.. 1920	W. S. Hall	.. 1925, 1927,
C. Thompson	.. 1921		1929
J. W. Taylor	.. 1922	G. Peart	.. 1926
G. Annable	.. 1923	J. Smith	.. 1927
W. A. Hipwood	1924, 1928	J. H. Harrison	.. 1930

GROUP 2

L. Lovett	.. 1920	Hugh Hughes	.. 1925, 1927
H. Dack	.. 1921	J. Williams	.. 1928
T. Cape	.. 1922		
E. Hughes	.. 1923	C. Gill ..	.. 1929
J. W. Smith	.. 1924, 1926	J. Elks ..	.. 1930

GROUP 3

W. Whitefield	.. 1920	W. Mansfield	.. 1925
A. Hassell	.. 1921	H. Dack	.. 1927, 1930
F. Swift	.. 1922		
W. K. Smith	.. 1923	C. Thompson	.. 1928
J. Williams	.. 1924	T. Gowdridge	.. 1929

GROUP 4

C. Thompson	.. 1924, 1926	H. Hughes	.. 1929
W. K. Smith	.. 1925, 1927	J. R. Barker	.. 1930
T. Cape	.. 1928		

GROUP 5

T. Cape	.. 1924	F. B. Varley	.. 1928
C. Gill ..	.. 1925	H. Buck	.. 1929
F. Swift	.. 1927	H. Booth	.. 1930

Note: The setting-up of Groups 1, 2, and 3 in 1920, and of Groups 4 and 5 in 1924 was a new form of representation of the smaller Districts and other constituents. As these varied from time to time, so names appear under different headings towards the end of the list.

(iii) LIST OF M. F. G. B. CANDIDATES AT FIVE GENERAL ELECTIONS

The candidates were elected to Parliament except where the name is in italic lettering

District	Constituency	Candidates				
		1918	1922	1923	1924	1929
Scotland	West Fife	W. Adamson	W. Adamson	W. Adamson	W. Adamson	W. Adamson
	Bothwell	*J. Robertson*	J. Robertson	J. Robertson	J. Robertson	J. Sullivan
	Hamilton	D. Graham	D. Graham	D. Graham	D. Graham	D. Graham
	South Ayrshire	J. Brown	J. Brown	J. Brown	J. Brown	J. Brown
	North Lanark	*J. Sullivan*	J. Sullivan	J. Sullivan	*J. Sullivan*	—
	South Midlothian	*J. Gold*	J. Westwood	J. Westwood	J. Westwood	J. Westwood
	Dunfermline Burghs	—	W. M. Watson	W. Watson	W. Watson	W. Watson
	Stirling					H. Murnin
Durham	Houghton-le-Spring	R. Richardson	R. Richardson	R. Richardson	R. Richardson	R. Richardson
	Barnard Castle	J. E. Swan	*J. E. Swan*	—	—	W. Lawther
	Blaydon	*W. Whiteley*	W. Whiteley	W. Whiteley	W. Whiteley	W. Whiteley
	Spennymoor	*J. Batey*	J. Batey	J. Batey	J. Batey	J. Batey
	Durham	*J. Ritson*	J. Ritson	J. Ritson	J. Ritson	J. Ritson
	Sedgefield	*J. Herriotts*	J. Herriotts	*J. Herriotts*	*J. Herriotts*	J. Herriotts
	Seaham	*J. Lawson*	J. Lawson	J. Lawson	J. Lawson	J. Lawson
	Chester-le-Street	—	*W. Lawther*	*W. Lawther*	*W. Lawther*	
Northumberland	Morpeth	J. Cairns	J. Cairns	R. Smillie	R. Smillie	E. Edwards
	Wansbeck	*E. Edwards*	G. Warne	G. Warne	G. Warne	G. W. Shields
	Hexham	*W. Weir*	—	—	—	—
	South Shields		*G. W. Shield*			
Yorkshire	Normanton	F. Hall	F. Hall	F. Hall	F. Hall	F. Hall
	Hemsworth	J. Guest	J. Guest	J. Guest	J. Guest	J. Guest
	Wentworth	G. Hirst	G. Hirst	G. Hirst	G. Hirst	G. Hirst
	Rother Valley	T. W. Grundy	T. W. Grundy	T. W. Grundy	T. W. Grundy	T. W. Grundy
	Rothwell	W. Lunn	W. Lunn	W. Lunn	W. Lunn	W. Lunn
	Don Valley	*C. Hough*	T. Williams	T. Williams	T. Williams	T. Williams
	Pontefract	*I. Burns*	T. Smith	T. Smith	*T. Smith*	T. Smith

Doncaster	—	W. Paling	W. Paling	W. Paling	W. Paling
Barnsley	*W. Gillis*	—	J. Potts	J. Potts	J. Potts
Penistone	*H. Dack*	—	—	—	—
Cleveland	*J. A. Parkinson*	—	—	—	—
Lancashire and Cheshire					
Wigan	—	*H. Dack*	—	*W. Mansfield*	W. Mansfield
Ince	*T. Greenall*	J. A. Parkinson	J. A. Parkinson	J. A. Parkinson	J. A. Parkinson
Farnworth	*J. E. Sutton*	*T. Greenall*	S. Walsh	S. Walsh	G. MacDonald
Clayton	—	*J. E. Sutton*	T. Greenall	T. Greenall	G. Rowson
Leigh	*J. McGurk*	H. Twist	J. E. Sutton	J. E. Sutton	J. E. Sutton
Darwen	—	*J. McGurk*	J. Tinker	J. Tinker	J. Tinker
South Wales					
Abertillery	*W. Brace*	G. Barker	G. Barker	G. Barker	G. Daggar
Ogmore	*V. Hartshorn*	V. Hartshorn	V. Hartshorn	V. Hartshorn	V. Hartshorn
Bedwellty	*C. Edwards*	C. Edwards	C. Edwards	C. Edwards	C. Edwards
Rhondda East	*D. W. Morgan*	D. W. Morgan	D. W. Morgan	D. W. Morgan	D. W. Morgan
Rhondda West	*W. Abraham*	W. John	W. John	W. John	W. John
Ebbw Vale	*T. Richards*	E. Davies	E. Davies	E. Davies	A. Bevan
Caerphilly	*A. Onions*	—	—	—	—
Gower	*J. Williams*	D. R. Grenfell	D. R. Grenfell	D. R. Grenfell	D. R. Grenfell
Pontypridd	*D. L. Davies*	T. I. M. Jones	T. I. M. Jones	T. I. M. Jones	T. I. M. Jones
Aberdare	*J. Winstone*	G. H. Hall	G. H. Hall	G. H. Hall	G. H. Hall
Neath	*F. Lee*	W. Jenkins	W. Jenkins	W. Jenkins	W. Jenkins
Merthyr Tydfil	*F. Hall*	—	—	—	—
Derbyshire					
N.E. Derby	—	F. Lee	F. Lee	F. Lee	F. Lee
Clay Cross	*G. A. Spencer*	*O. Wright*	*O. Wright*	—	—
Belper	*W. Carter*	G. A. Spencer	—	—	—
Notts					
Broxtowe	*S. Finney*	W. Carter	G. A. Spencer	G. A. Spencer	—
Mansfield	—	—	F. B. Varley	F. B. Varley	—
Midlands					
Burslem	*T. Riley*	—	—	—	—
Stoke-on-Trent	—	*W. J. French*	*J. Watts*	*J. Watts*	—
Lichfield	—	*J. Stevenson*	F. Hodges	F. Hodges	—
Nuneaton	—	—	—	—	—
Cumberland					
Workington	*T. Morris*	T. Cape	T. Cape	T. Cape	T. Cape
North Wales					
Oswestry	*E. Gill*	—	—	—	—
Somerset					
Frome	—	—	—	—	—

(iv) THE MINERS' SCHEME (1921)

DRAFT OF AGREEMENT PROPOSED TO BE ENTERED INTO BETWEEN THE MINING ASSOCIATION OF GREAT BRITAIN (FOR THE ONE PART) AND THE MINERS' FEDERATION OF GREAT BRITAIN (FOR THE OTHER PART), HEREINAFTER REFERRED TO AS THE "PARTIES."

Preamble

IT is hereby agreed in conformity with the terms of the Government Agreement with the parties dated November 3rd, 1920, Clause (1) (b) thereof, that the regulation of wages and profits in the coal industry of Great Britain shall be determined for the duration of this Agreement upon the basis set forth below:

1. For the purpose of securing the most effective means for the distribution of profits and wages in the industry there shall be established a National Board (to be known hereafter as the National Coal Board), and all powers and duties of the several District Conciliation Boards now in existence, relating to the fixing of the general district rates of wages, shall hereafter be exercised by the National Coal Board.

2. The National Coal Board shall consist of representatives of the owners and workmen, 26 of whom shall be representatives of the owners and 26 shall be representatives of the workmen; the manner of their election to be determined by the parties to this Agreement.

3. The National Coal Board shall determine all questions of wages and profits affecting the coal-mining industry as a whole.

NATIONAL REGULATION AND DISTRIBUTION OF WAGES

4. In lieu of the standard, basis, or minimum wage, of each workman prevailing at the respective collieries prior to the date of signing of this Agreement, a new standard wage for each workman shall be established by incorporating therein the whole of the existing district percentages, provided the alteration in such standard, basis, or minimum wage shall not in itself cause a change in wages.

5. The new standard thus created shall be known as the 1921 Standard Wage, which standard wage shall operate as a minimum wage during the life time of this agreement. In the case of those workmen for whom the advance in wages of 20 per cent (known as the March 12th, 1920, advance in wages) did not yield an advance of 2s. extra per shift in the case of adults, 1s. per shift for persons of 16 to 18 years of age, and 9d. per shift for persons under 16 years of age, upon the gross earnings, exclusive of the War Wage and Sankey Wage, a percentage shall be incorporated which will result in 2s., 1s., and 9d. respectively, being incorporated in the new standard before mentioned.

Wages known as the War Wage and Sankey Wage, and any other flat rate advances in addition to the 1921 standard, and which were in existence on or before the 31st March, 1921, shall be combined into one flat rate to be added to the 1921 standard until such combined flat rate is advanced or reduced in accordance with the terms of this Agreement.

That portion of the War Wage payable for time lost through circumstances at the colliery over which the workmen have no control, shall not be incorporated in the new combined flat rate, but shall be continued as heretofore in accordance with the rules governing the payment as set forth in the War Wage Agreement of September 17th, 1917, and any subsequent orders and decisions issued by the Coal Controller or the Ministry of Mines.

Where the customary number of War Wage or Sankey Wage payments are in excess of the actual number of shifts worked by the workmen, such additional War Wage or Sankey Wage payments shall be included in the combined flat rate payment hereafter to be paid in addition to the 1921 standard.

The 1921 Standard Wage shall be reckoned as the principal element of the cost of production, and to be payable before any profit is allocated to the coal-owners, additional wages in excess of the Standard Wage to be payable in accordance with the principles set forth in this Agreement.

Any advance in wages above the 1921 standard or reduction in wages to the standard made in accordance with the terms of this Agreement, shall be in the form of additions to or deductions from the combined flat rate in excess of the standard, as flat rate advances or flat rate reductions respectively.

NATIONAL REGULATION AND DISTRIBUTION OF PROFITS

The colliery owners shall receive in the aggregate as profits one-tenth of the amount paid as wages.

When wages are at or on the standard the owners shall receive as a minimum profit one-tenth of the aggregate wage paid at the aforesaid standard.

Where, however, the quarterly certificates of the joint auditors show that the balance available for distribution as profit, after costs have been met as set forth in the first schedule to this agreement, does not provide a sufficient sum to ensure a payment of one-tenth of the aggregate wages standard as profits, the owners agree to forego their minimum profit until subsequent ascertainments show available balances, sufficient to enable them to be paid any arrears of profit due from previous quarters.

The workmen undertake to make no application for wage advances above the standard as long as arrears of owners' minimum profit remain unpaid.

The amount payable in wages in excess of the standard, which standard is an element of cost as set forth in Schedule 1 of this agreement, shall be that proportion of the income above costs, which, with 10 per cent added thereto, equals such income. Such 10 per cent shall be payable to the owners as profits in addition to the minimum profit as set forth in paragraph 1.

The owners agree to maintain in production by the means of a National Profits Fund all the existing collieries and all collieries hereafter to be developed, until such times as the National Coal Board decide to the contrary.

(v) THE COAL-OWNERS' SCHEME (1921)
MINING ASSOCIATION OF GREAT BRITAIN

Heads of Proposed Scheme for the Future Regulation of Wages and Profits in the Coal Industry.

IT being agreed that wages in the industry must depend upon the financial ability to pay, the owners propose that the following principles be adopted by the Mining Association of Great Britain and the Miners' Federation of Great Britain for application to the determination of the wages payable in each district upon the financial position of such district:

1. That the base rates now existing at each colliery, with the percentages (or the equivalents in any district where there has been a subsequent merging into new standards) which were paid in July, 1914, shall be regarded as the point below which wages shall not be automatically reduced.

NOTE: All additions which have since been made to the base rates prevailing in July, 1914, shall be maintained, and the percentages which have been added to piece-workers' rates consequent upon the reduction in hours from eight to seven shall continue.

2. That the owners' aggregate standard profits in each district in correspondence with the above shall be taken as 17 per cent of the aggregate amount of wages payable as above.

3. That any surplus remaining of the proceeds of the sale of coal at the pit head after such wages and profits and all other costs have been taken into account shall be divisible as to 75 per cent to the workmen and 25 per cent to the owners, the workmen's share being expressed as a percentage upon the standard rate of the district.

NOTE: To meet the present abnormal situation the owners are prepared to accept a temporary departure from the strict application of the above principles to the extent of waiving their share of the surplus in favour of the workmen, on condition that ascertainments are made at monthly periods to determine the wages payable during such time as the above concession on the part of the owners continues to operate.

4. That if during any period of ascertainment the owners' standard profit is not realised, the amount of the deficiency shall be carried forward as a prior charge against any surplus available for the payment of wages in excess of the basis of wages provided in No. 1 above.

(vi) MINERS' EARNINGS

(*Not* Wage-rates)

Year	Per Man-Shift		Quarterly Average		
	s.	d.	£.	s.	d.
1921 (January to March)	19	2	58	5	2
1922	9	11¾	31	5	6
1923	10	1	33	11	6
1924	10	7¾	34	11	2
1925	10	6	32	18	11
1926 (January to April) ..	10	5	34	6	4
1927	10	0¾	30	13	1
1928	9	3½	28	9	2
1929	9	2½	29	11	7
1930	9	3½	28	9	7
1931	9	2¼	27	17	8
1932	9	2	27	7	1
1933	9	7½	27	11	6
1934	9	1¼	28	17	11
1935	9	3¼	29	12	0
1936	10	0¼	32	16	0
1937	10	8	36	0	10
1938	11	2¾	36	8	10

BIBLIOGRAPHY

SOURCES

As is stated in the Preface the main sources are the printed proceedings of the miners' trade unions and federations of unions together with Hansard and H.M. Stationery Office publications. These, already dealt with in the bibliographical note in volume one of this history (*The Miners*), are supplemented for this period of 1910 onwards by the records of the Labour Research Department and by its numerous publications, of which only a small selection are listed below.

For book lists see the references to bibliographies in *The Miners*. See also the note on books and sources in *Labour in the Coal-Mining Industry* 1914–21 by G. D. H. Cole whose compendious treatment has relieved me of the need to print many details and documents of the many joint committees and meetings of the 1914–18 period. The same may be said of Jevons' *British Coal Trade* (1915) as regards the administration of the Acts of 1911 and 1912. In addition I give below a short list of other books consulted.

LIST OF BOOKS

BRISSENDEN, P. F., The I.W.W.: a Study of American Syndicalism, Columbia, New York, 1919.

BURNS, E., The General Strike May 1926—Trades Councils in Action. L.R.D., 1926.

COLE, G. D. H., A Short History of the British Working Class Movement 1789–1947. Unwin, 1947.
British Trade Unionism Today, Gollancz, 1939.
Labour in the Coal Mining Industry (1914–21). Carnegie Endowment for International Peace. Clarendon Press, 1923.

COOK, A. J., The Nine Days (the story of the General Strike) Co-op Printing Society, 1927.
Is it Peace? Workers' Publications, 1926.

CROOK, W. H., The General Strike, O.U.P., 1931.

DUTT, R. P., The Meaning of the General Strike. C.P.G.B., 1926.
Socialism and the Living Wage. C.P.G.B., 1927.

FLYNN, C. R., Account of the Proceedings of the Northumberland and Durham General Council Joint Strike Committee, Newcastle, May, 1926.

FYFE, H., Behind the Scenes of the Great Strike. Labour Publishing Company, 1926.

GALLACHER, W., Revolt on the Clyde. Lawrence & Wishart, 1936.

GIBSON, W., Coal in Great Britain. Arnold, 1920.

GOULD, G., The Lesson of Black Friday. Labour Publishing Co., and Unwin, 1921.

GREAT WESTERN RAILWAY, General Strike, May 1926.

HALL, W. S., Durham Colliery Mechanics Association: A Historical Survey 1879–1929. J. H. Veitch & Sons, 1929.

HAMILTON, J., The Class Struggle in the Mining Industry. Plebs League, 1926.
A History of the Miners' Struggle. Plebs League.

HANNINGTON, W., Unemployment Struggles 1919–1936. Lawrence & Wishart, 1936.

HODGES, F., Nationalisation of the Mines. Parsons, 1920.
My Adventures as a Labour Leader. Newnes, 1925.

HORNER, A. L., Coal: The Next Round. Workers' Publications, 1926.

HORNER, A. L. and HUTT, G. A., Communism and Coal. C.P.G.B., 1928.

HUTT, G. A., The Post War History of the British Working Class. Gollancz, 1937.

JEFFREYS, J. Labour's Formative Years (History in the Making, Nineteenth Century), Vol. 2. Lawrence & Wishart, 1948.

JEVONS, H. S., The British Coal Trade. Kegan Paul, 1915.

KEYNES, J. M., The Economic Consequences of the Peace. Macmillan, 1919.
The Economic Consequences of Mr. Churchill. Hogarth Press, 1925.

LABOUR RESEARCH DEPARTMENT, Facts from the Coal Commission, and Further Facts from the Coal Commission (by R. P. Arnot). George Allen & Unwin, 1919.
The General Strike, May 1926: Its Origin and History (by R. P. Arnot, 1926).
Red Money (Foreword by A. J. Cook). 1926.
The Coal Crisis: Facts from the Samuel Commission, 1925–26 (Foreword by Herbert Smith). 1926.
The Workers' Register of Labour and Capital, 1923

LLOYD GEORGE, D., Coal and Power. Hodder & Stoughton, 1924.
The Truth About Reparations and War-Debts. Heinemann, 1932.

MARTIN, KINGSLEY, The British Public and the General Strike. Hogarth Press, 1926.

MELLOR, W., Direct Action 1920.

MURPHY, J. T., The Political Meaning of the Great Strike. C.P.G.B., 1926.

MURRAY, J., The General Strike of 1926. Lawrence & Wishart, 1951.

POSTGATE, R. W., WILKINSON, E., and HORRABIN, J. F., A Worker's History of the Great Strike. Plebs League, 1927.

REDMAYNE, Sir R., British Coal-Mining Industry during the War. O.U.P., 1923.

ROWE, J. W. F., Wages in the Coal Industry. King, 1923.

SIMON, Rt. Hon. Sir JOHN, Three Speeches on the General Strike. Macmillan, 1926.

SNOWDEN, P., Socialism and Syndicalism. Collins, 1913.

TRADES UNION CONGRESS, Official Report of British Trade Union Delegation to Russia and Caucasia, Nov. and Dec. 1924. Annual Reports.

WEARMOUTH, R. F., Some Working Class Movements of the 19th Century. The Epworth Press, 1948.

WOLFE, H., Labour Supply and Regulation. Clarendon Press, 1923.

GOVERNMENT PUBLICATIONS

Royal Commission on Mines, 2nd Report, 1909.

Coal Industry Commission (Sankey Commission), Vol. I and Vol. II. Reports and Minutes of Evidence, Vol. III. Appendices, Charts and Indexes, 1919.

Report of the Royal Commission on the Coal Industry (Samuel Commission), Vol. I, 1926.

Report by a Court of Inquiry Concerning the Wages Position in the Coal Mining Industry, 1924.

Report by a Court of Inquiry concerning the Coal Industry Dispute, 1925.

18th and 19th Abstract of Labour Statistics of the U.K.

INDEX OF NAMES

[other than those of Miners' Federation parliamentary candidates listed in General Appendices (iii)]

GENERAL INDEX

GEORGE ALLEN & UNWIN LTD
LONDON: 40 MUSEUM STREET, W.C.1
CAPE TOWN: 58–60 LONG STREET
SYDNEY, N.S.W.: 55 YORK STREET
TORONTO: 91 WELLINGTON STREET WEST
CALCUTTA: 17 CENTRAL AVE., P.O. DHARAMTALA
BOMBAY: 15 GRAHAM ROAD, BALLARD ESTATE
WELLINGTON, N.Z.: 8 KINGS CRESCENT, LOWER HUTT